WORLD ENCYCLOPAEDIA OF
THE
TANK

WORLD ENCYCLOPAEDIA OF

THE

TANK

An international history of the armoured fighting machine

Christopher Chant

SUTTON PUBLISHING

First published by Patrick Stephens Ltd in 1994

This revised edition published in the United Kingdom in 2002 by
Sutton Publishing Limited · Phoenix Mill
Thrupp · Stroud · Gloucestershire · GL5 2BU

British Library Cataloguing in Publication Data
A catalogue record for this book is available from the British Library.

ISBN 0 7509 3147 7

Typeset in 10/11 pt Helvetica.
Typesetting and origination by
Sutton Publishing Limited.
Printed and bound in England by
J.H. Haynes & Co. Ltd, Sparkford.

Contents

Introduction

It is a military truism that the survival and fighting efficiency of the soldier depends upon a combination of firepower, protection and mobility. The right blend of these three basic ingredients allows the soldier to close with his enemy and kill or disable him: without firepower the soldier can make efforts that are, at best, only raids or reconnaissances; without protection the soldier is all too liable to destruction before he can close with his enemy; and without mobility the soldier cannot bring his firepower to bear effectively.

History is littered with early examples of man's ingenuity in trying to produce such a blend, ranging from Egyptian war chariots and the Roman *testudo* (tortoise) formation of overlapping shields, to the protected and mobile siege engines of the mediaeval period and the Hussites' armoured wagons in Central Europe during the early 15th century. The advent of firearms and cannon marked a radical shift in man's approach to war, and emphasis then shifted from a blend of the three basic ingredients towards firepower and manoeuvre, it being thought that adequate protection against gunpowder weapons was impossible for all but increasingly impressive fortresses. The increasing capability of artillery in the 19th century was accompanied by an increase in weight, and this further reduced the mobility of armies' heavier firepower. Finally, the conditions leading to the static situation that prevailed in the First World War arrived, with the development of the magazine-fed repeating rifle and finally the machine-gun.

Some men were indeed aware of the deteriorating circumstances imposed by lack of mobility and protection against increasingly lethal firepower, but most armies were content to keep on their established courses. The great limitation was, of course, lack of power (except for the vulnerable and limited horse) for any type of genuine battlefield mobility. The

breakthrough came in 1885 with the German invention of the spark-ignition engine by Gottlieb Daimler. It took some years for the internal-combustion engine to reach any level of maturity and reliability, and in the interval there were many attempts to provide massive steam traction engines with protection so that they could be used on the battlefield, mainly as tractors for heavy artillery. From 1898, many inventors sought to produce battlefield vehicles on the basis of cars fitted with armour protection and one or more machine-guns, but the automotive state of the art had yet to reach the stage where such primitive armoured cars had any practical battlefield value. From 1910, however, the armoured car became increasingly feasible and reliable, though it was limited to road and undemanding cross-country movement.

What was needed was a true cross-country vehicle with an automotive system allowing it to tackle any type of going, with the power to carry a useful weight of protection and weapons, and with the size to accommodate the crew required to handle the vehicle and its armament. The first realistic proposal for such a 'landship' came from an Austro-Hungarian officer in 1911, and in the next few years comparable designs were evolved in Germany, Russia, the UK and the USA. The key to these efforts was caterpillar-tracked agricultural vehicles such as the Bullock Creeping Grip Tractor, the Holt Tractor, the Killen-Strait Tractor and the Diplock Pedrail. Though they differed considerably in reliability and overall efficiency, these marked a considerable advance in cross-country mobility, by adopting an endless-loop system of propulsion, a tracklaying concept that placed far greater propulsive area on the ground, for a combination of more traction and lower ground pressure. Developed to a fair degree of practicality in the USA and the UK, these tractors were an ob-

hundreds of yards only, and never once was there any chance of a genuine breakthrough and the unleashing of the cavalry. As the year progressed, the chances of the anticipated breakthrough became increasingly remote, but the generals remained optimistic. Another problem that they failed to consider was the nature of any breakthrough: even if the cavalry had been introduced through a rupture in the enemy's line, it is hard to see what success could have been achieved, even with the unlikely support of the plodding infantry.

Although the concept of a caterpillar-tracked 'landship' had enjoyed considerable currency in the period leading up to the First World War, it failed to find any measure of acceptance among military leaders, many of whom had little or no knowledge or appreciation of science and technology: indeed, many of the combatant nations' senior generals were still trying to come to grips with the nature and effect of technology which was already established, such as modern artillery and the machine-gun. One British convert of singular importance, however, was Lieutenant-Colonel E.W. Swinton, assistant secretary of the Committee of Imperial Defence. Serving in France as a reporter during 1914, Swinton soon appreciated that his existing fears about the machine-gun's role in defensive warfare had been realized. However, he also saw Holt caterpillar tractors being used as tow vehicles for heavy artillery, and envisaged the possibility of fitting such tractors with armoured bodies for the transport of assault parties (or light artillery) through no-man's land and over the barbed wire for direct assaults on the machine-guns that tore apart every infantry assault. Swinton reported back to his immediate superior, Lieutenant-Colonel Maurice Hankey, the secretary of the Committee of Imperial Defence, who passed on Swinton's notions to the Imperial General Staff and to Lord Kitchener. The IGS and Kitchener rebuffed the concept immediately, mostly on the grounds that any such 'Trojan horse' would be catastrophically vulnerable to artillery fire. To a certain extent the authorities were correct, for Swinton's concept envisaged a massive machine able to transport some 50 men: what the pundits ignored, however, was the difficul-

ty for the artillery of the period in engaging a moving target at all, except at such close ranges that the artillery would be left hopelessly exposed to counter-battery fire.

The problem faced by Swinton and other advocates of the embryonic tank concept was how to convince their sceptical superiors about the technical feasibility and tactical advantages of their novel concept. The decisive moment was perhaps the Christmas period of 1914, when Hankey wrote a memorandum on the progress of the war to date and included amongst his recommendations the desirability of some sort of armoured protection for infantry assaults. The memorandum was circulated within the Committee of Imperial Defence, which numbered amongst its members the First Lord of the Admiralty, Mr Winston Churchill. Ambitious for himself and for the service whose political fortunes he controlled, Churchill was an unorthodox thinker, ready to accept and develop apparently impossible ideas. Hankey's interim recommendation therefore found a ready supporter in Churchill, who was already aware of the progress being made by the Royal Naval Air Service in the development and procurement of armoured vehicles for use in northern France and Belgium by the Naval Armoured Car Division.

Churchill responded to the Hankey memorandum with a note of his own to the Prime Minister, Herbert Asquith, criticizing the army's apparent antipathy towards the notion of trench assault by the use of special cross-country vehicles carrying armour protection. In typical fashion, Churchill warned that the Germans might already be working along the lines eschewed by the War Office, and urged the creation of a committee of engineer officers and other experts to consider the concept of cross-country armoured vehicles. Asquith was impressed by Churchill's arguments (and indeed deliberately raised fears that the Germans might already be at work on the suggested lines, when there was no evidence either direct or indirect for this fear) and induced Kitchener to order such a committee into existence.

The committee comprised the War Office's directors of fortification, artillery and transport, and was tasked with a thorough evaluation of the suggestions made by Swinton and others. On 17 February 1915 the committee witnessed trials with a Holt tractor towing a trailer ballasted to simulate the weight of men, guns and armour: in fact Swinton had never proposed so unwieldy an arrangement, and in extremely wet conditions the trial was judged a failure. The committee therefore reported negatively, on the grounds that the tried system was too unwieldy and thus vulnerable, going on to claim that in any event the war would have ended before a practical system could be evolved. Having fulfilled the wishes of the politicians, the army allowed any current interest in the concept to lapse.

The torch now passed to the Royal Navy, in the form of the RNAS, which was already using powerful touring cars fitted with armour and machine-guns for the mobile defence of its air bases at Calais and Dunkirk. These vehicles were very limited by their origins, but the value of armour protection was sufficiently impressive for the RNAS commander, Captain Murray Sueter, to urge on Churchill the development of armoured vehicles on the Diplock Pedrail crawler chassis for greater cross-country mobility. The RNAS was alive with interesting concepts at this time: one of the most ambitious ideas, proposed by Flight-Commander Thomas Hetherington, transport officer of the RNAS Armoured Car Division,

was a 'land battleship', based on a tricycle chassis whose 800-hp (596.5-kW) diesel powerplant was to drive three 40-ft (12.2-m) diameter wheels to allow this massive machine to cross German trenches, which were 2.75 m (9 ft) wide. The 'land battleship' was to carry prodigious armament in the form of three turrets, each fitted with two 4-in (102-mm) naval guns.

Such a machine was clearly impractical, but on 15 February 1915, Hetherington was called to describe his concept to a receptive Churchill. Full of enthusiasm, on 20 February 1915 the First Lord of the Admiralty ordered the establishment of a Landship Committee, under the chairmanship of Mr Eustace Tennyson d'Eyncourt, the Director of Naval Construction. The committee included Hetherington and a number of engineer and transport specialists, with Lieutenant Albert Stern as its secretary, and its initial brief was the assessment of the two different 'land ship' concepts embodied in Sueter's tracked and Hetherington's big-wheel notions. While the committee was still assessing the two options, on 26 March the impetuous Churchill ordered prototypes of the two types, in the form of 12 tracked and six wheeled machines, the latter sensibly scaled down with 15-ft (4.57-m) diameter wheels. The development of the tracked prototype was entrusted to Colonel Crompton,

Coupled Bullock tractors were amongst the units investigated in the 1915 trials at Burton-on-Trent to assess the capabilities of various types of commercial tracked chassis. (*RAC Tank Museum*)

a highly capable, though elderly, engineer with a wealth of transport experience, aided by Lieutenant W.G. Wilson of the RNAS armoured car force, and a pre-war automotive engineer of great repute. The big-wheel prototype was contracted to a Lincoln firm, William Foster and Co. Ltd under the managing directorship of Sir William Tritton: the company's Foster-Daimler petrol-engined tractors were already in service with the Royal Marine Artillery as heavy gun tractors, and it was thought that the mechanical system and other components of these vehicles could be adapted for the proposed big-wheel machine.

One of the initial conclusions of the Crompton team was that the Diplock Pedrail could not be used as the basis of a machine for service in France, as its length of more than 40 ft (12.2 m) made it too unwieldy to negotiate the types of bend commonly encountered on French roads and, perhaps more importantly, country lanes. At the same time it was also appreciated that the Diplock Pedrail was mechanically complex and considerably underpowered. Work on adaptation of the first chassis was abandoned in May 1915, and the chassis was handed over to the army, which also abandoned the type.

The Crompton team deemed that an articulated chassis would be needed for a machine able to operate in France, and after trials with an ex-agricultural machine on Greenhithe marshes an order was placed in the USA for two Bullock Creeping Grip Caterpillar tractors. It was appreciated that the Bullock machine was too small to provide the 5-ft (1.52-m) trench-crossing and 2.5-ft (0.76-m) parapet-climbing capabilities which had been fixed as minima by the Landship committee, so at the same time additional track and suspension components were ordered so that larger machines could be developed. The two Bullocks were delivered in June 1915 to the new RNAS testing ground at Burton-on-Trent, where Wilson was in command of the test programme.

Meanwhile Fosters had completed their mock-up of the big-wheel proposal with 15-ft (4.57 m) diameter wheels. It was abundantly clear that the machine was too big and ponderous to have any real tactical value, and

would moreover be a considerable target for the enemy's artillery. In May 1915 the big-wheel concept was formally abandoned, and henceforward all development effort was devoted to the tracked machine. Early trials with the Bullock machine were essentially encouraging, but realistic assessment indicated that the vehicle was still unsuitable for France and, moreover, that the coupling between the two major units was too weak for service use, especially for tasks such as trench crossing.

Swinton had been working to overcome the army's inertia so far as armoured vehicles were concerned. Although at first his efforts had been unsuccessful on account of the opposition of the field army's chief adviser on military, engineering, dividends were finally paid by his close links with David Lloyd George, the head of the newly-created Inventions Department of the Ministry of Munitions who was becomingly increasingly distraught with the level of casualties in France: renewed army interest was finally evinced. At the same time a GHQ officer in France, Major Glyn, had been sufficiently impressed with Swinton's initial approach to press for army liaison with the Landship Committee. It was decided at the end of June to invite four army representatives on to the Landship Committee, which thus became a joint-service body with the army's Director of Fortifications as chairman. A number of RNAS personnel were transferred to the army to ease the task of bringing the new type of weapon to fruition and additional impetus was given to the work by an about-turn in the attitude of GHQ in France, which now saw the new machine as offering a sensible alternative to the head-on artillery and infantry assaults that were continuously proving themselves such costly failures.

Meanwhile Swinton had been evolving his particular concept, formalized in a series of memoranda reflecting the demands of a front-line machine. These thoughts were combined in a specification issued on 9 June for a machine with the following characteristics: a 4-mph (6.4-km/h) maximum speed on flat ground, a 20-mile (32-km) radius of action, the ability to make a sharp turn at maximum speed, a reversing capability, the ability to climb a 5-ft (1.52-m) parapet with a 1-in-1 slope, the ability to cross an 8-ft (2.44-m) trench, a crew of 10, and an armament of one light quick-firing gun plus two machine-guns. Swinton also called for armour up to 12 mm (0.47 in) thick, and ultimately a 6-pdr (57-mm) naval gun rather than the 2-pdr (40-mm) pom-pom originally envisaged.

The Landship Committee had now decided to end further exploration of the articulated chassis, in favour of a new vehicle roughly equivalent to one half of the articulated machine, but engineered for the specific military demands of service on the Western Front. On 2 July (confirmed on 24 July) the work was entrusted to Fosters, under the design leadership of Tritton with Wilson as his deputy and the Landship Committee's representative. This vehicle was to use the lengthened Bullock tracks and additional suspension units ordered during May, in combination with the standard 105-hp (78.3-kW) Foster-Daimler petrol engine.

At last real progress could be made and the new prototype, variously known as the Tritton Machine or No.1 Lincoln Machine, was soon taking shape after the start of construction on 11 August. The vehicle emerged as a box-like hull of boiler plate, the standard Foster powerplant and transmission driving the lengthened Bullock tracks low-mounted at the base of the hull on each side. Provision was made in the hull roof for a centrally-mounted turret accommodating a 2-pdr (40-mm) naval gun (though only a dummy turret was ever fitted) and steering was effected by a combination of differential braking and/or movement of the two 4.5-ft (1.37-m) diameter wheels projecting from the rear of the hull on a bogie frame. The vehicle had an overall length of 26.5 ft (8.08 m), and a height of 10.17 ft (3.10 m), and a fully-laden weight of some 32,480 lb (14,733 kg). With a crew of between four and six men, it could attain 3.5 mph (5.6 km/h) under favourable conditions. The No.1 Lincoln Machine was first run on 10 September 1915, but immediately encountered problems as a result of the inadequate Bullock tracks, which were easily shed and had poor grip, even in good going.

Tritton and Wilson realized that the tracks would have to be completely revised, and laun-

ched a high-priority effort to produce an effective type. Considerable experimental work was undertaken before the two men evolved a new and mechanically simpler type of track, based on lengthened track frames with rollers carrying the tracks proper, each comprising cast steel shoes riveted to links fitted with guides that engaged the inside of the track frames. Fitted with this radically improved type of track the No.1 Lincoln Machine became 'Little Willie', which emerged in December 1915 and immediately showed itself superior to the original: the tracks were more reliable, and allowed Little Willie to cross a 5-ft (1.52-m) trench and to climb a 4.5-ft (1.37-m) parapet: the equivalent figures for the machine in its original form were 4 ft (1.22 m) and 2 ft (0.61 m). In other respects, Little Willie was similar to the No.1 Lincoln Machine.

Little Willie was obsolescent even as it appeared, however, for even before the No.1 Lincoln Machine had started its trials, the ingenious Wilson had come up with a notion to overcome the original design's lack of stability when surmounting obstacles. Wilson's inspired idea was to combine the parapet-climbing capability of the original big-wheel notion with the advantages of the tracked concept: a new machine was planned on the basis of the existing hull, but with the tracks running round the full height of the hull and over 'horns' projecting forward and aft from the hull on

Shrouded in tarpaulins for security purposes, the epoch-making No.1 Lincoln Machine is seen at the Foster works in Lincoln. Note the Bullock tracks with negligible forward rise, and the rear bar connecting the tank with the twin steering wheels. (*RAC Tank Museum*)

13

Little Willie is seen during its trials at Burton Park surmounting a sharp rise exaggerated by a large sandbag. Notable is the considerably higher rise of the forward end of the trackwork. (*RAC Tank Museum*)

each side, to provide over the lower forward section an arc approximately equivalent to that of a 60-ft (18.3-m) diameter wheel.

The result was the rhomboidal- or lozenge-shaped tank that became standard in the First World War, combining the parapet-climbing superiority of the bigwheel concept with the trench-crossing, stability and silhouette advantages of the tracked chassis. The Land-ship Committee was shown a wooden mock-up of Wilson's design at the time of the No.1 Lincoln Machine's trials in September. As a further aid to stability in the revised concept, the roof-mounted turret was abandoned in favour of a heavier armament located in two hull-side sponsons. The specification for the vehicle, which was eventually called 'Big Willie', was settled on 29 September: frontal armour 10 mm (0.39 in) thick, side armour 8 mm (0.315 in) thick, a crew of eight (including four men for steering and gear changing), a speed of 4 mph (6.4 km/h), and a main armament of two 6-pdr (57-mm) guns backed by four 0.303-in (7.7-mm) machine-guns.

The building of the new machine was seriously hampered by labour problems at Fosters, where the secrecy of the work was such that the men could not be given war worker badges and began to leave when they

were accused of cowardice for not having volunteered for the services. During construction, the machine was variously called 'the Wilson Machine', 'the Centipede' and 'Big Willie', but finally emerged at the end of 1915 as 'Mother', weighing 62,720 lb (28,450 kg) and capable of 3.7 mph (5.95 km/h) on its 105-hp (78.3-kW) Foster-Daimler engine. Built of boiler plate, rather than the lightweight pressed steel proposed for the production version, the machine was 32.5 ft (9.91 m) long including the twin steering wheels at the rear, 13.75 ft (4.19 m) wide over the sponsons, and 8 ft (2.44 m) high. In the front of each sponson was a naval 6-pdr (57 mm) quick-firing gun, the four machine-guns being disposed one in the rear of each sponson, one in the bow and one at the rear. Naval guns were used, as the army's Master General of the Ordnance was opposed to the tank concept and therefore refused to release any weapons for use in the new machines.

Mother first ran on 3 December 1915, at about the time that the cover name 'water carrier' (soon amended to 'tank') was ordained at Swinton's instigation, in preference to the revealing 'landship'. After initial and successful running trials, Mother was fully completed on 26 January 1916 and moved, together with Little Willie, to Hatfield Park for two official trials

Mother (Tank Mk I)
(UK)

Type: battle tank prototype
Crew: 8
Combat weight: 62,720 lb (28,450 kg)
Dimensions: length overall with steering tail 32.50 ft (9.91 m); width over sponsons 13.75 ft (4.19 m); height 8.00 ft (2.44 m)
Armament system: two 6-pdr (57-mm) guns with 332 rounds and four 8-mm (0.315-in) Hotchkiss machine-guns with 6,272 rounds
Armour: between 6 and 10 mm (0.24 and 0.4 in)
Powerplant: one 105-hp (78.3-kW) Foster-Daimler petrol engine with 50 Imp. gal. (227 litres) of fuel
Performance: speed, road 3.7 mph (5.95 km/h); range, road 24 miles (38.6 km); gradient 24%; vertical obstacle 4.50 ft (1.37 m); trench 11.50 m (3.51 m) with steering tail, ground clearance 16 in (0.406 m)

and demonstrations. The first was attended only by those intimately involved in tank development, but four days later on 2 February the main demonstration was attended by such dignitaries as the Secretary of State for War (Field Marshal Lord Kitchener), the Minister of Munitions (Mr D. Lloyd George) and the Chancellor of the Exchequer (Mr R. McKenna). Both tanks were put through trials across terrain very similar to that of the Western Front (complete with British and German trench layouts), and Mother was judged worthy of production. As the Ministry of Munitions had in December refused to allow tank production, Kitchener ordered Lieutenant Stern of the RNAS to the War Office to oversee production on a direct basis, and this had the desired effect of forcing the ministry's hand: on 12 February the ministry ordered the production of 100 tanks based on Mother (25 by

Again seen during trials at Burton Park, this is the first true prototype tank, known as Mother, and noteworthy as the pioneer of the 'First World War shape', with a rhomboidal profile and side sponsons for the armament. (*RAC Tank Museum*)

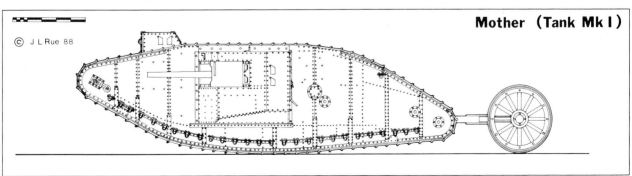

© J L Rue 88

Mother (Tank Mk I)

Fosters and the other 75 by the Metropolitan Carriage, Wagon and Finance Co.) in a programme to be overseen by the Landship Committee, now renamed the Tank Supply Committee and headed by Stern, and including Swinton as a member.

Churchill was now in France, having been forced to resign in May 1915 when a coalition government took over from the Liberal administration after the failure of the Dardanelles campaign, but had tried to keep up with developments. Though now 'only' a regimental officer, Churchill sent to Field Marshal Sir Douglas Haig, the British Commander-in-Chief in France, a paper entitled *Variants of the Offensive* which, while exaggerating the state of tank development, persuaded Haig to despatch Major Hugh Elles to report personally on the new weapon. It was Elles' approval that persuaded Haig to think in terms of an order for 40 tanks, which led to the initial plan for 100 vehicles, later increased to 150 vehicles.

In March 1916 the new tank arm was formed under Swinton, initially as the Armoured Car Section, Motor Machine Gun Service and then from May as the less revealing Heavy Section, Machine Gun Corps. After the tank had been used in action the name was changed again in November 1916 to the Heavy Branch, Machine Gun Corps, and finally in July 1917 to the Tank Corps. As the men for the new branch were being found and trained, production of the service version of Mother, the Tank Mk I, was being undertaken for the first deliveries to be made in June. At first it was planned that the production model should be all but identical with Mother, other than construction in mild steel rather than boiler plate and the installation of a frame of wood and chicken wire over the roof to prevent 'bombs' (grenades) from detonating on it. The armament sponsons projected about 3 ft (0.91 m) from each side of the tank, and were therefore designed to be removed for separate (or towed) carriage, to ease transport problems. Each sponson weighed some 3,920 lb (1,778 kg), and required about eight hours to remove or replace in the field with skids and levers (assuming that the hull had not been 'wrung' in transit, thereby moving out of alignment the bolt holes that had to be matched by those in

the sponsons).

In April 1916 Swinton decided that a proportion of the tanks (ultimately fixed at half of the production run) should be completed with the Hotchkiss 6-pdr (57-mm) guns replaced by two machine-guns. The more powerfully-armed variant was designated Tank Mk I Male, and at a combat weight of 62,720 lb (28,450 kg) carried an armament of two Hotchkiss L/40 guns (each with 166 rounds) in limited-movement mountings allowing traverse out to an angle of 120° from the centreline, plus three or four Hotchkiss machine-guns (with a total of 6,272 rounds of ammunition): the role of this variant was to tackle guns, emplacements and other fixed defences. The lighter variant, having a combat weight of 60,480 lb (27,434 kg), was designated Tank Mk I Female, and carried an armament of one or two Hotchkiss air-cooled machine-guns plus four water-cooled Vickers machine-guns (in place of the Male's guns and sponson-mounted machine-guns), with a total of 30,080 rounds of ammunition: the role of this variant was protection of the heavier Males from infantry attack, and pursuit of enemy infantry.

The men of the new army branch were soon coming to grips with their extraordinary new machines, which held great promise but were extremely uncomfortable: the Tank Mk I lacked any form of sprung suspension, vision of the outside world was limited by the small size of the few vision slits, the engine was unsilenced (meaning that internal communication had to undertaken largely by hand signalling) and ventilation was virtually non-existent. As operations were shortly to confirm, while the tank's construction (soft steel, cut and drilled and then hardened before being bolted together) may have provided protection from small arms fire, it was totally prone to spall and splash when struck on the outside: this meant that the crew had to wear thick clothing and face protection to avoid being wounded by the shards sent flying off the inside of the armour when it was struck on the outside (spall), or hit by the molten metal that penetrated between the tank's ill-fitting plates when bullets melted on hitting the tank (splash).

The Tank Mk I had a crew of eight comprising the commander/brakesman and driver in the front with their heads in the central cupola, four gunners in the central portion, and two gearsmen in the rear section. Modest steering capability was provided by the tail in good conditions, but major course corrections required a four-man effort in which the gear driving the track on the inside of the turn was put into neutral while that on the outside was operated in first or second gear until the turn had been accomplished, whereupon the same drive was applied to both tracks. The steering tail increased trench-crossing capability from 10 to 11.5 ft (3.05 to 3.51 m) but proved a great hindrance in operations, being easily damaged or clogged with mud, and from November 1916 was abandoned. Most of the vehicles so modified were then fitted with a substantial shelf between the rear horns, for the carriage of equipment such as a towing hawser.

The tank went into action for the first time on 15 September 1916 in one of the subsidiary battles of the Battle of the Somme, namely the Battle of Flers-Courcelette: here the British Reserve and 4th Armies were to punch a four mile (6.4-km) hole in the German line at Flers and Courcelette in the sector between Thiepval and Combles, the 10 assault divisions being supported by a proposed 50 tanks. Such was the technical infancy of the new weapon that some 18 Mk Is had broken down before the assault started, and the surviving 32 machines were allocated in penny packets (the largest mass being seven tanks) as what were in effect mobile pillboxes that could crush wire and lead the infantry into German positions. In the event the tanks did well, but their role was hopelessly wrong and their effect was thus small when the Battle of Flers-Courcelette fizzled out at the end of the day.

But though the tanks' actual successes had been poor, their use had finally persuaded the sceptical officers in France that here was a potentially decisive weapon, and tank orders were stepped up as the tank arm was increased in personnel size to 9,000 by February 1917 and 20,000 by the time of the Armistice in November 1918. After Flers-Courcelette Haig requested the production of another 1,000 tanks. Stern moved swiftly to order the required armour and powerplants, though the limited power of the Foster-Daimler petrol en-

gine led this astute pioneer to consider alternatives to this weakest feature of the Tank Mk I. That the army as a whole was still uncommitted to the tank found expression in the Army Council's 10 October cancellation of Haig's order, but this was reinstated when Stern went straight to Lloyd George, who was now a keen advocate of any device that could reduce the horific toll of head-on infantry battles. Lloyd George was to become prime minister on 6 December, and Stern persuaded him of the need not only for more tanks, but for better tanks. An improved machine was now under development as the Tank Mk IV, and to keep the production line open until this was ready Lloyd George allowed production of 100 examples of the Tanks Mk II and III, essentially Mk Is with detail modifications: the Mk II (50 built) had a revised roof hatch with raised coaming and wider track shoes at every sixth link for greater traction, while the Mk III (50 built) was the Mk II uparmoured to the standard of the Mk IV. The Mk II and III complemented the Mk Is in the trench battles of early 1917 at Arras (9–15 April), Messines (7 June) and Third Ypres (31 July to 10 November), but these first three models were rapidly superseded by the Mk IV during the second half of 1917. Once discarded as first-line tanks, the Mks I, II and III were used as training tanks or as wireless tanks (one sponson fitted out as a 'wireless office' and the other carrying the wireless equipment) or, with their sponsons removed and the resultant openings plated over, as supply tanks, known at the time as tank tenders, fitted with sponson-like side panniers each 3 ft (0.91 m) wide and made of mild steel: like the standard sponsons, these panniers were rectangular and all too prone to embedding themselves in the mud when the tank tipped sideways or forward. The Mk IV tank introduced sponsons with upward-swept lower sides, but this more practical design was not carried forward to the supply tenders' panniers. Each supply tank could also tow three sleds each carrying 22,400 lb (10,160 kg) of stores, and in the case of Mk IV conversions an uprated 125-hp (93.2-kW) engine was often fitted, to provide greater traction power. These supply tanks were generally used to ferry forward ammunition and fuel, and to carry back

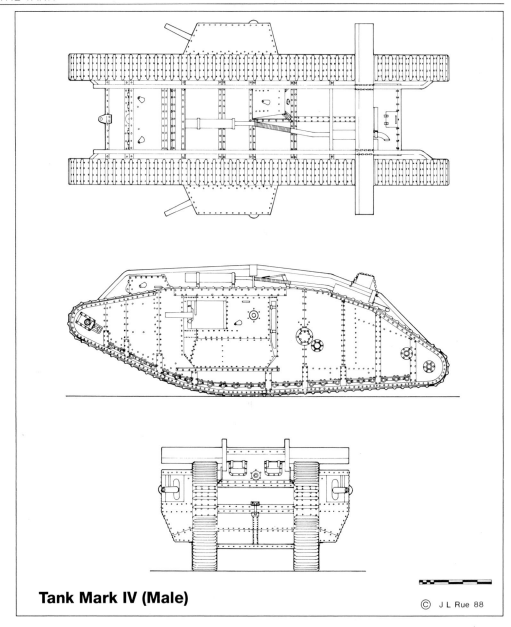

Tank Mark IV (Male)

© J L Rue 88

the most seriously wounded.

By February 1917 the Tank Mk IV was ready for production. The type still relied on the indifferent Foster-Daimler engine and its associated gear system, but was otherwise a much improved vehicle, incorporating the lessons of Flers-Courcelette and, as they were fought, the 1917 battles. Several of the earlier tanks had suffered because of the gravity feed From their 50-Imp. gal. (227-litre) internal fuel tank, which also leaked petrol over the inside of the tank if it was punctured, and failed to work if the tank was trying to climb up to or down from a steep parapet: in the Mk IV, therefore, the tank was moved to the outside of the vehicle between the rear horns, increased in capacity to 70 Imp. gal. (318 litres), provided with armour and fitted with a pump to

A British Tank Mk IV Male in First World War conditions typical of those it was designed to conquer. (*IWM*)

Tank Mk IV (Male)
(UK)

Type: battle tank
Crew: 8
Combat weight: 62,720 lb (28,450 kg)
Dimensions: length overall 26.42 ft (8.05 m); width 13.50 ft (4.115 m); height 8.17 ft (2.49 m) overall
Armament system: two 6-pdr (57-mm) Hotchkiss QF L/23 rifled guns (one in the forward part of each sponson) with 332 rounds and four 0.303-in (7.7-mm) Lewis machine-guns (one bow, one tail and one on the rear portion of each sponson) with 6,272 rounds; the main guns were stabilized in neither elevation nor azimuth (120° out from the forward centreline), and simple optical sights were fitted
Armour: riveted steel varying in thickness between 6.35 and 12.7 mm (0.25 and 0.5 in)
Powerplant: one 105-hp (78.3-kW) Daimler petrol engine with 70 Imp. gal. (318.2 litres) of fuel
Performance: speed, road 3.7 mph (6 km/h); range, road 35 miles (56.3 km); fording 4.5 ft (1.37 m) without preparation; gradient 47%; vertical obstacle 4.5 ft (1.37 m); trench 10.0 ft (3.05 m); ground clearance 16 in (0.41 m)

ensure an uninterrupted flow of petrol. Other major improvements were the use of thicker armour (16 mm/0.63 in at the front, and 12 mm/0.47 in declining to 8 mm/0.315 in elsewhere) to defeat the Germans' new anti-tank rifle bullets; steel 'spuds' bolted to every third, fifth or ninth track shoe to increase traction in heavy going; smaller sponsons that could be hinged inboard, rather than having to be re-moved for transport; an exhaust and external silencer for the engine; improved internal stowage, ventilation and cooling; shorter 6-pdr (57-mm) L/23 guns to prevent the muzzles digging into the ground; an unditching beam carried above the vehicle on special rails; and 0.303-in (7.7-mm) Lewis machine-guns in place of the original Hotchkiss weapons in ball-and-socket mountings that allowed 90° movement in elevation and traverse. Experience soon confirmed that the Lewis gun was unsuitable for tank use, as its air-cooling system filled the tank with fumes, the gun itself was vulnerable to enemy fire, and the need for a large opening in the sponson to accommodate the Lewis gun's air-cooling jacket increased the problem of splash: a revised Hotchkiss was then substituted, though without the original form of very limited-movement trunnion mounting.

After development from October 1916, Mk IV tanks were delivered from April 1917, and production of 1,015 tanks was undertaken in the ratio of three female to two male tanks. The Tank Mk IV Female was somewhat different to the earlier females, for the sponsons were shallower (allowing the incorporation of a pair of hatches on each side in the area previously covered by the sponson) and narrower at only 1.25 ft (0.381 m). The lighter weight of these sponsons contributed significantly to the reduction in combat weight to 58,240 lb (26,418 kg).

The growing sophistication of the tank is attested to by the development of several Mk IV variants, as dictated by the nature of combat experience. There had been some criticism of the November 1916 decision to eliminate the rear steering wheels, as this also reduced trench-crossing capability, and in an effort to improve this capability once more, Tritton in 1917 suggested the lengthening of the tank by 9 ft (2.74 m) through the extension of the rear horns. These extensions were of mild steel, strapped and riveted to the original structure, and braced diagonally by stays to provide a rigid frame for tracks, each lengthened by the insertion of 28 extra shoes and driven by a lengthened drive. Trials were also conducted with a 6-in (152-mm) Newton and Stokes mortar on a platform inserted between the rear horns to fire forward over the hull. Some interesting results were achieved with the 'tadpole tail' and mortars, but the lengthened horns lacked rigidity and were not put into production.

Even the tadpole tail could not offer much hope for the crossing of the extra-wide trenches built by the Germans in their so-called 'Hindenburg Line' defences, and to overcome this problem there was evolved the Mk IV Fascine Tank. In its original form this could carry wooden fascines on its unditching beam rails, these chain-bound bundles of brush-

A Tank Mk IV Female, converted as a fascine carrier, seen at the Plateau railhead in France during November 1917. (*RAC Tank Museum*)

wood, each 10 ft (3.05 m) in length and 4.5 ft (1.37 m) in diameter, being dropped over the nose under control of the driver; later versions carried hexagonal wood or steel cribs for the same purpose of filling the trench and providing a roadway for the tank's further progress.

Ditching was always a problem with the First World War British tanks and several experimental unditching systems were evaluated as alternatives to the standard beam. Some of these were promising, but none got past the evaluation phase. There were also salvage tanks of several patterns, developed in the field for recovery and maintenance work: these were generally fitted with a manually-operated jib crane for tasks such as engine changes.

When the Germans first began to put tanks in the field during April 1918, the British realized that their blend of male and female tanks was perhaps not ideal, for the female tank was distinctly vulnerable to the efforts of the German tanks. The result was the Tank Mk IV Hermaphrodite, essentially a standard Mk IV Female with one of its sponsons replaced by the gun-armed sponson of a Mk IV Male tank, to provide a blend of male and female firepower.

The key moment for the Tank Mk IV, and indeed for the tank in general, came on 20 November 1917 with the beginning of the Battle of Cambrai. This was the first occasion on which tanks were used in a homogeneous mass, and the practice nearly proved decisive. The British Third Army was entrusted with a surprise offensive against the German Second Army: in ideal terrain conditions to the south of Cambrai, the army was to attack without the protracted artillery bombardment that had previously been standard, this novel concept being designed to give the Germans no fore-warning of the offensive, and to prevent the ground from being churned up. This ensured excellent going for the 400 tanks that spear-headed the offensive behind a sharp creeping barrage that forced the Germans to keep their heads down. Tactical surprise was achieved by the new concept, and the tanks were instrumental in opening a six-mile (9.7-km) gap in the German line, through which the British ad-

Above A Tank Mk IV in pristine condition just after presentation to the British government by the president of the Federal Council of the Malay States. Well shown is the riveted construction of the hull and sponsons from comparatively small pieces of plate. (*IWM*)

Left A British Tank Mk IV in action during the First World War: this is a male tank, with a 6-pdr (57-mm) main gun in the forward part of each sponson, and carries an unditching beam above the hull.

Above Seen in a German army workshop near Cambrai in September 1918 are a pair of Beutepanzerwagen IV vehicles, captured British Tank Mk IVs fitted with German armament. (*Bundesarchiv*)

Right Two Beutepanzerwagen IVs, complete with trench-filling fascines, are put through their paces behind the German front in the summer of 1918. *Liesel* appears to be ditched, with *Fritz* about to tow her out of her predicament. (*Bundesarchiv*)

vanced to a depth of five miles (8 km). Two cavalry divisions were poised to exploit any advantage, but the extent of this success caught the British so unexpectedly that there were insufficient infantry and tanks in reserve to allow any rational exploitation. The Germans recovered with remarkable speed, and their counter-attacks of 30 November forced the British to fall back most of the way to their start line by 3 December. The Battle of Cambrai was thus a draw, but this fact cannot disguise the fact that the first mass use of tanks had in general secured unprecedented results.

As usual, however, the tanks had suffered large numbers of mechanical breakdowns, and many of these non-runners were captured by the Germans as they pushed back the British. Impressed with the capabilities of the tanks, and lacking their own counterparts, the Germans rushed the captured machines to their depot at Charleroi for refurbishment and rearming: in this latter aspect the 6-pdr (57-mm) guns were replaced by Sokol 57-mm guns captured from the Russians, and the 0.303-in (7.7-mm) machine-guns by 7.92-mm (0.31-in) MG08 weapons. The vehicles were then issued to the Germans' fledgling tank arm with the designation Beutepanzerwagen IV, the comparative extent of British and German tank production at this time being indicated by the fact that captured tanks equipped four of the Germans' seven tank companies in December 1917.

As noted above, Stern appreciated from the early days of the Mk I that the weakest point of the tank was its transmission/gearing and associated Foster-Daimler petrol engine. To meet operational requirements the Mk IV was rushed into production and service, even as Stern was investigating alternative power-plants, but from October 1917 the Tank Supply Department had a modest breathing space in which to consider other tank automotive systems. These included a Westinghouse petrol-electric drive with one-man control, via a separate petrol-electric generator on each track for infinitely variable speed control; a Daimler petrol-electric drive with similar capabilities; a Williams-Janney petrol-hydraulic drive, similar in concept to the petrol-electric drives, though using hydraulic rather than electric motors; a Wilkins multiple clutch drive of extraordinary complexity; and a Wilson mechanical system using epicyclic gears and brakes, instead of the standard change-speed gearing. The petrol-electric drives offered superior capabilities, but were sufficiently complex and expensive to urge on Stern the advantages of the Wilson system, which offered the possibility of one-man control without the potential problems of the petrol-electric systems.

Wilson was entrusted with the overall design of the tank to use his epicyclic gearbox,

and this emerged as the Tank Mk V with hull and armament based on those of the Mk IV but fitted with the Wilson gearbox and a new 150-hp (112-kW) Ricardo petrol engine commissioned by Stern. The Tank Mk V Male weighed 64,960 lb (29,466 kg) and the Tank Mk V Female 62,720 lb (28,450 kg), but the use of a more powerful engine boosted maximum speed to 4.6 mph (7.4 km/h), and combat radius was 45 miles (72 km) on 93 Imp gal (423 litres) of fuel in armoured external tanks. The Mk V went into production at the Birmingham works of the Metropolitan Carriage, Wagon and Finance Co. during December 1917, and began to reach service units in May 1918 in equal numbers of male and female tanks, of which a proportion were converted in the field to Tank Mk V Hermaphrodite stan-

---

Tank Mk V (Male)
(UK)

Type: battle tank
Crew: 8
Combat weight: 64,960 lb (29,466 kg)
Dimensions: length overall 26.42 ft (8.05 m); width over sponsons 13.5 ft (4.115 m) and hull 8.71 ft (2.65 m); height 8.67 ft (2.64 m)
Armament system: two 6-pdr (57-mm) guns with 332 rounds and four 8-mm (0.315-in) Hotchkiss machine-guns with 6,272 rounds
Armour: between 8 and 16 mm (0.315 and 0.63 in)
Powerplant: one 150-hp (111.8-kW) Ricardo petrol engine with 93 Imp. gal. (423 litres) of fuel
Performance: speed, road 4.6 mph (7.4 km/h); range, road 45 miles (72.4 km); vertical obstacle 4.5 ft (1.37 m); trench 10.0 ft (3.05 m); ground clearance 16 in (0.406 m)

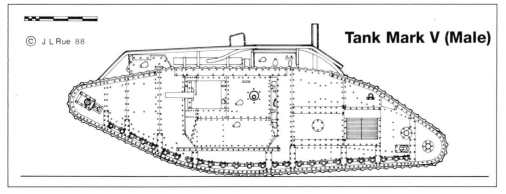

© J L Rue 88

Tank Mark V (Male)

dard. The initial 200 machines had tracks 20.5 in (521 mm) wide, but later examples had tracks 26.5 in (673 mm) wide for better performance in poor going. One-man control of the Mk V's automotive system made for considerable improvement in control and manoeuvrability, and the more powerful engine made a useful contribution to performance, but the Mk V was also a considerable advance over its predecessors in a number of ways; its better engine cooling and ventilation system; the provision of a cupola above the roof at the rear for the commander, who thus had far better fields of vision than in earlier tanks; and its facility for the underitching beam to be connected and disconnected from inside the vehicle, thereby obviating the need for at least two crew members to leave the vehicle in the fashion that had at times cost earlier tanks considerable casualties.

The Mk V first went into action at Hamel in July 1918, and thereafter partnered the more numerous Mk IV for the rest of the First World War. The tank was dimensionally similar to the Mk IV, and thus suffered the same limitations when faced with a wide trench. Not surprisingly, therefore, the Mk V was evaluated with a 'tadpole tail', but a better expedient was

A Tank Mk V Female of the 16th Battalion, Tank Corps, shows off the type's 13-ft (3.96-m) trench-crossing capability during British 1919 manoeuvres in occupied Germany. (*RAC Tank Museum*)

A Tank Mk V Male is put through its paces at the Tanks Corps' Central School at Bovington Camp shortly after the First World War. Clearly visible is the short-barrel 6-pdr (57-mm) main gun, the overhead stowage of the underitching beam, and the track-tensioning device associated with the forward idler. (*RAC Tank Museum*)

adopted after development by the Tank Corps Central Workshops in France from February 1918. This resulted in the Tank Mk V*, in which the vehicle was cut in half to allow the insertion of a 6-ft (1.83-m) armour section, comprising three 2-ft (0.61-m) panels, between the rear of the sponsons and the epicyclic gearbox, increasing ground length and so providing a 13-ft (3.96-m) trench-crossing capability, at an increase in weight of 8,960 lb (4,064 kg). The additional section carried two machine-gun positions to complement the standard fit based on that of the Mk IV, but already boosted by the provision of two positions in the new com-

mander's cupola. The extra weight inevitably reduced performance slightly, and manoeuvrability considerably, but the additional length had the incidental advantage of increasing internal volume to the extent that the Mk V* could be used to carry 25 troops (who suffered badly from the heat and the poor ventilation) or more usefully a substantial load of supplies. Production was undertaken by Metropolitan from May 1918, production reaching 579 examples by the time of the Armistice.

The Tank Mk V** was similar to the Mk V*, but designed as such and built in small numbers by Fosters for post-war service. The for-

In the closing stages of the First World War, the tank came into its own as an assault and exploitation weapon. These Tank Mk Vs of the 10th Battalion, Tank Corps, are passing infantry of the 37th and New Zealand Divisions near Grevillers on 26 August 1918. The Mk V lacked the differential housing (between the rear horns) of the earlier tanks, and this allowed the incorporation of a rear machine-gun. The rear vehicle has a platform between the horns for carriage of stores. (*IWM*)

In the Tank Mk V** Male the commander's cupola was brought well forward, for better fields of vision. Notable in front of this mud-spattered trials vehicle are sveral important tank pioneers, including Wilson and Ricardo (respectively first and second from left). Ricardo's 225-ph (168-kW) engine gave this vehicle useful cross-country performance. (*RAC Tank Museum*)

The sole Tank Mk VII Male used Williams-Janney hydraulic transmission for trials purposes, and was also fitted with an electric starter for its 150-hp (112-kW) Ricardo engine. (*RAC Tank Museum*)

ward rise was increased to provide better parapet-climbing capability, an uprated 225-hp (168-kW) Ricardo engine was located farther to the rear, and the commander's cupola was moved forward to a position just behind the driver's cupola. It is interesting to note that post-war development gave evidence of the tank's multiple uses: the Mk V** was developed as a Royal Engineer Tank in two forms as a carrier and launch vehicle for a 20-ft (6.1-m) bridge capable of supporting a tank, and as a mineclearing vehicle fitted with a forward roller to detonate pressure-activated mines.

The Mk V* was the ultimate version of British mainstream battle tank development to see service in World War I, no fewer than 324 Mk Vs and Mk V*s spearheading the decisive breakthrough offensive of 8 August in the Battle of Amiens, which the German commander, General Erich Ludendorff, characterized as 'the black day of the German army'. In this offensive the Mk IV and Mk V variants were partnered by a number of light tanks, but before turning to these it is perhaps sensible to complete a summary of British battle tank development in the First World War. Next in sequence came the Tank Mk VI, which was designed in December 1916 and reached mock-up form in February 1917. The type was designed to provide better cross-country performance than the Mk IV and Mk V, and the armament was

centred on a 6-pdr (57-mm) gun located in a limited-traverse mounting between the front horns, backed by four machine-guns carried in a substantial cupola above the hull roof and one machine-gun each in two small hull-side sponsons. Work was cancelled in favour of additional Mk V production to meet the German offensives in France from 21 March 1918.

The Tank Mk VII was built by Brown Brothers of Edinburgh, the sole prototype completing successful trials between October

Far right The prototype of the Tank Mk VIII, otherwise known as the International, is seen on trials in the USA. The lengthened rhomboidal shape is notable, as is the long roof turret with separate commander's cupola. (*RAC Tank Museum*)

Tank Mk VIII Liberty (or International)
(UK/USA)

Type: battle tank
Crew: 8–11
Combat weight: 82,880 lb (37,594 kg)
Dimensions: length overall 34.21 ft (10.43 m); width 12.33 ft (3.76 m); height 10.25 ft (3.12 m)
Armament system: two 6-pdr (57-mm) guns with 208 rounds and seven 8-mm (0.315-in) Hotchkiss machine-guns with 13,484 rounds
Armour: between 6 and 16 mm (0.24 and 0.35 in)
Powerplant: one 300-hp (224-kW) Ricardo or Liberty petrol engine with 200 Imp. gal. (909 litres) of fuel
Performance: speed, road 5.2 mph (8.4 km/h); range, road 55 miles (88.5 km); fording 2.83 ft (0.86 m); gradient 84%; vertical obstacle 4.50 ft (1.37 m); trench 16.00 ft (4.88 m); ground clearance 21 in (0.53 m)

and November 1917. The Mk VII was based on the Mk V but with a 3-ft (0.91-m) longer tail for improved trench-crossing capability, and the electrically started 150-hp (112-kW) Ricardo petrol engine was used to power twin William-Janney hydraulic motors. The cross-country performance and agility of the type were most encouraging, and early in 1918 an order was placed for 75 production vehicles. Production of the Williams-Janney hydraulic motors proved troublesome, however, and only one production machine was completed before the Armistice and the wholesale cancellation of production orders.

Up to the Mk VII, British tank design had followed a linear line from the Mk I. With the Tank Mk VIII, however, all the lessons of earlier development and combat use were melded into a completely new design by the army's Mechanical Warfare Department, for joint Anglo-American production of an initial 1,500 machines. The hulls and armament were to have been provided from the UK, to be assembled with American-supplied engines, transmission systems and controls on a special assembly line in France. The tank was variously known as Anglo-American Tank, the Liberty, the International and the Allied, and the hopes vested in the machine are evidenced by the fact that the 1,500 joint-venture tanks were to be supplemented by 1,450 purely British examples and 1,500 purely American examples, for a grand total of 4,450 Mk VIIIs.

The Mk VIII design was modelled on the standard rhomboidal shape that had proved generally successful in previous British tanks,

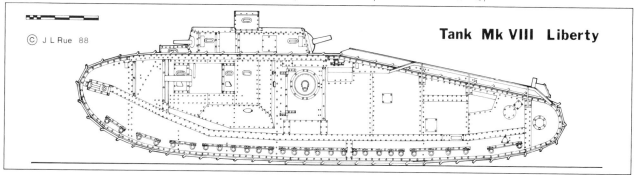

© J L Rue 88

Tank Mk VIII Liberty

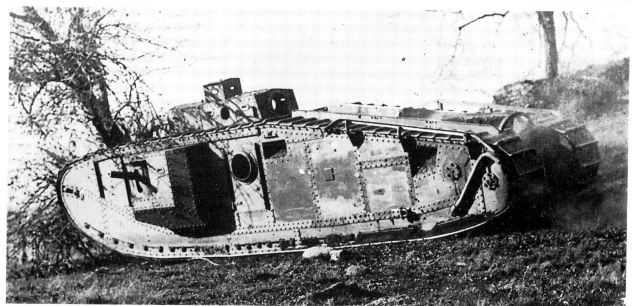

but provided with lower contours that allowed 7.5 ft (2.29 m) of contact area with the ground, by comparison with the Mk V's 4.5 ft (1.37 m), and ground clearance of 1.75 ft (0.533 m) by comparison with the earlier tanks' 1.33 ft (0.406 m). The result was a considerably heavier machine, with a combat weight of 82,880 lb (37, 594 kg). The Mk VIII was also a generally larger machine, with an overall length of 34.208 ft (10.43 m) to the Mk V's 26.417 ft (8.05 m), a width of 12.33 ft (3.76 m) to the Mk V Male's 12.83 ft (3.91 m), and a height of 10.25 ft (3.12 m) to the Mk V's 8.67 ft (2.64 m). In terms of battlefield capabilities, the additional length reduced manoeuvrability, but provided an impressive trench-crossing capability of 15 ft (4.57 m).

The crew remained the standard eight men, and the armour thicknesses were the same as those of the Mk V. The larger dimensions of the Mk VIII allowed a useful compartmentalization of the interior, with the engine and transmission in the rear section cut off from the rest of the tank by a bulkhead, for considerable improvement in terms of noise and fumes. The main armament comprised two 6-pdr (57-mm) Hotchkiss L/23 guns in the side sponsons with 104 rounds each, and the secondary armament was seven machine-guns with a total of 13,484 rounds: the machine-guns were located as one in the bow, one in each of the doors behind the sponsons, and four in the centrally-mounted main fighting turret (one in each side, one on the front left and one on the rear right). The sponsons were hinged and fitted on roller bearings, so that they could be hand-pulled into the main fighting compartment for transport, and each machine-gun was carried into a ball-and-socket mounting (itself carried in a spherical mounting) to allow 130° movement. The main fighting turret was also fitted with a commander's rotating sub-turret offering a 360° field of vision.

Considerable difficulties were encountered with the design and final development of the Mk VIII, the most troublesome individual component being the 300-hp (224-kW) engine. In the joint and American versions, this was a V-12 Liberty, adapted from the standard aeroplane engine by lowering the compression ratio and using cast iron rather than steel

cylinders. In the British version the engine was a V-12 Ricardo, produced by mounting two 150-hp (112-kW) Ricardo V-6 engines on a common crankcase. Under good conditions the Ricardo unit provided a maximum speed of 7 mph (11.25 km/h) in a lightly-loaded Mk VIII. Some 200 Imp. gal. (909 litres) of fuel were carried in three armoured tanks at the rear, and pump-fed to a gravity tank above the engine, surplus fuel being vented back into the main tankage by an overflow pipe. This fuel tankage provided a 55-mile (88.5-km) combat radius. Considerable thought was given to engine cooling, and the location of the engine in its own compartment greatly aided the designers, who opted for a system in which air was drawn in through a roof louvre to pass round the engine and through the rear-mounted radiator before being expelled by a fan through a rear louvre. Compartmentalization also allowed proper ventilation of the fighting section, by means of an electrically-powered fan that created a slight internal overpressure, that was vented through any available opening to take with it any gun fumes.

Mild steel prototypes had been successfully trialled by the end of the war, and a large number of components had been produced for assembly in the unfinished French factory at Nervy-Pailloux. The programme was cancelled at the end of the war, but in 1919 and 1920 the Americans used existing components to build 100 tanks at the Rock Island Arsenal: these differed from the wartime standard only in having 0.3-in (7.62-mm) Browning machine-guns instead of Hotchkiss machine-guns, and formed the mainstay of the US tank arm up to 1932, when they were placed in storage and finally used by Canada as training machines in the early days of the Second World War.

The final designations in the mainstream of British battle tanks during World War I were the Tank Mk IX and Tank Mk X. The Mk IX was really a supply tank based mechanically on the Mk V, and at a combat weight of 60,480 lb (27,434 kg) could carry 50 troops or 22,400 lb (10,161 kg) of supplies, with access through four large side hatches; only three prototypes were completed. In 1919 one of these was modified for amphibious trials, being fitted with a raised cab, high exhausts and ex-naval 'camel' flotation chambers. The Mk X was schemed as a revised Mk V, with modifications intended to increase habitability, reliability and manoeuvrability. If the war had continued into 1919, some 2,000 Mk Xs would have been ordered as the backbone of the tank army around which the assault into Germany was being planned.

The Allied concept of military operations after November 1914 had been posited, without any significant deviation, on a breakthrough of the German line and exploitation into the enemy rear. Even before the battle tank had begun to prove itself as a weapon for the breakthrough phase, tank advocates had begun to work on a lighter and more mobile tank suitable for the exploitation phase, for the battle tank was clearly too slow and too short-ranged for any but the most direct battlefield tasks. In 1916 Tritton designed a high-speed tank with light armour for the task of co-operating with the cavalry, and this initial 'Whippet' scheme was revised from December 1916 as the Tritton Chaser or, more prosaically, the Tritton No.2 Light Machine. The type first ran in February 1917, and trials were generally successful. Various changes were required before a firm order was placed in June 1917. The definitive version became the Medium Tank Mk A, generally named the Whippet, and deliveries from Foster's works in

Lincoln began in October 1917, to meet the initial requirement for 200 machines. This order was subsequently increased to 385 machines, and then reduced once more to 200 when it became clear that the double automotive system of the Mk A was both expensive to produce and difficult to maintain at a reasonable standard of reliability.

The overall design of the Whippet was totally different from that of the battle tanks, with long, low-set unsprung tracks whose shoes were based on those of battle tanks, but of lighter construction and fitted with provision for spuds: the tracks were long enough to provide a 7-ft (2.13-m) trench-crossing capability. The track units were fitted on each side with four chutes along much of the length of the top run to keep the tracks clear of mud, and thus lighter. The long forward section of the hull above the upper run of the tracks accommodated two 45-hp (33.6-kW) Taylor four-cylinder in-line engines (used mainly for lorries), located side-by-side and each provided with its own clutch and gearbox to drive one track. Twin throttles were located on the steering wheel, their movement together controlling acceleration to a maximum speed of 8.3 mph (13.4 km/h) in this 31,360-lb (14,225-kg) vehicle. Steering was effected by the driver's steering wheel, whose movement worked on the throttles to increase the power of one engine and decrease that of the other (to a

This painting of a Medium Tank Mk A 'Whippet' reveals the salient design features of this pioneering British cavalry tank. (*IWM*)

maximum variation of 12 hp/8.95 kW) and so provide additional power to one track or the other: the system was complex and extremely demanding on the driver, who could easily stall one engine in a tight turn and then shed a track, thus immobilizing the vehicle. An armoured tank in the extreme nose held 70 Imp. gal. (318 litres) of petrol, fed to the engines by a pump, and this capacity was sufficient for a combat radius of 80 miles (129 km).

The crew of three or four was located in the fighting compartment at the rear of the vehicle. This compartment was essentially a fixed barbette (the original notion of a rotating turret having been abandoned to simplify production), and, in addition to the driver, was occupied by the commander and one or two gunners, with between them three or four Hotchkiss machine-guns (plus 5,400 rounds of ammunition) for all-round fire. The second gunner and the Hotchkiss in the rear of the barbette were generally omitted by operational units, to mitigate the appalling conditions inside the barbette. Armour varied from a minimum of 6 mm (0.24 in) to a maximum of 12 mm (0.47 in).

The type first saw action in March 1918 near Herbertune in northern France, and was used up to the end of the war. The type's greatest moment came in the Battle of Amiens on 8 August 1918, involving the 3rd Tank Brigade's two battalions, which were fully equipped with 96 Mk As. The brigade was tasked with support of the Cavalry Corps, and though liaison was poor, some useful results were gained. The major tactical problem was that in good conditions the cavalry was faster than the tank brigade, but had to wait for the tanks to catch up and deal with opposition armed with anything but small arms. The result was that the tanks were not employed in a homogeneous mass that might have completely destroyed the German rear areas to a depth of 10 miles (16 km) or more. The Mk As were used in small numbers attached to specific cavalry units, but nonetheless achieved successes that fully vindicated their overall capabilities.

Obviously the type was limited by its use of two low-powered engines and unsprung tracks, and in an effort to overcome this limitation Major Philip Johnson, an Army Service

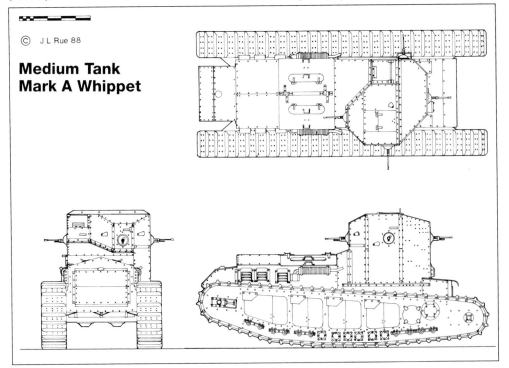

© J L Rue 88

**Medium Tank
Mark A Whippet**

Medium Tank Mk A
(UK)

Type: medium tank
Crew: 3–4
Combat weight: 31,360 lb (14,225 kg)
Dimensions: length overall 20.00 ft (6.10 m); width 8.58 ft (2.62 m); height overall 12.60 ft (2.74 m)
Armament system: three or four 0.303-in (7.7-mm) Hotchkiss machine-guns (for use in the four ball mountings located one in each face of the fixed barbette) with 5,400 rounds
Armour: riveted steel varying in thickness between 5 and 14 mm (0.2 and 0.55 in)
Powerplant: two 45-hp (33.6-kW) Tylor JB petrol engines with 70 Imp. gal. (318.2 litres) of fuel
Performance: speed, road 8.3 mph (13.4 km/h); range, road 80 miles (128.75 km); fording 3.0 ft (0.91 m); gradient 84%; vertical obstacle 2.625 ft (0.8 m); trench 7.0 ft (2.13 m); ground clearance 22 in (0.56 m)

Corps officer serving at the Tank Corps Central Workshops in France, reworked the design with sprung tracks and a 360-hp (268-kW) Rolls-Royce Eagle aero engine working through the transmission of a Mk V battle tank: speeds well over 20 mph (32 km/h) were achieved, but this important advance failed to find favour.

As noted above, production of the Mk A was limited to just 200 machines, a fact ensured by the development of the Medium Tank Mk B, whose arrival in service was anticipated in good time for the grand tank offensive designed to finish off Germany in 1919 (see below). The Mk B was also called the Whippet, but in this instance was designed by Wilson and bore closer conceptual affinities to current battle tanks than to the Mk A, though intended for the same cavalry or exploitation role.

The Mk B was based on a new automative system using a 100-hp (76-kW) four-cylinder version of Harry Ricardo's 150-hp (112-kW) six-cylinder battle tank engine, located at the rear of the hull in the first instance of a tank engine in its own compartment. The fan-cooled engine drove the twin tracks via epicyclic gearing, and provided greater levels of manoeuvrability with much improved reliability and reduced production cost. The rest of the vehicle was also different from the Mk A, being based on the rhomboidal shape of contemporary battle tanks with the tracks running right round the hull and its projecting front and rear horns. On each side of the Mk B were three large chutes to clear mud from the upper run of the tracks.

At 7 and 2.5 ft (2.13 and 0.76 m) respectively, the Mk A's trench-crossing and parapet-climbing capabilities were notably poor: the shape of the Mk B improved these figures considerably, the trench-crossing figure to 8.5 ft (2.59 m). Inevitably the Mk B was a larger and, at a combat weight of 40,320 lb (18,289 kg), heavier tank. The crew of four comprised the driver, commander and two gunners, all accommodated in a large barbette at the front of the tank. The Mk B was proposed in two forms, a female with the standard armament of four Hotchkiss machine-guns plus a total of 7,500 rounds of ammunition, and a male with a revolving turret carrying a 2-pdr (40-mm) gun: only the female type was produced. Armour was comparable to that of the Mk A, though the thinnest plates were to a 6- rather than 5-mm (0.24- rather than 0.2-in) basis.

Medium Tank Mk A 'Whippet' of the 3rd Battalion, Tank Corps, near Maillet Mailly on 26 March 1918 with infantry of the New Zealand Division. This was a crisis period for the Allies, and the Whippet had been used in action for the first time earlier on the same day. (*IWM*)

As this painting conveys, the Medium Tank Mk A was not best suited to the rough terrain of the First World War's front-line areas, as it was designed for fast movement after a breakthrough by heavier tanks. (*IWM*)

Other features of the Mk B were removable rear decking to provide access to the engine compartment, a crude smoke-generation system, whereby sulphonic acid was dripped onto the hot exhaust from a special tank, and provision for electric or hand starting. Design work was completed late in 1917, but it was mid-1918 before the first production order was placed with the Metropolitan Carriage, Wagon and Finance Co. for 450 vehicles: this delay was caused in part by the need for modifications to the original design, and in part by the caution of the army, which wished to assess the capabilities of the first medium tank (the Mk A), before committing scarce production facilities to a successor. The first vehicle appeared in September 1918, and only 45 had been completed by the time of the Armistice, when all further production was cancelled. The Mk B displayed a maximum speed of only 6.1 mph (9.8 km/h) and a combat radius of 65 miles (105 km) on 85 Imp. gal. (386 litres) of fuel, so outright performance was well down on that of the Mk A. Other criticism of the Mk B centred on the engine installation: all appreciated the fact that its separation from the rest of the tank by a bulkhead reduced the problem of engine noise and fumes in the fighting compartment, but the compact nature of the engine compartment meant that the entire engine had often to be lifted out for even the most minor of maintenance tasks.

As Wilson worked on the development of

the Mk B, Tritton was involved on his own successor to the Mk A, in the form of the Medium Tank Mk C, generally known as the Hornet and judged to have been the best medium tank design evolved in the First World War. The Mk C bore a strong conceptual similarity to the Mk B (a rear engine, all-round tracks and a forward fighting compartment, complete with a rotating cupola for the commander), and the basic design was completed at about the same time, in December 1917. Again like the Mk B, the Mk C was offered in male and female forms, the male with a 6-pdr (57-mm) gun located in the hull front and the female with four Hotchkiss machine-guns plus 7,200 rounds. The engine was the 150-hp (112-kW) six-cylinder version of the Ricardo tank engine,

Medium Tank Mk C Hornet (UK)

Type: medium cavalry tank
Crew: 4
Combat weight: 44,800 lb (20,321 kg)
Dimensions: length overall 26.00 ft (11.79 m); width 8.33 ft (2.54 m); height 9.50 ft (2.90 m)
Armament system: four 8-mm (0.315-in) Hotchkiss machine-guns with 7,200 rounds
Armour: between 6 and 14 mm (0.24 and 0.55 in)
Powerplant: one 150-hp (111.8-kW) Ricardo petrol engine with 150 Imp. gal. (682 litres) of fuel
Performance: speed, road 7.9 mph (12.7 km/h); range, road 140 miles (225 km); vertical obstacle 4.50 ft (1.37 m); trench 10.00 ft (3.05 m)

driving the tracks by means of epicyclic gears. Tritton gave considerable attention to the engine and transmission installation, to ensure easy access for maintenance, and planned the whole design for rapid manufacture, making maximum use of sub-assemblies.

The Mk C prototype was completed in the summer of 1918 and underwent a highly successful evaluation programme, before a production order for 200 Mk C Females was placed at the beginning of October. Faith in the type was considerable, and longer-term plans called for production of 6,000 Mk Cs (4,000 females and 2,000 males) for the proposed 'Plan 1919'. Building of the Mk C was drastically curtailed at the time of the Armistice, and only 48 Mk Cs were completed, serving with considerable distinction up to 1925.

Weighing 44,800 lb (20,321 kg) the Mk C had a length of 26 ft (7.92 m) in comparison with the Mk B's 22.75 ft (6.93 m), a width of 8.33 ft (2.54 m) in comparison with 8.83 ft (2.69 m) and a height of 9.5 ft (2.90 m) in comparison with 8.5 ft (2.59 m). The Mk C's additional length contributed to a trench-crossing capability of 10 ft (3.05 m), and the type's other main performance figures included a maximum speed of 7.9 mph (12.7 km/h) and a combat radius of 140 miles (225 km) on 150 Imp. gal. (682 litres) of fuel.

The ultimate British tank design of the First World War was the Medium Tank Mk D, which was designed by the same Johnson responsible for development of the Mk A with leaf-sprung suspension and (from February 1918) a modified Eagle aero engine. It was not thought practical to modify in-service Mk As in this fashion, but the capabilities of the single experimental vehicle did not go unremarked. With the support of the corps' chief engineer, in May 1918 the Tank Corps' chief-of-staff, Colonel J.F.C. Fuller, produced his now-classic *Tactics of the Attack as Affected by the Speed and Circuit of the Medium D Tank*. This was the direct inspiration for 'Plan 1919', which envisaged a breakthrough on a 90-mile (145-km) front by concentrated masses of battle tanks (mostly Mk V** and Mk VIII types) to allow an exploitation by Mk C and Mk D medium tanks, supported by lorried infantry and close-support aircraft.

The core of the concept was the Medium Tank Mk D, the development of which was entrusted to Johnson, who capitalized on his Whippet experimental programme to suggest a machine capable of high cross-country speed as a result of its automotive system, which was to comprise a converted aero engine and sprung tracks that had two-axis freedom of movement. In basic shape the Mk D was similar to the Mk A, but convention was flouted by the fact that Johnson's layout was exactly opposite to the Mk A, with the lower end of the track at the front to provide good fields of vision and fire for the four men in the front-mounted barbette, which was well shaped and fitted for an armament of perhaps three Hotchkiss machine-guns in the female version, that was later to be supplemented by a male version with a short 6-pdr (57-mm) gun.

Medium Tank Mk C Hornet

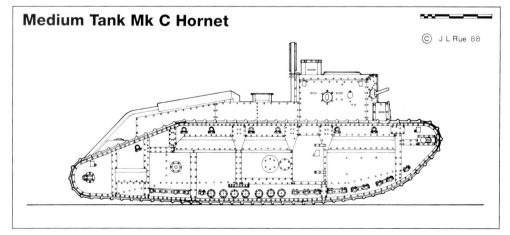

© J L Rue 88

The unusual shape of the Medium Tank Mk D was designed to provide the crew with superior fields of vision to the front, and the type also had the Johnson combination of wire rope suspension and articulated tracks for high cross-country speed. This vehicle is seen on trials in India, where asbestos cladding was added in an effort to reduce the effect of heat on the crew. (*RAC Tank Museum*)

Development was protracted, and four prototypes (the first appearing in May 1919) were followed by only two production machines before the programme was cancelled in 1921. Powered by a 240-hp (179-kW) Armstrong Siddeley Puma aero engine driving through epicyclic gears, the Mk D weighed 44,800 lb (20,321 kg) and was 30 ft (9.14 m) long. Maximum speed was 25 mph (40 km/h), and the tank's combat radius was about 200 miles (322 km).

At much the same time that Colonel Swinton was first pleading his case to the War Office for armoured fighting vehicles, the same pattern of events was emerging in France, where Colonel J.E. Estienne had seen the cross-country capability of the Holt tractor and, working from this conceptual basis, advocated the development of what he called a *cuirasse terrestre* (land battleship) to unlock the static nature of trench warfare. Estienne's ideas found ready acceptance by General Joseph Joffre, the French field commander, who saw great tactical utility for Estienne's original concept for a 4,000-kg (8,818-lb) armoured tractor with a crew of four and able to drag a 7,000-kg (15,432-lb) armoured sled carrying 20 infantrymen. The similarity to Swinton's original thinking is strong, and Estienne's tactical notion was that such an armoured force could 'sandwich' the occupants of the desired trench by pushing half its strength across the trench to isolate it and keep it under machine-gun fire.

As noted above, Joffre saw the advantages of such a combination, but was sufficiently astute to realize its impracticality. Ultimately the French army reached the same conclusions as the British about the need for a tracked armoured vehicle that could cross barbed-wire and knock out the German machine-gun posts, and so open the way for the attacking infantry. Joffre therefore ordered Estienne to Paris, there to liaise in the development of France's first tank with Eugene Brillié of the Schneider-Creusot company. Schneider-Creusot was the French licensee of the American Holt company, which had supplied one 45-hp (33.6-kW) and one 75-hp (55.9-kW) machine for trials purposes in May 1915. The basic design made extensive use of Holt components and practices, and was completed towards the end of 1915: on 31 January 1916 an order was placed for 400 of these tanks, to be designated Char d'Assaut 1 (CA 1) Schneider and delivered by November 1916. August 1916 saw the creation of the Artillerie d'Assaut, as the French tank arm was named, and in September the first CA 1 Schneiders were delivered, just before Estienne was appointed commander of the tank arm at the end of the month.

The CA 1 Schneider was based on the Holt track system, which in this application was sprung by vertical coil springs, but was notable for its short overall length and very limited forward rise. The all-important trench-crossing and parapet-climbing capabilities were therefore an indifferent 1.75 and 0.8 m (5.74 and 2.62 ft) respectively, and ground clearance was also too small to give the tank useful performance under adverse conditions. The hull was basically rectangular, with a boat-hull nose section to aid parapet-climbing and reduce the tank's chances of embedding its nose in mud, and terminated at its front in a large serrated wire cutter. At the rear were a pair of upward-curving projections, designed to improve trench-crossing capability by increasing the tank's effective length. The CA 1 Schneider was armoured to a maximum thickness of 11.5 mm (0.45 in).

The vehicle weighed 13,500 kg (29,762 lb) under combat conditions, and was powered by a 55-hp (41-kW) Schneider petrol engine located at the front left of the vehicle (with the driver to its right), driving the tracks via a crash gearbox: steering was effected by clutches and brakes on the half shafts. As in the British Mk I, the petrol tank was located internally, feeding the engine by gravity. The CA 1 Schneider had a crew of six (an officer as commander/driver, an NCO as second-in-command, and four enlisted men in the forms of gunner, loader and two machine-gunners), who entered and left the tank via large double doors in the rear. The armament was planned originally as one 37-mm gun and machine-guns, but the definitive fit comprised one short-barrel 75-mm (2.95-in) Schneider gun with 90 rounds and two 8-mm (0.315-in) Hotchkiss machine-guns with a total of 4,000 rounds. The gun was located in a narrow embrasure on the right towards the front of the vehicle, which allowed traverse of only 60° and elevation in an arc between − 10° and + 30°, severely limiting the capabilities of this otherwise useful main armament. The machine-guns were located in substantial ball-and-socket mountings on the hull sides, each mounting allowing traverse of 106° and elevation in an arc between − 45° and + 20°.

The CA 1 Schneider first saw action at Berry-au-Bac near the Chemin des Dames on 16 April 1917: of the 132 tanks committed, no fewer than 57 were destroyed and many others were damaged beyond economical

Schneider Char d'Assaut 1
(France)

Type: assault tank
Crew: 6
Combat weight: 14,600 kg (32,187 lb)
Dimensions: length overall 6.32 m (20.735 ft); width 2.05 m (6.73 ft); height 2.30 m (7.55 ft)
Armament system: one 75-mm (2.95-in) gun with 90 rounds and two 8-mm (0.315-in) machine-guns with 4,000 rounds
Armour: 11.5 mm (0.45 in) maximum
Powerplant: one 41-kW (55-hp) Schneider petrol engine
Performance: speed, road 7.5 km/h (4.6 mph); range, road 48 km (30 miles); gradient 57%; vertical obstacle 0.787 m (2.58 ft); trench 1.75 m (5.74 ft)

Bottom The Char d'Assaut Schneider CA 1 was France's first tank, its 'boat' front being designed to provide adequate climbing ability. The nosepiece was a wire-cutting device, and the very limited traverse of the 75-mm (2.95-in) gun is notable. (*RAC Tank Museum*)

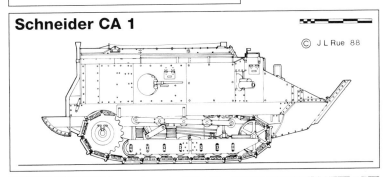

Schneider CA 1

© J L Rue 88

repair. The primary cause of this disaster was a combination of poor design and the Germans' special 'K' bullet with its tungsten carbide core, which could penetrate the French armour without undue difficulty. The poor design concerned mainly the dismal ventilation and the location of the fuel tankage right next to the machine-guns, and after several tanks had blown up the CA 1 Schneider was dubbed the 'mobile crematorium', an epithet that it was slow to lose, even after the internal tankage had been replaced by two armoured external tanks, each holding 100 litres (22 Imp. gal.); ventilation was also improved, but remained problematical under certain conditions. Protection was enhanced by the addition over the most vulnerable areas of rudimentary spaced armour 5.5 mm (0.22 in) thick and located some 40 mm (1.57 in) from the base armour; this added about 500 kg (1,102 lb) to the tank's combat weight.

The CA 1 Schneider remained in service up to the Armistice, but was neither popular nor successful. Developments were planned as the CA 2 (with the 75-mm/2.95-in embrasure gun replaced by a 47-mm gun in a rotating roof turret) and the CA 3 (with twin roof turrets in a longer hull and powered by a 100-hp/76-kW engine): the CA 2 attained prototype form, but the CA 3 did not reach even this stage. Later in the war the CA 1 Schneider found additional employment as a supply tank, the embrasure gun being removed and another door fitted in its place to create the Schneider Char de Ravitaillement.

Development and production of the CA 1 Schneider had bypassed the French army's normal vehicle procurement executive, the Service Technique Automobile, which was sufficiently piqued to instigate the design and construction of another battle tank. This was the Char d'Assaut Saint Chamond, designed by Colonel Rimailho and ordered from the Compagnie des Forges et Aciéries de la Marine et Homecourt (FAMH) at Saint Chamond. The first prototype was completed in February 1916, and two months later the STA ordered 400 of the type. Like the CA 1 Schneider, the CA Saint Chamond was based on the Holt sprung tractor system, though in this application with the track length increased by

Char d'Assaut St Chamond
(France)

Type: assault tank
Crew: 8
Combat weight: 22,000 kg (48,501 lb)
Dimensions: length overall 8.687 m (21.94 ft); width 2.667 m (8.75 ft); height overall 2.362 m (7.75 ft)
Armament system: one 75-mm (2.95-in) Canon de 75 Modèle 1897 L/36 rifled gun with 106 rounds and four 8-mm (0.315-in) Hotchkiss machine-guns (one bow, one rear and two beam), with 7,488 rounds; the main gun was stabilized in neither elevation nor azimuth, and simple optical sights were fitted
Armour: riveted steel varying in thickness from 5.5 to 17 mm (0.22 and 0.67 in)
Powerplant: one 67.1-kW (90 – hp) Panhard petrol engine with 250 litres (55 Imp. gal.) of fuel driving one Crochat-Collardeau electrical generator powering one motor attached to each drive sprocket
Performance: speed, road 8 km/h (4.9 mph); range, road 60 km (37.3 miles); gradient 57%; vertical obstacle 0.381 m (1.25 ft); trench 2.45 m (8.04 ft); ground clearance 0.33 m (13 in)

about 0.3 m (0.98 ft). This was clearly a basic improvement over the trackwork of the CA 1 Schneider, but was totally offset by the superimposition of an extraordinarily long hull, increasing overall length from the 6.32 m (20.75 ft) of the CA 1 to 8.69 m (28.51 ft): the result was cross-country performance still worse than that of the CA 1, with the tendency to ditch even on only slightly undulating ground: in terms of performance in front-line conditions this translated into trench-crossing and parapet-climbing capabilities of only 2.4 and 0.38 m (7.87 and 1.25 ft) respectively.

Two unusual features of the CA Saint Chamond were its provision for a rear driving position (the only time this has been featured in a tracked fighting vehicle) and its use of electric drive for the tracks. The Crochat-Collardeau electric generator was driven by a 90-hp (67.1-kW) Panhard petrol engine, and current was supplied to the electric motors attached to each track's drive sprocket. Differential powering of the tracks provided considerable agility within the limitations imposed by the hull, and despite a combat weight of 22,000 kg

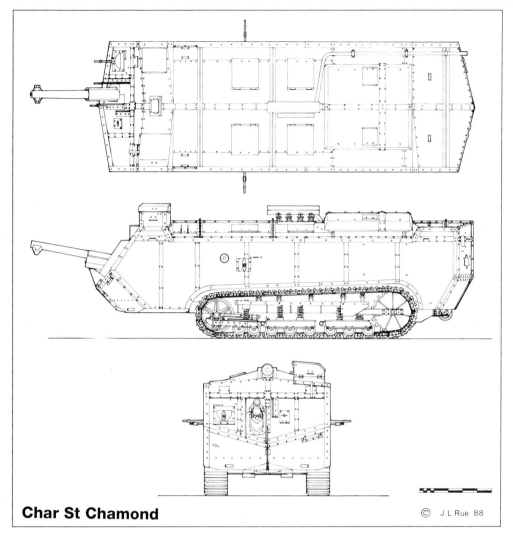

Char St Chamond

© J L Rue 88

(48,501 lb) the CA Saint Chamond had useful performance, including a maximum speed of 8 km/h (4.9 mph), but a range of only 60 km (37 miles). The primary disadvantage of the electric drive system was its weight, which added to the mobility problems engendered by the long hull. The hull was armoured to a maximum thickness of 11.5 mm (0.45 in), and terminated at its forward end in a well-sloped glacis plate above an angled-back vee-shaped lower surface designed to help the tank ride over earth banks and the like.

The CA Saint Chamond possessed a crew of eight, including the driver and commander who each had a small cupola at the front of the vehicle, and access to the vehicle was provided by a door in each side plus a third in the tail plate. The armament comprised one 75-mm (2.95-in) Saint Chamond TR commercial gun (first 165 vehicles) or one 75-mm (2.95-in) Modèle 1897 gun (last 235 vehicles) with 106 rounds, and four 8-mm (0.315-mm) Hotchkiss machine-guns with a total of 7,488 rounds. The TR main gun was located in a limited-traverse mounting in the glacis plate, and the machine-guns were placed one in the bow (on the lower right-hand side), one in the tail plate, and one on each side of the hull.

Deliveries of the CA Saint Chamond began in late 1916, and the type was first used in ac-

Though it had its good points, the French Char d'Assaut St Chamond had inadequate tracks and far too long a forward overhang to give the vehicle adequate climbing ability for trench warfare or even cross-country mobility. This is a model from late in the production run, with a sloping rather than flat roof. (*RAC Tank Museum*)

tion on 5 May 1917 at Moule de Laffaulx. In this first engagement the limitations of the design became all too apparent: of 16 CA Saint Chamonds committed, 15 ditched in the first line of German trenches. Further action confirmed the need for modification, successive efforts increasing the armour to a maximum thickness of 17 mm (0.67 in) against the effect of the German 'K' anti-tank bullet, a raised forward section of the hull, the elimination of the commander's cupola, the replacement of the original flat roof with a pitched roof so that grenades would roll off, and the use of wider tracks. These improved the CA Saint Chamond's capabilities, but nothing could be done about the basic design flaw in the vehicle's configuration, and from May 1918, when the final deliveries were made, the type was increasingly stripped of its main gun and used for supply tasks as the Char Saint Chamond de Ravitaillement.

Both the French *chars d'assaut* were perhaps ahead of their British contemporaries in gun calibre, and in the location of this single weapon on a central mounting, but the French designers had been too impressed with the cross-country capabilities of the Holt tractor to realize that a long track length combined with a large forward rise were essential to adequate trench performance. The two French tanks were thus little more than incidentals to the French army's war effort, though they did play an important part in the development of 'tank consciousness' and in the evolution of tank tactics and organization. However, the most important French tank of the First World War was an altogether different machine, the Renault FT light tank, the designation indicating Faible Tonnage (light weight). The concept stemmed from Estienne's desire for a lightweight partner to his CA 1: the heavy tank would crush barbed wire and deal with the German strongpoints, and the lightweight machine would accompany the attacking infantry to suppress any surviving pockets of German resistance and develop the exploitation phase of any breakthrough.

Estienne's first choice as partner in the design and development of the CA 1 had been the company headed by Louis Renault, but Renault had declined Estienne's invitation on the grounds that the company lacked any experience in heavy tracked vehicles and was, in any case, heavily committed to other efforts.

However, by 1916 Renault had become involved in production of tracked vehicles (mainly tractors for the French artillery), and was more receptive when Estienne proposed a collaborative venture to produce the desired light tank. There remains some doubt as to the exact design parentage of the resulting FT, though Renault and a subordinate (Serre) were certainly involved, and its seems likely that Estienne exercised more than a watching brief over the project.

Yet again Estienne bypassed the normal channels of procurement, and in October 1916 went straight to Joffre with his scheme for 1,000 examples of a 4,000-kg (8,818-lb) light tank carrying one 8-mm (0.315-in) machine-gun or, in a small number, one 37-mm gun in a 360° traverse turret, possessing a maximum height of 1.75 m (5.74 ft), armoured against small arms fire and possessing a maximum speed of 12 km/h (7.5 mph). Estienne also proposed, in a very far-sighted manner, that a number of the machines should be completed with wireless equipment to allow communication between commanders and their mobile forces. Though there was considerable resistance from some parts of the French war ministry apparatus, Estienne's notion found sufficient favour to secure authorization of prototype production after a mock-up had been completed at the end of 1916. The first prototypes appeared in February and March 1917, and immediately displayed excellent qualities in trials at the Champlieu camp. An initial order for 150 FTs was placed on 22 February 1917, but at the insistence of General Henri Pétain, the French Commander-in-Chief, this was to total 3,500 vehicles for delivery by the end of 1918, and additional orders then increased the planned production run to more than double this figure. It was clear that Renault could not handle the orders on its own, and this important programme soon involved Belleville, Berliet, Delaunay, Renault and SOMUA (Société d'Outillage Mécanique et d'Usinage d'Artillerie) as manufacturers with a large number of other companies (including some in the UK) as sub-contractors.

The FT was an unusual, but interesting and successful tank in its technical and tactical features. Technically, the tank lacked a conventional chassis but was rather a monocoque of riveted armour plate between 6 and 16 mm (0.24 and 0.63 in) thick, a box-like structure to which were attached the major internal and external components, terminating at the tail in an upswept plate that increased the effective length of the vehicle as an aid to trench crossing, which was 1.35 m (4.43 ft) without and 1.8 m (5.91 ft) with the tailplate. The hull accommodated the driver at the front, the turret in the centre, and the combined engine and transmission assembly at the rear. The driver gained access to his position via twin frontal doors, and the other crew member, the commander/gunner, used rear doors to enter the turret, which had a maximum thickness of 22 mm (0.87 in). The turret, surmounted at its rear by a mushroom-shaped observation cupola, was the world's first to offer 360° traverse, resting on a ball race for ease of manual movement, with a neat handbrake to lock the turret on the desired bearing. The armament in the first machines to enter service was an 8-mm (0.315-in) Hotchkiss machine-gun capable of elevation in an arc between −20° and +35°. Some 4,800 rounds of ammunition were carried. The engine was a 35-hp (26.1-kW) Renault petrol unit, driving the tracks by means of a crash gearbox, with a clutch-and-brake system used for steering. Suspension of the tracks was achieved by coil and leaf springs for the four bogies (nine road wheels), and at the front of each track was a large idler to provide sufficient track rise for the FT to climb a 0.6-m (1.97-ft) parapet. The idlers comprised a steel rim over laminated wood centres, and there were six track-return rollers.

The first production tanks were completed in September 1917, but the whole programme was hampered by shortages of the special cast steel turret and by arguments within the army about the precise nature of the armament to be fitted. By the end of the year Renault had delivered only 83 examples of the initial variant, which was designated the Char Mitrailleuse Renault FT 17 and first used in combat on 31 May 1918 in the Forêt de Retz. The turret problem proved impossible to solve in the short term, and after the delivery of some pre-production vehicles with cast turrets, the producers designed their own eight-sided turret of riveted plate construction, allowing larger-scale production from about the middle of 1918 for the delivery of 3,177 tanks before the Armistice, against orders that currently totalled 7,820, including 3,940 from Renault. When the cast turret began to arrive in useful numbers it was installed on a version generally designated FT 18. In 1921 the French army still deployed the FT in substantial quantities: of the total of 3,728 such vehicles, 2,100 were armed with a machine-gun 1,246 were armed with a 37-mm gun, 39 were armed with a 75-mm (2.95-in) gun, 188 were fitted with wireless equipment, and 155 were training tanks.

The second FT version to appear was the Char Canon Renault FT 17, in which the turret accommodated a 37-mm Puteaux gun capable of elevation in an arc between − 20° and + 35°. Ammunition stowage was provided for 200 HE, 25 armour-piercing and 12 shrapnel rounds (237 rounds in all). Production orders for the gun-armed version totalled 1,830 units, and together with the standard model with a machine-gun, it was used by countries including Belgium, Brazil, Canada, China, Czechoslovakia, Finland, Greece, Italy (with modification as the Fiat 3000), Japan (Type 79 Ko-Gata Sensha), Manchuria, the Netherlands, Poland, Spain, the UK, the USA

Char Canon Renault FT17
(France)

Type: light tank
Crew: 2
Combat weight: 6,800 kg (14,991 lb)
Dimensions: length overall 4.10 m (13.45 ft) or 5.00 m (16.40 ft) with optional tail; width 1.74 m (5.71 ft); height overall 2.14 m (7.02 ft)
Armament system: one 37-mm SA Canon rifled gun with 237 rounds; the turret was manually operated, the gun was stabilized in neither elevation (−20 to +35) nor azimuth (360), and simple optical sights were fitted
Armour: riveted steel varying in thickness between 6 and 16 mm (0.24 and 0.63 in)
Powerplant: one 26-kW (35-hp) Renault petrol engine with 100 litres (22 Imp. gal. of fuel)
Performance: speed, road 7.7 km/h (4.8 mph); range, road 35 km (21.75 miles); fording 0.7 m (2.3 ft); gradient 50%; vertical obstacle 0.6 m (1.97 ft); trench 1.35 m (4.43 ft) or 1.8 m (5.91 ft) with optional tail; ground clearance 0.435 m (17.1 in)

(6-Ton Tank M1917), the USSR (KS, and with modification MS-1 and MS-2) and Yugoslavia.

The other two initial variants were the Char Canon Renault 75S with a short-barrel 75-mm (2.95-in) gun in a riveted heptagonal turret with a bustle to accommodate the gun recoil, and the three-man Char Renault Télégraphe San Fil with a boxlike superstructure and tall aerial

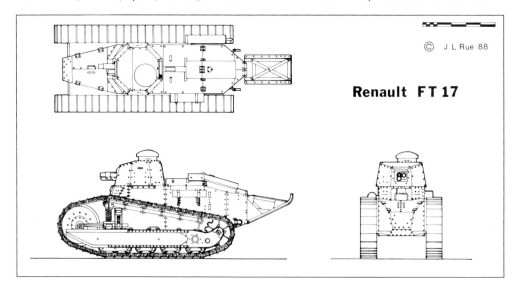

© J L Rue 88

Renault FT 17

for the wireless equipment needed in the command role. The variant with the 75-mm (2.95-in) gun was really a self-propelled gun, and though orders were placed for 970 units, the type was so delayed that it did not appear until after the Armistice, thereafter being produced only in very small numbers, mainly for service in North Africa.

The FT was also developed after the war in a number of largely experimental forms as the Char Fascine (trench-filler with up to three fascines), Char Démineur (mine clearer, with two ploughs on hinged forward arms), Char Projecteur (internal-security searchlight vehicle, with a tall mast supporting twin searchlights), a smoke-laying vehicle, an amphibious vehicle, a bridgelayer, a bulldozer, and a cargo carrier with a largely redesigned

hull. The FT was also used as the basis for experimental work with the Citroen-Kégresse suspension and rubber-band track system for higher speeds and quieter running. Trials with continuous rubber tracks were undertaken in 1924 and 1925, and though much interesting data was collected, nothing came of the system. From 1931 the remaining FT 17 and FT 18 vehicles were refitted with the new 7.5-mm (0.295-in) Hotchkiss Modèle 31 machine-gun, and redesignated Char Mitrailleuse Renault FT 31: this variant's ammunition stowage was 4,050 rounds, including 400 armour-piercing rounds.

The FT remained in widespread service between the two world wars, seeing service in Morocco, Syria and Tunisia, before meeting its end in the German invasion of France during

An American tank unit with French Renault FT17 light tanks just before the opening of the Meuse-Argonne offensive in 1918. The front vehicle has a riveted flat-plate turret with a 37-mm Puteaux cannon, while the vehicle behind it has the moulded conical turret that proved so troublesome to produce. (IWM)

41

May and June 1940. Machines captured by the Germans were used for internal security duties, with the designation PzKpfw 18R 730(f).

It is worth noting that even in the 1920s the French sought to capitalize on the capabilities of the basic FT design by producing an upgraded model as the Char NC 1, otherwise designated the Char NC27 and intended as an infantry support tank. This was considerably uparmoured from the standard of the FT, with a maximum of 34 mm (1.34 in) on the turret front and 30 mm (1.18 in) on the hull front for a combat weight of 8,500 kg (18,730 lb). Power was provided by a 60-hp (44.7-kW) Renault petrol engine for a maximum speed of 18 km/h (11.2 mph), and on each side the suspension comprised three coil-spring columns combined with six-hydro-pneumatic shock absorbers for three four-wheel bogies; there was also an independent wheel at the front. Armament was either one machine-gun or one 37-mm gun, and though the type was not adopted by the French army, it was exported to Japan as the Otsu-Gata Sensha, and to Yugoslavia.

The NC 1 was followed by the Char NC 2, otherwise designated the Char NC31. This was similar to the NC 1 (NC27), but weighed 9,500 kg (20,944 lb), was fitted with heavier tracks and powered by a 75-hp (55.9-kW) Renault petrol engine, and carried an armament of two 7.5-mm (0.295-in) machine-guns. Small sales were made to the Greek army.

This was the mainstream of French tank development in the First World War, and though a few experimental types were developed, these generally failed to lead anywhere. The exception was the Char 1, developed in two forms as a *char de rupture* (breakthrough tank) for the planned 1919 offensives, and most important as the precursor of the Char 2C discussed in the next chapter.

Given the dominant role played by German armour in the first half of the Second World War, it is interesting to note that in the First World War, Germany was most decidedly an 'also ran' in the tank stakes. An overly cautious approach to the tank was not for lack of prodding, for many army officers and civilians had advocated the development of tracked armoured vehicles. The army was not without sympathy for the concept, but having decided

that no civilian tracked chassis were immediately useful as a development origin, opted to concentrate its limited effort on armoured versions of cars and trucks. By 1915 it was clear that these offered no real utility in trench conditions, and German efforts were concentrated on a tracked version of the Bremen Marien Wagen, essentially a version of the Daimler 4,000-kg (8,818-lb) truck with its rear wheels replaced by tracked units. By October 1916 the front wheels had also been replaced by undriven tracked units, and in March 1917 an armoured body was installed. Plans envisaged an armed version, but any rational appraisal confirmed the type's lack of combat value.

By this time the British Tank Mk I had been used in combat, and the German army was now fully aware of the possibilities of the true tank, even in its most rudimentary form. A major effort was launched towards the creation of a German tank superior in all significant capabilities to the British tank. Initial contracts were placed on 13 November 1916 and finalized on 22 December of the same year for the new vehicle. Herr Steiner, the German representative of the Holt company, was called in as adviser on the tracks, and the initial specification called for a Geländespanzerwagen (all-terrain armoured vehicle) weighing 30,000 kg (66,138 lb) and powered by a 100-hp (74.6-kW) engine for road and cross-country speeds of

Sturmpanzerwagen A7V
(Germany)

Type: battle tank
Crew: 18
Combat weight: 32,510 kg (71,671 lb)
Dimensions: length overall 8.00 m (26.25 ft); width 3.20 m (10.50 ft); height 3.50 m (11.48 ft)
Armament system: one 57-mm gun with 500 rounds and six 7.92-mm (0.312-in) MG08/15 machine-guns with 18,000 rounds
Armour: between 10 and 30 mm (0.39 and 1.18 in)
Powerplant: two 74.6-kW (100-hp) Daimler 165204 petrol engines
Performance: speed, road 9 km/h (5.6 mph); range, road 80 km (49.7 miles); gradient 30°; vertical obstacle 0.455 m (1.49 ft); trench 2.2 m (7.22 ft); ground clearance 0.2 m (8 in)

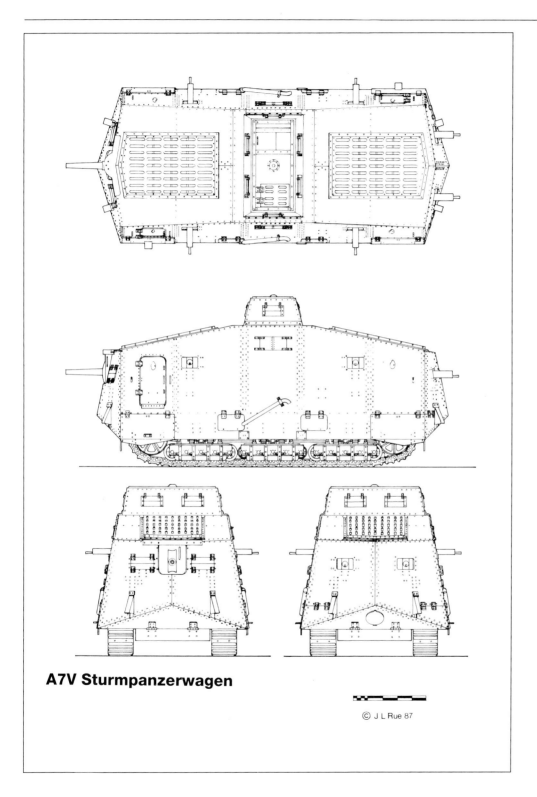

A7V Sturmpanzerwagen

© J L Rue 87

A veritable strongpoint on tracks, the Germans' A7V was tactically disadvantaged by its size, dismal performance and unwieldy crew drawn from several army branches. (*Bundesarchiv*)

12 and 6 km/h (7.5 and 3.7 mph) respectively with an armament of two guns (one in the front and the other in the rear) plus flank-mounted machine-guns or, in unarmed form, a payload of 4,000 kg (8,818 lb).

The specification was hopelessly unrealistic, and failed to take into significant account the actualities of front-line terrain. The Germans had an enormous technical effort to make in their attempt to catch up with the British, but like the French they made a great mistake in relying on the existing Holt track system as the core of their new vehicle, regardless of the fact that it lacked the cross-country capabilities manifestly required for parapet climbing and trench crossing. Working with Steiner, who was primarily tasked with the much-lengthened Holt track system, Josef Vollmer designed a truly massive machine with a crew of 18 that first ran in prototype form in April 1917. A wooden mock-up of the definitive version was inspected by the German general staff representatives on 14 May 1917, and the design was accepted for production as the Sturmpanzerwagen A7V, the alphanumeric portion being the abbreviated form of the responsible department of the German war ministry, Allgemeine Kriegsdepartment 7 Abteilung Verkehrswesen (General

War Department 7, Transport Section). The prototypes were thoroughly tested during the summer, providing striking evidence of the design's failings, particularly in the track and engine-cooling systems.

On each side the track ran on 15 road wheels in three bogies with coil spring suspension. The tracks were powered by rear sprockets driven via half-shafts (each with a steering brake) from the final transmission placed at the rear of the A7V's large single interior compartment. The final transmission was itself driven by an extension shaft projecting from a gearbox taking power from the two 100-hp (74.6-kW) Daimler 165204 petrol engines in the centre of the vehicle under the driver and commander, who sat with shoulders and heads in the large cupola on the tank roof. It was a practical, though heavy, drive system, but decidedly lacking in power for a vehicle weighing 29,900 kg (65,917 lb) unladen and 32,510 kg (71,671 lb) laden. This led to limited engine life and to overheating under all but the best of road conditions.

The tracks had a ground length of 4.5 m (14.76 ft), compared with an overall vehicle length of 8.0 m (26.25 ft), and the return run of the tracks was usefully protected by the lower edges of the rolled steel armour, which varied in thickness from a minimum of 10 mm (0.39 in) to a maximum of 30 mm (1.18 in). However, the tracks lacked significant rise at their forward ends, limiting the A7V's parapet-climbing capability to a mere 0.455 m (1.49 ft); the vehicle's trench-crossing capability was also disappointing at 2.2 m (7.22 ft), and the ground clearance of 0.2 m (7.87 in) meant that the tank bellied on all but the levellest of hard surfaces; its performance on soft ground was of course poorer still.

In short, the A7V had been designed as an armoured fort to co-operate with the infantry, but the German designers concentrated on the armoured fort notion to the virtual exclusion of the mobility aspect. And in fortress terms the huge A7V was good: the main armament, located in the bow plate with a traverse of 25° left and right, was a 57-mm Sokol cannon (from captured stocks) plus 500 rounds, while the secondary armament comprised six 7.92-mm (0.312-in) MG08 machine-guns with a total of 36,000 rounds. The machine-guns were located two in each side and two in the rear. The large crew was drawn from three separate army branches, rather than from a homogeneous tank corps: the driver and two mechanics were engineers, the two men on the 57-mm gun were artillerymen, and the commander and 12 machine-gunners were infantrymen.

The first vehicle was delivered in September 1917, the first fully-armoured example following on 1 October of the same year. Daimler of Berlin was responsible for manufacture, the armour coming from Krupp in Essen and from Steffens & Noelle in Berlin. There were considerable variations in the quality and nature of the armour plate supplied, some A7Vs having a hull made of a few large plates, but most having hulls in which smaller plates were riveted together; splash was a particular problem with the latter. There were still a large number of problems with the type, but the German general staff decided that it could wait no longer for improvements and ordered 100 A7Vs on 1 December 1917, with delivery to be completed by the time of the great spring offensives planned for 1918. Daimler, on the other hand, thought that a delivery rate of five per month was more prac-

tical, and in fact only 35 or fewer machines had been delivered by the time of the Armistice. The type was first used operationally in the Battle of St Quentin on 21 March 1918, and proved next to useless for any task other than boosting the morale of the German infantry. On 24 April the first tank-versus-tank engagement saw the pitting of one A7V against two Tanks Mk IV Female, which were forced to pull back before a Mk IV Male arrived and knocked out the A7V. The Mk IV Male was then engaged by two more A7Vs that had arrived: one was knocked out by the Mk IV Male's 6-pdr (57-mm) fire, and the other climbed a bank and overturned. After the war a number of A7Vs were supplied to Poland, which used the type for the defence of Warsaw in the Russo-Polish War of 1920.

The only A7V variant was the A7U (Uberlandwagen), developed as a supply tank with the load carried inside the erstwhile fighting compartment. This variant had a mild steel rather than rolled plate body. About 30 of these machines were built, but like the A7Vs they suffered from their inherently bad cross-country capability.

This deficiency in mobility was fully appreciated by the Germans, and in an effort to ameliorate the problem the A7V design team produced the A7V/U (Umlaufende Kette, meaning all-round tracks) with a configuration modelled on the British Mk IV, though on a larger scale for a length of 8.5 m (27.89 ft). This seven-man machine was ordered into production during September 1918 but appeared only in prototype form, and with an armament of two sponson-mounted 57-mm guns plus four MG08 machine-guns turned the scales at some 39,600 kg (87,302 lb) for a maximum speed of 12 km/h (7.5 mph) on the 210 hp (157 kW) provided by two petrol engines. The maximum armour thickness was 30 mm (1.18 in). The type was also projected in two variants as the A7V/U2 with smaller sponsons and a machine-gun in the large roof cupola, and the A7V/U3 as a female with armament limited to machine-guns.

The ultimate expression of Germany's desire for massive tanks in the First World War is the 'K-Wagen', otherwise called the Grosskampfwagen, and at a weight of 150 tonnes one of

the heaviest tanks ever projected. The design was by Vollmer, and was intended to provide the German army with a 22-man break-through tank for service in 1919. The whole machine broke into four parts for rail transport, and comprised a hull on four roller-type track units, and two large sponsons. The armament was to have been four 77-mm (3.03-in) guns with 800 rounds and seven MG08 machine-guns with 21,000 rounds, and the maximum armour thickness was 30 mm (1.18 in). Power was provided by two 650-hp (485-kW) Daimler-Benz aero engines via electro-magnetic clutch transmissions, for a maximum speed of 7.5 km/h (4.7 mph), and this vast machine was 13.0 m (42.65 ft) long. The two incomplete prototypes were broken up by the Allies in 1919.

Despite his involvement in these programmes for the German army's heavyweight tanks, Vollmer was more interested in light tanks, which he saw as more useful, and also better suited to Germany's declining ability to produce sophisticated equipment. The spur for the final development of light tanks was the arrival in action of the British Medium Tank Mk A Whippet. Vollmer's initial efforts resulted in the Leichte Kampfwagen I, which appeared in prototype form during 1918. The 7,000-kg (15,432-lb) LK I used the chassis of a Daimler car (with the existing axles for the front-mounted idlers and rear-mounted drive sprockets) with a 60-hp (44.7-kW) petrol engine to drive the simple tracks. The engine was located at the front, with the compartment for the three crewmen at the rear. Maximum armour thickness was 8 mm (0.315 in), and ar-mament a single MG08 machine-gun. The LK I was designed as an experimental cavalry tank, and paved the way for the definitive LK II to meet the specification of the A7V commit-tee. In June 1918 two prototypes were trialled, and this led to an order for 580 production machines with a rear barbette carrying one 57-mm gun. Like the LK I, this three-man LK II was based on a Daimler car chassis, but the tracks were revised to provide a higher rise at the front, and were fitted with twin mud chutes. The maximum armour thickness was 14 mm (0.55-in), and at a weight of 8,900-kg (19,621-lb) the vehicle could achieve a maximum speed of 18 km/h (11.2 mph) on its 55-hp (41-kW)

Daimler petrol engine. For the same level of protection, the LK II was lighter than the Mk A, and was thus both faster and more manoeuvrable than the British tank. No production machines were completed before the end of the war, but the LK II then became the basis of the Swedish Strv m/21, which was fitted with a rotating turret for its 37-mm gun, had a crew of four, and often carried radio.

There was also to have been a female version of the LK II with a rotating turret and machine-gun armament, while the projected LK III would have revised the family's layout on a custom-designed chassis to accommodate a turret at the front. The turret would have accommodated a 57-mm gun or 20-mm Becker cannon, and an order for 1,000 machines was placed.

The only other countries to develop tanks to the hardware stage during the First World War were Italy and the USA, which made determined efforts but achieved little success. The Italians were slow to get into the 'armour act', for the conditions in which the Italians were fighting the Austro-Hungarians were totally unlike those of the Western Front and therefore not particularly suitable for the armoured concept developed by the British and French for their theatre.

After the cancellation of an initial project, designed by Capitano Luigi Cassali and built by Pavesi as a cross-country machine with two turrets, each accommodating a single machine-gun, the Italians devoted effort to the Fiat Tipo 2000 Modello 1917 heavy tank, which was more akin to the 'mobile fortress' concept embodied in the A7V than to the notions of the Italians' main allies, the British and French. Like the German tank, the Italian effort suffered from lack of mobility, but, surprisingly, possessed adequate trench performance including parapet-climbing and trench-crossing capabilities of 1.0 and 3.0 m (3.28 and 9.84 ft) respectively, conferred by the large radius of the track front and the overall length of 7.4 m (24.28 ft). The 10-man Tipo 2000 was innovative in its use of a roof-mounted cylindrical turret accommodating one 65-mm (2.56-in) gun. This was a short L/17 weapon, but the turret provided 360° traverse and the mounting allowed gun elevation in an arc between

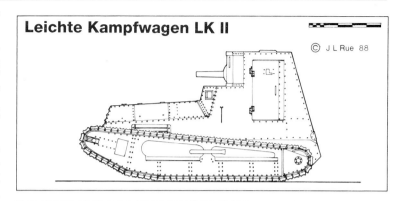

Leichte Kampfwagen LK II

© J L Rue 88

Leichte Kampfwagen LK II
Germany

Type: light (cavalry) tank prototype
Crew: 3
Combat weight: 8,900 kg (19,261 lb)
Dimensions: length overall 5.06 m (16.60 ft); width 1.95 m (6.40 ft); height 2.50 m (8.20 ft)
Armament system: one 57-mm gun or two 7.92-mm (0.312-in) MG08/15 machine-guns
Armour: between 8 and 14 mm (0.315 and 0.55 in)
Powerplant: one 44.7-kW (60-hp) Daimler four-cylinder petrol engine
Performance: speed, road 16 km/h (10 mph); range, road 65 km (40 miles); gradient 45°; trench 2.04 m (6.5 ft)

− 10° and + 75°; this initial turret was later replaced by a hemispherical unit fitted with a 14-mm (0.55-in) machine-gun in addition to the 65-mm (2.56-in) gun. Additional firepower was conferred by the exceptional secondary battery of seven 6.5-mm (0.256-in) Fiat machine-guns located in 100°-traverse mountings, one at each corner of the boxlike armoured superstructure, one in each side and one in the rear panel. Armour thickness varied from a minimum of 15 mm (0.59 in) to a maximum of 20 mm (0.79 in), and this substantial protection contributed significantly to the overall weight of 40,000 kg (88,183 lb). Power was provided by a 240-hp (179-kW) Fiat A12 aero engine, which gave the modestly-sprung vehicle a maximum speed of 6 km/h 3.7 mph). The Tipo 2000 appeared in 1918, and was produced to the extent of only two prototypes and four pre-production machines, the latter remaining in service up to 1934.

Top far left Though of poor quality, this photograph of a German K-Wagon under construction in 1918 reveals the basic layout of this massive type with its two roller-type tracks and external sponsons for a quartet of 77-mm (3.03-in) guns.

Far left Germany too was interested in the concept of the cavalry or exploitation tank, this pioneering vehicle being the Vollmer-designed LK I based on the chassis of a Daimler car. The rear-mounted turret accommodated a single 7.92-mm (0.312-in) machine-gun. (*RAC Tank Museum*)

Right The Fiat Tipo
2000 was notable for its
central turret and heavy
secondary armament, but
was high and unwieldy, as
well as too large for
Italy's limited production
capability. (*RAC Tank
Museum*)

Below The Fiat Tipo
3000 was modelled on the
Renault FT17, but
introduced improvements
and refinements such as a
transverse engine
mounted lower in the hull.
This is a Tipo 3000A
Modello 1921 with twin
turret-mounted machine-
guns rather than the
Modello 1930's 37-mm
gun. (*RAC Tank Museum*)

The Tipo 2000 was an advanced design for its time, but by any realistic assessment, was too big and cumbersome for Italian tactical needs, let alone Italian industry. Far better suited to Italy's needs and capabilities, therefore, was the Renault FT. It was originally planned that Italy should manufacture a copy of the French original, but in the process of launching Italian production, the type was considerably improved as the Fiat Tipo 3000 Modello 1921, with reduced weight (5,500 kg/12, 125 lb) and higher performance, including a maximum speed of 24 km/h (15 mph). As can be inferred from the designation, the Italian programme resulted in considerable delay, and the prototype appeared only in June 1921, being accepted for production during 1921 and entering service in 1923. Externally the Tipo 3000 was similar to the FT, but the 50-hp (37.3-kW) petrol engine was located in a lower, transverse position in the hull rear, and the armament comprised a pair of turret-mounted 6.5-mm (0.256-in) machine-guns with 2,000 rounds: gun elevation was an arc between −17° and +24°. The type was later upgraded as the 6,000-kg (13,228-lb) the Tipo 3000B Modello 1930 with improved suspension, a 63-hp (47-kW) engine and a turret-mounted 37-mm gun with 68 rounds, capable of elevation in an arc between −10° and +20°. Most surviving Modello 1921s were reworked to Modello 1930 standard, and the type remained in steadily reducing service up to 1943.

Despite overseas interest in US-designed tracked agricultural vehicles as the basis of armoured fighting vehicles, the US Army was initially uninterested in the concept, and it was 1916 before the first American tank designs were produced as private ventures. These were the C.L. Best Tractor Company's CLB 75 (an agricultural tractor with a simulated armour body and a revolving turret fitted with two light guns), the Holt Tractor Company's HA 36 (a diminutive one-man machine of rhomboidal shape and powered by a motorcycle engine), the Holt Tractor Company's G–9 (an armoured boxlike body with two turrets, mounted on the chassis of the Holt 10-ton tractor powered by a 75-hp/55.9-kW petrol engine) and, perhaps most significantly of all, the Holt Tractor Company's Gas-Electric Tank. This last was the first American vehicle designed specifically as a tank, and used a petrol-electric drive system with a Holt 90-hp (67.1-kW) petrol engine to drive a General Electric generator supplying current to the single electric motor that powered each track. The vehicle weighed 56,000 lb (25,402 kg) and was 16.5 ft (5.03 m) long, the drive system providing good manoeuvrability and a maximum speed of 6 mph (9.6 km/h). Armament comprised a 75-mm (2.95-in) Vickers mountain howitzer located low in the nose in a limited-traverse mounting, and two Vickers machine-guns in side sponsons.

The USA came into the war against Germany in April 1917, and in July of the same year it was decided that the American Expeditionary Forces being prepared for despatch to France should have an armoured component from a newly-created Tank Corps. It was planned to provide the Tank Corps with heavy and light vehicles, the British Mk VI being selected as the heavy machine and the French Renault FT as the light machine. After the Battle of Cambrai, however, the Tank Corps decided to switch its heavy tank requirement to the Mk VIII, with Mk IVs, Mk Vs and Mk V*s as interim vehicles. The FT (including the American M1917, originally known as the 'Six-Ton Special') and Mk VIII are discussed above, and it is

A dramatic climax to the 1929 trials of a Fiat Tipo 3000B Modello 30 with a 37-mm L/40 turret gun. (*IWM*)

worth recording that the Americans also buckled down to the task of developing an indigenous tank design in a large-scale programme launched in 1917 and enthusiastically pursued in 1918. The programme caught up the Gas-Electric Tank, which had first run in the month that the USA entered the war, and also produced the US Engineer Corps' Steam Tank, the Holt Three-Wheeled Steam Tank and the Pioneer Tractor Company's Skeleton Tank.

The Steam Tank was an impractical effort to produce a massive machine, modelled conceptually on the Mk IV but turning the scales at 112,000 lb (50,803 kg) and measuring 34.75 ft (10.59 m) in length. Each track was driven by its own 250-hp (186-kW) two-cylinder steam engine. The main armament was a flame gun, and the kerosene-fuelled boilers of the powerplant were also designed to provide the steam pressurization for flame projection: the system proved ineffective, and a separate 35-hp (26.1-kW) petrol engine was provided for this task, allowing the projection of the flame to a range of 90 ft (27.4 m). As may well be imagined, the Steam Tank was not successful. No more success attended the Three-Wheeled Steam Tank, which used a tricycle arrangement of two massive forward wheels and a triple steering roller at the back: the front wheels were each powered by a 75-hp (55.9-kW)

Right One of several ingenious but unsuccessful American tanks of the First World War period was the Holt Three-Wheeled Steam Tank. Each of the two front wheels had its own 75-hp (56-kW) steam engine, and the rear of the vehicle was supported by a triple-disc steering roller fitted with a trailing steel structure to improve trench-crossing capability. (*RAC Tank Museum*)

A fascinating but ultimately futile attempt to produce a light tank with good trench-crossing ability was the so-called Skeleton Tank, seen here during its trials at the Aberdeen Proving Ground in Maryland, USA. (*RAC Tank Museum*)

steam engine using kerosene-fuelled boilers. The armament comprised one 75-mm (2.95-in) howitzer in a nose mounting, and 0.5-in (12.7-mm) Browning machine-guns in the hull sides. The Skeleton Tank was intended to combine the trench performance of larger (and thus heavier) tanks with the logistic advantages of the light tank: the result is well summed up by the type's development name, with the tracks running round a lozenge-shaped skeletal frame 25 ft (7.62 m) in overall length. Inside this frame of iron pipes was a small box-like fighting compartment accommodating the two 50-hp (37.3-kW) Beaver petrol engines, the two crewmen and the high-set rotating turret fitted with a single 0.3-in (7.62-mm) Browning machine-gun. The machine weighed 20,160 lb (9,145 kg), and attained a maximum speed of 5 mph (8 km/h). Only single prototypes of all three designs were built for trials in 1918.

The only other armed tank designed in the USA during this period was the Ford 3-Ton Tank, evolved by the US Ordnance Department for manufacture by Ford as a machine-gun carrier or ammunition supply vehicle. Extensive use was made of standard Ford car components, to facilitate production on a massive scale, and the result was a 6,950-lb (3,153-kg) vehicle, reminiscent in general outline to the Renault FT and powered by two 20-hp (14.9-kW) Ford Model T petrol engines for a maximum speed of 8 mph (12.9 km/h). The armament of this two-man type comprised a single 0.3-in (7.62-mm) machine-gun in a bow mounting with 21° traverse, but of 15,015 ordered in 1918, only 15 were ever completed and then for use mainly as tractors for the 75-mm (2.95-in) artillery equipment. From the 3-Ton Tank the Ordnance Department evolved the Ford Three-Man Tank Mk 1. This was powered by a single 60-hp (44.7-kW) Hudson petrol engine, allowing an increase in length from 13.67 to 16.5 ft (4.165 to 5.03 m), and in weight to 16,800 lb (7,620 kg) with an arma-

The Ford Three-Man Tank Mk 1 was developed from the two-man Ford 3-Ton tank with a tactically disastrous turret accommodating a 37-mm main gun. The type was cancelled in 1919. (*RAC Tank Museum*)

ment of one bow-mounted 0.3-in (7.62-mm) machine-gun and one turret-mounted 37-mm gun. Trials showed the type to be generally unsatisfactory, and in 1919 development was halted.

Popularly thought to have been the 'war to end all wars', the conflict known at the time as the Great War had shown the value of the tank as a versatile weapon that could break the deadlock of trench warfare. Trench warfare was dominated by barbed wire, the machine-gun and artillery, but was essentially infantry warfare: the tank had thus been schemed at first as an infantry support weapon, as used at Flers-Courcelette in September 1916. This basic concept did not alter much in the rest of the war, but Cambrai in November 1917 showed what could be achieved by a mass of 300 tanks (an advance in a single morning greater than that achieved by infantry alone in the four-month Third Battle of Ypres, culminating in the Battle of Passchendaele), while Amiens in August 1918 intimated the course of future possibilities when a mixed force of more than 600 medium and light tanks took the dominant part with infantry and air support to create a gap about 11 miles (17.7 km) wide and up to 8 miles (12.9 km) deep in the German lines.

Yet while the civilians were looking forward to a peaceful future, more sombre and indeed more sober military minds knew that war could not possibly be at an end. Tank advocates were already analysing the results of tank warfare in the First World War and finding in their assessments the results that showed how the tank could be developed mechanically and evolved conceptually to become the decisive weapon of a new type of warfare. So at one end of the spectrum there were the tank protagonists, who saw in the new weapon a machine that could dominate the battlefield and to which the other arms would be subordinate. At the other end there were the senior officers who had learned their soldiering in the established arms, and now occupied the highest positions of command: these men generally saw the tank as an upstart, and their position was ably put by General Sir Louis Jackson in his celebrated statement that 'The tank-proper was a freak. The circumstances which called it into existence were exceptional and not likely to recur. If they do they can be dealt with by other means.' With hindsight it is easy to see the fallacy of Jackson's argument, especially as it is arguable that greater attention should have been devoted to the implications of the American Civil War (1861–65) and the Russo-Japanese War (1904–05), and to the inevitable consequences of technological developments resulting in accurate, quick-fire artillery and the machine-gun. But it is more appropriate to look at Jackson's assertion from the viewpoint of the time: trench warfare had indeed been a divergence from the established norms of warfare, and it was therefore almost inevitable that professional soldiers should persuade (or with hindsight delude) themselves into the belief that the old order would return.

A Troubled Adolescence

The task faced by the world's new tank arms was first to survive, and then to secure emancipation from their positions subordinate to one of the armies' other arms. It was to be a difficult task, occupying the 1920s and most of the 1930s. To the politicians, the tank could embody the concept of 'an engine of war' and thus smacked too strongly of militarism; to the economists, the tank represented a high level of development cost, followed by high production and operating costs; and to the professional heads of the world's most important armies, the tank was an inessential embarassment. Among the soldiers, the more far-sighted were content to see the retention of the tank in small numbers as an adjunct of the infantry (medium tank) and of the cavalry (light tank), while, as noted above, the majority wished to return to the pre-1914 pattern in which they had trained and gained most of their experience of practical soldiering. As a young arm, the tank service in most countries had attracted relatively junior officers with an interest in the mechanization that was becoming important in the period up to the First World War but without 'entrenched' attitudes to military operations: these men were able and eloquent, but had generally risen only into the lower levels of field rank, and were therefore able to achieve little but keep up a constant but carefully-controlled stream of propaganda to keep their arm alive, pending the day it could prove itself.

In the type of perverse reversal for which they are famous, the British squandered the technical and tactical lead they had established in the First World War, by a programme of parsimony so extreme that it could well have led to extinction. Yet the British tank arm was saved by the twin efforts of men working solely within the professional confines of the army (middle-ranking officers such as P. Hobart, G.Q. Martel and Ernest Swinton) and a smaller number of men such as Colonel J.F.C. Fuller and Captain B.H. Liddell Hart, working mainly on the outside of the army framework to develop and bring wider attention to their theories of armoured warfare.

Within the army, the middle-ranking advocates of armoured warfare worked to convince their largely sceptical superiors that the era of fully-mechanized warfare was the tank: the army protagonists urged as strongly as they could the concept of the tank as embodying the primary virtues of firepower, protection and mobility in a package of unrivalled versatility; and at the same time they urged that the army open its mind to the possibility of merging the new weapon with a new set of tactical doctrines, whose absence would negate all the advantages of a tank force.

This tied in neatly with the role played by Fuller and Liddell Hart, who were concerned not just with the practicalities of armoured warfare with the weapons to hand and under development, but with the 'ideal' of armoured warfare and therefore the course in which the long-term development of tanks should be directed. At the core of the thinking of both Fuller and Liddell Hart was the concept that the tank was a new weapon, perhaps presaged in other weapons, but in its post-First World War form, a weapon different from those of the infantry, cavalry and artillery, and as such requiring the formulation of a new set of tactical precepts.

Fuller was the tactical thinker *par excellence*, and his ideas stemmed directly from the British experience at Cambrai and Amiens: if it made full use of its mobility, the tank was unstoppable, possessing the ability to strike at will against different points in the enemy's line; this would force the enemy on to the defensive, and dilute his strength to the point that he would find it impossible to counter the tank attack and consequent breakthrough at the offensive's chosen point; the threat thus posed to the enemy's lines of communication would in turn force the enemy to retreat, the accumulation of such retreats leading inevitably to the enemy's defeat. Fuller was the great advocate of the 'all-tank' school of thinking, which averred that the evolution of the tank had rendered obsolete all other combat arms: cavalry had been rendered manifestly obsolete by the advent of mechanization, infantry was required merely to garrison that which the tanks captured, and artillery should be replaced by special versions of tanks fitted with large-calibre ordnances (self-propelled artillery) yet able to match the tank force for speed and mobility. In this latter concept Fuller went too far, and in the process so threatened (or appeared to threaten) the established arms that they banded together to stem the further acceptance of Fuller's notions. In the long run, therefore, Fuller had a partially counterproductive effect on the development of the British tank arm when he moved out of the province of tactics into the more difficult intellectual and moral terrain of operational doctrine.

Working from the same basis of operational experience as Fuller, Liddell Hart moved more easily from the field of tactics to the terrain of operations and strategy based on exploitation of the tank's speed (mobility) combined with its shock effect (firepower and protection). The key to Liddell Hart's concept was tactical and operational surprise: thus the initial offensive could be a hammer blow by massed armour into and through the enemy's front line, followed by an unrelenting exploitation in which the key was outright speed to keep the enemy off balance. Tanks must therefore be organized to push straight through opposition or, if the latter was too strong, bypass and isolate it for elimination by the follow-up forces. By maintaining its impetus, Liddell Hart showed, the tank force could punch through to the enemy's rear areas on a narrow front and then fan out in an 'expanding torrent' that would prevent the enemy's reserves from moving up in effective support, and then by destroying, capturing or incapacitating his command and logistic centres, crush the enemy's capability to sustain the defence. It is worth noting here that Liddell Hart saw the full

potential of the aeroplane for a battlefield role: Fuller had rightly realized the value of the aeroplane for reconnaissance and communication, but Liddell Hart had gone farther, to recognize the fact that the aeroplane was the ideal substitute for artillery in his 'expanding torrent', possessing yet greater mobility than the tanks they were to support and having the three-dimensional agility to negate the effect of the enemy's anti-aircraft artillery, while delivering attacks of pinpoint accuracy.

Liddell Hart's concept was remarkably farsighted, but was little accepted in his own country as anything but an idealized picture of future warfare. This was a failing with immense consequences.

The overall failure of the army advocates, Fuller and Liddell Hart, should not be construed, however, as failing in smaller objectives. The most important successes gained by the tank advocates were in the development of new vehicles possessing far greater mobility than their predecessors in terms of agility, speed and range. The development programme was severely limited by lack of funds, but evolved via two main streams, namely the one- or two-man tankettes from the Morris-Martel and Crossley-Martel stables, and the two- or three-man light tanks from the Carden-Loyd and Vickers stables.

The tankette concept can most readily be traced back to 1915, when Colonel J.E. Estienne proposed that conventional infantry could be replaced by large numbers of skirmishers mounted in small cross-country vehicles carrying sufficient armour to defeat small arms fire. This concept finally resulted in the development of the excellent Renault FT, to which the British had no equivalent. After the First World War, however, Fuller became an enthusiastic proponent of the idea of a skirmishing and reconnaissance tank. Fuller soon secured a significant following within the Tank Corps (from 1923, the Royal Tank Corps), including Major Gifford Martel. Because of lack of official interest or funds, Martel undertook the design and construction of a prototype at his own expense during 1925, using commercial components from a number of sources, tracks provided by the Roadless Traction

The Crossley-Martel One-Man Tankette is in some respects typical of the cost-cutting expedients tried during the 1920s to provide some experience towards armoured warfare, but was also unusual in being a hybrid type featuring front steering wheels and a rear track unit of the Citroen-Kegresse type with rubber tracks. (*RAC Tank Museum*)

The definitive Carden-Loyd One-Man Tankette was the Mk VI that appeared in 1928 and exerted a considerable influence on tankette design in most parts of the world. The variant has a mortar in place of the standard 0.303-in (7.7-mm) Vickers machine-gun. (*RAC Tank Museum*)

Company, and a wooden body. Trials of the Martel One-Man Tankette were modestly successful, and persuaded the army to order four pre-production versions from Morris Commercial Motors. Three of these were Morris-Martel One-Man Tankettes, and the fourth the sole Morris-Martel Two-Man Tankette. Like the Martel original, these used commercial components including the 16-hp (11.9-kW) Morris car engine to drive the short tracks in front of the twin steering wheels at the rear; the maximum speed was 20 mph (32 km/h). At 9.1 ft (2.77 m), the one-man version was the same length as the Martel prototype, but was fitted with light armour and a single machine-gun for a weight of 4,925 lb (2,234 kg), rather than 4,500 lb (2,041 kg). Another one-man machine was developed by Crossley as the Crossley-Martel One-Man Tankette, but both one-man designs proved impractical: the operator could not drive and operate the machine-gun effectively, so greater emphasis was placed on the more versatile two-man version, of which eight examples were ordered in 1927 as scouting machines with the Experimental Mechanized Force then being created to evaluate the tactical and conceptual notions of British tank enthusiasts.

The Morris and Crossley variants of the Martel theme paved the way, but were in themselves unsuitable for anything but the most limited experimental and development work. Greater success attended the efforts of Carden-Loyd Tractors Ltd, who in 1925 produced the Carden-Loyd One-Man Tankette prototype and then capitalized on the interest in the Martel prototypes to approach the War Office. A single official prototype followed, this having a box body that left the operator's shoulders and head exposed, but offered performance advantages over the Martel types in having longer tracks without separate steering wheels, plus, on each side, 14 coil-sprung road wheels instead of the Morris's two and Crossley's four road wheels. The prototype was followed by Carden-Loyd Mk I, Mk I*, Mk II and Mk III versions with a number of developments and refinements, but these single-man machines suffered the same tactical limitations as the Morris and Crossley one-man tankettes.

In 1926 the company had produced the Carden-Loyd Two-Man Tankette prototype, with a wider and lower hull to accommodate the second man. The revised hull added to tactical capabilities and also improved the stability of the basic design. Development then produced the Carden-Loyd Mk IV, with a number of mechanical improvements and provision for a single 0.5-in (12.7-mm) Vickers machine-gun. Next in numerical sequence appeared the Carden-Loyd Mk V, a tricycle wheel/track machine, of which eight were ordered to support the eight Morris-Martel Two-Man Tankettes, so next in the main stream of the company's tankette developments was the Carden-Loyd Mk VI, built by Vickers-Armstrongs Ltd after its purchase of Carden-Loyd in 1928. The Mk VI was designed as a machine-gun carrier for one 0.303- or 0.5-in (7.7- or 12.7-mm) Vickers machine-gun, which could be fired from the vehicle, or dismounted for installation on the tripod that was accommodated on the carrier. Just under 400 Mk VIs were built for the British army and for export, but with this variant, tankette design veered away from the mainstream of tank development towards the 'weapon platform' concept that led to the British Bren and Universal Carriers of the 1930s and the Second World War. The Mk VI was in its way an important and highly influential machine, serving to confirm the practicality of tracked vehicles for cross-country mobility, and inspiring comparable developments in Czechoslovakia (the MU4), France (the UE), Italy (the CV33 and CV35), Poland (the TK3) and the USSR (the T27).

The development of the Carden-Loyd Mk VI was the first result of the Royal Tank Corps' 1927 decision that, while the turretless tankette might have an application as a weapons-carrier for the infantry, the exigencies of armoured warfare called for turreted armament, so that at all times the crew was protected. The Royal Tank Corps therefore replaced the tankette with the light tank as the reconnaissance element of its tactical thinking. The first of the breed had been the 1925 Royal Ordance Factory Light Tank A3E1, an experimental machine designed to test the feasibility of using a commercial engine and

---

Carden-Loyd Tankette Mk VI
(UK)

Type: tankette
Crew: 2
Combat weight: 3,360 lb (1,524 kg)
Dimensions: length overall 8.08 ft (2.46 m); width 5.75 ft (1.75 m); height 4.00 ft (1.22 m)
Armament system: one 0.303-in (7.7-mm) Vickers machine-gun
Armour: between 5 and 9 mm (0.2 and 0.35 in)
Powerplant: one 40-hp (29.8-kW) Ford Model T petrol engine
Performance: speed, road 25 mph (40.2 km/h); range, road 90 miles (145 km); vertical obstacle 1.33 ft (0.41 m); trench 4.0 ft (1.22 m)

Carden - Loyd Mark VI

The A3E1 was developed in 1925 by the Royal Ordnance Factory as a three-man light tank of low cost through use of a bus engine and cheap cast steel tracks, but was unsuccessful. The type had front and rear machine-gun turrets, each carrying a single 0.303-in (7.7-mm) Vickers weapon. The type was later redesignated Carrier, Machine-Gun No.1. (*RAC Tank Museum*)

cast steel track shoes to reduce manufacturing costs, and carrying fore and aft machine-gun turrets.

The first practical light tank design was the Carden-Loyd Mk VII, a two-man vehicle that appeared in 1929 for evaluation as the A4E1. Though evolved from the earlier Carden-Loyd vehicles, the Mk VII provided striking proof of the pace of armoured vehicle development in the later 1920s, for it was a machine markedly superior to its predecessors in all respects. The armament was still a single 0.303-in (7.7-mm) Vickers machine-gun, but this was located in an exceptionally trim turret with bevelled edges on its top to reduce its silhouette. More notable, perhaps, was the increase in performance generated by the new running gear and more powerful engine. The former comprised four large road wheels in leafsprung pairs connected by an external girder, and the latter a 59-hp (44-kW) Meadows petrol engine: the result was a maximum speed of 35 mph (56 km/h) for this 5,600-lb (2,540-kg) vehicle. Trials confirmed the overall suitability of the A4E1, which was developed for small-scale production as the Carden-Loyd/Vickers Light Tank Mk VIII and accepted as the British army's first light tank in 1930, under the designation Light Tank Mk I. The running gear was revised and the engine was a 58-hp (43-kW) Meadows EPT petrol unit providing a maximum speed of 30 mph (48.3 km/h) in a vehicle that weighed 10,750 lb (4,876 kg)

and possessed armour varying in thickness from 4 to 14 mm (0.16 to 0.55 in). The Light Tank Mk I was then developed in variants designated between A4E2 and A4E5 for use in running trials and experiments, paving the way for the Light Tank Mk IA. This first appeared in October 1930, and was generally similar to the Mk I, apart from its better-sloped armour. Again the type was produced in various forms with designations varying from A4E6 to A4E10 to evaluate features such as Horstmann coil-spring suspension, laminated-spring suspension with shorter tracks and no idler wheels, different armament fits (including a tall turret with two machine-guns in superimposed mountings) and a different engine.

Further development of the Mk IA produced the Light Tank Mk II, of which 16 were built in 1931. The type had the hull of the Mk IA, Horstmann suspension and a 66-hp (49.2-kW) Rolls-Royce petrol engine for a maximum speed of 30 mph (48.3 km/h) at a weight of 9,500 lb (4,309 kg). The type was produced in A4E13 to A4E15 variants, and important trials were undertaken into the amphibious employment of such vehicles. Mechanical and tactical development was rampant during the early 1930s as the British army came fully to grips with the concept of total mechanization, and the Mk II was rapidly joined by the Light Tank Mk IIA (29 A4E16 and A4E18 vehicles built by the Royal Ordance Factory, Woolwich) and the Light Tank Mk IIB (21 A4E17 vehicles built by

57

Vickers-Armstrongs Ltd). The two variants were essentially similar, and were in essence an upgraded Mk I with the Horstmann suspension of the Mk II, though with two rather than three track-return rollers. There was also a Light Tank Mk IIB (India Pattern) with the Meadows EPT engine and a non-rotating cupola atop the turret.

In production terms, the family evolved directly from the Carden-Loyd Mk VII ended with the Light Tank Mk III and Light Tank Mk IV. The Mk III entered service in 1933 as a Mk II with its superstructure lengthened to the rear. The ultimate developments from this were the Light Tank Vickers Experimental Model 1933 India Pattern No. 1 (A4E19) and No. 2 (A4E20), with features such as a shorter and wider hull, lighter armour and a 90-hp (67.1-kW) Meadows EST engine to reduce weight, facilitate production and increase speed. The Mk IV series was produced in 1934 on the basis of the two model 1933 experimental variants. In the Mk IV the hull was made of armour varying in thickness from 5 to 12 mm (0.2 to 0.47 in) and, for the first time in British practice, used as a monocoque chassis, with components attached directly to it. An important feature adopted from the Model 1933 variants was the omission of the rear idler wheels: this track layout, combined with Horstmann suspension and an 88-hp (65.6-kW) Meadows ESTE engine provided the 10,300-lb (4,672-kg) Mk IV with a max-

imum speed of 36 mph (57.9 km/h).

By this time the Royal Tank Corps had amassed a considerable volume of experimental and operational data with its first series of light tanks. On the whole it was satisfied that the light tank has a valuable role to play, though operational experience was limited to parts of the world where there was no effective opposition. It was clear, though, that while the monocoque hull, powerplant and running gear of the Mk IV still had value, the vehicle was limited in operational capacity by its one-man turret and its single machine-gun. An important step was thus taken with the 1935 adoption of the Light Tank Mk V. This was another Vickers-Armstrongs product, and was in practical terms the hull of the Mk IV with an enlarged fighting compartment surmounted by a new two-man turret. This was the first such unit fitted on a light tank, and for ease of traverse it was mounted on a ball race: the armament comprised two Vickers machine-guns, one of 0.303-in (7.7-mm) and the other of 0.5-in (12.7-mm) calibre, and the turret was surmounted by a commander's cupola. The Mk IV had been criticized for being nose heavy, and in the Mk V the weight was redistributed to remove the problem. Power was provided by a Meadows ESTL engine, whose 88 hp (65.6 kW) provided the 9,300-lb (4,218-kg) Mk V with a maximum speed of 32 mph (51.5 km/h).

For a number of reasons (including the cost factor) many countries adhered to the light tank concept long after it had become obsolete. Typical were the British, whose Light Tank Mk V was introduced in 1935. Amongst the type's useful features, however, was the first two-man turret fitted on a light tank. (*RAC Tank Museum*)

In 1936 the Light Tank Mk VI entered service, and with it the stream of development by Vickers-Armstrongs on the basis of the Carden-Loyd Mk VII came to an end. The Mk VI was modelled closely on the Mk V, with the turret increased in length rearwards to allow the installation of a radio set. The hull was also lengthened, and with an 88-hp (65.6-kW) Meadows ESTL engine this 10,750 lb (4,876-kg) tank had a maximum speed of 35 mph (56.3 km/h). The type was mechanically reliable and cheap to produce, a combination that prompted large-scale orders: indeed, during the first month of the Second World War in September 1939 the British army fielded about 1,000 examples of the Mk VI family. Given the army's lack of recent combat experience against a high-quality enemy, these modest little vehicles were extensively used in Europe, the Middle East and North Africa, suffering heavy losses because of their poor offensive and defensive capabilities.

As procurement of the Mk VI proceeded, improvements were incorporated as and when possible, to produce a number of variants. These started with the Light Tank Mk VIA with a more powerful engine, a revised commander's cupola, and modified suspension with the single track-return roller attached to the hull rather than to the forward bogie unit. Then came the Light Tank Mk VIB, which was the most extensively used British light tank of the Second World War: this reverted to the circular commander's cupola from the octagonal unit of the Mk VIA or, in its Light Tank Mk VIB (India Pattern) subvariant, had no cupola. The ultimate model was the Light Tank Mk VIC, with wider tracks and suspension units, roof hatches in place of the commander's cupola, and armament comprising two Besa machine-guns, one of 15-mm (0.59-in) and the other of 7.92-mm (0.312-in) calibre.

The final pair of British three-man light tanks were both Vickers-Armstrongs designs, the Light Tank Mk VII Tetrarch of 1938, and its successor the Light Tank Mk VIII Harry Hopkins of 1941. The two types were built only in small numbers, and were similar in concept, being based on four independently-sprung road wheels of which the rear units served as drive sprockets and the front units as idlers; the

Light Tank Mark VIB

Light Tank Mk VIB
(UK)

Type: light tank
Crew: 3
Combat weight: 11,648 lb (5283 kg)
Dimensions: length overall 13.17 ft (4.01 m); width 6.83 ft (2.08 m); height 7.42 ft (2.26 m)
Armament system: one 0.5-in (12.7-mm) Vickers machine-gun with 400 rounds, one 0.303-in (7.7-mm) Vickers machine-gun with 2,500 rounds and one 4-in (102-mm) smoke-discharger
Armour: between 4 and 15 mm (0.16 and 0.59 in)
Powerplant: one 88-hp (65.6-kW) Meadows petrol engine
Performance: speed, road 35 mph (56.3 km/h); range, road 125 miles (201 km); gradient 60%; vertical obstacle 2.0 ft (0.61 m); trench 5.0 ft (1.52 m)

steering was unusual, sharp turns being effected by the standard skid occasioned by braking of the inside track, but gentle turns being provided by pivoting of the road wheels to curve the tracks. The Mk VII was armed with a 2-pdr (40-mm) main gun plus a coaxial 7.92-mm (0.312-in) Besa machine-gun in a trim turret. The armour thickness ranged from 4 to 16 mm (0.16 to 0.63 in) for a vehicle weight of 16,800 lb (7,620 kg), and the 165-hp (123-kW) Meadows petrol engine provided a maximum speed of 37 mph (59.5 km/h). The Mk VII had little practical application in the Second World War, its only real use being the provision of armoured support for airborne forces, after arrival in the specially-designed General Aircraft Hamilcar glider. The type was also used in small numbers as the Tetrarch Infantry Close Support (ICS) with a 3-in (76.2-mm) howitzer

Light Tank Mk VII Tetrarch

Light Tank Mk VIII Harry Hopkins

A17 Light Tank Mk VII Tetrarch Mk I
(UK)

Type: light tank
Crew: 3
Combat weight: 16,800 lb (7,620 kg)
Dimensions: length, gun forward 14.125 ft (4.31 m) and hull 13.50 ft (4.11 m); width 7.58 ft (2.31 m); height 6.92 ft (2.10 m)
Armament system: one 2-pdr (40-mm) gun with 50 rounds, one 7.92-mm (0.312-in) Besa machine-gun with 2,025 rounds and two 4-in (102-mm) smoke-dischargers
Armour: between 4 and 16 mm (0.16 and 0.63 in)
Powerplant: one 165-hp (123-kW) Meadows MAT petrol engine with 45 Imp. gal. (205 litres) of fuel
Performance: speed, road 40 mph (64.4 km/h); range, road 140 miles (224 km); fording 3.0 ft (0.91 m) without preparation; gradient 60%; vertical obstacle 1.67 ft (0.51 m); trench 5.0 ft (1.52 m)

Light Tank Mk VIII Harry Hopkins
(UK)

Type: light tank
Crew: 3
Combat weight: 19,040 lb (8,637 kg)
Dimensions: length overall 14.25 ft (4.35 m); width 8.875 ft (2.705 m); height 6.917 ft (2.108 m)
Armament system: one 2-pdr (40-mm gun) and one 7.92-mm (0.312-in) Besa machine-gun
Armour: between 6.4 and 38.1 mm (0.25 and 1.5 in)
Powerplant: one 149-hp (111-kW) Meadows petrol engine
Performance: speed, road 30 mph (48.3 km/h); range, road 125 miles (201 km)

rather than 2-pdr (40-mm) turret gun.

The Mk VIII was intended to overcome the Mk VII's vulnerability, by the adoption of armour that was both thicker and of superior ballistic shape: the maximum thickness was 38 mm (1.5 in), but the result was an increase in weight to 19,050 lb (8,641 kg) and decrease in speed to 30 mph (48.3 km/h) on the 149-hp (111-kW) Meadows engine. Mk VIII production amounted to 100 machines, but fortunately for their crews these were never issued for service.

Such, then, was the mainstream of British light tank development in the period between the two world wars. It is worth noting though, that in addition to its Carden-Loyd derivatives for the British army, Vickers-Armstrongs also developed and produced two private-venture series of light tanks that enjoyed considerable export success. The first of these was the Sixton Tank Mk E, powered by an 87-hp (64.8-kW) Armstrong-Siddeley engine: the Mk E was built in two basic forms: as the Type A with two side-by-side turrets each fitted with a single Vickers machine-gun (generally two 0.303-in/7.7-mm weapons but sometimes one 0.303-in/7.7-mm and one 0.5-in/12.7-mm weapon), armour to a 13-mm (0.51-in) basis and a weight of 16,125 lb (7,314 kg); and as the Type B, with a two-man turret accommodating one 3-pdr (47-mm) gun and a coaxial machine-gun, armour to a 17-mm (0.67-in) basis and a weight of 16,575 lb (7,518 kg). Examples of this series were sold to Bolivia, Bulgaria, China, Estonia, Finland, Greece, Japan, Poland, Portugal, Romania, Siam and the USSR, and overseas development and construction resulted in the Polish 7TP, the Soviet T-26 and the US T1

Vickers Six-Ton Tank Mk E Type A

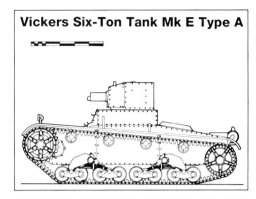

7 TP jw

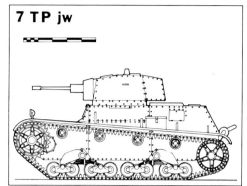

Vickers Six-Ton Tank Mk E Type A
(UK)

Type: medium tank
Crew: 3
Combat weight: 15,680 lb (7,112 kg)
Dimensions: length overall 15.00 ft (4.57 m); width 7.917 ft (2.41 m); height 6.83 ft (2.08 m)
Armament system: two Vickers 0.303-in (7.7-mm) machine-guns, or one Vickers 0.5-in (12.7-mm) and one Vickers 0.303-in (7.7-mm) machine-gun
Armour: between 5 and 14 mm (0.2 and 0.55 in)
Powerplant: one 80-hp (59.6-kW) Armstrong Siddeley petrol engine
Performance: speed, road 22 mph (35.4 km/h)

series.

The second series was similar to the Light Tank Mk IV, though fitted with a bewildering array of armaments. Examples of the Light Tank Model 1933 were sold to Finland, Lithuania and Latvia; of the Model 1934 to Argentina, Belgium and Switzerland; and of the Model 1936 to China, the Dutch East Indies and the Netherlands.

Further up the weight scale was the medium tank, for which the light tank provided reconnaissance and support: thus, while the light tank was the inheritor of the First World War medium tank's mantle, the medium tank succeeded the (battle) tank of that war. Initial British efforts in the period after the First World War were the Medium Tank Mk D, continuing the effort already well under way in the war, and the Light Infantry Tank. The latter was again the work of Colonel P. Johnson of the government's Tank Design Department, and similar to the Mk D, though smaller and lighter: its role was machine-gun support of infantry

assaults, but work was ended in 1923 when the Tank Design Department was closed down as part of the government's financial retrenchment programme.

By this time, Vickers-Armstrongs had been invited to join the medium tank development programme, and its first design in this important field was the five-man Vickers Tank, produced in Nos 1 and 2 variants during 1921 and 1922. The overall configuration was akin to that of the Medium Tank Mk B, but the Vickers Tank sported a roof-mounted turret of domed shape, surmounted by a commander's cupola. The Vickers Tank was thus the first British armoured fighting vehicle with its main armament in a 360° traverse turret: in the No. 1, the turret accommodated three 0.303-in (7.7-mm) Hotchkiss machine-guns in ball mountings, including one for anti-aircraft fire. Based on 0.5-in (12.7-mm) armour and weighing 19,600 lb (8,891 kg), the Vickers Tank was

7 TP jw (7 TP Improved)
(Poland)

Type: light tank
Crew: 3
Combat weight: 11,000 kg (24,250 lb)
Dimensions: length overall 15.08 m (15.08 ft); width 2.413 m (7.92 ft); height 2.159 m (7.08 ft)
Armament system: one 37-mm gun and one 7.92-mm (0.312-in) machine-gun
Armour: 40 mm (1.575 in) maximum
Powerplant: one 82-kW (110-hp) Saurer diesel
Performance: speed, road 32 km/h (19.9 mph); range, road 160 km (100 miles); gradient 60%; vertical obstacle 0.6 m (1.97 ft); trench 1.825 m (6.0 ft)

The Vickers Six-Ton Tank was a considerable export success in the 1930s, this being a Chinese Mk 'F' similar to the single-turret Six-Ton Tank Type B but fitted with radio in a bulged turret rear. (*RAC Tank Museum*)

powered by an 86-hp (64.1-kW) engine and proved mechanically unreliable.

Experience with the Vickers Tank was important for the company, however, and its next design was a winner, and one of the most notable steps in the evolution of tank design: the new vehicle was the world's first fast tank, allowing the type's use in the manoeuvres that validated the tactical and operational concepts originating from Fuller and Liddell Hart. The body was located above the tracks so that adequate armament could be located in a revolving turret without loss of fields of fire, and reduction of length and weight thus achieved allowed higher performance on the same power as earlier tanks. Designed in 1922 as the first British tank of genuinely postwar concept, the five-man Light Tank Mk I was redesignated the Vickers Medium Tank Mk I after the army's decision to buy the Carden-Loyd/Vickers Mk VIII (the Light Tank Mk I). The Medium Tank Mk I entered production in 1923 and service in 1924, and in its various forms was built to a total of about 160 machines that formed the mainstay of the Royal Tank Corps in the later 1920s and early 1930s, and remained in service until the period just before the Second World War. The Mk I was the first British service tank to have a 360° traverse turret and geared elevation for the main armament, and

is also notable for the high speed made possible by the sprung suspension and the 90-hp (67.1-kW) Armstrong Siddeley petrol engine: officially 16 mph (25.75 km/h), this speed was in reality just under 30 mph (48.3 km/h). The armour was to a 6.5-mm (0.26-in) basis, mainly of riveted plate, resulting in a box-like hull in which the driver was located at the front of the vehicle, next to the engine. The other four crew members were located in the fighting compartment and turret to deal with command, operation of the radio, and the handling of the armament. This had both advanced and obsolescent features: on the advanced side was the powerful 3-pdr (47-mm) Mk 1 L/31.4 main gun, a 217-lb (98.4-kg) weapon firing a 3-lb (1.36-kg) shot with a muzzle velocity of 1,750 ft (533 m) per second to pierce 25 mm (1 in) of armour angled at 30° at a range of 500 yards (457 m); and on the obsolescent side was the secondary armament, comprising four 0.303-in (7.7-mm) Hotchkiss guns in the turret plus a pair of 0.303-in (7.7-mm) Vickers guns in the hull sides.

Given the type's longevity of service, it is not surprising that the basic machine was developed into variants with a number of mechanical and operational improvements. First of these, appearing in 1924, was the Medium Tank Mk IA with slightly thicker armour, in-

creasing weight to 26,655 lb (12,091 kg), and a revised secondary armament arrangement, including an anti-aircraft mounting on a newly bevelled turret rear. The Medium Tank Mk IA* was basically similar to the Mk IA, but fitted with a 0.303-in (7.7-mm) Vickers coaxial machine-gun and a commander's cupola on the turret. The Medium Tank Mk I ICS was the infantry close support version, the standard 3-pdr (47-mm) ordance of the gun tank being replaced by a 3-in (76-mm) Mk 1 L/25 howitzer, a 256-lb (116.1-kg) weapon firing its 13.75-lb (6.24-kg) projectile to a range of 2,000 yards (1,830 m). There were also two experimental variants, in the forms of the Medium Tank Mk I (Ricardo C.I) and the Medium Tank Mk I Wheel-and-Track: the former was powered by a 90-hp (67.1-kW) Ricardo diesel engine, and the latter had nose- and tail-mounted wheels. These were twin-wheel units power-lowered (via a gearbox take-off) in about one minute, the object being to reduce track wear by removing them from road contact whenever possible.

In 1925 Vickers-Armstrongs introduced the improved Medium Tank Mk II with armour on an 8.25-mm (0.325-in) basis for improved protection, at the penalty of a weight increase to 29,575 lb (13,415 kg), the longer 3-pdr (47-mm) Mk 2 L/40.05 gun with an additional 100 ft (30.5 m) per second of muzzle velocity for

Medium Tank Mk I
(UK)

Type: medium tank
Crew: 5
Combat weight: 26,208 lb (11,888 kg)
Dimensions: length overall 17.50 ft (5.33 m); width 9.125 ft (2.78 m); height 9.25 ft (2.82 m)
Armament system: one 3-pdr (47-mm) gun, four 0.303-in (7.7-mm) Hotchkiss machine-guns and two 0.303-in (7.7-mm) Vickers machine-guns
Armour: 6.25 mm (0.25 in)
Powerplant: one 90-hp (67.1-kW) Armstrong Siddeley petrol engine with 72 Imp. gal. (327 litres) of fuel
Performance: speed, road 15 mph (24.1 km/h); range, road 120 miles (193 km); fording 2.3 ft (0.7 m); trench 6.5 ft (2.0 m)

A Vickers design, the Light Tank Mk I was then redesignated Medium Tank Mk I, and amongst its advanced features were fully sprung suspension for higher speeds, a turret capable of 360° traverse, and a main gun with geared elevation. These are Mk I and Mk IA tanks, the latter differing only in detail from the former. (*RAC Tank Museum*)

Vickers Medium Tank Mk I

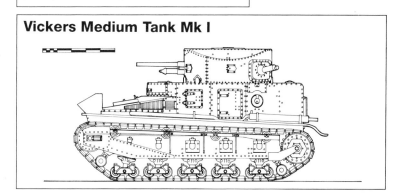

slightly more armour penetration, the driver located farther forward for better fields of vision, and the suspension protected by skirt armour.

Variations of this basic theme were the Medium Tank Mk II* with a Vickers coaxial machine-gun and no turret-mounted Hotchkiss machine-guns; the 1932 Medium Tank Mk II** produced by converting Mk IIs to a standard approximating to that of the Mk II* but with the addition of an armoured radio installation and a commander's cupola; the 1930 Medium Tank Mk IIA with a number of detail improvements and revised tracks; the Medium Tank Mk IIA* basically similar to the Mk IIA but with radio in an armoured installation; the Medium Tank Mk IIA Close Support based on the Mk IIA but with a 3-in (76.2-mm) howitzer in place of the gun tank's 3-pdr (47-mm) quick firing gun; and the 1931 Medium Tank Mk II Command with a fixed turret (complete with dummy gun barrel) carrying additional radio equipment. There were also tropical and bridge carrier versions, and for the USSR a small number of 'English Workman' tanks were built to a standard similar to that of the Mk IIA.

As the Medium Tank Mk II was entering service, Vickers-Armstrongs was involved during 1925 in the design of the Vickers Independent Tank, which pioneered a number of advanced features and had a profound effect on tank design outside the UK. This tank inaugurated the new British system of tank nomenclature, being officially designated the A1E1, and was delivered to the Mechanical Warfare Experimental Establishment in 1926 for exhaustive trials that did not lead to a production order, because of financial restrictions rather than any major problem with the tank itself. Amongst the Independent Tank's more advanced features were intercommunication between the eight-man crew by throat-mounted laryngaphone, a long wheelbase with the hull built up between the suspension assemblies, hydraulically powered controls, and wheel steering for all but the sharpest turns. For its time, the Independent was a massive machine, weighing 70,560 lb (32,006 kg) and measuring 25.42 ft (7.75 m) in overall length. Power was provided by a 398-hp (267-kW) Armstrong Siddeley petrol engine for a maximum speed of 25 mph (40.2 km/h), and the armour varied in thickness between 13 and 28 mm (0.51 and 1.1 in). Most unusual (and widely copied, largely in Germany and the USSR) was the armament system, which comprised one main turret with four subsidiary turrets clustered round it. The main turret was fitted with a 3-pdr (47-mm) Mk 2 gun and incor-

The most important British tank of the later 1920s and early 1930s was the Vickers-designed Medium Tank Mk II. This is a Mk II**, the designation applying to 44 Mk IIs converted in 1934 with a commander's cupola, radio in a rear bulge of the turret, and a twin mountings for the turret's 3-pdr (47-mm) gun and Vickers machine-gun. (*RAC Tank Museum*)

A1E1 'Independent'

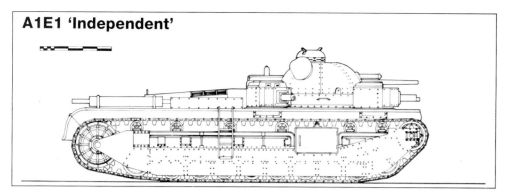

porated a cupola for the commander, whose laryngaphone communication with all other crew members was complemented by a pointer system to indicate targets to any of the turrets. The subsidiary turrets were each fitted with a single 0.303-in (7.7-mm) Vickers machine-gun.

Elements of this innovative machine were evident in the two other British medium tanks of the period between the world wars, namely the A6 and the A7.

Only prototypes of the A6 were built between 1928 and 1930, with engines ranging from a 180-hp (134-kW) Armstrong Siddeley petrol engine (A6E1) and a similarly rated Ricardo C.1 diesel (A6E2) to the 500-hp (373-kW) Thorneycroft RY-12 diesel. The tanks were well armoured, fitted as standard with radio and protection against gas attack, and armed with three turrets: the main turret accommodated one 3-pdr (47-mm) gun and one 0.303-in (7.7-mm) Vickers coaxial machine-gun, and each of the two forward-mounted subsidiary turrets accommodated twin Vickers guns. The production version was to have been the Medium Tank Mk III, of which three prototypes were built in 1930 with a number of improvements, and reduction of the secondary armament to three machine-guns.

The A7 was an official design by the Chief Superintendent of Design for construction at the Royal Ordnance Factory, Woolwich. The first two examples were the A7E1 (3-pdr/47-mm main gun plus two Vickers machine-guns) and A7E2 (2-pdr/40-mm main gun plus two Vickers machine-guns), and trials confirmed that the basic design was excellent. There were a number of mechanical failings,

Vickers A1E1 'Independent' (UK)

Type: heavy tank prototype
Crew: 8
Combat weight: 70,560 lb (32,006 kg)
Dimensions: length overall 24.42 ft (7.747 m); width 10.50 ft (4.76 m); height 8.83 ft (2.69 m)
Armament system: one 3-pdr (47-mm) gun and four 0.303-in (7.7-mm) Vickers machine-guns
Armour: between 12.7 and 29 mm (0.5 and 1.14 in)
Powerplant: one 398-hp (297-kW) Armstrong Siddeley petrol engine
Performance: speed, road 25 mph (40.25 km/h)

though, and by the time these had been overcome in 1936, the design was obsolescent. Similar mechanical problems dogged the 1937 trials of the single A7E3, which was based on the A7E2 but powered by twin AEC diesels, and incorporated features of the A6E3 and Medium Tank Mk III.

Up to the early 1930s the British had remained confident that they had the right 'mix' of armoured vehicles, in the form of the light tank for reconnaissance, and the medium tank for independent mobile operations and support of the infantry. But when the failure of the A6 and A7 programmes coincided with the realization of a rapid rearmament programme forced by Germany's growing strength and belligerence, the army decided that it could best cater for the independent mobile and infantry support roles with different tank types. Thus the medium tank gave way to the cruiser tank for mobile operations, and the infantry tank for support operations.

The first cruiser tank was the A9, otherwise

65

Cruiser Tank Mark I CS (A9)

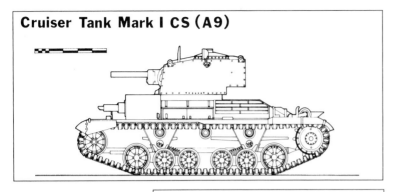

A9 Cruiser Tank Mk I CS
(UK)

Type: cruiser tank (close support)
Crew: 6
Combat weight: 28,068 lb (12,732 kg)
Dimensions: length overall 19,00 ft (5.79 m); width 8.42 ft (2.57 m); height 8.67 ft (2.64 m)
Armament system: one 3.7-in (94-mm) howitzer and three 0.303-in (7.7-mm) Vickers machine-guns with 3,000 rounds
Armour: between 6 and 14 mm (0.24 and 0.55 in)
Powerplant: one 150-hp (111.8-kW) AEC Type 179 petrol engine with 72 Imp. gal. (327 litres) of fuel
Performance: speed, road 25 mph (40.2 km/h); range, road 150 miles (241 km); vertical obstacle 3.0 ft (0.91 m); trench 8.0 ft (2.43 m); ground clearance 18 in (0.46 m)

known as the Cruiser Tank Mk I and designed by Sir John Carden of Vickers-Armstrongs in 1934 as a simpler and cheaper derivative of the A6/Medium Tank Mk III. The type entered small-scale production in 1937 as a 28,000-lb (12,701-kg) vehicle with a crew of six, a 150-hp (112-kW) AEC Type 179 petrol engine for a maximum speed of 23 mph (37 km/h), armour between 4 and 16 mm (0.16 and 0.63 in) thick, and an armament of one 2-pdr (40-mm) gun and one 0.303-in (7.7-mm) machine-gun in the power-traversed main turret and one Vickers machine-gun in each of two subsidiary turrets. The use of a 2-pdr (40-mm) gun in place of the previously standard 3-pdr (47-mm) weapon may appear to have been a retrograde step, but it was in fact a highly sensible move as the smaller-calibre weapon had far higher muzzle velocity than the larger weapon, and thus greater armour-penetrating capability. Whereas the 3-pdr (47-mm) weapon fired its 3-lb (1.36-kg) shot with a muzzle velocity of 1,850 ft (564 m) per second to pierce 27 mm (1.06 in) of armour at an angle of 30° at a range of 500 yards (457 m), the 2-pdr (40-mm) weapon fired its 2.375-lb (1.08-kg) shot with a muzzle velocity of 2,800 ft (1,270 m) per second to pierce 57 mm (2.24 in) of armour at an angle of 30° at a range of 500 yards (457 m). The 2-pdr (40-mm) ordnance was slightly longer and heavier than the 3-pdr (47-mm)

The A9 Cruiser Tank was developed in the UK as replacement for the Medium Tank Mk I and Mk II family. The work was carried out by Vickers on the basis of the cancelled A6, and this is a Cruiser Tank Mk I CS with a 3.7-in (95-mm) howitzer in place of the original turret-mounted 2-pdr (40-mm) high-velocity gun. (*RAC Tank Museum*)

weapon, but this was more than offset by its considerably greater lethal effect.

Production of the A9 amounted to only 125 vehicles, and the type remained in service up to 1941, seeing operational use in France and North Africa.

At the same time as developing the A9, Vickers-Armstrongs undertook design of the A10 as an infantry tank, using the A9 as its basis, but increasing the armour thickness to a maximum of 30 mm (1.18 in): the additional armour took the form of plates attached to the hull (the first use of appliqué armour on a British tank), and increased the weight of the vehicle to 30,800 lb (13,971 kg). The engine remained unaltered, and this meant a reduction in maximum speed to 16 mph (25.75 km/h). The subsidiary turrets of the A9 were not retained, and in 1940 the Vickers coaxial machine-gun was replaced by a 7.92-mm (0.312-in) Besa, a weapon of the same type sometimes being added in the nose in place of some of the ammunition stowage. By the time the A10 was ready for production, it was clear that it lacked adequate protection for the infantry role, and the type was classified as the Heavy Cruiser Tank Mk II. There was also a Mk IIA with detail improvements (and in later vehicles improved armour, including additional thickness over the mantlet), and as with the A9, an infantry close support version with a 3.7-in (94-mm) howitzer, this Mortar Mk 1 being a 222-lb (100.7-kg) weapon whose L/15 barrel fired a 10.5-lb (4.76-kg) projectile with a muzzle velocity of only 620 ft (189 m) per second.

There now came a turning point in British tank design, with the 1936 decision to develop new cruiser tanks on the basis of the suspension system devised in the USA by J. Walter Christie and already adopted with a high degree of success by the Soviets for their BT series. The Christie suspension used large-diameter road wheels attached to swinging arms supported by long coil springs: this gave the individual road wheels great vertical movement. In its basic form the Christie suspension system provided for high speed over adverse terrain, but considerable work had to be undertaken to turn the system into a battleworthy suspension for the new cruiser tanks. The

Cruiser Mark IIA (A10)

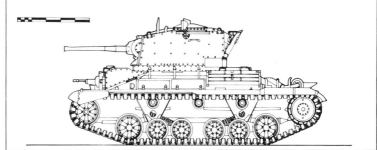

A10 Cruiser Tank Mk IIA
(UK)

Type: heavy cruiser tank
Crew: 5
Combat weight: 30,800 lb (13,971 kg)
Dimensions: length, gun forward 19.25 ft (5.87 m) and hull 18.08 ft (5.51 m); width 8.29 ft (2.53 m); height 8.5 ft (2.59 m)
Armament system: one 2-pdr (40-mm) gun and two 7.92-mm (0.3-in) Besa machine-guns
Armour: 30 mm (1.18 in)
Powerplant: one 150-hp (111.8-kW) AEC petrol engine
Performance: speed, road 16 mph (25.75 km/h); range, road 100 miles (161 km)

Designed by Vickers, the A10 Cruiser Tank Mk II was a much improved version of the Cruiser Tank Mk I with sufficient armour to allow the type's use as an infantry tank when required. This is a Mk IIA of the main production sequence, with the hull machine-gun omitted from some earlier vehicles. (*RAC Tank Museum*)

result was incorporated in the A13 designed under the auspices of the Mechanisation Board by Nuffield Mechanisations and Aero Ltd, a branch of the Nuffield industrial organization. The prototype was completed in 1937 and immediately displayed excellent performance as a result of the Christie suspension combined with a high power-to-weight ratio: the A13 was powered by a 340-hp (253.5-kW) derivative of the Liberty aero engine and weighed 31,810 lb (14,429 kg) for a ratio of 23.9 hp per ton (17.57 kW per tonne), which compares interestingly with the Cruiser Tank Mk II's 10.9 hp per ton (8.006 kW per tonne). This produced a maximum speed of more that 30 mph (48.3 km/h) combined with unprecedented cross-country performance. Only moderate armour was provided, with minimum and maximum thicknesses of 6 and 14 mm (0.24 and 0.55 in) as the tank was intended to rely on performance and agility as the main platforms of its protection, and the araries-

A13 Mk I Cruiser Tank Mk III
(UK)

Type: cruiser tank
Crew: 4
Combat weight: 31,808 lb (14,428 kg)
Dimensions: length overall 19.75 ft (6.02 m); width 8.33 ft (2.54 m); height 8.50 ft (2.59 m)
Armament system: one 2-pdr (40-mm) gun and one 0.303-in (7.7-mm) Vickers machine-gun
Armour: between 6 and 14 mm (0.24 and 0.55 in)
Powerplant: one 340-hp (253.5-kW) Nuffield Liberty petrol engine
Performance: speed, road 30 mph (48.3 km/h); range, road 90 miles (145 km)

Cruiser Tank Mark III (A13 Mk I)

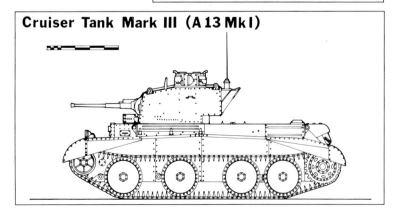

mament was also modest. This comprised a turret-mounted 2-pdr (40-mm) gun and 0.303-in (7.7-mm) Vickers coaxial machine-gun. The reduction in the number of machine-guns did not seriously affect the tank's ability to defend itself against infantry attack, and had the very useful advantage of allowing a reduction in crew number to a mere four men. Deliveries of the resultant Cruiser Tank Mk III began in December 1938 and were completed in 1939, when the improved Cruiser Tank Mk IV began to appear. The Mk III was used in France during 1940 and in North Africa during 1941, and proved a failure because of its wholly inadequate armour.

It was this failing that the Mk IV (otherwise the A13 Mk II) was designed to overcome through the addition of additional armour to increase the protective basis to 20 or 30 mm (0.79 or 1.18 in) in the more important areas. Even so, the Mk IV was decidedly underarmoured by the standards of its contemporaries. The Mk IVA introduced a 7.92-mm (0.312-in) Besa coaxial machine-gun in place of the original Vickers, and also featured a Wilson combined gearchange and steering gearbox. As with the Mk III, range was too limited for effective independent operations, and the angular design of the box-like hull and vee-sided turret provided many shot traps.

During this period the British learned of the Soviet T-28 tank, and decided to investigate more fully the concept of a heavy cruiser tank with the A14, built by the London, Midland & Scottish Railway Co., and the A16 built by Nuffield Mechanisations and Aero. It was government policy in this period to allocate the design and construction of less important tanks to companies with heavy engineering capability but no previous experience of armoured fighting vehicles: the country's capacity for tank production was thereby expanded, and the failure of the design would have minimal operational consequences, while still providing the company with useful experience. The A14 had Horstmann suspension and the A16 was designed round Christie suspension, but both were unsuccessful and cancelled in 1939, the A16 even before the prototype had been completed.

The next British cruiser tank was therefore

the A13 Mk III, otherwise known as the Cruiser Tank Mk V Covenanter. This resulted from official dissatisfaction with the speed of the A14 prototype, and the LMS Railway Co. was therefore asked to develop, on the basis of the A13 Mk II, a cruiser tank with considerably better speed than the 66,080-lb (29,974-kg) A14. The Covenanter was essentially the A13 Mk II with a purpose-designed 300-hp (224-kW) Meadows engine, armour thicknesses increased to between 7 and 40 mm (0.28 and 1.575 in), and a low-silhouette turret designed to optimize ballistic protection by increasing armour angles. The tank was a combat vehicle of some potential, and production eventually amounted to 1,771: but the type was beset by intractable problems with engine cooling and, despite evolution through four marks in an effort to overcome these difficulties, was never used in combat. The Covenanter nevertheless proved invaluable as a training tank. The standard armament was one 2-pdr (40-mm) gun and a 7.92-mm (0.312-in) Besa coaxial machine-gun, but the close-support variant of each of the four marks was fitted with a 3-in (76.2-mm) howitzer.

The next British cruiser tank was the A15, otherwise the Cruiser Tank Mk VI Crusader. Design of this important tank was started in 1938 but completed only in 1940, and is described more fully in a later chapter.

As noted above, the cancellation of the A6 and A7 medium tanks in the mid 1930s coincided with the realization that, whereas previous tanks had been fitted with the 14-mm (0.55-in) armour deemed sufficient to stop the anti-tank projectiles fired by small arms, the advent of specialist anti-tank guns in calibres of 37 mm or greater posed a new threat. The cruiser tank was evolved as successor to the medium tank in its mobile independent role, with only modest armour as it was to rely on agility and speed for its main protection. The infantry support role demanded a new type of tank, with considerably greater armour protection, as agility and speed would not be appropriate to the operational task envisaged. The division of the medium tank role into the cruiser and infantry roles coincided with the appointment to the position of Master General of the Ordnance of General Sir Hugh Elles,

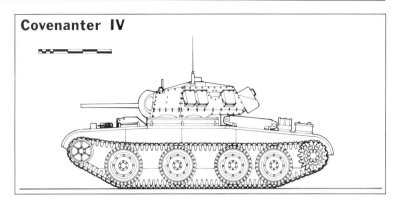

Covenanter IV

A13 Mk III Cruiser Tank Mk V**
Covenanter IV
(UK)

Type: heavy cruiser tank
Crew: 4
Combat weight: 40,320 lb (18,289 kg)
Dimensions: length overall 19.00 ft (5.79 m); width 8.58 ft (2.62 m); height 7.33 ft (2.23 m)
Armament system: one 2-pdr (40-mm) gun and one 7.92-mm (0.312-in) Besa machine-gun
Armour: between 7 and 40 mm (0.28 and 1.575 in)
Powerplant: one 300-hp (224-kW) Meadows DAV petrol engine
Performance: speed, road 31 mph (49.9 km/h); range, road 100 miles (161 km)

commander of the Tank Corps in the First World War. Elles thus had considerable operational experience of the direct infantry support role, and despite the technical and financial objections of many interested parties, Elles was insistent that a new breed of infantry tank should be evolved: the primary requirements were to be invulnerability to the fire of 37-mm anti-tank guns, and good performance in adverse conditions.

The task was entrusted to Sir John Carden of Vickers-Armstrongs, but the predetermined unit cost of each vehicle meant that Carden had to work to very fine limits and forget all possibility of 'frills'. The resulting A11, or Infantry Tank Mk I Matilda, gave every indication of having been designed down to a price, rather than up to a specification, yet managed to achieve one of the concept's primary requirements: invulnerability to the anti-tank weapons of the day, thanks to the use of armour varying in thickness between 10 and 60 mm (0.39 and 2.36 in). Indeed, it is rightly pointed out that up to the end of 1940, the A11 was amongst the world's most heavily armoured tanks, and this helped to reduce losses. This was perhaps just as well, for on the other side of the coin the A11 was not adequately planned in terms of armament, the limiting price having forced Carden to design a small vehicle whose two-man crew dictated the use, for the first time on a British tank, of a one-man cast turret armed with just one 0.303-in (7.7-mm) Vickers machine-gun, later altered to one 0.5-in (12.7-mm) Vickers machine-gun in a move that increased firepower but further cramped the already uncomfortable turret. The armament was thus wholly inadequate right from the beginning of the tank's service career in 1938, the tracks and running gear were based on those of the Vickers Six-Ton Light Tank, and were thus vulnerable and limited in capability to low speeds and modest power, as they carried at least twice their designed load. The 70-hp (52.2-kW) Ford engine proved inadequate for this 24,640-lb (11,177-kg) vehicle, without considerable gearing down.

Even as the A11 was starting prototype trials in 1936, the War Office was concluding that the infantry tank should not only be well protected, but also sufficiently well armed to deal with enemy positions as well as infantry. A cursory examination showed that the A11 could not be evolved in such a fashion, and it was decided to limit A11 production to 139 machines that would serve as interim types, pending the arrival of a superior infantry tank. This was the A12, otherwise known as the Infantry Tank Mk II Matilda II, and designed by the Tank Design Department of the Mechanisation Board on the basis of the 1932 A7 prototype, using the same running gear (strengthened for higher weights) and powerplant of two 87-hp (64.9-kW) AEC diesels, driving through a Wilson gearbox. The design was ordered straight into production, and for lack of tank-experienced companies with the capability for making large armour castings, manufacture was entrusted to the Vulcan Foundry of Warrington, with other companies brought in as the programme expanded. Most of the castings for the heavy hull and turret armour, varying in thickness between 20 and 78 mm (0.79 and 3.08 in), were produced by Vulcan, which was responsible for final assembly. Production eventually

The very small size of the Infantry Tank Mk I is readily apparent in this illustration of a Romanian inspection of vehicles belonging to the 4th Battalion, Royal Tank Corps. (*RAC Tank Museum*)

A12 Infantry Tank Mk IIA* Matilda III (UK)

Type: infantry tank
Crew: 4
Combat weight: 59,360 lb (26,926 kg)
Dimensions: length overall 18.42 ft (5.61 m); width 8.50 ft (2.59 m); height overall 8.25 ft (2.515 m)
Armament system: one 2-pdr (40-mm) QF Mk IX or X L/50 rifled gun with 93 rounds, one 7.92-mm (0.312-in) Besa coaxial machine-gun with 2,925 rounds, one 0.303-in (7.7-mm) Bren AA machine-gun with 600 rounds, and two smoke-dischargers on the right of the turret; the turret was hydraulically operated, the main gun was stabilized in neither elevation (−15° to +20°) nor azimuth (360°), and simple optical sights were fitted
Armour: bolted and cast steel varying in thickness between 13 and 78 mm (0.51 and 3.07 in)
Powerplant: two 95-hp (70.8-kW) Leyland E148/148 or E164/165 diesel engines with 46.5 Imp. gal. (211.4 litres) of fuel
Performance: speed, road 15 mph (24.1 km/h); range, road 160 miles (257.5 km); fording 3.0 ft (0.91 m) without preparation and 3.5 ft (1.02 m) with preparation; vertical obstacle 2.0 ft (0.61 m); trench 7.0 ft (2.13 m); ground clearance 14 in (0.36 m)

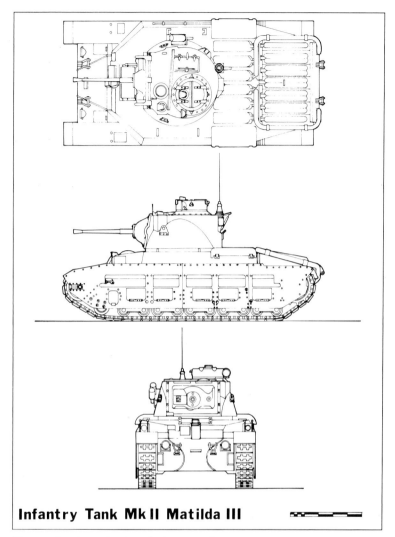

Infantry Tank Mk II Matilda III

amounted to 2,987 vehicles, and the risky decision to order the type 'off the drawing board' was validated by generally successful capabilities from the beginning of trials. The 59,360-lb (26926-kg) Matilda II was of course heavier than its precedessor, but this allowed the carriage of a four-man crew and the installation of a larger turret accommodating a 2-pdr (40-mm) gun and one coaxial machine-gun (0.303-in/7.7-mm Vickers in the Mk II Matilda II and 7.92-mm/0.312-in Besa in the Mk IIA Matilda II and later marks). Improvement during the Second World War was undertaken wherever possible, resulting in the Mk IIA* Matilda III with two 95-hp (70.8-kW) Leyland diesels, the Matilda III CS with a 3-in (76.2-mm) howitzer, the Matilda IV with mechanical improvements over the Matilda III, the Matilda IV CS with mechanical improvements over the Matilda III CS, and the Matilda V identical with the Matilda IV but with a directly-operated pneumatic gearbox. Other improvements centred on features such as a 0.303-in (7.7-mm) Bren light machine-gun on an overhead mounting above the commander's cupola for anti-aircraft fire, and the Matilda was also developed for the mine-clearing role as the Matilda Scorpion flail tank, the Matilda AMRA Mk IA roller tank and the Matilda Carrot roller/explosive tank.

Third in the sequence of British support tanks was the Infantry Tank Mk III Valentine. Like the Cruiser Tank Mk VI Crusader, this was originated before World War II (in this instance on the basis of the A9 and A10 cruiser tanks with thicker armour) but matured during the war and is treated in a later chapter. So far as

71

Matilda Scorpion

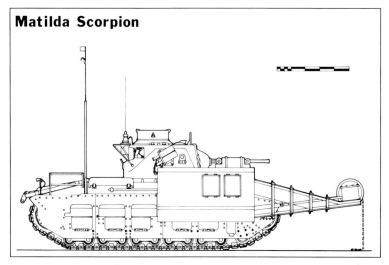

Valentine III

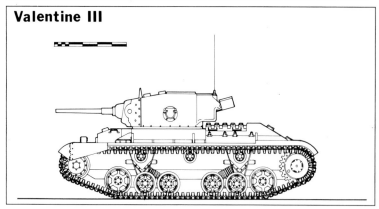

Matilda Scorpion Mk I
(UK)

Type: mineclearing flail tank
Crew: 4–5
Combat weight: not known
Dimensions: length overall 23.25 ft (7.09 m); height 8.25 ft (2.51 m)
Armament system: one 2-pdr (40-mm) gun with 93 rounds, one 7.92-mm (0.312-in) Besa machine-gun with 2,925 rounds, one 0.303-in (7.7-mm) Bren machine-gun with 600 rounds, and two 4-in (102-mm) smoke-dischargers
Armour: between 20 and 78 mm (0.79 and 3.07 in)
Powerplant: two 95-hp (70.8-kW) Leyland E-series petrol engines with 46.5 Imp. gal. (211 litres) of fuel, plus one 30-hp (22.4-kW) Bedford or Ford truck engine in the external compartment on the right of the tank to drive the flail mechanism by a cardan shaft and bevel gears
Performance: (gun tank) speed, road 15 mph (24.1 km/h); range, road 160 miles (257.5 km); fording 3.5 ft (1.07 m); vertical obstacle 2.0 ft (0.61 m); trench 7.0 ft (2.13 m)

Infantry Tank Mk III Valentine III
(UK)

Type: infantry tank
Crew: 4
Combat weight: 35,840 lb (16,257 kg)
Dimensions: length overall 17.75 ft (5.41 m); width 8.625 ft (2.63 m); height 7.46 ft (2.27 m)
Armament system: one 2-pdr (40-mm) gun with 60 rounds, one 7.92-mm (0.312-in) Besa machine-gun with 3,150 rounds, one 0.303-in (7.7-mm) Bren machine-gun with 600 rounds and one 2-in (50.8-mm) bomb thrower with 18 rounds
Armour: between 8 and 65 mm (0.315 and 2.56 in)
Powerplant: one 131-hp (97.7-kW) AEC Type A.190 diesel engine with 36 Imp. gal. (164 litres) of fuel
Performance: speed, road 15 mph (24.1 km/h); range, road 90 miles (145 km); fording 3.0 ft (0.91 m);
gradient 60%; vertical obstacle 3.0 ft (0.91 m); trench 7.75 ft (2.36 m)

the situation in 1939 is concerned, one must conclude that official indifference and lack of funding had resulted in a parlous tank position: the light reconnaissance tank was available in

Char FCM 2C

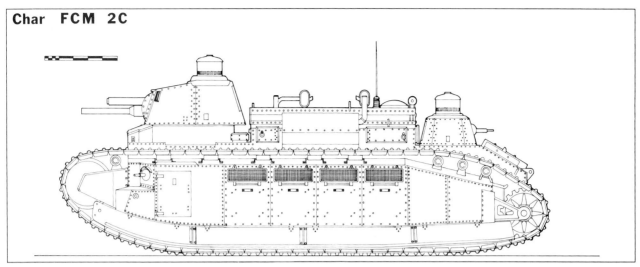

useful numbers but obsolete, the medium tank was outdated, the cruiser tank was unproven in concept as well as too lightly armed and armoured, and the infantry tank was also unproved, as well as too slow. This dangerous situation was compounded by lack of adequate design and manufacturing capabilities, and by the failure of the higher authorities to grasp the nettle of German tank superiority when this became evident.

Like the UK, France was faced with problems of how to develop its armoured force after the First World War, especially as financial resources were again scarce and the role of the tank was in question. Most production orders were cancelled at the end of the war and much of the in-service tank fleet was in fact unserviceable, because of the cumulative mechanical defects of designs that had been rushed too hastily into production. General J.E. Estienne meanwhile set to work on the tactical and operational roles of an independent tank arm evolved from the Artillerie d'Assaut of the war using as its first major vehicle a derivative of the Char 1, but in 1920 the Artillerie d'Assaut was disestablished and the tank arm subordinated to the infantry, tank units thereafter serving as components of infantry formations.

In 1921 the French formulated their first programme for tank development, calling for a *char de rupture* (breakthrough tank) and a *char de bataille* (battle tank) to succeed the Renault

Char FCM 2C
(France)

Type: heavy tank
Crew: 12–13
Combat weight: 70,000 kg (154,321 lb)
Dimensions: length overall 10.27 m (33.69 ft); width 2.95 m (9.68 ft); height 4.01 m (13.16 ft)
Armament system: one 75-mm (2.95-in) gun with 125 rounds and four 8-mm (0.315-in) machine-guns with 10,000 rounds
Armour: between 13 and 45 mm (0.51 and 1.77 in)
Powerplant: two 134.2-kW (180-hp) Mercedes petrol engines
Performance: speed, road 12 km/h (7.5 mph); range, road 160 km (100 miles); gradient 50%; vertical obstacle 1.22 m (4.0 ft); trench 4.115 m (13.5 ft)

FT in the infantry support role. Under the auspices of the Section Technique des Chars de Combat, headed by the *Inspecteur des Chars* (inspector of tanks, General Estienne), this programme produced one breakthrough tank (the Forges et Chantiers de la Mediterranée 2C) and five possible battle tanks from Delaunay-Belleville, FAMH (Saint Chamond), FCM and Renault/Schneider.

The origins of the Char 2C in fact lie deep in the First World War, when the evident limitations of the Chars d'Assaut Schneider and Saint Chamond persuaded FCM to inaugurate the design under Jammy and Savatier of a

Far left The British army's most successful tank design of the period leading up to the Second World War was the A12 Infantry Tank Mk II Matilda II, which combined excellent protection with adequate performance, but was let down by its small turret, which in the tank's basic role could be fitted with nothing larger than the 2-pdr (40-mm) high-velocity gun or 3-in (76-mm) close-support howitzer. (*RAC Tank Museum*)

73

The Char 2C was a monstrous tank by anyone's standards, and had its origins in the breakthrough tank designed by FCM for service in 1919. This is one of six surviving vehicles knocked out on their rail cars by German air attack in 1940, the side view emphasizing the size of the vehicle and its multi-turret armament: the front turret accommodated a 75-mm (2.95-in) gun, and the rear turret an 8-mm (0.315-in) machine-gun; there were three other machine-guns of the same calibre located one each in the front and the sides. (*IWM*)

considerably larger and more capable *char lourd* (heavy tank) using a rhomboidal hull shape reminiscent of the Medium Tank Mk C but with a sloping top run, fitted with a rotating turret for the main armament, and having sufficient armour for the breakthrough role. Two prototypes of the Char 1A were ordered in October 1916, one with mechanical and the other with electric transmission. Powered by one 240-hp (179-kW) Renault petrol engine, each of these seven-man tanks weighed 40,000 kg (88,183 lb) complete with armour varying in thickness up to 35 mm (1.38 in), and could achieve 6 km/h (3.7 mph): the armament comprised one turret-mounted 75-mm (2.95-in) gun and two 8-mm (0.315-in) Hotchkiss machine-guns. There was also a single Char 1B with a 105-mm (4.13-in) rather than 75-mm (2.95-in) main gun, but like its companions this potentially excellent tank was let down by its dismal turning performance, and further effort towards development of a major tank type for the planned 1919 Allied offensives was turned to the Char 2C with operational improvements and petrol-electric transmission.

It was planned to build 300 Chars 2C in time for the 1919 push, but in the event only 10 tanks had been started by the time of the Armistice and the cancellation of further orders. Each 12-man machine weighed 70,000 kg (154,321 lb) with armour up to a maximum thickness of 45 mm (1.77 in) and was powered by two 180-hp (134-kW) Mercedes petrol engines, later replaced by 250-hp (186-kW) Maybach petrol engines, each driving a generator and electric motor for one track. The type's size, including a length of 10.27 m (33.69 ft) and large forward rise, provided good front-line performance, including trench-crossing and parapet-climbing figures of 4.15 and 1.22 m (13.62 and 4.0 ft) respectively. The size also allowed the installation of comprehensive armament in what was thus the world's first multi-turret tank: the front turret was fitted with a 75-mm (2.95-in) gun, the rear turret was armed with an 8-mm (0.315-in) machine-gun, and three other machine-guns were located in ball mountings (one in the front hull and one on each side). The Char 2C ran on 24 double roller wheels in six flat-sprung bogies, and possessed a maximum speed of 13 km/h (8.1 mph). The last of the 10 tanks was delivered in 1922, one year after the Char 2C became operational, and the type remained in service right up to the Second World War. The only variant appeared in 1926, when FCM modified one machine as the Char 2C-bis with two 250-hp (186-kW) Sautter-Harie engines, thicker armour and a short-barrel 155-mm (6.1-in) howitzer as its main armament.

After assessment of the five *char de bataille* proposals and examination of four mock-ups in 1924, the Section Technique des Chars de Combat in 1927 ordered single Char B prototypes from FAMH, FCM and Renault/ Schneider. The specification had called for a weight of 15,000 kg (33,069 lb), a crew of four, and a main armament of one hull-mounted 47-mm or 75-mm (2.95-in) gun: the prototypes appeared between 1929 and 1931 with a weight of 25,000 kg (55,115 lb), a hull-mounted 75-mm (2.95-in) SA 35 main gun, and a secondary armament of four 7.5-mm (0.295-in) Chatellerault machine-guns (two fixed in the forward hull and two flexible in the turret). After exhaustive trials in the 1932 French army manoeuvres, the Char B was ordered into production in a revised form as the Char B1. This began to enter service in 1935, and was armoured to a maximum thickness of 60 mm (2.36 in): in this model the main gun was fixed in traverse (the whole tank having to be slewed via a Naeder hydrostatic pump drive to bring the gun to bear on the target) and capable of elevation through an arc between -15° and +35°, while the turret accommodated one 37-mm gun plus a 7.5-mm (0.295-in) coaxial machine-gun. Only 36 Chars B1 had been produced before the considerably revised Char B1-bis was introduced with heavier armour, revised armament, and a more powerful engine. The Char B1-bis weighed 30,000 kg (66,138 lb), was armoured more extensively with bolted-together castings to the maximum of 40 mm (1.575 in), had a revised turret accommodating one 47-mm gun and one 7.5-mm (0.295-in) coaxial machine-gun, and featured a 250- rather that 180-hp (186- rather than 134-kW) Renault petrol engine: production amounted to 365 vehicles by June 1940. The last development of this potent armoured fight-

Above The Char B1-bis entered production in 1937 after development from the Char B1 of 1935, itself the production version of the Char B prototypes of 1929. The type employed an FCM development of the Holt suspension used in French tanks of the First World War. (*MARS*)

Left One of the best tanks in service with the French army in 1940, the Char B1-bis was well protected, but its armament disposition included a 75-mm (2.95-in) gun mounted low in the hull and a 47-mm gun and coaxial machine-gun in the APX4 turret. (*MARS*)

Char B1-bis
(France)

Type: heavy tank
Crew: 4
Combat weight: 32,000 kg (70,547 lb)
Dimensions: length overall 6.52 m (21.39 ft); width 2.50 m (8.20 ft); height overall 2.79 m (9.15 ft)
Armament system: one 75-mm (2.95-in) SA 35 L/17.1 rifled gun fixed in azimuth in the hull front with an elevation arc of − 15° to + 25° and provided with 74 rounds, one 47-mm SA 35 L/34 rifled gun with 50 rounds, and two 7.5-mm (0.295-in) Chatellerault Modèle 1931 machine-guns (one coaxial with the 47-mm gun and one bow) with 5,100 rounds; the turret was manually operated, its main gun was stabilized in neither elevation (− 18° to + 18°) nor azimuth (360°), and simple optical sights were fitted
Armour: bolted and cast steel varying in thickness between 20 and 60 mm (0.79 and 2.36 in)
Powerplant: one 134-kW (180-hp) Renault petrol engine
Performance: speed, road 28 km/h (17.4 mph); range, road 150 km (93 miles); fording 1.5 m (4.92 ft);
gradient 50%; vertical obstacle 0.93 m (3.05 ft); trench 2.75 m (9.02 ft); ground clearance 0.48 m (18.9 in)

A Char B1-bis captured from the French in the 1940 Battle of France. The armour of this type was virtually impervious to the Germans' current anti-tank rounds. (*IWM*)

ing vehicle, still one of the most formidable weapons of its type in 1940, was the Char B1-ter of which five were produced with a 310-hp (231-kW) Renault engine, a maximum armour thickness of 70 mm (2.76 in), the crew increased to five by inclusion of a mechanic in the enlarged fighting compartment, and the main gun provided with traverse of 10° (5° left and right of the centreline).

In 1926 the French produced a new tank programme providing for three tank types in the form of the *char léger* (light tank with one 37-mm gun and 7.5-mm/0.295-in machine-guns), the *char de bataille* (battle tank with a main gun of 47-mm calibre or more) and the *char lourd* (heavy tank with thicker armour than the *char de bataille*). Little money was available to the French army in this and slightly later periods, most available resources being devoted to the fixed defences of the 'Maginot Line', and the programme was generally unsuccessful. The main results were the Renault Chars NC1 and NC2 (evolved from the FT series and discussed in the previous chapter), which secured export orders but failed to win French approval. Considerable development of tactical ideas followed in the early 1930s as the infantry and cavalry expanded their thinking about the nature and employment

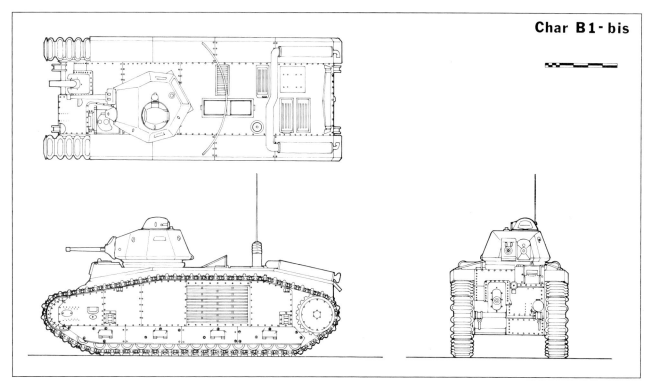

Char B1-bis

of armour, but France's sole armoured warfare visionary, Colonel Charles de Gaulle, fell into political oblivion after the publication of his *Vers l'Armée de Métier*. This called for a professional rather than conscript army of mechanized shock troops, centred on armoured divisions, and ran counter to all the tenets of France's pacifist government.

In 1931 the infantry organized its armoured force by type of equipment in service or under development, all such infantry vehicles being designated *chars*: the *chars légers* (light tanks) were the Renault R-35 and R-40, the FCM-36 and the Hotchkiss H-35; the *chars moyens* (medium tanks, a new category) were the Renault D1 and D2, and the AMX-38; the *chars de bataille* (battle tanks) were the Char B series; and the *chars lourds* (heavy tanks) were the Char 2C series. In 1932 the cavalry followed suit with a wider-ranging classification of *auto-mitrailleuses* (machine-gun cars) that included wheeled armoured cars: the AMD (*Auto-Mitrailleuse de Découverte*) category comprised long-range armoured cars; the AMR (*Auto-Mitrailleuse de Recon-*

naissance) category comprised cross-country light reconnaissance tanks with machine-gun armament, such as the Renault Type VM and Type ZT; the AMC (*Auto-Mitrailleuse de Combat*) category comprised gun-armed tanks such as the Renault Type YR and Type ACG1; and the *char de cavalerie* category added in 1935 covered heavier gun-armed tanks such as the Hotchkiss H-35 and H-38/39, and the SOMUA S-35 and S-40.

This classification system lasted until after the Second World War and it is convenient to treat the tanks filling each niche (other than those already discussed) in the order mentioned above. The Char Léger R-35 originated from a 1934 requirement for a light tank to replace the FTs, still serving in substantial numbers despite their total obsolescence. The specification demanded a two-man light tank weighing no more than 8,000 kg (17,637 lb) with armour to a maximum thickness of 45 mm (1.77 in), a road speed of 20 km/h (12.5 mph) and turreted armament of one 37-mm or two 7.5-mm (0.295-in) machine guns.

77

Proposals were received from the Compagnie Générale de Construction des Locomotives, Delaunay-Belleville, FCM and Renault, the last's Type ZM being selected in 1935 for a 300-vehicle production run. The prototype was armed with twin machine-guns and used scissors-type horizontal coil-spring suspension based on that of the Type ZT. The production vehicle had a revised turret of superior shape and fitted with one 37-mm gun and a 7.5-mm (0.295-in) coaxial machine-gun, and the 82-hp (61.1-kW) Renault petrol engine drove this 9,800-kg (21,605-lb) vehicle at a maximum speed of 20 km/h (12.4 mph). Production amounted to between 1,600 and 1,900 vehicles (including export versions for Poland, Romania, Turkey and Yugoslavia), making this the most prolific of French tanks in the Second World War. The armament and armour were adequate, but the small one-man cast turret was a hindrance to operational utility, and the type was too slow for its intended reconnaissance role. Another criticism was the short-barrel SA 18 main gun, and to overcome

A Renault R-35 light tank preserved at Satory in France. Visible are the 'scissors' type of horizontal coil-spring suspension and hand-operated one-man turret armed with a 37-mm gun and coaxial machine-gun. (*MARS*)

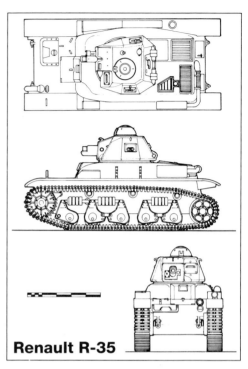

Renault R-35

Char Léger Renault R-35
(France)

Type: light tank
Crew: 2
Combat weight: 10,000 kg (22,046 lb)
Dimensions: length overall 4.20 m (13.78 ft); width 1.85 m (6.07 ft); height overall 2.37 m (7.78 ft)
Armament system: one 37-mm SA 18 L/21 or SA 38 L/33 rifled gun with 100 rounds, and one 7.5-mm (0.295-in) Chatellerault Modèle 1931 coaxial machine-gun with 2,400 rounds; the turret was manually operated, the main gun was stabilized in neither elevation (−18° to +18°) nor azimuth (360°), and simple optical sights were fitted
Armour: cast steel varying in thickness to a maximum of 45 mm (1.77 in)
Powerplant: one 61.1-kW (82-hp) Renault petrol engine with 170 litres (37.4 Imp. gal.) of fuel
Performance: speed, road 20 km/h (12.4 mph); range, road 140 km (87 miles); fording 0.6 m (1.97 ft); gradient 60%; vertical obstacle 0.5 m (1.64 in); trench 1.6 m (5.25 ft) increasing to 2.0 m (6.56 ft) with optional tail; ground clearance 0.32 m (12.6 in)

this limitation to muzzle velocity (and thus to armour penetration, the R-40 was introduced with a long-barrel SA 38 gun of the same calibre, a weight of 10,500 kg (23,148 lb) and provision for a detachable tail unit modelled on that of the FT for greater effective length and therefore an improved trench-crossing capacity. Despite its one-man limitations, the turret was thought generally satisfactory, as attested by the fact that it was also used on the H-35 and H-38/39 tanks.

Next in this category came the Char Léger FCM-36, designed as an infantry support vehicle, as initially developed, France's first diesel-engined tank, using a Berliet-built version of the Ricardo engine. This design was produced in parallel with the R-35 with the same armament, but differed considerable in using all-welded armour varying in thickness up to 40 mm (1.57 in). The FCM-36's combat weight was about 10,500 kg (23,148 lb), allowing the 90-hp (67.1-kW) diesel to produce a maximum speed of 25 km/h (15.5 mph). This was significantly better than the speed of the R-35, as too was the combat range of 320 km (199 miles). But only 100 FCM-36s had been produced by 1940, and the FCM-36 therefore played only a modest part in French operations.

Last of this initial trio was the Char Léger H-35. The origins of this tank lay with an infantry requirement of 1933 for a light tank to partner the S-35. The Hotchkiss 1934 prototype to meet this requirement was rejected by the infantry in favour of the R-35, but the design was then accepted by the cavalry (Char de Cavalerie 35H) and finally accepted by the infantry as the H-35. Total production of the H-35, together with its H-39 and H-40 successors, amounted to about 1,000 vehicles. The armament was identical with that of the other *chars légers*, but at a maximum of 34mm (1.34 in) the armour was considerably thinner than that of its two companions. To counterbalance this potential deficiency, however, the H-35 was powered by a 75-hp (55.9-kW) Hotchkiss petrol engine that gave this 11,400-kg (25,132-lb) vehicle the high maximum speed of 28 km/h (17.4 mph). It was appreciated soon after the H-35's service debut that despite its speed, the type would prove vulnerable, and the H-38 was developed with armour up to a

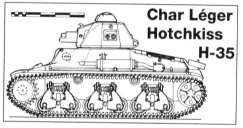

Char Léger Hotchkiss H-35

Though in many respects a useful light tank, the Char Léger R-35 (Renault Type ZM) was decidedly hampered by its one-man turret with manual traverse system and low-velocity 37-mm gun. (*Musée de l'Armée*)

Char Léger Hotchkiss H-38
(France)

Type: light (cavalry) tank
Crew: 2
Combat weight: 12,000 kg (26,455 lb)
Dimensions: length overall 4.22 m (13.85 ft); width 1.85 m (6.07 ft); height 2.14 m (7.02 ft)
Armament system: one 37-mm SA 18 gun with 100 rounds and one 7.5-mm (0.295-in) machine-gun with 2,400 rounds
Armour: between 12 and 40 mm (0.47 and 1.57 in)
Powerplant: one 89.5-kW (120-hp) Hotchkiss petrol engine
Performance: speed, road 36 km/h (22.4 mph); range, road 150 km (93.2 miles); gradient 60%; vertical obstacle 0.5 m (1.64 ft); trench 1.8 m (5.9 ft)

maximum thickness of 40 mm (1.57 in): this increased weight to about 12,000 kg (26,455 lb), though performance was maintained, and indeed improved, by the installation of a 120-hp (89.5-kW) Hotchkiss engine for a maximum speed of 36 km/h (22.4 mph). Further development produced the H-39, modelled on the H-38 but featuring armour increased to a maximum thickness of 45 mm (1.77 in) and with the long-barrel SA 38 L/33 main gun in place of the original short-barrel SA 18 L/21 weapon: firing the same projectile, the short-barrel gun produced a muzzle velocity of 388 m (1,273 ft) per second and the long-barrel weapon a muzzle velocity of 701 m (2,300 ft) per second for much improved armour penetration. The H-38 and H-39 were produced only in modest numbers, and were used by the cavalry.

Compared with their German opponents in 1940, the PzKpfw I and II, the French tanks had generally superior armament and protection, but were let down tactically by their two-man crews, their use in small non-homogeneous units, and (with exception of the R-35 series) their comparatively small numbers.

Next up the weight and capability ladder were the *chars moyens*, intended as medium-weight infantry support tanks. The most important of these was the Char D, produced by Renault in response to the 1926 new tank programme and based mechanically on the Renault NC 1 (NC27) light tank, that secured export rather than domestic sales. The first prototype appeared in 1931, and production of 160 tanks was undertaken between 1932 and 1935. The key to this model was the use of a two-man cast turret (one of the first such units in French service) on a riveted hull with skirt armour to protect the running gear. The crew of three was well provided with vision devices, and a radio with a distinctive triangular antenna was standard. The Char D1A was armed with a 37-mm main gun and coaxial 7.5-mm (0.295-in) machine-gun, plus a fixed machine-gun of the same calibre fired by the driver, and at a weight of 12,000 kg (26,455 lb) had a maximum speed of 18 km/h (11.2 mph) on its 65-hp (48.5-kW) Renault petrol engine. The armour varied in thickness from 12 to 30 mm (0.47 to 1.18 in), and the tank's range was 80 km (50 miles). The Char D1A was regarded as an interim step only, and the definitive early variant was therefore the Char D1B, with armour increased to a maximum of 40 mm (1.57 in), the main gun increased to 47-mm calibre, and a 100-hp (74.6-kW) engine installed to increase the maximum speed to 20 km/h (12.5 mph) despite an increase in weight to 12,800 kg (28,219 lb).

But even the Char D1B was clearly inadequate by the standard of the early 1930's, and Renault therefore developed the considerably enhanced Char D2 with greater protection and greater power. The prototype appeared in 1932 and production of 100 examples began in 1934. The Char D2 was powered by a 150-hp (112-kW) Renault petrol engine, and this gave the vehicle a maximum speed of 25 km/h (15.5 mph), despite the increase in overall weight to 16,000 kg (35,273 lb) by the increase in minimum armour thickness to 20 mm (0.79 in). The armament remained essentially unaltered from the standard of the Char D1B,

---

Char Renault D1B
(France)

Type: medium (infantry) tank
Crew: 3
Combat weight: 14,225 kg (31,360 lb)
Dimensions: length overall 5.77 m (18.94 ft); width 2.16 m (7.08 ft); height 2.39 m (7.84 ft)
Armament system: one 47-mm gun with 35 rounds and two 7.5-mm (0.295-in) machine-guns with 2,000 rounds
Armour: between 14 and 40 mm (0.55 and 1.575 in)
Powerplant: one 74.6-kW (100-hp) Renault petrol engine
Performance: speed, road 20 km/h (12.4 mph); range, road 100 km (62.1 miles)

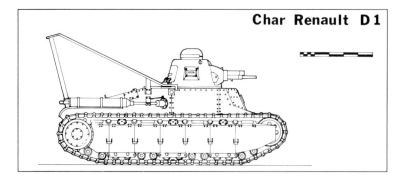

Char Renault D1

Delivered by Renualt from 1934, the Char D2 was essentially an uparmoured and upengined derivative of the Char D1 infantry tank with an APX1 cast turret. Substantial production was anticipated, but in 1936 the total was trimmed back to just 50 after the emergence of the clearly superior SOMUA S-35. (*IWM*)

though 47-mm ammunition stowage was considerably improved from 35 to 108 rounds. The Char D series was not particularly successful, and further production was curtailed in favour of the impressive SOMUA S-35 and the planned Char Moyen AMX-38. This latter was a 16,250-kg (35,825-lb) machine powered by a 150-hp (112-kW) Aster diesel for a maximum speed of 25 km/h (15.5 mph) and a range of 145 km (90 miles). In a retrograde move the French reduced the crew to two, but the armament was the standard fit for *chars moyens*, though the 47-mm gun had 120 rounds. The protection was well designed and substantial, however, with minimum and maximum thicknesses of 15 and 60 mm (0.59 and 2.36 in). A small number of production machines had been built by the time the Second World War erupted in September 1939, but the French sensibly decided to concentrate on larger-scale production of the in-service types, rather than efforts to bring the AMX-38 into service.

The French infantry's *chars de bataille* (Char B series) and *chars lourds* (Char 2C series) have been discussed above as they were early machines stemming from First World War programmes and experience, so it is time to turn to the cavalry tanks designed for

longer-range operations. The lightest of these vehicles were the *auto-mitrailleuses de reconnaissance*, a category in which only the Renault Type VM and Type ZT entered service as the AMR 33R and AMR 35R respectively. Since 1921 the French army had being trying to secure such a reconnaissance vehicle, with a crew of two and an armament of two machine-guns, but the various projects had all failed for a variety of reasons. Thus it was only after the 1931 reorganization of the French tank forces that significant progress was made in the form of the Type VM, designed in 1932 and ordered initially as five prototypes with differing suspensions based on leaf or even rubber springs. Evaluation followed, and the first order for 123 AMR 33R vehicles stipulated four rubber-tyred road wheels mounted as a freely-pivoting central pair on a vertical coil spring and end units on bellcrank scissors with horizontal rubber springing. The vehicle was of riveted construction with minimum and maximum armour thicknesses of 5 and 13 mm (0.2 and 0.51 in), and at a weight of 5,000 kg (11,023 lb) was driven by an 84-hp (62.6-kW) Reinastella petrol engine at a maximum speed of 60 km/h (37.3 mph). This excellent road performance was matched by

81

AMR 33

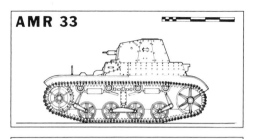

AMR 35

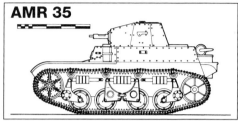

Auto-Mitrailleuse de Reconnaissance 33 (Renault Type VM) (France)

Type: light (cavalry) tank
Crew: 2
Combat weight: 5,000 kg (11,023 lb)
Dimensions: length overall 3.504 m (11.50 ft); width 1.60 m (5.25 ft); height 1.727 m (5.67 ft)
Armament system: one 7.5-mm (0.25-in) machine-gun with 2,500 rounds
Armour: between 5 and 13 mm (0.2 and 0.51 in)
Powerplant: one 62.6-kW (82-hp) Reinastella petrol engine
Performance: speed, road 60 km/h (37.3 mph); range, road 200 km (124 miles); vertical obstacle 0.61 m (2.0 ft); trench 1.5 m (4.92 ft)

Variously known as the AMR 33 and Renault Type VM, this trim light tank was notable for its good road and cross-country performance but was let down by its light armament, comprising just one 7.5-mm (0.295-in) machine-gun. (*RAC Tank Museum*)

very good cross-country performance and agility. The poorest features were the two-man crew, the driver being located in the front of the hull and the commander/gunner in the small turret armed with a single 7.5-mm

(0.295-in) machine-gun. The turret was offset to the left to allow the installation of the engine on the right.

The AMR 33R proved successful, but the cavalry felt that improvement was possible in terms of suspension, powerplant, armament and vision. This paved the way for the Type ZT, which was accepted for service as the AMR 35R. This was powered by an 85-hp (63.4-kW) Renault engine, but as the weight had increased to 6.5000 kg (14,330 lb) the tank's outright performance suffered: maximum speed, for example, dropped to a still respectable 55 km/h (34.2 mph). The suspension was revised so that the central pair were mounted on horizontally-sprung bellcranks. The success of this suspension is attested by its later use on Renault and Hotchkiss light and medium tanks. Many detail improvements were made to the hull to improve fields of vision and maintainability, but the main development came in the armament, which could

Auto-Mitrailleuse de Reconnaissance 35 (Renault Type ZT) (France)

Type: light (cavalry) tank
Crew: 2
Combat weight: 6,600 kg (14,550 lb)
Dimensions: length overall 3.85 m (12.63 ft); width 1.63 m (5.34 ft); height 1.88 m (6.18 ft)
Armament system: one 13.2-mm (0.52-in) Hotchkiss machine-gun with 1,750 rounds (or one 25-mm cannon with 75 rounds, or one 7.5-mm/ 0.295-in machine-gun and one 13.2-mm/0.52-in machine-gun, or one 78.5-mm/0.295-in machine-gun with 1,750 rounds)
Armour: between 5 and 13 mm (0.2 and 0.51 in)
Powerplant: one 59.7-kW (80-hp) Renault petrol engine
Performance: speed, road 55 km/h (34.2 mph)

comprise a single 25-mm Hotchkiss anti-tank gun, or a combination of one 13.2-mm (0.52-in) and one 7.5-mm (0.295-in) machine-guns, or one machine-gun of either calibre. Production amounted to 200 vehicles.

Next up in capability was the *automitrailleuse de combat* intended for the combat rather than reconnaissance role, but with emphasis on hit-and-run tactics rather than head-on confrontations. The cavalry used the Schneider P16 halftrack in this role, but more important were two Renault light tanks, the Type YR and the Type ACG1. The 1933 prototype was fitted with the FT's turret and thus had only a two-man crew, but was unsuccessful in evaluation trials and rapidly superseded by a more capable version with a hull and suspension modelled on those of the AMR 33 but carrying a two-man turret accommodating a 25-mm main gun and coaxial 7.5-mm (0.295-in) machine-gun. This was the first time a two-man turret had been installed on a French light tank, and offered a considerable improvement in capability as the commander could concentrate his efforts on

supervision of the tactical situation, leaving the gunner to deal with targets. As befitted its role, the production AMC 34R was lightly armoured to a maximum of 20 mm (0.79 in), but the use of a 120-hp (89.5-kW) Renault petrol engine produced quite sprightly performance, including a maximum speed of 40 km/h (24.9 mph) at a combat weight of 10,800 kg (23,810 lb). In overall terms the AMC 34R was a three-man version of the two-man AMR 33R with heavier armour and armament, but poorer performance despite the installation of a more powerful engine. The type also inherited some of the AMR 33R's suspension limitations, and was thus supplanted without delay by the Type ACG1, which entered service as the AMC 35R.

Designed and built initially by Renault, the AMC 35R was produced in largest numbers by the Atelier de Construction d'Issy-les-Moulineaux. And as the AMC 34R was modelled on the AMR 33R, the AMC 35R was derived from the AMR 35R with the same basic hull and suspension, though considerably uparmoured and upengined, and fitted with a more

An AMR 33 (Renault Type VM) light tank at speed on a French road. (*IWM*)

83

AMC 35

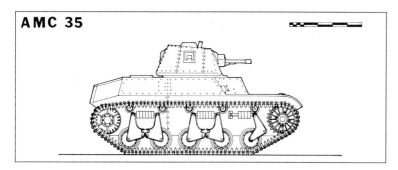

Auto-Mitrailleuse de Combat 35 (Renault Type ACG1)
(France)

Type: light (cavalry) tank
Crew: 3
Combat weight: 14,500 kg (31,966 lb)
Dimensions: length overall 5.57 m (14.9 ft); width 2.235 m (7.33 ft); height 2.335 m (7.66 ft)
Armament system: one 47-mm gun and one 7.5-mm (0.295-in) machine-gun
Armour: between 14 and 20 mm (0.55 and 1.575 in)
Powerplant: one 134.2-kW (180-hp) Renault petrol engine
Performance: speed, road 40 km/h (24.9 mph); range, road 160 km (99 miles); gradient 60%; vertical obstacle 0.6 m (1.97 ft); trench 1.825 m (5.99 ft)

capable two-man turret. The armour varied from a minimum of 14 mm (0.55 in) to a maximum of 25 mm (0.98 in), and the provision of more than double the power in the form of a 180-hp (134-kW) Renault petrol engine produced good performance, including a maximum speed of 40 km/h (24.9 mph), despite a combat weight of 14,500 kg (31,967 lb). The standard armament was a short-barrel 47-mm gun and 7.5-in (0.295-in) coaxial machine-gun, but some French tanks were fitted with a long-barrel 25-mm anti-tank gun plus coaxial machine-gun, while the Belgians fitted their version with a locally-designed turret carrying a 47-mm gun and 13.2-mm (0.52-in) coaxial machine-gun.

The last cavalry tank category was the *char de cavalerie*, essentially a subdivision of the AMC category to encompass the cavalry's most potent light tanks. The three Hotchkiss tanks already described (the H-35, H-38 and H-39) were important vehicles in this category, but the best was clearly the S-35 produced by the Société de'Outillage Mécanique et d'Usinage d'Artillerie (SOMUA). This was the world's first tank with all-cast hull and turret construction, and arguably one of the ablest armoured fighting vehicles of its day anywhere in the world. The hull comprised three large castings to a maximum thickness of 41 mm

The world's first tank with cast hull and turret, the SOMUA S-35 was perhaps the best tank available to France at the beginning of the Second World War, because of the high level of protection, good performance and the electrically-powered turret carrying a useful 47-mm gun. (*RAC Tank Museum*)

(1.61 in), that comprising the lower hull accommodating on its interior the engine, gearbox, power train, radiators, fuel tanks, ammunition racks, batteries etc, and on its exterior the suspension, springs, wheels and rollers. Onto this were attached the rear upper casting over the powerplant, and the forward upper casting including the turret ring. All three sections were bolted together, and this was the S-35's weakest point, as the impact of the high-velocity projectile on a join line could shatter the bolts and cause the vehicle to fall apart.

The suspension comprised 18 road wheels (nine on each side, in the form of four twin units and one singleton) with combined coil and semi-elliptical leaf springs. The whole assembly was protected by skirt armour.

The turret was an electrically-traversed unit with a maximum thickness of 56 mm (2.2 in), and was identical with the turret used by the Char B1-bis and Char D2: the main armament was the 47-mm SA 35 gun with an elevation arc between -18° and +18°, firing armour-piercing and HE projectiles with a muzzle velocity of 670 m (2,198 ft) per second, and the secondary armament comprised a 7.5-mm (0.295-in) coaxial machine-gun in an unusual mounting that allowed a total of 20° traverse (10° left and right) independently of the turret;

there was also provision for mounting a second 7.5-mm (0.295-in) machine-gun on the commander's cupola for anti-aircraft defence.

With a crew of three, the S-35 had a combat weight of 20,050 kg (44,202 lb). The engine

Char SOMUA S–35
(France)

Type: medium tank
Crew: 3
Combat weight: 20,050 kg (44,202 lb)
Dimensions: length overall 5.38 m (17.65 ft); width 2.12 m (6.96 ft); height overall 2.63 m (8.63 ft)
Armament system: one 47-mm SA 35 L/34 rifled gun with 18 rounds and one 7.5-mm (0.295-in) Reibel coaxial machine-gun with 3,000 rounds; the turret was manually operated, the main gun was stabilized in neither elevation (−18° to +18°) nor azimuth (360°), and simple optical sights were fitted
Armour: cast steel varying in thickness between 20 and 56 mm (0.79 and 2.2 in)
Powerplant: one 141.7-kW (190-hp) SOMUA petrol engine with 410 litres (90.2 Imp. gal.) of fuel
Performance: speed, road 40 km/h (24.9 mph); range, road 260 km (162 miles); fording 1.0 m (3.28 ft); gradient 65%; vertical obstacle 0.75 m (2.46 ft); trench 2.13 m (6.99 ft); ground clearance 0.42 m (16.5 in)

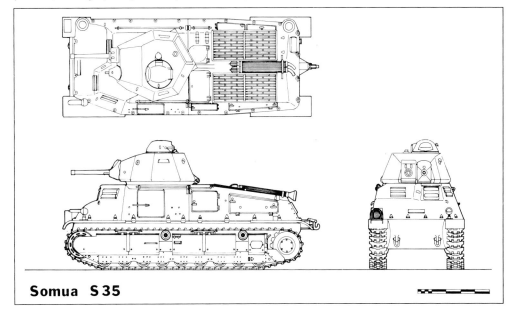

Somua S 35

The SOMUA S-35 had a fairly roomy fighting compartment with large entry/exit hatches, and a power-traversed turret with separate commander's cupola. (*IWM*)

was a 190-hp (142-kW) SOMUA petrol engine, and this made possible a maximum speed of 37 km/h (23 mph) and the useful range of 260 km (162 miles). In 1940 an improved version, the S-40 with modified suspension and a 220-hp (164-kW) engine, began to enter production. Total manufacture comprised about 500 S-35s and just a few S-40s.

Of the countries which were to become the Allied powers of the Second World War, that making the greatest strides in the development of armoured fighting vehicles in the interwar period was without doubt the USSR. As in other countries, ideas for armoured fighting vehicles abounded in the years before and during the First World War, considerable numbers of armoured cars being placed in service and some development towards genuine tanks being undertaken, as supplies were received of British and French tanks. But the first tanks were not produced until after the war, by which time revolution had replaced Tsarist Russia with the Soviet state. The Reds were impressed with the capabilities of tanks and avidly seized those left by the departing 'interventionist' Allied forces. The Renault FT suited the Reds' requirements admirably, and in 1919 they ordered an FT clone into indigenous production as the Krasno-Sormova (KS), which was identical to the FT in exterior

detail, but featured an American gearbox and 45-hp (33.6-kW) Fiat engine. Production was limited by lack of Soviet industrial capacity, and this also affected the Reds' thinking towards the development of other tanks. However, the Soviet authorities readily agreed to the establishment, in direct violation of the 1919 Treaty of Versailles, of a secret German tank centre at Kazan in the USSR, and thereby kept abreast of German developments. Combined with overt purchases of the best of foreign tanks, this allowed the Soviets to keep their tactical and technical thinking fully apprised of modern developments, without the risks and costs of an indigenous tank programme. Some wholly-Soviet design was also attempted, but nothing came of this effort before the Central Armoured Force Command was dissolved in the early 1920s and further design entrusted to the War Department Tank Bureau created in 1923.

From the KS the Soviets evolved the Maliy Soprovozhdieniya (MS, or small support tank) series, which was very similar to the French NC 1 (NC27) and the first Soviet tank to enter production, to the extent of 960 examples. The first version was the MS-1, produced between 1928 and 1931, and placed in service as the T-18. This resembled the KS, but had a completely new suspension and a more compact installation for the transversely mounted 35-hp (26.1-kW) petrol engine. Weight declined from the 7,000 kg (15,432 lb) of the KS series to 5,500 kg (12,125 lb), and subsequent models were the MS-2 with detail improvements and an uprated engine, and finally the MS-3 with a 40-hp (29.8-kW) engine and a redesigned hull front to provide a full-width glacis. The KS and MS series allowed the Red Army to develop its concept of armoured warfare during the 1920s, and this was not seriously affected by the failure of a proposed medium tank development, the T-12 tested in 1930 and found to lack the required mechanical reliability.

The consolidation of the Soviet state continued steadily during the 1920s, allowing the promulgation in 1929 of the wide-ranging First Five-Year Plan. This included the notion of mechanizing the Red Army, and also of developing tanks in all categories now deemed essential for a modern army. The plan called for each division to have a supporting group of tanks, and the MS series was thought to be an adequate basis for the first generation. These vehicles included the T-17 one-man tankette, the T-19 and T-20 two-man light tanks, the T-21 two-man light tank, the T-23 two-man tankette, the T-24 three-man medium tank and the TG five-man heavy tank. All were failures for a variety of reasons, lack of mechanical reliability proving the single most significant factor. The TG heavy tank was of notably advanced concept with low silhouette, armament of one 75-mm (2.95-in) gun and four machine-guns, and a 300-hp (224-kW) petrol engine sufficient to drive this 25,400-kg (55,996- lb) machine at a maximum road speed of 40 km/h (24.9 mph).

That the Soviets had appreciated the possible failure of this programme is given credence by the contemporary purchase of much of Vickers-Armstrongs' tank range, including Carden-Loyd tankettes, Six-Ton Light Tanks, Medium Tank Mk IIs, Carden-Loyd A4E11 amphibious tanks and tractors. A thorough technical and tactical analysis of these vehicles provided the Soviets with the starting point for a new generation of designs based on sound principles rather than the assumptions of the First World War. Just as significantly, however, several of these British tanks were passed to the Germans for evaluation at

Kazan, and it is not surprising, therefore, that Carden-Loyd and Vickers-Armstrongs features appeared in several German tank designs of the early 1930s. It is also worth noting that at this time the Soviets were astute enough to investigate tank developments of other sorts, in 1930 buying licences for German BMW engines and the US Christie suspension.

Evaluation of these tanks and associated components was completed at the beginning of 1931, and the decision was made to cancel production of the T-19 to T-24 series, in favour of the Six-Ton Light Tank as the T-26 light tank, the Carden-Loyd Mk VI as the T-27 tankette, and the Carden-Loyd A4E11 as the T-37 and improved T-38 light amphibious tanks. All were produced in large numbers and several steadily improving variants, providing the Soviets with a first-rate introduction to modern design, manufacturing and operating principles. The

T-24
(USSR)

Type: medium tank
Crew: 5
Combat weight: 18,800 kg (41,446 lb)
Dimensions: length overall 6.55 m (21.50 ft) and hull 6.45 m (21.16 ft); width 3.00 m (9.85 ft); height 2.80 m (9.20 ft)
Armament system: one 45-mm gun with 45 rounds and four 7.62-mm (0.3-in) machine-guns with 3,000 rounds
Armour: between 8 and 20 mm (0.315 and 0.79 in)
Powerplant: one 186-kW (250-hp) M-5 petrol engine with 95 litres (20.9 Imp. gal.) of fuel
Performance: speed, road 22 km/h (13.7 mph); range, road 70 km (43.5 miles); fording 0.7 m (2.3 ft); vertical obstacle 0.66 m (2.18 ft); trench 2.5 m (8.2 ft); ground clearance 0.73 m (24 in)

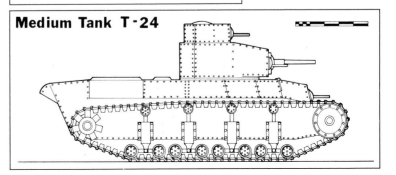

Medium Tank T-24

The Soviet T-26 series of light tanks was essentially the Vickers Six-Ton Light Tank built under licence in the USSR and then developed in T-26A and T-26B strains with twin or single turrets respectively. This is the T-26B-2(V) command tank, a variant of the T-26B-2 with a larger proportion of welding in its construction than the mostly riveted T-26B-1. The frame aerial for the radio is missing from the turret. (*RAC Tank Museum*)

T-26A-2 Model 1931 (USSR)

Type: light tank
Crew: 3
Combat weight: 7,125 kg (15,708 lb)
Dimensions: length overall 4.80 m (15.76 ft); width 2.40 m (7.85 ft); height 2.06 m (6.75 ft)
Armament system: two 7.62-mm (0.3-in) machine-guns
Armour: between 6 and 15 mm (0.24 and 0.59 in)
Powerplant: one 67-kW (90-hp) GAZ T-26 petrol engine with 180 litres (40 Imp. gal.) of fuel
Performance: speed, road 35 km/h (21.75 mph); range, road 140 km (87 miles); fording 0.87 m (2.85 ft) without preparation; gradient 32°; vertical obstacle 0.73 m (2.4 ft); trench 1.8 m (5.9 ft); ground clearance 0.365 m (14.4 in)

T-26 Model 1931

Christie M1931 (T-3) medium tank was also accepted for production as the BT-1, the first variant of the BT (Bistrokhodny Tank, or fast tank) series, though the Soviets were mindful that this was clearly not a tank well suited to operational use: modest production was undertaken, however, to provide Soviet designers with a data base of experience with the Christie suspension, which unlike the complete Christie tank was clearly well suited to the nature and extent of the theatres likely to be forced on the Soviets in any future war.

Hand in hand with these moves the Soviets developed their production capacity, during the 1930s commissioning additional factories so that by the end of the decade there were about 30 specialist tank-building factories that had built perhaps 10,000 tanks of all types in the previous 10 years. One of the major efforts was concerned with the evolution of the BT-1, firstly into an effective fighting machine as the primary equipment of long-range tank forces designed to operate in the enemy's rear areas, and secondly into the starting point of a new generation of medium tanks with excellent cross-country capability and a very high turn of speed across country as well as on roads.

The initial three-man BT-1 was modelled very closely on the Christie original, with riveted construction of armour varying in thickness between 6 and 13 mm (0.24 and 0.51 in), a turret accommodating two 7.62-mm (0.3-in) machine-guns, the ability to run on its tracks or on its large rubber-tyred road wheels, and a 343/400-hp (256/298-kW) Liberty aero engine to provide this 10,350-kg (22,817-lb) vehicle with a very respectable maximum cross-country speed of 63 km/h (39.1 mph) on its tracks, rising to an extraordinary road speed of 110 km/h (68.4 mph) on its wheels. From the BT-1 was developed the BT-2, which was basically similar to its predecessor in all respects but armament, which comprised a turret-mounted 37-mm M1930 anti-tank gun and secondary 7.62-mm (0.3-in) machine-gun, increasing combat weight to 11,175 kg (24,636 lb). Further development produced the BT-3 with solid rather than spoked road wheels, and main armament increased to a 45-mm anti-tank gun. A variant of the BT-3 was produced in prototype form as the BT-4 with

T–26TU Model 1933
(USSR)

Type: light command tank
Crew: 3
Combat weight: 10,060 kg (22,178 lb)
Dimensions: length overall 4.80 m (15.76 ft); width 2.40 m (7.85 ft); height 2.42 m (7.95 ft)
Armament system: one 45-mm gun with 92 rounds and one 7.62-mm (0.3-in) DT machine-gun with 3,000 rounds
Armour: between 6 and 15 mm (0.24 and 0.59 in)
Powerplant: one 67.1-kW (90-hp) GAZ T–26 petrol engine with 285 litres (63 Imp. gal.) of fuel
Performance: speed, road 28 km/h (17.4 mph); range, road 225 km (140 miles); fording 0.87 m (2.85 ft) without preparation; gradient 32°; vertical obstacle 0.73 m (2.4 ft); trench 1.8 m (5.9 ft); ground clearance 0.36 m (14 in)

T–37
(USSR)

Type: amphibious light tank
Crew: 2
Combat weight: 3,225 kg (7,110 lb)
Dimensions: length overall 3.75 m (12.30 ft); width 2.00 m (6.56 ft); height 1.68 m (5.50 ft)
Armament system: one 7.62-mm (0.3-in) DT machine-gun with 2,520 rounds
Armour: between 4 and 9.5 mm (0.16 and 0.37 in)
Powerplant: one 29.8-kW (40-hp) GAZ (Ford) AA petrol engine with 110 litres (24.2 Imp. gal.) of fuel
Performance: speed, road 35 km/h (21.75 mph) and water 4 km5h (2.5 mph); range, road 185 km (115 miles); fording amphibious; gradient 40°; vertical obstacle 0.5 m (1.64 ft); trench 1.6 m (5.25 ft); ground clearance 0.3 m (11.8 in)

BT–2
(USSR)

Type: fast medium tank
Crew: 3
Combat weight: 11,175 kg (24,636 lb)
Dimensions: length overall 5.52 m (18.11 ft); width 2.23 m (7.33 ft); height 2.20 m (7.22 ft)
Armament system: one 37-mm gun with 96 rounds and one 7.62-mm (0.3-in) DT machine-gun with 2,709 rounds
Armour: between 6 and 13 mm (0.24 and 0.51 in)
Powerplant: one 256-kW (343-hp) Liberty petrol engine with 400 litres (88 Imp. gal.) of fuel
Performance: speed, road 64 km/h (39.8 mph) on tracks and 111 km/h (69 mph) on wheels; range, road 300 km (186 miles) on wheels; fording 1.21 m (3.97 ft); gradient 40°; vertical obstacle 0.2 m (8 in) on wheels and 0.76 m (29.9 in) on tracks; trench 2.1 m (6.9 ft); ground clearance 0.27 m (10.6 in) on tracks

Amphibious Tank T-37

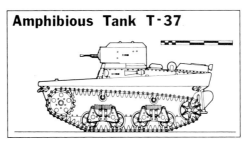

T-26TU Model 1933

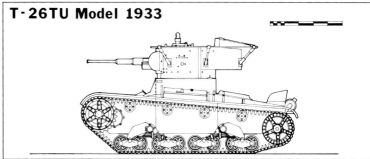

BT-2

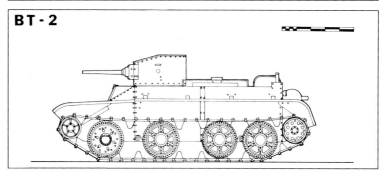

the twin-turret armament arrangement of the T-26A series, the left-hand turret accommodating one 7.62-mm (0.3-in) machine-gun and the right-hand turret carrying a 27-mm gun.

These early variants paved the way for the first large-scale production model, the 1935 BT-5, with the same three-man crew but featuring a 350-hp (261-kW) M-5 petrol engine (the 'sovietized' version of the Liberty) and a larger turret for one 45-mm L/46 anti-tank gun and a

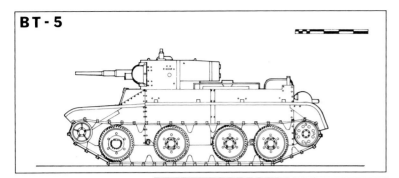

BT-5

BT-5
(USSR)

Type: fast medium tank
Crew: 3
Combat weight: 11,685 kg (25,761 lb)
Dimensions: length overall 5.52 m (18.11 ft); width 2.23 m (7.33 ft); height 2.21 m (7.25 ft)
Armament system: one 45-mm gun with 72 rounds and one 7.62-mm (0.3-in) DT machine-gun with 2,394 rounds
Armour: between 6 and 13 mm (0.24 and 0.51 in)
Powerplant: one 261-kW (350-hp) M-5 petrol engine with 400 litres (88 Imp. gal.) of fuel
Performance: speed, road 65 km/h (40.4 mph) on tracks and 111 km/h (69 mph) on wheels; range, road 300 km (186 miles) on wheels; fording 1.2 m (3.94 ft); gradient 40°; vertical obstacle 0.2 m (8 in) on wheels and 0.76 m (29.8 in) on tracks; trench 2.7 m (8.85 ft); ground clearance 0.23 m (9 in) on wheels and 0.27 m (10.6 in) on tracks

7.62-mm (0.3-in) coaxial machine-gun. This model also introduced the type of radio antenna that became standard on Soviet tanks until after the Second World War: running round the turret on short supports, this served secondarily as a hand rail for the infantry often carried into action on Soviet tanks. A close support version was developed in 1938 as the BT-5A with a 76.2-mm (3-in) L/16.5 howitzer in place of the 45-mm gun. The BT-5 was also developed in flamethrower and command versions, the former with the OT-130 flame gun and the latter with superior radio equipment.

With the BT-5 the Soviets knew they had the makings of a highly effective machine, and further development yielded the BT-7 with tactically advantageous features such as welded construction, an uprated engine, a more flexible gearbox, greater fuel capacity, thicker armour and enhanced armament. Power was provided by a 450-hp (336-kW) development of the Liberty with 790 litres (174 Imp. gal.) of fuel for a range of 500 km (311 miles) rather than the 400 litres (88 Imp. gal.) of earlier models for a range of 300 km (187 miles). Protection was improved by fitting the hull front with 22 mm (0.87 in) of armour in place of the earlier models' 13 mm (0.51 in): this increased weight to 14,000 kg (30,864 lb) from the BT-5's 11,685 kg (25,761 lb), and thereby contributed to a certain loss of outright performance in terms of speed, which declined to 53 and

4503.41

The BT series was one of the most successful applications of the Christie design philosophy, this BT-7 variant of the Soviets' most important medium tank family of the 1930s being a BT-7-1 (V) command tank. It is seen here with its tracks removed from road running, and without its radio's frame aerial, which would fit into the sockets visible on the turret sides and rear. (*RAC Tank Museum*)

73.5 km/h (32.9 and 45.6 mph) across country and on roads respectively. The original BT-7-1 retained the conical turret of the BT-5 with its 45-mm L/46 anti-tank gun, though the secondary armament was boosted from a single 7.62-mm (0.3-in) coaxial machine-gun to a pair of these weapons in the form of the coaxial gun and, in most tanks, a similar gun in the rear of the turret. There was also a command version of the BT-7 in the form of the BT-7-1V.

The BT-7-1 was soon supplanted by the definitive BT-7-2 with a conical turret offering superior ballistic protection. The armament remained unaltered in the basic gun tank, though there was also a BT-7A close support version armed with a 76.2-mm (3-in) L/16.5 howitzer. The gun tank had stowage for between 132 and 146 main armament rounds or between 172 and 188 main armament rounds with or without radio, and the comparable figures for the close support version were 40 or 50 rounds.

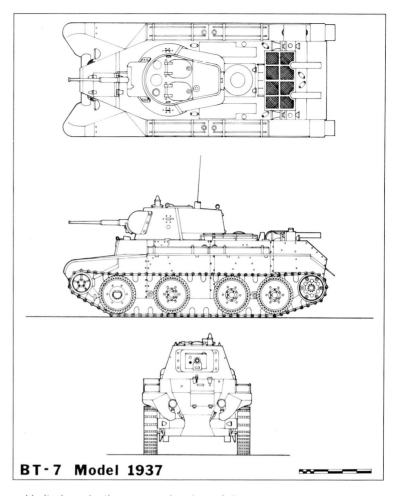

BT-7 Model 1937

BT-7-2
(USSR)

Type: fast medium tank
Crew: 3
Combat weight: 14,000 kg (30,864 lb)
Dimensions: length overall 5.68 m (18.64 ft); width 2.43 m (7.97 ft); height overall 1.93 m (6.33 ft)
Armament system: one 45-mm M1935 L/46 rifled gun with 188 rounds (reduced to 146 rounds when a radio was installed), two 7.62-mm (0.3-in) DT machine-guns (one coaxial and one bow) with 2,394 rounds; the turret was manually operated, the main gun was stabilized in neither elevation (−4° to +45°) nor azimuth (360°), and simple optical sights were fitted
Armour: riveted and welded steel varying in thickness between 6 and 22 mm (0.24 and 0.87 in)
Powerplant: one 335.5-kW (450-hp) M–17T petrol engine with 790 litres (173.8 Imp. gal.) of fuel
Performance: speed, road 73.4 km/h (45.6 mph) on wheels; range, road 500 km (311 miles) on wheels; fording 1.2 m (3.98 ft); gradient 63%; vertical obstacle 0.2 m (0.66 ft) on wheels and 0.76 m (2.5 ft) on tracks; trench 1.85 m (6.07 ft); ground clearance 0.27 m (10.6 in) on wheels and 0.3 m (1.0 ft) on tracks

Limited production was undertaken of the BT-7M (otherwise known as the BT-8) with the hull redesigned to accommodate a 500-hp (373-kW) diesel, a full-width glacis plate and the turret of the T-28 tank with its 76.2-mm (3-in) L/26 gun and two 7.62-mm (0.3-in) machine-guns. Weighing 14,900 kg (32,848 lb), the BT-7M had 790 litres (174 Imp. gal.) of fuel for a range of 700 km (435 miles). The final development of the BT series was the BT-IS of 1936. This appeared only in prototype form, and was essentially the BT-7M with sloping side armour in addition to the full-width sloping glacis plate, and also featured removable skirt armour over the upper portion of the running gear. Though the type did not enter service, it was of great importance in Soviet tank development, as it paved the way for the next generation of highly mobile and well-protected Soviet medium tanks with considerably greater gun power.

The BT series derived wholly from the Christie concept, and was paralleled by a Soviet medium tank family of heavier construction with specific features adopted from a variety of foreign sources. Whereas the BT series had been designed for exploitation of any breakthrough, the heavier type of medium tank was designed to co-operate with heavy tanks in the creation of the breakthrough. Development of this vehicle was entrusted to a team at the Kirov factory in Leningrad, and the team's starting point was the British A6E1, whose details the Soviets discovered through espionage rather than outright purchase, as the British tank was still secret when the Soviet specification was issued in 1931. This specification was difficult to fulfil, calling for a five-man tank armed with one 45-mm gun and one 7.62-mm (0.3-in) coaxial machine-gun in the main turret, plus one 7.62-mm (0.3-in) machine-gun in each of the two subsidiary turrets, armour between 20 and 30 mm (0.79 and 1.18 in) thick, and a maximum speed of 60 km/h (37.3 mph) on a 500-hp (373-kW) petrol engine. Based on the Vickers-Armstrongs type of vertical springing for 12 small road wheels on each side, the first prototype was completed in 1932, and weighed 17,575 kg (38,746 lb). Trials confirmed that the vehicle was basically satisfactory, but the Red Army called for heavier protection and armament, the latter to include a 76.2-mm (3-in) low-velocity main gun. The redesigned tank was accepted in August 1933 for service as the T-28, which featured a frame antenna for the

radio when fitted, smoke emitters and, in later vehicles, a gun stabilization system that considerably improved the accuracy of fire from the main gun when the tank was moving. The last was a singularly advanced development that presaged a main stream of future development.

The T-28 proved reliable and quiet in operation, despite the installation of a 500-hp (373-kW) M-17L engine. Just as importantly for the breakthrough role, the tank could climb a 1.05-m (3.44-ft) obstacle and cross a 2.9-m (9.5-ft) gap. The type began to enter service in 1934 as the T-28, with a 76.2-mm (3-in) L/16.5 main gun and three 7.62-mm (0.3-in) machine-guns located as one coaxial weapon and one in each of the two subsidiary turrets placed

---

T-28
(USSR)

Type: medium tank
Crew: 6
Combat weight: 28,960 kg (63,845 lb)
Dimensions: length overall 7.40 m (24.28 ft); width 2.80 m (9.19 ft); height 2.82 m (9.25 ft)
Armament system: one 76.2-mm (3-in) gun with 70 rounds, one 47-mm gun with 35 rounds or one 7.62-mm (0.3-in) DT machine-gun in the subsidiary turret, and two 7.62-mm (0.3-in) DT machine-guns with 7,938 rounds
Armour: between 11 and 40 mm (0.43 and 1.575 in)
Powerplant: one 373-kW (500-hp) M-17L petrol engine with 650 litres (143 Imp. gal.) of fuel
Performance: speed, road 37 km/h (23 mph); range, road 220 km (137 miles); fording 0.8 m (2.62 ft) without preparation; gradient 42°; vertical obstacle 0.95 m (3.12 ft); trench 2.7 m (8.85 ft); ground clearance 0.54 m (21.25 in)

T-28

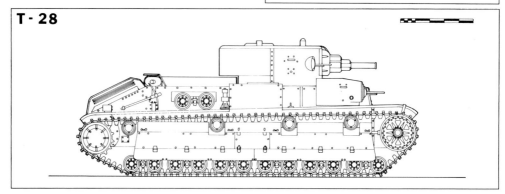

Inspired by British and German multi-turret tanks, the Soviets' T-28 medium tank featured a high rear superstructure, a central turret accommodating a 76.2-mm (3-in) low-velocity gun, and two forward turrets flanking the main turret and each fitted with one machine-gun. This is a 1938 variant, the T-28(V) command tank fitted with radio and a frame aerial round the turret sides and rear.

Complementing the T-23 medium tank, the Soviets' T-35 heavy tank was again of the multi-turret type, but in this instance with four subsidiary turrets grouped round the central turret and its low-velocity 76.2-mm (3-in) gun: two of these featured 37-mm high-velocity guns, and the other two 7.62-mm (0.3-in) machine-guns for local defence. (RAC Tank Museum)

forward and to each side of the main turret. The armour ranged in thickness from a minimum of 10 mm (0.39 in) to a maximum of 30 mm (1.18 in), and at a weight of 28,960 kg (63,845 lb) the T-28 had a maximum speed of 37 km/h (23 mph), well below requirement but still an impressive figure for so substantial a tank. The basic model was improved as the T-28A with a weight of 31,500 kg (69,444 lb) with thicker armour in key points, and the right-hand subsidiary turret modified to take a 47-mm anti-tank gun in place of the machine-

gun. Further evolution continued during the mid-1930s, and in 1938 the tank was revised as the T-28B, sometimes known as the T-28M: this had detail modifications, such as a turret basket and driver's visors, but the most important tactical development was the use of the L10 L/26 gun in place of the original L/16.5 weapon.

The T-28 was blooded against the Japanese in 1939 and the Finns in 1939-40, proving to be too thinly armoured to sustain hits by modern anti-tank weapons. The Soviets therefore pro-

93

duced the T-28C with much improved armour: the front of the turret and hull were increased in thickness from 50 to 80 mm (1.97 to 3.15 in), and of the turret sides and rear to a maximum of 40 mm (1.575 in) through the addition of 'screen' plates. This increased combat weight to 32,000 kg (70,547 lb), but had little effect on performance. Protection was judged to be excellent, however, and the T-28C was decisive in the Soviets' eventual defeat of the Finns in April 1940, with the breakthrough of the Mannerheim Line's fixed defences. The basic chassis was also developed as a bridgelayer, flamethrower, mineclearer and hull for various types of self-propelled artillery, but perhaps the most important variant was the T-29-5, produced in 1934 as a prototype with Christie track/wheel suspension to constitute, with the BT-IS, a development link towards the classic T-34, discussed in a later chapter.

T–32
(USSR)

Type: heavy tank
Crew: 10
Combat weight: 45,520 kg (100,353 lb)
Dimensions: length overall 9.30 m (30.51 ft); width 3.20 m (10.50 ft); height 3.05 m (10.00 ft)
Armament system: one 76.2-mm (3-in) gun with 96 rounds, two 37-mm guns with 220 rounds and six 7.62-mm (0.3-in) DT machine-guns with 8,230 rounds
Armour: between 11 and 25 mm (0.43 and 1 in)
Powerplant: one 257-kW (345-hp) M-17L petrol engine with 590 litres (130 Imp. gal.) of fuel
Performance: speed, road 20 km/h (12.4 mph); range, road 150 km (93 miles); fording 1.2 m (3.95 ft) without preparation; gradient 40°; vertical obstacle 1.2 m (3.94 ft); trench 4.6 m (15.1 ft); ground clearance 0.53 m (21 in)

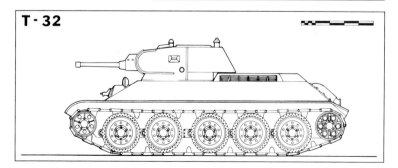

T - 32

While the Soviets directed their energies mainly towards the creation of a substantial armoured force based initially on light and then medium tanks, they were conscious all along in the 1920s that there was a place for the heavy tank once industry was capable of producing such a weapon to the right quality and in sufficient numbers. In 1930 the Red Army finalized its plans for a heavily armoured tank with powerful armament in multiple turrets, the object being to provide breakthrough forces with a potent shock weapon. Though developed on the conceptual basis of the British A1 Independent heavy tank, the resulting T-32 was evolved from the design of the TG to complement the T-28. The T-32 was based on armour varying in thickness from a minimum of 11 mm (0.43 in) to a maximum of 25 mm (0.98 in), and at an overall length of 9.3 m (30.5 ft) turned the scales at a combat weight of 45,500 kg (100,309 lb), complete with its crew of 10 and maximum ammunition for its diverse armament: this comprised a central turret accommodating one 76.2-mm (3-in) L/16.5 gun plus 96 rounds, right-hand forward and left-hand rear secondary turrets each accommodating one 37-mm gun plus 110 rounds, and left-hand forward and right-hand rear tertiary turrets each accommodating one 7.62-mm (0.3-in) machine-gun. Each of the main turrets was fitted with a coaxial machine-gun, and a sixth machine-gun was located in the bow; the machine-gun ammunition totalled 8,230 rounds. The T-32 was powered by a 345-hp (257-kW) M-17L engine for a maximum speed of 29 km/h (18 mph), while the 590-litre (130-Imp. gal.) fuel capacity provided a range of only 150 km (93 miles). But this was perhaps more than adequate for such a tank, which could also climb a 1.2-m (3.94-ft) obstacle and cross a 4.6-m (15.1-ft) gap.

Comparatively few T-32s were built, greater emphasis being placed on the T-35 with superior capabilities. The initial T-35A, sometimes known as the T-35-1, had a longer L/24 main gun, two 45-mm secondary guns and five machine-guns, the last with 10,000 rounds. Armour thickness was improved by 5 mm (0.2 in) on the hull front, and this 45,725-kg (100,805-lb) monster was driven by the more

T - 35

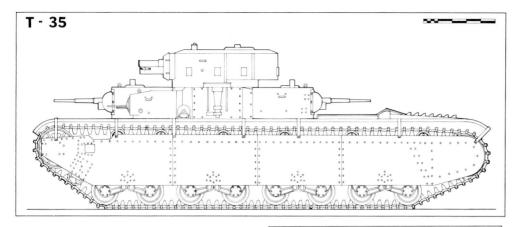

powerful 500-hp (373-kW) M-17T engine so that performance would not be degraded. The T-35 also differed from the T-32 in its road wheels, numbering eight medium-sized units on each side of the T-35 to the six larger wheels on each side of the T-32. Total production was only about 30 machines, later examples being of a variant generally known as the T-35B but alternatively as the T-35-2. This was generally fitted with radio, but its most important advantage over the T-35A was its considerably thicker armour: the maximum turret thickness was 35 mm (1.38 in) rather than 20 mm (0.79 in), and the hull sides and front were all increased by 5 mm (0.2 in). The last vehicles had welded conical rather than riveted slab-sided turrets, and in service some of the turrets were removed to save weight and so increase mobility.

The ultimate heavy tanks of Soviet design before the Second World War were two quite extraordinary designs, the T-100 and SMK (Sergius Mironovich Kirov) of 1938, which were both developed as possible successors to the T-35. Each type was powered by a 400-hp (298-kW) petrol engine, the 56,900-kg (125,441-lb) T-100 achieving a maximum speed of 30 km/h (18.7 mph) and the 45,725-kg (100,805-lb) SMK a slightly faster 32 km/h (19.9 mph). Both tanks were moderately well armoured, with minimum and maximum thicknesses of 30 and 60 mm (1.18 and 2.36 in) respectively, and were of multi-turret concept with the main turret on a tall barbette to provide superfiring capability over the secondary turret. In each case the 360° trav-

T-35
(USSR)

Type: heavy tank
Crew: 11 when all turrets were installed and manned
Combat weight: 50,000 kg (110,229 lb) with all turrets installed
Dimensions: length overall 9.72 m (31.89 ft); width 3.20 m (10.50 ft); height 3.43 m (11.25 ft)
Armament system: one 76.2-mm (3-in) gun with 96 rounds, two 45-mm guns with 220 rounds, and up to seven 7.62-mm (0.3-in) machine-guns (six DTs and one P-40) with 10,000 rounds
Armour: between 11 and 35 mm (0.43 and 1.38 in)
Powerplant: one 373-kW (500-hp) M-17T petrol engine with 590 litres (130 Imp. gal.) of fuel
Performance: speed, road 30 km/h (18.6 mph); range, road 150 km (93 miles); fording 1.2 m (3.95 ft) without preparation; gradient 20°; vertical obstacle 1.2 m (3.94 ft); trench 3.5 m (11.5 ft); ground clearance 0.53 m (21 in)

erse main turret was armed with a 76.2-mm (3-in) L/24 gun and the 300° traverse subsidiary turret with a 45-mm gun, while the tertiary armament comprised three 7.62-mm (0.3-in) machine-guns. The six-man T-100 was no less than 3.25 m (10.66 ft) and the seven-man SMK 3.2 m (10.5 ft) high, both therefore being so tall that they were tactically unwieldy and highly visible. Both types were evaluated operationally in the Russo-Finnish War of 1939-40, and proved disastrously vulnerable to artillery fire.

The T-35 series saw service in the Second World War, but was unsuccessful because of its multi-turreted design and comparatively thin armour in so lengthy a machine. The Soviets saw the continued virtues of a heavy tank for breakthrough tasks, but also appreciated that a single-turret design offered far greater promise. The result was the powerful KV discussed in a later chapter.

Like the USSR, the USA ended the First World War with no indigenous tank in production, and its small armoured forces equipped with British and French tanks. But again like the USSR, the American industrial machine proved capable of developing useful armoured fighting vehicles, though not in numbers as great as its Soviet counterpart. The Soviets started from a small industrial base and succeeded, by a combination of sensible design and monolithic effort, in producing a large armoured force. The Americans started from an altogether larger and more sophisticated industrial base but were almost totally stymied by lack of financial support and by the basic isolationist antipathy of the administrations that controlled the US forces.

The vast production orders that had been placed with US manufacturers in the First World War were cancelled after the Armistice as the enormously expanded US forces were cut back towards their pre-war norms. An early casualty of this retrenchment was the US Army's Tank Corps, which was disbanded in 1920. Tanks thereupon became the responsibility of the infantry, whose main asset in the armoured field was a force of 100 Tank Mk VIIIs. Some development work was continued, but it was the establishment in 1922 of a Tank Board that allowed constructive work to resume. The board was tasked with the definition of American tank policy, within the overall context of infantry-dominated war. The board therefore called for the development of two primary types: an 11,200-lb (5,080-kg) light tank suitable for truck transport in long-distance movements, and a medium tank armed with a 37-mm gun and a 0.3-in (7.62-mm) machine-gun, capable of a maximum speed of 12 mph (19.3 km/h), but limited in maximum weight by the 15-ton capacity of the army's bridging equipment. This latter limitation at a stroke rendered obsolete the various medium tanks being developed in prototype form (see

below), though prototype testing was continued for technical reasons. Between 1922 and 1926 several medium tank designs were evolved, for construction and evaluation between 1926 and 1931, while the light tank notion was dropped in 1926 as the army felt the single type would satisfy all its tactical requirements. American tank developments can be divided into two main design streams (one stemming from official design authorities and the other from private enterprise in the form of J. Walter Christie and the Marmon-Herrington company) in the standard light and medium categories: the USA produced no heavy tanks in the period up to 1940, its first such vehicle being the Heavy Tank M6, which was designed in 1940 and is discussed in a later chapter.

As the US Army could not afford to produce substantial numbers of tanks, its efforts were sensibly devoted to maintaining a cadre tank force that could be used to explore the tactical organization and applications of armour, and the evolution of tank designs to keep the US tank force up to the technical level reached by other advanced nations. Within this latter requirement the army was careful to demand tank designs that were capable of mass production by the USA's heavy machinery industry, should the world situation deteriorate to a position such that rapid rearmament was desirable: this was a particularly important factor, that paid handsome dividends in the mid- and late 1930s.

In purely numerical terms, the most important US tank at the end of the First World War was the Renault FT. It was planned that American industry should supply these vehicles, after the delivery of pattern vehicles from France, but this proved too optimistic a plan and the American Expeditionary Forces serving on the Western Front used French-supplied examples. Production finally got under way in the USA, though the orders for 4,400 vehicles were curtailed to an eventual total of 950 tanks, designated Six-Ton Tank M1917. These were very similar to the FT in overall appearance, but had been completely re-engineered to suit American production practices. The type was powered by a 42-hp (31.3-kW) Buda engine with a self-starter, and had a revised turret able to accommodate either a 0.3-in (7.62-mm) machine-gun or a 37-mm gun. The M1917 served the US tank arm well, right through the 1930s, and from 1929 was updated as the M1917A1 with a 100-hp (74.6-kW) Franklin air-cooled engine in place of the original water-cooled unit, which had never proved entirely satisfactory. The new engine increased maximum speed from 5.5 to 10 mph (8.9 to 16.1 km/h), to the great pleasure of the newly-created Mechanized Force, but further development was halted by the Chief of Industry, who rightly appreciated that scarce resources would be better applied to the development of new vehicles than to the updating of a design already 15 years old. In the event only seven M1917A1 light tanks were delivered.

Already under development by J. Cunningham Sons and Co. on the basis of a design by the US Ordnance Department, the Light Tank T1 was a 15,000-lb (6,804-kg) machine with a crew of two and a turret fitted with one 37-mm gun and one 0.3-in (7.62-mm) coaxial machine-gun. Power was provided by a front-mounted 105-hp (78.3-kW) Cunningham engine for a maximum speed of 20 mph (32.2 km/h), and the armour varied from a minimum of 0.25 in (6.35 mm) to a maximum of 0.375 in (9.53 mm). Development continued into the mid-1930s, the final variant being the 19,900-lb (9,027-kg) T1E6 with its 240-hp (179-kW) La France engine, for the same maximum speed despite the greater weight of the thicker armour; the armament remained unaltered from that of the original T1. Though production of the T1E1 variant was planned with the designation Light Tank M1, the series did not enter production, but proved significant in the evolution of later designs, starting with the Light Tank T2 based in the T1E4.

Design of this more advanced machine began in 1933, and the construction of T2E1 and T2E2 prototypes was undertaken by the Rock Island Arsenal in 1934. The suspension was of the Vickers-Armstrongs pattern with articulating two-wheel bogies and leaf springs, and the design produced a trim four-man machine with a comparatively high superstructure to support the cylindrical turret armed with one 0.5-in (12.7-mm) and one 0.3-in (7.62-mm) machine-gun. Power was provided

The first light tank developed in the USA was the Light Tank T1, a development type designed to a maximum weight of 5 tons and the ability to be moved over strategic distance by truck. The 105-hp (78-kW) engine was located in the box projecting forward of the tracks. (*RAC Tank Museum*)

by a 260-hp (194-kW) Continental radial, modified from a standard aircraft engine, and this was to become a common practice in light and medium tanks of US design. Trials confirmed the overall suitability of the type, which was produced in very small numbers as the Light Tank M2A1 and Light Tank M2A2: the former introduced volute springing, and at a weight of 18,790 lb (8,523 kg) could reach 45 mph (72.4 km/h), while the latter had paired machine-gun turrets. The M2A2 went through a large series of experimental developments, including different petrol and diesel powerplants, thicker armour and modified turrets.

In 1938 there appeared the M2A3, and in 1939 the M2A4. Amongst several detail modifications, the former featured a longer wheelbase, with repositioned bogies, while the latter resembled the M2A3 in all respects but the armament: the M2A4 was fitted with a single turret and one 37-mm gun (plus two 0.3-in/7.62-mm machine-guns in side sponsons), instead of the previous pair of machine-gun turrets. The maximum armour thickness was increased to 1 in (25.4 mm), and the tank weighed 23,000 lb (10,432 kg), allowing a road speed of 34 mph (54.7 km/h) on a 250-hp (186-kW) Continental radial. The M2A4 was produced to the extent of 375 examples, and became the mainstay of the US Army's expanding armoured force in 1940 and 1941. The

M2A4 was thus the first wholly-American tank to enter large-scale production, and though overshadowed by later light tanks, was in fact used operationally by the Americans at the beginning of the war against Japan; some were also supplied to the UK for training. The type was, at best, obsolescent at the beginning of the Second World War, but proved useful against the Japanese as they lacked an anti-tank gun able to defeat its armour, which was considerably thicker than the norm accepted for light tanks elsewhere.

The same basic vehicle was used by the US cavalry as the Combat Car M1, a deliberately misleading designation adopted to circumvent the 1920 law that allocated tanks exclusively to the infantry. The decision to develop a cavalry scouting vehicle came in 1932, when General Douglas MacArthur became the US Army chief-of-staff and launched a programme to turn the US Army into a fully mechanized force. As early as 1929 the cavalry had decided in favour of increased mechanization, and had in the short term turned to Christie (see below), whose Medium Tank T3 was ordered for evaluation as the Combat Car T1. The Christie type of suspension was used in the following Combat Cars T2 to T4, but the first production vehicle for the

cavalry was the Combat Car M1, developed from the Combat Car T5, itself a modified T2E1 with a barbette superstructure, to the T5E2 which was placed in production as the Combat Car M1 with a turret accommodating two machine-guns. In 1940 the type was redesignated Light Tank M1A2. The Combat Car M1A1 was fitted with revised transmission, radio and a turret offset to the right, and the Combat Car M2 was basically similar, though fitted with an improved turret and a 250-hp (186-kW) Guiberson T-1020 diesel; in 1940 the M2 was redesignated the Light Tank M1A1. This completed the mainstream of US light tank development in the period between the world wars. The next offering was to be the Light Tank M3, known to the British as the General Stuart and nicknamed 'Honey': this was developed in the late 1930s and standardized for the still-neutral US Army in 1940, but is discussed below in Chapter Five, together with other light tanks of the Second World War period.

American development of medium tanks was initially dominated by a lateral extension of the recommendations expressed in 1918 by the Caliber Board, otherwise known as the Westervelt Board and established to make proposals about the development of the US Army's artillery. The board recommended the

Standardized in 1939 after development at the Rock Island Arsenal, the M2A4 was the final version of the M2 light tank series to enter US service, and was similar to the preceding M2A3 apart from having a single turret armed with a 37-mm gun rather than twin turrets each fitted with one 0.3-in (7.62-mm) machine-gun. Further evolution led to the classic M3 series. (*RAC Tank Museum*)

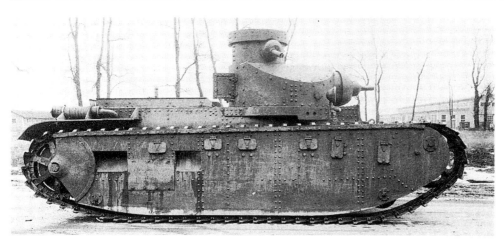

The Medium Tank T1 was evolved from the Medium Tank M1921, and after trials in 1928 was recommended for standardization as the Medium Tank M1. Approval was granted but then withdrawn. (*RAC Tank Museum*)

creation of a new medium tank that would supplant both the French FT (M1917) and the British Mk VIII International. Under the auspices of the Chief of the Tank Corps, the designers set to work on a new four/five-man tank weighing no more than 40,000 lb (18,144 kg), carrying a 57- or 76-mm main gun, provided with protection sufficient to halt a 0.5-in (12.7-mm) armour-piercing bullet at short range, and able to cross a 9-ft (2.74-m) trench.

The result was the Medium Tank M1921, otherwise known as the Medium Tank A. This was powered by a 250-hp (186-kW) Murray and Tregurtha marine engine, and at a weight of 41,000 lb (18,598 kg) could reach 10 mph (16.1 km/h). The armament system comprised a main turret with a 57-mm gun and 0.3-in (7.62-mm) coaxial machine-gun, and a superimposed turret with a second 0.3-in (7.62-mm) machine-gun. This all-riveted machine was obsolete even as it appeared, and gave way to the Medium Tank M1922, which appeared from the Rock Island Arsenal in 1923 with features of the M1921 but also with the flexible track/cable suspension of the British Medium Tank Mk D on a lengthened hull shape that was considerably higher at the back than at the front, with the object of providing greater traction as the vehicle climbed out of trenches. The armament and power-plant were identical with those of the M1921, but speed was increased to 15 mph (24.1 km/h), despite an increase in all-up weight to 49,500 lb (22,453 kg).

The M1921 and M1922 were clearly suitable only for trial work, so in 1924 the Ordnance Department designed the Medium Tank T1, which was built at the Rock Island Arsenal in 1925. This was essentially an improved version of the M1921 with a 200-hp (149-kW) Packard petrol engine for a speed of 14 mph (22.5 km/h), and was standardized in 1928 as the Medium Tank M1. Production plans were then scrapped, and the T1 was used for trials with features such as better ventilation and the 338-hp (252-kW) Liberty engine.

The same basic engine was used, in 312-hp (233-kW) form, as the engine of the Medium Tank T2, built by Cunningham within the constraints of the army's bridging equipment. The type emerged with armour varying in thickness between 0.25 and 1 in (6.35 and 25.4 mm), a crew of four, a maximum speed of 25 mph (40.2 km/h), and armament comprising one 47-mm gun and one 0.5-in (12.7-mm) coaxial machine-gun in the turret, and one 37-mm gun and one 0.3-in (7.62-mm) machine-gun in the bow. The T2 was produced in prototype form only, but exemplifies many of the trends in US armour design, most notably the good protection, the mixed armament with turret and hull guns of fairly large size, and a high power-to-weight ratio for good performance under adverse conditions.

The US Army's first production medium tank was therefore the Medium Tank M2, which was standardized in June 1939 on the basis of the Medium Tank T5 Phase III evaluation model. The T5 series first appeared in

Clearly inspired by the Vickers Medium Tank series, the American T2 medium tank was built down to a weight limit of 15 tons. The type is seen here without its 47-mm turret gun. (*RAC Tank Museum*)

26 mph (41.8 km/h) at a weight of 38,000 lb (17,237 kg), a crew of six, and an armament comprising one 37-mm gun and no fewer than eight 0.3-in (7.62-mm) machine-guns. The M2 was superseded in production during 1940 by the M2A1 with 1.25-in (31.75-mm) armour and a supercharged 400-hp (298-kW) Wright engine for a speed of 30 mph (48.3 km/h), despite a weight increase of 46,000 lb (20,865 kg). By this time, however, the first lessons of the new armoured warfare in Europe were reaching the USA, and the obsolescence of the M2 series was plainly evident, leading to plans for more ambitious vehicles, that matured as the M3 and M4.

One of the great names in tank design is J. Walter Christie, an American who came to tanks via the Wheel-and-Track 8-in Gun Motor Carriage during the First World War. An innovative thinker with many sound technical capabilities, Christie firmly appreciated that while the tanks of the period might be suited to the particular conditions of trench warfare, by being matched to this peculiar set of circumstances they were prohibited from any utility in the prophetic breakthrough tactics developed and so eloquently expounded in the 1920s by Fuller and Liddell Hart. Christie was convinced that the future of the tank lay in far-ranging operations, by modestly protected tanks with the suspension and power-to-weight ratio for high-speed mobility over adverse terrain.

As a first step, this far-sighted man designed the Christie Medium Tank M1919, the USA's first tank of post-First World War concept. The vehicle was built by the Front Drive Motor Company, and was planned round a chassis suitable for use as a tank or as a cross-country truck. The boxlike hull accommodated the driver in a compartment at the front, the payload (fighting compartment or freight, depending on variant) in the centre, and the powerplant and transmission compartment at the rear. Tested as a tank, the M1919 had a large circular turret some 5 ft (1.52 m) in diameter and fitted with a 57-mm gun; on top of this main turret was an independent dome-shaped sub-turret fitted with a 0.3-in (7.62-mm) machine-gun. Both turrets could be traversed through 360°, and were

1938 from the Rock Island Arsenal in succession to the Medium Tanks T3 and T4 inspired by the Christie M1928 (see below). The T5 was designed to use as many components of the Light Tank M2 as possible, and was fitted with vertical volute suspension and a 250-hp (186-kW) Continental radial engine. Oddly enough, the T5 was developed with armour on a 1-in (25.4-mm) basis, which was less than that of contemporary US Army light tanks, and the concept of the vehicle was still infantry support: this resulted in a main armament of one turret-mounted 37-mm gun, but no fewer than six 0.3-in (7.62-mm) machine-guns located in a high barbette that formed the structural base for the turret. With a crew of five, the T5 weighed 30,000 lb (13,608 kg) and possessed a maximum speed of 20 mph (32.2 km/h). The US Army was now conscious of the impending war in Europe and wished to explore its options in the development of medium tanks, so the T5 was developed in a number of alternative forms before production was ordered. Thus the T5E1 had twin 37-mm guns, and the T5E2 had a 75-mm (2.95-in) pack howitzer on the right of the vehicle front, while the T5 Phase III pilot model of the M2 had wider tracks, and greater power in the form of a 346-hp (258-kW) Wright radial.

Production started in June 1939, the initial model being the Medium Tank M2 with a 350-hp (261-kW) Wright engine for a speed of

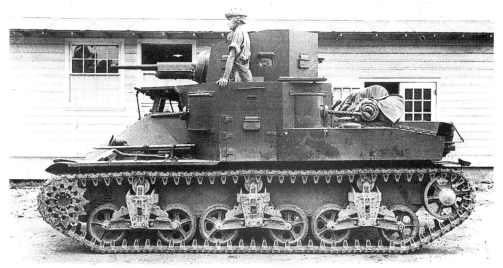

Featuring considerable commonality of parts with the M2 light tank series, the M2 medium tank offered greater protection at the expense of performance. This is an M2A1 with a supercharged rather than normally aspirated radial engine, and an armament comprising one turret-mounted 37-mm gun and eight 0.3-in (7.62-mm) machine-guns. The crew required was six, and when it was standardized in 1940 it was clearly obsolete by comparison with the Germans' PzKpfw III and IV medium tanks. (*RAC Tank Museum*)

manned by the second and third crew members. Protective armour varied in thickness from 0.25 to 1 in (6.35 to 25.4 m), and power was provided by a 120-hp (89.5-kW) Christie engine to provide this 27,000-lb (12,247-kg) vehicle with a maximum speed of 7 mph (11.25 km/h). Evidence of what was to come from Christie was provided by the running gear. As a cross-country vehicle, the machine ran on twin tracks: on each side these ran over large front and rear rubber-tyred wheels, as well as a centrally-placed unit with two coil-sprung road wheels, and a single return roller. For road running the tracks were removed and stowed on the hull sides, the two central road wheels were raised, and the vehicle moved on its front and rear wheels like an ordinary wheeled vehicle.

The M1919 was revised as the Christie Medium Tank M1921, with a crew of four and a rearrangement of the forward compartments to locate the two-man fighting compartment at the front with the driver and commander in a separate compartment in the centre of the vehicle. The 57-mm main gun was installed in a ball mounting in the front plate, with two 0.3-in (7.62-mm) coaxial machine-guns, and the armour was thinned to a maximum of 0.75 in (19 mm). The effect of this major revision was a far lower silhouette, the M1921 having an overall height of 7.08 ft (2.16 m), compared with the M1919's 8.75 ft (2.67 m):

Medium Tank M2A1
(USA)

Type: medium tank
Crew: 6
Combat weight: 51,520 lb (23,369 kg)
Dimensions: length overall 17.83 ft (5.44 m); width 8.75 ft (2.67 m); height 9.50 ft (2.90 m)
Armament system: one 37-mm gun with 200 rounds and eight 0.3-in (7.62-mm) Browning machine-guns with 12,250 rounds
Armour: 32 mm (1.25 in) maximum
Powerplant: one 350-hp (261-kW) Continental R–985 petrol engine with 136 US gal. (515 litres) of fuel
Performance: speed, road 30 mph (48.3 km/h); range, road 130 miles (209 km); fording 3.5 ft (1.07 m);
gradient 60%; vertical obstacle 2.0 ft (0.61 m); trench 7.6 ft (2.32 m); ground clearance 17 in (0.43 m)

M2A1

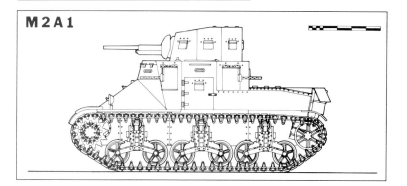

The first tank designed and built in the USA after the First World War, the Christie M1919 medium tank has wheel-or-track running gear, road operation requiring the removal of the tracks and the raising of the central pair of wheels. (*RAC Tank Museum*)

Far right The Christie Model 1931 was typical of the designer's needle-nosed track-or-wheel tanks, and was evaluated as the Medium Tank T3. This vehicle is seen without its tracks, which would normally be stowed on the shelf-like projections along the sides of the hull rear, and also lacks its cylindrical turret carrying a 37-mm gun and coaxial machine-gun.(*IWM*)

the tactical penalty to be paid was a less effective armament with far smaller fields of fire. The suspension was revised slightly to allow the installation of larger road wheels, but the M1919's track or wheel capability was retained. The same engine was used, but the suspension revisions allowed a maximum speed of 15 mph (24.1 km/h), despite a slightly higher weight.

These were experimental vehicles, and some time elapsed before the advent of the next machine, the Christie M1928 built by the US Wheel and Track Layer Corporation. The M1928 was a turretless vehicle designed to validate the new type of Christie suspension designed to allow the vehicle to run at high speed on roads without its tracks (carried on shelves on the hull sides), and at a lower but still very high speed across country with its tracks. The key to this performance was the first version of the definitive Christie suspension with four large road wheels on each side, each mounted on an arm connected to a long and adjustable spring located inside the hull side. This development vehicle was arranged as a tank (with the driver at the front in a characteristic pointed nose section, fighting compartment in the centre and the powerplant at the rear) and weighed 17,200 lb (7,802 kg). Power was provided by a 338-hp (252-kW) Liberty engine, and the M1928 achieved the

prodigious speeds of 70 mph (112.7 km/h) on its wheels and 42 mph (67.6 km/h) on its tracks. The effect of this prototype and its trials was enormous, leading to considerable revision of many nations' thinking about tank mobility in the 1930s. By far the most important consequence was the Soviets' purchase of two such vehicles as the precursor of the BT series and thus of the superb T-34 and its descendants.

The M1928 formed the basis of the Christie M1931, which was fitted with a 360° traverse turret accommodating one 37-mm gun and one 0.3-in (7.62-mm) coaxial machine-gun. The installation of a turret and thicker armour

Christie Model 1928
(USA)

Type: medium tank prototype
Crew: 3
Combat weight: 17,200 lb (7,802 kg)
Dimensions: length overall 17.00 ft (5.18 m); width 7.00 ft (2.13 m); height 6.00 ft (1.83 m)
Armament system: only dummies were fitted, comprising one bow gun and one pedestal-mounted machine-gun
Armour: 12.7 mm (0.5 in)
Powerplant: one 338-hp (252-kW) Liberty petrol engine with 89 US gal. (337 litres) of fuel
Performance: speed, road 42 mph (67.6 km/h) on tracks and 70 mph (112.7 km/h) on wheels

increased weight to 22,000 lb (9,979 kg), and with other modifications to make the type suitable for production and service use, this reduced maximum wheel and track speeds to 46 and 27 mph (74 and 43.5 km/h) respectively. Considerable evaluation of the type was undertaken by the infantry and cavalry, which designated the vehicle Medium Tank T3 and Combat Car T1 respectively. Christie and the US Army eventually fell out with each other, and subsequent development of the basic idea was pursued by the Ordnance Department as the Medium Tank T4 for the infantry and as the Combat Cars T4 and T7 for the cavalry: a considerable official effort was made, and the type was built in modest development batches, but failed to enter full-scale production. Christie persevered with his private-venture designs right into the 1940s, but these failed to attract production orders. These included the M1932, the extraordinary M1932 Flying Tank with detachable biplane wings and boom-mounted empennage/propeller unit, the M1935, the M1936, the M1937, the M1938 and M1942. These took the Christie suspension to its limits in terms of high-speed movement across country, but were not viable as the starting points for service tanks, as their pneumatic tyres were clearly vulnerable to small arms fire, and the concept of a nose-mounted main

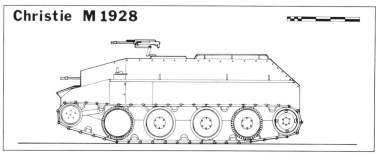

Christie **M 1928**

Christie's Model 1937 contributed strongly to the development of the British cruiser tanks from the Mk III onwards, and was itself intended as the versatile basis for a number of armament options. The driver was seated under a conical cupola, the space behind it being left open for the installation of a barbette or light turret. (*IWM*)

gun was increasingly obsolescent, even though it provided lower overall weight and silhouette.

In the period from 1939 to the entry of the USA into the Second World War in 1941, a number of tanks were produced by Marmon-Herrington as commercial ventures into the export market, and several of these secured modest success. The basic configuration used four small road wheels: the light two-man CTL tanks without a turret were based on components from the company's tractor range, had leaf springs and rubber tracks with steel cable reinforcement, while the heavier three- and four-man turreted types had steel tracks and, in many cases, suspension modified to the vertical volute spring type.

Of the other countries that fell into the orbit of the Allied nations in the Second World War, the only two that produced tanks in the period between the world wars were Czechoslovakia and Poland. The Czechs produced several excellent designs, and as these were absorbed into the German army after Czechoslovakia's occupation in 1939, it is perhaps more rational to deal with them with German armour in the next chapter. Polish tank development was

less ambitious, reflecting the obsolescence of Poland's tactical thinking and the country's relative lack of industrialization when it came into being in 1919. Poland's forces were initially equipped with French and ex-German machines, and these played a useful part in the Russo-Polish War of 1920, which seriously threatened the continued existence of a sovereign Poland. Useful development work could begin only after the end of this war and the inevitable period of consolidation and reconstruction that followed. In the short term, efforts were made to improve the reliability and firepower of the Renault FT. These efforts continued up to the end of the decade, but in 1924 it was decided to press ahead with the design of a light tank and also an infantry support/breakthrough tank. From 1925, however, the main effort was devoted to the WB-10 concept, which called for a vehicle with a maximum weight of 12,000 kg (26,455 lb), a main armament of one 47-mm gun backed by one heavy and one medium machine-gun, a speed of 25 km/h (15.5 mph) and a range of between 200 and 250 km (124 and 155 miles). Various trials failed to produce a viable machine, and the concept was abandoned.

In 1928 the attention of the Polish army was drawn (as was that of many other armies) to the Carden-Loyd Mk VI tankette. One example was bought from the UK, and this led to the Polish TK series. The TK.1 and TK.2 development models paved the way for an initial production model, of which 300 were built. This 2,450-kg (5,401-lb) TK.3 had an enclosed superstructure, a crew of two, and armament of one 7.92-mm (0.312-in) machine-gun, armour thicknesses ranging from 3 to 8 mm (0.12 to 0.315 in), and a maximum speed of 45 km/h (28 mph) on the 40 hp (29.8 kW) of its Ford Model A petrol engine. An extraordinary development of the TK.3 resulted in a four-wheel trailer that could be pulled behind the tankette: when the TK.3 had to move long distances on roads, the tankette was driven onto this wheeled chassis, its tracks were removed, and a chain drive was used to connect the tankette's drive sprockets to the rear wheels of the combined tankette/trailer, which was steered by the tankette driver from his standard driving position. Between 1936 and

Used as the Light Tank T16 for training, the Marmon-Herrington CTLS-4TA was designed and produced in 1941 for export to China and the Dutch East Indies with the three hull machine-guns supplemented by a fourth gun in a small turret offset to the right in the CTLS-4TAC with left-hand drive (illustrated) or to the left in the CTLS-TAY with right-hand drive. Production amounted to 240 vehicles. (*MARS*)

1939 some TK.3s were upgunned with a 20-mm cannon in the front plate, but other developments were more far-reaching.

The TKS of 1933 had armour between 3 and 10 mm (0.12 and 0.39 in) thick, wider tracks, strengthened suspension and a Polish-built Fiat engine of 40 hp (29.8 kW), which drove the 2,650-kg (5,842-lb) vehicle at 40 km/h (24.9 mph). Production of the TKS amounted to 390. The TKW of 1934 was developed only in prototype form, and had a turret accommodating the commander and a single heavy machine-gun, with the driver located in a separate compartment. The TKS-D of 1936 was another variant that again reached only prototype form, in this instance with a 27-mm Bofors anti-tank gun located in a semi-exposed position on the strengthened front plate. The final development of the TK.3 was the TKF with a 46-hp (34.3-kW) Polish-built Fiat engine and a combination gun mounting for one 7.92-mm (0.312-in) machine-gun and one 9-mm (0.35-in) machine-gun, the latter for the engagement of low-flying aircraft.

The Poles were also impressed with the Vickers-Armstrongs Six-Ton Tank Mk E with twin turrets. This was further developed as the

Poles' considerably more capable 7 TP light tank with 17-mm (0.67-in) armour and a 110-hp (82-kW) Saurer diesel for a speed of 32 km/h (19.9 mph) at a weight of 9,550 kg (21,054 lb). With a crew of three and an armament of two 7.92-mm (0.312-in) machine-guns, this variant entered production in 1934 and was the world's first production tank with a diesel powerplant. The initial model was succeeded in 1937 by a revised model with a single turret carrying a 37-mm Bofors anti-tank gun plus 7.92-mm (0.312-in) coaxial machine-gun. The latter version had armour to a maximum thickness of 15 mm (0.59 in), and was clearly suitable for employment only as an interim type, pending the arrival of the 7 TP light tank. Improved with a revised turret, welded armour to a maximum thickness of 40 mm (1.575 in), wider tracks, strengthened suspension and a weight of 11,175 kg (24,636 lb).

Several other Polish tanks were developed in the last years of peace, but none of these reached service use. Among these were the four-man 10 TP fast tank modelled on Christie wheel/track running gear and carrying a turreted 37-mm gun, the four-man 14 TP medium tank with track-only Christie running gear and thicker armour, the multi-turret 20/25 TP heavy tank, and the 4 TP small tank with its Pz.Inz. 130 small amphibious derivative. These indigenous designs showed the capabilities and inventiveness of the Polish designers, and much of significance to armoured warfare might have followed, had Poland not fallen foul of German aggression in September 1939.

Developed in Poland during the late 1930s, the Fast Tank 10 TP used Christie-type track-and-wheel running gear, seen here in its wheel form with the two forward road wheels turned to the right for steering. (RAC Tank Museum)

TK.3
(Poland)

Type: tankette
Crew: 2
Combat weight: 2,500 kg (5,511 lb)
Dimensions: length overall 2.577 m (8.455 ft); width 1.778 m (5.83 ft); height 1.307 m (4.29 ft)
Armament system: one 7.92-mm (0.312-in) machine-gun
Armour: between 3 and 8 mm (0.12 and 0.315 in)
Powerplant: one 40-hp (29.8-kW) Ford Model A petrol engine
Performance: speed, road 45 km/h (28 mph); range, road 200 km (124 miles); gradient 60%; vertical obstacle 0.43 m (1.41 ft); trench 1.22 m (4.0 ft)

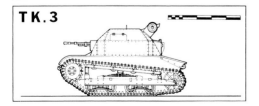

TK.3

Precocious Germany

After the Armistice of 11 November 1918 the German army's tank force was disbanded, and the Treaty of Versailles of June 1919 included amongst its provisions a total ban on the development of tanks. Yet the German army was already well established in its programme of intelligence-gathering about foreign developments, clandestine evaluation of tank-capable components in Germany, and secret links with countries not unsympathetic to German liaison in the development of their own tank forces. In this last respect the Swedes were the Germans' most important 'allies' in the early 1920s, when the LK.II was readied for Swedish production and service as the Strv m/21 under the leadership of Vollmer and a German army team. As the 1920s progressed, the Germans became increasingly involved with the Soviets, both parties thinking that a fair deal had been struck when the Germans were given use of the Kazan tank school as an experimental and proving ground, in return for technical information and training provided to the fledgling Soviet tank arm.

Between 1926 and 1929 the Germans broke the strictures of the Treaty of Versailles to produce a number of experimental tanks. These were commissioned in great secrecy from major engineering and arms companies as a means of evaluating trends in the design of armoured fighting vehicles, and also of regaining a manufacturing capability, pending the day that Germany would move into the field as a major armoured force.

Hand in hand with this technical and manufacturing effort there was a great volume of theoretical thinking about the operational and tactical employment of armour. By a paradox typical of military history, the Germans were well served by their lack of armour in this period: it left them without the entrenched thinking and existing hardware that inevitably accompanies the existence of the in-service weapons, and opened the way for radical though professionally competent thought about the nature and employment of a future tank force. Coupled with a realistic analysis of the German army's performance in the First World War, this paved the way for the adoption of the *Blitzkrieg* (lightning war) concept of operations, derived ultimately from the thinking of Fuller and, more significantly, Liddell Hart towards massive breakthroughs (or rather bypassing) of the enemy's major front-line assets by massed armour with substantial air support as the first step in fast-moving operations into the enemy's rear areas.

But while these tactical and operational concepts were still in their embryonic phases, the Germans were moving towards the creation of new hardware with the Leichte Traktor VK31 and Grosstraktor, so designated to convey the impression of an agricultural role not contrary to the provisions of the Treaty of Versailles. Limited design work had been undertaken since 1921, but it was 1926 before definitive work was started and 1928 before the first of six Leichte Traktor prototypes (three each from Krupp and Rheinmetall) were delivered for trials at Kazan. The Leichte Traktor was a light tank built of mild steel varying in thickness between 8 and 14 mm (0.315 and 0.55 in) thick, and weighed about 9,650 kg (21,274 lb). The type was armed solely with a 37-mm gun in a 360° traverse turret located at the rear of the vehicle, and the front-mounted engine provided a speed of 20 km/h (12.4 mph). In general configuration the Leichte Traktor was reminiscent of the British Medium Tank Mk II, and though an order for 289 was placed, this was cancelled in the light of subsequent developments. Details of the Leichte Traktor are lacking, a situation even more pronounced with the Grosstraktor series.

The Grosstraktor series comprised separate

designs from Daimler-Benz (Grosstraktor I), Rheinmetall (Grosstraktor II) and Krupp (Grosstraktor III), each designed to the same specification and built to the extent of two mild steel prototypes. Each was of semi-rhomboidal configuration with mud chutes (very large on the Grosstraktor I), weighed about 20,000 kg (44,092 lb) and in basic shape resembled the British Medium Tank III. Powered by a 300-hp (224-kW) engine, the tanks were each armed with one 75-mm (2.95-in) gun in the main turret together with three 7.92-mm (0.312-in) machine guns, including one in a subsidiary turret to the rear of the main turret to deter infantry assaults on the tanks' exposed flanks and rear. The Grosstraktor I is believed to have possessed another subsidiary turret forward of the main gun and to have been amphibious, whilst the Grosstraktor II was basically similar in overall layout but had less advanced suspension and thus an inferior cross-country performance. Some lessons were learned from the design, construction and evaluation of these types, but even the most cursory assessment convinced the Germans that they were obsolescent in basic concept.

By the time that the various Grosstraktor prototypes had been evaluated, the German army was well advanced with its plans for re-armament and growth, and a new series of tactical tanks was already under development as the planned armoured force's initial mass-production vehicles. But in common with other such services, the German army still saw the need for a heavy tank, and appreciated the apparent armament advantages of main and subsidiary turrets along the lines of the British A1E1 Independent. This feeling was formalized in a January 1934 meeting to consider a new medium tank: the meeting decided in favour of a fairly large machine with a medium-velocity main gun of large calibre to fire HE shell, in support of the more numerous light and medium tanks equipped with high-velocity anti-tank guns. The consequent specification produced the six-man Panzer Kampfwagen NbFz, or Neubaufahrzeug (new construction vehicle), which was developed in prototype form as the PzKpfw NbFz A with a Krupp turret and as the PzKpfw NbFz B with a Rheinmetall turret. The Krupp, MAN and Rheinmetall companies undertook design studies for the hull, the successful Rheinmetall type showed some evidence of the concept's long-toothed pedigree in its retention of a slightly rhomboidal aspect in the high rise to the forward idler and the long downward slope of the upper track run's rear portion: the definitive hull was based closely on that of the Rheinmetall Grosstraktor II. Construction of all six or eight prototypes was of mild steel varying in thickness from 10 to 70 mm (0.39 to 2.76 in), and the installation of a 500-hp (373-kW) petrol engine provided for

The Rheinmetall Grosstraktor II was designed to the same specification as the Daimler-Benz Grosstraktor I and Krupp Grosstraktor III as an experimental heavy tank intended to provide design and manufacturing experience rather than to form the basis of an operational tank. (RAC Tank Museum)

Designed to provide the PzKpfw V heavy tank component in a family that also encompassed the PzKpfw I light training tank, the PzKpfw II light reconnaissance tank, the PzKpfw III medium tank and PzKpfw IV support tank, the PzKpfw NbFz proved unsuccessful. This is the Model A with a Krupp main turret between front and rear machine-gun turrets. (*RAC Tank Museum*)

good cross-country performance and a maximum speed in the order of 35 km/h (21.5 mph) in combination with a suspension arrangement based on that of VK2001(Rh) prototype for the PzKpfw IV medium tank and consisting of 10 road wheels on each side: these were arranged as five articulated twin-wheel bogies on sprung trailing arms for considerable vertical movement;

The PzKpfw NbFz A concept included a main turret armed with one 105-mm (4.13-in) medium-velocity gun and one 37-mm high-velocity gun in a superimposed coaxial mounting, while the PzKpfw NbFz B was more realistically armed with one 75-mm (2.95-in) KwK L/24 medium-velocity gun and one 37-mm KwK L/45 high-velocity gun in a side-by-side coaxial mounting at the front of an advanced turret with low silhouette and lines that were moderately well sloped for ballistic protection. Both types featured a secondary battery comprising two turrets (identical with that of the PzKpfw I light tank), each armed with two 7.92-mm (0.312-in) machine-guns and located to the front right and rear left of the main turret. By the time the prototypes had been delivered, the German army had concluded that the day of the multi-turret tank was over, and that in any case such vehicles did not fit well with the new generation of medium tanks in service with or under development for the German army's new Panzer (armoured) divisions. The vehicles were thus used for

trials, and with the designations PzKpfw V (NbFz A) and PzKpfw VI (NbFz B) for propaganda purposes in the Norwegian campaign of April 1940. They were then used for training, before being broken up in 1941.

Discussion of the NbFz has introduced elements of the Germans' complex system of military designation, and before proceeding to the main stream of German tank development in the 1930s under the driving leadership of the Nazi government that came to power in January 1933, it is useful to look at this system. Up to the beginning of the Spanish Civil War in 1936, the German designation system for tanks under design, development and construction included, in order of size from smallest to largest, the cover terms LaS (*Landwirtschaftlicher Schlepper*, or agricultural tractor), *Zugführerswagen*, (or platoon/troop commander's vehicle) and BW (*Bataillonsführerswagen*, or battalion commander's vehicle). Experimental vehicles were designated by the letter prefix VK (*Vollkettenkraftfahrzeug*, or fully-tracked motor vehicle) followed by a four-digit suffix in which the first two digits expressed the vehicle's nominal weight in tonnes, and the last two the prototype number in the sequence: thus the VK1601 was the first prototype in the 16-tonne fully-tracked class. This VK system was often completed by a bracketed letter indicating the manufacturer. Once the vehicle had been accepted for service, it was allocated a service designation based on the abbreviation PzKpfw (*Panzer Kampfwagen*, or armoured vehicle) followed by a roman number, and when it entered service it was also given the ordnance list designation based on the abbreviation SdKfz (*Sonder Kraftfahrzeug*, or particular vehicle) followed by an arabic number. Variants of the basic machine were indicated in the cover name system by an arabic numeral prefixed to the name by an oblique stroke, in the PzKpfw system by the abbreviation Ausf (*Aüsfuhrung*, or model) followed by a letter or alphanumeric combination, and less commonly in the SdKfz system (to indicate a major variation) by an arabic number separated from the main designation by an oblique stroke.

It is also worth noting at this point that German gun calibres are properly quoted in centimetres, but are here translated into millimetres to facilitate comparison with the tank guns of other countries. German tank guns were generally designed in the KwK series, the abbreviation standing for *Kampfwagen Kanone* (fighting vehicle gun) and being followed by a two-digit number to denote year of acceptance, or by an L/-type indication of bore length in calibres.

The German army began to plan its overt growth to world capacity in 1932 and an accelerating implementation and indeed augmentation of this plan followed the Nazis' rise to power. Plans had already been laid for the development of a tank force based on existing prototypes, but the recommendations of men such as Oberst Heinz Guderian for a massive force of comparatively light armour used in the *Blitzkrieg* concept of fast-moving operations found favour with the army's political masters, who saw both military and propaganda value in a multitude of smaller vehicles that could be obtained for the same financial and industrial outlay as a considerably smaller number of heavier vehicles. In 1933, therefore, the German army started to plan a family of tactically interrelated armoured fighting vehicles for development over the next few years. However, the need to train large numbers of tank crews and support personnel, and also to develop the appropriate tactical doctrines through practical training, coincided with

political demands that Germany must be seen to be developing a tank force: the result was a requirement for a nominal 5-tonne light tank with a crew of two and an armament of two turret-mounted 7.92-mm (0.312-in) MG13 machine-guns. Designs were commissioned from Daimler-Benz, Henschel, Krupp, MAN and Rheinmetall for a light tank weighing between 4,000 and 7,000 kg (8,818 and 15,432 lb), the Krupp LKA I design (with features of the Carden-Loyd Mk VI tankette in its running gear being accepted) and construction by Henschel of three LaS prototypes beginning in December 1933. The first mild steel prototype was running in February 1934, and after successful prototype trials an initial production contract for 150 vehicles was placed in July 1934, later contracts raising the total to about 1,800. Of this number about 300 were of the initial PzKpfw I Ausf A (Sdkfz 101) model with four road wheels, and the remainder of the more powerfully engined PzKpfw I Ausf B (SdKfz 101) variant with five road wheels. The Ausf A was powered by a 60-hp (44.75-kW) Krupp M 305 engine for a speed of 37 km/h (23 mph), while the 0.43-m (1.4-ft) longer Ausf B had the 100-hp (74.6-kW) Maybach NL 38 TR

By comparison with the Ausf A, the PzKpfw I Ausf B was slightly longer and had five rather than four wheels on each side. The armament remained unaltered at two turret-mounted 7.92-mm (0.312-in) machine-guns. (*Bundesarchiv*)

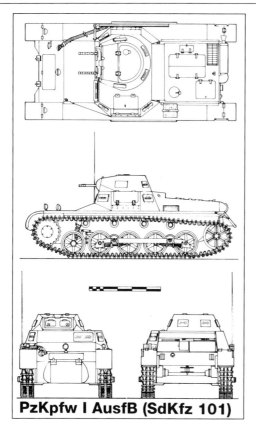

PzKpfw I AusfB (SdKfz 101)

PzKpfw I Ausf B (SdKfz 101)
(Germany)

Type: light tank
Crew: 2
Combat weight: 5,900 kg (13,007 lb)
Dimensions: length overall 4.44 m (14.58 ft); width 2.08 m (6.83 ft); height 1.73 m (5.67 ft)
Armament system: two 7.92-mm (0.312-in) machine-guns with 3,125 rounds
Powerplant: one 74.6-kW (100-hp) Maybach NL 38 TR petrol engine with 145 litres (31.9 Imp. gal.) of fuel
Performance: speed, road 40 km/h (24.9 mph); range, road 145 km (90 miles); gradient 58%; vertical obstacle 0.355 m (1.16 ft); trench 1.4 m (4.6 ft)

engine for a speed of 40 km/h (24.9 mph). The PzKpfw I was the main vehicle used by the German tank force up to the beginning of the Second World War, and was largely instrumental for the high quality of German tank tactics, maintenance and overall capability at the beginning of that war. The type was also used operationally in the Spanish Civil War (1936-39), achieving much, but also confirming the tactical limitations imposed by the two-man crew and armament of only two

The PzKpfw I light tank was designed mainly as a training vehicle for Germany's emergent armoured force, and also served to build tank production experience in German industry. This is an example of the first production variant, the PzKpfw I Ausf A with four rather than five road wheels as fitted on the Pzkpfw I Ausf B. (*RAC Tank Museum*)

machine-guns. The armour varied from 7 to 13 mm (0.28 to 0.51 in) in thickness, and this too was confirmed as too thin for genuine operational capability. Variants of the PzKpfw I included the SdKfz 265 three-man command vehicle with thicker frontal armour, a fixed turret and only one machine-gun; an explosive demolition vehicle; a flamethrower vehicle; and most interestingly of all, the VK601 prototype for the proposed PzKpfw I Ausf C reconnaissance and airborne variant, with armour increased to minimum and maximum thicknesses of 10 and 30 mm (0.39 and 1.18 in), a revised turret accommodating one 20-mm cannon and a 7.92-mm (0.312-in) coaxial machine-gun, a 150-hp (112-kW) engine, and a running gear arrangement based on five large-diameter interleaved road wheels for a speed of 65 km/h (40.4 mph). Nothing came of this project, and as the total obsolescence of the design led to the PzKpfw I's retirement from front-line roles from 1941, some chassis were then converted to other roles. In general, however, the small size and light weight of the chassis made it difficult to instal heavier armament, even on exposed limited-traverse mountings.

In 1934 it became clear that the German army's definitive PzKpfw III battle and PzKpfw IV medium tanks would take longer to develop than anticipated, and it was decided to produce another interim type to succeed the PzKpfw I and offer superior operational qualities through an increase in crew to three and of nominal weight to 10 tonnes. Designs and prototypes were tendered by Henschel, Krupp and MAN, that eventually selected for development as the LaS 100 being the MAN design with a 130-hp (96.9-kW) engine to provide a maximum speed of 40 km/h (24.9 mph) with armour to a maximum thickness of 14.5 mm (0.57 in) and a turret-mounted armament of one 20-mm KwK 30 cannon and one 7.92-mm (0.312-in) MG13 coaxial machine-gun. Basically similar prototype series were produced as the LaS 100 a1 and LaS 100 a2 (25 vehicles each, alternatively designated PzKpfw II Ausf a1 and PzKpfw II Ausf a2) with six road wheels on each side in paired bogies with an equalizing beam, before the arrival in 1936 of the pre-production LaS 100 a3 (PzKpfw II Ausf a3) and

improved PzKpfw II Ausf b with 30-mm (1.18-in) armour and a 140-hp (104-kW) Maybach HL 62 TR engine. Extensive trials were continued in this period, together with operational trials in the Spanish Civil War, and this resulted in the 1937 arrival of the PzKpfw II Ausf c with a full-width superstructure, a revised turret and completely remodelled suspension based on five larger-diameter road wheels with independent elliptical springing.

This led to the first service model, the 7,305-kg (16,104-lb) PzKpfw II Ausf A (SdKfz 121) with improved protective features but otherwise similar to the Ausf C. The PzKpfw II Ausf B introduced a slightly more powerful engine and revised tracks, while the PzKpfw II Ausf C was very similar but had thicker frontal armour for a weight of 9,500 kg (20,944 lb). Full-scale deliveries began in 1937, and such was the pace of production that 1,000 PzKpfw IIs were available for the Polish campaign that started the Second World War. The type was clearly as good as any light tank in the world in the late 1930s, but by the beginning of the 1940s the position was changing. Thus when the PzKpfw II was used in the Western campaigns of May and June 1940, it proved itself to retain an admirable reconnaissance capability, but was a liability when it was forced to fight: even the frontal armour was too thin to stop the British 2-pdr (40-mm) shot, and the KwK 30 cannon projectile could not penetrate the armour of British and French medium tanks.

Development of the basic machine was still continuing, however, and in 1939 Daimler-Benz produced the PzKpfw II Ausf D and PzKpfw II Ausf E variants with revised running gear: this was on the Christie pattern, with four large road wheels using torsion bar rather than vertical springing, and allowed an increase in maximum speed to 55 km/h (34.2 mph) under good conditions. But cross-country performance was inferior to that of the Ausf A to Ausf C variants, and in 1940 most surviving vehicles were taken in hand for conversion to other roles: 95 became flamethrower tanks with the designation Flammpanzer II (SdKfz 122), and the rest were used for self-propelled artillery chassis. The main stream of development therefore evolved from the Ausf C, resulting in

Panzerkampfwagen II Ausf C (SdKfz 121)
(Germany)

Type: light tank
Crew: 3
Combat weight: 9,650 kg (21,274 lb)
Dimensions: length overall 4.64 m (15.22 ft); width 2.24 m (7.35 ft); height overall 1.98 m (6.50 ft)
Armament system: one 20-mm KwK 30 or KwK 38 L/97 gun with 180 rounds and one 7.92-mm (0.312-in) MG34 coaxial machine-gun with between 1,425 and 2,250 rounds; the turret was manually operated, the main gun was stabilized in neither elevation (−9.5° to +20°) nor azimuth (360°), and simple optical sights were fitted
Armour: welded steel varying in thickness between 10 and 30 mm (0.39 and 1.18 in)
Powerplant: one 96.9-kW (130-hp) Maybach HL 62 TR petrol engine with 200 litres (44 Imp. gal.) of fuel
Performance: speed, road 40 km/h (24.9 mph); range, road 190 km (118 miles); fording 0.92 m (3.02 ft); gradient 50%; vertical obstacle 0.43 m (1.41 ft); trench 1.7 m (5.58 ft); ground clearance 0.345 m (13.6 in)

the 1940 introduction of the PzKpfw II Ausf F with solid conical-hubbed rear idlers in place of the previous open spoked type, and frontal armour increased to a maximum of 35 mm (1.38 in) by the addition of spaced appliqué plates to defeat the hollow-charge anti-tank warhead that was becoming increasingly lethal to battlefield tanks. Further evolution of the same basic theme resulted in the PzKpfw II Ausf G and PzKpfw II Ausf J variants with a stowage box on the turret bustle and other detail modifications. Production of the PzKpfw II series continued into 1941, but in that year the start of the war against the USSR displayed beyond doubt that the type was obsolete. A planned development with a 300-hp (224-kW) Maybach HL-P engine for a speed of 65 km/h (40.4 mph), 30 mm (1.18 in) of armour and the higher-velocity KwK 38 20-mm cannon was therefore cancelled, and from 1942 the PzKpfw II disappeared from front-line service in its original role. Surplus chassis were extensively reworked for other roles. The final development of the basic vehicle was the PzKpfw II Ausf L Luchs (lynx), developed as the SdKfz 123 fast reconnaissance machine. This was derived from the VK1303 experimental model, itself produced after experience with the

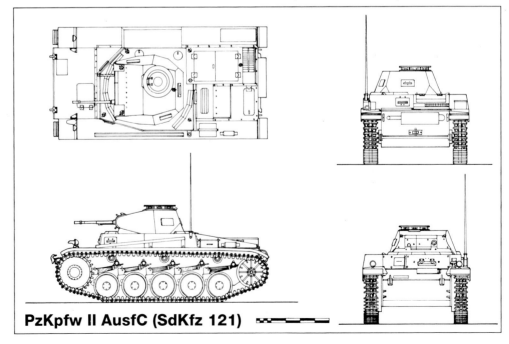

PzKpfw II AusfC (SdKfz 121)

heavily-protected VK1601, upgunned VK1602 and high-speed VK901 prototypes. The Ausf L used the Christie-type running gear and the Ausf D had spaced armour, a 180-hp (134-kW) engine for a speed of 60 km/h (37.3 mph) and a main armament of one KwK 38 20-mm cannon in the first 100 examples, and one KwK 39 50-mm gun in the last 31 examples.

With hindsight, it is easy to criticize the PzKpfw I and PzKpfw II as inadequate for their roles in the Second World War. However, this conveniently omits the fact that the two were developed as interim types, and were never intended for full-blown war operations, being forced into them only by the limitations of the German production system that failed to deliver adequate numbers of the PzKpfw III battle tank and PzKpfw IV medium tank in time for a war that was originally planned to begin in 1942 but it was brought back to 1939 by Hitler's ambitions. When one makes allowances for this factor, the PzKpfw I and PzKpfw II emerge in a truer light as the important machines they were in the development of the German armoured force.

By 1935 the German designers and industrialists had gained sufficient experience with the PzKpfw I and PzKpfw II light tanks to embark with a realistic hope of success upon the first of Germany's definitive battle tanks, the five-man PzKpfw III with a nominal weight of 15 tonnes. The German army's plan at this time was to field a force based on two main types, one a battle tank with a high-velocity anti-tank gun backed by machine-guns, and the other a medium tank with a medium-velocity gun backed by machine-guns and intended mainly for the support role: the battle tank became the PzKpfw III with a 37- and later a 50-mm gun, while the medium tank became the PzKpfw IV with a 75-mm (2.95-in) gun. The standard tank battalion had four companies, and it was planned that three of these would field the PzKpfw III battle tank.

Development of the battle tank was undertaken with the cover designation ZW, and prototype orders were placed with Daimler-Benz, Krupp, MAN and Rheinmetall during 1936. The Inspectorate for Mechanized Troops wished the ZW to be fitted with a 50-mm gun, but the Ordnance Department pointed out that the infantry's standard anti-tank gun was a 37-mm weapon: the compromise eventually thrashed out was that the type would carry the 37-mm KwK L/45 gun, but have a turret ring of adequate diameter to allow later substitution of

The PzKpfw II Ausf B and C were distinguishable from the Ausf A by the provision of a commander's cupola. This is a machine of the 21st Panzer Division in North Africa. (*RAC Tank Museum*)

the 50 mm KwK 39 gun if tactical conditions altered. This was an extremely far-sighted move, and allowed the PzKpfw III to be retained as an effective weapon for about two years longer than would otherwise have been the case. It is odious to make comparisons, but it is inevitable that one should think of the A12 Matilda II, a potentially formidable British tank that could have played a decisive role if the turret ring had not been sized exactly to the 2-pdr (40-mm) tank gun of the late 1930s and thereby precluded from development with a larger-calibre gun of the type that operations soon revealed to be essential.

It proved impossible to design a battle tank down to the desired limit of 15 tonnes, so the upper limit was raised to the 24-tonne rating of Germany's road bridges, and the selection battle settled down to a choice between the Krupp and Daimler-Benz offerings, before the latter was selected for production as the PzKpfw III Ausf A (SdKfz 141) after features of the Krupp MKA prototype had been incorporated into the design. In overall layout, the PzKpfw III followed the pattern finalized in the PzKpfw I, with the driving compartment at the front, the fighting compartment in the centre and the engine compartment at the rear. Crew dispositions were the driver and radio operator/bow gunner in the forward compartment, and the commander, gunner and loader in the fighting compartment/turret. The crew were favoured with considerable working space, by comparison with contemporary tanks of the same basic type, and the driver had the useful advantage of a preselector gearbox: this required more maintenance than the crash gearbox used in most other tanks, but offered greater flexibility of operation in conjunction with the 230-hp (171.5-kW) Maybach HL 108 TR petrol engine. The drive sprockets were located at the front, the track on each side passing under the six coil-sprung road wheels before returning via the rear idler and two track-return rollers: this arrangement provided a good cross-country ride and a maximum speed of 32 km/h (19.9 mph). The sensible layout of the vehicle was echoed in the construction of high-grade chrome/molybdenum steel armour: the hull was a bolted-together assembly of three welded sub-assemblies (the lower hull, the forward upper hull and the rear upper hull), and the turret was another welded assembly. The minimum and maximum armour thicknesses in the prototype were 10 and 14.5 (0.39 and 0.57 in), resulting in a weight of 15,400 kg (33,951 lb). The armament rather let down the potential of the tank, being the 37-mm KwK L/45 gun and three 7.92-mm (0.312-in) MG34 machine-guns (two coaxial with the main armament and the third in the bow): the main gun had the useful ammunition stowage of 150 rounds, but its indifference as an anti-tank weapon is indicated by its ability to penetrate only 36 mm (1.42 in) of armour angled at 30° at a range of 500 m (545 yards) with its 0.75-kg (1.65-lb) shot fired at a muzzle velocity of 760 m (2,493 ft) per second.

The Ausf A was in reality a pre-production type, and only 10 were built before production switched to the PzKpfw III Ausf B in 1937. This was identical to the Ausf A in all respects but its running gear, which now consisted on each side of eight small road wheels: these were arranged in two-wheel bogies, which were supported in pairs by large horizontal leafsprings; there were also three track-return rollers. Production of this variant amounted to 15 tanks, which were supplanted by the PzKpfw III Ausf C in which the suspension was revised once more, in this instance so that each two-wheel bogie was supported by an individual leafspring. The next pre-production variant was the PzKpfw III Ausf D, evolved from the Ausf C but with the armour increased to a 30-mm (1.18-in) basis: again, 15 of these 19,800-kg (43,651-lb) vehicles were built. The final pre-production model (or perhaps initial production model, since 440 were built) was the PzKpfw III Ausf E, which appeared in 1938. This had a more powerful engine, in the form of the 320-hp (239-kW) Maybach HL 120 TR, a revised transmission and, most significant of all, new running gear. On each side this consisted of six road wheels independently sprung by transverse torsion bars.

At about this time the Ordnance Department finally appreciated its short-sightedness in pressing for a 37-mm main armament, and instructed Krupp to proceed with the design of a new turret to accommodate the 50-mm KwK 39 gun. The development had not been com-

The main 1942 production variant of the PzKpfw III was the Ausf L with spaced frontal armour and the L/60 version of the 50-mm main gun, the KwK 39. The vehicles were often retrofitted with skirt armour. (*RAC Tank Museum*)

pleted, however, when the next variant of the tank III was being readied for production in early 1940 as the PzKpfw III Ausf F. This 20,300-kg (44,753-lb) variant had therefore to retain the 37-mm gun, so its main improvements over the Ausf E were better ventilation, five smoke emitters on the rear decking, a stowage box on the turret and the HL 120 TRM engine rated at 300 hp (224 kW). The main armament was still not ready when the PzKpfw III Ausf G was introduced later in 1940, so again this variant retained the 37-mm main gun. It had the same weight and improvements as the Ausf F, but also featured a revised commander's cupola with improved protection for the vision ports.

All three of these variants were retrofitted with the new KwK L/42 gun as this became available, to the annoyance of Hitler, who appreciated the pace of armoured warfare development and thus demanded the longer and more powerful KwK 39 L/60 gun of the same calibre: firing the same round with a 2.05-kg (4.52-lb) shot, the L/42 weapon generated a muzzle velocity of 685 m (2,247 ft) per second, sufficient to penetrate 49 mm (1.93 in) of armour at an angle of 30° at a range of 500 m (545 yards), whereas the L/60 weapon

generated a muzzle velocity of 825 m (2,707 ft) per second to penetrate 60 mm (2.35 in) of armour at the same inclination and range. Stowage of 50-mm ammunition amounted to 99 rounds. Development of the PzKpfw III continued after 1940, and details of this ultimate extension of the PzKpfw III's capabilities are discussed in the next chapter.

The last of Germany's main tanks with a pre-war pedigree was the PzKpfw IV, which also possesses the distinction of being the only German tank to have remained in production right through the Second World War for an overall total of more than 8,500 examples. The type was planned at the same time as the PzKpfw III, and was essentially similar, other than in its main armament, which was the 75-mm (2.95-in) KwK L/24 designed to provide the lighter PzKpfw III with HE fire support. The ordnance weighed 285 kg (628.3 lb) compared with the 37-mm KwK L/45's 195 kg (429.9 lb) and the 50-mm KwK L/42's 225 kg (496 lb); it fired its 6.75-kg (14.9-lb) APCBC projectile with a muzzle velocity of 385 m (1,263 ft) per second, sufficient to penetrate 41 mm (1.61 in) of armour at an angle of 30° at a range of 500 m (545 yards). In addition to this armour-piercing round, the KwK L/24 ordnance could fire HEAT, HE, Smoke and Case rounds. The standard tank battalion had four companies, and it was planned that while three of these would field the PzKpfw III battle tank, the fourth would operate the PzKpfw IV medium tank in the support role.

The design was fixed at a weight not exceeding 24 tonnes, and in 1934 prototype vehicles were ordered under the cover designation BW from Krupp as the VK2001(K), MAN as the VK2002(MAN), and Rheinmetall as the VK2001(Rh). The Krupp submission had large-diameter interleaved road wheels, and this was considered the best basis for a production tank, though only after incorporation of features from the Rheinmetall prototype, including the simpler running gear consisting on each side of eight small road wheels in two-wheel bogies with leafsprings; the drive sprocket was at the front and the idler at the rear, and there were four track-return rollers. In 1936 production contracts were let to Krupp for a vehicle to be designated PzKpfw IV (SdKfz 161), and in overall configuration similar to the PzKpfw III. The crew was disposed

in much the same way as the PzKpfw III, but whereas the battle tank had a manually-operated turret, that of the medium tank was traversed electrically. Before the PzKpfw IV entered large-scale production, a number of features were trialled in small pre-production batches, of which the first was the PzKpfw IV Ausf A, built to the extent of 35 examples. This weighed 17,300 kg (38,139 lb), was armoured from a minimum of 8 mm (0.315 in) to a maximum of 20 mm (0.79 in), and was armed with the 75-mm (2.95-in) main gun plus a secondary battery of two 7.92-mm (0.312-in) MG34 machine-guns (one in the bow and the other coaxial). The Ausf A was powered by a 250-hp (186-kW) Maybach HL 108 TR petrol engine for a maximum speed of 30 km/h (18.6 mph), and its features included the distinctive air inlets on the rear decking and the commander's cupola projecting vertically through the rear of the angular but moderately well shaped turret.

Next came the PzKpfw IV Ausf B of 1938 with a modified cupola, a straight-fronted rather than recessed superstructure, no bow machine-gun, a 320-hp (239-kW) engine and a number of detail modifications; production

Produced in 1940, and seen here during the Battle of France in that year, the PzKpfw IV Ausf D introduced a more powerful engine, a stepped front to the superstructure, and an external mantlet for the short-barrel 75-mm (2.95-in) gun intended to provide the tank with a support rather than anti-tank role. (*MARS*)

Panzerkampfwagen IV Ausf D (4/BW) (SdKfz 161)
(Germany)

Type: battlefield support tank
Crew: 5
Combat weight: 20,000 kg (44,092 lb)
Dimensions: length overall 5.91 m (19.39 ft); width 2.92 m (9.58 ft) over steps; height overall 2.59 m (8.50 ft)
Armament system: one 75-mm (2.95-in) KwK L/24 rifled gun with 80 rounds and two 7.92-mm (0.312-in) MG34 machine-guns (one coaxial and one bow) with 2,800 rounds; the turret was electrically operated, the main gun was stabilized in neither elevation nor azimuth (360°), and simple optical sights were fitted
Armour: welded steel varying in thickness between 10 and 30 mm (0.39 and 1.18 in)
Powerplant: one 224-kW (300-hp) Maybach HL 120 PRM petrol engine with 470 litres (103.4 Imp. gal.) of fuel
Performance: speed, road 42 km/h (26.1 mph); range, road 200 km (124 miles); fording 0.8 m (2.62 ft); gradient 57%; vertical obstacle 0.6 m (1.97 ft); trench 2.3 m (7.55 ft); ground clearance 0.4 m (15.75 in)

amounted to 42 machines. The Ausf B formed the basis for the PzKpfw IV Ausf C, which followed in 1939 with a 300-hp (224-kW) engine, an armoured sleeve for the turret machine-gun, and armour increased in maximum thickness to 30 mm (1.18 in), so increasing weight from the 17,700 kg (39,021 lb) of the Ausf B to 20,000 kg (44,092 lb).

Full-scale production began late in 1939 with the PzKpfw IV Ausf D, which was based on the Ausf C but restored the bow machine-gun and introduced a stepped front to the superstructure. Other changes were an increase in the armour thickness of the glacis plate, hull sides and hull rear from 14.5 to 20 mm (0.57 to 0.79 in), an external rather than internal gun mantlet of 30-mm (1.18-in) thickness, eyelid shutters over the five vision ports in the commander's cupola, a new pattern of track and slightly larger overall dimensions. The uparmouring of the Ausf D indicated that the German army was now becoming seriously worried about the comparatively thin armour of its primary tanks, and this process was continued with the PzKpfw IV Ausf E that was identical to the Ausf D in all but

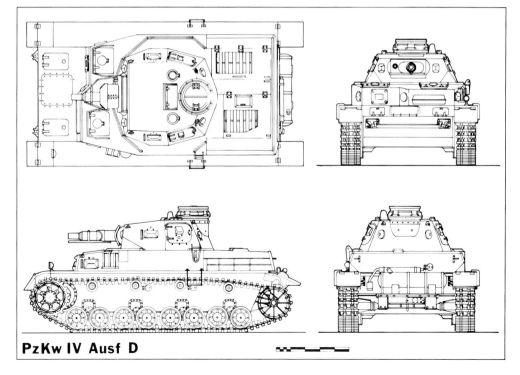

PzKw IV Ausf D

117

its improved protection and its new turret. The protective features included the thickening of the nose plate from 30 to 50 mm (1.18 to 1.97 in), but though it had been planned to increase the front plate to the same thickness, the design of the bow machine-gun installation precluded this until a new mounting had been designed. Increased protection was afforded to the fighting compartment by the addition of 20-mm (0.79-in) face-hardened armour plate on the sides, and in service the tank was often provided with additional protection by the addition of spaced armour of various types: this generally comprised 30-mm (1.18-in) panels attached over a 75-mm (2.95-in) gap to reduce the effect of the hollow-charge warheads.

The Ausf E introduced the type of turret that remained standard on production vehicles for the rest of the Second World War. Some criticism had been levelled at the inadequate protection offered by the 20-mm (0.79-in) thickness of the commander's cupola, and in the revised turret this was increased to a minimum of 30-mm (1.18-in) and a maximum of 67-mm (2.64-in). The cupola was also moved forward, allowing the installation of a smoothly curved back plate without the distinctive cut-out previously necessary to accommodate the rear of the cupola. Finally the turret was fitted with an electrical ventilation fan to provide better fighting conditions than had prevailed with the original ventilator flap. The PzKpfw IV went through later marks and developments, but these fall completely within the context of the Second World War and are therefore treated in the next chapter.

Germany's design and industrial capabilities were severely tested by the virtually simultaneous development and production of four major service tanks, and despite a prodigious effort, could not satisfy the army's requirement in terms of volume and speed of production. To this extent, therefore, the army was extremely fortunate that Hitler's territorial ambitions encompassed the overrunning of Czechoslovakia's rump in March 1939, after the ignominious British and French abandonment of the Czech Sudetenland to German demands in the Munich agreement of September 1938: the German army was able to absorb much of the Czech army's capable tank fleet, and the Czech production capabilities were completely at the disposal of the German war machine.

Czechoslovakia was split off from Austria-Hungary as an independent country in October 1918, and immediately set about building up its armed forces. Here the new country had the considerable advantage of containing, in addition to large iron-producing capacity, one of the world's largest armament concerns in the form of Skoda, located at Pilsen. This was joined in 1927 by the CKD (Ceskomoravska Kolben Danek) formed by the amalgamation of four large companies, including the car manufacturer Praga, and a further addition to the potential for armoured fighting vehicles was Tatra, another major manufacturer of cars and trucks. What was lacking to the Czechs in the short term was indigenous experience of tank operation and design. In common with many other countries, the Czechs surmounted this initial obstacle by the import of Renault FT light tanks. These provided the Czech tank force with the basis of an operational doctrine, and gave fledgling designers the chance to examine and learn from the French practice in light armoured vehicles. This led to the design of armoured cars in the early 1920s and, with the aid of J. Vollmer after his departure from Sweden, the Skoda/Tatra KH.50 wheel/track light tank, prototypes of which were built in 1925. The abbreviation KH stands for *Kolohousenka* (wheel track), and these two-man vehicles weighed 6,800 kg (14,991 lb) on a 13-mm (0.51-in) armour basis, and with a 50-hp (37.3-kW) petrol engine could attain 12 km/h (7.5 mph) on their tracks or 35 km/h (21.75 mph) on their wheels. The armament was located in a small 360° traverse turret, and comprised one 37-mm gun or one machine-gun. After service evaluation the type was rejected by the Czech army, and the designers moved forward to the KH.60 of 1928-29 with slightly thicker armour and a 60-hp (44.7-kW) engine, and the ultimate KH.70 of 1930 with an improved wheel/track change system and a 70-hp (51.2-kW) engine. The wheel/track concept clearly appealed to Czech designers, for despite problems with the concept, it was 1934 before the notion was finally abandoned.

Another vehicle that spurred considerable overseas interest was the Carden-Loyd tankette, several examples of which were obtained by Czechoslovakia for evaluation and analysis. Impressed with the capabilities and simple construction of the type, the Czechs saw this as an ideal starting point for fully-tracked vehicles, and two design streams resulted: the P-I from CKD/Praga and the S-I (T-1/MU-4) from Skoda. The P-I was an unexceptional vehicle that was criticized for its poor cross-country ride, but ordered to the extent of 70 T-33 vehicles, the prefix standing for *Tancik* (tankette). The two-man T-33 weighed 2,500 kg (5,511 lb), had 12 mm (0.47 in) of armour, and was armed with two 7.92-mm (0.312-in) machine-guns in limited-traverse mountings at the front of the crew compartment; the type was powered by a 31-hp (23.1-kW) Praga petrol engine, and could reach 35 km/h (21.75 mph). Whereas the T-33 was an all-riveted machine, the competing S-I was all-welded to a maximum thickness of 5.5 mm (0.22 in). The S-I (T-1/MU-4) was a two-man tankette weighing 2,300 kg (5,071 lb), and with its 40-hp (29.8-kW) Skoda petrol engine could reach 45 km/h (28 mph). The armament was identical to that of the T-33, but in spite of its overall superiority in performance, the vehicle was turned down by the Czech army for its lack of adequate protection, abetted by the fact that the P-I (T-33) had already been ordered. The T-33 gained a small contract but was a design and evolutionary dead-end. The Skoda design was more fortunate, for despite the failure of the S-I (T1/MU-4) the type had some growth potential and was evolved into the two-man S-Id heavy tankette with a 60-hp (44.7-kW) Skoda engine for a speed of 45 km/h (28 mph), despite a weight of 4,500 kg (9,921 lb), protection to a maximum of 15 mm (0.59 in), and an armament of one 47-mm gun and one 7.92-mm (0.312-in) machine-gun. This model entered production in 1938 for Yugoslavia, and was later used by Romania.

The production success of the P-I in 1933 persuaded CKD/Praga to develop a genuine light tank as the P-II, which was the first tank of Czech origin to be ordered in production quantities (50 tanks) as the TNHB. To the company the vehicle was also known as the LTL-H or,

CKD/Praga LT-34

CKD/Praga P-II (LT-34)
(Czechoslovakia)

Type: light tank
Crew: 4
Combat weight: 7,625 kg (16,810 lb)
Dimensions: length overall 4.02 m (13.25 ft); width 2.03 m (6.67 ft); height 1.83 m (6.00 ft)
Armament system: one 37-mm gun and two 7.92-mm (0.312-in) machine-guns
Armour: 15 mm (0.59 in) maximum
Powerplant: one 46.2-kW (62-hp) Praga petrol engine
Performance: speed, road 40 km/h (21.1 mph);

for export, as the LT-34, the prefix standing for *Lekhy Tank* (light tank) and the suffix for the year of introduction (1934). This was a four-man machine weighing a modest 7,500 kg (16,534 lb) as it was armoured to a maximum of only 15 mm (0.59 in), and was 4.04 m (13.25 ft) long. In layout the tank was conventional, with the driving compartment at the front, the fighting compartment in the centre and the engine compartment at the rear. The suspension was based on comparatively small road wheels (later revised to four large road wheels on cranked stub axles and controlled in pairs by free-pivoting semi-elliptic springs), the drive sprockets were at the front with the idlers at the rear, and there were four unequally spaced track-return rollers (later revised to three). The armament comprised one 37-mm gun and two 7.92-mm (0.312-in) machine-guns, the latter located as one coaxial and one bow weapon. Careful design made the TNHB reliable and easy to maintain, but considerable criticism was made of the fact that it was noisy and tiring to drive. Located under a high rear decking, the Praga petrol engine developed 62 hp (46.2 kW), sufficient to give this vehicle a

Strv m/42

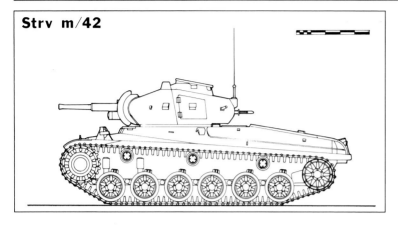

Strv m/42
(Sweden)

Type: medium tank
Crew: 4
Combat weight: 22,860 kg (50,397 lb)
Dimensions: length overall 6.10 m (20.01 ft); width 2.45 m (8.04 ft); height 2.60 m (8.53 ft)
Armament system: one 75-mm (2.95-in) gun and three 8-mm (0.315-in) machine-guns
Armour: between 40 and 80 mm (1.575 and 3.15 in)
Powerplant: one 306-kW (410-hp) Scania-Vabis petrol engine
Performance: speed, road 45 km/h (28 mph); gradient 60%; vertical obstacle 0.6 m (1.97 ft)

The m/37 light tank was the CKD/Praga AH-IV-Sv produced in Sweden from Czech-supplied components. (*Försvarets Materielverk, Sweden*)

speed of 34 km/h (21.1 mph).

The LT-34 enjoyed considerable success in the export market, the basic vehicle being sized up or down to suit particular customer requirements. These export variants were the R-I (35 for Romania), the AH-IV-Sv (50 for Sweden, with the local designation Strv m/37), the TNH (for Persia), the TNH-Sv (for Sweden, with the local designation Strv m/42), the LTH (24 for Switzerland, with the local designation Pz 39), the LTP (24 for Peru) and the LTL (21 for Latvia). The R-I was a scaled-down two-man machine weighing 4,000 kg (8,818 lb), armoured to a maximum of 12 mm (0.47 in), armed with two machine-guns, powered by a 60-hp (44.7-kW) Praga engine for 45 km/h (28 mph), and 3.2 m (10.5 ft) long. The AH-IV-Sv was another scaled-down version, in this instance built under licence in Sweden, operated by a two-man crew, weighing 4,500 kg (9,921 lb), armoured to a maximum of 15 mm (0.57 in), armed with two 8-mm (0.315-in) machine-guns, powered by an 80-hp (59,6-kW) Volvo engine for 48 km/h (29.8 mph), and 3.4 m (11.15 ft) long. The TNH was a slightly scaled-up three/four-man version with modifications for desert operations, weighing 8,500 kg (18,739 lb), armoured to a maximum of 25 mm (0.98 in), armed with one 37-mm gun and two machine-guns, powered by a 100-hp (74.6-kW) Praga engine for 42 km/h (26.1 mph), and 4.5 m (14.76 ft) long. The TNH-Sv was another slightly scaled-up three/four-man version which was produced under German licence in Sweden by Scania Vabis after Czechoslovakia had been occupied and the vehicles on the CKD/Praga production line impressed by the Germans: the Swedish model weighed 10,500 kg (23,148 lb), was armoured to a maximum of 25 mm (0.98 in), was armed with one Bofors 37-mm gun and two 8-mm (0.315-in) machine-guns, and was powered by a 160-hp (119-kW) Scania Vabis engine for 45 km/h (27.9 mph). The LTH was a similar three-man version weighing 7,500 kg (16,534 lb), armoured to a maximum of 32 mm (1.26 in), armed with one Oerlikon 24-mm cannon and two machine-guns, powered by a 125-hp (93.2-kW) Saurer Arbon diesel engine for 45 km/h (28 mph), and 4.3 m (14.1 ft) long. The LTP was a slightly modified version of the

TNH with a three-man crew, weighing 7,500 kg (16,534 lb) armed with one Skoda 37-mm gun and two machine-guns, and powered by a 125-hp (93.2-kW) Praga engine for 45 km/h (28 mph). And the LTL was another TNH version with a three-man crew, weighing 7,200 kg (15,873 lb), armoured to a maximum of 25 mm (0.98 in), armed with one Skoda 37-mm gun or Oerlikon 20-mm cannon and two machine-guns, and powered by a 125-hp (93.2-kW) Praga engine for 54 km/h (33.6 mph).

The real importance of the TNHB and its scaled-up/scaled-down offshoots lies in the fact that they paved the way for the CKD/ Praga TNHP, otherwise known as the LT-38 or, to the Germans, as the PzKpfw 38(t). The spur for this vehicle was the Czech army's reaction to a rapidly worsening European situation, by the creation in October 1937 of a committee to evaluate current Czech tank production capability and to recommend a new type of high-performance light tank to complement and then to supplant the Skoda LT-35, a 1935 type of exceptional performance but notable mechanical complexity.

To meet this requirement several companies submitted designs and prototypes, the two most important competitors being CKD/Praga and Skoda. CKD/Praga offered

three prototypes based on the TNH (a re-worked version of the TNHB, a basically similar LTL-P modelled on the export variant and a TNH derivative with upgraded protection, more capable armament and a host of in-

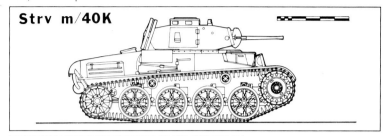

Strv m/40K

Strv m/40K
(Sweden)

Type: light tank
Crew: 3
Combat weight: 10,900 kg (24,030 lb)
Dimensions: length overall 4.90 m (16.08 ft); width 2.11 m (6.92 ft); height 2.08 m (6.82 ft)
Armament system: one 37-mm gun and two 8-mm (0.315-in) machine-guns
Armour: 24 mm (0.94 in) maximum
Powerplant: one 119.3-kW (160-hp) Scania-Vabis petrol engine
Performance: speed, road 49 km/h (29.8 mph); gradient 60%, vertical obstacle 0.6 m (1.97 ft); trench 1.675 m (5.5 ft)

For its time the Czech LT-35 (Skoda S-IIa) light tank was singularly advanced, pneumatically-assisted steering and gear changing doing much to ease the task of the driver and so make possible more effective combat operations. (*RAC Tank Museum*)

Right The LTL-H (TNHP) prototype paved the way for the highly successful LT-38 series of Czech light tanks and their export derivatives. The LT-38 is now better known by the PzKpfw 38(t) designation afforded to it by the Germans. (*RAC Tank Museum*)

Below After the overrunning of Czechoslovakia by Germany in 1939, the vehicles of the Czech tank arms were absorbed into Germany's growing Panzer force. These are LT-38s in service as PzKpfw 38(t) light tank with Generalmajor Erwin Rommel's 7th Panzer Division during the Battle of France.(*IWM*)

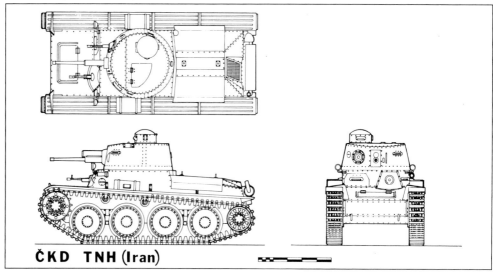

ČKD TNH (Iran)

ternal modifications to improve both reliability and crew habitability). This last factor was of singular importance in promoting the type's fighting capabilities by keeping the crew in better morale and physical shape. The prototypes were thoroughly evaluated in some 5,000 km (3,105 miles) of running trials, including 1,500 km (930 miles) across country, and emerged with virtually no problems. All who had partaken in the trials were impressed with the CKD/Praga prototypes' good reliability, low maintenance needs and high performance. Some minor modifications were incorporated into the TNHS (the LTL-P prototype) before it received a production order for 150 examples as the TNHP, soon increased by orders for the LT-38 export version.

The TNHP is the classic light tank of the period immediately before the Second World War, with a beautifully balanced blend of firepower, protection and mobility to optimize its capabilities in the twin roles of recon-

CKD/Praga TNHP-S or LT-38
(Czechoslovakia)

Type: light tank
Crew: 4
Combat weight: 9,700 kg (21,384 lb)
Dimensions: length overall 4.54 m (14.91 ft); width 2.02 m (6.62 ft) for early vehicles and 2.05 m (6.74 ft) for late vehicles; height overall 2.365 m (7.76 ft)
Armament system: one 37.2-mm Skoda A7 L/47.8 rifled gun with 90 rounds and two 7.92-mm (0.312-in) vz37 machine-guns (one coaxial and one bow) with 2,550 rounds; the turret was manually operated, the main gun was stabilized in neither elevation ($-6°$ to $+12°$) nor azimuth (360°), and simple optical sights were fitted
Armour: riveted and bolted steel varying in thickness between 8 and 30 mm (0.315 and 1.18 in)
Powerplant: one 93.2-kW (125-hp) EPA Model I, II or III (early variants) or 111.8-kW (150-hp) EPA/AC Model IV (last variant) petrol engine with 225 litres (49.5 Imp. gal.) of fuel
Performance: speed, road 56 km/h (34.8 mph) in early vehicles and 42 km/h (26.1 mph) in late vehicles; fording 0.9 m (2.95 ft); gradient 58% in early vehicles and 48% in late vehicles; vertical obstacle 0.8 m (2.6 ft); trench 1.85 m (6.1 ft); ground clearance 0.28 m (11 in)
(Illustration: TNH (Iran))

naissance and support for the more powerfully-armed medium tank; the weakest points of the design were riveted construction (with the exception of the bolted-on upper surfaces to the superstructure) and the modest 37-mm Skoda A7 gun. In layout the tank was conventional, with the driver in the forward compartment, the commander, gunner and loader/radio operator in the fighting compart-

THe CKD/Praga company designation LTL was given to the light tank known to the Czech military as the TNH. This particular variant is the LTL-P (TNHS). (*RAC Tank Museum*)

An LTL-P is put through its impressive paces on the obstacle course. (*RAC Tank Museum*)

Kept in service until the 1950s, the Pz 39 was in fact a pre-Second World War design, the CKD/Praga LTH built under licence in Switzerland. The basic similarity to the TNH/LT-38 series is evident, but the type carried a 24-mm Oerlikon cannon as main armament. (*Eidgenössische Konstrucktionswerkstatte, Berne*)

ment, and the powerplant in the rear compartment under a comparatively high rear decking. The minimum and maximum armour thicknesses were 8 mm (0.315 in) on the belly and 25 mm (0.98 in) on the front via 15 mm (0.59 in) at the rear and 19 mm (0.75 in) at the sides, and the tank weighed 8,000 kg (17,637 lb) in this form. The turret was surmounted by a fixed cupola, and its weapons comprised one 37-mm gun with 90 rounds of armour-piercing and HE ammunition, and one 7.92-mm (0.312-in) vz37 coaxial machine-gun; another vz37 machine-gun was located in the bow for operation by the driver, and 2,550 rounds of ammunition were carried for these two guns. The turret could be traversed through 360° mechanically, and allowed the main gun an elevation arc between -6° and +12°; the elevation gear was designed to provide an accurate fire capability when locked and with the vehicle halted. The running gear was modelled closely on that of the definitive TNHB, the arrangement on each side comprising four large-diameter rubber-tyred road wheels (controlled in pairs by pivoting semi-elliptical leafsprings), the drive sprocket was at the front, the idler at the rear, and two track-return rollers located towards the front of the track run. The engine was a 125-hp (93.2-kW) Praga EPA unit.

When Czechoslovakia was occupied by Germany in 1939, the TNHP was just entering service with the Czech army and was taken in-to German service as the PzKpfw 38(t). Manufacture was continued against German plans for 40 such vehicles per month, ending only in 1942 after the production of 1,168 vehicles for the Germans, within an overall chassis production figure of 1,590. The Germans were concerned with the TNHP's comparatively light protection, and ordered an increase to 50 mm (1.97 in) on the front by the addition of a 25-mm (0.98-in) plate over the existing 25-mm (0.98-in) armour, and to 30 mm (1.18 in) on the sides, thereby increasing combat weight to 9,700 kg (21,384 lb) in the variant known as the TNHP-S, the suffix standing for *Schwer* (heavy). In many vehicles the German 37-mm KwK L/45 gun was used in place of the L/47.8 Skoda weapon, and considerable revisions were made to the internal equipment to modify the vehicle to German standards. In the last 500 chassis an uprated powerplan was installed in the form of the 150-hp (112-kW) EPA/AC engine.

The PzKpfw 38(t) was a welcome addition to the German army's light tank inventory, and was used most extensively by the 7th and 8th Panzer Divisions right into 1942. By that time the basic vehicle was obsolescent as a tank, but the capabilities of the chassis rightly convinced the Germans that the core vehicle could form the automotive core for a whole series of self-propelled mountings that played a prominent part in German operations for the rest of the war.

Skoda Model T-11 or LT-35 (LTM-35) S-IIa
(Czechoslovakia)

Type: light tank
Crew: 4
Combat weight: 10,500 kg (23,148 lb)
Dimensions: length overall 4.54 m (14.88 ft); width 2.14 m (7.03 ft); height overall 2.20 m (7.21 ft)
Armament system: one 37.2-mm Skoda A3 L/40 rifled gun with 90 rounds and two 7.92-mm (0.312-in) vz37 machine-guns (one coaxial and one bow) with 2,550 rounds; the turret was manually operated, the main gun was stabilized in neither elevation (− 10° to + 25°) nor azimuth (360°), and simple optical sights were fitted
Armour: riveted and bolted steel varying in thickness between 12 and 35 mm (0.47 and 1.38 in)
Powerplant: one 89.5-kW (120-hp) Skoda T-11 petrol engine with 155 litres (34.1 Imp. gal.) of fuel
Performance: speed, road 40 km/h (24.9 mph); range, road 200 km (124 miles); fording 0.8 m (2.6 ft); gradient 54%; vertical obstacle 0.8 m (2.6 ft); trench 2.0 m (6.56 ft); ground clearance 0.35 m (13.8 in)

The LT-35 (sometimes LTM-35) was designed by Skoda in the light of its experience with the S-I tankette, and the S-IIa/T-11 basic design for a light tank was evolved to satisfy operational requirements, such as rear drive to leave the fighting compartment uncluttered by transmission elements, a short engine to leave as much floor area as possible for the fighting compartment, a pneumatically-operated gearbox for transmission flexibility and ease of driving, pneumatically-powered steering to permit the coverage of long distances without excessive driver fatigue, new running gear to ensure equal pressure on all road wheels, and duplication of all major accessories to increase system reliability in sustained operations. For its time the design was highly advanced, but suffered the consequences of its mechanical complexity in low serviceability. Nonetheless, the performance of the type in prototype trials was so impressive that at the end of 1935 the tank was ordered into production for the Czech army. The hull and turret were of riveted and bolted construction, protection being afforded by ar-

mour varying in thickness from a minimum of 12 mm (0.47 in) on the belly to a maximum of 35 mm (1.38 in) on the hull nose and gun mantlet. The driver and bow gunner were located in the forward compartment, the latter to operate the 7.92-mm (0.312-in) bow machine-gun, and the commander/gunner and loader/radio operator were placed in the first 360° traverse turret to be installed on a Skoda tank. The turret was fitted with a fixed cupola, and was armed with a 37-mm Skoda A3 L/40 semi-automatic gun plus 90 rounds, and with a 7.92-mm (0.312-in) coaxial machine-gun; some 2,550 rounds of ammunition were carried for the two machine-guns. The main gun had an elevation arc between -10° and + 25°, and the turret was traversed mechanically. An obvious limitation with the turret was its re-

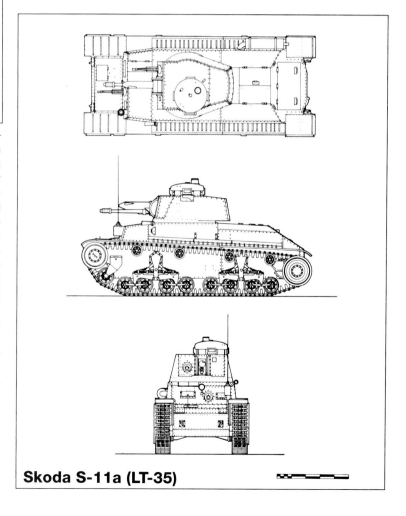

Skoda S-11a (LT-35)

striction to two men, requiring the commander to double as the gunner, seriously affecting the tank's tactical flexibility. The 120-hp (89.5-kW) Skoda engine was located in the rear compartment. The drive sprockets were at the rear and the idlers at the front, and on each side the running gear comprised eight small road wheels coupled into two-wheel bogies attached to the hull in four-wheel pairs on rocker arms with semi-elliptical leafsprings; a small guide wheel was located between the idler and the forward road wheel, and there were four track-return rollers.

The advanced design of the steering, transmission and suspension made the LT-35 an excellent driver's tank, and reliability permitted daily runs of 200 km (125 miles) at an average speed of between 20 and 25 km/h (12.4 and 15.5 mph) to be common. This cruising speed is the more remarkable given that the maximum speed was limited to only 40 km/h (24.9 mph) by the comparatively low power of the engine. After German occupation of Czechoslovakia the LT-35 was taken into German service as the PzKpfw 35(t) and used to equip the 6th Panzer Division right into 1942. The type continued to suffer reliability problems, and the Germans redesigned the tank's transmission and steering systems. From 1942, however, the type was phased out of front-line service for a less exacting but still important role as a mortar and artillery tractor.

From the same basic design Skoda evolved the S-IIb medium tank, but this suffered still worse problems of reliability, and was rejected for service. Further work resulted in the S-IIr/T-21 medium tank prototype, which was sufficiently improved for the Hungarian army to order the type for licence production in modified form as the 40 M Turan I. This weighed 16,000 kg (35,273 lb), had a five-man crew (including three in the turret), was armed with one 40-mm Skoda gun and two 8-mm (0.315-in) machine-guns, and was powered by a 260-hp (194-kW) engine. The same basic chassis/hull combination was later fitted with a modified turret accommodating a 75-mm (2.95-in) main gun to produce the Turan II.

In competition with the S-IIb CKD/Praga developed its V-8-H medium tank, which was a much superior vehicle ordered for Czech ser-

vice as the ST-39 in a 300-vehicle production programme involving CKD/Praga and Skoda. Only the prototypes had been produced by the time Czechoslovakia was occupied, and further development of this four-man 16,500-kg (36,376-lb) tank effectively ceased. The type was armed with one 47-mm gun and two 7.92-mm (0.312-in) machine guns, and was armoured to a maximum thickness of 50 mm (1.98 in).

After the rise of the Fascist party under Benito Mussolini, Italy increasingly swayed from its First World War alliance with France and the UK towards a political adherence to Germany, especially after the rise of the Nazi party in Germany. This commonality of right-wing political beliefs led to a formal alliance between Germany and Italy in May 1939. As noted above, Italy had perceived little utility for the tank in the context of its particular opera-

Carro d'Assalto Fiat Tipo 3000 Modello 21
(Italy)

Type: light assault tank
Crew: 2
Combat weight: 5,500 kg (12,125 lb)
Dimensions: length overall 4.17 m (13.68 ft) including removable tail or 3.61 m (11.84 ft) without tail; width 1.64 m (5.38 ft); height 2.19 m (7.185 ft)
Armament system: two 6.5-mm (0.256-in) SIA or Fiat machine-guns with 2,000 rounds
Armour: between 6 and 16 mm (0.24 and 0.63 in)
Powerplant: one 37.3-kW (509-hp) Fiat petrol engine with 90 litres (20 Imp. gal.) of fuel
Performance: speed, road 24 km/h (14.9 mph); range, road 95 km (59 miles); fording 1.1 m (3.6 ft); gradient 60%; vertical obstacle 0.6 m (1.97 ft); trench 1.50 m (4.9 ft); ground clearance 0.35 m (13.8 in)

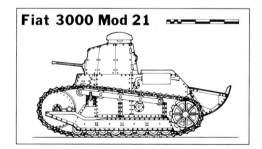

Fiat 3000 Mod 21

The principal production version of the CV.33 family was the CV.33/II (otherwise CV.35 or CV.3/35) with twin 8-mm (0.315-in) machine-guns. (*RAC Tank Museum*)

tional scenario in the First World War, but nevertheless developed one important type (the limited-production Fiat 2000 heavy tank), improved on the Renault FT and imported others. With the end of the First World War, Italian orders were immediately curtailed from 1,400 to a mere 100 examples of Italy's modified FT, the Fiat 3000. This served the Italian army well right into the 1930s, and it was the late 1920s before serious consideration was given to a successor.

For a variety of economic, tactical and industrial reasons, Italy was drawn to the example of the Carden-Loyd Mk VI tankette, which offered useful though limited capabilities but the possibility of large-scale production at modest cost by an automotive and armament industry with only small capacity for heavy engineering. The result was the CV.29, the prefix standing for *Carro Veloce* (fast vehicle, otherwise a tankette) and the suffix for the year of design (1929). The CV.29 was very similar to the Mk VI, and was built in small numbers (25 examples) largely as a trials variant. The vehicle was produced by Ansalso with a 40-hp (29.8-kW) Fiat-built Ford Model T petrol engine for a maximum speed of 40 km/h (24.9 mph) at a weight of 1,700 kg (3,748 lb). An open-topped vehicle with a crew of two, the CV.29 was armoured to thicknesses between 4 and 9 mm (0.16 and 0.35 in), and the armament was a single 6.5-mm (0.26-in) machine-gun, the original water-cooled weapon being rapidly replaced by an air-cooled version of the same basic design. Practical experience in

building and operating the CV.29 paved the way for an improved version of Italian origin, produced in prototype form as the CV.3 and, after evaluation in 1932 and 1933 with different running gear and water- or air-cooled machine-gun armament, standardized for service as the CV.33 (sometimes rendered CV.3-33). The order was for 1,300 vehicles, of which 1,100 were armed with a 6.5-mm (0.26-in) machine-gun under the designations CV.33 Serie I and the other 200 with two 8-mm (0.315-in) machine-guns under the designation CV.33 Serie II. Most Serie I tankettes were later brought up to Serie II standard, but this could not disguise the overall obsolescence of the type. The CV.33 was admittedly light enough for air-portability and possessed a commendably low silhouette, but had all the operational limitations of a tankette in terms of minimal armament and armour: yet this was all that Italian industry could manage in the mid-1930s, and the type did provide experience in the operation and maintenance of tracked vehicles. Considerable development was undertaken on the basis of this simple vehicle. The CV.35 (sometimes rendered CV.3-35) had a redesigned hull of bolted rather than riveted construction and slightly revised suspension, but was otherwise unaltered from the CV.33, while the L.38 of 1938 was a more ambitious updating of the basic concept, with strengthened suspension, new tracks, improved vision devices, and an armament of one 13.2-mm (0.52-in) Breda machine-gun, revised in 1940 to one 20-mm Solothurn

127

The flamethrower version of the CV.33 series was the L.35/Lf, later known as the L.3-35Lf, with the flame fuel carried in an armoured trailer. (*RAC Tank Museum*)

s13-1000 cannon. The 1938 system of nomenclature led to the redesignation of the CV.33 as the L.3-33 and the CV.35 as the L.3-35 in the L-series of *Leggero* (light) tanks. The CV.33 was intended primarily for security and reconnaissance duties in association with heavier tanks, but the nature of the Italian industrial machine meant that when Italy entered the Second World War in June 1940, her armoured forces were still equipped largely with the L.3, which had therefore to be used

Carro Veloce L.3–33
(Italy

Type: tankette
Crew: 2
Combat weight: 3,250 kg (7,165 lb)
Dimensions: length overall 3.20 m (10.50 ft); width 1.40 m (4.59 ft); height 1.28 m (4.20 ft)
Armament system: one 6.5-mm (0.256-in) Fiat machine-gun with 2,240 rounds
Armour: between 6 and 13.5 mm (0.24 and 0.53 in)
Powerplant: one 32-kW (43-hp) Fiat CV3-005 petrol engine with 62 litres (13.6 Imp. gal.) of fuel
Performance: speed, road 42 km/h (26.1 mph); range, road 120 km (74.6 miles); fording 0.7 m (2.3 ft); gradient 100%; vertical obstacle 0.65 m (2.13 ft); trench 1.45 m (4.75 ft); ground clearance 0.23 m (9.1 in)

Carro Veloce L.3-33

for combat roles of a type for which it had never been designed: losses were high, the 5- to 15-mm (0.2- to 0.59-in) armour not being proof against British armoured car projectiles, let alone anti-tank weapons. The L.3 series was also developed for other roles in variants such as the Carro d'Assalto Lanciafiamme 35 (or from 1940 as the L.3-35/Lf) flamethrower with an armoured trailer containing 500 litres (110 Imp gal) of flame fuel that could be fired to a range of 100 m (110 yards); the L.3-35/r command version with extra radio equipment, and often no armament to allow the installation of a mapboard; the Carro Veloce Passerella armoured vehicle-launched bridge; the Carro Veloce Recupero armoured recovery vehicle; a radio-controlled demolition vehicle; an anti-aircraft vehicle with an 8-mm (0.315-in) machine-gun; and the Semovente L.3 da 47/32 self-propelled anti-tank mounting with a 32-calibre 47-mm anti-tank gun in a limited-traverse mounting in the forward part of the hull.

Private-venture developments in this period were unsuccessful, the two most notable examples being the Ansaldo Carro Armato Modello 32 12,000-kg (26,455-lb) medium tank and its 8,000-kg (17,637-lb) light tank development. The Modello 32 was a turretless design armed with a 45-mm howitzer and four machine-guns, and was powered by a 75-hp (55.9-kW) Fiat truck engine, while the light tank had a purpose-designed diesel engine, a 40-mm gun in a limited-traverse mounting in the hull superstructure, and two 8-mm (0.315-in) machine-guns in a small turret. These designs paved the way for another unsuccessful type, the Fiat-Ansaldo Carro Cannone. This was a 5,000-kg (11,023-lb) machine with a 42-hp (31.3-kW) petrol engine, and was developed through three forms: the first prototype had a high superstructure accommodating a hull-mounted 37-mm anti-tank gun, and was then revised to include a turret armed with two 8-mm (0.315-in) machine-guns, while the second prototype was fitted with a turret-mounted 37-mm gun. This led to the Fiat-Ansaldo L.6/40 light tank, of which 283 were ordered to begin a programme of L.3 replacement. The first prototype ran in 1940 and production began in 1941, lasting into 1942. Prototypes were evaluated with different turrets, one accommodating two 8-mm (0.315-in) machine-guns, and the other one 37-mm gun plus an 8-mm (0.315-in) coaxial machine-gun. The production standard was one Breda 20-mm cannon and one 8-mm (0.315-in) coaxial machine-gun in a riveted turret manned by a single commander/gunner. The only other crew member was the driver sitting at the front of the 6,800-kg (14,991-lb) vehicle, which was powered by a 70-hp (52.2-kW) SPA 180 petrol engine for a maximum speed of 42 km/h 26.1 mph). The armour protection was modest but adequate, varying in thickness from 6 to 30 mm (0.24 to 1.18 in). The chassis was also used as the basis for the Semovente L.40 self-propelled mounting fitted with a 47-mm anti-tank gun in a limited-traverse mounting.

Another stream of development from the Ansaldo light tank of 1935 resulted in the Carro Armato M.11/39, which was the first of the M-series of *Medio* (medium) tanks and destined to become Italy's most important tank of the Second World War. The design was started in 1936, and then pursued with considerable vigour after combat experience in the Spanish Civil War had revealed to the Italians the total inadequacy of the CV.35 in the face of even moderate anti-tank capability. The first prototype was completed in 1937, and used running gear modelled on that of the CV.33/CV.35 series combined with the 105-hp (78.3-kW) SPA 8T diesel engine and armament layout of the 8,000-kg (17,637-lb) 1935 light tank. In 1938 a revised prototype introduced the running gear of the production model, and this running gear was also used on subsequent Italian tracked vehicles in the Second World War: on each side it comprised eight small road wheels

Carro Armato L.6/40

Carro Armato L.6/40
(Italy)

Type: light tank
Crew: 2
Combat weight: 6,900 kg (15,212 lb)
Dimensions: length overall 3.78 m (12.40 ft); width 1.92 m (6.30 ft); height 2.03 m (6.66 ft)
Armament system: one 20-mm Breda cannon with 296 rounds and one 8-mm (0.315-in) Breda machine-gun with 1,560 rounds
Armour: between 6 and 30 mm (0.24 and 1.18 in)
Powerplant: one 52.2-kW (70-hp) SPA 18 D petrol engine with 145 litres (32 Imp. gal.) of fuel
Performance: speed, road 42 km/h (26.1 mph); range, road 200 km (124 miles); fording 0.8 m (2.6 ft); gradient 60%; vertical obstacle 0.7 m (2.3 ft); trench 1.7 m (5.6 ft); ground clearance 0.35 m (13.8 in)

Though based on the chassis of the L.3 (CV.33) tankette, L.6/40 was a true if ineffective light tank with a 360 traverse turret accommodating a 20-mm cannon. (*RAC Tank Museum*)

The M.11/39 was obsolete even as it entered service, and after a severe mauling by British armour and anti-tank guns in its debut engagements was withdrawn from service in 1941. (*RAC Tank Museum*)

Carro Armato M.11/39
(Italy)

Type: medium tank
Crew: 3
Combat weight: 11,175 kg (24,636 lb)
Dimensions: length overall 4.73 m (15.52 ft); width 2.18 m (7.15 ft); height 2.30 m (7.55 ft)
Armament system: one 37-mm gun with 80 rounds and two 8-mm (0.315-in) Breda machine-guns with 2,808 rounds
Armour: between 6 and 30 mm (0.24 and 1.18 in)
Powerplant: one 78.3-kW (105-hp) SPA 8 T diesel with 145 litres (32 Imp. gal.) of fuel
Performance: speed, road 33.3 km/h (20.7 mph); range, road 200 km (124 miles); fording 1.0 m (3.3 ft); gradient 70%; vertical obstacle 0.8 m (2.6 ft); trench 2.0 m (6.56 ft); ground clearance 0.36 m (14.2 in)

Carro Armato M.11/39

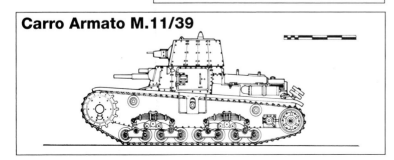

in two-wheel bogies sprung by semi-elliptical leafsprings; the drive sprocket was at the front and the idler at the rear, and there were three track-return rollers. The armour was still too thin for the type of armoured operations that were now becoming inevitable, but the armament was adequate in overall terms, though distinctly hampered by its specific layout. The turret's only occupant was the commander, who thus had to undertake all the responsibilities of tactical control and also operate the two 8-mm (0.315-in) Breda machine-guns, while the hull accommodated at the front the driver and behind him the gunner for the 37-mm main gun, which could be moved in elevation through an arc between -8° and +12°, but in traverse through the distinctly small arc of only 30°. The M.11/39 entered service in 1940, and was immediately revealed by an alarming loss rate as totally obsolete in basic concept. The Italians were at this time planning a new series of armoured fighting vehicles for the Second World War, and these are covered in the next chapter.

The third of the Axis powers was Japan, which had fought on the Allied side in the First World War, but then fell under the sway of increasingly right-wing military administrations and so drifted with an apparent inexorability into the same political arena as Germany and Italy; in 1940 the three countries signed the German-Italian-Japanese Axis agreement, a 10-year mutual assistance pact. Japan was slow to enter the field of armoured warfare, though in 1918 she received small quantities of tanks from France (Renault FT) and the UK (Tanks Mk V and Medium Tank Mk A). These were adequate for Japanese purposes until well into the 1920s, though an effort was made to keep abreast of major development through small-scale purchases of tanks such as the Renault NC 1 (with the Japanese designation Otsu-Gata Sensha, in succession to the Ko-Gata Sensha used for the FT with the 37-mm gun turret) from France, the Vickers Medium Tank Mk C, the Carden-Loyd Amphibious Tank and Carden-Loyd Mk VI tankette from the UK, and some Christie tanks from the USA.

In 1925 the Japanese army established two specialist tank companies (one of them attached to the infantry school for tactical evaluations) and instituted an indigenous tank development programme. The first fruit of this effort was the Experimental Tank No. 1, produced in 1927 at the Osaka Arsenal as a five-man multi-turret machine weighing some 20,000 kg (44,092 lb). The running gear of this machine was made up on each side of 19 small road wheels, grouped mainly in pairs and supported by two-stage leafsprings: the tank was powered by a 140-hp (104-kW) petrol engine, and this allowed a maximum speed of only 20 km/h (12.4 mph). The main turret was modelled on that of the NC 1, but featured a short-barrel 57-mm gun, while the two subsidiary turrets were located fore and aft of the main turret and each featured a single 6.5-mm (0.256-in) machine-gun. Unhappy with the performance of this first effort, the Japanese reworked the concept as the Experimental Heavy Tank, which emerged from the Osaka Arsenal in 1930 with its weight reduced by 2,000 kg (4,409 lb) through the use of thinner armour, but the main armament improved by the use of a 70-mm (2.76-in) main gun and the addition of another 6.5-mm (0.256-in) machine-gun in the left-hand side of the main turret. The running gear was modified (the number of road wheels on each side being reduced to 17), but there was no appreciable increment in performance or cross-country agility. The Japanese thought that the multi-turret heavy tank retained a tactical value, and therefore continued development right up to 1935, by which time a new designation system had been adopted. This was based on a two-digit (from 1940 a one-digit) type number indicating the relevant date, based on the founding of the Japanese empire in the year 0 (660 BC by Western dating), and in-service types were retrospectively redesignated: for example, the Ko-Gata Sensha became the Medium Tank Type 79. The official type designation was often suffixed by a manufacturer's name and, in some instances, by an official name: the Light Tank Type 95 was thus given the manufacturer's name Ha-Go, and the official name Ke-Go.

The first heavy tank in the new system was the Heavy Tank Type 91, indicating the Japanese year 2591 (1931 AD). This was similar to the Experimental Heavy Tank, but had a new gearbox and wider tracks, and a revised turret without the stroboscopic vision cupola of the earlier models. The ultimate expression of the concept was the Heavy Tank Type 95, a 24,000-kg (52,910-lb) machine with armour varying in thickness from 12 to 30 mm (0.47 to 1.18 in), and its armament in three turrets: the main unit sported a 70-mm (2.76-in) gun and a single 6.5-mm (0.256-in) machine gun, the forward unit had a 37-mm gun, and the rear unit was armed with a single 6.5-mm (0.256-in) machine-gun. The running gear was revised to nine leaf-sprung road wheels on each side, and in concert with a 290-hp (216-kW) petrol engine this provided a maximum speed of 22 km/h (13.7 mph).

By 1935 the Japanese had come to appreciate at last that the multi-turret tank was obsolescent as a concept, and also did not fit in with the plans for either Asian or Pacific operations. At the same time it was clear that Japanese industry was not adequate for the development and construction of such land behemoths in useful numbers, and accordingly the decision was taken to concentrate on light and medium tanks, together with a number of tankettes that could double as tractors for armoured ammunition resupply trailers. The inspiration for this requirement was found in the small number of Carden-Loyd

The Type 91 heavy tank was developed at the Imperial Japanese Army's Osaka Arsenal, and is sometimes known as the Type 92 as it was completed in the Japanese year 2592 (1932). It paved the way for the ultimate multi-turret Japanese tank, the Type 95, which was then abandoned as the army decided to concentrate limited resources and production facilities on lighter tanks. (*RAC Tank Museum*)

Mk VI tankettes which the Japanese army had bought from the UK in the late 1920s. After extensive evaluation of these vehicles the Japanese decided in 1933 to produce their own equivalent to meet the trailer-tractor requirement, and this emerged as the Tankette Type 94 (frequently known in the West as the Type 92, in perpetuation of a US intelligence failure). Weighing 3,400 kg (7,496 lb) and powered by a 32-hp (23.85-kW) Type 94 petrol engine for a maximum speed of 40 km/h (24.9 mph), the Type 94 was of riveted construction, with armour varying in thickness between 4 and 12 mm (0.16 and 0.47 in). The driver and engine were located at the front, and the commander/gunner sat in a small turret towards the rear of the vehicle over a compartment accessed by a rear door for the simple loading/unloading of stores. The turret was armed with a single 6.5-mm (0.256-in) machine-gun, later replaced by a 7.7-mm (0.303-in) weapon. The running gear on each side of the vehicle consisted of four rubber-tyred road wheels in two-wheel bellcranked bogies separated by a horizontal compression spring, the whole arrangement providing moderately good cross-country performance. Even so it was felt that improvements were both necessary and feasible, and this led to an updated model with greater track length in

The Japanese Type 94 tankette was modelled on the Carden-Loyd Mk VI, and the one-man turret was traversed by pressure on the commander/gunner's shoulders against the machine-gun mounting. (*RAC Tank Museum*)

contact with the ground. The Type 94 began to enter service in 1934, and was widely used as a front-line vehicle into 1943, thereafter fading into second-line roles during 1944 and 1945.

Experience with these two Type 94 variants proved highly important in the development of Japanese tactics for light armour, and also paved the way for the Tankette Type 97 Te-Ke, which entered service in 1938 and remained in service with the Japanese army up to the end of the Second World War. One Type 94 had been trialled with a 65-hp (48.5-kW) diesel engine for greater operational safety, as well as improved range on a given fuel load, and such an engine was specified for the Type 97, which emerged as a substantially larger vehicle than the Type 94, with an overall length of 3.682 m (12.08 ft) compared with the Type 94's 3.08 m (10.1 ft). The weight of the Type 97 was 4,750 kg (10,471 lb), and the 65-hp (48.5-kW) Ikega diesel engine provided for a maximum speed of 42 km/h (26.1 mph) and a range of 250 km (155 miles), compared with the Type 94's 210 km (130 miles). The suspen-

sion and tracks were basically similar to those of the Type 94, but the turret was generally armed with a 37-mm Type 94 anti-tank gun, provided with 96 rounds; in some vehicles, however, this weapon was replaced by a 7.7-mm (0.303-in) machine-gun. With a crew of two the Type 97 was tactically impoverished, because the commander was also the gunner and loader. The Japanese army appreciated that the Type 97 was obsolete by the beginning of the Second World War, but the type remained in production for lack of an adequate replacement, and in fact performed usefully against the Chinese until the end of the war.

In parallel with its tankette interests, the army was also concerned with the development and introduction of amphibious tanks: the generally poor land communications of mainland Asia meant that there was a dearth of bridges and modern ferries, so sustained land operations called for an amphibious capability of significant size. The starting point for this effort was the Combat Car Type 92, essentially a three-man heavy tankette designed for the support of cavalry in deep tactical operations. The running gear suspension was again based on four road wheels per side, located like those of the tankettes in two-wheel bogies, but here attached on a longer and wider hull with the drive sprockets at the extreme front and the idlers at the rear: the result was a long track length of bowed appearance,

The Type 97 was the last tankette developed in Japan, and somewhat larger than its predecessors, allowing the use of a turret-mounted 37-mm gun rather than a machine-gun. (*RAC Tank Museum*)

Type 97 Te-Ke

Tankette Type 97 (Te-Ke)
(Japan)

Type: tankette
Crew: 2
Combat weight: 4,750 kg (10, 472 lb)
Dimensions: length overall 3.68 m (12.08 ft); width 1.803 m (5.92 ft); height 1.773 m (5.82 ft)
Armament system: one 37-mm gun with 96 rounds
Armour: between 4 and 16 mm (0.16 and 0.63 in)
Powerplant: one 48.5-kW (65-hp) Ikega diesel engine with 90 litres (19.8 Imp. gal.) of fuel
Performance: speed, road 42 km/h (26 mph); range, road 250 km (155 miles); gradient 60%; vertical obstacle 0.81 m (2.67 ft); trench 1.7 m (5.58 ft)

The Type 92 combat car was a heavy tankette for the Japanese cavalry. This in an early model with six small bogie wheels, rather than the four larger road wheels of later production examples. (*RAC Tank Museum*)

with only a comparatively short section in contact with the ground, in the centre. Weighing 3,200 kg (7,055 lb) and armoured to a maximum thickness of only 6 mm (0.24 in), the Combat Car Type 92 was one of the world's first all-welded armoured fighting vehicles: in appearance it was very angular, and its armament comprised a ball-mounted 6.5-mm (0.256-in) machine-gun in the bulged forward edge of the hull superstructure, and either one 13.2-mm (0.52-in) and one 6.5-mm (0.256-in) machine-gun, or two 6.5-mm (0.256-in) machine-guns in the 360° traverse turret. The Type 92 was powered by a 45-hp (33.6-kW) Ishikawajima petrol engine for a maximum speed of 40 km/h (24.9 mph). The prototype described above performed adequately, but the production variant was revised with different running gear, based on three pairs of road wheels on each side for greater ground contact length. Weight rose to 3,500 kg (7,716 lb) and as the engine was unaltered this reduced speed to 35 km/h (21.75 mph) with a standard turret armament of one 13.2-mm (0.52-in) and one 6.5-mm (0.256-in) machine-gun. That the running gear was still not satisfactory is indicated by the fact that in late-

production examples of the Type 92, the running gear reverted to four road wheels on each side, though these wheels were somewhat larger than those of the prototype, and spoked rather than solid.

From the Combat Car Type 92 the army sought to develop an amphibious version, the Amphibious Combat Car Type 92 (A-I-Go). The welded hull was waterproofed and increased in volume, while a propeller and floats were added, but the variant did not proceed past the prototype stage. Instead the experience gained with this machine was used for the Amphibious Tank SR-I (I-Go), a 1933 development with buoyancy chambers, two two-wheel bogies on each side, and armament of one 6.5-mm (0.256-in) machine-gun in a light turret. The type was powered by a Mitsubishi diesel, and of the two prototypes one was water-propelled by a pumpjet. This experimental model was succeeded by the Amphibious Tank SR-II (Ro-Go), a 4,000-kg (8,818-lb) machine with Horstmann suspension on the two twin-wheel bogies on each side, and powered by a petrol engine for a land speed of 40 km/h (24.9 mph) and a water speed of 8 km/h (4.9 mph), driven by two propellers. The much

A Japanese Type 95 light tank knocked out in the December 1941 fighting for Malaya. Well displayed on the turret, which is traversed to the tank's left, are the 37-mm main gun and the 7.7-mm (0.303-in) machine-gun in the turret rear. Not so evident is the built-out nature of the compartment for the hull machine-gun. (*IWM*)

improved octagonal turret was fitted with two 7.7-mm (0.303-in) machine-guns. At this point the army became disenchanted with the amphibious tank concept, and further development fell to the navy, who saw a greater need for such vehicles within the context of the amphibious operations planned for its marine corps in the island campaigns of the Second World War.

Greater attention was devoted to the light tank by the Japanese than by most Western nations. From the Western point of view this Japanese interest may seem backward, but the nature of Far Eastern operations in fact fully validated the Japanese army's primary premise, and it was only when these vehicles were required to face American and British medium tanks that their shortcomings became crucial. Japan's first essay into the light tank design field was the Light Tank Type 89 Experimental Tank No.2, evolved largely from the Vickers Medium Tank Mk C bought from the UK in 1927. The Type 89's running gear comprised nine leafsprung road wheels and five track-return rollers on each side, and the forward-mounted turret was fitted with a 37-mm or, according to some sources, 57-mm

gun and a rearward-firing 6.5-mm (0.256-in) machine-gun, a second machine-gun of the same type being located in the bow. The crew was four men, and at a weight of 9,800 kg (21,605 lb) the vehicle was driven at a maximum speed of only 25 km/h (15.5 mph) by its 105-hp (78.3-kW) Daimler petrol engine. The prototype appeared in 1929, but it soon became clear in trials that it was better suited to the medium tank role.

First into production, therefore was the Light Tank 95 (Ha-Go), without doubt the best tank produced and deployed in quantity by the Japanese in the Second World War. The prototype was built by either the Sagami Arsenal or Mitsubishi, and extensively evaluated in Japan and under the operational conditions encountered in China before production was entrusted to Mitsubishi, which built about 1,250 examples from its own and sub-contracted assemblies. The type began to enter service in 1935, and for its time was a capable machine, as good as any light tank in the world, the provision of an interior layer of asbestos proving useful in reducing interior heat and protecting the crew from damage as the tank moved at speed across country.

135

The machine was based on a welded and riveted hull made of armour varying in thickness from 9 to 12 mm (0.35 to 0.47 in), and locating in its forward compartment the driver and the gunner for the 6.5-mm (0.256-in) bow machine-gun. Behind them was the 360° traverse turret, which was again of welded and riveted construction: here was the third crew member, the commander, who had in addition to his command responsibilities the task of loading, aiming and firing the 37-mm Type 94 main gun. At the rear were the Mitsubishi NVD 6120 diesel engine and its transmission, the 120 hp (89.5 kW) of this powerplant being sufficient to propel the 7,400-kg (16,314-lb) Type 95 at the respectable speed of 45 km/h (28 mph). By this time the Japanese had considerable practical experience with the bellcrank type of suspension, and this was used in the Type 95: on each side the running gear comprised two bogies, each of two rubber-tyred road wheels, resisted by a horizontally mounted compression spring. The drive sprockets were at the front and the idlers at the rear, and on each side there were two track-return rollers. In Manchuria it was found that the Type 95 suffered severe pitching in cross-country operations, and some vehicles were modified to Light Tank Type 95 Special standard, with the wheels of each bogie coupl-

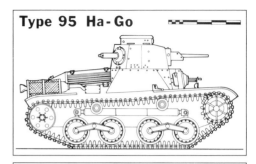

Type 95 Ha-Go

Light Tank Type 95 (Ha-Go)
(Japan)

Type: light tank
Crew: 3
Combat weight: 7,400 kg (16,314 lb)
Dimensions: length overall 4.38 m (14.375 ft); width 2.057 m (6.75 ft); height 2.18 m (7.17 ft)
Armament system: one 37-mm gun with 19 rounds and two 7.7-mm (0.303-in) Type 97 machine-guns with 2,940 rounds
Armour: between 6 and 12 mm (0.24 and 0.47 in)
Powerplant: one 89.5-kW (120-hp) Mitsubishi NVD diesel engine with 100 litres (22 Imp. gal.) of fuel
Performance: speed, road 45 km/h (28 mph); range, road 245 km (152 miles); fording 1.0 m (3.28 ft); gradient 45°; vertical obstacle 0.81 m (2.67 ft); trench 1.8 m (5.92 ft); ground clearance 0.39 m (15.4 in)

Well camouflaged Type 95 light tanks of the Imperial Japanese army on the move in Malaya during January and February 1942. (*Fujifotos, Tokyo*)

ed by an inverted triangular bogie bolster. Operations also confirmed that better armament was desirable, and the 6.5-mm (0.256-in) bow machine-gun was replaced by a 7.7-mm (0.303-in) weapon, another 7.7-mm (0.303-in) machine-gun was added on the right-hand side of the turret rear for use by the already overworked commander/gunner, and finally the original Type 94 main gun was replaced by a Type 98 weapon of the same calibre but higher muzzle velocity.

The Type 95 was a major improvement over the Japanese army's previous light tanks, but was soon involved in a major programme to produce improved variants. The first of these was the Light Tank Type 98 (Ke-Ni), which was schemed with two alternative types of running gear and built by Mitsubishi and Hino: the Type 98-Ko (Type 98-A) used three two-wheel bogies (plus three track-return rollers) on each side and had front-sprocket drive controlled by the driver's steering wheel, while the Type 89-Otsu (Type 98-B) had Christie-type running gear, comprising on each side four large-diameter road wheels individually coil-sprung via bellcranks and a rear drive sprocket. The Type 98-Otsu did not progress beyond the prototype stage, but the Type 98-Ko finally entered production in 1942 for construction to a maximum of perhaps 200 vehicles though some sources suggest only 100 vehicles. The Ke-Ni used a greater proportion of welding than the Ha-Go, and was armoured to a maximum thickness of 14 mm (0.55 in). The armour was also better shaped, and the armament comprised one 37-mm Type 100 high-velocity gun and two 7.7-mm (0.303-in) machine-guns. A 150-hp (112-kW) supercharged diesel engine was fitted, and this provided the 7,200-kg (15,873-lb) tank with a maximum speed of 50 km/h (31.1 mph). The Ke-Ni's production and service debuts had been delayed by user satisfaction with the original Ha-Go, and by the time the type began to appear in 1942, shortly after Japan's entry into the Second World War, the day of the light tank was effectively over except in the peculiar conditions of Japanese army operations in mainland China, to which the Ke-Ni was admirably suited. Essentially similar to the Ke-Ni was the Light Tank Type 2 (Ke-To) with a 37-mm Type 1

main gun, secondary armament limited to one 7.7-mm (0.303-in) machine gun, and armour varying in thickness between 6 and 16 mm (0.24 and 0.63 in). Only a few were built after the start of production in 1944.

Closer to the original Ha-Go were the Light Tank Type 3 (Ke-Ri) and Light Tank Type 4 (Ke-Nu). Both were based on the hull of the Type 95, the Type 3 having the standard turret reworked to accommodate the 57-mm gun of the Medium Tank Type 97, and the Type 4 being fitted with the complete turret/gun assembly of the Medium Tank Type 97. The Light Tank Type 3 weighed 7,400 kg (16,314 lb) and proved impractical because of its extremely cramped turret, and the Light Tank Type 4 was too unwieldy at a weight of 8,400 kg (18,519 lb).

Properly speaking, Japan's last light tank falls into the purview of the next chapter, but is discussed here for the sake of completeness, as it never entered full-scale production. This was the Light Tank Type 5 (Ke-Ho), which was designed in 1942 and evaluated in prototype form with first-class results, but was not considered for production unitl too late. It was a four-man machine turning the scales at 10,000 kg (22,046 lb) with armour varying in thickness from 8 to 20 mm (0.315 to 0.79 in). The tank was armed with one 47-mm Type 1 anti-tank gun and one 7.7-mm (0.303-in) machine-gun, and powered by a 150-hp (112-kW) diesel engine could reach 50 km/h (31.1 mph).

The Type 2 light tank was little more than the Type 98-Ko fitted with Type 1 rather than Type 100 37-mm main gun. (*RAC Tank Museum*)

Next up the size scale comes the medium tank, which the Japanese saw as a battle tank with modest armour, good armament and only limited performance as a battlefield support weapon for the infantry. Mention has been made above of the Light Tank Type 89 Experimental Tank No. 2, the 1929 prototype passed over in its designed cavalry role. This was thought to form the basis of an adequate infantry support tank, however, and further development produced the Medium Tank Type 89, which was evolved in two forms as the Type 89-Ko (Type 89-A) and Type 89-Otsu (Type 89-B). Of these the Type 89-Ko was powered by a 105-hp (78.3-kW) Mitsubishi petrol engine adapted from an aircraft powerplant. The armour varied in thickness between 10 and 17 mm (0.39 and 0.67 in), giving the tank an overall weight of 12,700 kg (27,998 lb), and the armament was basically similar in disposition to that of the Light Tank Type 89 but comprised one 57-mm Type 90 main gun and two 6.5-mm (0.256-in) machine-guns. The crew was four, and the maximum speed 25 km/h (15.5 mph).

The main theatres envisaged for operations by the Type 89 were China and Manchuria. In the latter, the Japanese faced the armour-rich Soviets, and extensive trials were undertaken to test the Type 89's battlefield performance in the terrain and climate of Manchuria. These trials confirmed the tank's adequacy in terms of battlefield agility, but revealed the limitations of the petrol engine under conditions of extreme cold. This resulted in the development of the Type 89-Otsu with a 115-hp (85.7-kW) Mitsubishi diesel engine for greater safety, better range and easier starting. The tank is sometimes known as the Medium Tank Type 94, as production started in 1934. Construction was undertaken by Mitsubishi and other manufacturers, resulting in a diversity of detail, such as one- or two-piece front plates, different skirt armour configurations and modified cupolas. The weight was generally in the order of 13,000 kg (28,660 lb), the additional weight being balanced by greater power for performance essentially unaltered from that of the Type 89-Ko. Many tanks serving in Machuria were fitted with an unditching tail of the type first seen on the Renault FT, in an ef-

The Type 89-Otsu medium tank was the diesel-engined version of the Type 89-Ko petrol-engined model. The variant was produced at different factories in Japan and Manchuria, and this resulted in differences such as the driver on the left and the 57-mm gun on the right, or *vice versa*. (*RAC Tank Museum*)

fort to provide better trench-crossing capability.

The Type 89 provided the Japanese army with valuable operational experience and lessons in the operation of medium tanks, and remained in service up to 1943, seeing service in the Philippines as well as in China. But it was clear from the comparatively early stage of the Type 89's career that the type was distinctly limited by its obsolescent layout and clumsy arrangement of nine small road wheels. In the mid-1930s the Japanese launched a competitive programme to find a new and considerably more advanced medium tank. The two main competitors were the Experimental Medium Tank Chi-Ni designed by the army general staff and built by the Osaka Arsenal, and the Experimental Medium Tank Chi-Ha designed by the army engineering department and built by Mitsubishi.

The three-man Chi-Ni appeared in 1937, at a weight of 10,000 kg (22,046 lb) with armour up to 25 mm (0.98 in) thick. On each side the running gear comprised four twin-wheel bogies with bellcranks to horizontal compression springs, and there were three track-return rollers. The engine was a 135-hp (101-kW) petrol unit for a speed of 30 km/h (18.6 mph), and the armament comprised one turret-mounted 57-mm Type 90 gun and one 7.7-mm (0.303-in)

bow machine-gun. The single prototype was successfully evaluated, and production was on the cards and the army was still persuaded of the advantages of a lighter, cheaper and more easily manufactured tank. But with the outbreak of full-scale war in China during 1937 the production decision finally went to the larger and heavier Chi-Ha.

The Chi-Ha was thus standardized as the Medium Tank Type 97, a four-man machine weighing 15,000 kg (33,069 lb) and armoured to thicknesses varying from a minimum of 8 mm (0.315 in) to a maximum of 25 mm (0.98 in). In basic concept the Type 97 was a scaled-up version of the Light Tank Type 95 with a two-man turret, more potent armament, thicker armour and greater power to maintain performance, despite the considerably greater weight. The hull was of riveted and welded construction, with the driver and gunner for the 7.7-mm (0.303-in) bow machine-gun in the forward compartment, the fighting compartment in the centre, and the engine and transmission in the rear compartment. The turret was surmounted by the commander's cupola, and its weapons comprised one 57-mm Type 97 short-barreled tank gun and, in the rear face, one 7.7-mm (0.303-in) machine gun. The turret provided 360° traverse, but the main gun had a second pair of trunnions allow-

Far left (top) Japanese Type 89-Otsu medium tanks on the move in China during the sino-Japanese war of the late 1930s (*IWM*)

Far left (bottom) A Japanese Type 89-Otsu tank crosses a partially-demolished bridge in China. (*US Army*)

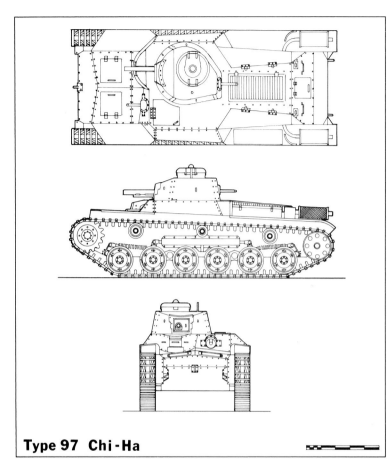

Type 97 Chi-Ha

Medium Tank Type 97 (Chi-Ha)
(Japan)

Type: medium (light) tank
Crew: 4
Combat weight: 15,000 kg (33,069 lb) with 57-mm gun or 16,000 kg (35,273 lb) with 47-mm gun
Dimensions: length overall 5.516 m (18.10 ft); width 2.33 m (7.64 ft); height overall 2.23 m (7.32 ft)
Armament system: one 57-mm Type 97 or, in Type 97 (Special) one 47-mm Type 1 rifled gun with 120 or 104 rounds respectively, two 7.7-mm (0.303-in) Type 97 machine-guns (one bow and one turret rear) with 2,350 or, in Type 97 (Special), 2,575 rounds; the turret was manually operated, the main gun was stabilized in neither elevation (−9° to +11°) nor azimuth (360°) with a secondary pair of internal trunnion's giving an independent main armament traverse of 5° left and right, and simple optical sights were fitted
Armour: riveted steel varying in thickness between 8 and 25 mm (0.315 and 0.98 in)
Powerplant: one 126.75-kW (170-hp) Mitsubishi diesel engine with 197 litres (43.3 Imp. gal.) of fuel
Performance: speed, road 38 km/h (23.6 mph); range, road 210 km (130.5 miles); fording 1.0 m (3.28 ft); gradient 57%; vertical obstacle 0.8 m (2.625); trench 2.5 m (8.2 ft); ground clearance 0.36 m (14.2 in)

The Type 97 (Shinhoto Chi-Ha) medium tank was essentially the Type 97 (Chi-Ha) carrying the turret of the Type 1 (Chi-He) complete with long-barrel 47-mm gun. (*RAC Tank Museum*)

ing a maximum 10° traverse independently of the turret; it could also be elevated in an arc between -9° and +11°. The running gear on each side comprised six medium-diameter road wheels grouped into pairs of two-wheel bogies in the centre (with bellcrank suspension to a horizontal coil spring) and two singleton units at the ends, three track-return rollers, a front drive sprocket and a rear idler. Power was provided by a 170-hp (127-kW) Mitsubishi Type 97 diesel engine for a maximum speed of 38 km/h (23.6 mph). The Type 97 entered service in 1938 and remained in major service right to the end of the Second World War. The type marked a significant improvement over earlier Japanese tanks in its use of a two-man turret to leave the commander free for his primary task, and was well up to the standard of contemporary light/medium tanks. It was destined to come up against increasingly powerful American and British tanks, however, and was found wanting in the three key areas of firepower, protection and mobility. The major reason for this failing was a combination of poor industry capacity for the production of better medium tanks, and of the Japanese army's predilection for infantry support rather anti-armour operations. This fact is confirmed by the use of comparatively short-barrelled guns firing their shells at modest velocities, and the devotion of most ammunition stowage to HE rather than armour-piercing rounds: in the Type 97 the main ammunition stowage of 120 rounds was allocated in the ratio two HE to one armour-piercing, whereas Western and Soviet tanks reversed this ratio in favour of armour-piercing ammunition.

But the Japanese were not totally blind to the progression of tank tactics, and sensibly provided the Type 97 with a turret ring of greater diameter than strictly required by the 57-mm medium-velocity gun. This allowed the later development of the Type 97 (Shinhoto Chi-Ha), which was essentially the hull of the Type 97 fitted with the turret of the Medium Tank Type 1 complete with its 47-mm Type 1 long-barrelled gun. This increased combat weight to 16,000 kg (35,273 lb), but the longer gun provided for a muzzle velocity of 825 m (2,707 ft) per second, giving the projectile an armour-penetration capability of 70 mm (2.76 in) at a range of 500 m (545 yards). Some 104 rounds of 47-mm ammunition were carried, some of them HE rounds for the standard infantry support role. The basic hull of the Chi-Ha was judged excellent by the Japanese, and was used for a number of other tasks. These variants included the Command Tank (Shi-Ki) which had additional vision and communication equipment, and a 37- or 57-mm short-barrelled gun in place of the bow machine-gun. The Recovery Tank (Se-Ri) had a conical turret armed with a single 7.7-mm (0.303-in) machine-gun, and its recovery equipment comprised a light jib at the rear. The Mine-clearing Tank G was essentially a standard Type 97 fitted with arms projecting from the front of the tank to carry two chain-fitted rotating drums. The Observation Tank (Ka-So) was the Shi-Ki equivalent based on the Shinhoto Chi-Ha with a dummy main gun. The Bulldozer Tank was again based on the Shinhoto Chi-Ha, with a front-mounted dozer blade. Other models included self-propelled guns, a self-propelled anti-aircraft mounting, a ram tank for the creation of paths through Manchurian forests, and an armoured bridgelayer.

The Blitzkrieg Years

Such, then, was the main stream of tank development in the period between the two world wars. There had been some armoured conflict during the period, mostly notably between the Soviets and the Japanese in a number of border clashes in eastern Asia, and between the Nationalist and Republican forces in the Spanish Civil War, but these had lacked the sustained intensity to allow the drawing of valuable long-term conclusions. It was clear from these conflicts, however, that armour had a potentially decisive part to play, if reliability could be improved, numbers increased and offensive power boosted. The two countries that took these implications closest to heart were Germany and the USSR: the former used the Spanish Civil War to validate the basic premises of its new *Blitzkrieg* concept, and the latter decided that its considerable capacity for tank design and production would be best used in the development of a new generation of high-speed tanks with superb cross-country performance, hard-hitting main armament, good protection and reliability enhanced by the ruthless elimination of less essential items of equipment.

During the months leading to the Second World War, the German army mustered six armoured divisions (the 1st to 5th, and 10th Panzer Divisions) and four light divisions. The Panzer divisions each had an establishment of one tank brigade comprising two tank regiments, each of two four-company tank battalions, and one motorized infantry brigade comprising either one three-battalion infantry regiment plus one motorcycle battalion, or two two-battalion infantry regiments: on mobilization these divisions were modified, each tank battalion being reduced to three companies (two with light tanks and one with medium tanks), the erstwhile fourth company being used for training and depot duties and so reducing the company balance from 16 of

tanks to 12 of infantry, to a wartime norm of 12 of tanks to 12 of infantry. The light division was the cavalry equivalent of the Panzer division, having the same infantry strength but only a single three-battalion regiment of tanks: after the Polish campaign these light divisions became the 6th, 7th, 8th and 9th Panzer Divisions. The Panzer divisions and the 4th Light Division were equipped with German tanks, and the 1st, 2nd and 3rd Light Divisions with Czech tanks. The German equipment in service with these first-line divisions were the PzKpfw I and PzKpfw II light tanks, the small number of PzKpfw III battle and PzKpfw IV medium tanks being allocated mainly to the Panzer-Lehr Bataillon (the ordnance department's evaluation and demonstration unit) and the Aufklarungs-Lehr Bataillon (reconnaissance demonstration unit).

For the beginning of the campaign in the West (10 May 1940), the 10 Panzer divisions had 35 tank battalions, and these were equipped with a total of 2,574 tanks, comprising 523 PzKpfw I, 955 PzKpfw II, 349 PzKpfw III, 278 PzKpfw IV, 106 PzKpfw 35(t) and 228 PzKpfw 38(t) machine-gun/gun tanks plus 135 command tanks (96 and 39 on the chassis of the PzKpfw I and PzKpfw II respectively). After the completion of the French campaign the number of Panzer divisions was increased to 20: there were inadequate tank supplies for the creation of these new divisions on the original 1935 pattern, so the tank brigade was reduced to a single regiment (in six divisions with three tank battalions and in the others with only two tank battalions) balanced by a doubling of the infantry strength to two two-battalion infantry regiments plus one motorcycle battalion. Armoured strength was maintained, however, by the upgrading of equipment, the battalion having two light companies with PzKpfw IIIs and one medium company with PzKpfw IVs. This gave a tank strength of

150 per three-battalion tank regiment (1st to 6th Panzer Divisions) and 100 per two-battalion tank regiment (7th to 20th Panzer Divisions).

Of the 19 available Panzer divisions, 17 were used in the opening moves of the German campaign against the USSR (21 June 1941), organized largely into four Panzer armies (Panzerarmee) with about 3,200 tanks between them. This was the high point in the fortunes of Germany's tank force, though on paper the establishment later rose to a peak of 25 army and eight SS Panzer divisions in 1944. The army designation sequence included the 1st to 27th Panzer Divisions, the 116th Panzer Division and the Panzer-Lehr Division, of which the 10th, 22nd and 27th were destroyed and not re-formed, and the 18th disbanded before 1944. The army divisions had a strength of two tank battalions (one of PzKpfw IVs and the other of PzKpfw V Panthers) each nominally of four 22-tank companies, but generally of three 17-tank companies, while the more favoured SS Panzer divisions had a strength of three or even four tank battalions.

From late 1940 the mainstay of the Panzer battalions became the PzKpfw III battle tank and the PzKpfw IV medium tank, as the obsolescence of the PzKpfw I and PzKpfw II forced the earlier tanks' relegation to secondary roles. The PzKpfw III was designed as the German army's standard battle tank, and entered its stride as a production weapon with the PzKpfw III Ausführung H, the main production variant in the period between late 1940 and the end of 1941. The first large-scale production variant, the PzKpfw III Ausf E, had been allocated for production to several companies with little experience in the manufacture of armoured fighting vehicles, and had suffered in terms of production quantity and quality because of the comparatively complex manufacturing techniques required: therefore the PzKpfw III Ausf H had features to ease mass production, the most important being new idlers and drive sprockets, and a transmission arrangement with a six-speed manual gearbox in place of the original 10-speed pre-selector box. As a result of combat experience in Poland and the Western campaign, extra protection was added in the form of bolt-on plates, as well as a measure of spaced armour to defeat hollow-charge warheads. This boosted the PzKpfw III Ausf H's combat weight to 21,600 kg (47,619 lb), and to reduce ground pressure from the 0.99 kg/cm^2 (14.1 lb/sq in) of the Ausf F and Ausf G to the 0.95-kg/cm^2 (13.5-lb/sq in) figure of the Ausf E,

Two PzKpfw Is and one PzKpfw III move through a devastated French village during June 1940. (MARS)

Seen with supporting infantry during the German drive into the USSR, this is a PzKpfw III Ausf F with a 50-mm high-velocity gun in place of the earlier PzKpfw III variants 37-mm weapon. (*MARS*)

wider 400-mm (15.75-in) rather than 360-mm (14.17-in) tracks were fitted. The 300-hp (224-kW) Maybach HL 120 TRM petrol engine introduced on the Ausf E was used in this and all later variants. Early examples of the PzKpfw III Ausf H retained the 50-mm KwK L/42 gun, but later examples were produced with the more capable KwK 39 L/60 weapon of the same calibre (see previous chapter), and this was retrofitted to tanks already in service. By the beginning of the campaign against the USSR in June 1941 some 1,500 PzKpfw III tanks were in service, and these performed creditably in the opening stages of the campaign. Here the experience of the crews and the relative maturity of the basic design swept Soviet armour away without difficulty. But from the end of 1941 the new breed of Soviet tanks, epitomized by the T-34 medium and KV heavy types, began to appear in growing numbers: the Soviet tanks crews were now of better tactical quality, but more importantly the protection of their vehicles proved too thick for effective penetration by the L/42 gun. A crash programme was launched to retrofit the German tanks with the L/60 gun, which entailed a reduction in ammunition capacity from 99 to 84 rounds. To the dismay of the German authorities this longer version of the 50-mm gun also proved inadequate to the task of

tackling the T-34 and KV at all except the point-blank ranges that were seldom achievable on the Eastern Front. A longer-term implication was that Hitler, on learning that his earlier instructions to fit the L/60 weapon had not been obeyed immediately, started to take a more personal interest in the design and manufacture of German tanks, as well as in their deployment and tactical use.

The comparatively small diameter of the PzKpfw III's turret ring now proved the decisive factor in developing a more capable variant: the 50-mm Krupp gun never proved entirely satisfactory, and the turret ring diameter effectively prohibited the installation of a high-velocity gun of greater calibre. All the Germans could do, therefore, was to step up production of better-protected models, in the hope that numbers would provide the Panzer arm with an edge over the Soviet tank force. It was an impossible task, and the PzKpfw III was rapidly overhauled in quality and quantity by Soviet production. At the same time the German tank crews found themselves steadily matched in tactical capability by the USSR's increasingly experienced men. The next production variant was the PzKpfw III Ausf J, which was similar to the Ausf H apart from a reduction in hull and turret vision slots to ease manufacture, and an increase in armour protection from a 30-mm (1.18-in) to a 50-mm (1.97-in) basis, resulting in an increase in weight to 22,300 kg (49,162 lb). The addition of another 700 kg (1,543 lb) of weight without any increase in installed power inevitably entailed a slight but nonetheless significant degradation in cross-country performance and agility.

The next PzKpfw III variant was the PzKpfw III Ausf L, which entered production in 1942, the year in which PzKpfw III production attained 2,600 machines. The PzKpfw III Ausf L was similar to the late-production Ausf J with the L/60 main gun in every external respect but armour, which now included a 20-mm (0.79-in) layer 100 mm (3.94 in) above the superstructure and mantlet. This further increased the nose heaviness already evident in the Ausf J and earlier models retrofitted with the L/60 gun, and a torsion bar compensator was added to the suspension as the coil springs used in addition to the torsion bars of the front road wheels were inadequate for the task. Weight was reduced slightly by the limitation of this model to a maximum of 78 50-mm rounds. The exigencies of the war, especially on the Eastern Front, are reflected in the fact that the photographic record shows the Ausf L with a wide assortment of field modifications designed to provide improved protection. Intended to detonate incoming hollow-charge warheads before the latter reached the critical focus distance from a vulnerable point, skirt armour was a firm favourite: large rectangular plates were attached to the hull sides, extending far enough downward to protect the running gear and sufficiently high to protect the hull/turret junction line, while curved plates were often added round the turret and over the mantlet as additional protection.

In 1942 the PzKpfw III Ausf M also appeared, this being a variant of the Ausf L optimized for mass production by the elimination of the hull vision ports and escape doors. Though the elimination of the hull escape doors might be thought a retrograde step, it should be remembered that these were generally inoperable when essential skirt armour was fitted: at the same time this move allowed a redistribution of ammunition stowage, increasing 50-mm rounds to 98 at the expense of machine-gun rounds, which fell in number from 4,950 to 2,550 rounds. Other features of the Ausf M were a wading capability to a depth of 1.5 m (4.92 ft), and a valve system to allow hot engine coolant to be passed to other tanks with the same system. This was introduced in response to conditions on the Eastern Front, and made it possible for the engine of one tank to warm up that of another as a means of facilitating start-up in cold conditions: it took between 12 and 15 minutes to raise the engine temperature of the cold vehicle by 80° at an exterior temperature of -30°.

Production of the Ausf M continued into the beginning of 1943, but in 1942 the first examples of the ultimate PzKpfw III variant had appeared. This was the PzKpfw III Ausf N, identical to the deep-wading Ausf M in all respects but armament. In July 1942 Hitler had ordered that the Ausf L should be fitted with the obsolescent 75-mm (2.95-in) KwK L/24 gun in place of its existing 50-mm weapon. The German leader's intention was to provide a support tank for heavier tanks such as the PzKpfw VI Tiger, and the designated weapon was the ordnance of early models of the PzKpfw IV, weighing 285 kg (628 lb) and able to fire a 6.75-kg (14.9-lb) APCBC projectile with a muzzle velocity of 385 m (1,263 ft) per second, sufficient to penetrate 41 mm (1.61 in) of armour at an angle of 30° at a range of 500 m (545 yards). But whereas the 50-mm weapon was limited to HE and armour-piercing ammunition, the 75-mm (2.95-in) weapon could fire armour-piercing, HEAT, HE,

A PzKpfw III of the 18th Panzer Division emerges from a Russian river during the summer of 1942. (*MARS*)

The last production version of the PzKpfw III was the Ausf N, similar to the Ausf L in all basic respects except armament, which was a short-barrel 75-mm (2.75-in) weapon suited better to the support than to the anti-tank role. These are Ausf N tanks en route to Germany's Panzer divisions in North Africa. (*MARS*)

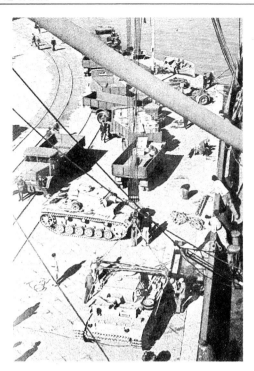

Smoke and Case projectiles, of which 56 rounds were carried in addition to 3,450 machine-gun rounds. The same ordnance was used in the Ausf N, which had revised ammunition stowage for 64 75-mm (2.95-in) rounds. Production amounted to 660 Ausf N tanks in the period from July 1942 to August 1943, the 213 vehicles built in 1943 being modified in production with the definitive *Schürzen* (aprons): this comprised 8-mm (0.315-in) skirts over the running gear and 5-mm (0.2-in) panels round the turret. Further protection was afforded by *Zimmerit* paste, a 100-kg (220-lb) coating of which provided protection against magnetically-attached mines.

Produced in parallel with the PzKpfw III from 1939, and remaining in production to the end of the war, when more than 10,500 had been built, was the Sturmgeschütz III (SdKfz 142/1), an assault gun version of the PzKpfw III with its armament in a fixed superstructure for simplified manufacture and lower overall height. This was armed with a 75-mm (2.95-in) StuK 37 L/24, L/43 or L/48 gun, or in its Sturmhaubitze

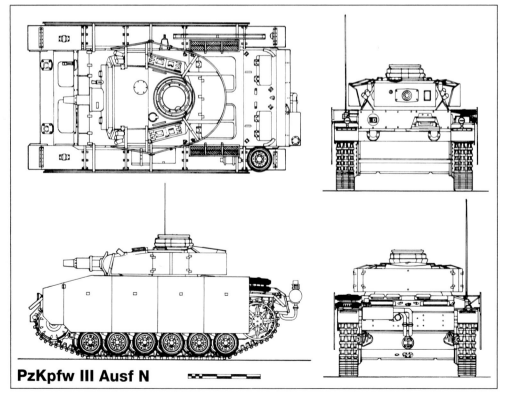

PzKpfw III Ausf N

42 (SdKfz 142/2) form a 105-mm (4.13-in) L/28 howitzer. The PzKpfw III was also adapted for other roles as the Flammpanzer III (SdKfz 141/3) flamethrower with 1,000 litres (220 Imp. gal.) of flame fuel, the Panzerbefehlswagen III (SdKfz 266, 267 and 268) command tank with dummy main armament, and the Panzerbeobachtungswagen III (SdKfz 143) armoured observation vehicle for use by self-propelled artillery units. There was also a submersible version, the PzKpfw III (Tauchfähig) developed for Unternehmen 'Seelöwe' (Operation 'Sealion', the proposed invasion of Southern England): this had all openings sealed with rubber compound, a one-way exhaust valve and a buoyant rubber air hose leading into the turret. The variant was designed to allow the tank to move across the seabed at depths of 7.5 m (24.6 ft), before emerging on to the assault

Panzerkampfwagen III Ausf N (11/ZW) (SdKfz 141/2)
(Germany)

Type: close-support medium tank
Crew: 5
Combat weight: 21,300 kg (46,958 lb)
Dimensions: length overall 5.78 m (18.96 ft) for production vehicles and 5.52 m (17.06 ft) for Ausf L conversions; width 2.97 m (9.74 ft) without skirts and 3.41 m (11.19 ft) with skirts; height overall 2.50 m (8.20 ft)
Armament system: one 75-mm (2.95-in) KwK L/24 rifled gun with 64 rounds in production vehicles and 56 rounds in Ausf L conversions, two 7.92-mm (0.312-in) MG34 machine-guns (one coaxial and one bow) with 3,450 rounds, and six 90-mm (3.54-in) smoke-dischargers; the turret was manually operated, the main gun was stabilized in neither elevation (−8.3° to +20°) nor azimuth (360°), and simple optical sights were fitted
Armour: welded steel varying in thickness between 16 and 70 mm (0.63 and 2.76 in) plus varying levels of additional armour
Powerplant: one 224-kW (300-hp) Maybach HL 120 TRM petrol engine with 320 litres (70.4 Imp. gal.) of fuel
Performance: speed, road 40 km/h (24.9 mph); range, road 155 km (93.3 miles); fording 0.8 m (2.62 ft); gradient 57%; vertical obstacle 0.6 m (1.97 ft); trench 2.2 m (7.22 ft); ground clearance 0.385 m (15.2 in)

beach with great tactical surprise. Some of these vehicles were converted with 3-m (9.84-ft) steel pipes instead of flexible hoses, for river crossing in the first stages of the war against the USSR. Total production of the PzKpfw III was 5,644, and the type's importance in the development of armoured warfare cannot be exaggerated, as it was the primary weapon of the Panzer divisions in their heady days of triumph between 1939 and 1941: the PzKpfw III led the Panzer divisions as they swept through Poland in 1939, the Low Countries and France in 1940, and the Balkans, North Africa and USSR in 1941. For the first time in armoured warfare there was a mass-production battle tank design that could be upgunned without undue difficulty, and the type's combat record speaks for itself in terms of the results that were secured. The lesson was absorbed to the fullest extent by the Americans and British, who had hitherto lagged in considering armoured fighting vehicles as mass-production vehicles, and in the future far greater thought was given to the longer-term production values that allowed the introduction of improved variants with heavier armament. The PzKpfw III also validated the

Production of the PzKpfw III battle tank was halted in late 1943, though the chassis was kept in production as the basis for weapons such as these Sturmgeschütz III assault guns, whose fixed superstructure with limited-traverse mounting for the main armament was simpler and cheaper to produce than the turret of the battle tank. (*MARS*)

147

concept of a common chassis for multiple applications; of the 15,000 or so chassis produced, nearly 9,500 were used as the automotive/structural basis of vehicles other than tanks proper.

The PzKpfw III's partner through the first half of the war was the PzKpfw IV, whose development up to the Ausf E has been covered in the previous chapter. The PzKpfw III had been designed as the spearhead tank of the Panzer divisions, with the PzKpfw IV in support to deal with heavier obstacles: but as the tide of the war began to sway against the Germans, the limitations of the PzKpfw III's armament became clearer: whereas the original concept of relying on a 37-mm main gun but

Details of the running gear and track of a PzKpfw IV medium (support) tank. (*MARS*)

allowing for subsequent revision to a 50-mm weapon had seemed sufficient in the mid-1930s, the situation in 1942 revealed without doubt that the original concept should have called for a 50-mm gun, with subsequent revision to a 75-mm (2.95-in) weapon. By 1942, therefore, the Allies were fielding substantial numbers of tanks with armour generally impervious to 50-mm projectiles at all but the shortest ranges, and as a result the PzKpfw IV with its 75-mm (2.95-in) main gun came increasingly to the fore.

The first definitive variant of the PzKpfw IV was the PzKpfw Ausf F, its importance compared with the earlier SdKfz 161 variants being marked by the allocation of a revised inventory designation, SdKfz 161/1. Though modelled on the preceding Ausf E, this variant was planned with thicker armour and a longer-barrelled 75-mm (2.95-in) main gun. The armour was to a 50-mm (1.97-in) rather than 30-mm (1.18-in) basis with maxima of 60 and 50 mm (2.36 and 1.97 in) respectively on the hull and turret, but the longer ordnance was not ready in time and the standard KwK L/24 gun had to be fitted. The variant was built right through 1941, and weighed 22,300 kg (49,162 lb). When the far superior KwK 40 L/43 gun became available, it was introduced on an Ausf F variant known as the PzKpfw IV Ausf F_2, earlier models being retrospectively redesignated PzKpfw IV Ausf F_1. The Ausf F_2 weighed 23,600 kg (52,028 lb), and its advent marked a high-point in German tank capability. The L/43 ordnance weighed 472 kg (1,041 lb), and fired its 6.8-kg (15-lb) armour-piercing projectile with a muzzle velocity of 740 m (2,428 ft) per second: this provided the projectile with the power to penetrate 89 mm (3.5 in) of armour at an angle of 30° at a range of 500 m (545 yards), translating into just over twice the penetration capability of the L/24 weapon at the same range. German gun power had in the period (1941-1942) fallen below the best provided in American and Soviet tanks, but the L/43 gun restored parity at a time which was crucial to the German war effort. The German army was more than thankful for the restoration of parity, but quite rightly demanded tank gun superiority in the standard 75-mm (2.95-in) calibre: Krupp therefore produced an L/48 version of the KwK 40, the additional five calibres of barrel length adding 24 kg (53 lb) in weight and 38 cm (14.86 in) in overall length. The L/48 weapon thus weighed 496 kg (1,093 lb) and was 3.9 m (153.5 in) long, but as projectile muzzle velocity was boosted to only 750 m (2,461 ft) per second, the armour penetration capability was increased by only 3 mm (0.12 in), to 92 mm (3.62 in) at standard angle and range. The PzKpfw IV was still seen as a dual-role weapon, with anti-tank and support roles to undertake, and this duality is reflected in the KwK 40's ammunition types, which included APCBC, APCR, HEAT, HE and Smoke.

The Ausf F2 was succeeded by the PzKpfw IV Ausf G, which was basically similar to its predecessor apart from detail modifications and improved armour, the latter including a thicker top to the superstructure. Field additions often included spaced frontal armour and *Schürzen* of the types also used in the PzKpfw III's later variants for protection against the hollow-charge warheads carried by Allied weapons such as Soviet anti-tank grenades, American 'bazooka' rocket-launchers and British PIAT spigot-mortar projectors. The L/48 version of the KwK 40 gun was introduced on the PzKpfw IV Ausf H version of this increasingly important tank, which received the revised inventory designation SdKfz 161/2 in recognition of its importance. The Ausf H began to leave the production lines in March 1943, and was similar to the Ausf F2 and Ausf G apart from its use of the longer gun, a revised turret hatch cover, cast rather than fabricated drive sprockets, improved frontal armour of the spaced type, and as a measure of protection for the increasingly vulnerable flanks, 8-mm (0.315-in) turret and 5-mm (0.2-in) skirt armour. This resulted in an increase in combat weight to 25,000 kg (55,115 lb), but the retention of the same 300-hp (224-kW) engine inevitably caused a loss of performance, with the maximum speed 38 km/h (23.6 mph), down slightly from the 40 km/h (24.9 mph) of the preceding models.

By the beginning of 1943 the limitations of the PzKpfw III and PzKpfw IV were clear to field commanders and procurement authorities alike, and in February of that year it was proposed that the PzKpfw IV be entirely sup-

planted in production by the new PzKpfw V Panther and PzKpfw VI Tiger tanks. In essence the notion was correct, but as men such as General Heinz Guderian were swift to point out, production rates of the newer vehicles were so slow that the PzKpfw IV should have been retained to maintain the numerical strength of the Panzer arm in the decisive year of 1943, which in the event saw the strategic initiative swing firmly to the Allied nations, in events such as the German defeat at Stalingrad (February 1943), in North Africa (May 1943), at Kursk and in Sicily (July 1943), and at Salerno (September 1943). Hitler therefore decided that production of the PzKpfw IV should continue at least to the beginning of 1944, and this paved the way for the evolution of the final production variant, the PzKpfw IV Ausf J, that began to reach combat units in March 1944.

The designers had taken the lessons of combat firmly to heart and produced a variant which was easier to produce and more effective in combat, yet lighter than its predecessors, and thus possessed of higher performance combined with greater cross-country agility. The Ausf J had thicker frontal armour, including 80 mm (3.15 in) for the front plate, driver's plate and mantlet, combined with flank protection by wire mesh screens, in place of the heavy skirts of the Ausf F, G and H

The PzKpfw IV Ausf F2 was a comparatively simple evolution from the Ausf F with thicker armour and, most importantly, a long-barrel 75-mm (2.95-in) gun for much enhanced anti-tank capability. This vehicle is somewhat unusual in having a single- rather than double-baffle muzzle brake. (*RAC Tank Museum*)

149

variants. A revised exhaust system was incorporated, as too were a new transmission and provision for wading to a depth of 1.2 m (3.94 ft). Earlier models had been provided with a power system plus manual back-up for turret traverse, but in the Ausf J the power traverse system was removed (and the manual system made a two-speed geared unit) to provide greater fuel capacity. The Ausf J was thus a more capable machine than the Ausf H, and remained in production right to the end of the Second World War, the total for the two models reaching almost 6,000 chassis (from a total of 9,000 PzKpfw IV tanks) in the last two years of the war. The PzKpfw IV fought on every German front in the Second World War, and proved itself one of the most important tanks ever produced. Though it was always armed with a 75-mm (2.95-in) main gun, the adoption of longer-barrelled ordnance of this calibre allowed the designers to keep the tank current with most Western and many Soviet tanks, and when properly handled the PzKpfw IV was still a capable adversary right to the end of the war. Like the PzKpfw III, the PzKpfw IV is also of significance for its well-proved chassis, which was adopted for many other tracked vehicles such as the StuPz 43 (Sturmpanzer IV Brummbär, SdKfz 166) heavy assault gun with a 150-mm (5.91-in) assault howitzer, the Jagdpanzer IV (SdKfz 162/1) tank destroyer with a 75-mm (2.95-in) high-velocity gun, the Flakpanzer IV Wirbelwind anti-aircraft vehicle with four 20-mm cannon, and a number of self-propelled artillery mountings.

As early as 1937 the Germans had begun to consider a new generation of tanks to succeed the PzKpfw III and PzKpfw IV. Conscious that contemporary development was leading to heavier tanks with thicker armour and more powerful armament, the Germans thought in terms of a 30-tonne successor to the 24-tonne PzKpfw IV, thereby taking the new tank into the category which at the time was considered heavy. A vehicle in this weight bracket had already found expression in the VK6501 prototype, designed in 1936 and 1937 and built in uncompleted prototype form between 1938 and 1940, as the basis of a proposed assault tank with a 75-mm (2.95-in) gun in the main turret and 7.92-mm (0.312-in) machine-guns in auxiliary turrets. The project was to have led to a PzKpfw VII heavy tank, but was cancelled in 1940 and is most interesting for its running gear, which included seven interleaved road wheels of medium diameter. At this time the German army was highly satisfied with the versatility of the new PzKpfw IV, and was content to opt for the exploitation of this major type's development potential, rather than the creation of a wholly-new type. The army had little reason to doubt the wisdom of its decision until the last quarter of 1941, when the German forces driving towards Moscow began to encounter small but increasing numbers of a new Soviet tank designated T-34, which immediately displayed itself superior to the PzKpfw IV in all aspects of firepower, protection and mobility. It was also clear to a worried German army that this was a new tank, already mature in its mechanical aspects, yet still full of development potential in terms of firepower and protection.

On 20 November 1941 a German investigation team assessed a captured T-34 and came to the conclusion that the Soviet tank had significant advantages over German tanks in its sloped armour, its large road wheels and its long gun. The sloping of the armour offered an effective increase in thickness, without the weight penalty of vertical protection of that actual thickness; the large road wheels offered a superior ride, especially across country; and the long gun, hitherto rejected by the Germans as impractical for a number of reasons, offered very high muzzle velocity and therefore a devastating armour-penetration capability. The inevitable conclusion was that all current German tanks were obsolete in the technical sense, and an immediate programme was launched to produce a counter to the T-34: within five days the German armaments ministry contracted with Daimler-Benz and MAN for VK3002 designs to meet a specification that demanded a 30/35-tonne battle tank with a 75-mm (2.95-in) main gun, well-sloped armour to a maximum thickness of 40 mm (1.57 in) on the sides and 60 mm (2.36 in) on the front, and a maximum speed of 55 km/h (34.1 mph). In January 1942 the specification was revised to include a 60-km/h (37.3-mph) maximum speed and frontal armour of 60 mm

The PzKpfw IV Ausf G was modelled on the Ausf F$_2$ but had improved armour including a thickened upper surface to the superstructure. (*IWM*)

(2.36 in) on the hull and 100 mm (3.94 in) on the turret.

The VK3002(DB) and VK3002(MAN) designs were completed in April 1943. The VK3002(DB) was essentially a Germanicized copy of the T-34, with the turret located so far forward that the driver sat inside the turret cage and had to use a hydraulically operated remote steering system. The gun mantlet was effectively a continuation of the glacis plate, the fighting compartment was large and uncluttered, and the Daimler-Benz MB 507 diesel engine was located in the rear compartment: the use of a diesel offered considerable advantages in terms of range, safety and continued availability of fuel, should Germany's supply problem with more refined petrol become acute (as of course it did). External but jettisonable fuel tanks were envisaged for the combination of range with safety, the drive sprockets were at the rear, and to ease production the interleaved road wheels were designed without rubber tyres and fitted with leafspring rather than torsion bar suspension. All in all, the VK3002(DB) was a design of great potential, and an order for 200 was placed at the express instruction of Hitler, whose only demand was that the planned 75-mm (2.95-in) L/48 gun of Krupp design should be replaced

by a Rheinmetall L/70 weapon of the same calibre. Prototype construction was started soon after the placement of the order, but was cancelled in the later months of 1942.

The armament ministry, on the other hand, preferred the VK3002(MAN), which was a more specifically German solution to the requirement, was powered by a proved petrol engine and, in the short term at least, was better suited to German production practices.

The VK3002(MAN) had a basic layout similar to that of the PzKpfw IV, with the driver and radio operator/bow machine-gunner in the forward compartment, the commander, gunner and loader in the fighting compartment located in the centre of the vehicle, and the Maybach HL 210 engine in the rear compartment but powering forward drive sprockets for the comparatively wide tracks, which ran over an assembly, on each side, of eight interleaved road wheels with torsion bar suspension. The new vehicle was considerably more powerful than earlier German tanks, having more than twice the horsepower of the PzKpfw IV, and a special gearbox was developed to allow optimum use to be made of this potential for high speed and good cross-country performance. The rubber-tyred road wheels were of sufficiently great diameter that there was no

151

range of 1,000 m (1,095 yards)

Mild steel prototypes of the MAN design were ordered in May 1942, and such was the importance allocated to the programme that the army ministry's chief tank designer, Dipl. Ing. Kniepkampf, was seconded to MAN to supervise the whole project.

The first prototype of the VK3002(MAN) appeared in September 1942. It was immediately launched on a large-scale evaluation programme, and such was the seriousness of Germany's armour position on the Eastern Front (compounded by technical problems with the new PzKpfw VI Tiger heavy tank) that the type was ordered into immediate production as the PzKpfw V Panther (SdKfz 171). The first production Panther appeared in November 1942, and though production was envisaged at the rate of 250 vehicles per month, this already ambitious figure was almost immediately raised to 600 Panthers per month. This figure was never achieved, despite the launch of a large-scale co-production system involving four major manufacturers, and the 1944 monthly average was 330, leading to an overall total of 5,590 Panthers by the end of the Second World War, including 1,850 in the first year of production and 3,740 between January 1944 and May 1945. An additional 679 chassis were completed for use in roles such as recovery (the Bergepanzer Panther, or Bergepanther), command (Befehlspanzer Panther), artillery observation (Beobachtungspanzer Panther) and tank destroying (Panzerjäger Panther, or Jagdpanther).

The German army's maximum weight limit of 35 tonnes had proved impossible to meet, and the Panther turned the scales at a weight of 45,500 kg (100,309 lb) from its service debut, remaining at about this figure throughout its career. This weight was attributable mostly to Hilter's insistence on thicker armour, and as a result plans were laid for use of the bored-out HL 230 in place of the originally specified HL 210 engine: even so the reduced maximum speed of 45 km/h (28 mph) had to be accepted.

The first 20 Panthers were designated PzKpfw V Panther Ausf A, and were in reality pre-production machines with the 60-mm (2.36-in) frontal armour demanded by the

need for track-return rollers. The turret was located as far back as possible to reduce the type of mobility and tactical problems that might otherwise have been caused by a long barrel overhang of the L/60 gun originally planned for the vehicle: this problem would have been acute with the forward-mounted turret of the VK3002(DB), especially when the failure of the L/60 gun led to the adoption of the yet-longer L/70 main armament derived from that which had been under development for the PzKpfw VI Tiger since July 1941: the armament specification called for an armour-penetration capability of 140 mm (5.51 in) at a

original specification, a 642-hp (479-kW) HL 210 engine, a ZF-7 rather than the definitive AK 7-200 gearbox, an early model of the L/70 main gun, and the commander's cupola at the extreme left of the Rheinmetall turret. Considerable development work was undertaken with these first Panthers, which were redesigned PzKpfw V Panther Ausf D_1 early in 1943. The proposed second and third production models were the Ausf B with a Maybach Olvar gearbox, and the Ausf C, of which no details have been found. Trials with the Ausf A revealed a number of problems, but the importance of the programme was such that no delay in the overall production programme was authorized to allow a full examination and rectification of the deficiencies before they were built into service tanks. The problem stemmed mostly from the rushed development of the Panther, which was considerably heavier and more powerful than first planned, without significant modification of the gearbox, cooling system and running gear. The most important of these problems were failures in the bolts attaching the rubber tyres to the road wheels (entailing the removal of up to

five complete wheels when an inner wheel failed), failure of the final drive gears (often causing transmission gear, differential and steering failures) and engine overheating.

The first real production variant was therefore the PzKpfw V Panther Ausf D, which was redesignated PzKpfw V Panther Ausf D_2 at the same time that the Ausf A became the Ausf D_1. The type appeared in January 1943, and featured the standard type of 'dustbin' cupola, a vision port and machine-gun port in the glacis plate, the definitive L/70 main gun with a double-baffle muzzle brake to reduce recoil distance in an already cramped turret, smoke-dischargers on each side of the turret and, on later-production examples, skirt armour added during construction, together with a coating of *Zimmerit* anti-mine paste; these later vehicles also had a grenade-launcher above the turret (operated by the loader) in place of the flanking smoke-dischargers.

The next variant appeared in July 1943, and should have been the Ausf E, but for reasons which remain unexplained was in fact designated the PzKpfw V Panther Ausf A. This incorporated features that had been omitted to

Far left An overhead view of a German production facility reveals the basically simple lines of the PzKpfw V Panther battle tank. The hull was made of panels of machinable-quality homogeneous armour plate, whose separate panels were mortised together and welded. The heaviest armour was the glacis plate, which was 80-mm (3.15-in) thick and angled at 33° to the horizontal. (*Bundesarchiv*)

Allied infantrymen in Italy during 1944 pause for an interested examination of a captured PzKpfw Panther Ausf D_2. This has the later pattern of commander's cupola with lifting and swinging hatch but no hull machine-gun mounting. Notable are the coating of *Zimmerit* anti-magnetic mine paste, and the 75-mm (2.95-in) projectile resting on the glacis plate. (*RAC Tank Museum*)

speed production of the Ausf D_2 in preparation for the Germans' last-throw effort in July 1943 to regain the strategic initiative on the Eastern Front in the Battle of Kursk, the world's largest-ever tank battle. Kursk was the Panther's combat debut, most available vehicles serving with one army and three SS divisions of the 4th Panzerarmee: when they ran properly the Panthers were more than a match for the Soviets' T-34s, but they seldom ran for more than a few miles without a mechanical problem. The Panthers had been rushed into service so quickly that there was no adequate recovery vehicle, and as many as three large half-tracks were required to extricate a broken-down Panther. Hitler's insistence on use of the Panthers at Kursk was a profound error, forced on a reluctant army: used in small numbers by crews inexperienced with the type and therefore little able to overcome the type's lack of mechanical maturity, the Panthers had little tactical impact, but were revealed prematurely as the potent weapons they were to become, allowing the Soviets to develop counter-tactics in good time.

The Ausf A introduced the definitive commander's cupola, with better ballistic shaping and armoured periscopes, a fully-engineered ball mounting for the hull machine-gun, a monocular rather than binocular gunner's sight in the turret, and elimination of all turret pistol spent-case ejection ports.

The final production variant of the original Panther series was the PzKpfw Panther Ausf G, designated simply thus as Hitler had on 27 February 1944 ordered the roman numeral in the original designation to be omitted. The origins of this model lay with the February 1942 instruction of the German armaments ministry that MAN was to co-operate with Henschel in the development of a Panther variant incorporating as many PzKpfw VI Tiger components as possible. The programme would have resulted in the Panther II Ausf F with the interleaved steel wheels of the Tiger II, thicker armour on the hull top, a turret modelled on that of the Tiger Ausf B with stereoscopic rangefinder and gun stabilization system, the higher-rated AK 7-400 gearbox, and greater power in the form of the HL 230 rated to 800 hp (596 kW) with petrol injection

and a higher compression ratio, and to 900 hp (671 kW) with a supercharger. The *Panzerturm schmal* (small tank turret) was designed by Daimler-Benz to accommodate L/70 or even L/100 versions of the KwK 42, or the 88-mm (3.46-in) KwK 43 L/71 gun as used in the Tiger II.

The Panther II would have entered production in the summer of 1945, and would probably have been a truly devastating weapon had the war gone into the autumn and winter of that year. Fortunately for the Allies, Germany was defeated before the Panther II could be developed, and its only feature to appear in the interim Panther Ausf G was the Tiger's resilient steel wheel, which finally solved the Panther's long-term problem with shed tyres. Other modifications were revised and thicker hull sides, inclined at a greater angle, a modified mantlet of simpler construction, elimination of the driver's vision port, revised stowage arrangements (including main am-

---

Panzerkampfwagen Panther Ausf G (SdKfz 171)
(Germany)

Type: battle tank
Crew: 5
Combat weight: 45,300 kg (88,868 lb)
Dimensions: length, gun forward 8.86 m (29.07 ft) and hull 6.935 m (22.75 ft); width 3.27 m (10.73 ft); height overall 2.995 m (9.83 ft)
Armament system: one 75-mm (2.95-in) KwK 42 L/70 rifled gun with 79 rounds, two or three 7.92-mm (0.3-in) MG34 machine guns (one coaxial, one bow and one optional AA) with 4,500 rounds, and one 92-mm (3.62-in) Nahverteidgunswaffe bomb/grenade launcher; the turret was hydraulically operated, the main gun was stabilized in neither elevation (–4° to +20°) nor azimuth (360°), and simple optical sights were fitted
Armour: welded steel varying in thickness between 13 and 120 mm (0.51 and 4.72 in)
Powerplant: one 522-kW (700-hp) Maybach HL 230 P30 petrol engine with 730 litres (160.6 Imp. gal.) of fuel
Performance: speed, road 45.7 km/h (28.4 mph); range, road 200 km (124 miles); fording 1.9 m (6.23 ft); gradient 70%; vertical obstacle 0.9 m (2.95 ft); trench 2.45 m (8.04 ft); ground clearance 0.56 m (22 in)

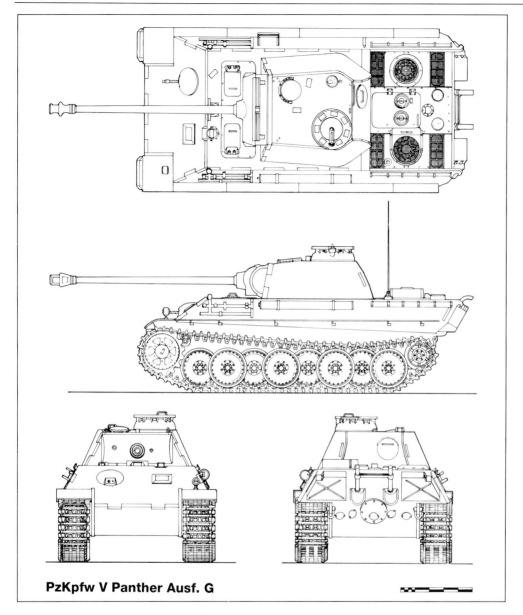

PzKpfw V Panther Ausf. G

munition capacity increased from 79 to 82 rounds) and a number of detail modifications, such as better attachments for the skirt armour, which had often been pulled off in woods.

The most famous of the Panther's variants was the Jagdpanther, more formally known as the Panzerjäger Panther (SdKfz 173), a potent tank destroyer with the classic 88-mm (3.46-in) PaK 43/3 anti-tank gun mounted in a limited-traverse mounting in the forward face of the fixed superstructure.

It is hard to overestimate the importance of the Panther to armoured warfare in the Second World War, or to the development of the tank since that time. An indication of the Panther's capabilities is that its frontal armour was impenetrable to the projectiles of the Allies' main gun tanks, while its own manoeuvrability and gun power allowed it to knock out the

155

Allied tanks from stand-off range. One American estimate suggests that one Panther required the attentions of at least five M4 Sherman tanks if it was to be successfully engaged, with a decisive flank or rear shot by one of the US tanks: otherwise the Allies' best course of action when facing a Panther was to try for a mobility kill, halting the tank with a blow to its trackwork.

The largest German tanks to see combat in the Second World War were the variants of the PzKpfw VI Tiger series, which first appeared before the PzKpfw V Panther but are treated after it because of their later numerical designation. In 1937 the German army appreciated the high qualities of its new PzKpfw III battle and PzKpfw IV medium tanks, but also realized that a heavier tank might form a useful adjunct in the assault role. In that year, therefore, Henschel received an order for two prototypes of a 30/33-tonne heavy tank designated DW.1 (the prefix standing for *Durchbruchswagen* or breakthrough vehicle). The design emerged as a massive machine with interleaved road wheels, and testing of the first prototype hull was well under way when Henschel was instructed to drop the concept and devote its energies instead to a truly huge design, the VK6501. This was to be a 65-tonne machine armed with a 75-mm (2.95-in) main gun plus a secondary armament of machine-guns in separate turrets: evolved conceptually and mechanically from the PzKpfw NbFz (PzKpfw V), the VK6501 was planned for production as the PzKpfw VII, but was cancelled in 1940 even as the two prototype chassis were being tested. The emphasis now returned to a heavy tank derived from the DW.1, which Henschel had refined into the DW.2 with a weight of 32,000 kg (70,547 lb), a crew of five, and an armament of one short-barrel 75-mm (2.95-in) gun and two 7.92-mm (0.312-in) machine guns. Trials with the DW.2 continued into 1941, but more definitive plans had already matured with the German official hierarchy during 1940, which made the DW.2 obsolete as a contender for production orders. These plans called for a 30-tonne breakthrough tank armed with a 75-mm (2.95-in) main gun, and after design proposals had been solicited from Daimler-Benz,

Henschel, MAN and Porsche, orders were placed with two companies for eight prototypes (four from each company): the Henschel machine was the VK3001(H) and the Porsche machine the VK3001(P).

The VK3001(H) was a logical development from the DW.2, and the four prototypes appeared in March 1941 (first two) and October 1941 (last two), differing from each other only in detail. The superstructure was similar to that of the PzKpfw IV, and the running gear comprised, on each side, seven interleaved road wheels with three track-return rollers. The armament was the 75-mm (2.95-in) KwK 40 L/48 gun, but as the prototypes were being evaluated, the T-34 made its appearance on the Eastern Front and at a stroke rendered obsolete any German plans for a new tank with the 75-mm (2.95-in) gun, which was patently inferior to the 76.2-mm (3-in) weapon of the Soviet tank. Whereas the VK3001(H) was competely orthodox in its concept and mechanical features, the same cannot be said of the VK3001(P) from the innovative Dr Ferdinand Porsche, who called his creation the Typ 100 Leopard. This resembled the VK3001(H) in overall design, but its running gear on each side comprised six road wheels and two track-return rollers, the suspension was of the longitudinal rather than transverse torsion bar type, and power was provided by a novel petrol-electric drive system. Daimler-Benz and MAN also produced prototypes, but these are believed not to have progressed as far as the Henschel and Porsche types, which were in any event never fitted with their turrets. The VK3001 concept was shown to be obsolete by the advent of the T-34, and the Germans sensibly cancelled further work on the prototypes.

The Germans had been working concurrently on a heavier tank concept largely to satisfy the demands of Hitler, who was developing into a firm advocate of heavy tanks with powerful armament and protection. The German leader had been impressed by aspects of the technical reports about the British and French infantry-support tanks encountered by the German forces in the Western campaign of May and June 1940, especially the extent of their armour protection. This had proved invulnerable to the German tank guns of the period, and Hitler now sought to provide the German forces with tanks providing a comparable level of protection with decisively heavier firepower and adequate mobility. For firepower, Hitler's demand was a weapon capable of penetrating 100 mm (3.94 in) of armour at a range of 1,500 m (1,640 yards), and in line with the standard German practice of the time the tank was to be protected against a comparable weapon. The German leader's first choice for the main gun was a tank development of the 88-mm (3.46-in) FlaK 36 dual-role anti-aircraft and anti-tank gun, while the German ordnance department held out for a smaller-calibre weapon using the tapered-bore concept of barrel and ammunition design to provide the same armour-penetration capability: the use of a 60- or 75-mm (2.36- or 2.95-in) weapon, the department argued, would allow stowage of a larger number of rounds in any given volume, and also allow a reduction in tank size and weight, with consequent advantages in cost and performance.

It was decided to produce a 36-tonne prototype with the tapered-bore gun and the designation VK3601(H). But the tapered-bore gun required considerable quantities of increasingly scarce tungsten, and was cancelled by Hitler at about the time the VK3001 and VK3601 concepts were halted in favour of an altogether larger 45-tonne tank ordered in the form of competing VK4501(H) and VK4501(P) prototypes in May 1941. The contracts stipulated that the prototypes should be ready for Hitler's birthday on 20 April 1942: each type was to use a Krupp-designed turret accommodating the 88-mm (3.46-in) KwK 36 L/56 gun. Henschel used features of its VK3001 and VK3601 prototypes in the VK3601(H), which was proposed as the VK3601(H1) with the Krupp turret and an 88-mm (3.46-in) gun, and as the VK3601(H2) with a Rheinmetall turret and a 75-mm (2.95-in) KwK 42 L/70 gun. The H2 variant was never built and the first prototypes of the VK3601(H1) variant appeared in March 1942. The tank was modelled on the VK3001, though the road wheels were of larger diameter, thereby removing the need for track-return rollers.

The VK4501(P) appeared in the following month, and was modelled on the VK3001(P)

with the same type of petrol-electric drive and longitudinal torsion bar suspension. Comparative trials confirmed the overall superiority of the VH4501(H), though it was as much as 11,000 kg (24,250 lb) over legend weight, and in August 1942 the type was ordered into production under the designation PzKpfw VI Tiger Ausf H (SdKfz 181) with the KwK 36 gun. This weighed 1,330 kg (2,932 lb), and its L/56 barrel provided for a muzzle velocity of 810 m (2,657 ft) per second, sufficient to give the 9.4-kg (20.72-lb) APCBC projectile the ability to penetrate 112 mm (4.4 in) of armour at an angle of 30° at a range of 500 m (545 yards). Combined with stowage for 92 rounds, this provided the Tiger with an anti-tank capability unmatched anywhere in the world at that time.

A back-up order was placed for 90 examples of the Porsche design as the PzKpfw VI VK4501(P) Tiger (P), in case the Henschel type should encounter problems. Once it had become clear that the Henschel Tiger was proceeding without difficulty, these chassis were modified during construction into tank destroyers, with the designation Panzerjäger Tiger (P) Ferdinand (SdKfz 184), though the name was subsequently changed to Elefant. This was armed with an 88-mm (3.46-in) PaK 43/2 L/71 gun in a fixed superstructure, and made its debut in the Battle of Kursk. Here it suffered heavy losses due to mechanical failures and its total lack of defensive machine-gun armament, which allowed Soviet pioneers to attack it with virtual impunity.

Production of the Tiger lasted exactly two years from August 1942 to August 1944, and in that time production totalled 1,350 vehicles. Production peaked in April 1944, when 104 vehicles were delivered: the original rate planned by the armaments ministry had been 12 vehicles per month, but at Hitler's insistence this had been increased to 25 vehicles per month by November 1942, increasing as the type proved itself in combat as an exceptional gun tank. In February 1944 the designation was revised, and the vehicle then became the PzKpfw Tiger Ausf E (SdKfz 181), this change being contemporary with a modification of the production standard to include a new cupola, simplified fittings and resilient steel wheels in place of the original type with rubber tyres.

The Tiger was a truly massive machine, and its design epitomizes the design of the classic 'German tank' of the Second World War: this was evolved before the T-34 hammered home the advantages of sloped armour (as copied by the Germans in the Panther), and the Tiger was thus the next in logical sequence from the PzKpfw IV with basically upright armour. In so large and heavy a machine, the designers were faced with acute problems of hull rigidity, especially against the torsional effect of recoil when the gun was fired at any angle off the centreline. For this reason the basic structure made use of the largest possible one-piece plates: the 26-mm (1.02-in) belly plate, for example, was a single piece some 1.8 m (5.9 ft) wide and 4.85 m (15.9 ft) long, and the interlocking armour plates were all welded. The curved sides and rear of the turret were made of a single piece of armour 80 mm (3.15 in) thick bent into a horseshoe shape and connected across the front by a 100 mm (3.94 in)

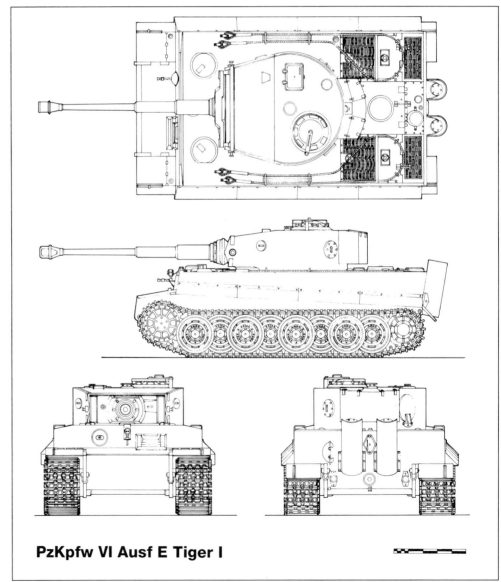

PzKpfw VI Ausf E Tiger I

Panzerkampfwagen Tiger Ausf E (SdKfz 181)
(Germany)

Type: heavy battle tank

Crew: 5

Combat weight: 56,900 kg (125,441 lb)

Dimensions: length, gun forward 8.46 m (27.76 ft) and hull 6.32 m (20.73 ft); width 3.73 m (12.24 ft); height overall 2.90 m (9.51 ft)

Armament system: one 88-mm (3.46-in) KwK 36 L/56 rifled gun with 92 rounds, two or three 7.92-mm (0.312-in) MG34 machine-guns (one coaxial, one bow and one optional AA) with 5,100 rounds, and three smoke-dischargers on each side of the turret or one 92-mm (3.62-in) Nahverteidgunswaffe bomb/grenade launcher; the turret was hydraulically operated, the main gun was stabilized in neither elevation (− 6.5° to + 17°) nor azimuth (360°), and simple optical sights were fitted

Armour: welded steel varying in thickness between 26 and 110 mm (1.02 and 4.33 in)

Powerplant: one 478.7-kW (642-hp) Maybach HL 210 P45 (first 250 vehicles) or 517.4-kW (694-hp) Maybach HL 230 P45 petrol engine with 567 litres (124.7 Imp. gal.) of fuel

Performance: speed, road 37 km/h (23 mph); range, road 117 km (72.7 miles); fording 1.22 m (4.0 ft) without preparation or 4.0 m (13.1 ft) with snorkel; gradient 70%; vertical obstacle 0.79 m (2.59 ft); trench 2.3 m (7.55 ft); ground clearance 0.43 m (16.9 in)

Above The scene in a German tank factory as the hull of a PzKpfw Tiger is inched forward towards its tracks. (*MARS*)

Left Seen in the form of a captured vehicle under test in the USA, the PzKpfw Tiger Ausf E was a highly impressive heavy tank. The blocky hull and cylindrical turret offered excellent protection through weight of metal rather than careful ballistic shaping, but the dominant feature is the large 88-mm (3.46-in) gun with its muzzle brake. (*RAC Tank Museum*)

front plate whose opening for the gun was protected by a 110-mm (4.33-in) mantlet. The whole impression conveyed by the vehicle was of angular strength, and this impression is confirmed by the armour inclination (at the most, 24° from the vertical) and thickness, varying from 26 mm (1.02 in) on the belly and hull roof via 60 mm (2.36 in) on the lower sides, and 82 mm (3.23 in) on the upper sides and rear, to 100 mm (3.94 in) on the nose and front plate. This gives a good indication of how a combat weight of 55,000 kg (121,252 lb) or more was reached. The movement of this mass required considerable power: the first 250 vehicles had the 642-hp (479-kW) Maybach HL 210 P45 petrol engine, and the rest the 694-hp (517.5-kW) HL 230 P45 from the same manufacturer. The engine drove the forward drive sprockets via the coupled preselector gearbox/regenerative steering system, and in each side the running gear comprised eight large-diameter road wheels, with the idler to their rear. These were the first interleaved road wheels used on a German service tank, and provided an admirable ride: their main fault appeared in the winter, when the slush and mud, caught between the wheels, tended to freeze overnight and thus immobilize the tank at a time the Soviets therefore found tactically advantageous for any attack. The driver and bow machine-gunner/radio operator were located in the forward compartment, the commander, gunner and loader in the centrally-located fighting compartment, and the engine in the rear compartment. Other tactical limitations with the Tiger were the use of hydraulic power from an engine-driven motor for turret traverse, meaning that the heavy turret had to be moved in secondary manual mode when the engine was shut down, and the prodigious thirst of the engine, which consumed the maximum 570 litres (125 Imp. gal.) of petrol in only 120 km (74 miles) on roads, or 70 km (43.5 miles) across country. This short range was an added inducement to use the Tiger as an ambush rather than mobile warfare tank, and the high points of its career were thus in the close-country campaigns, such as those waged in Normandy (June and July 1944) and the Ardennes (December 1944).

Impressed with the offensive potential of the new vehicle, Hitler overruled his army commanders and demanded that the Tiger should be rushed into action as soon as possible, even if this meant its deployment in penny packets and the sacrifice of surprise at all but the very lowest tactical level. Given its weight and high ground pressure of 1.04 kg/cm^2 (14.8 lb/sq in), even on its 715-mm (28.15-in) wide combat tracks, rising to 1.43 kg/cm^2 (20.4 lb/sq in) on the special 515-mm (20.28-in) wide transport tracks, the Tiger was best suited to operations on firm ground offering the possibility of ambush positions where the Tiger's powerful protection and devasting armament would give it a decided tactical advantage over numerically superior Allied types. As it was, the Tiger was first committed in unsuitable terrain outside Leningrad in September 1942, and suffered a high proportion of losses to the Soviets' carefully sited and extremely potent anti-tank defences. The Tigers were organized in 30-strong battalions, at first under command of corps or army headquarters; it was later planned to provide all Panzer divisions with an organic Tiger battalion, but in fact only the more favoured of SS Panzer divisions received such a battalion.

The only three Tiger variants were the Panzerbefehlswagen Tiger Ausf E command tank, which was produced in SdKfz 267 and SdKfz 268 variants with additional radio equipment, the Bergepanzer Tiger Ausf E (SdKfz 185) recovery vehicle, and the Sturmtiger assault weapon with a 380-mm (14.96-in) mortar in a fixed superstructure

At about the time that the Tiger entered production, the Germans decided to develop a new model with better armament and protection, in case the Soviets produced another surprise after the T-34. Again Henschel and Porsche were asked to develop competing designs with sloped armour and the new KwK 43 88-mm (3.46-in) gun. This weapon was considerably heavier and longer than the KwK 36, at a weight of 1,690 kg (3,726 lb) and a length of 6.68 m (263.0 in) compared with 5.32 m (209.45 in), but its L/71 barrel provided for a muzzle velocity of 1,020 m (3,346 ft) per second for the ability to penetrate 182 mm (7.17 in) of armour at an angle of 30° at a

The PzKpfw VI Tiger II Ausf B, otherwise known as the Köningstiger (King Tiger) was magnificently armed and armoured, but suffered from its great weight in terms of agility and performance. (*RAC Tank Museum*)

range of 500 m (545 yards) with its 10.2-kg (22.49-lb) APCBC projectile.

Porsche responded with the VK4502(P), based on the VK4501(P) but carrying a beautifully-shaped turret offering excellent ballistic protection and at first intended for a 150-mm (5.91-in) L/37 or 105-mm (4.13-in) L/70 gun, but then revised in line with the army's thinking of the period to an 88-mm (3.46-in) L/71 gun. The VK4502(P) was thought the likely winner by Porsche, who organised the casting process for the turret before the receipt of any production order: but whereas the petrol-electric drive of the VK4501(P) had been rejected largely for its novelty, the basically similar system of the VK4502(P) was now rejected because the copper required for its electric motors was, by late 1943, in very short supply, and likely to get still scarcer.

The winning design was therefore Henschel's VK4503(H), though the first 50 production vehicles were fitted with the Porsche turret before the comparable Henschel type became standard: the Porsche turret was recognizable by the cut-away lower edge of the turret front, which created a dangerous shot trap between the gun and the roof of the hull; the Henschel turret had a straight front dropping right down to the hull roof, without the Porsche turret's dangerous re-entrant. The Henschel design had been completed later than anticipated, the delay to October 1943 being attributable mainly to the armament

ministry's desire to standardize as many parts as possible between the new tank and the planned Panther II. Henschel thereby lost a considerable amount of time in liaison with MAN. Production finally began in December 1943 alongside the Tiger (now sometimes known as the Tiger I to differentiate it from its more powerful companion), and the type began to enter service in spring 1944, first seeing action on the Eastern Front in May 1944. Production continued to the end of the Second World War, and amounted to 485 vehicles known to the Allies as the Royal Tiger or King Tiger, to the German soldiers as the Königstiger (King Tiger), and to German officialdom as the PzKpfw VI Tiger II Ausf B (SdKfz 182), revised at about the time of the tank's introduction, to PzKpfw Tiger II Ausf B (SdKfz 182).

To a certain extent the Tiger II should be regarded as the heavyweight counterpart to the Panther, rather than as a successor to the Tiger, and certainly the Tiger II had similarities to the Panther in its configuration, sloped armour and similar powerplant. This comprised a 694-hp (517-kW) Maybach HL 230 P30 petrol engine for a 69,700-kg (153,660-lb) vehicle, considerably heavier than the Panther at 45,500 kg (100,309 lb) and the Tiger I at 55,000 kg (121,252 lb). The results were inevitable: reduced performance and agility as the power-to-weight ratio was poorer than those of the Panther and Tiger, unreliability as

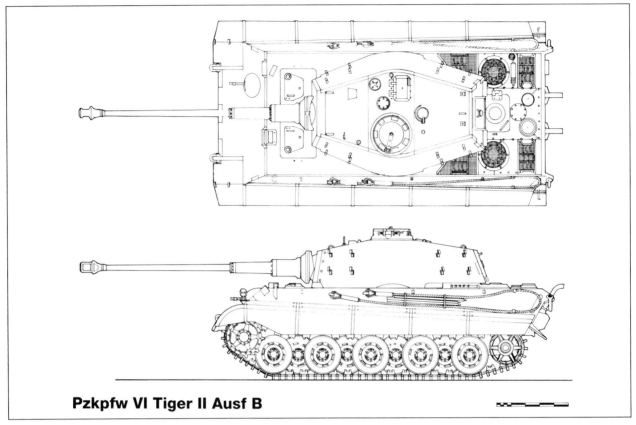

Pzkpfw VI Tiger II Ausf B

PzKpfw VI Tiger Ausf B (SdKfz 182 Königstiger)
(Germany)

Type: heavy battle tank
Crew: 5
Combat weight: 69,750 kg (153,770 lb)
Dimensions: length, gun forward 10.43 m (34.21 ft) and hull 7.25 m (23.79 ft); width 3.72 m (12.20 ft); height 3.27 m (10.73 ft)
Armament system: one 88-mm (3.46-in) gun with 84 rounds and two 7.92-mm (0.3-in) MG34 machine-guns with 4,800 rounds
Armour: between 40 and 185 mm (1.57 and 7.28 in)
Powerplant: one 447-kW (600-hp) Maybach HL 230 P30 petrol engine with 865 litres (190 Imp. gal.) of fuel
Performance: speed, road 38 km/h (24 mph); range, road 110 km (68.4 miles); fording 1.625 m (5.33 ft); gradient 70%; vertical obstacle 0.85 m (2.79 ft); trench 2.5 m (8.2 ft); ground clearance 0.49 m (19.3 in)

the engine and transmission were overstressed, and a dismal maximum range of 110 km (68 miles). These failings were perhaps excusable in a tank now used for defensive warfare, its sole offensive outing being the 'Battle of the Bulge' of December 1944, when many Tiger IIs were abandoned by their crews when they broke down or ran out of petrol.

On the credit side, however, the Tiger II was the best-armed and best-protected tank of the Second World War. The construction of the vehicle was of welded and well-sloped armour, varying in thickness from a minimum of 25 mm (0.98 in) on the belly to a maximum of 150 mm (5.91 in) on the hull upper front; the turret was also welded of armour up to 100 mm (3.94 in) thick. The internal layout was standard, with the driver and bow machine-gunner/radio operator in the forward compartment, the commander, gunner and loader in the central fighting compartment, and the engine plus associated transmission in the rear compartment. As in the Tiger I, the massive turret was

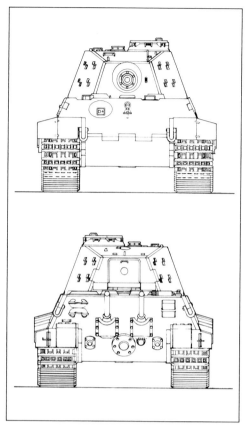

hydraulically powered from the engine, with manual operation for back-up and on those occasions on which the engine was shut down.

The only Tiger II variant was the almost incredibly powerful Panzerjäger Tiger Ausf B, a tank destroyer with armour to a maximum thickness of 250 mm (9.84 in) and a fixed superstructure accommodating a 128-mm (5.04-in) PaK 44 L/55 high-velocity gun firing a 28.3-kg (62.4-lb) armour-piercing shell. This vehicle weighed 71,700 kg (158,069 lb) but retained the standard HL 230 P30 engine, resulting in yet further problems of reliability and mobility. Only a few were placed in service, but these proved truly formidable weapons when they had fuel and worked properly. Fuel was a constant problem for the Germans in the last year of the war, and the problem became decisively acute in the five months of war during 1945. Germany's massive tanks of the Panther and Tiger series were good vehicles, using their firepower and protection to counter the Allies' numerical

superiority in armoured vehicles of all types, but were finally immobilized for want of petrol. The significance of these operational tanks is proved by the interest with which captured examples were examined by the victorious Western Allies, their many good features being assessed for incorporation into the new generation of post-war tanks demanded by the American and British tanks.

A not inconsiderable proportion of Germany's tank development effort in the Second World War was absorbed by projects that were patently non-starters in the tactical sense. The two projects that got furthest along the development road were also the largest tanks proposed in Germany during the war: the PzKpfw Maus (mouse) and the PzKpfw E100. The Maus started life in 1942 as the Mammut (mammoth), a super-heavy tank urged on Hitler by the head of the German tank commission, Dr Porsche, as a 150-tonne vehicle with armour ranging in thickness from a minimum of 40 mm (1.58 in) to a maximum of 350 mm (13.78 in), and turret-mounted armament of one 150-mm (5.91-in) KwK 44 L/38 or 128-mm (5.04-in) KwK L/55 gun with 50 rounds plus one 75-mm (2.95-in) L/36.5 coaxial gun with 200 rounds. Orders were placed for six prototypes, made of flat-rolled plate mortised and welded together, and power was to be provided by a 1,200-hp (895-kW) petrol or diesel engine, though the prototypes used a 1,080-hp (805-kW) Daimler-Benz MB 509 petrol engine as part of the petrol-electric drive system. With a crew of six, a weight of 188,000 kg (414,462 lb) and an overall length of 10.1 m (33.14 ft) including the main gun, the Maus first appeared in December 1943 and proved surprisingly successful in its running trials. The running gear comprised rear drive sprockets, front idlers and 48 partially-interleaved road wheels arranged in four-wheel bogies with longitudinal torsion bar suspension, and a maximum speed of 20 km/h (12.5 mph) was attained. The type was far too large and heavy for Germany's bridges, and was thus designed for wading to a depth of 8 m (26.25 ft) with the aid of tall snorkels for the crew and engine compartments. Development of this massive type, for which no coherent tactical use was ever formulated, continued to

163

Panzerkampfwagen Maus

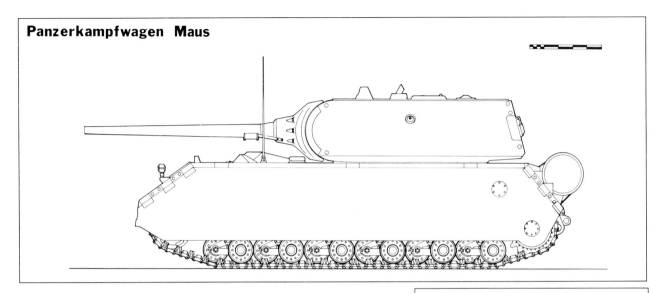

the end of the Second World War, by which time nine prototypes had been or were being built, and plans had been laid for the production of 150 Maus tanks.

The Maus had been placed in development against the recommendations of the army. The service therefore riposted with the E100 designed by Henschel, which had earlier proposed a development of the Tiger II as the VK7001 with a 128-mm (5.04-in) gun in a rear-mounted turret. The only one of the later *Entwicklungtypen* (standard types) series to reach the hardware stage, the six-man E100 bore more than a passing resemblance to the Tiger II, but had eight interleaved road wheels on each side and was considerably larger: overall length with the gun was 10.4 m (34.12 ft) and the gross weight was 140,000 kg (308,642 lb). The armament comprised one 150-mm (5.91-in) KwK 44 L/38 gun with 50 rounds and one 75-mm (2.95-in) KwK L/36.5 coaxial gun with 200 rounds, and the armour varied from a minimum of 50 mm (1.98 in) to a maximum of 200 m (7.87 in). Only one prototype was under construction at the end of the war, remaining unfinished, and the type was proposed initially in Ausf A form with a 700-hp (522-kW) Maybach P230 petrol engine, so the planned Ausf B variant would have used a 1,200-hp (895-kW) HL 234 petrol engine for a speed of 40 km/h (24.9 mph). The E100 was the better of two wholly fascinating but wholly imprac-

Panzerkampfwagen Maus
(Germany)

Type: super-heavy tank prototype
Crew: 6
Combat weight: 188,000 kg (414,462 lb)
Dimensions: length, gun forward 10.10 m (33.14 ft); width 3.67 m (12.04 ft); height 3.63 m (11.91 ft)
Armament system: one 128-mm (5.04-in) gun with 50 rounds, one 75-mm (2.95-in) coaxial gun with 200 rounds, one 20-mm cannon and two 7.92-mm (0.312-in) machine-guns
Armour: between 40 and 350 mm (1.57 and 13.78 in)
Powerplant: one 895-kW (1,200-hp) Daimler-Benz MB 509 petrol engine
Performance: speed, road 20 km/h (12.4 mph); range, road 185 km (115 miles); gradient 30°; vertical obstacle 0.72 m (2.36 ft); trench 4.50 m (14.76 ft)

tical designs that diverted much effort from the task of giving the German army adequate numbers of effective tanks in 1944 and 1945.

Germany's primary allies in the Second World War were Italy and Japan, but these fell far behind Germany in the development and employment of armour as the cornerstone of their land operations. It has to be admitted that both countries lacked an industrial base comparable in size with that of Germany, but this merely compounded the problem that neither country had seriously considered the tank as

The sole prototype of the PzKpfw Maus is seen under test. (*RAC Tank Museum*)

One of the largest tanks ever designed, the E100 was never completed in even its prototype form. (*RAC Tank Museum*)

an offensive weapon in its own right, and therefore laid the organizational and tactical groundwork for significant armoured forces in the early to mid-1930s.

During the war Italy deployed a maximum of 70 divisions, only four of which were armoured: the 131st Centauro, 132nd Ariete and 133rd Littorio Armoured Divisions of the 1940 establishment, and the 135th Ariete Armoured Cavalry Division added in April 1943. Plans were laid for the conversion of the 2nd Emanuele Filberto Testa di Ferro Cavalry Division into the 134th Freccia Armoured Division, but this conversion was never undertaken. The

136th Giovanni Fascisti Division has sometimes been called an armoured formation, but the nearest it came to such elevation was the use of truck-mounted artillery! After Italy's armistice with the Allies in 1943, the Fascist forces co-operating with the Germans in northern Italy created two armoured groups (the Gruppo Corazzato Leoncello and the Gruppo Corazzato Leonessa), while the Italian force co-operating with the Allies had no armoured units at all.

Mussolini's desire to bring Italy into the Second World War in June 1940, largely to capture parts of southern France and the British posessions in North Africa, resulted in greater effort to complete the rearmament planned for that year. The Carro Armato M.11/39 medium tank was already entering service, as noted in the previous chapter. But a production run of only 100 examples of this essentially interim type was planned, and development of the new Carro Armato M.13/40 medium tank was therefore pushed ahead under the programme leadership of General di Feroleto, the inspector of mechanized forces.

It was thought that the hull of the M.11/39 was adequate, so this was retained, despite its high silhouette, bolted construction, modest power and comparatively thin armour. The location of the main gun in the sponson on the M.11/39 was clearly an anachronism of disastrous tactical consequences, and on the M.13/40 the small machine-gun turret of the M.11/39 was replaced by a larger unit to accommodate the new 47 mm high-velocity gun adopted in this vehicle. This L/32 gun fired a 1.5-kg (4.92-lb) armour-piercing projectile with a muzzle velocity of 630 m (2,067 ft) per second, sufficient to penetrate 50 mm (1.97 in) of armour at 400 m (435 yards) declining to 32 mm (1.26 in) at 1,000 m (1,095 yards); the ordnance could also deliver a 2.45-kg (5.4-lb) HE shell to a maximum range of 7,000 m

(7,655 yards), though such a range capability with a simple sight system and a small shell was next to useless. More important was the greater field of fire provided by a turret location: the 30° traverse and 20° total elevation arcs of the M 11/39's 37/40 main gun were improved to 360° traverse and 30° total elevation arcs, the elevation arc being more precisely from -10° to + 20°. The secondary armament comprised four 8-mm (0.315-in) machine-guns, disposed as a single anti-aircraft weapon on the turret roof, a single weapon coaxial with the main gun, and twin forward-firing weapons in the hull superstructure. The driver and bow machine-gunner/wireless operator sat in the forward compartment, and the turret was occupied by the commander/gunner and loader: the limitation on crew size to four men, requiring the commander to double as the gunner, was a singular tactical failing.

Total production of the 14,000-kg (30,864-lb) M.13/40 was 799, and the type entered combat for the first time during December 1940 in North Africa. The gun was thought barely adequate, though incapable of pushing its projectile through the armour of British infantry tanks, and the protection was clearly inadequate, but the primary failing of the M.13/40

The M.13/40 medium tank was the best fighting vehicle available in quantity to the Italians during the Second World War, but was still not a match for contemporary British tanks. This is an M.13/40 knocked out in the desert fighting of North Africa. (*RAC Tank Museum*)

was its powerplant, which developed too little power and was prone to failure in North African conditions.

The M.13/40 was therefore succeeded in production by the almost identical Carro Armato M.14/41, which was built to a total of 1,103 examples with the 145-hp (108-kW) SPA 15 TM41 engine, sand-removing air filters and a weight of 14,500 kg (31,966 lb). The final development in this design sequence was the 15,500-kg (34,171-lb) Carro Armato M.15/42, which began to enter service in 1943. This was modelled closely on the M.14/41, but had a hull lengthened from 4.92 m (16.14 ft) to 5.04 m (16.54 ft), allowing the installation of a 192-hp (143-kW) SPA 15 TBM42 petrol engine to increase road speed from 33.3 km/h (20.7 mph) to 40 km/h (24.9 mph), despite the greater weight. Several detail modifications (such as additional attachment points for external stowage, a revised exhaust system, etc.) were introduced and the turret was provided with a power traverse system. At the same time, the armament was modernized, the 47/32 gun of the M.13/40 and M.14/41 being replaced in the M.15/42 by a 47/40 gun whose additional eight calibres of barrel length provided a muzzle velocity of 820 m (2,690 ft) per second, for greater armour penetration without any sacri-

fice of fire rate, which remained about seven or eight rounds per minute. Production of the M.15/42 reached a maximum of 90 examples (perhaps less) by March 1943, when the

Carro Armato M.13/40
(Italy)

Type: medium tank
Crew: 4
Combat weight: 14,000 kg (30,864 lb)
Dimensions: length overall 4.92 m (16.14 ft); width 2.20 m (7.22 ft); height 2.37 m (7.78 ft)
Armament system: one 47-mm Modello 37 L/32 rifled gun with 104 rounds, and four 8-mm (0.315-in) Breda Modello 38 machine-guns (one coaxial, two bow and one AA) with 3,048 rounds; the turret was manually operated, the main gun was stabilized in neither elevation (−10° to +20°) nor azimuth (360°), and simple optical sights were fitted
Armour: riveted steel varying in thickness between 6 and 42 mm (0.24 and 1.65 in)
Powerplant: one 93.2-kW (125-hp) Fiat-Ansaldo SPA 8 TM40 diesel engine with 180 litres (39.6 Imp. gal.) of fuel in main and reserve tanks
Performance: speed, road 31.8 km/h (19.75 mph); range, road 200 km (124 miles); fording 1.0 m (3.28 ft); gradient 70%; vertical obstacle 0.8 m (2.625 ft); trench 2.1 m (6.9 ft); ground clearance 0.41 m (16.1 in)

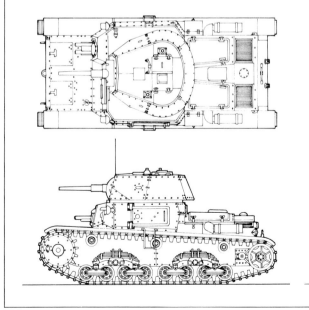

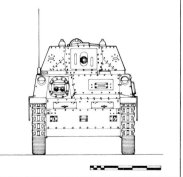

Fiat-Ansaldo M.13/40

Italy was quick to appreciate that its limited resources in raw materials and production capability would be better used in the manufacture of self-propelled artillery than of genuine tanks, and this results in the Semovente da 75/18 carrying a short-barrel gun/howitzer. These are such vehicles based on the chassis of the M.13/40 or upengined M.14/41 medium tank. (*IWM*)

Italians decided to halt production of this class of tank in favour of increased availability of the chassis for use in 75-mm (2.95-in), 90-mm (3.54-in) and 149-mm (5.87-in) self-propelled ordnances.

Up to 1940 the Italian army had been quite content with the tactical blend of its armoured force: the primary battlefield role was undertaken by medium tanks and the reconnaissance/scouting role was performed by light tanks and tankettes. Mussolini had more grandiose ambitions for his forces, and decided that a heavy tank was essential. This led to the P-series, whose prefix (standing for *Pesante*, or heavy) was followed by a numerical suffix indicating main armament calibre (in millimetres) or nominal weight (in tonnes) and after an oblique stroke the year of introduction (final two digits). The operational plan seems to have been that the new tanks would first supplement and then replace the M-series medium tanks. It is worth noting here that Italian tank classifications corresponded with neither the British nor the German systems of the period, and the P-series would have been considered either a medium tank or a light battle tank by the British and Germans.

Designs for the proposed Carro Armato P.75 were commissioned from the army's mechanization department and from Ansaldo (two competing projects from each), and after these had been carefully evaluated one of the Ansaldo designs was selected for full-scale development. A full-scale wooden mock-up was approved in December 1940, and the type was ordered into production with the revised designation Carro Armato P.26/40 and a nominal weight of 26 tonnes. Though still of bolted construction and based on the standard type of running gear (four twin-wheel bogies coupled in pairs with semi-elliptic leafspringing), in appearance this was an altogether more modern vehicle than the Italian medium tanks of the period. Initial plans called for frontal armour 40 mm (1.575 in) thick, a 330-hp (246-kW) diesel engine, and a 75-mm (2.95-in) 75/18 gun/howitzer as main armament, with a 20-mm cannon mounted coaxially. Development and testing of the engine was an arduous process, taking most of 1941, and the prototype finally ran only in October of that year, with 50-mm (1.97-in) frontal armour and the 75/18 ordnance, which had a muzzle velocity of only 430 m (1,411 ft) per second. The latter was soon changed to the more capable 75/32 gun with a muzzle velocity of 610 m (2,001 ft) per second, and then again to the newer 75/34 gun used with an 8-mm (0.315-in) coaxial machine-gun. The P.26/40 was finally authorized for production in May 1942 with a 420-hp (313-kW) petrol engine instead of the problematical diesel, whose replacement was first mooted as an Italian copy of the diesel used in the Soviets' T-34 medium tank. The integration of the new engine consumed further invaluable time, and it was 1943 before production finally began, the order having been increased from the original 500 to 1,000. But it was now too late for Italy, and only 21 vehicles

had been completed by the time Italy capitulated in September 1943. By this time, in any case, the P.26/40 was beginning to show signs of obsolescence, and plans had been laid for 30-tonne successors, in the forms of the Carro Armato P.43 with a larger but lower turret characterized by sloped side armour and a commander's cupola, and of the P.40bis with a wider but less sloped turret that lacked the cupola.

Potentially the finest Italian tank of the Second World War was the Carro Armato Celere Sahariano, a high-speed medium tank modelled closely on the Crusader cruiser tank encountered and admired by the Italians when

The M.14/41 was the late-production version of the M.13/40 medium tank.(*RAC Tank Museum*)

The late-production version of the M.13/40 was designated M.14/41, and from this latter was developed the M.15/42 illustrated here. This used a petrol engine for higher performance, featured a higher velocity 47-mm gun, and had the hull access hatch moved from the left to the right. (*RAC Tank Museum*)

they met this British type in the North African fighting. The 18-tonne Italian tank was designed for desert operations, and was a long, low type with Christie running gear, a 250-hp (186-kW) petrol engine for a maximum speed of 70 km/h (43.5 mph), a crew of four and a main armament of one 75-mm (2.95-in) gun, though only a 47-mm weapon was carried in the prototype. The North African fighting had ended by the time the first prototype appeared in spring 1943, and the Sahariano was cancelled.

The Japanese attitude to armour was not dissimilar from that of the Italians, though armoured divisions did not exist as such at the beginning of the war. Tanks were organized in special units comprising one light company with 20 tanks, and two medium tank companies with a total of 48 tanks. Such a unit was organic to the so-called strengthened divisions and to some of the so-called modified divisions, other divisions making do with the 13 tankettes of the single armoured company belonging to their single organic cavalry regiment. As the war progressed the Japanese grouped their tanks into tank regiments, brigades and finally divisions: in mid-1945 there were four armoured divisions (one in

China, one in the Philippines and two in Japan) and a number of lesser units allocated at corps and army levels (designated army and area army levels by the Japanese)

The bulk of Japan's limited armour strength was provided by types designed before the country's entry into the Second World War. With hindsight this may seem a short-sighted move by the Japanese, but factors other than Japan's final conflict with the Western Allies have to be taken into account. The most important of these is a general lack of production capacity, as indicated by the fact that total Japanese tank production between 1931 and 1945 amounted to only 6,450, of which 3,300 were produced by the giant Mitsubishi company, which had heavy commitments in aircraft, warship and other war construction fields. Second is the fact that Japan's main reason for war was the subjugation of China, so that the latter's raw materials could be seized and her vast markets opened to Japanese trade: and for the war against the indifferently-led and poorly-equipped Chinese, Japan's 1930s' vintage light and medium tanks were more than adequate. Next in Japan's priority list was the protection of Manchukuo (Manchuria) from Soviet ambitions:

Though rated by the Italians as a heavy tank, the P.26/40 was by Allied and German standards little more than a medium tank. Only a few had been completed by the time of the Italian armistice of September 1943, and several of these were taken over by the Germans.

the Soviets were known to possess large numbers of tanks, but the Japanese felt (with some justification up to 1944) that these could not be deployed in numbers decisive enough to deal with Japan's numerically stronger forces. And finally, the war against the Western Allies was to be fought in areas considered by the Japanese to be wholly unsuitable for operations by all but modest numbers of light and medium tanks: this expectation proved to be completely false, and in both the mainland and island campaigns the Allies were able to bring to bear large numbers of light and medium tanks of types considerably more advanced than the Japanese could have imagined in their plan for a short war.

The most modern tank in service with the Japanese at the beginning of their participation in the war was the Medium Tank Type 1 (Chi-He), a development of the Type 97 (Shinhoto Chi-Ha) discussed in the previous chapter. The Chi-He was basically similar to the Type 97 but had a slightly longer hull and was fitted with a longer-barrelled main gun, the 47-mm Type 1 high-velocity weapon with improved armour-penetration capability. This was installed in a redesigned and slightly taller turret that provided room for a gunner, in addition to the commander/gunner and loader of the Type 97, and the other main modifications included a revised front superstructure, welded rather than riveted armour to a maximum thickness of 50 mm (1.97 in), and a 240-hp (179-kW) Type 100 diesel for a speed of 44 km/h (27.3 mph) at a combat weight of 17,475 kg (38,525 lb). The turret modification was most important, the separation of the commander and gunner functions doing much to ensure that the Type 1 gun was usable to maximum effect. The Chi-He medium battle tank was complemented by the Gun Tank Type 2 (Ho-I), a support version fitted with a short-barrel 75-mm (2.95-in) gun in a 360° traverse turret. The Ho-I weighed 17,300 kg (38,139 lb) and was standardized for service in 1942; however, production was undertaken on only the most limited of scales.

By 1942 the Japanese were beginning to appreciate the tactical limitations of 37- and 47-mm anti-tank guns as the primary armament of their light and medium tanks: such weapons had been able to deal with the older light tanks fielded by the Allies in the Far East during 1942, but would clearly be inadequate against the newer generation of light and indeed medium tanks encountered at the end of the year and likely to become increasingly numerous in succeeding years. The 47-mm Type 1 gun, for example, had an L/54 barrel and fired its 1.4-kg (3.09-lb) armour-piercing projectile with a muzzle velocity of 825 m (2,707 ft) per second, giving the shot sufficient energy to penetrate 50 mm (1.98 in) of armour at an angle of 30° at a range of 500 m (545 yards): this was adequate by the standards of late 1941 and early 1942, perhaps, but offered no hope against the newer Allied tanks. The problem here faced by Japanese tank designers was the lack of a suitable anti-tank weapon in a calibre greater than 47 mm, so they turned instead to a 'tankified' version of the 75-mm (2.95-in) Type 90 field gun, which was a Japanese development of a French weapon, the 85-mm (3.35-in) Schneider Modèle 1927. This was an L/38.4 weapon and fired its 6.025-kg (13.28-lb) armour-piercing or HE projectile with a muzzle velocity of 700 m (2,297 ft) per second, providing quite respectable armour-penetration capability in its Type 3 tank version.

The hull of the Chi-He was thought adequate, so a new turret was designed round the Type 3 gun and installed on the basic hull to produce the Medium Tank Type 3 (Chi-Nu). The larger main gun and its turret (without a machine-gun in its rear face) added considerably to combat weight, which rose to 18,800 kg (41,446 lb) and overall height, which increased from the 2.39 m (7.83 ft) of the Type 1 and 2.565 m (8.4 ft) of the Type 2 to a figure of 2.62 m (8.6 ft). The 240-hp (179-kW) diesel engine remained unchanged, and the overall effect was a slight reduction in performance, as indicated by a maximum speed of 38 km/h (23.6 mph). Production started in 1944, but Japan's increasingly acute production problems limited manufacture to between 50 and 60 of these significantly improved tanks.

The same story applies to the later medium tanks developed by Japan. The Medium Tank Type 4 (Chi-To) had a lengthened 6.325-m (20.75-ft) hull with seven rather than six road wheels, and at a weight of 30,500 kg

171

The Japanese Type 3 medium tank was little more than the Type 1 fitted with a larger turret to accommodate the 75-mm (2.95-in) Type 3 high-velocity gun to provide useful anti-tank capability. (*RAC Tank Museum*)

that on a one-to-one basis this would have been equal to American and British medium tanks.

Although the Japanese army was involved in the Pacific campaign of the Second World War, mainly on the larger islands such as New Guinea, Formosa and those of the East Indies and Philippines groups, its main interests lay on the Asian mainland. For this reason, therefore, in 1940 the army was happy to abandon development of its adventurous amphibious light tank series to the Japanese navy, whose marine forces were tasked with primary responsibility for operations on the smaller islands and island chains in the Pacific. The navy found its starting point for this development stream not in the army's SR-series, but rather in the army's Light Tank Type 95 (Ha-Go), whose primary components were used in a redesigned, all-welded and water-proofed hull to create the Amphibious Light Tank Type 2 (Ka-Mi). This was fitted with large 3-mm (0.12-in) steel pontoons at the front and rear for additional buoyancy: the front pontoon was shaped like the bow of a boat and sub-divided internally into eight compartments to minimize the effects of shell splinters, should the vehicle be hit as it approached the shore. With its pontoons the Type 2 weighed 11,300 kg (24,912 lb). Water propulsion at a maximum speed of 9.5 km/h (5.6 mph) was provided by two propellers driven via a transfer case from the 120-hp (89.5-kW) diesel engine, whose decking was fitted with a tall snorkel to ensure uninterrupted and water-free aspiration, and water steering was in turn provided by a pair of rudders. Once the tank had climbed up onto the assault beach, the pontoons could be released from inside the vehicle, leaving the tank unencumbered for its land tasks. In this arena the standard running gear came into its own, this being based on that of the Type 95 but with the compression springs located inside rather than outside the hull: maximum speed was 37 km/h (23 mph). A crew of between four and six could be carried, the number being large for a vehicle whose main armament was a single 37-mm Type 1 gun with 132 rounds in a 360° traverse turret; the secondary armament comprised two 7.7-mm (0.303-in) machine-guns with 3,500 rounds, one of these weapons being mounted

(67,240 lb) carried armour varying in thickness from 12 to 75 mm (0.47 to 2.95 in) thick. The armament was again improved, the 75-mm (2.95-in) Type 4 tank gun being a development of the Type 88 anti-aircraft gun with an L/44.1 barrel, which could fire its 6.6-kg (14.55-lb) shell with a muzzle velocity of 720 m (2,362 ft) per second. It is believed that about six pro-totypes were built.

The final expression of Japan's tank philosophy in the Second World War was the Medium Tank Type 5 (Chi-Ri). This was based closely on Japan's previous medium tanks, but was again lengthened, to 7.31 m (23.98 ft), by the addition of an eighth road wheel on each side. Armour protection was provided on the same basis as that of the Chi-To, resulting in a weight of 37,600 kg (82,892 lb), and a 500-hp (373-kW) diesel engine was planned. However, this latter was still under development as the first Chi-Ri prototypes were approaching com-pletion, and these were therefore engined with a 550-hp (410-kW) BMW aero engine using petrol rather than diesel oil. Maximum speed was 45 km/h (28 mph). The armament layout was also unusual for a tank of this period, the turret accommodating a 75-mm (2.95-in) Type 4 tank gun and the superstructure front a 37-mm Type 1 tank gun in a limited-traverse mounting. As with the Chi-To, there were also two 7.7-mm (0.303-in) machine-guns. Develop-ment of the Chi-Ri was incomplete at the end of the Second World War, but it seems likely

coaxially with the main gun and the other in the hull front. The Type 2 was admirably suited for Pacific island campaigns, for they could be launched well offshore in comparative safety, approach the target island at moderately high speed, cross any reefs with their tracks, and then become standard light tanks on discarding the buoyancy pontoons and engine-breathing snorkel after climbing ashore on the target island. The armament was adequate for 1941 and 1942, but at minimum and maximum thicknesses of 9 and 13 mm (0.35 and 0.51 in) the protection was decidedly scanty.

These failings of firepower and protection were remedied in the Amphibious Medium Tank Type 3 (Ka-Chi), a 29,250-kg (64,484-lb) vehicle based on the Medium Tank Type 1 (Chi-He) in much the same way as the Ka-Mi had been derived from the Type 95 (Ha-Go). The running gear comprised eight road wheels (two four-wheel bogies) and four track-return rollers per side, and power was provided by a 240-hp (179-kW) Type 100 diesel that provided a land speed of 32 km/h (19.9 mph) and a water speed of 10.5 km/h (6.5 mph) via two propellers. Engine aspiration was ensured on the water by a snorkel (complete with escape hatch) located above the turret and discarded,

together with the front and rear buoyancy pontoons, after the tank had come ashore. A maximum crew of seven was carried, the armament was one 47-mm gun and two 7.7-mm (0.303-in) machine-guns, and armour to a maximum thickness of 50 mm (1.98 in) was carried.

The ultimate Japanese amphibious tank was the Amphibious Medium Tank Type 5 (To-Ku), an odd 29,500-kg (65,035-lb) type with a 47-mm gun and a 7.7-mm (0.303-in) machine-gun in the hull front, and a 25-mm cannon and another 7.7-mm (0.303-in) machine-gun in the turret. In terms of its mechanical systems, water-borne features and performance the Type 5 was similar to the Type 3, but it appeared too late for any serious consideration of production.

Given their failure to appreciate the true course of development in armoured warfare in the 1930s, the Italian and Japanese tank arms could not emulate that of Germany, either operationally or technically. Italian and Japanese tanks were therefore of limited use only, in the Second World War, and were technical dead ends that generally failed to inspire post-war trends.

The Japanese Type 2 amphibious tank was a development of the Type 95 light tank with detachable bow and stern flotation units. (*RAC Tank Museum*)

Allied Dominance

At the outbreak of war in September 1939, the British army possessed only two regular armoured divisions: in the UK was the 1st Armoured Division (formerly the Mobile Division) and in Egypt was the Armoured Division (Egypt), which was renamed the 7th Armoured Division on 16 February 1940. These were organized on the May 1939 pattern with a divisional headquarters (three light cruiser and five heavy cruiser tanks), one light armoured brigade headquarters (six light cruiser tanks and four heavy cruiser tanks) controlling three light armoured regiments (each having 36 light and 22 light cruiser tanks), one heavy armoured brigade headquarters (six light cruiser and four heavy cruiser tanks) controlling three heavy armoured regiments (each having 26 light cruiser, eight close support cruiser and 15 heavy cruiser tanks) and a support group: this gave a divisional strength of 349 tanks. The overall establishment of armoured divisions was changed eight times up to the end of the Second World War, and brief details of these modifications are provided in the diagrams in the Appendix.

The bulk of British tank strength was still mustered in army tank brigades controlled by higher-level formations (army and occasionally corps). Operations in the period from May 1940 finally convinced the army that this penny-packet distribution of armoured strength was not effective, and as the situation allowed, the brigades (increasingly strengthened by new units and the transformation of cavalry brigades) were allocated to newly-formed armoured divisions. Surviving brigades were eventually organized into independent armoured brigade groups for operation in areas that did not require or could not accommodate a full armoured division. Thus the British army's muster of armoured divisions grew steadily throughout the war: the Guards Armoured Division was created in June 1941,

the 2nd Armoured Division in December 1940, the 6th Armoured Division in September 1940, the 8th Armoured Division in November 1940, the 9th Armoured Division in December 1940, the 10th Armoured Division in August 1941, the 11th Armoured Division in March 1941, the 42nd Armoured Division in November 1941 and the 79th Armoured Division in August 1942. Armoured formations of British dominions, most notably Australia, Canada, India and South Africa, were generally organized on British lines, with similar equipment.

At the beginning of the war British armoured regiments were equipped with tanks developed in the 1930s, but the increasingly rapid pace of rearmament since 1936 was beginning to pay dividends in newer tank types which the army hoped would be better suited to the type of operations likely to be encountered in warfare of the global nature that had to be considered by the British. These far-flung commitments required tanks that could operate in terrains, climates and logistical situations as disparate as those of the cold and wetness of northern Europe, the heat and dryness of North Africa and the Middle/Near East, and the heat and wetness of South-East Asia.

The tank types serving in greatest numbers at the beginning of the Second World War were the Light Tank Mk VI, the Infantry Tanks Mk I and Mk II, and the Cruiser Tanks Mk I, Mk II, Mk III and Mk IV: best of these, without any shadow of a doubt, were the A13 Cruiser Tank Mk III and A13 Mk II Cruiser Tank Mk IV, and the A12 Infantry Tank Mk II Matilda II, which were all discussed in Chapter Two.

In the cruiser field, great things had been hoped of the A13 Mk III Cruiser Tank Mk V Covenanter, but as discussed above these hopes failed to materialize. The basic design was taken in hand during 1937 for development into the A15 Cruiser Tank Mk VI Crusader, first of the so-called heavy cruiser tanks but retaining the same 2-pdr (40-mm) main armament as the earlier tanks, together with the 340-hp (253.5-kW) Liberty Mk III engine used in the A13. Even as it appeared, the type was recognized as being too lightly armed and, with its 40-mm (1.57-in) maximum thickness, too poorly armoured. The Crusader was nonetheless ordered 'off the drawing board' in July 1939, with Nuffield Mechanisations and Aero heading a consortium of nine companies involved in manufacture of an eventual 5,300 examples in various marks.

The hull was basically similar to that of the Covenanter, with a long low decking and a well-angled glacis, and the Christie type of running gear was again similar to that of the Covenanter, though with the addition of an extra road wheel on each side and the springs located inside rather than outside the hull. The running gear proved excellent, and the Crusader was able to exceed its legend speed of 27 mph (43.5 km/h) by a considerable margin: some Crusaders were capable of speeds over 40 mph (64.4 km/h), but high speeds not infrequently caused mechanical failure in the engine. The forward compartment was occupied by the driver and bow machine-gunner,

the latter operating a single 7.92-mm (0.312-in) Besa machine-gun in a small turret to the left of the driver. The rear compartment was occupied by the Liberty engine, a derated version of the aero engine designed in the First World War as a 400-hp (298-kW) unit. The centre of the vehicle was the fighting compartment, with the multi-side and angular (though well sloped) turret above it: this power-traversed turret was extremely cramped with its complement of commander, gunner and loader/radio operator, yet carried only a 2-pdr (40-mm) main gun, whose limitations were becoming apparent even in 1939. A 7.92-mm (0.312-in) Besa machine-gun was mounted coaxially with the main armament, and there was also a 0.303-in (7.7-mm) Bren light machine-gun on the roof for anti-aircraft defence. In the Cruiser Tank Mk VICS Crusader ICS the 2-pdr (40-mm) gun was replaced by a 3-in (76.2-mm) howitzer for use in the close support role.

The Crusader was rushed into production and service before all its mechanical problems had been eliminated, and it is known that in its first combat operations, the 'Battleaxe' fighting of June 1941, more Crusaders were immobilized by mechanical failure than by enemy

An A15 Cruiser Tank Mk VI Crusader I in the Western Desert. Notable features are the cramped, multi-faceted turret and the later-production bulbous mantlet for the 2-pdr (40-mm) main gun. (*IWM*)

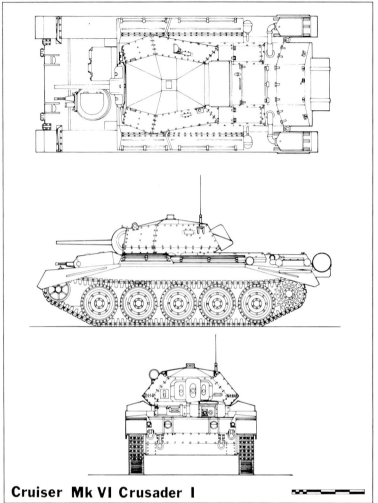

Cruiser Mk VI Crusader I

The ultimate development of the Crusader gun tank was the Cruiser Tank Crusader III with much improved armament and the improved Liberty Mk IV engine, at a weight of 44,240 lb (20,067 kg). In this model all provision for the machine-gun turret was removed, the frontal armour was thickened to 51 mm (2 in) and the main gun became a 6-pdr (57-mm) weapon. The 6-pdr (57-mm) Mk 3 gun weighed 768 lb (348 kg) and possessed an L/42.9 barrel: this fired its 6.28-lb (2.85-kg) armour-piercing shot with a muzzle velocity of 2,800 ft (853 m) per second, giving it sufficient momentum to penetrate 81 mm (3.19 in) of armour at an angle of 30° at a range of 500 yards (455 m), a performance comfortably exceeding the 57-mm (2.24-in) penetration of the 2-pdr (40-mm) shot. But the 6-pdr (57-mm) gun was both longer and heavier than its predecessor, and this meant revision of the turret for two-man operation by the gunner and commander/loader/radio operator. The Crusader III was available in time for the decisive 2nd Battle of El Alamein in October and November 1942, but was severely hampered by the overtaxing of the commander. Nevertheless the Crusader was a vital element of the eventual British success in the North African campaign, and though a few were used in the opening stages of the Italian campaign, from mid-1943 the Crusader disappeared rapidly as a firstline gun tank.

Crusader variants worthy of note were command versions of the standard gun tank with additional radio equipment, the Crusader III (OP) artillery observation vehicle with dummy main armament, the Crusader III AA anti-aircraft vehicle delivered to artillery units in Mk I form with a single 40-mm Bofors gun and to armoured formations in Mks II and III forms with twin 20-mm Oerlikon cannon and coaxial 0.303-in (7.7-mm) Vickers machine-gun, the Crusader ARV recovery vehicle, the Crusader Bulldozer with a front-mounted dozer blade, and the Crusader Gun Tractor for the 17-pdr (3-in/76.2-mm) anti-tank gun with accommodation in the hull for eight men and 40 rounds of ammunition.

The Covenanter and Crusader provided invaluable data on cruiser tank design and operations, resulting in the development of

action. There was also criticism of the Crusader's cramped interior and thin armour, resulting in the Cruiser Tank Mk VIA Crusader II. The former criticism was alleviated by omission of the machine-gun turret, though the space was frequently used to increase the 2-pdr (40-mm) ammunition stowage from the notional 110 rounds; and the latter was ameliorated by increasing the maximum armour thickness on the frontal arc to 49 mm (1.93 in). The loss of the turret was balanced by the thicker armour, and the combat weight therefore remained steady at 42,560 1lb (19,305 kg). There was also a Cruiser Tank Mk VIA Crusader IICS with a 3-in (76.2-mm) close-support howitzer instead of the 2-pdr (40-mm) gun.

A15 Cruiser Tank Mk VI Crusader I
(UK)

Type: cruiser tank
Crew: 5
Combat weight: 42,560 lb (19,305 kg)
Dimensions: length overall 19.67 ft (5.60 m) or 20.71 ft (6.31 m) with jettisonable fuel tank; width 8.67 ft (2.64 m); height 7.33 ft (2.23 m)
Armament system: one 2-pdr (40-mm) QF Mk IX or X rifled gun with 110 rounds, two 7.92-mm (0.312-in) Besa machine-guns (one co-axial and one in the auxiliary turret) with 4,500 rounds, one 0.303-in (7.62-mm) Bren AA machine-gun with 600 rounds, and one 2-in (51-mm) bomb thrower with 26 rounds; the turret was hydraulically powered, the main gun was stabilized in neither elevation ($-15°$ to $+20°$) not azimuth (360°), and an optical fire-control system was fitted
Armour: riveted and bolted steel varying in thickness from 7 to 40 mm (0.28 to 1.575 in)
Powerplant: one 340-hp (254-kW) Nuffield Liberty Mk III petrol engine with 110 Imp. gal. (500 litres) of internal fuel plus 30 Imp. gal. (136 litres) of external fuel in a jettisonable tank
Performance: speed, road 27.5 mph (44.25 km/h); range, road 200 miles (322 km); fording 3.25 ft (0.99 m); gradient 60%; side slope 30%; vertical obstacle 2.0 ft (0.61 m); trench 7.5 ft (2.29 m); ground clearance 15.7 in (0.40 m)

more capable machines better able to deal with German tanks. The 6-pdr (57-mm) gun was in all respects superior to the 50-mm KwK L/42 and L/60 weapons used in the PzKpwf III, and to the 75-mm (2.95-in) L/24 weapon of first generation PzKpfw IVS; it was also comparable in most respects to the longer 75-mm (2.95-in) KwK 40 L/43 weapon of second-generation PzKpfw IVs. It was sensible, therefore to keep the 6-pdr (57-mm) gun, which even in 1944 was only marginally inferior to the 75-mm (2.95-in) KwK 40 L/48 gun of the third-generation PzKpfw IVs. The origins of the cruiser concept lay with the lightweight cavalry tank, designed for reconnaissance and deep penetration, using its speed and mobility to avoid trouble other than that which could be handled by thin armour and light armament. The Crusader was the last cruiser tank to be designed to this concept, whose fallacies were evidenced by the efforts made to step up the Crusader's protection and firepower.

As noted above, the 6-pdr (57-mm) gun was beginning to mature as a weapon in 1940, although it entered production only in 1941 because of the need to keep the current 2-pdr (40-mm) gun in production so that the losses suffered in the French fighting of May 1940 could be made up. The 6-pdr (57-mm) gun

An A15 Cruiser Tank Mk VI Crusader I with the small auxiliary machine-gun turret at the front of the hull. (*RAC Tank Museum*)

Never used operationally, the A24 Cruiser Tank Mk VI Cavalier used a development of the Crusader's basic hull with an angular turret mounting a 6-pdr (57-mm) gun.

offered the firepower required, so the main problem to be addressed in the next cruiser tank was the deficiency in protection. By 1940 the War Office had decided on its next move, and early in 1941 issued a requirement for a new heavy cruiser tank, to be called the Cromwell.

This requirement demanded armour on a 2.75-in (70-mm) basis, thereby offering some 50 per cent more protection than the Crusader, and a 6-pdr (57-mm) main armament in a turret using a 60-in (1.524-m) diameter turret ring so that there would be adequate volume for the commander, gunner and loader. The requirement specified a combat weight of about 56,000 lb (25,240 kg) for the new tank, which was to be powered by a Rolls-Royce Meteor (a derivative of the Merlin aero engine) to provide cruiser-type performance. The stumbling block to rapid progress was the Meteor, which was still at an early stage of development by Leyland and Rolls-Royce. As an interim measure, therefore, Nuffield Mechanisations and Aero was commissioned to produce the A24 Cruiser Tank Mk VII with the hull and turret of the proposed Cromwell but the power train and other mechanical features of the Crusader. The type was initially called the Cromwell I, but this was soon changed to Cavalier. The design was ordered into production 'off the drawing board' to the extent of 500 tanks, and the prototype appeared in January 1942. This 59,360-lb (26,926-kg) vehicle was powered by a 410-hp (306-kW) Liberty, but was so grossly

underpowered that consistent use of the maximum 24-mph (38.6-km/h) speed resulted in frequent engine failures. The Cavalier was never used in action as a gun tank, but served with modest success for training, and with greater success as the basis of specialist derivatives such as an observation post vehicle for the Royal Artillery. Perhaps most importantly of all, its lack of success finally persuaded the War Office to cease its practice of ordering tanks 'off the drawing board'.

Continued delays with the Meteor engine led to a second interim model, the A27L Cruiser Tank Mk VIII Centaur, which was originally called the Cromwell II, until it was decided to retain the name Cromwell exclusively for the definitive Meteor-engine variant. The Centaur first appeared in prototype form in June 1942, and was in effect the Cromwell apart from its use of a 395-hp (295-kW) Liberty engine, and since the type was designed with an engine compartment that could accept either engine, many Centaurs were re-engined with the Meteor when this became available in 1943, to become Cromwell Xs. Primary design responsibility for the Centaur was allocated in November 1941 to Leyland rather than Nuffield Mechanisations and Aero, and the comparatively greater reliability and success of the Centaur resulted in Leyland becoming 'parent' to the Cromwell development and production programme, in succession to the Birmingham Railway Carriage and Wagon Company, which had accepted temporary parentage in September 1941. The other main contractors for the Cromwell were Morris Engines (power-plant) and David Brown (transmission), Leyland having been responsible for the running gear and tracks since the beginning of the program-me.

The Centaur weighed 61,600 lb (27,942 kg) and attained a speed of 27 mph (43.5 km/h), and was similar to the Cavalier in protection and armament: the former varied from a minimum of 20 mm (0.79 in) to a maximum of 76 mm (3 in), and in the initial Centaur I and Centaur II variants the latter comprised one 6-pdr (57-mm) gun plus one or two 7.92-mm (0.312-in) Besa machine-guns located as one coaxial weapon and one optional bow weapon. The Centaur III introduced a 75-mm (2.95-in) Mk 5 gun in place of the 6-pdr (57-mm) weapon, and the Centaur IV was the close-support model with a 94-mm (3.7-in) Tank Howitzer Mk 1. This was a short L/21.5 weapon weighing 867 lb (393 kg) and firing a 25-lb (11.34-kg) projectile with a muzzle velocity of 1,075 ft (328 m) per second; a hollow-charge projectile was one of the ammunition options, and this could penetrate 110 mm (4.33 in) of armour at an angle of 30° at a range of 500 yards (455 m). The Centaur was also used for artillery obser-vation with a dummy gun to allow the incorp-oration of additional radio equipment in the turret.

The scene was finally set for the A27M Cruiser Tank Mk VIII Cromwell, the suffix to the A-series designation indicating that this was the Meteor- rather than Liberty-engined variant of the basic A27 type. Development had been very protracted, in part because of delays with the Meteor engine and in part due to the exhaustive evaluation programme demanded by the War Office after the problems with the Crusader and Cavalier production runs. Though the first Cromwell prototype had run in January 1942, it was January 1943 before the first Cromwell I gun tanks began to come off the production line. The first vehicles had the 600-hp (447-kW) Meteor engine built by Rolls-Royce, though production of this important tank engine was switched as rapidly as possible to other sources, so that Rolls-Royce could concentrate on its aero engine develop-ment and production programmes. The availa-bility of the new engine finally gave British tanks the performance fillip they so despe-rately needed: there was now great reliability and ample power, and this latter meant that the engine rarely needed to be run at the high power settings that had caused the less powerful Liberty to break down with alarming regularity.

The Cromwell had been planned with the 6-pdr (57-mm) gun, but during 1942 there was a gradual switch in user preference from the dedicated anti-tank gun to a dual-capable weapon capable of firing anti-tank and HE rounds. Officers with experience of the Ameri-can M3 Grant and M4 Sherman tanks were unanimous in their praise for the 75-mm (2.95-in) M2 and M3 weapons used in these

The A27L Cruiser Tank Mk VII Centaur was an interim type between the Crusader/Centaur and A27M Cromwell, and used the elderly Liberty engine. (*RAC Tank Museum*)

The UK's best cruiser tank to serve in substantial numbers in the Second World War was the A27M Cromwell, seen here as a Cromwell IV reworked with reduced-ratio final drive, wider tracks and additional armour: in this form the type was known as the Cromwell VII. (*RAC Tank Museum*)

vehicles, and their pressure finally convinced the War Office. In January 1943 it was decided that the majority of medium tanks should be fitted with a dual-capable weapon, and be supported in action by smaller numbers of tanks with role-specific anti-tank and close-support weapons. The result in the armament field was the rapid creation of the 75-mm (2.95-in) Mk 5/5A gun using many parts from the 6-pdr (57-mm) gun and firing the standard range of US ammunition for the M2/M3 gun. The British 75-mm (2.95-in) gun was derived from the 6-pdr (57-mm) weapon with the barrel bored out, shortened and fitted with a single-baffle muzzle brake: it weighed 692 lb (314 kg), and the L/36.5 barrel fired the 13.75-lb (6.24-kg) projectile with a muzzle velocity of 2,030 ft (619 m) per second. Several other types of projectile could be carried, adding considerably to the tactical versatility of the tank, and as well as a capable HE projectile these included an anti-tank type which could penetrate 68 mm (2.68 in) of armour at an angle of 30° at a range of 500 yards (455 m).

It was therefore planned to fit this weapon in the Cromwell, whose generous turret ring diameter made such a move possible without undue modification. But as the weapon did not become available until October 1943, the first Cromwells were delivered with the 6-pdr (57-mm) gun. In overall configuration the Cromwell was similar to the Cavalier and Centaur, and thus of typical British tank layout. The construc-

tion was of armour plates of varying thicknesses riveted together, though some variants of the Mks V and VII had all-welded hulls, the suffix 'w' being added to the designation in these cases. The forward compartment was occupied by the driver and bow machine-gunner, the centrally located turret (traversed by hydraulic power) provided accommodation for the commander, gunner and loader/radio operator in a turntable basket that moved with the turret, and the rear compartment contained the engine and transmission to the rear drive sprockets. The Christie running gear was derived from that of the A13, with suitable strengthening, and comprised five large and independently-sprung road wheels but no track-return rollers; the idler was at the front. The transmission included a Merritt-Brown combined gearbox and steering unit of the type validated in the Churchill infantry tank (see below), and this provided driving flexibility, reliability and maintenance simplicity far superior to those of the Merritt-Maybach system used in most American and German tanks.

The Cromwell remained in service right up to 1950, and went through an extensive development programme. The Cromwell I was the baseline model and had an armament of one 6-pdr (57-mm) gun and two 7.92-mm (0.312-in) Besa machine-guns. The Cromwell II was similar to the Mk I but was fitted with tracks 15.5 in (394 mm) rather than 14 in (356 mm) wide, to reduce ground pressure and thus promote agility in poor going. The Cromwell III was originally designated Cromwell X, and was produced by converting the Centaur I with the Meteor engine. The Cromwell IV was the result of a similar process, and was produced by converting the Centaur III with the Meteor engine and a 75-mm (2.95-in) gun. The Cromwell V marked a significant improvement in the basic tank, as it was the first production model to be fitted with the 75-mm (2.95-in) gun; there was also a Cromwell Vw with a welded rather than riveted hull. The Cromwell VI was a close-support version fitted with a 94-mm (3.7-in) howitzer in place of the 75-mm (2.95-in) gun. The Cromwell VII was based on the Mk IV but fitted with wider tracks, a reduced ratio final drive to decrease maximum speed from 40 to 32 mph (64.4 to 51.5 km/h), and had increased armour thicknesses, including the upgrading of the frontal protection to 101 mm (3.98 in), thereby increasing combat weight to 62,720 lb (28,450 kg); there was also a Cromwell VIIw variant with the welded hull. The final production variant was the Cromwell VIII, which was essentially the Cromwell VI close-support version with the improvements of the Cromwell VII.

Several experimental variants were produced, these including a Cromwell II with a cast turret, a Cromwell II with skirt armour, a Cromwell with appliqué armour for enhanced protection, and the Cromwell CIRD with the Canadian Indestructible Roller Device for mine-clearing. There were also hybrid types, these being designated by the suffixes D (a side-opening door for the hull gunner), E (final

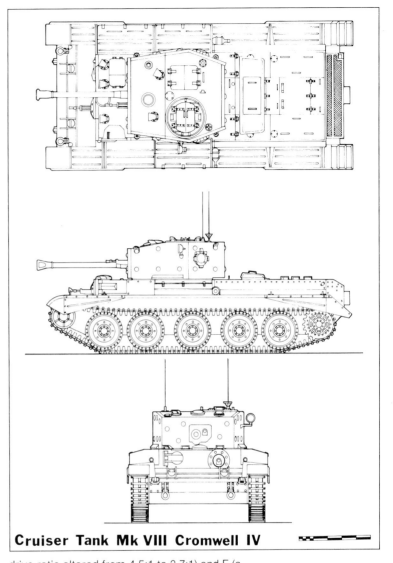

Cruiser Tank Mk VIII Cromwell IV

A27M Cruiser Tank Mk VIII Cromwell IV
(UK)

Type: cruiser tank
Crew: 5
Combat weight: 61,600 lb (27,942 kg)
Dimensions: length, gun forward 21.06 ft (6.42 m) and hull 20.46 ft (6.24 m); width 10.00 ft (3.05 m); height 8.17 ft (2.49 m) over aerial mountings
Armament system: one 75-mm (2.95-in) QF Mk V or VA L/36.5 rifled gun with 64 rounds, two 7.92-mm (0.312-in) Besa machine-guns (one coaxial and one bow) with 4,952 rounds, two 0.303-in (7.7-mm) Vickers Type K or Bren AA machine-guns with 2,000 or 600 rounds respectively, one 2-in (50.8-mm) bomb thrower with 30 rounds, and two smoke-dischargers on each side of the hull rear; the turret was hydraulically operated, the main gun was stabilized in neither elevation (− 12.5° to + 20°) nor azimuth (360°), and simple optical sights were fitted
Armour: riveted, welded and steel varying in thickness between 8 and 76 mm (0.315 and 3 in)
Powerplant: one 600-hp (447.4-kW) Rolls-Royce Meteor petrol engine with 116 Imp. gal. (527 litres) of fuel
Performance: speed, road 38 mph (61.2 km/h); range, road 173 miles (278 km); fording 3.0 ft (0.91 m) without preparation or 4 ft (1.22 m) with preparation; gradient 47%; vertical obstacle 3.0 ft (0.91 m); trench 7.5 ft (2.29 m); ground clearance 16 in (0.41 m)

drive ratio altered from 4.5:1 to 3.7:1) and F (a side-opening door for the driver).

The Cromwell proved itself an excellent tank in terms of protection and mobility, and when properly handled could evade the more powerfully armed German tanks. But this could not disguise the fact, recognized as early as the beginning of 1942, that the type would shortly lack the firepower anticipated for the German tanks likely to appear in service from late 1942 onwards. This resulted in a development known as the A30 Cruiser Tank Challenger designed to carry the extremely powerful

181

17-pdr (3-in/76.2-mm) anti-tank gun in a new and somewhat larger turret. This latter was characterized by its height rather than its width, but despite the lengthening of the Cromwell's basic hull by the addition of a sixth road wheel on each side, the 70,560-lb (32,006-kg) Challenger was too small for its turret, and performance suffered as a consequence. The pressures of the situation demanded production, however, and in 1943 some 260 Challengers were ordered: these were generally used to strengthen the capabilities of Cromwell cruiser tank regiments in the North-West European campaign of 1944-45. To remedy the Challenger's limitations a Challenger II version was produced with a shallower turret and thus less top weight, but this did not proceed past the prototype stage. There was also the A30 Avenger, which was more akin to a self-propelled gun than to a tank, despite its 360° traverse turret. This turret had only a splinter-proof steel roof, and the vehicle weighed 69,440 lb (31,498 kg).

The Centaur and Cromwell series also led to the A33 Heavy Assault Tank, which was built in prototype form by English Electric during 1943. This was basically a heavyweight development of the A27 series with additional armour, new running gear and wider tracks. The crew was five, the armament comprised one 75-mm (2.95-in) gun and one 7.92 (0.312-in) Besa machine-gun, and the protection varied in thickness up to a maximum of 114 mm (4.5 in). The engine was the standard 600-hp (47-kW) Meteor, giving this substantial 100,800-lb (45,723-kg) vehicle the useful maximum speed of 24 mph (38.6 km/h).

The last operational cruiser tank was another heavy type, the A34 Cruiser Tank Comet. The specific spur for the specification that led to development of the Comet was the nature of the armoured battles fought in the Western Desert in early 1942, when it became clear that current British tanks lacked a gun capable of defeating the armour of Germany's latest tanks. Just as worrying, moreover, was the fact that the new generation of British tanks was designed round the 6-pdr (57-mm) gun, which was possessed of only marginal superiority to current German protection and was therefore likely to fall short of the protection

---

A34 Cruiser Tank Comet
(UK)

Type: cruiser tank
Crew: 5
Combat weight: 73,248 lb (33,225 kg)
Dimensions: length, gun forward 25.125 ft (7.66 m) and hull 21.50 ft (6.55 m); width 10.08 ft (3.07 m); height 8.77 ft (2.67 m)
Armament system: one 77-mm (3.03-in) gun with 61 rounds, two 7.92-mm (0.312-in) Besa machine-guns with 5,175 rounds, one 0.303-in (7.7-mm) Bren machine-gun with 600 rounds, one 2-in (50.8-mm) bomb-thrower with 20 rounds, and two pairs of smoke-dischargers
Armour: between 14 and 101 mm (0.55 and 4 in)
Powerplant: one 600-hp (447-kW) Rolls-Royce Meteor Mk 3 petrol engine with 116 Imp. gal. (527 litres) of fuel
Performance: speed, road 32 mph (51.5 km/h); range, road 123 miles (198 km); gradient 35°; vertical obstacle 3.0 ft (0.91 m); trench 8.0 ft (2.43 m)

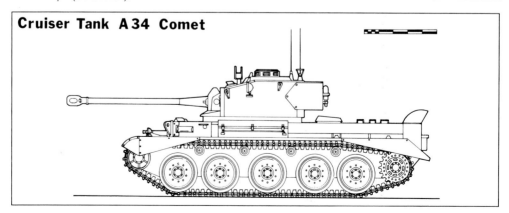

Cruiser Tank A 34 Comet

likely to appear on newer tanks. The answer was a larger-calibre gun, and the ideal weapon was found in the 17-pdr (3-in/76.2-mm) towed anti-tank gun, whose 17-lb (7.71-kg) shot was fired with ,a muzzle velocity of 2,900 ft (884 m) per second to penetrate 130 mm (5.12 in) of armour at 30° at a range of 1,000 yards (915 m). The 17-pdr (3-in/76.2-mm) gun was adapted for tank use by Vickers-Armstrongs as the OQF 77-mm Mk 2, a 1,502-lb (681-kg) weapon with a shorter barrel (L/49.2 rather than L/55.1) and a revised chamber for the shorter and wider (but more manageable) case: this fired the standard armour-piercing shot with a muzzle velocity of 2,600 ft (792 m) per second to penetrate 109 mm (4.29 in) of armour at an angle of 30° at a range of 500 yards (455 m). Plans to upgrade the Cromwell with this weapon proved impossible, and the hybrid Challenger was also unsuccessful. Just one month after the appearance of the prototype Challenger in August 1942 the decline of the British situation in North Africa further emphasized the need for an upgunned cruiser tank, and in September Leyland was commissioned for a new A34 heavy cruiser tank with the 17-pdr (3-in/76.2-mm) gun and good armour on a chassis that was to use as many Cromwell features as possible, to reduce costs and speed development.

Leyland had completed its A34 mock-up by September 1943 after starting definitive work in July of the same year, and production was scheduled for mid-1944. The hull was based on that of the Cromwell (and thereby perpetuated the vertical front plate and bow machine-gun that had caused a certain amount of justified criticism), but the armour was thickened to a maximum of 76 mm (3 in) and the construction was all-welded. The same 600-hp (447-kW) Meteor engine and associated transmission were used, and the running gear was ultimately revised to included four track-return rollers on each side. The major improvement, however, was the welded turret with a cast front plate and mantlet to a thickness of 102 mm (4 in): this turret was roomier, had better access, supported a 360° vision cupola for the commander, was fitted with an electrical traverse system, and had provision for the ready-use rounds to be stowed in armoured bins for additional protection.

The prototype appeared in February 1944 with running gear akin to that of the Cromwell. But the need to strengthen the suspension for the Comet's weight of 73,500 lb (33,340 kg) combined with other modifications to delay production into the late summer, the first production tanks reaching regiments in September 1944. Thereafter the Comet proved itself an excellent machine that remained in British service up to 1958, its most notable features apart from the high-quality main armament being its cross-country speed and agility: these latter, indeed, were often too great for the crew to endure, and the tank therefore has the distinction of being limited by crew rather than mechanical considerations.

The British army's first two infantry tanks, the Matilda I and Matilda II, had resulted from official requirements and specifications. The same cannot be said for their successor, which was a private venture by Vickers-Armstrong based on the A10 Cruiser Tank Mk II with components from a number of other Vickers-Armstrongs tanks of the period, notably the A9 Cruiser Tank Mk I and A11 Infantry Tank Mk I. The result was a vehicle that was something of a cross between the pure infantry tank and the cruiser tank: the protection and armament were to infantry tank standards, but the performance fell half-way between infantry and cruiser tank requirements: this last was an unfortunate feature that led the hard-pressed War Office to regard the machine as a well-protected cruiser, and thus to allocate the comparatively easily-manufactured Valentine to the new armoured divisions being raised in expectation of the open warfare for which the Valentine really lacked the performance.

The company presented its design to the War Office in February 1938, but it was July 1939 before a production order for the Infantry Tank Mk III Valentine was placed and, given the exigencies of the situation, this order demanded 275 tanks delivered in the shortest possible time. No prototype was required as the basic features of the design had already been well proved, and the first Valentine I entered service in May 1940 just as the German offensive against the West was unleashed. Production ended in the early months of 1944 after some 8,275 had been built: of

183

these just under 2,700 (including all but 30 of the 1,420 Canadian-built machines) were supplied to the USSR. The Red Army approved the Valentine's simplicity, reliability and protection, but found the main armament hopelessly inadequate: the standard 2-pdr (40-mm) gun of the British tanks was not infrequently replaced in Soviet service by a 76.2-mm (3-in) weapon, which boosted offensive performance to a considerable degree but made the already small turret yet more cramped.

Mention has been made above of some of the Valentine's virtues, and to these must be added the type's enormous advantage of easy upgrading in terms of armament and motive power. The basic vehicle was constructed of riveted armour plate, with hardly a curve in sight: the driver sat in a cramped compartment at the front of the vehicle, the fighting compartment was in the centre together with the hydraulic turret-traverse system, and the spacious engine compartment was at the rear. Protection over the frontal arc was good, the hull having 60-mm (2.36-in) front and side plates plus a well-angled 30-mm (1.18-in) glacis. At the rear and on top, however, the protection was only 8 mm (0.315 in) thick: this was perhaps acceptable in 1940, but was hopelessly thin by the standards of 1944, when the type finally went out of production. The turret was made of castings riveted or bolted together, offering 65-mm (2.56-in) frontal and 60-mm (2.36-in) flank protection. As the Valentine was designed for infantry use, it was carried fairly high above the ground by a suspension system that provided, on each side, two three-wheel bogies, each sprung by a large obliquely-located coil spring: the inner four wheels on each side were smaller than the leading and trailing wheels, giving a distinctive appearance to the Valentine. The suspension was designed only for modest speeds, and the running gear was completed by rear drive sprockets, front idlers and, on each side, three track-return rollers.

Up to the Mk VIII, all Valentines weighed 35,840 lb (16,257 kg). The Valentine I was powered by a 135-hp (101-kW) AEC petrol engine and could reach 15 mph (24.1 km/h); fuel amounted to a mere 36 Imp. gal. (164 litres) for a range of only 90 miles (145 km), which was adequate by the obsolescent standards of the infantry tank but far too small for the tank when it began to be used in open warfare as a semi-cruiser tank. The Valentine I had a crew of three, and the small turret thus accommodated the commander and the gunner for the 2-pdr (40-mm) main gun, which was supported by a 7.92-mm (0.312-in) Besa coaxial machine-gun: the commander had to double up as gunner and radio operator, and this proved a serious hindrance to the proper exercise of his basic function, which was also hampered by lack of adequate vision devices. The Infantry Tank Mk III* Valentine II had a 131-hp (97.7-kW) AEC diesel engine, but was otherwise similar to the Valentine I, though often fitted with sand shields for desert operations. The Valentine III was identical with the Valentine II in everything except its turret, which was a modified type allowing a three-man fighting crew: the turret had the appearance of the original turret, but was modified internally by pushing the front plate forward and the rear plate backward, turret weight being increased from 6,160 lb (2,794 kg) to 7,280 lb (3,302 kg). The Valentine IV and Valentine V were identical with the Mk II and Mk III respectively except in the engine, which was a 138-hp (103-kW) GMC diesel. The Valentine VI and VII were produced in Canada, and were in effect versions of the Valentine IV with a General Motors diesel engine, a cast rather than riveted nose plate and a 0.3-in (7.62-mm) Browning rather than Besa coaxial machine-gun: the Mk VII differed from the Mk VI in having a remote-control system for the machine-gun. The Valentine VIIA was a derivative of the Mk VII with studded tracks and jettisonable external fuel tanks.

The Valentine VIII saw a considerable improvement in firepower by the adoption of a 6-pdr (57-mm) main gun, though the installation meant the sacrifice of the coaxial machine-gun in the two-man turret; the 6-pdr (57-mm) gun was controlled in elevation via a geared manual system, the original 2-pdr (40-mm) weapon having been operated directly via a gunner's shoulder rest. Weight was increased to 38,080 lb (17,273 kg), and power was provided by the AEC diesel, switched in the otherwise identical Valentine IX to the General Motors diesel. Some Mk IXs were later fitted with a 165-hp (123-kW) General Motors diesel, and this engine was also used in the last two production models, the Valentine X with a 6-pdr (57-mm) main gun and Besa coaxial machine-gun, and the Valentine XI with a cast nose plate and a 75-mm (2.95-in) gun in place of the 6-pdr (57-mm) weapon.

The large number of Valentines built and the excellent reputation for reliability enjoyed by the basic vehicle both contributed to the extensive use of the type for a number of different roles. The most important of these developments were an armoured vehicle-launched bridge, roller and flailer mine-clearers, a flamethrower, a dozer and an artillery observation vehicle. The type was also used for development and training in the Straussler DD (Duplex Drive) system for amphibious operations. The tank was supported in the water by a fabric screen, which ran round the hull and was both raised and made rigid by compressed air, and powered by a propeller driven off the main transmission by a transfer case. The Valentine was also used as the basis for two widely-used self-propelled guns: the Bishop had a 25-pdr (3.45-in/87.6-mm) gun/howitzer, and the Archer carried a 17-pdr (3-in/76.2-mm) anti-tank gun.

The Valentine was also the inspiration for the A38 Infantry Assault Tank Valiant, whose development was undertaken by Ruston and Hornsby to allow the running trials of a prototype to begin in mid-1944. The type had been planned with the fixed defences of Germany's 'Siegfried Line' in mind, and though many features and components of the Valentine were used, the Valiant had many cast armour sections in the turret and hull. The protection varied in thickness from 14 to 110 mm (0.55 to 4.33 in), and the armament comprised a turret-mounted 6-pdr (57-mm) or 75-mm (2.95-in) gun with a 7.92-mm (0.312-in) Besa coaxial machine-gun. The vehicle turned the scales at 60,480 lb (27,433 kg), and the use of a General Motors diesel of only a 210-hp (157-kW) limited speed to 12 mph (19.3 km/h). The concept was clearly obsolete by the time the prototype appeared, and only limited trials were undertaken before the type was cancelled.

After the Valentine came the UK's most important infantry tank of the Second World War, the A22 Infantry Tank Mk IV Churchill. This vehicle was planned in 1939 as a replacement for the Matilda II, the operational scenario envisaged by the War Office comprising a Western Front not dissimilar to that in France during the First World War: this scenario called for a tank that was in essence a modern version of the rhomboidal tanks of that war, with thick armour, good but not exceptional armament and the ability to move without undue difficulty

The Infantry Tank Mk III Valentine went through a large number of variants, this being a Valentine XI with all-welded construction and a 75-mm (2.95-in) gun. (*RAC Tank Museum*)

in a heavily shelled area. In September 1939 the specification for an A20 infantry tank was issued, and design work was entrusted to Harland and Wolff in Belfast as part of the government's sensible (but long overdue) policy of diversifying tank design and construction capability. Harland and Wolff built four prototypes by June 1940, and these revealed a striking similarity to First World War practices, with a generally rhomboidal shape for good trench-crossing capability, and a main armament of two 2-pdr (40-mm) guns located in side sponsons. The type was also planned with a central turret, but in the event none of the prototypes was ever fitted with turret or armament.

In June 1940 the French campaign ended, and with it the War Office discarded its notions of latter-day trench warfare and thus the A20's *raison d'être*. The design had good features in its hull and running gear, however, and these formed the basis of the vehicle designed by Dr. H.E. Merritt, the director of tank design, when the revised A22 specification was released to Vauxhall Motors. The country's desperate situation after the defeat at Dunkirk was reflected in the War Office's stipulation that production of the A22 begin within one year, even though it realized that so rushed a programme would necessarily entail a number of inbuilt faults in the first model. Design began in July 1940 and the first A22 prototype appeared in December 1940, with the initial Churchill I production tanks coming off the line in June 1941 to inaugurate a programme that finally produced 5,640 Churchill tanks before production was completed in October 1945.

Results of tank development in the late 1930s, and the lessons of the Polish and Western campaigns waged and won by the Germans in 1939 and 1940 had resulted in a tank that was both lower and better protected than its predecessors: in the first Churchills, the armour varied in thickness from a minimum of 16 mm (0.63 in) to a maximum of 102 mm (4 in). But two short-term limitations were the inadequate armament and the problem-prone engine.

By 1940 it had been realized that the 2-pdr (40-mm) gun was too feeble a weapon for effective anti-tank employment, and lacked a significant HE shell capability: a considerably more effective weapon, the 6-pdr (57-mm) gun, was already in existence but was not in production, and in the days after Dunkirk the decision was made to keep the obsolescent gun in large-scale production rather than phase in the 6-pdr (57-mm) weapon. So far as the Churchill was concerned, this meant that a substantial 86,240-lb (39,118-kg) vehicle was fitted with a turret carrying obsolescent armament. The situation was partially remedied in the Churchill I by the installation of a 3-in (76.2-mm) howitzer in the front plate of the hull: this howitzer had a useful support capability, though the installation can be regarded only as poor, because of the limited traverse imposed by the semi-recessed position of the front plate behind the projecting forward horns of the running gear. Compensating in part for the armament deficiency was the excellent ammunition stowage, amounting to 150 2-pdr (40-mm) rounds and 58 3-in (76.2-in) rounds without hampering the space left for the crew of five (driver and gunner in the nose compartment, and the commander, gunner and loader in the spacious turret).

The other major limitation was the engine, a custom-designed Bedford petrol unit that was essentially a pair of six-cylinder truck engines lying on their sides and married to a common crankcase. This petrol unit developed only 350 hp (261 kW), giving the Churchill a distinctly modest power-to-weight ratio, and was also plagued with reliability problems in its first year of service. Unreliability was of course a disadvantage in itself, but it was exacerbated by the Churchill's poor engine installation. The War Office had demanded a readily accessible engine compartment, but this failed to materialize and even comparatively minor problems demanded the removal of the entire engine. Development and service experience gradually eliminated the engine problems, and this in turn reduced the adverse effect of the poor engine installation. Ultimately the Churchill became a notably reliable tank.

The engine's power was transmitted to the rear drive sprockets by a flexible transmission system, and driving was both easier and more precise than on other British tanks of the period, through the use of hydraulics in the clutch and steering systems. The latter was also the first operational use of the Merritt-Brown regenerative system, which was less tiring for the driver and also allowed increasingly sharp turns with reducing speed, until in neutral the driver could turn the tank in its own length. The running gear was also good, given the obvious constraints of the tank's design for the infantry role. There were 11 small independently-coilsprung road wheels on each side. These made for a fairly bumpy ride, but were cheap to manufacture and install; they also meant that the tank could survive the loss of several road wheels without loss of mobility, and could be repaired without difficulty in the field.

The Churchill remained in service with the British army from 1941 to 1952, and in this period underwent considerable development, especially during the Second World War. The Churchill I has already been described in basic detail, and there was also a Churchill ICS with a second 3-in (76.2-mm) howitzer in the turret in place of the 2-pdr (40-mm) gun. The Churchill II was similar to the Churchill I in all but armament, where the hull-mounted howitzer was replaced by a 7.92-mm (0.312-in) Besa machine-gun to complement the coaxial weapon in the turret. These first two marks may be regarded as pilot models, and the A22 design began to reach maturity in the Churchill III, which was a much improved 87,360-lb (39,626-kg) model that appeared in March 1942 with an all-welded turret accommodating the 6-pdr (57-mm) gun for greater anti-tank capability; the Mk III also introduced the large mudguards that were fitted on all later marks and retro-fitted to the first two variants. The Churchill IV was similar to the Mk III except for its turret, which was a cast rather than welded unit; in North Africa some Mk IVs were revised to the so-called Churchill IV (NA 75) standard with the 75-mm (2.95-in) main gun and 0.3-in (7.62-mm) Browning coaxial machine-gun of the M3 Grant medium tank. The Churchill V was the first genuine close-support version of the series, and was armed with a 94-mm (3.7-in) Tank Howitzer Mk 1, the same weapon as that installed in the Centaur IV. The final variant of the initial Churchill series was the Churchill VI, another gun tank and modelled on the Mk IV

with the exception of the main armament, which was a 75-mm (2.95-in) Mk 5 weapon of the type installed on the Centaur III and on the Cromwell V, VI and VII.

The use of this weapon is an interesting commentary on the state of British tank gun development, for it compared generally unfavourably with the contemporary 75-mm (2.95-in) KwK 42 L/70 weapon used in the PzKpfw V Panther. The British Mk 5 weapon was 112.576 in (2.86 m) long and weighed 692 lb (314 kg), firing its 13.75-lb (6.24-kg) projectile with a muzzle velocity of 2,030 ft (619 m) per second; by comparison the KwK 42 gun was 5.54 m (218 in) long and weighed 630 kg (1,389 lb), but fired its 6.8-kg (15-lb) projectile with a muzzle velocity of 935 m (3,068 ft) per second. The German gun was thus longer and heavier than the British weapon, but this translated into higher muzzle velocity with a larger projectile, producing an armour penetration of 92 mm (3.62 in), compared with only 68 mm (1.73 in) for the British gun.

The Churchill VI was essentially an interim variant pending deliveries of the considerably upgraded A22F (later A42) Infantry Tank Churchill VII. The origins of the variant reach back to the War Office's realization that appliqué armour (additional thicknesses of plate attached over key areas) was not the optimum solution to the problem of improving protection. The A22F specification therefore called for a maximum armour thickness of 152 mm (6 in), though this was to be of the integral rather than appliqué type. The resultant Churchill VII retained the basic configuration and indeed shape of the earlier marks, but was extensively revised to allow the incorporation of thicker armour in the structure, and also to incorporate the many features that had been shown to be desirable in earlier variants. The armour varied in thickness from a minimum of 25 mm (0.98 in) to a maximum of 152 mm (6 in), and this increased the tank's basic weight to 89,600 lb (40,643 kg). The engine remained unaltered, and the tank's maximum speed was reduced from 16 to 12.75 mph (25.75 to 20.5 km/h): this was a governed speed produced by a gearbox with lower ratios to avoid overtaxing the strengthened suspension. The main armament was the same 75-mm (2.95-in) gun as fitted in

187

The A22F Churchill VII was a major redesign of the basic Churchill with a new hull/turret combination and a 75-mm (2.95-in) gun. This was the major Churchill variant in British post-war services. (*RAC Tank Museum*)

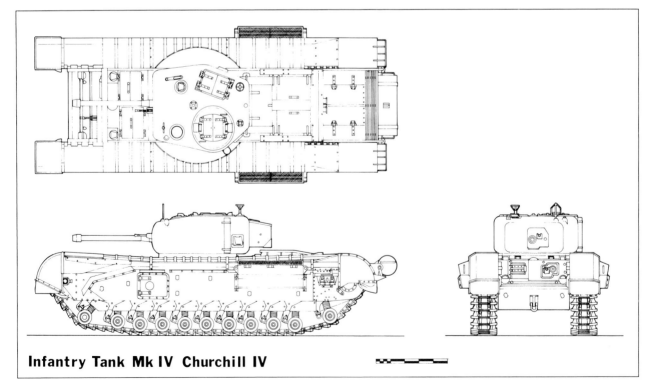

Infantry Tank Mk IV Churchill IV

A22 Infantry Tank Mk IV Churchill IV (UK)

Type: infantry tank
Crew: 5
Combat weight: 87,360 lb (39,626 kg)
Dimensions: length overall 25.17 ft (7.67 m); width 10.67 ft (3.25 m); height overall 8.17 ft (2.49 m)
Armament system: one 6-pdr (57-mm) QF Mk III L/43 or Mk V L/50 rifled gun with 84 rounds, two 7.92-mm (0.312-in) Besa machine-guns (one coaxial and one bow) with 9,450 rounds, one 0.303-in (7.7-mm) Bren AA machine-gun with 600 rounds, and one bomb thrower with 30 rounds; the turret was electrically operated, the main gun was stabilized in neither elevation (– 12.5° to + 20°) nor azimuth (360°), and simple optical sights were fitted
Armour: cast, bolted and welded steel varying in thickness between 16 and 104 mm (0.63 and 4.1 in)
Powerplant: one 350-hp (261-kW) Bedford Twin-six petrol engine with 150 Imp. gal. (682 litres) of fuel plus provision for 32.5 Imp. gal. (147.7 litres) of additional fuel in a jettisonable external tank
Performance: speed, road 15.5 mph (24.9 km/h); range, road 120 miles (193 km) with external fuel; fording 3.33 ft (1.01 m) without preparation; gradient 58%; vertical obstacle 2.5 ft (0.76 m); trench 10.0 ft (3.05 m); ground clearance 20 in (0.51 m)

the Mk VI, with a single-baffle muzzle brake, but the turret was a composite unit with the horizontal roof welded to the cast vertical sections and, perhaps most importantly, the first British example of a commander's cupola providing a 360° field of vision in the closed-down mode. The close-support version of the Mk VII was the Churchill VIII, which was in fact the last production variant of the Churchill. This was identical to the Mk VII in all but its armament, which was the same as that of the Mk V: one 94-mm (3.7-in) howitzer and two 7.92-mm (0.312-in) Besa machine-guns, one coaxial and the other in the bow plate.

The last three marks were earlier Churchills reworked to improved standards with appliqué armour and the cast turret of the Mk VII complete with the 75-mm (2.95-in) gun. The designations Churchill IX, X and XI were used for Mks III and IV, Mk VI and Mk V tanks

respectively, while the suffix LT (light turret) was used for those that retained their original turrets (revised for the heavier main gun) but featured appliqué armour.

The roomy nature of the Churchill's hull combined with its reliability and good cross-country performance to promote its use for a large number of the specialist roles. Several of these developments failed to pass the experimental stage, or to achieve more than very limited use, but others were important armoured vehicles that paved the way for future developments and additionally played a key part in the success of the British forces' final offensives against Germany. The Churchill AVRE (Armoured Vehicle Royal Engineers) was a specialist conversion of Mk III and Mk IV gun tanks to the standard required for assault engineer operations: the standard gun was replaced by a 290-mm (11.42-in) Petard spigot mortar, which could fire its 40-lb (18.14-lb) 'Flying Dustbin' bomb over an effective range of 80 yards (75 m) for the clearance of obstacles; the interior of the tank was stripped of gun tank appurtenances to allow storage of special assault engineer stores, and the hull front was fitted with attachment points for special equipment. The Churchill Mk II SBG AVRE (Standard Box Girder Armoured Vehicle Royal Engineers) was a 1943 Canadian development of the Churchill AVRE with a 34-ft (10.36-m) box girder bridge on quick-release mountings. The bridge was controlled from a winch at the rear of the vehicle, and the practice when faced with high obstacles was for one Mk II SGB AVRE to place its bridge at an angle against the obstacle and pull back, allowing a second vehicle carrying fascines to climb the ramp thus created before dropping its fascines on the far side of the obstacle and then climbing down. The Churchill was also developed as a straighforward armoured vehicle-launched bridgelayer in forms such as the Churchill ARK and as the carrier and launcher for mobile and Bailey bridges.

To cross sand and heavy concentrations of obstacle-laced barbed wire, the Churchill was developed as a carpet-layer with one wide or two narrow strips of matting carried on arm-supported rollers in front of the tank. When required, the weighted end of the matting was

gun armament, that of the Crocodile being a trainable weapon located in the position of the bow machine-gun to fire jets to a maximum range of 120 yards (110 m), though a more practical range was 80 yards (75 m).

Minefields were extensively laid by the Germans to slow and channel the advance of the Allied armies, and all combatants developed their own systems to deal with this threat. So far as the Churchill was concerned, the type was trialled or used with roller, plough and explosive devices. Light obstacles were also a problem to the Allies, and here the Churchill came into its own with mechanical charge-placers such as the Light Carrot, Jones Onion, Goat, and Bangalore Torpedo.

Finally in the Churchill story come the Churchill 3-in Gun Carrier Mk I and the A43 Infantry Tank Black Prince. The gun carrier was a self-propelled mounting for the 3-in (76.2mm) Mk 3 AA gun in a limited-traverse mounting in the heightened front plate that now formed the forward edge of the boxlike supers-

Below The A22 Infantry Tank Mk ICS Churchill was developed in an amazing number of variants in addition to its primary gun tank form. This is a Churchill Bridgelayer midway through launching its 30-ft (9.14-m) 80-ton capacity bridge, which remained horizontal throughout the operation. (*IWM*)

dropped to the ground, the tank then moving forward over the matting, which unrolled automatically; the spent bobbin was then discarded. Another obstacle-clearing device was the highly-feared flamethrower, and the Churchill was developed in initial Churchill Oke and later Churchill Crocodile forms with this weapon. The Oke had an internal fuel tank for the flamethrower, but in the Crocodile used a 400-Imp. gal. (1,818-litre) two-wheel trailer tank that could be jettisoned. In both cases the flame gun was carried in addition to the main

Churchill Crocodile
(UK)

Type: flamethrower infantry tank
Crew: 5
Combat weight: 89,600 lb (40,643 kg) excluding flame-throwing equipment
Dimensions: length overall 24.42 ft (7.44 m) excluding flame fuel trailer; width 10.67 ft (3.25 m); height 8.17 ft (2.49 m)
Armament system: one 75-mm (2.95-in) gun, one flame gun in the hull with 400 Imp. gal. (1,818 litres) of flame fuel, one 7.92-mm (0.3-in) Besa machine-gun, one 0.303-in (7.7-mm) Bren machine-gun with 600 rounds, and one 2-in (50.8-mm) bomb thrower with 30 rounds
Armour: between 25 and 152 mm (1 and 6 in)
Powerplant: one 350-hp (261-kW) Bedford Twin-six petrol engine with 182.5 Imp. gal. (830 litres) of fuel including 32.5 Imp. gal. (147.75 litres) in a jettisonable tank, and flame fuel (see above) in a 20,160-lb (9,145-kg) armoured two-wheeled trailer for up to 100 seconds of flame-firing in short bursts
Performance: (basic Churchill VII) speed, road 12.75 mph (20.5 km/h); range, road 90 miles (145 km); fording 3.33 ft (1.01 km) without preparation; vertical obstacle 2.5 ft (0.81 m); trench 10.0 ft (3.05 m)

Far left The Churchill Bobbin, or Churchill AVRE Carpetlayer Type C Mk II, laid a carpet of scaffolding-reinforced hessian matting to create going resilient enough for movement over soft sand in amphibious assault operations. (*PRO*)

The Churchill AVRE was fitted with a large-calibre demolition mortar and could also carry a fascine for filling trenches and other gap obstacles. (*IWM*)

tructure. The type was developed as an emergency measure in the *matériel*-poor days after Dunkirk, but the 50 production examples were delivered only from July 1942. The A43 was designed between 1943 and 1945 by Vauxhall as an enlarged version of the Churchill with a turret large enough to carry the 17-pdr (3-in/76.2-mm) gun, and protection to the same scale as that of second-generation Churchills. The type was unofficially known as the Super Churchill, and was powered by the same Bedford unit as the standard Churchill:

the weight was 112,000 lb (50,803 kg), so performance was dismally low.

It remains only to mention briefly the other two British tanks of the Second World War, the Heavy Tank TOG and the A39 Heavy Assault Tank Tortoise. The TOG was created by a committee of First World War tank designers (hence the acronym TOG, for The Old Gang), and not surprisingly resembled the rhomboidal machines of that period, complete to the proposal for armament in side-mounted sponsons. The tactical need for such a tank seemed

Churchill Crocodile

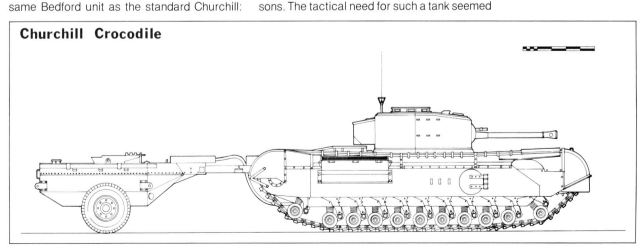

to be indicated by the defences of the 'Siegfried Line', and Sir Albert Stern called together his team (General Sir Ernest Swinton, Sir Eustace Tennyson d'Eyncourt and Mr Harry Ricardo) to create a machine capable of crossing shell-torn ground without difficulty, of absorbing the effects of 37- and 47-mm anti-tank projectiles and 105-mm (4.13-in) HE shells without significant damage, and conversely of inflicting substantial damage with its own bow-mounted field piece (firing shells able to deal with concrete 7 ft/2.13 m thick) and sponson-mounted 2-pdr (40-mm) anti-tank guns. Detail design was entrusted to another First World War 'veteran', in the form of William Foster and Co. Ltd of Lincoln. Design began in February 1940, and the first prototype TOG I was ready for trials in October of the same year: the sponsons had been abandoned, the turret of an A12 Matilda II being added on top, and the bow-mounted armament had been fixed as one 75-mm (2.95-in) howitzer or 17-pdr (3-in/76.2-mm) anti-tank gun, depending on specific role. The vehicle carried a crew of six, had armour varying in thickness between 12 and 62 mm (0.47 and 2.44 in), and at a weight of 179,200 lb (81,285 kg) was powered by a 600-hp (447-kW) Paxman-Ricardo diesel driving an electric system for a speed of 8.5 mph (13.7 km/h). The design was too long for adequate mobility, and was also very slow.

Nonetheless some development work was undertaken with the two prototypes. The original TOG I was modified as the TOG IA with hydraulic drive, and the TOG II was an improved model with lower tracks and a dummy turret carrying a 6-pdr (57-mm) gun, subsequently modified to TOG II* form with the turret and 17-pdr (3-in/76.2-mm) gun of the A30 Challenger.

The Tortoise was developed to outmatch the heaviest German armoured fighting vehicles, such as the Tiger II and Jagdtiger. The result was in effect a tank destroyer with a massive fixed superstructure of cast armour, carrying a development of the 3.7-in (94-mm) anti-aircraft gun in a mounting that allowed traverse to a maximum of only 20° on each side of the centreline. The ordnance fired a 32-lb (14.51-kg) shot with a muzzle velocity of 3,050 ft (930 m) per second. As the seven-man machine was armoured to thicknesses between 35 and 225 m (1.38 and 8.86 in) it weighed 174,720 lb (79,253 kg), and attained a speed of 12 mph (19.3 km/h) on its 600-hp (447-kW) Meteor engine. The design was begun in 1942 by Nuffield Mechanisations and Aero, but the six prototypes were not delivered until 1947, when trials confirmed the complete obsolescence of the type.

On the other side of the Atlantic Ocean, the UK's lack of enthusiasm for the large-scale

Though its lower tracks helped to make the TOG II less obviously related to First World War types than the original TOG I, it was still an obsolescent concept, seen here with a dummy turret and 6-pdr (57-mm) gun. The left-hand aperture for the proposed sponson is visible. (*RAC Tank Museum*)

A 39 Tortoise

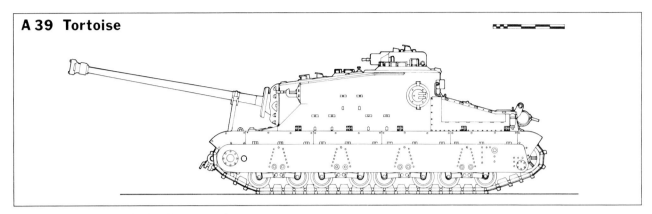

technical and tactical development of armoured warfare in the 1920s and 1930s had been mirrored and indeed exceeded by the USA. During the late 1930s, however, the rapid worsening of the world situation prompted a re-evaluation. As noted in Chapter Two, the US Army had sought in the 1930s to mitigate the worst effects of the USA's isolationist foreign policy and its lack of financing for the services by pursuing an adventurous design philosophy with limited production allocated to industrial concerns capable of rapid expansion in times of need. This policy helped to keep the US Army abreast of overseas developments up to the mid-1930s, and the organization of the army's tank arm was also modified to mirror tactical thinking. The establishment of the First World War had been a Tank Corps modelled on that of the UK, with its tank brigades each comprising one heavy and two light battalions. This structure had been abandoned in 1920, however, when the Tank Corps was disbanded and tanks became part of the infantry arm. In 1928 a new type of armoured force was created as prototype for an expanded mobile formation: comprising single battalions of light tanks, heavy tanks, infantry and artillery, this establishment was not successful, and was abandoned in the same year. A revised armoured force was formed in 1930, but this too enjoyed only a short career before being disbanded in 1932, when the 1st Cavalry Regiment (Mechanized) was tasked with the conceptual development of US armour organization and tactics. A number of organizations resulted, and by 1939 there was a 7th Cavalry Brigade of two light tank battalions and one

A39 Heavy Assault Tank Tortoise (UK)

Type: heavy assault tank prototype
Crew: 7
Combat weight: 179,200 lb (81,285 kg)
Dimensions: length overall 33.00 ft (10.06 m) and hull 23.75 ft (7.24 m); width 12.83 ft (3.91 m); height 10.00 ft (3.05 m)
Armament system: one 32-pdr (3.7-in/94-mm) gun with 60 rounds, three 7.92-mm (0.312-in) Besa machine-guns with 7,500 rounds, one 2-in (50.8-mm) bomb thrower with 30 rounds and two sextuple smoke-dischargers
Armour: between 35 and 225 mm (1.38 and 8.86 in)
Powerplant: one 600-hp (447-kW) Rolls-Royce Meteor Mk V petrol engine
Performance: speed, road 12 mph (19.3 km/h); range, road 28 miles (45 km); fording 4.5 ft (1.38 m); gradient 30°; vertical obstacle 3.0 ft (0.91 m); trench 8.0 ft (2.43 m); ground clearance 15 in (0.38 m)

mechanized artillery regiment. Unfortunately for the Americans this brigade was cavalry-inspired towards light roles such as reconnaissance, raiding and exploitation of successes by other arms.

During 1939 and 1940 the German successes in Poland and the West prompted a complete re-evaluation of the Americans' armoured policy, and resulted in the creation of the Armored Force, based on the new 1st and 2nd Armored Divisions, together with the 70th GHQ Tank Battalion. The diagram in the Appendix reveals the basic structure of the armoured division at this time. This organiza-

193

tion was thoroughly trialled in 1940 and 1941, but found deficient in a number of respects. These were most notably the imbalance of the division and the existence of too many head-quarters, so the 1941 establishment rectified the situation. This was found an altogether more wieldy structure, and though the number of tanks in each division was reduced slightly, the division was stronger in firepower as the balance of armour now favoured medium rather than light tanks. Tactical flexibility was also enhanced by the availability in each armored division of two Combat Command headquarters, each able to control any blend of tanks, mechanized infantry and self-propelled artillery, which gave the Armored Force a division of potent structure.

Unfortunately for the Armored Force, it fell within the organizational purview of the Army Ground Forces, and as a result slightly more than half of the growing number of armoured battalions were allocated to direct infantry-support roles at infantry division level, the armoured divisions proper being controlled at corps level within an organization that combined two infantry divisions with one armored division: this effectively tied American armour to its slower-moving companion, infantry. Greater flexibility was provided to the armoured division by its 1943 reorganization with three combat command headquarters (the third smaller than the original two) for a smaller establishment. This organization survived to the end of the Second World War, and confirms the Americans' predilection for balanced all-arms combat teams, rather than armoured forces with a preponderance of tanks supported by infantry and artillery, as was the norm in the German Panzer and, to a lesser extent, the British armoured divisions.

The main tank types in service with the Armored Force in 1941 were the Light Tank M3 and the Medium Tank M3, both introduced to service in that year, after standardization in 1940. The M3 was a straightforward development of the Light Tank M2A4, which had been standardized in 1939 as the final expression of the basic concept pioneered in the M2A1 of 1935. The Americans had wished to develop a more capable light tank, perhaps armed with a 75-mm (2.95-in) main gun, but the need to press

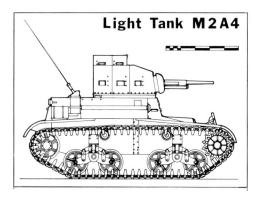

Light Tank M2A4

Light Tank M2A4
(USA)

Type: light tank
Crew: 4
Combat weight: 24,125 lb (10,943 kg)
Dimensions: length overall 14.58 ft (4.44 m); width 8.33 ft (2.54 m); height 8.33 ft (2.54 m) to top of commander's cupola
Armament system: one 37-mm gun with 106 rounds and five 0.3-in (7.62-mm) Browning machine-guns with 7,220 rounds
Armour: between 6.1 and 25.4 mm (0.24 and 1 in)
Powerplant: one 250-hp (186-kW) Continental W–670–9A petrol engine with 54 US gal. (204 litres) of fuel
Performance: speed, road 37.5 mph (60.4 km/h); fording 3.58 ft (1.09 m); gradient 50%; vertical obstacle 2.17 ft (0.66 m); trench 6.0 ft (1.83 m); ground clearance 14.5 in (0.37 m)

ahead with development as rapidly as possible to match the numerical superiority of potential enemies meant that an M2 update rather than a new vehicle was inevitable: this removed any possibility of a larger-calibre main gun, because of the M2's narrow hull, itself dictated by the width capability of the Engineer Corps' pontoon bridging equipment.

The M2A4 was a moderately useful machine. The mobility and firepower were considered just about adequate. The 37-mm M5 gun was 77.35 in (1.965 m) long, and the L/50 barrel fired its 1.92-lb (0.87-kg) shot with a muzzle velocity of 2,545 ft (776 m) per second, giving it the ability to penetrate 48 mm (1.89 in) of armour at an angle of 30° at a range of 500 yards (455 m). The M6 weapon used in the

M3A3 final variant was marginally better, having an overall length of 82.5 in (2.096 m) and a weight of 185 lb (84 kg): the L/53.5 barrel gave the 1.92-lb (0.87-kg) APCBC shot a muzzle velocity of 2,900 ft (1,315 m) per second for the ability to penetrate 61 mm (2.4 in) of armour at an angle of 30° at a range of 500 yards (455 m). But there was less satisfaction about the level of protection of riveted plate varying in thickness between 9.5 and 32 mm (0.37 and 1.25 in): overall thickness was marginally adequate, but serious reservations were expressed about the protection offered against air attack, which the opening operations of the Second World War had shown to be considerably more devastating than had been supposed, even on the evidence of *Blitzkrieg*-type operations in the Spanish Civil War. Thus the M2 was taken in hand for development with thicker armour on the upper surfaces, though the overall level of protection was improved to a minimum of 25 mm (1 in) and a maximum of 38 mm (1.5 in) of reliable homogeneous armour, rather than the brittle face-hardened armour of the M2 series. This better armour was used for the all-riveted construction of the baseline M3A1, raising weight from the M2A4's 25,760 lb (11,685 kg) to 27,550 lb (12,497 kg) in the M3A1 that was standardized in July 1940. The additional weight necessitated the incorporation of a weight-supporting rather than merely track-tensioning idler at the rear of the track run on each side: this idler was carried on a trailing arm and was entirely independent of each

side's arrangement of two volute-sprung twin-wheel bogies inherited from the M2A4's basic design.

Production of the M3 series lasted until August 1942, the American Car and Foundry Company delivering some 5,811 M3 tanks in this period of just over two years. The Americans failed to fall into the trap of three-man crews, and the M3's four-man complement consisted of a driver, assistant driver/hull gunner, commander and gunner. Thus the turret had a crew of only two, a situation ameliorated by the comparatively light weight of the ammunition for the 37-mm main gun (the complete APCBC round weighed 3.4 lb/1.54 kg), which did not impose too great a burden on the gunner. Apart from the 37-mm M5 or M6 main gun, the M3A1's armament comprised no fewer than five 0.3-in (7.62-mm) Browning machine-guns, located as a single coaxial weapon, a single bow weapon, a single anti-aircraft weapon on the commander's fixed turret-roof cupola, and two weapons in side sponsons fixed to deliver forward fire; these last were often omitted, especially in British service, where sandshields were generally installed in place of the machine-guns. The ammunition supply amounted to 103 37-mm and 8,270 0.3-in (7.62-mm) rounds.

Development of the M3 was undertaken on a constant basis, and the major improvements added to this light tank were centred on structure and armament. In order of introduction, these improvements included an all-

An M3A1 light tank of the 47th Armored Regiment on manoeuvres at Camp Chaffer, Arkansas, in February 1943. This variant had provision for a 0.3-in (7.62-mm) machine-gun in the forward edge of each sponson. (*US Army*)

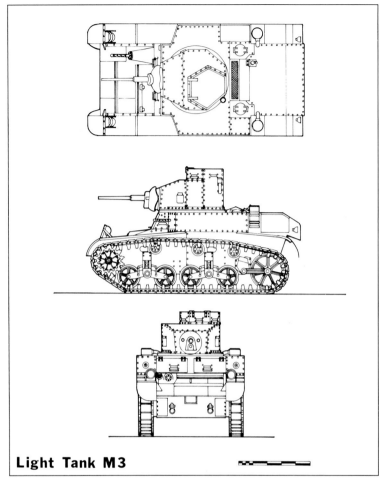

Light Tank M3

used in preference to the official British name. The first production variant was the M3, which was called General Stuart I by the British: the 5,311 examples of this model were powered by a 250-hp (186-kW) Continental W-970-9A petrol engine developed from a radial aero engine. It became clear early in the production programme that there would be insufficient quantities of the Continental engine, however, so a 500-tank batch was authorized with a 220-hp (164-kW) Guiberson T-1020 diesel engine: this was still designated M3 by the Americans, but was called the General Stuart II by the British. The next variant was the Continental-engined M3A1 (General Stuart III), introduced in August 1941 with the cast/welded power-traversed turret and a stabilized main gun. This variant weighed 28,450 lb (12,905 kg), reducing maximum road speed from 35 to 34 mph (56.3 to 54.7 km/h), though cross-country speed remained substantially unaltered at a maximum of 20 mph (32.2 km/h). The 4,410 petrol-engined

---

Light Tank M3 (Stuart I or II)
(USA)

Type: light tank
Crew: 4
Combat weight: 27,400 lb (12,429 lb)
Dimensions: length overall 14.875 ft (4.53 m); width 7.33 ft (2.23 m); height overall 8.25 ft (2.515 m)
Armament system: one 37-mm M5 L/50 or M6 L/55 rifled gun with 103 rounds, and five 0.3-in (7.7-mm) Browning M1919A4 machine-guns (one coaxial, one bow, one in each hull sponson and one AA) with 8.270 rounds; the turret was manually operated, the main gun was stabilized in neither elevation ($-10°$ to $+20°$) nor in azimuth (360°), and simple optical sights were fitted
Armour: riveted steel varying in thickness between 10 and 64 mm (0.375 and 2.5 in)
Powerplant: (Stuart III) one 250-hp (186.4-kW) Continental W–970–9A petrol engine or (Stuart II) one 220-hp (164-kW) Guiberson Buda T–1020–4 diesel engine with 56 US gal (212 litres) of fuel plus provision for 45 US gal (170.3 litres) of additional fuel in jettisonable external tanks
Performance: speed, road 36 mph (57.9 km/h); range, road 70 miles (112.7 km); fording 3.0 ft (0.91 m); gradient 60%; vertical obstacle 2.0 ft (0.61 m); trench 6.0 ft (1.83 m); ground clearance 16.5 in (0.42 m)

---

welded heptagonal turret of homogeneous armour in place of the original face-hardened riveted type (June 1941), a stabilizer for the main gun in elevation (mid-1941), a new cylinder turret of cast and welded construction (second half of 1941), hydraulic turret traverse and a turret basket (second half of 1941), two jettisonable 22.5-US gal. (85-litre) fuel tanks to increase the M3's poor range in open-warfare conditions (early 1942), and an all-welded hull (just before the end of production).

The M3 series was widely used by the British and dominion forces, and was given the name General Stuart in British service. The tank was widely admired for its high level of protection, reliability, high speed and good agility in difficult going, and this admiration was reflected in the nickname 'Honey', generally

M3A1s were complemented by 211 examples of the Guiberson diesel-engined variant, known to the British as the General Stuart IV. The M3A2 was to have been a variant of the M3A1 with a welded hull, but as this was not put into production, the final M3 variant was the 31,750-lb (14,402-kg) M3A3, known to the British as the General Stuart V. This introduced the all-welded hull, whose plates were better sloped than those of the riveted M3 and M3A1. Other modifications included a larger driver's compartment, elimination of sponson provision in favour of increased fuel and ammunition capacities, engine air cleaners, and a revised rear to the turret to allow carriage of a radio. The M3A3 was built to the extent of 3,427 examples before production ended in October 1943. Total production of the M3 series amounted to 13,859 tanks, making this the most prolific light tank series of the Second World War. The type was extensively used in most Allied theatres, and thanks to features such as its stabilized gun was still an effective weapon against Japanese tanks in 1945. What cannot be ignored, however, are the type's several limitations, most notably its high silhouette and angular lines, the latter contributing in no small measure to the creation of several shot traps.

The next stage in US light tank development was inspired by the car industry, rather than by the Ordnance Department or the heavy engineering companies upon which the Ordnance Department had relied for tank production until it became clear that mass-production capability was more significant than heavy engineering experience. The Light Tank M5 was suggested by Cadillac, which proposed to a sceptical Ordnance Department that the M3 could be revised without difficulty to accept a different powerplant and transmission: the powerplant was to be a pair of Cadillac V-8 car engines, and the transmission the Cadillac Hydra-Matic automatic type. Cadillac converted an M3 to this standard as the M3E2 with a raised rear decking, an increase in internal fuel capacity from 56 to 89 US gal. (212 to 337 litres), a longer superstructure, an angled rather than a vertical front plate, and elimination of the machine-gun sponsons.

The conversion was completed in October

An M5 light tank on desert manoeuvres during August 1942 reveals the compact shape of this important armoured vehicle. Notable features are the welded hull and turret, the gyrostabilized 37-mm main gun and the two hull-mounted 0.3-in (7.62-mm) machine-guns. (US Army)

1941, and the revised model was standardized in February 1942 as the Light Tank M5 with a welded hull and the hull front thickened to a maximum of 64 mm (2.5 in). The turret was that of the M3A1, and the ammunition capacities were 123 37-mm and 6,250 0.3-in (7.62-mm) rounds. This model weighed 33,000 lb (14,969 kg), and with 220 hp (164 kW) available from the ganged Cadillac engines had much the same performance as the M3A3, apart from greater range. The M5 was called the General Stuart VI by the British, and was succeeded in production from September 1942 by the M5A1 (also called the General Stuart VI). This final version weighed 33,910 lb (15,382 kg), and differed from the M5 in having the turret of the M3A3 with radio bulge, improved main gun mounting, larger hatches for the driver and co-driver, and an escape hatch in the belly. Production of the M5 series amounted to 8,884 (2,074 M5s and 6,810 M5A1s) before production terminated in October 1944.

The main variant of the M5 series was the Howitzer Motor Carriage M8, a 34,600-lb (15,695-kg) vehicle based on the M5 but carrying a turret armed with one 75-mm (2.95-in) M2 or M3 pack howitzer. The M8 carried 46 howitzer rounds (plus further stocks in a small two-wheeled towed limber), and its secondary armament comprised one 0.5-in (12.7-mm) Browning machine-gun with 400 rounds for anti-aircraft defence. The M8 was placed in production in September 1942, and 1,778 were built before the line closed in January 1944. The M8 was generally used to provide medium tank battalions with fire support.

The Americans sought to replace the M3/M5 series with a light tank of more modern concept, notably lower silhouette and 38-mm (1.5-in) armour. In typically lavish US fashion the T7 was developed in E1 to E4 prototypes by the Rock Island Arsenal to evaluate different features: the T7E1 was not built, but would have featured all-riveted construction and horizontal volute spring suspension; the T7E2 had all-cast construction; the T7E3 was not built, but would have had all welded construc-

tion; and the T7E4 was also not built. Development of the T7E2 proceeded apace, but the potential of the design combined with a shift in operational requirements to alter the concept to more heavily armed configuration with a 57-mm gun, a calibre requested by the British, who had an interest in the tank. Thus armed, and powered by a 400-hp (298-kW) Wright R-975 petrol engine for a speed of 34 mph (54.7 km/h), the T7E2 weighed 51,000 lb (23,134 kg) and thereby moved into the medium tank class, which called for rearmament with a 75-mm (2.95-in) main gun. After reclassification as a medium tank in August 1942, the tank was standardized as the Medium Tank M7. However, in February 1943 the order for 3,000 M7s was cancelled to allow all US medium tank production to be concentrated on the M4 series.

The next US light tank of the Second World War was therefore the Light Tank M22 developed as the T9 to meet a requirement for a 16,800-lb (7,620-kg) armoured fighting vehicle suitable for deployment with airborne forces. The specification drew submissions from J.

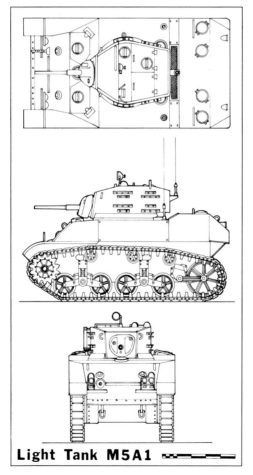

Light Tank M5A1

Light Tank M5 (Stuart Mk VI) (USA)

Type: light tank
Crew: 4
Combat weight: 33,000 lb (14,969 kg)
Dimensions: length overall 14.23 ft (4.34 m); width 7.375 ft (2.25 m); height overall 7.54 ft (2.30 m)
Armament system: one 37-mm M6 L/55 rifled gun with 123 rounds and three 0.3-in (7.62-mm) machine-guns (one coaxial, one bow and one AA) with 6,250 rounds, the turret was hydraulically operated, the main gun was gyyrostabilized in elevation (−10° to +20°) but not in azimuth (360°), and simple optical sights were fitted
Armour: welded steel varying in thickness between 10 and 64 mm (0.375 and 2.5 in)
Powerplant: two 110-hp (82-kW) Cadillac Series 42 petrol engines with 89 US gal. (337 litres) of fuel
Performance: speed, road 36 mph (57.9 km/h); range, road 100 miles (161 km); fording 3.5 ft (1.07 m); gradient 60%; vertical obstacle 1.5 ft (0.46 m); trench 5.33 ft (1.62 m); ground clearance 15 in (0.38 in)

Light Tank (Airborne) M22 Locust
(USA)

Type: light tank
Crew: 3
Combat weight: 16,400 lb (7,439 kg)
Dimensions: length overall 12.92 ft (3.94 m); width 7.3125 ft (2.23 m); height 5.71 ft (1.74 m)
Armament system: one 37-mm gun with 50 rounds and one 0.3-in (7.62-mm) Browning machine-gun with 2,500 rounds
Armour: between 10 and 25 mm (0.4 and 1 in)
Powerplant: one 162-hp (121-kW) Lycoming O–435T petrol engine with 57 US gal. (216 litres) of fuel
Performance: speed, road 40 mph (64.4 km/h); range, road 135 miles (217 km); fording 3.5 ft (1.07 m); gradient 63%; vertical obstacle 1.03 ft (0.315 m); trench 5.4 ft (1.65 m); ground clearance 9.5 in (0.24 m)

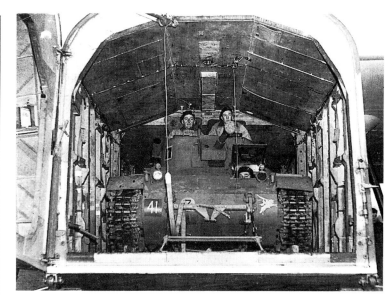

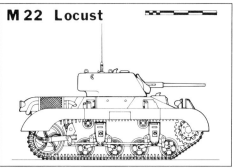

The M22 Locust light tank was designed for airborne forces' use, and one of the few aircraft that could accommodate the type was the RAF's special General Aircraft Hamilcar glider. (*RAC Tank Museum*)

Walter Christie, the General Motors Corporation and the Marmon-Herrington Company, the submission of the last being accepted for further development with standard Marmon-Herrington running gear and an Avco Lycoming air-cooled engine. The Light Tank T9 (Airborne) prototype was delivered in autumn 1941 but at a weight of 17,700 lb (8,029 kg) was found to be in need of further refinement during 1942 as the T9E1 with a welded hull and cast turret, a new nose without a machine-gun, removal of the turret power traverse and main armament stabilization systems, and provision of a removable turret (complete with turret basket) for enhanced air-portability. The T9E1 was ordered into production in April 1942 as the Light Tank M22 with a crew of three, a weight of 17,025 lb (7,723 kg) with armour varying in thickness between 9 and 25 mm (0.33 and 1 in), a maximum speed of 40 mph (64.4 km.h) on its 162-hp (121-kW) Lycoming 0-435T engine, and an armament of one 37-mm M6 gun and one 0.3-in (7.62-mm) coaxial machine-gun. The M22 was surprisingly roomy, but the demands of air-portability (in American service under a Douglas C-54 Skymaster four-engined transport) meant that armour and armament were both too light to give the M22 any worthwhile role in the European theatre. As it turned out, production ended in February 1944 after the delivery of

only 830 of a planned 1,900 M22s, and the only combat operator of the type was the British army, which called the tank the Locust. In British service the Locust was carried by the General Aircraft Hamilcar glider in operations such as the airborne crossing of the Rhine river in April 1945.

Because of its peculiar operation requirement, the M22 can be described as adequate in mobility but woefully deficient in firepower and protection. These attributes were clear from an early stage of the T9/M22 programme, and the next American light tank was carefully planned as an altogether more operational vehicle in its task of replacing the M3 and M5 series. This was the Light Tank M24, which emerged as without doubt the best light tank of the Second World War: firepower was superior to that of all medium tanks of 1939 through the

Lacking an effective tank destroyer, which was a tank-based vehicle carrying a light turret armed with a specialized anti-tank gun, the US Army promoted the development of the M36 90-mm Gun Motor Carriage that entered service late in the Second World War. This was the hull of the obsolescent M10A1 tank destroyer (itself based on the M4 Sherman medium tank fitted with an open-topped turret carrying a 3-in/76-mm gun) with a turret carrying a potent anti-tank gun derived from the 90-mm (3.54-in) M1 anti-aircraft gun. (*US Army/MARS*)

use of a lightweight 75-mm (2.95-in) T13E1 gun with concentric recoil mechanism derived from the M5 aircraft weapon, protection was provided by a considerable lowering of silhouette in combination not so much with great thickness of armour but rather with careful design of thinner (and thus lighter) armour to provide, a high level of ballistic protection with few shot traps, and mobility was at least equal to that of the highly praised M5.

Since the mid-1930s the US Army had planned its structure with parallel tank and tank-destroyer forces, the latter being the Tank Destroyer Command. This sought to provide itself with vehicles carrying the same basic armament as the Armored Force's tanks, but allowing greater tactical mobility by the use of

thin frontal and side armour plus minimal overhead protection: the need for such vehicles was enshrined in the 'shoot-and-scoot' tactics practised by the command. When the Armored Force began development of a medium tank armed with a 75-mm (2.95-in) main gun, therefore, the Tank Destroyer Command sought to develop a tank destroyer with comparable firepower. The first result was the Howitzer Motor Carriage T17, based on the Combat Car M1E3 and standardized as the Howitzer Motor Carriage M8 fitted with the 75-mm (2.95-in) M3 gun.

The programme that led to the M24 was launched in April 1943, the object being a successor to the M5 with the features listed above plus a combat weight of 35,840 lb

An M24 Chaffee light tank at range practice in France during March 1945 with its 75-mm (2.95-in) M6 main gun. (*US Army*)

(16,257 kg) with maximum 25-mm (1-in) armour, greater accessibility and improved
buoyancy. Initial consideration was given to a
Light Tank T21, but at a projected weight of
48,160 lb (21,845 kg) this was clearly too
heavy. Obvious starting points were the engine
and transmission that had proved so successful in the M5, and the running gear of the
76-mm Gun Motor Carriage M18 'Hellcat', a
high-mobility tank destroyer using torsion bar
suspension for five medium-diameter road
wheels on each side. Such a vehicle was
proposed by the Cadillac Motor Car Division of
the General Motors Corporation, and two
prototypes were ordered under the designation
Light Tank T24. These were delivered in
October 1943, and proved so successful
during initial running trials that 1,000 were
ordered even before the full service trials had
been started. The tank was standardized as the
Light tank M24 in July 1944, and production
orders eventually totalled 5,000 units, of which
4,070 had been built by June 1945. The M24
entered service with the US Army in 1944, and
in 1945 a small quantitiy was supplied to the
British army, which gave the name Chaffee to
the type. In combat the M24 Chaffee proved
useful, despite the fact that the day of the light
tank was clearly over, so far as the world's
most advanced armies were concerned: the
gun proved accurate and powerful, and for its
thickness the armour was effective. The overall
success of the tank may be gauged from the
fact that the type remained in extensive service
with many armies into the late 1970s, and is still
fielded in modest numbers by several armies in
the late 1980s, many current examples have
been upgraded in various ways.

There were no variants of the M24 in its
basic tank role, but as the vehicle had been
planned as the baseline model of the original
'Lightweight Combat Team' there were a
number of specialist vehicles on the same
chassis, the most important of these being a
sextuple 0.5-in (12.7-mm) heavy machine-gun
mounting, two armoured utility vehicles, three
cargo carriers, a dozer and a tank recovery
vehicle.

Next up in size and capability from the light
tank is the medium tank, and here the US Army
expended enormous development and produc-

M 24 Chaffee

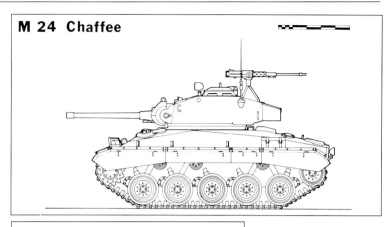

Light Tank M24 Chaffee
(USA)

Type: light tank
Crew: 4–5
Combat weight: 40,500 lb (18,371 kg)
Dimensions: length, gun forward 18.00 ft
(5.49 m) and hull 16.50 ft (5.03 m); width 9.67 ft
(2.95 m); height 8.08 ft (2.46 m) including commander's cupola
Armament system: one 75-mm (2.95-in) gun with
48 rounds, one 0.5-in (12.7-mm) Browning
machine-gun with 440 rounds and two 0.3-in
(7.62-mm) Browning machine-guns with 3,750
rounds
Armour: between 12.7 and 38 mm (0.5 and 1.5 in)
Powerplant: two 110-hp (82-kW) Cadillac 44T24
petrol engines with 110 US gal. (416 litres) of fuel
Performance: speed, road 34 mph (54.7 km/h);
range, road 175 miles (281 km); fording 3.33 ft
(1.02 m); gradient 60%; side slope 30%; vertical
obstacle 3.0 ft (0.91 m); trench 8.0 ft (2.44 m);
ground clearance 18 in (0.46 m)

tion effort, as such tanks were the mainstays of
the service's armoured divisions in the Second
World War. In the late 1930s the US Army's
principal vehicle in this class was the Medium
Tank M2 and basically similar M2A1 armed
with a 37-mm main gun, but in 1940 it was
realized that despite their recent development,
these were obsolete by the standard now set
by German tank development and operations.
In August 1940, therefore, the heads of the
Armored Force and Ordnance Department
decided on the specification for a new medium
tank with armour on a 38-mm (1.5-in) basis and
a 75-mm (2.95-in) main gun. So far as these
features were concerned, the specification

was adequate: the trouble came with the realization that the US Army had lagged behind the European nations in developing large-diameter turrets of the type required for a 75-mm (2.95-in) gun, and that an alternative installation would have to be considered. Such a mounting had already been trialled in a Medium tank T5 Phase III (the final precursor of the M2), which had been fitted with a 75-mm (2.95-in) pack howitzer in a limited-traverse mounting carried in a sponson on the right-hand side of the hull. It was decided, therefore, to upgrade the M2 with thicker armour and a 75-mm (2.95-in) sponson-mounted gun in addition to the existing 37-mm weapon (in a cast rather than welded turret surmounted by a secondary turret accommodating the commander and a 0.3-in/7.62-mm machine-gun) as the new Medium Tank M3. Late in August 1940 a recently-placed order for 1,000 M2A1s was modified to the same number of M3s in a programme co-ordinated by William Knudsen, president of the General Motors Corporation and a co-opted member of the National Defense Advisory Committee. It was Knudsen who was largely instrumental in persuading the US military authorities that tank production was better entrusted to the car industry than to the heavy engineering industry (in the forms of the American Locomotive Company and the

Baldwin Locomotive Company for medium tanks), and production of the new M3 was allocated to a new government-owned facility run by the Chrysler Corporation.

The key to the new tank was the M2 gun, a 783-lb (355-kg) weapon derived by the Watervliet Arsenal from the celebrated French Modèle 1897 field gun. This weapon was 91.75 in (2.33 m) long, and its L/28.5 barrel allowed the 14.96-lb (6.79-kg) armour-piercing projectile to be fired with a muzzle velocity of 1,860 ft (567 m) per second, providing a penetration capability of 60 mm (2.36 in) of armour angled at 30° at a range of 500 yards (455 m): this translates as a 25 per cent improvement over the capabilities of the 37-mm M6 gun, and the M2 could also fire a useful HE as well as other rounds. The M2 was an interim model, the definitive weapon in this calibre being the M3 weighing 910 lb (413 kg) and measuring 118.375 in (3.01 m) in overall length: this had an L/37.5 barrel, which gave the standard armour-piercing projectile a muzzle velocity of 2,300 ft (701 m) per second for a penetration capability of 70 mm (2.76 in) of armour at an angle of 30° at a range of 500 yards (455 m). The M3 gun was ready for installation on later M3 tanks, and was also earmarked for the M3's successor, the legendary M4. The primary limitation of the 75-mm (2.95-in) gun mounting in the M3 was its small traverse (15° left and right of the centreline) while a useful feature was the provision (for the first time in an operational tank) of a Westinghouse stabilization system for the main and secondary guns in elevation. This latter allowed moderately accurate fire, even with the tank on the move, a feature imposssible with previous shoulder- or gear-controlled guns. In tactical terms, the location of the main gun in a sponson meant that much of the tank's already considerable height had to be exposed to bring the gun into action, while the engagement of targets more than 15° off the centreline meant manoeuvring the whole vehicle.

Prototypes of the new M3 were delivered in January 1941 by Chrysler, additional vehicles following from American Locomotive (Alco) and Baldwin by April. Production was launched in August 1941, and 6,258 M3s were built before production ceased in December 1942: 3,352 came from Chrysler, and smaller

The first Chrysler-built M3 medium tank leaves the production facility for delivery on 12 April 1941. This was an event of great moment, marking a milestone in the US car industry's move towards becoming the US Army's main tank supplier. (*Chrysler Historical Collection*)

numbers from Alco, Baldwin, Pressed Steel and Pullman, fully vindicating the decision to allocate medium tank production mainly to the car industry.

The six-man M3 bore a marked similarity to the M2, retaining from its predecessor the massive and angular hull, the aero engine-derived powerplant, and the running gear that comprised on each side three twin-wheel bogies with vertical volute spring suspension, three track-return rollers (located at the upper end of each bogie attachment), a front drive sprocket and a rear idler. Oddly enough, given the fact that the 51,520-lb (23,369-kg) M2A1 was powered by a 400-hp (298-kW) Wright radial, the M3 had only a 340-hp (253.5-kW) version of the same unit to move its 60,000-lb (27,216-lb) mass, which resulted in a maximum speed of 26 mph (41.8 km/h) rather than the 30 mph (48.3 km/h) of the M2A1.

The M3 entered US service in 1941, and was also delivered in substantial numbers to the British under the terms of the Lend-lease programme, largely for service in North Africa and the Far East. Though the M3 medium tank's production life was comparatively short, there appeared several important variants reflecting the rapid pace of development in the first half of the Second World War, and also the ability of American manufacturing companies to respond to these developments without undue delay.

The original M3 (General Lee I in British service) had a riveted hull and a Wright R-975 radial petrol engine, though some M3 (Diesel) tanks were fitted with a Guiberson T-1400 diesel engine to overcome shortages of the Wright engine. Next came the M3A1 (General Lee II), mechanically identical with the M3 with Wright or Guiberson engine but built exclusively to the extent of 300 vehicles by Alco, the only company in the programme able to produce this variant's cast upper hull whose side hatches were later eliminated to provide extra strength, an escape hatch then being added in the belly. The M3A2 was not used by the British, though the designation General Lee III had been allocated, and the variant was mechanically identical with the M3 but based on a welded rather than riveted hull. M3A2 production amounted to only 12 vehicles

before Baldwin switched to the 63,000-lb (28,577-kg) M3A3 (General Lee IV) with a welded hull and completely revised power-plant. This latter comprised two General Motors 6-71 diesels, coupled to deliver 375 hp (280 kW): the larger engine installation reduced fuel capacity from 175 to 150 US gal. (662 to 568 litres), but the efficiency of the diesel powerplant boosted range from 120 to 160 miles (193 to 257 km). Production was by Baldwin to a total of 322 vehicles, and some British-operated M3A3s were re-engined with the Wright radial and given the designation General Lee V. The M3A4 (General Lee VI) was identical to the original M3 in everything but its engine, which was a 370-hp (276-kW) Chrysler A-57 multibank petrol unit, made by combining five car cylinder blocks on a common crank-shaft; the engine was longer than the earlier units, and to provide an adequate engine compartment the hull had to be increased in length by 14 in (0.356 m) to an overall figure of 19.67 ft (5.99 m), increasing weight to 64,000 lb (29,030 kg). Production of 109 vehicles was undertaken by Chrysler. The final production variant was the M3A5, identical to the M3A3 in every respect but its hull, which was riveted rather than welded, for a weight of 64,000 lb (29,030 kg), and had the side doors either welded shut or eliminated: Baldwin delivered

The M3A1 medium tank was mechanically identical with the M3 but has a cast rather than riveted upper hull. Notable features are the 75-mm (2.95-in) main gun in a sponson, a 37-mm gun in the turret and a 0.3-in (7.62-mm) machine-gun in the cupola, as well as a side access hatch that was eliminated from later production examples. (*RAC Tank Museum*)

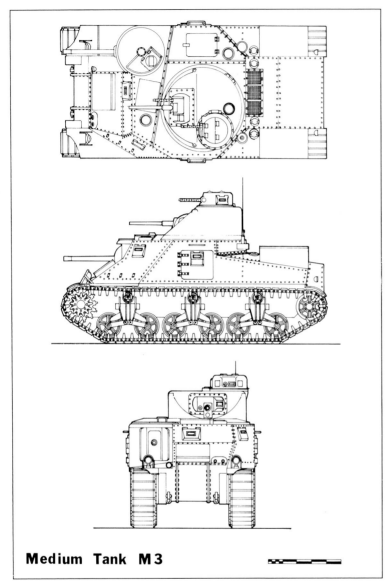

Medium Tank M3

stripped of its secondary turret to reduce overall height. Similar modification was later made to the M3A5 to produce the General Grant II, whereupon the original variant became the General Grant I. It was as the General Grant that the type made its combat debut in the Battle of Gazala in May 1942. Here for the first time the British had a tank with a gun matching that of the Germans' PzKpfw IV. The importance of the Lee/Grant to the British was considerable, and though there were problems with the fuses and filling of the type's HE shell earlier in 1942, the tank played a significant part in the British success at the 2nd Battle of El Alamein in October and November of 1942.

The interim nature of the M3 series is confirmed by the speed at which it disappeared from service once the M4 began to arrive in significant numbers: the US Army declared the type obsolete in March 1944, and the basic

---

Medium Tank M3 (Lee Mk I)
(USA)

Type: medium tank
Crew: 6
Combat weight: 60,000 lb (27,216 kg)
Dimensions: length overall 18.50 ft (5.64 m); width 8.92 ft (2.72 m); height overall 10.25 ft (3.12 m)
Armament system: one 75-mm (2.95-in) M2 L/28.47 or M3 L/37.5 rifled gun with 46 rounds in a right-hand hull sponson allowing gyrostabilized elevation, and azimuth movement of 60°, one 37-mm M5 L/50 or M6 L/55 gun with 178 rounds, and four 0.3-in (7.62-mm) Browning M1919A4 machine-guns (one coaxial, two bow and one commander's) with 9,200 rounds; the turret was hydraulically operated (with manual reversion), the 37-mm gun was gyrostabilized in elevation but not in azimuth (360°), and simple optical sights were fitted
Armour: riveted steel varying in thickness between 12.7 and 57 mm (0.5 and 2.25 in)
Powerplant: one 340-hp (253.5-kW) Continental R–975–EC2 or C1 petrol engine with 185 US gal. (700 litres) of fuel
Performance: speed, road 26 mph (41.8 km/h); range, road 120 miles (193 km); fording 3.33 ft (1.01 m); gradient 60%; vertical obstacle 2.0 ft (0.61 m); trench 6.2 ft (1.89 m); ground clearance 17 in (0.43 m)

591 such vehicles, the last of them with the longer M3 gun fitted with a counterbalance weight at the muzzle.

As noted above, tanks of the M3 series were delivered to the UK under Lend-Lease with the name General Lee. The British also bought a variant of the basic M3 with a number of modifications as the General Grant. The most notable of these modifications was to the 360° traverse turret, which was lengthened to the rear so that a radio could be installed, and

chassis thereafter remained in service only in alternative roles. The two most important operational variants were the Howitzer Motor Carriage M7 'Priest' with a 105-mm (4.13-in) M2 howitzer in a limited traverse mounting located at the front of an open superstructure, and the Tank Recovery Vehicle M31. The chassis was also used for a wide assortment of experimental and limited-service variants in a number of roles. The British also used the Lee/Grant for alternative roles such as mine-clearing (as the Grant Scorpion with forward-mounted flails).

The M3 was of tactical importance in its own right, but was also of significance in buying time for the development of the Americans' most important medium tank of the Second World War. It had been appreciated from the beginning of the M3 programme that the sponson-mounted main gun was a significant limitation, and on 29 August 1940 (just one day

after the first production order for the M3 had been placed) design work began on an M3 successor with its 75-mm (2.95-in) main gun in a 360° traverse turret: this would in itself provide great tactical improvements, while the elimination of sponsons reduced the volume requiring armour protection, thereby allowing a lighter weight of armour for a more sprightly vehicle or, more practically, greater weight of armour over the protected volume, that now accommodated five rather than six men. As much as possible of the M3 was retained, and the result was the Medium tank T6 development model with a short-barrel M2 gun in a cast turret on a cast hull. The machine weighed 67,200 lb (30,482 kg), was powered by a 400-hp (298-kW) Wright radial petrol engine for a speed of 26 mph (41.8 km/h), and in addition to its main gun possessed an armament of four 0.3-in (7.62-mm) machine-guns located as one coaxial, one bow and two fixed foward-firing

An immaculate M3A5 medium tank with twin General Motors 6-71 diesels is seen in its British form as the General Grant V with its British cast turret without cupola. (*RAC Tank Museum*)

nose guns. Prototype vehicles were delivered in September 1941, and trials confirmed the expectations of the designers and the army: in October 1941 a slightly modified version of the T6 (with a belly hatch and an additional driver's hatch in place of the the side doors) was standardized as the Medium Tank M4, better known by the name Sherman, bestowed initially by the British within their system of naming US tanks after famous American generals. The M4 was planned to supersede the M3 on all current medium tank production lines, with additional sources coming on stream as production tempo increased. It was then realized that adequate casting facilities were not available for the anticipated number of hulls (at one time planned as 2,000 vehicles per month!), and a more boxy upper hull of welded construction was developed as an alternative. Vehicles with the welded hull were designated M4, and those with the cast hull M4A1: both used the same one-piece cast turret, which had a maximum frontal thickness of 76 mm (3 in), and Oilgear hydraulic or Westinghouse electric power traverse system, and a stabilization system for the main gun in elevation. The main gun was the longer-barrel M3 weapon rather than the M2 used in the T6.

In overall layout the Sherman was typical of its era, with a forward compartment for the driver and co-driver/nose gunner (the two fixed guns of the T6 being abandoned as superfluous soon after the M4A1's production life had started), a central fighting compartment for the commander, gunner and loader, and a rear compartment for the engine. On each side the running gear comprised three twin-wheel bogies with vertical volute spring suspension, three track-return rollers located one at the top of each bogie attachment unit ('first-type suspension'), a front drive sprocket and a rear idler. The standard engine was the 400-hp (298-kW) Wright R-975 radial petrol engine.

The Sherman ran through a large number of variants and sub-variants, and these are listed below in order of designation rather than of production by the M3 manufacturers, who were joined by Federal Machine and Welder, Fisher Body, the Ford Motor Company, and Pacific Car and Foundry. First in the designation sequence was the M4, designated Sher-

man I by the British: 8,389 of this model were built, 6,748 of them with the standard 75-mm (2.95-in) M3 gun and the other 1,641 with the 105-mm (4.13-in) M4 howitzer in the close-support role; the British designated the latter version with the Sherman IB, and the suffix 'B' was used thereafter to denote Shermans with the howitzer. The M4 was a very useful weapon, and was fitted in a mounting that allowed elevation to a maximum of 35° rather than the 25° of the M3 gun: the ordnance weighed 973 lb (441 kg) and was 101.3 in (2.57 m) long, its L/22.5 barrel firing a 33-lb (14.97-kg) HE shell (or alternatively HEAT and Smoke projectiles) to give the projectile a muzzle velocity of 1,550 ft (472 m) per second. The M4 was standardized in October 1941, but became only the third model to go into production, and was distinguishable by its all-welded hull. Early production models had a differential housing comprising three cast sections bolted together, and later models (designated Hybrid Sherman I by the British) had a combination cast and rolled hull front together with a one-piece cast differential housing. This evolution of the hull front and differential was also a characteristic of other Sherman variants.

Next in designation sequence, but actually the first to enter production, was the M4A1 (Sherman II in British terms) with a cast hull. During the course of production the M4A1

Medium Tank M4A1 (Sherman II) (USA)

Type: medium tank
Crew: 5
Combat weight: 66,500 lb (30,164 kg)
Dimensions: length overall 19.17 ft (5.84 m); width 8.58 ft (2.62 m); height 9.00 ft (2.74 m)
Armament system: one 75-mm (2.95-in) gun with 89 rounds and two or three 0.3-in (7.72-mm) Browning machine-guns with 7,750 rounds
Armour: between 25 and 51 mm (1 and 2 in)
Powerplant: one 400-hp (298-kW) Continental R–975–C1 petrol engine with 175 US gal. (662.5 litres) of fuel
Performance: speed, road 22 mph (35.4 km/h); range, road 100 miles (161 km); fording 3.33 ft (1.01 m); gradient 60%; vertical obstacle 2.0 ft (0.61 m); trench 7.5 ft (2.29 m); ground clearance 17 in (0.43 m)

received differential and hull front modifications parallel to those of the M4, and the track-return rollers were later shifted to the rear of the bogie attachment units ('second-type suspension'). Like the M4, the combat weight was 66,500 lb (30,164 kg). Production of this variant amounted to 9,677 tanks, of which 6,281 were completed with the M3 gun and the other 3,396 with the 76.2-mm (3-in) M1 high-velocity gun, whose installation was signified in British terminology by the designation Sherman IIA. This gun resulted from the realization by both the Armored Force and the Ordnance Department that the M3 was comparatively indifferent in armour-penetration capability, by comparison with the guns of contemporary German tanks, which moreover were appearing with thicker armour. The M1 was evolved in two months from an anti-aircraft weapon, and tested during September 1942 in a standard M4 turret. This proved too small for the more powerful weapon, which was then installed in the cylindrical turret designed for the 90-mm (3.54-in) gun of the Medium Tank T23. This turret proved excellent, and could be installed on the M4 without modification. The gun/turret combination was authorized for the M4A3 in February 1944, deliveries beginning in the following month; the gun/turret combination was also used on the M4, M4A1 and M4A2, all signified in British usage by the suffix 'A' after the roman mark number. The M1 weighed 1,141 lb (518 kg) and was 163.75 in (4.16 m) long, its L/52 barrel giving the 15.4-lb (6.98-kg) APCR shot a muzzle velocity of 3,400 ft (1036 m) per second for an armour-penetration capability of 102 mm (4 in) at a range of 1,000 yards (915 m).

The M4A2 was called Sherman III or Sherman IIIA by the British depending on armament, and after standardization in December 1941 became the second Sherman variant to enter production. The type was basically similar to the M4 with a welded hull, but had a different powerplant in the form of a 410-hp (306-kW) General Motors 6046 diesel engine, comprising two General Motors 6-71 diesels geared to a common propeller shaft, giving this 69,000-lb (31,298-kg) vehicle a 29-mph (46.7-km/h) maximum speed in comparison to the 24-mph (38.6-km/h) speed of the two

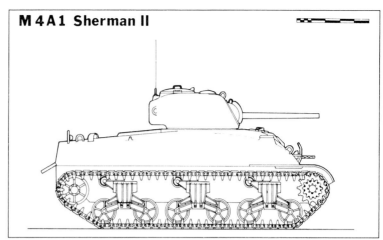

M4A1 Sherman II

previously-mentioned variants. Production amounted to 11,283 tanks, 8,053 of them with the 75-mm (2.895-in) gun and the other 3,230 with the 76.2-mm (3-in) gun. Late-production examples had a more steeply inclined hull front that greatly simplified manufacture and also provided marginally better protection.

In January 1942 a new variant was standardized as the M4A3, which was designated Sherman IV by the British. This was again similar to the M4 with a welded hull, but was fitted with a custom-designed tank engine, the 500-hp (373-kW) Ford GAA. This powerful and reliable petrol unit was instrumental in making the M4A3 the most important single Sherman

A war-weary M4A1 Sherman in Italy. This type is distinguishable by its cast hull and turret, and the fact that it is an early-production machine is attested by its three-piece differential housing. (US Army)

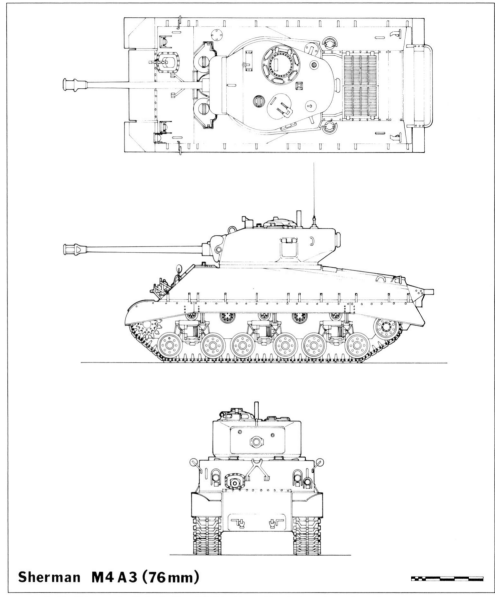

Sherman   M4 A3 (76 mm)

variant: 11,424 were built, including 5,015 with the 75-mm (2.95-in) gun, 3,370 with the 76.2-mm (3-in) gun and the other 3,039 with the 105-mm (4.13-in) howitzer. Once the M4A3 was available, the Americans generally reseved this model for themselves and disbursed the types with other engines to their Lend-Lease allies. Included in the total of M4A3s with the 75-mm (2.95-in) gun were 254 examples of the special M4A3E2 variant, which was nicknamed 'Jumbo' and produced specifically for assault operations in the invasion of France during June 1944. It had been anticipated that in this invasion and the subsequent break-out operations the Allies would face heavy concentrations of powerful artillery and tank destroyers, so the 'Jumbo' was fitted with extra protection in the form of 102-mm (4-in) plate welded to the hull front, a new turret with 152-mm (6-in) frontal thickness, and rolled plate added to the

Medium Tank M4A3E8 Sherman
(USA)

Type: medium tank
Crew: 5
Combat weight: 71,175 lb (32,285 kg)
Dimensions: length, gun forward 24.67 ft (7.5128 m) and hull 20.58 ft (6.273 m); width 8.75 ft (2.667 m); height 11.25 ft (3.43 m) to turret top
Armament system: one 3-in (76-mm) M1A1/2 rifled gun with 71 rounds, two 0.3-in (7.62-mm) Browning M1919A4 machine-guns (one coaxial and one bow) with 6,250 rounds, and one 0.5-in (12.7-mm) Browning M2HB AA machine-gun with 600 rounds; the turret is hydraulically powered, the main gun is stabilized in neither elevation (−10° to +25°) nor azimuth (360°), and an optical fire-control system is fitted
Armour: cast and welded steel varying in thickness between 1 and 3 in (25.4 and 76.2 mm)
Powerplant: one 450-hp (336-kW) Ford GAA petrol engine with 168 US gal. (636 litres) of fuel
Performance: speed, road 30 mph (48 km/h); range, road 100 miles (161 km); fording 3 ft (0.91 m); gradient 60%; vertical obstacle 24 in (0.61 m); vertical obstacle 2.0 ft (0.61 m); trench 7.4 ft (2.26 m); ground clearance 17 in (0.43 m)

hull top for a weight of 84,000 lb (38,102 kg) rather than the 68,500 lb (31,072 kg) of the standard M4A3, reducing maximum speed to 22 mph (35.4 km/h) on the 500 hp (373 kW) of the GAA engine. In the field some 'Jumbos' were revised with the 76.2-mm (3-in) gun.

The M4A4 was called Sherman V by the British, and was indeed the main type supplied to the UK. The type was standardized in February 1942 as an M4 variant with a 425-hp (317-kW) Chrysler multibank engine created by marrying five car engine cylinder blocks to a common crankcase. This was the same engine as used in the M3A4, and required a 6-in (0.152-m) lengthening of the rear hull and an additional four track shoes on each side. The type was phased out of production in September 1943, and all 7,499 examples had the 75-mm (2.95-in) gun and three-piece differential housing.

The designation M4A5 was used in the USA for the Canadian Ram tank, so the next production Sherman was the M4A6, which was designated Sherman VII by the British. The type was standardized in October 1943, and may be considered a variant of the M4A4 with the

Like the M4A4 version of the Sherman, the M4A6 had a slightly lengthened hull to allow insertion of the RD-1820 air-cooled diesel powerplant. The vehicle has a cast and rolled upper hull, and used vertical volute spring suspension. Production amounted to only 75 vehicles, which were hampered by the turret traverse limitations imposed by the bolstering of the hull top plates to accommodate the diesel. (*RAC Tank Museum*)

Sherman VC Firefly
(USA/UK)

Type: medium tank
Crew: 4
Combat weight: 77,840 lb (35,308 kg)
Dimensions: length, gun forward 25.50 ft (7.77 m); width 9.50 ft (2.90 m); height 9.33 ft (2.84 m)
Armament system: one 17-pdr (3-in/76.2-mm) gun with 78 rounds, one 0.5-in (12.7-mm) Browning machine-gun with 500 rounds and one 0.3-in (7.62-mm) Browning machine-gun with 5,000 rounds
Armour: between 19 and 76 mm (0.75 and 3 in)
Powerplant: one 425-hp (317-kW) Chrysler A57 petrol engine with 150 US gal. (568 litres) of fuel
Performance: speed, road 22.25 mph (35.8 km/h); range, road 125 miles (201 km); fording 3.5 ft (1.07 m); gradient 60%; side slope 30%; vertical obstacle 2.0 ft (0.61 m); trench 8.0 ft (2.44 m); ground clearance 16 in (0.41 m)

An overhead view emphasizes the barrel length of the Sherman VC Firefly's 17-pdr gun as well as the simple shape of the turret with additional hatch for the loader and the small bustle for the radio. (*IWM*)

497-hp (371-kW) Caterpillar D-200A diesel engine: the longer hull, more widely-spaced bogies, extended tracks and 71,000-lb (32,206-kg) weight were retained, and the 75-mm (2.95-in) gun was standard. Production amounted to only 75 tanks, for at the end of 1943 it was decided to cease powerplant experimentation and concentrate all production effort on the Wright- and Ford-engined models. Total production of Sherman gun tanks was thus 48,347, but this is by no means the whole of the Sherman story (or even of the

Sherman gun tank story), for there were a large number of important variants produced by production-line, depot or even field modification.

The best known of these is perhaps the Sherman 'Firefly', a British conversion with the 17-pdr (3-in/76.2-mm) high-velocity anti-tank gun (indicated by the suffix 'C') for enhanced tank-destroying capability. Most Fireflies were of the Sherman VC variety, but there were also Sherman IC, IIC, IIIC and IVC versions, and the family proved highly important in the

Sherman VC Firefly

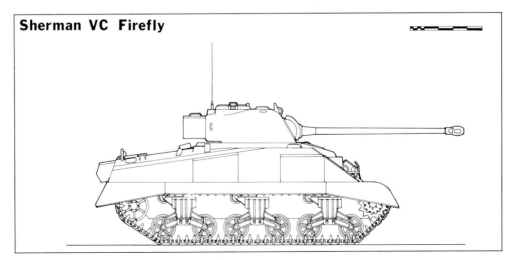

Normandy and subsequent North-West European campaigns as the Allied tanks best able to tackle the Panther and Tiger on anything approaching an equal firepower footing. For installation in the Sherman turret the 17-pdr (3-in/76.2-mm) gun had to be turned on its side and adapted for left-hand loading, and was provided with new mounting, recoil and elevating gear. The long breech section of the gun occupied so much room that the radio had to be shifted into an armoured box suspended from the rear of the turret, and this served the useful purpose of balancing the long barrel section of the gun. To provide maximum stowage for main armament ammunition, the bow machine-gun and its gunner's position were eliminated, allowing the accommodation of 78 rounds.

Other major modifications were less obvious but also important. Typical of these, and coincident with the more sharply angled 47°

hull front on the M4A3, was wet stowage for the main armament ammunition inside the vertical superstructure faces: the original stowage arrangement of dry racks had resulted in many disastrous fires and explosions, so the wet stowage used a hollow casing filled with a water/glycerine mixture to reduce the chance of combustion. Provision of such stowage was costly financially and in terms of manufacturing time, but proved well worth the expense. Another important change was horizontal rather than vertical volute spring suspension (indicated in the US and British terminologies by the suffix 'E8' and 'Y' respectively): this was introduced to provide greater flotation and simplified maintenance, though the system's use of tracks 23 in (584 mm) rather than 16.5 in (419 mm) wide also did much to reduce ground pressure and so improve cross-country mobility in poor going. The HVSS suspension used bogies with four wheels arranged in lateral

Known to its British developers as the Sherman VC Firefly, this was an American M4A4 fitted with the British 17-pdr high-velocity gun for much improved anti-tank capability by comparison to the M4/Sherman's standard 75- and 76-mm (2.95- and 3-in guns. (*PRO*)

An important British development for amphibious assault was the Duplex Drive arrangement to provide amphibious capability. This is a Sherman DD with its collapsible flotation screen locked in position by metal struts. The screen was permanently attached to a deck welded to the Sherman's hull, and was erected by the inflation (from two compressed-air bottles on the rear decking) of 36 rubber air pillars.

Far right   The other component of the Duplex Drive was the double propeller arrangement, driven from the bevel drive of the vehicle for a water speed of 4.6 mph (7.4 km/h). (*IWM*)

A Sherman DD with its flotation screen lowered. (*PRO*)

pairs, and the track-return rollers were attached directly to the hull sides. Field modifications were usually concerned with protection, and generally consisted of appliqué armour and additional track shoes welded to potentially vulnerable spots.

The Sherman was also used for a number of specialist roles, being developed in different forms by the Americans and the British to meet their particular requirements for armoured recovery vehicles, rocket-launchers, flame-throwers, mine exploders, self-propelled weapons and other role-dedicated vehicles too numerous to list. The Sherman proved as successful in these alternative roles as in its primary gun tank role, and the importance of the tank in the Allied victory of the Second World War cannot be overemphasized. The Sherman may not have been a qualititive match for the best German tanks (it lacked the all-round fighting capabilities of the Panther, and was not as heavily armed and protected as the Tiger), but it was adequate to its tasks and was produced in the vast numbers that allowed Allied tank formations to overwhelm the Germans and, to a lesser extent, the Japanese. The Sherman remained in widespread service into the 1970s, and is still used by a number of armies.

The Americans were well satisfied with the M4 in the early stages of the war, but were wise enough to appreciate that a successor would be necessary. Early in 1942, therefore, work began on a potential successor. The Americans were looking for a more potent medium tank with optimized exploitation capability, and reworked the M4 concept to include rear drive sprockets and in the longer term a 90-mm (3.54-in) main gun. The larger-calibre gun was left for potential production models, and the development series concentrated on improved versions of the current armament fits, together with new transmission systems. The M4 successor programme spawned three development models as the T20, T22 and T23.

The Medium Tank T20 was projected with different armaments (a 75-mm/2.95-in automatic gun, a 76.2-mm/3-in gun and a 3-in/76.2-mm gun) and different running gear (HVSS or torsion bar suspension), but in all variants was powered by the 470-hp (350-kW) Ford GAN

petrol engine driving the tracks via a Torquematic automatic transmission. The T20 eventually appeared in June 1943 with the 76.2-mm (3-in) M1 gun, an early form of horizontal volute spring suspension for the three two-wheel bogies on each side, and armour varying in thickness between 38 and 64 mm (1.5 and 2.5 in) for a weight of 67,500 lb (30,616 kg). Trials confirmed that the transmission was still underdeveloped for tank use, and the type was

Below An important special-purpose vehicle was the mineclearing tank. This is a British-developed Sherman Crab in France during 1944. Based on the Sherman V, and retaining the full armament capability of that tank, the Crab used a whirling arrangement of flails to detonate pressure mines in front of the tank. (*IWM*)

abandoned. The same fate befell the T20E3, which used the same power train but had torsion bar suspension for its arrangement of six independently-sprung road wheels on each side. The T20 achieved a maximum speed of 25 mph (40.2 km/h), but the T20E3 managed 35 mph (56.3 km/h) on the same engine.

The Medium Tank T22 was a Chrysler-developed alternative to the T20, and two prototypes were delivered in June 1943. The vehicles resembled the T20 in all respects but the transmission, which was a five-speed mechanical system. This proved better than the T20's automatic type, but still unsatisfactory. One of these 69,000-lb (31,298-kg) machines was subsequently modified as the T22E1 with a 75-mm (2.95-in) gun and automatic loader, but the real need of the Armored Force was for a reliable tank with a larger-calibre gun, and the programme was terminated.

First of the trio to appear was the Medium Tank T23, the initial prototype of which was delivered in January 1943. This 73,500-lb (33,340-kg) machine had the same armour and powerplant as the T20 and T22, but the engine drove an electric drive system developed by General Electric for a speed of 35 mph (56.3 km/h), and the running gear was of the VVSS type. The prototype was armed with the 76.2-mm (3-in) M1 gun, and T23E1 and T23E2 variants were projected with an automatically-loaded 75-mm (2.95-in) and 3-in (76.2-mm) gun respectively. Trials of the basic T23 proved highly successful, and an initial production order for 250 tanks was placed. These were built between November 1943 and December 1944, but never entered operational service. The type was very important in the development of current as well as future medium tanks, however: the turret and its 76.2-mm (3-in) gun, were incorporated on later M4s, as was the 47° front. The production models were also used in an extensive test programme that paved the way for the T25 and T26 medium tanks, which also profited from experience with the only T23 development to reach the hardware stage. This was the T23E3, which resulted from official dissatisfaction with the heavy ground pressure and poor weight distribution of the T23, as well as worries about the reliability of the petrol-electric drive system. The 75,000-lb (34,020-kg) T23E3 in fact retained the standard T23-series power train, the armament and protection were essentially those of the production T23 (though the turret basket was removed to allow an increase in main armament ammunition stowage from 64 to 84 rounds), but the running gear was derived from the torsion bar type of the T25E1. The T23E3 was completed in August 1944, and though standardization had been proposed as the M27 as long ago as July 1943 (at the same time that standardization of the T20E3 was proposed as the M27B1), no further production was ordered.

One of the main reasons for the abandonment of the T20, T22 and T23 series was its limitation to current gun calibres at a time when the US Army was moving towards a classification system (formalized after the Second World War) that designated tanks with guns up to 76.2-mm (3-in) calibre as light tanks, those with 90-mm (3.54-in) guns medium tanks, and those with 120-mm (4.72-in) guns heavy tanks. As noted above, the desired M4 successor was to be armed with a 90-mm (3.54-in) gun, and this finally became available as the M3, a weapon weighing 2,300 lb (1,043 kg) and measuring 202 in (5.13 m) in overall length. This possessed an L/50 barrel, giving the 24-lb (10.89-kg) APCBC shot a muzzle velocity of 3,350 ft (1,021 m) per second. Development of this weapon had started in September 1942, at the same time that the T20 series was being planned, and the first weapon appeared in March 1943, being mounted in a converted T23E3 for trials. In April 1943 authorization was granted for the development of two tank types with the 90-mm (3.54-in) gun as the Medium Tank T25 and the Medium Tank T26.

The T25 was based on the T23E3 with armour varying in thickness between 38 and 89 mm (1.5 and 3.5 in), horizontal volute spring suspension for 23-in (584-mm) tracks, and a 470-hp (350-kW) Ford GAF engine with petrol-electric drive for a maximum speed of 30 mph (48.3 km/h) at a weight of 82,000 lb (37,195 kg). The two prototype models were delivered in January and April 1944, and though generally satisfactory, were considered too heavy. The

T25E1 was therefore developed with armour limited to a maximum thickness of 76 mm (3 in), Torquematic transmission, torsion bar suspension and a weight of 77,590 lb (35,195 kg). This last was within the 80,000-lb (36,288-kg) limit set for the vehicle, but left little room for the inevitable growth in weight that would characterize combat-configured vehicles. A total of 40 T25E1s was produced between January and April 1944, but as greater potential was being shown by the T26, further development of the T25 ceased in the middle of the year.

The T26 was close kin to the T25, but was planned from the beginning with 25-mm (1-in) thicker armour, and thus with greater weight. This called for the use of torsion bar suspension for 24-in (610-mm) rather than 19-in (483-mm) tracks. The estimated weight was 90,000 lb (40,824 kg), and this in turn dictated a change from petrol-electric to Torquematic drive, and in this guise the vehicle was redesignated T26E1, of which 10 examples were built. The armour of this model varied in thickness from a minimum of 51 mm (2 in) to a maximum of 102 mm (4 in) over the more vulnerable areas, and this generated a weight of 86,500 lb (39,236 kg) for a maximum speed of 25 mph (40.2 km/h). Trials showed the T26E1 to be generally satisfactory, but a number of modifications were demanded: refined in this fashion with a muzzle brake, strengthened suspension, redesigned differential and cooling system etc, in June 1944 the tank was redesignated the Heavy Tank T26E1, whose history is resumed below.

In its original form, the T26 was the last American medium tank developed in the Second World War, leaving the M4 to bear the brunt of operations in Europe, Asia and the Pacific. The last category of American tank to be discussed is therefore the heavy tank. The US Army had seen the possible need for such a tank in the 1920s and 1930s, but lacked the finance and total commitment to produce even development models in the austere days of the early and mid-1930s. The decline of the world political situation in 1939 prompted a reconsideration of this position in 1939, however, and in May 1940 agreement was reached on development of the Americans' first vehicle in this class, the Heavy Tank T1. This was seen as a substantial machine weighing some 100,000 lb (45,360 kg) with a maximum 76-mm (3-in) thickness of armour, a speed of 25 mph (40.2 km/h) on the 925 hp (690 kW) provided by a Wright Whirlwind G-200 radial engine, and a turreted armament of one 76.2-mm (3-in) main gun and one 37-mm coaxial gun.

Design of the basic vehicle was largely completed in 1940, and in February 1941 authorization was granted for prototypes of four variants: the T1E1 with a cast hull and petrol-electric drive, the T1E2 with a cast hull and torque-converter drive, the T1E3 with a welded hull and torque-converter drive, and the T1E4 with a welded hull and Torquematic transmission for a four-diesel powerplant. The T1E4 was later cancelled, and the first of the prototypes to be delivered was that of the T1E2 in December 1941, just as the USA became embroiled in the Second World War. Trials were generally successful, but revealed the need for a complete revision of the brake and cooling systems to produce the version standardized in May 1942 as the Heavy tank M6.

While trials of the T1E2 were under way, the T1E3 was completed and evaluated, leading to the variant's standardization in May 1942 as the Heavy Tank M6A1, which was externally identical to the M6, apart from its welded rather than cast hull. The last of the variants to appear in prototype form was the T1E1, which was not delivered until June 1943 and was not ordered into production, although the single development machine was often designated Heavy Tank M6A2, as though it had been standardized. The original plan had envisaged 5,500 tanks of the M6 series, but after representations by the Armored Force to the Ordnance Department this was curtailed in September 1942 to 115 machines and finally in March 1943 to the 40 machines (eight M6s, 12 M6A1s and 20 M6A2s) that had been built. The M6 used horizontal volute spring suspension with four two-wheel bogies and three track-return rollers on each side, weighed 126,500 lb (57,380 kg) with armour varying in thickness between 25 and 102 mm (1 and 4 in), and on the 800 hp (596 kW) of its Wright Whirlwind G-200 could attain 22 mph (35.4 km/h). The crew of six men (commander, driver, assistant driver, gunner, loader and ammunition handler) was

M 26 Pershing

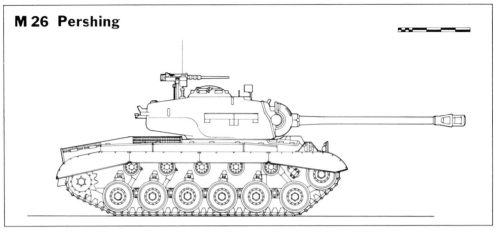

small, given the diversified armament of the vehicle: the main armament was one 76.2-mm (3-in) T12 gun with 75 rounds plus one 37-mm M6 coaxial gun with 340 rounds. The machine-gun armament varied, the nearest to a standard fit being a forward-firing battery or two 0.5-in (12.7-mm) and two 0.3-in (7.62-mm) machine-guns, a single 0.3-in (7.62-mm) machine-gun in the turret cupola, and a single 0.5-in (12.7-mm) machine-gun in an anti-aircraft mounting in the rear of the turret.

At the time of its development the M6 was the world's most powerful tank, but given the production and logistical factors associated with the programme as originally envisaged, the Armored Force was right to question the real utility of the type. The M6 was declared obsolete late in 1944, though not before a T1E1 had been fitted with a turret based on that of the T26 complete with 90-mm (3.54-in) T7 gun, and an M6A2 with a heavily protected turret armed with the 105-mm (4.13-in) T15E1 gun as a heavy assault tank for European operations; the two types were cancelled in March and September 1944 respectively.

The next heavy tank to enter US service was therefore the T26, which had been designed as a medium tank (see above) but had grown in weight to the point at which it had to be reclassified as a heavy tank during June 1944. This vehicle was the culmination of a development programme that had encompassed the T20, T22, T23, T25, and T26 medium tanks in all their variations, and to avoid confusion the first heavy tank model was classified Heavy Tank

T26E3 and standardized for limited procurement in November 1944. The T26 was subjected to intensive combat evaluation, and in January 1945 was declared battle-worthy, leading to the type's standardization in March 1945 as the Heavy Tank M26 General Pershing. The M26 was considered as the primary US tank in the armoured battle with the Germans' Tiger tanks, though experience in Europe confirmed that while the M26 was equal to the Tiger in protection and superior in mobility, it was decidedly inferior in firepower, where the German 88-mm (3.46-in) KwK 36 and 43 weapons reigned supreme.

Heavy Tank M26 Pershing (USA)

Type: heavy tank
Crew: 5
Combat weight: 92,355 lb (41,891 kg)
Dimensions: length, gun forward 28.42 ft (8.66 m) and hull 21.33 ft (6.50 m); width 11.50 ft (3.51 m); height 9.08 ft (2.78 m)
Armament system: one 90-mm (3.54-in) gun with 70 rounds, one 0.5-in (12.7-mm) Browning machine-gun with 600 rounds, and two 0.3-in (7.62-mm) Browning machine-guns with 5,000 rounds
Armour: between 13 and 102 mm (0.51 and 4 in)
Powerplant: one 373-kW (500-hp) Ford GAF petrol engine with 191 US gal. (723 litres) of fuel
Performance: speed, road 30 mph (48.3 km/h); range, road 100 miles (161 km); fording 4.0 ft (1.81 m); gradient 60%; vertical obstacle 3.83 ft (1.17 m); trench 8.0 ft (2.44 m); ground clearance 17.7 in (0.45 m)

The ultimate US heavy tank of the Second World War was the M26 Pershing, which was reclassified as a medium tank almost immediately after the end of the war. (*RAC Tank Museum*)

There were a number of variants of the M26 in its basic gun tank role, and just as there was a 'Lightweight Combat Team' derived from the M24 Chaffee, there was a 'Heavyweight Combat Team' derived from the M26 Pershing. In the basic line of development as a gun tank, the M26 spawned five derivatives. The M26A1 was very similar to the M26 but had a revised M3A1 main gun with bore evacuator and single-baffle muzzle brake; some of the type were fitted with

The M26 Pershing remained in US service after the Second World War as a medium tank, but was increasingly unpopular for its short range. (*US Army*)

a system to stabilize the main gun in elevation. The M26E1 was the basic vehicle fitted with the 90-mm (3.54-in) T54 gun: this had a concentric recoil system and used fixed rather than separate-loading ammunition, requiring that the ammunition stowage inside the tank be revised. The T26E2 was a close-support version with a 105-mm (4.13-in) howitzer as stabilized main armament; in July 1945 the T26E2 was standardized for limited production as the M45. The T26E4 was again very similar to the M26 but had a 90-mm (3.54-in) T15E2 gun in place of the M26's M3 of the same calibre: this weapon weighed 3,270 lb (1,483 kg) and had an overall length of 272.9 in (6.93 m), its L/70 barrel allowing the standard 24-lb (10.89-kg) armour-piercing shot to be fired with a muzzle velocity of 3,200 ft (975 m) per second. And the T26E5 was the heavy tank counterpart to the M4A3E2 'Jumbo', a dedicated assault version with the frontal armour thickened to a maximum of 279 mm (11 in) on the mantlet, 190.5 mm (7.5 in) on the turret and 152 mm (6 in) on the hull, increasing weight to 102,000 lb (46,267 kg); production amounted to only 27 vehicles.

Production of the M26 reached 2,432, but the type saw only limited service in the Second World War. In May 1946 it was reclassified as a medium tank once again, and served with considerable distinction in the Korean War (1950-53). The Pershing was a decisive turning-point in the design of American medium tanks: it marked the culmination of the evolutionary design process from the M2 series, yet its divergence from the main sequence in terms of its large road wheels, torsion bar suspension, hull-mounted track-return rollers and rear drive sprockets marked the beginning of the post-Second World War series of medium and battle tanks from the M47 to the M60.

Further development of the M26 led to the Heavy Tank T32, which was designed to provide firepower, performance and reliability comparable with that of the M26, with superior protection. The basic M26 chassis was lengthened to 23 ft 2.5 in (7.07 m) by the insertion of an additional road wheel on each side, and on this was located armour thickened to 127 mm (5 in) on the 54° front and 76 mm (3 in) on the sides; the turret was also uparmoured to 203

mm (8 in) on the front and 152 mm (6 in) on the sides, and fitted with a 90-mm (3.54-in) T15E1 gun. A 770-hp (574-kW) Ford GAC engine was fitted, and this drove a cross-drive combined transmission/steering system to give the 120,000-lb (54,432-kg) vehicle a maximum speed of 22 mph (35.4 km/h). Four vehicles were ordered in February 1945, two of them with welded rather than cast hull fronts, under the designation T32E1. With the end of the Second World War, only limited trials were undertaken.

Further development of the heavy tank concept during the Second World War produced five more types, the Assault Tank T14, the Super-Heavy Tank T28, the Heavy Tank T29, the Heavy Tank T30 and the Heavy Tank T34. The origins of the T14 can be traced back as far as December 1941, when the British and US tank commissions agreed on the development to a British specification and the construction to the extent of 8,500 examples of a heavy assault tank based as far as possible on the M4 but with hull and turret armour to maximums of 76 and 102 mm (3 and 4 in) respectively, a 6-pdr (57-mm) or 75-mm (2,95-in) gun, a weight of 92,000 lb (41,731 kg), and a speed of 18 mph (29 km/h) on a 470-hp (350-kW) Ford GAZ petrol engine. Two 93,930-lb (42,607-kg) prototypes were built, but in 1944 the British lost interest and the concept was cancelled.

The same basic concept led to the T28, which was really an assault gun of mammoth proportions and armour to a maximum of 305 mm (12 in) for a weight of 190,000 lb (86,184 kg). Power was provided by a 410-hp (306-kW) Ford GAF petrol engine for a speed of only 8 mph (12.9 km/h), and the running gear on each side comprised four twin-wheel bogies with horizontal volute spring suspension. A highly unusual feature was the provision of a complete set of additional trackwork: for movement over soft ground these were attached outside the standard units to double the track area on the ground, and when not needed they could be detached and coupled together to be towed behind the parent vehicle as a dumb unit. The main armament was a 105-mm (4.13-in) T5E1 high-velocity gun in hull-front mounting for traverse 10° left and right of the centreline: this ordnance weighed 6,300 lb (2,858 kg) and had an overall length of 295 in (7.49 m), its L/65 barrel giving the 39-lb (17.69-kg) armour-piercing shot a muzzle velocity of 3,000 ft (914 m) per second. In March 1945 the type was rightly redesignated as the 105-mm Gun Motor Carriage T95, and after the end of the war with Germany the order for five prototypes was reduced to two. These were trialled in 1946, but as the T29 heavy tank offered the same firepower in a 360° traverse turret, the programme was cancelled in October 1947.

The T29 began life in September 1944 as a specialist vehicle for attacks on fortified positions and Germany's heaviest tanks. The hull was basically that of the M26 lengthened to 25 ft 0 in (7.62m) by the addition of two more road wheels on each side. The new turret was a singularly massive unit with a 105-mm (4.13-in) T5E2 gun and two 0.5-in (12.7-mm) coaxial machine-guns, a crew of four (commander, gunner and two loaders) and its own 5-hp (3.73-kW) traversing motor. A 770-hp (574-kW) Ford GAC petrol engine with cross-drive transmission gave this 139,000-lb (63,050-kg) vehicle a maximum speed of 22 mph (35.4 km/h), but development ceased with the end of the war in Europe.

The T30 was produced in parallel with the T29 to meet the same requirement, and differed from the T29 principally in its engine and armament: the engine was an 810-hp (604-kW) Continental AV-1790-3 petrol engine, giving this 145,000-lb (108,112-kg) giant a speed of 22 mph (35.4 km/h), and the main armament was a 155-mm (6.1-in) T7 gun, fitted with a power rammer for the massive separate-loading ammunition. The T34 used the same chassis as the T30, but fitted with a revised turret that featured an additional 102 mm (4 in) of frontal armour and a 120-mm (4.72-in) T53 high-velocity gun developed from an anti-aircraft weapon.

American tanks made an enormous contribution to the Allied victory in the Second World war. The Americans themselves fielded large numbers of armoured divisions and independent tank battalions, but perhaps just as importantly, provided their allies with enormous numbers of tanks, allowing these manpower-rich but *matériel*-poor countries to make most effective use of their strengths. The importance of the American tanks was initially their availability, reliability and comparatively heavy armament. But as the war progressed, the capabilities of American tank designers and the vast industrial machine that supported them gave an increasingly free rein to develop

Super-Heavy Tank T28
(USA)

Type: heavy tank prototype
Crew: 4
Combat weight: 188,000 lb (85,227 kg)
Dimensions: length overall 34.67 ft (10.57 m); width 14.92 ft (4.55 m); height 9.46 ft (2.88 m)
Armament system: one 105-mm (4.13-in) gun with 62 rounds and one 0.5-in (12.7-mm) Browning machine-gun with 660 rounds
Armour: between 25 and 305 mm (1 and 12 in)
Powerplant: one 500-hp (373-kW) Ford GAF petrol engine with 480 US gal. (1,817 litres) of fuel
Performance: speed, road 7 mph (11.3 km/h); fording 3.92 ft (1.2 m); gradient 48.2%; vertical obstacle 2.0 ft (0.61 m); trench tested to only 6.0 ft (1.83 m); ground clearance 19.5 in (0.5 m)

T 28 Heavy Tank

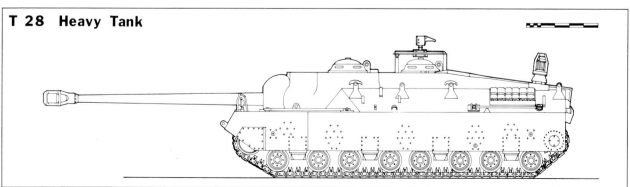

better designs that were then put into production without hampering the flow of existing designs.

The nation that stands out as the most important exponent of armoured warfare in the Second World War, however, must be the USSR. As noted in Chapter Two, the Soviets had devoted their energies in the 1920s and early 1930s to absorbing as much imported technology as possible, while at the same time pursuing a policy of limited indigenous development. By the mid-1930s the Soviets had built up a considerable armoured force, backed by a substantial industrial machine capable of supporting and expanding the in-service tank fleet. In the later 1930s the Soviets consciously turned away from their policy of mass production virtually regardless of quality, and there after turned their attention towards the development of tanks that were the qualitative equal of, or indeed the qualitative superior to, the best of Western tanks. This should not be construed, however, as meaning that quantity was sacrificed: Soviet tactical thinking still emphasized the overwhelming importance of numerical superiority, but this was now seen as being complemented by qualitative improvement. The philosophy of Soviet tank designers therefore became one of producing an easily produced baseline tank that was in itself a good combat vehicle yet possessed the capacity for technical growth that would turn it into an increasingly more potent type as major qualitative improvements were added at a limited number of points in the type's production life. This meant that low cost and increasing quality could be ensured in large blocks of standardized tanks.

Hand in hand with this design and production philosophy went a development in tactical thinking. In common with the Western nations that were developing their tank forces in the 1920s and early 1930s, the Soviets suffered a dichotomy of tactical thinking: one school saw tanks as infantry-support weapons, and the other as the constituents of an independent force that could strike deep into the enemy's rear. By comparison with the Western nations, however, the Soviets had the physical space and the number of tanks to allow the development of both concepts. In the early 1930s,

therefore, Soviet rifle divisions included in their establishment a single battalion of light tanks, while frontier-based rifle battalions had attached battalions of tankettes. To give these primary infantry formation's additional support, the higher command echelons controlled a number of tank brigades, each comprising three battalions of light or medium tanks: these brigades could be allocated to specific sectors of the front as the tactical situation demanded. Extensive manoeuvres allowed the thorough integration of the infantry-support armour with its rifle divisions, whose men were trained to move forward into combat on their tanks.

For the exploitation (cavalry) role, the Soviets organized two types of armoured formation. The tank brigade had three battalions of BT fast tanks (about 100 in all), a motor rifle unit and the appropriate support units: these were designed to exploit the chaotic situation attendant on any breakthrough, paving the way for the tank corps, which combined two or three brigades, a motor rifle brigade, an artillery unit and the appropriate support and service unit.

The Soviets carefully analysed the implications of armoured warfare (such as it was) in the Spanish Civil War (1936-39), and came to the tentative conclusion that the proponents of major armoured formations for deep penetration were partially wrong: some moves towards a closer integration of armour and infantry were inaugurated, but these were incomplete when the campaigns against the Japanese (1938 and 1939), the Poles (1939) and the Finns (1939-40) were fought. These campaigns produced some armoured warfare and a larger volume of armoured manoeuvre, serving to force another change of heart on the Soviet civilian and military authorities: there was clearly a tactical space for infantry-support tanks, but there was just as clearly the operational space for larger tank formations in the deep penetration role.

In the summer of 1940, therefore, the Soviets set about a thoroughgoing reform of their armoured strength, and in the process took much to heart of the German successes in Poland and the West. At the operational level the Soviets envisaged their basic formation as the tank corps (of which there were to be at least 20!) each comprising one motor rifle and

The Modern Tank

Flamethrower tanks came to play a prominent part in assault operations against heavily defended areas, and the best-known M4 Sherman variant in this role was the M3-4-3. The flamethrower was supplied as a kit for field installation, and comprised a flame gun fitted in place of the bow machine-gun, and a flame fuel tank fitted in the right sponson. (*US Army*)

Snorkel-fitted M48s of the US Marine Corps move ashore during an assault landing exercise. (*MARS*)

Far left M48A2G MBT of 2nd BN *Heimat-schutzbrigade* of the West German army, on exercise near Pfullendorf. (*MARS*)

Below left M60A1 main battle tank comes ashore in Vietnam. (*US Army*)

Left M60A1 of 3rd Brigade (Bulldog), 1st US Armored Div. preparing to cross the Danube on exercise. (*MARS*)

Below The ultimate Centurion tank of the original British series was the Mk 13 with infra-red driving lights and a 12.7-mm (0.5-in) ranging machine-gun for its 105-mm (4.13-in) main gun. Experience with the Centurion was instrumental in the development of the Chieftain (seen here) that followed it into British service. (*MARS*)

This page Two views of the AMX-30 with its elegant turret and 105-mm (4.13-in) GIAT rifled gun. (*SOFRESA*)

Opposite page The Creusot-Loire AMX-13 light tank with 105-mm (4.13-in) gun. (*Creusot-Loire*)

Above Chieftain main battle tank of the Royal Tank Regiment, on exercise in 1978. (*MOD*)

Above left Combining features of the Centurion and Chieftain, the Vickers Main Battle Tank has a 105-mm (4.13-in) main gun and an advanced fire-control system. (*MARS*)

Far left A Chieftain tank travelling at speed, Sennelager, West Germany. (*MOD*)

Left Chieftain main battle tank of the 4th/7th Dragoon Guards on winter exercises in Germany, 1979. (*MOD*)

Above Challenger MBT of A Sqn, Royal Hussars in Germany during Exercise 'Lionheart'. (*MARS*)

Right A Scimitar on Exercise 'Spearpoint' in Germany. (*MOD*)

Above right A Scimitar of the 13th/18th Royal Hussars during an exercise in Germany. (*COI*)

Far right A Scorpion of 1 Sqn RAF Regiment. (*B. Ellson*)

Right A Scorpion on exercises with the Saudi Arabian army. (*Alvis*)

Far right A Leopard 1A2 battle tank of the Belgian army. This Leopard has a turret of stronger steel, an improved NBC system, and passive night-vision equipment for the commander and driver. (*NATO*)

Below right A Leopard 2 main battle tank of the West German army. (*Krauss-Maffei AG*)

Below A Leopard 1 of the West German army during night-firing exercises. The enormous muzzle flash at once reveals the location of the firing tank, which must move immediately if it is to avoid retribution. (*Bundeswehr*)

Right AN M1 Abrams of 3rd Infantry Div. crossing a bridge during Exercise 'Certain Fury'. (*MARS*)

Far right A Swedish Strv 103B battle tank uses its permanently attached dozer blade to dig itself into a fire position, further reducing its already very low silhouette. (*Swedish Army*)

Right An M1 Abrams of 3/61st Tiger Brigade during Exercise 'Lionheart'. (*MARS*)

Far right The OF40 battle tank capitalizes on OTO Melara experience in building the Leopard 1 for the Italian army, and has secured modest export success. (*OTO Melara*)

Right   EE-T1 OSORIO
main battle tank seen
during desert trials.
(*Engesa, Brazil*)

Below   The French
AMX-40. (*SOFRESA*)

Left The TAM tank was designed in West Germany for production in Argentina, and uses the basic chassis/hull combination of the Marder mechanized infantry combat vehicle with a new turret carrying a 105-mm (4.13-in) gun to provide battle tank firepower at little more than light tank weight. (*Thyssen Henschel, Kassel*)

Below A Russian T-62 MBT, part of an Opposing Forces Concept Demonstration in the USA, 1977. A typical Soviet design feature is the high rise of forward track run to the forward idler. (*US Army*)

Above and right T-72 main battle tanks of the Soviet army. The type is identifiable by the exhaust outlet on the vehicle's left rear side, and by the sighting arrangement on the turret. (*MARS*)

two tank divisions, whose establishments are detailed in the appendixed diagrams. The German invasion caught the Soviets only part way through their reorganization, yet even so the beginning of Operation 'Barbarossa' on 21 June 1941 matched 17 German Panzer divisions against no fewer than 30 Soviet tank divisions. But whereas the Panzer divisions were massed into four armour-heavy *Panzergruppen* tasked with deep encirclement manoeuvres in strategic regions, the Soviet tank divisions were allocated on a penny-packet basis to armies disposed along the whole length of the front: the only bodies of massed armour were to be found in the 5th, 6th, 12th and 26th Armies of the South-West Front (army group) shielding the Ukraine, and these proved ineffective against the five Panzer divisions of the 1st Panzergruppe. German estimates suggest that by the end of 1941 the Soviets had lost 60 tank divisions: 30 destroyed completely and the other 30 so heavily handled that they were broken up to strengthen new formations. Up to the end of 1941, the Germans also estimated, the Soviets had lost about 15,000 of the 20,000 or so tanks available to them.

Yet the Germans failed in their strategic effort to break the USSR in a single campaign, and their exhaustion between December 1941 and June 1942 gave the Soviets the time to replan and re-establish their armoured forces. In an enormous upheaval of industrial capacity the Soviets had managed to dismantle and remove most of their production facilities in the western USSR before it was overrun by the Germans, and in a logistical effort almost beggaring the imagination they shifted this plant to virgin sites east of the Urals, reassembled their factories and resumed production in time to support the revitalization of the Soviet armies in the first half of 1942.

At the heart of this revitalization was a tank brigade whose revised establishment is detailed in the Appendix: the inclusion of one mortar company provided mobile but exceptionally heavy fire support by the standard of the day. Up to mid-1943 there were insufficient tank battalions for the number of tank brigades fielded, and a motor rifle battalion was generally used instead of the third mixed tank

battalion. By 1944, all tank brigades were up to establishment strength, each tank battalion having two tank companies each of 10 T-34 medium tanks, but the motor rifle battalion was retained. The Germans had identified at least 250 such brigades by 1945.

Tank brigades were allocated to tank corps, whose establishment is described in another diagram. The tank corps possessed about 300 tanks, making it equivalent in this respect to a Western armoured division. Of particular note, however, is the tank corps' additional strength of support weapons by comparison with the Western division. The Soviets also fielded a large number of mechanized corps, in which the ratio of armour to infantry was reversed to three motor rifle brigades and one tank brigade, the other parts of the establishment remaining unaltered.

The tank corps were the breakthrough and exploitation arm of the Red Army, though they remained closely tied to the infantry in the very highly organized Soviet plan of attack, which saw no place for genuinely independent operations by deep-thrusting tank forces. For the purely infantry-support role, however, there were independent tank brigades and independent heavy tank regiments. The independent tank brigades had 107 T-34 medium tanks but no organic infantry, though the infantry of the division being supported often rode on the tanks. The independent heavy tank regiments generally had 32 IS or KV heavy tanks each, and were allocated to motor rifle units tasked with breaking through heavily-defended positions.

At the beginning of the Second World War in 1939, the Soviets were just beginning a complete overhaul of their tanks with the development and introduction of a new generation to replace the derivative designs of the 1930s. Given the nature of the USSR, with its poor road and rail communications over vast tracts cut by large rivers and split by extensive marshes, it was inevitable that the Soviets would place great emphasis for reconnaissance on the light tank, preferably an amphibious type. In the late 1930s the most important in-service types were the T-27, T-37A and T-38, and to replace these the two-man T-40 light amphibious tank was developed, its

237

The Soviet T-37 light amphibious tank was modelled on the British Carden-Loyd A3E11. The T-33 prototype has balsa wood side floats, but these were omitted from the T-37A and T-37M initial and final production models, each armed with just a single 7.62-mm (0.3-in) machine-gun. (*RAC Tank Museum*)

prototype apppearing in 1936: this resembled the BT-IS in overall configuration, and was a complete departure from earlier Soviet light tank design in its welded construction, independent torsion bar suspension for the arrangement of four road wheels on each side, and truncated conical turret accommodating the commander and the armament of one 12.7-mm (0.5-in) and one 7.62-mm (0.3-in) coaxial machine-gun. Standard components were used wherever possible, as in the 85-hp (63.3-kW) GAZ-202 petrol engine, and the type was buoyant without aid, being propelled in the water by a single propeller. Weight was 5,590 kg (12,234 lb) with a maximum armour thickness of 13 mm (0.51 in). The original T-40 had a blunt nose, but the later T-40A had a more streamlined nose and the non-amphibious T-40S of 1942 had slightly thicker armour and provision for a 20-mm main gun. The T-40 series served from 1941 to 1946.

The T-40 was planned for only modest service, as the Soviets envisaged that the T-60 light tank should supplement and then supplant all in-service light tanks from 1942. Design of this vehicle was already under way when the lessons of the Germans' 1941 invasion began to be digested. These suggested that the primary requirements of the light tank should not be mobility (including amphibious capability) to the exclusion of firepower and protection, but rather a more judicious blend of all three components. The design of the two-man T-60 was therefore revised to produce a more capable machine of all-welded construction. The armour varied in thickness from 7 to 20 mm (0.28 to 0.79 in), and greater firepower was provided. In this latter category the Soviets had hoped to install a 37-mm gun, but the recoil forces of this weapon could not be absorbed by the small turret ring: in its place the designers therefore fitted the exceptional 20-mm ShVAK cannon, whose projectile incorporated a sub-calibre slug of heavy metal to produce a penetration capability all but identical with that of the 37-mm weapon, namely 38 mm (1.5 in) of armour at an angle of 30° at a range of 400 m (435 yards). A 7.62-mm (0.3-in) machine-gun was installed coaxially. The T-60 entered production in November 1941, and nearly 6,000 were built before the type was superseded in production by the T-70 light tank during 1943. The T-60 weighed 5,150 (11,354 lb), and with its 85-hp (63.3-kW) GAZ-202 petrol engine could attain 45 km/h (28 mph) on running gear similar to that of the T-40. The only tank variant was the T-60A of 1942 with 35-mm (1.38-in) frontal armour and solid rather than spoked road wheels, though after the introduction of the T-70, surplus T-60s were converted as mountings for Katyusha rockets or as tractors for 57-mm anti-tank guns.

Designed where possible around car components to ease problems of manufacture, the T-40 amphibious light tank was designed to replace the T-27, T-37 and T-38 series. This is a T-40A version with a streamlined nose and folding trim vane. (*RAC Tank Museum*)

T–40A
(USSR)

Type: amphibious light tank
Crew: 2
Combat weight: 6,300 kg (13,889 lb)
Dimensions: length overall 4.27 m (14.00 ft); width 2.33 m (7.65 ft); height 1.98 m (6.48 ft)
Armament system: one 12.7-mm (0.5-in) DShK machine-gun or 20-mm ShVAK cannon with 550 rounds and one 7.62-mm (0.3-in) DT machine-gun with 2,016 rounds
Armour: between 6 and 14 mm (0.24 and 0.55 in)
Powerplant: one 63.4-kW (85-hp) GAZ-202 petrol engine with 207 litres (45.5 Imp. gal.) of fuel
Performance: speed, road 42 km/h (26.1 mph); range, road 340 km (211 miles); fording amphibious; gradient 34°; vertical obstacle 0.65 m (2.15 ft); trench 1.7 m (5.6 ft); ground clearance 0.36 m (14.2 in)

Amphibious Tank T-40

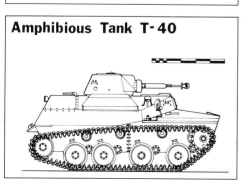

Despite its improvement over the T-40 in firepower and protection, the T-60 was soon seen by the Red Army to be inadequate in these respects for the military requirements of the Eastern Front. The result was the T-70 light tank, which retained the basic chassis of the T-60, but with the drive sprockets shifted from the rear to the front and the armour revised in shape and angle to generate better protection. But on this hull was fitted a modified turret which still accommodated only the single and therefore tactically overtaxed commander/gunner/loader: this one man had to command the tank and also work the armament of one 45-mm L/46 high-velocity gun and a 7.62-mm (0.3-in) coaxial machine-gun, for which 70 and 945 rounds respectively were provided. Firing a 1.43-kg (3.15-lb) shot with a muzzle velocity of 760 m (2,493 ft) per second, the main gun provided the same armour-penetration capability as the 37-mm and 20-mm ShVAK weapons but at a range of 1,000 m (1,095 yards) rather than 400 m (435 yards). With armour varying in thickness from 10 to 45 mm (0.39 to 1.77 in), the T-70 weighed 9,960 kg (21,958 lb) but had better performance than its predecessor, thanks to the use of improved running gear (five independently torsion-sprung road wheels on each side) and as powerplant two 70-hp (52.2-kW) ZIS-202 petrol engines for a speed of 50 km/h (31.1 mph). Production of the T-70

239

The T-60A light tank was the 1942 production version of the T-60, with improvements such as thicker frontal armour and disc rather than spoked wheels. (*RAC Tank Museum*)

started late in 1941, and ended in the autumn of 1943 after the delivery of 8,225 vehicles, including the improved T-70A with thicker armour. The T-80 was a T-70 development with additional hull armour in the form of welded plates, a revised turret to a maximum thickness of 60 mm (2.36 in) and possibly accommodating a third crew member, as a commander's cupola was provided, two 63.4-kW (85-hp) engines and a weight of 11,785 kg (25,981 lb). Only a few T-80s were produced: by late 1943 Soviet production of medium tanks was running at such a high rate that these considerably more capable tanks could be used for reconnaissance, ending for the time Soviet development of light tanks.

The medium tank that made this possible was the T-34, which was without doubt the most important tank of the Second World War and arguably the most influential tank ever developed. By Western standards the tank was mechanically unsophisticated, with its four-speed gearbox and clutch/brake steering, but the power train and running gear/suspension were utterly reliable, the armament was formidable and the protection far superior to that of the German PzKpfw IV tank. Small-scale encounters with the T-34 units began to be recorded by the Germans as early as 22 June 1941, but fully operational T-34 units were encountered with increasing frequency in the autumn of the same year. The advent of the T-34 was an enormous and thoroughly unpleasant surprise to the Germans: up to this point in the Second World War, their Panzer divisions had enjoyed an unequalled blend of tactical superiority and technical advantage; from this moment the Germans' technical edge was gone, and their tactical expertise was slowly matched, even if never excelled, by the Soviets.

The origins of the T-34 are evolutionary, lying firmly with the BT series of fast tanks using the Christie running gear/suspension. The main development centre for the BT series was Kharkov, and in 1936 the brilliant designer M.I.Koshkin was sent to the Komintern plant in this city to continue development of the BT series with the assistance of A.A. Morozov, N.A. Kucherenko and M. I. Tarshinov. The first result of Koshkin's labours was the A-20 medium tank that appeared at the beginning of 1938. This was modelled on the BT-IS and weighed 20,000 kg (44,092 lb). The armament was the medium-calibre 45-mm L/46 gun, which weighed 125 kg (276 lb), but this was fitted in a turret of inclined rolled armour for enhanced protection, and the hull (based on that of the BT-7M) was also fitted with well inclined armour as pioneered by the BT-IS to provide better ballistic protection against incoming projectiles. The crew was four (driver,

T-70
(USSR)

Type: light tank
Crew: 2
Combat weight: 9,200 kg (20,282 lb)
Dimensions: length overall 4.65 m (15.26 ft); width 2.34 m (7.68 ft); height 2.29 m (7.50 ft)
Armament system: one 45-mm gun with 70 rounds and one 7.62-mm (0.3-0in) DT machine-gun with 945 rounds
Armour: between 10 and 60 mm (0.39 and 2.36 in)
Powerplant: two 52.2-kW (70-hp) ZIS-202 petrol engines with 460 litres (101 Imp. gal.) of fuel
Performance: speed, road 51.5 km/h (32 mph); range, road 450 km (280 miles); fording 0.9 m (2.95 ft); gradient 34°; vertical obstacle 0.66 m (2.18 ft); trench 1.8 m (5.9 ft); ground clearance 0.3 m (11.75 in)

T-70

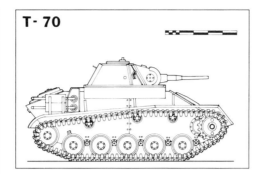

bow machine-gunner, commander/gunner and loader), and the running gear was the standard Soviet wheel/track derivative of the Christie type, with four large-diameter road wheels (with torsion bar suspension) on each side.

The engine was a 450-hp (336-kW) V-2 diesel, which provided a maximum speed of 65 km/h (40.4 mph). This diesel was produced in prototype form during 1936, and marks a significant milestone in the development of tanks. Even in its early form the V-2 was powerful yet reliable, and offered the virtually priceless advantages of greater range on a given volume of fuel, the ability to run on easily produced (and thus cheaper and more readily available) diesel fuel, and lower volatility. This last was of particular interest to tank crews, who became all too aware during the Second World War of the alarming tendency of the fuel to ignite when a petrol-engined tank was hit, causing a perhaps survivable hit to turn virtually instantly into an inferno from which few men were

The T-70 was closely related to the T-60 but had better protection and greater firepower, and the two truck engines were fitted in place of the T-60's single engine for greater performance and agility. By comparison with the T-60, the drive sprockets were at the front and the idlers at the rear. (*RAC Tank Museum*)

likely to emerge, and then only with severe burns.

The A-20 was evaluated against the T-III (otherwise T-46-5) prototype, which used a Christie-type suspension comprising six smaller-diameter road wheels on each side, together with three track-return rollers. The T-III was powered by a 300-hp (224-kW) diesel for a speed of 45 km/h (28mph) at a weight of 28,500 kg (62,832 lb), and though armour thicknesses and armament were similar to those of the A-20 the latter was judged superior in all operational aspects, largely as a result of its superior running gear and the considerably better protection offered by its well-sloped armour. The only major criticism levelled at the A-20 was its modest armament, and this was improved in the A-30 that appeared at the beginning of 1939 by the adoption of a 76.2-mm (3-in) L/26.5 weapon. The A-30 was heavier than the A-20, and was hampered by a number of problems associated with the armament.

Koshkin had meanwhile moved forward to a revised concept, based on an analysis of the small amount of time spent on their wheels rather than tracks by Christie-suspended Soviet tanks. Koshkin was confirmed in his belief that the need for combined wheel and track capability was small (and added weight as well as mechanical complexity), and therefore moved forward to the development of the T-32 based on the A-20 and A-30 but without any provision for the tank to be stripped of its tracks so that it could run on its rubber-tyred road wheels. This allowed the use of wider tracks for reduced ground pressure and improved traction, and also permitted broadening of the hull for yet further sloped protection. The armour varied in thickness up to a maximum of 30 mm (1.18 in) on the hull and 45 mm (1.77 in) on the turret, and other details were basically those of the A-20 and A-30, with the notable exception that the running gear now comprised five road wheels on each side. At a weight of 19,300 kg (42,549 lb) and with a standard crew of four the T-32 could reach 'only' 60 km/h (37.3 mph), but in competitive trials with the A-20 was preferred for its greater firepower and protection.

Thus was the scene set for the T-34 (often called the T-34/76 in Western terminology for the calibre of its main gun), which appeared in prototype form at the end of 1939 for exhaust-ive evaluation and proving trials in the first half of 1940. Just after the beginning of these prototype trials, Koshkin succumbed to pneumonia and died, his place as chief designer being taken by Morozov and later by V.V. Krylov for the much improved T34/85 variant that appeared in 1943. The T-34/76 was a further development of the T-32 with a number of detail modifications and slightly thicker armour on the least protected areas for a weight of 26,725 kg (58,918 lb). The hull and turret were of welded construction, the latter fitted with an L/30.5 version of the 76.2-mm (3-in) gun, which fired its 6.25-kg (13.78-lb) shot with a muzzle velocity of 610 m (2,001 ft) per second. The T-34 was powered by a 500-hp (373-kW) diesel, which provided for a maximum speed of 51.5 km/h (32 mph), and the fuel capacity of 615 litres (135 Imp. gal.) offered the exceptional range of 450 km (280 miles).

The hull was divided into three compartments. The forward compartment provided side-by-side seating for the driver and bow machine-gunner, who doubled as radio operator, in the company and platoon commanders' vehicles that were the only tanks fitted with this equipment. The fighting compartment was just behind the short forward compartment rather than in the centre, and the engine compartment at the rear. The transmission to the rear drive sprockets was also located in the rear compartment, and proved the least reliable single component of the T-34 (vehicles were often seen with a spare transmission unit lashed down on the rear decking). The running gear comprised five unequally spaced road wheels, each mounted on a trailing arm whose coil spring suspension unit was located inside the hull: the two leading wheels had double concentric springs, and the other three had single springs.

The least successful tactical feature of the T-34/76 in its initial form was the turret, a small unit with manual or electric traverse through 360° and provision for manual geared elevation of the main armament through an arc between $+30°$ and $-3°$. Mounted coaxially with the main armament was a 7.62-mm (0.3-in) DT machine-gun, and the bow machine-gun was a similar weapon. Ammunition stowage comprised 77 main-armament rounds (a mixed complement of armour-piercing, HE and shrapnel as required) and up to 3,000 machine-gun rounds, the latter in magazine rather than belted form.

The T-34/76 entered production towards the middle of 1940 at factories located in Kharkov, Leningrad and Stalingrad, the first machines being delivered in June 1940. Germany's advance after the beginning of Operation 'Barbarossa' immediately threatened the Kharkov and Leningrad production facilites, and these were part of the USSR's heavy industrial and war-making capability uprooted for movement into the safety of Siberia: the Kharkov and Leningrad facilities were combined with the tractor factory at Chelyabinsk east of the Ural mountains, to create what became known as Tankograd, which is still one of the USSR's main centres for tank production. Exact production figures are uncertain, but the figures appear to be in the order of 115 machines in 1940, 2,800 in 1941, 5,000 in 1942, 10,000 in 1943, 11,750 in 1944 and 10,000 in 1945, giving a grand total of about 39,665 T-34s of all types.

The first production variant has the Western designation T-34/76A, and is the version described above with a welded turret carrying the Model 1939 L-11 main gun. The welded turret was somewhat complex to build, and as the Soviets possessed a good capability for the production of large castings, a cast turret (still with the same L/30.5 gun in a rolled plate mounting) was introduced, to allow turret production to match the steadily increasing tempo of hull production. During 1941 the Germans began to field an increasing number of 50-mm PaK 38 anti-tank guns, whose projectiles could pierce the T-34's armour at short ranges, and in response the Soviets increased the frontal armour of the T-34 to 47 mm (1.85 in) on the hull and 60 mm (2.36 in) on the turret; at much the same time the original steel-tyred wheels were supplanted by rubber-tyred wheels, offering greater ride comfort for the crew.

In 1942 the Soviets introduced to the T-34 series the improved Model 1940 F34 gun with a longer barrel, a weapon that had been pioneered in the 1930s for the T-28 and T-35 tanks. This piece weighed 455 kg (1,003 lb) and had an overall length of 3.165 m (124.6 in), its L/41.2

The Soviets' T-34/76 was an altogether superlative tank, but like all other armoured vehicles was prone to bogging down in wet conditions. (MARS)

T-34 Model 1940

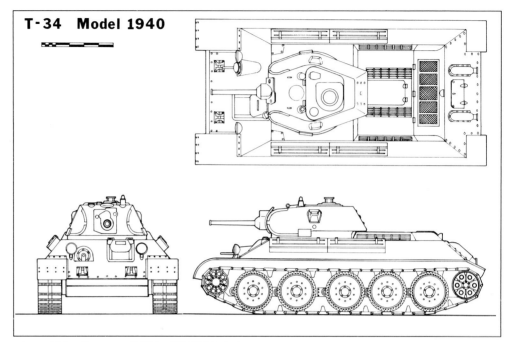

barrel firing the same 6.25-kg (13.78-lb) shot as the Model 1939 gun, but with the higher muzzle velocity of 680 m (2,231 ft) per second, for armour-penetration figures of 69 mm (2.72 in) at 500 m (545 yards), 61 mm (2.4 in) at 1,000 m (1,095 yards), 54 mm (2..13 in) at 1,500 m (1,065 yards) and 48 mm (1.89 in) at 2,000 m (2,185 yards). These figures compared favourably with the equivalents for the 75-mm (2.95-in) KwK L/24 and KwK 40 L/43 weapons carried by the Germans' contemporary PzKpfw IV tanks, but where the T-34 still scored decisively over its German adversaries was in protection, range and cross-country performance. The use of the longer 76.2-mm (3-in) gun in the T-34 is signalled in Western terminology by the designation T-34/76B, and T-34/76Bs are associated with welded as well as cast turrets. Thicker armour and the cast turret increased the T-34/76B's weight to 28,500 kg (62,831 lb) without any serious degradation of performance.

Some criticism had been levelled at the provision in these first models of a single large forward-hingeing hatch in the turret roof, and this deficiency was remedied in the T-34/76C that began to appear in 1943. This variant had twin hatches, increasing overall height from

T-34/76A
(USSR)

Type: medium tank
Crew: 4
Combat weight: 26,725 kg (58,918 lb)
Dimensions: length, overall 6.10 m (20 ft 0 in); width 3.00 m (9.85 ft); height overall 2.45 m (8.04 ft)
Armament system: one 76.2-mm (3-in) M1938 L-11 L/30.5 rifled gun with 80 rounds and two 7.62-mm (0.3-in) DT machine-guns (one coaxial and one bow) with 2,394 rounds; the turret was electrically operated, the main gun was stabilized in neither elevation (−3° to +30°) nor azimuth (360°), and simple optical sights were fitted; smoke could be generated by injecting diesel fuel into the exhaust
Armour: welded steel varying in thickness between 15 and 45 mm (0.59 and 1.77 in)
Powerplant: one 373-kW (500-hp) V-2-34 diesel engine with 420 litres (92.4 Imp. gal.) of internal fuel plus provision for 140 litres (30.8 Imp. gal.) of fuel in jettisonable tanks
Performance: speed, road 51.5 km/h (32 mph); range, road 450 km (280 miles) with external fuel; fording 1.1 m (3.6 ft); gradient 70%; vertical obstacle 0.9 m (2.95 ft); trench 3.0 m (9.85 ft); ground clearance 0.41 m (16.1 in)

The T-34/76D medium tank appeared in 1943, and by comparison with the T-34/76C had a hexagonal turret that eliminated the previous shot trap under the rear of the turret. The gun was the same 76.2-mm (3-in) L/41.2 weapon used in the T-34/76C. (*RAC Tank Museum*)

the 2.49 m (8.17 ft) of the previous models to 2.69 m (8.825 ft). Weight was boosted to 30,500 kg (67,240 lb), with a consequent decrease in speed to 48 km/h (29.8 mph). Other features of the T-34/76C were spudded tracks, improved vision devices and an armoured sleeve for the bow machine-gun.

By the time the T-34/76C was beginning to enter service the Soviets were well advanced with the development of the upgunned T-34/85 version, but saw considerable merit in maintaining the combat capability of the T-34/76 series with a number of improved features. The first of these was a revised hexagonal turret with a wider gun mounting/mantlet in a version known to the West as the T-34/76D: the importance of the new turret is that it provided greater internal volume and, perhaps just as significantly, removed the earlier turrets' rear overhang, whose slight horizontal separation from the rear decking had given German assault pioneers an ideal spot for the placement of anti-tank mines. The new turret increased tank weight to 31,400 kg (69,224 lb), and another feature intorduced on this variant but then retrofitted without delay on earlier marks was provision for jettisonable external fuel tanks, to increase the T-34/76's already

considerable range. The T-34/76E was basically similar, but had a welded turret complete with a commander's cupola. The final T-34/76F had a cast turret with the commander's cupola, and also introduced a five-speed gearbox; only very limited production was undertaken before the T-34/76 series was superseded by the T-34/85.

In autumn 1943 there appeared the T-34/85 with the new 85-mm (3.35-in) gun designated initially as the D-5T85 or in upgraded form as the ZIS-S53; the gun was used with a turret adapted from that of the KV-85 heavy tank. The D-5T85 weighed 582 kg (1,283 lb) and possessed an overall length of 4.42 m (173.9 in): its L/51.5 barrel allowed the 9.36-kg (20.635-lb) armour-piercing shot to be fired with a muzzle velocity of 792 m (2,599 ft) per second, with APCBC, HE and HEAT rounds as alternatives. The ZIS-S53 weighed 1,148 kg (2,531 lb) and possessed an overall length of 4.641 m (173.9 in): its L/54.6 barrel allowed the 9.36-kg (20.635-lb) armour-piercing shot to be fired with a muzzle velocity of 800 m (2,625 ft) per second, thereby giving it sufficient kinetic energy to penetrate 102 mm (4 in) of armour at a range of 1,000 m (1,095 yards). With either of these weapons the T-34/85 was a devastating

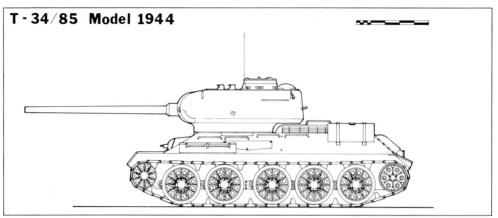

T-34/85 Model 1944

T-34/85 Model 1944
(USSR)

Type: medium tank
Crew: 5
Combat weight: 32,000 kg (70,547 lb)
Dimensions: length, gun forward 7.50 m (24.61 ft) and hull 6.00 m (19.70 ft); width 2.92 m (9.58 ft); height 2.39 m (7.84 ft)
Armament system: one 85-mm (3.35-in) gun with 55 rounds and two 7.62-mm (0.3-in) DT machine-guns with 2,394 rounds
Armour: between 18 and 75 mm (0.71 and 2.95 in)
Powerplant: one 373-kW (500-hp) V–2–34 diesel engine with 635 litres (140 Imp. gal.) of fuel, excluding a 135-litre (30-Imp. gal) jettisonable tank
Performance: speed, road 50 km/h (31.1 mph); range, road 300 km (186 miles) on internal fuel; fording 1.3 m (4.3 ft) without preparation; gradient 30°; vertical obstacle 0.79 m (2.59 ft); trench 2.5 m (8.2 ft); ground clearance 0.4 m (15.75 in)

tank, completely outclassing the PzKpfw IV and providing a match for the Panther and Tiger in all but outright firepower at medium and long ranges. The main gun was provided with 55 rounds, and the secondary armament of two 7.62-mm (0.3-in) machine-guns (one bow and the other coaxial) had 2,394 rounds available to them. The larger turret had the considerable advantage of allowing a tactical crew of three, the availability of a gunner and loader permitting the commander to concentrate on his primary function.

The T-34/85 was authorized for production in December 1943, and by the year's end 283 had been built in convincing proof of the advantage of combining well-proved features (the hull of the T-34 with the turret/armament of the KV-85). By the end of 1944 some 11,000 T-34/85s had been delivered, and production continued into the post-war period: the type served with the Soviet armies until the mid-1950s, and is still in fairly widespread use in many parts of the world today.

As noted in Chapter Two, the Soviets were long-term advocates of the heavy tank, and during the 1930s travelled along much the same design path as the heavy tank advocates of other countries, until they reached the massive T-100 and SMK types with their main turrets on barbettes to give them a superfiring capability over the auxiliary turret. The fallacy of this practice was fully revealed in the Russo-Finnish 'Winter War' (1939-40); yet at the beginning of the Second World War in 1939, the USSR was the only country to have placed such monsters into full-scale production, the initial type being the KV-1, named after Klimenti Voroshilov. Design of the KV-1 began during February 1939 at the Kirov factory in Leningrad, the intention of the design team being a heavy tank less tall than its predecessors, and therefore lacking their stability and visibility problems. The KV-1 was modelled on the T-100 and SMK (especially in the design and structure of the hull, and the nature of the running gear with torsion bar suspension) but did away with the auxiliary turret and its 45-mm gun, thereby removing the need for the main turret's barbette and allowing a general reduction in overall dimensions and weight.

The prototype KV-1 was built between April and September 1939, and ordered into production at the same time as the T-34 medium tank, in December of the same year. The machine had a crew of five, and at a weight of 47,500 kg (104,719 lb) with a maximum 77-mm (3.03-in) thickness of hull armour attained a speed of 35 km/h (21.75 mph) on its 600-hp (447-kW) V-2K diesel. The massive turret was made of welded armour between 30 and 75 mm (1.18 and 2.95 in) thick with a 25-mm (0.98-in) cast mantlet, and was fitted with the same main armament as the T-34/76; the secondary armament was three 7.62-mm (0.3-in) machine-guns.

The KV-1 entered production in Leningrad in February 1940, and some 245 had been produced by the end of the year. A few were sent for operational evaluation in the Finnish campaign, proving successful in the breakthrough of the Finns' Mannerheim Line defences. After the German invasion, the Kirov factory was evacuated to Chelyabinsk, in whose Tankograd all subsequent production

was undertaken, to the extent of 13,500 chassis used for assault guns as well as heavy tanks. Variants of the KV-1 were the KV-1A of 1940 with the L/41.2 main gun, resilient road wheels, an additional 20 mm (0.79 in) of armour on the nose, and a cast mantlet with 25-mm (0.98-in) welded armour strengthening; the KV-1B of 1941 with an additional 25 to 35 mm (0.98 to 1.38 in) of armour bolted and later welded to the hull front and sides, and later with a cast turret, increasing weight to 48,775 kg (107,520 lb); the KV-1C of 1942 with the cast turret, wider tracks, and uprated engine and maximum armour thicknesses increased to 130 mm (5.12 in) on the hull and 120 mm (4.72 in) on the turret; and the KV-1s (*skorostnoy*, or fast) of 1942 with weight reduced to 43,185 kg (95,205 lb) by the omission of the appliqué armour used on the previous models, to increase speed from 34 to 44.5 km/h (21.2 to 27.7 mph).

Running in parallel with KV-1 production was that of the KV-2 artillery fire-support version with an enormous and slab-sided turret accom-

Retaining the well-proved hull/powerplant combination of the T-34/76 series, the T-34/85 added the KV-1's larger turret housing a powerful 85-mm (3.35-in) gun. (*RAC Tank Museum*)

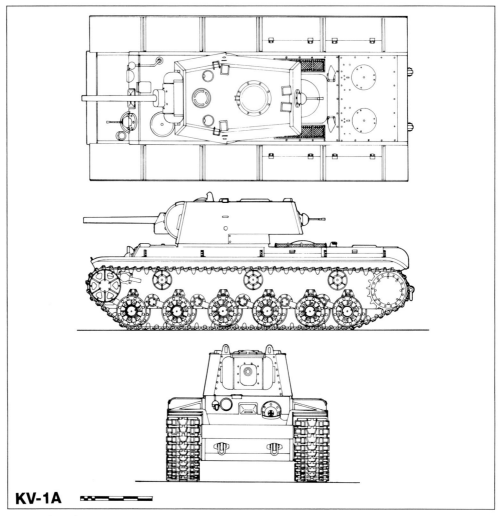

KV-1A

The KV-1B heavy tank was an uparmoured version of the KV-1, and this is an example of the 1942 production variant with a cast rather than welded turret. (*RAC Tank Museum*)

KV-1A
(USSR)

Type: heavy tank
Crew: 5
Combat weight: 47,100 kg (103,836 lb)
Dimensions: length overall 6.89 m (22.60 ft); width 3.25 m (10.66 ft); height overall 2.67 m (8.76 ft)
Armament system: one 76.2-mm (3-in) M1938/1939 L/40 rifled gun with 111 rounds and three 7.62-mm (0.3-in) DT machine-guns (one coaxial, one bow and one turret rear) with 3,024 rounds; the turret was electrically operated, the main gun was stabilized in neither elevation (−4° to +24.5°) nor azimuth (360°) and simple optical sights were fitted
Armour: welded steel varying in thickness between 30 and 77 mm (1.18 and 3.03 in)
Powerplant: one 410-kW (550-hp) V–2–K diesel engine with 595 litres (130.9 Imp. gal.) of fuel
Performance: speed, road 35 km/h (21.75 mph); range, road 225 km (140 miles); fording 1.45 m (4.76 ft); gradient 70%; vertical obstacle 1.2 m (3.9 ft); trench 2.7 m (8.86 ft); ground clearance 0.3 m (1.0 ft)

modating a 152-mm (6-in) howitzer. The size of this turret was a severe tactical hindrance, as too was the weight of 53,850 kg (118,717 lb) without any increase in power, and the KV-2's short production life was mirrored by its brief operational career. It had been planned to develop a KV-3 heavy tank on the same basic chassis but fitted with a turret able to accept a 107-mm (4.21-in) gun, but this did not proceed

past the prototype stage, so the final variant of this family was the KV-85 of 1943 with a large cast turret for an 85-mm (3.35-in) gun. Most KV-85s were produced by converting KV-1s, at a weight of 46,750 kg (103,064 lb).

The ultimate development of the Soviets' enthusiasm for the heavy tank was the Iosef Stalin (IS, sometimes rendered JS) series, which resulted in the short term from the knowledge in August 1942 that the Germans were developing new tank types with heavy protection and powerful armament. It was appreciated by the Soviets that their current service and development tanks might not be

KV-85
(USSR)

Type: heavy tank
Crew: 4
Combat weight: 46,740 kg (103,042 lb)
Dimensions: length, gun forward 8.50 m (28.89 ft) and hull 6.80 m (22.31 ft); width 3.25 m (10.66 ft); height 2.90 m (9.51 ft)
Armament system: one 85-mm (3.35-in) gun with 71 rounds and three 7.62-mm (0.3-in) DT machine-guns with 3,276 rounds
Armour: between 30 and 110 mm (1.18 and 4.33 in)
Powerplant: one 447-kW (600-hp) V–2K–s diesel engine with 550 litres (121 Imp. gal.) of fuel
Performance: speed, road 35 km/h (21.75 mph); range, road 250 km (155 miles); fording 1.6 m (5.25 ft); gradient 36°; vertical obstacle 1.2 m (3.94 ft); trench 2.7 m (8.86 ft); ground clearance 0.4 m (15.75 in)

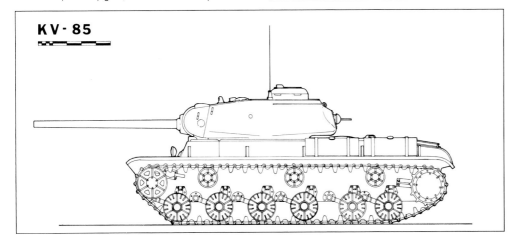

KV-85

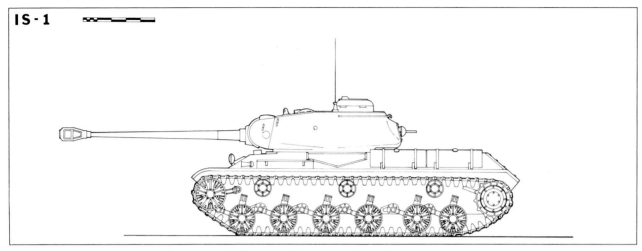

IS-1

able to cope with these new German tanks, and early in 1943 a novel IS series was planned at the Kirov factory. Design was entrusted to the KV team, who therefore used features of the KV series wherever possible, to reduce technical risk and to speed the design and development programme. Weight no greater than that of the KV was demanded, and as initial plans called for an 85-mm (3.35-in) main gun, the designation IS-85 was allocated. The first of three prototypes appeared in the autumn of 1943, and though clearly derived from the KV series in its hull, powerplant and running gear, it was an altogether more formidable machine, with highly sloped armour that was also extremely thick: that of the hull was welded, and varied in thickness from 19 to 120 mm (0.75 to 4.72 in), while the turret was the same cast unit as fitted on the KV-85 and provided thicknesses between 30 and 100 mm (1.18 and 3.94 in). By comparison with the KV-85 the hull of the IS-85 had lower running gear to permit the use of a superstructure that overhung the tracks and so made possible a larger turret ring. The care taken in component as well as overall design is indicated by the fact that the IS-85 emerged with 50 mm (1.98 in) more armour than the KV-85, but weighed some 2,000 kg (4,409 lb) less, allowing a slightly higher maximum speed on a slightly less powerful engine. It is thought likely that the IS-85 saw very limited operational service as the IS-1.

At the same time it was considered in-

IS-1
(USSR)

Type: heavy tank
Crew: 4
Combat weight: 45,215 kg (99,680 lb)
Dimensions: length, gun forward 10.00 m (32.81 ft) and hull 6.63 m (21.75 ft); width 3.11 m (10.25 ft); height 2.71 m (8.9 ft)
Armament system: one 122-mm (4.8-in) gun with 28 rounds, one 12.7-mm (0.5-in) DShK machine-gun with 945 rounds and three 7.62-mm (0.3-in) DT machine-guns with 2,330 rounds
Armour: between 19 and 120 mm (0.75 and 4.72 in)
Powerplant: one 382-kW (513-hp) V–2–IS (V–2K) diesel engine with 525 litres (115 Imp. gal.) of fuel
Performance: speed, road 37 km/h (23 mph); range, road 185 km (115 miles); fording 1.3 m (4.25 ft) without preparation; gradient 36°; vertical obstacle 1.0 m (3.3 ft); trench 2.5 m (8.2 ft); ground clearance 0.37 m (14.6 in)

appropriate that a heavy tank should have the same armament as the current medium tank, so it was proposed that a variant should be developed as the IS-100 with a 100-mm (3.94-in) main gun, in a process made very straightforward by the initial adoption of a large turret ring. A small number of IS-100 tanks were put in hand for evaluation purposes, but the type proceeded no further as General F. Petrov, talented designer of the turret used in the KV-85, T34/85 and IS-1, had proposed an altogether more formidable machine with a new turret of superior ballistic shape and fitted with the 122-mm (4.8-in) D-25 gun: this was 5.92 m (233 in) long, and its L/43 barrel fired a 24.95-kg (55-lb) armour-piercing shot with a muzzle velocity of 780 m (2,559 ft) per second. After development as the IS-122, the type was placed in production as the IS-2, and the considerably more potent turret/armament combination was also retrofitted to the small number of IS-100s that had been built to create the variant known in the West as the IS-1B, the original IS-1 being redesignated IS-1A to avoid confusion. The IS-2 was accepted for production at the end of October 1943 after an extremely rapid development programme, and by the end of the year some 100 IS-2 tanks had been delivered.

Operational experience with the IS-2 in the first half of 1944 showed that the type was truly formidable in firepower and protection, but that the latter factor could still be improved. The result was the IS-3 that appeared towards the end of the year: the hull was basically that of the IS-2 revised in thicker rolled plate for better ballistic protection, while the totally new turret introduced the smooth inverted-bowl shape

that is still used by the Soviets, with thickness varying from a minimum of 25 mm (0.98 in) to a maximum of 230 mm (9.06 in). The weight was still only 46,535 kg (102,590 lb), somewhat lower than that of the Germans' Tiger series, yet the firepower and protection were immeasurably superior, without adversely affecting mobility. The IS-3 can thus be seen as the ultimate expression of the design philosophy first seen in the T-34, taken to so great an extreme that it marked the advent of a new philosophy pursued with great determination by the Soviets in their tanks on the period after the Second World War.

To conclude this assessment of the Allied nations' tanks of the Second World War, it is necessary to backtrack to two British dominions, namely Australia and Canada. Australia ultimately enjoyed a good supply of American tanks to replace its original establishment of British machines (largely pre-war types). But fearing that supplies from the UK and USA might be impossible, Australia produced an indigenous tank, in the form of the Australian Cruiser Tank Sentinel. Design was started in late 1940, using locally available resources and

The IS-2 heavy tank was a much improved development of the IS-1 with usefully reduced weight yet better protection resulting from the optimization of the hull's ballistic shaping. (*RAC Tank Museum*)

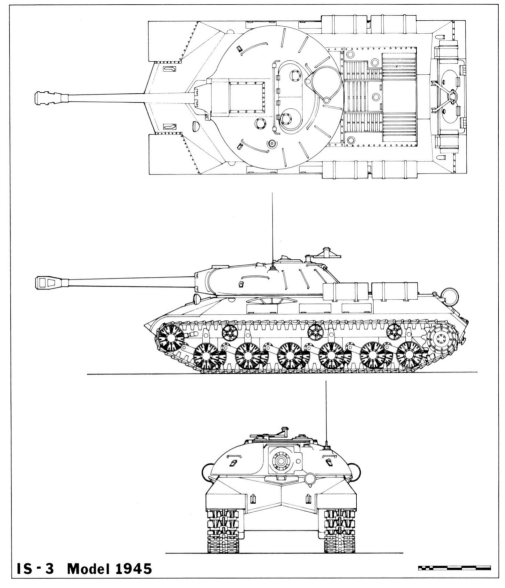

IS-3 Model 1945

techniques, and the Sentinel AC I's design was completed in September 1941 with a power-plant comprising three 117-hp (87.2-kW) Cadillac engines driving a transmission modified from that of the Americans' Medium Tank M3, and a cast turret armed with a 2-pdr (40-mm) gun. Only 66 production tanks, were made, and these were used for training. Developments that did not enter production included the AC III close-support version with a 25-pdr (2.35-in/87.6-mm) gun/howitzer in place of the 2-pdr

(40-mm) weapon, and the AC IV with a 17-pdr (76.2-mm/3-in) anti-tank gun.

Canada's only indigenously-developed tank was the Cruiser Tank Ram I, which used the lower hull, running gear and powerplant of the Medium Tank M3 married to a new cast upper hull and turret mounting a 2-pdr (40-mm) gun, though a 6-pdr (57-mm) weapon had been planned. Production of 50 vehicles was undertaken between late 1941 and summer 1943, by which time the Ram II had introduced the

IS-3
(USSR)

Type: heavy tank
Crew: 4
Combat weight: 46,500 kg (102,513 lb)
Dimensions: length, gun forward 10.00 m (32.81 ft) and hull 6.66 m (21.85 ft); width 3.20 m (10.50 ft); height overall 2.71 m (8.89 ft)
Armament system: one 122-mm (4.8-in) D–25 (M1943) L/43 rifled gun with 28 rounds, two 7.62-mm (0.3-in) DT machine-guns (one coaxial and one bow) with 1,000 rounds and one 12.7-mm (0.5-in) DShK AA machine-gun with 945 rounds; the turret was electrically operated, the main gun was stabilized in neither elevation (−3° to +20°) nor azimuth (360°), and simple optical sights were fitted
Armour: cast and welded steel varying in thickness between 20 and 230 mm (0.79 and 9.06 in)
Powerplant: one 387-kW (519-hp) V–2–IS diesel engine with 480 litres (105.6 Imp. gal.) of fuel
Performance: speed, road 37 km/h (23 mph); range, road 210 km (130.5 miles); fording 1.3 m (4.27 ft); gradient 70%; vertical obstacle 1.0 m (3.28 ft); trench 2.5 m (8.2 ft); ground clearance 0.45 m (17.7 in)

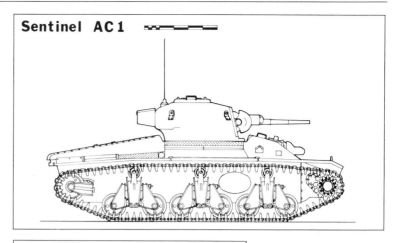

Sentinel AC 1

Cruiser Tank Sentinel AC 1
(Australia)

Type: cruiser tank
Crew: 5
Combat weight: 62,720 lb (28,450 kg)
Dimensions: length overall 20.75 ft (6.32 m); width 9.08 ft (2.77 m); height 8.40 ft (2.56 m)
Armament system: one 2-pdr (40-mm) gun with 130 rounds and two 0.303-in (7.7-mm) Vickers machine-guns with 4,250 rounds
Armour: between 25 and 65 mm (1 and 2.56 in)
Powerplant: three 117-hp (87.2-kW) Cadillac '75' petrol engines with 140 Imp. gal. (636 litres) of fuel (excluding a 44-Imp. gal. (200-litre) jettisonable tank)
Performance: speed, road 30 mph (48.3 km/h); range, road 200 miles (322 km); trench 8.0 ft (2.44 m)

stabilized 6-pdr (57-mm) gun plus a host of mechanical and operational improvements. Production amounted to 1,899 Ram IIs in 1942 and 1943. Canada also produced the Medium Tank M4A1 (Sherman II) with slight modifications as the Cruiser Tank Grizzly I.

Like the Canadian Ram, based mechanically and automotively on the US M3 medium tank but fitted with a powerplant derived from commercial truck engines, the Cruiser Tank Sentinel was a bold Australian attempt to develop a self-sufficiency in tank design and production. This is a Sentinel AC I with 360° traverse turret and 2-pdr (40-mm) gun. (*IWM*)

Ram Mk I

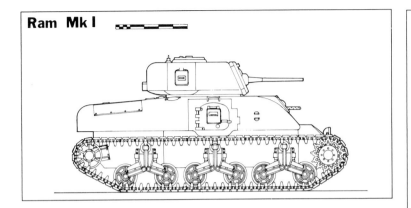

Cruiser Tank Ram Mk I
(Canada)

Type: cruiser tank
Crew: 5
Combat weight: 64,000 lb (29,030 kg)
Dimensions: length overall 19.00 ft (5.79 m); width 9.83 ft (3.00 m); height 8.75 ft (2.67 m)
Armament system: one 2-pdr (40-mm) gun with 171 rounds, three 0.3-in (7.62-mm) Browning machine-guns with 4,275 rounds and one 2-in (50.8-in) bomb thrower with 44 rounds
Armour: between 25 and 76 mm (1 and 3 in)
Powerplant: one 400-hp (298-kW) Continental R–975–EC2 petrol engine with 121.5 Imp. gal. (552 litres) of fuel
Performance: speed, road 25 mph (40.2 km/h); range, road 144 miles (232 km); fording 3.33 ft (1.01 m); gradient 60%; vertical obstacle 2.0 ft (0.61 m); trench 7.4 ft (2.26 m); ground clearance 17 in (0.43 m)

The Canadian Cruiser Tank Ram Mk II was based mechanically and automotively on the US Medium Tank M3, but had a 360° traverse turret with a 6-pdr (57-mm) gun. (*IWM*)

The Years of Consolidation

After the Second World War, the victorious Allies combined an intensive analysis of armoured warfare during the recent conflict with an avid picking over of the bones of German technical research into all aspects of tank technology. The Soviets were well content with the tactical and technical performance of their armoured forces in the last two years of the war and continued along the same basic lines, but the Western Allies had cause for considerable revision in their thinking, though there were clearly many good features that could be retained as the basis for new development.

The Second World War had nearly bankrupted the UK, and the vast demobilization after the end of the war in 1945 forced economies on the army at the same time that it further straitened the situation at home. This position was worsened after 1947, when the grant of independence to India signalled the start of a rapid dissolution of the British Empire: the departure from India removed the need for many of the imperial 'way stations' on the sea and air routes to the old viceroyalty, and within about 15 years the British possessions in Africa and in the Near, Middle and Far East had gone, further reducing the UK's need for a large military capability. This capability had never been as large as that which many other countries would have used for the same task, but demanded a high-quality regular army supported by a territorial force and designed for high levels of strategic mobility, so that the eruption of trouble could be met by adequate strength with minimum delay. The dissolution of the empire led to a reassessment of the role of the British army, the inevitable conclusion being that while the dwindling imperial commitment had still to be met, the new role of the army was in Europe as part of the NATO alliance. Like the imperial role, this demanded a modest but high-quality

army, though in this instance fielding the best of heavy weapons, rather than ordnance designed for easy mobility over strategic distances before use against an unsophisticated enemy. The projected foe was now the USSR, and the vast tank fleet mustered and constantly improved by the Soviets demanded a very high-quality counter.

The light tank concept had fallen out of favour with the British during the Second World War, and in the period immediately after the war the reconnaissance role was entrusted to wheeled scout cars and wheeled armoured cars. So far as tracked vehicles were concerned, in the short term the British kept in service the best of the cruiser and infantry tanks of World War II while working on replacements. These two types were the A41 Cruiser Tank Centurion and the A45 Infantry Tank Conqueror, both launched on their development careers in 1944. These were seen as complementary vehicles incorporating all the lessons of armoured warfare learned so painfully since 1940 by the Royal Armoured Corps, which had been created in April 1939 to control all mechanized cavalry regiments (with the exception of the Household Cavalry) and the Royal Tank Corps, which thereupon became the Royal Tank Regiment.

After basic formulation by the Department of Tank Design in 1943, the A41 was entrusted to AEC for detail design with the object of producing a high-mobility cruiser tank, characterized by improved Horstmann suspension, better protection through the adoption of armour that was both thicker and better sloped, and heavier firepower through the use of the 17-pdr (76.2-mm/3-in) high-velocity gun in a mounting that would be readily adaptable to larger-calibre weapons as these became available; the secondary armament was also increased in the prototypes to a 20-mm Polsten coaxial cannon, but it was eventually decided to revert to the standard 7.92-mm (0.312-in) Besa machine-gun, which was then replaced by a 0.3-in (7.62-mm) Browning machine-gun. Not included in the original concept were high road speed and anything more than minimal range, and these two factors have been the Centurion's main limitations throughout its highly successful and lengthy service career.

Production of the Centurion was entrusted to the Royal Ordnance Factory at Leeds, Vickers-Armstrongs at Elswick and Leyland Motors at Leyland: by the time Centurion production ended in 1962 these companies had built just over 4,400 of the series including about 2,500 for export to countries as diverse as Australia, Canada, Denmark, India, Iraq, Israel, Jordan, Kuwait, Lebanon, the Netherlands, South Africa, Sweden and Switzerland. The type is still in service with several of these countries, such is the worth of the basic design, and, indeed it is still being upgraded to maintain it as a viable weapon with a better fire-control system, modern armament and (in many cases) a diesel powerplant. Though limited in speed to 21.5 mph (34.6 km/h) and in the range of early models to 65 miles (105 km) by its 650-hp (485-kW) Rolls-Royce Meteor Mk IVB petrol engine and miserly 100-Imp. gal. (458-litre) internal fuel capacity, the Centurion has proved a remarkably long-lived weapon because of its capability for uparmouring and upgunning, as indicated below.

In overall design the Centurion is unexceptional, with the driver's compartment at the front behind moderately sloped frontal armour, the fighting compartment in the centre (complete with turret for the commander, gunner and loader), and the engine compartment at the rear. The engine drives rear drive sprockets, and on each side the running gear comprises three pairs of road wheels, each sprung by one set of concentric springs, and six track-return rollers, of which the front and rear units support only the inner sides of the track. Provision is made for the installation of skirt plates over the upper halves of the tracks to provide a measure of protection against the hollow-charge warheads that proved so effective in the Second World War and which have been spectacularly improved since that time.

Construction of the hull is welded, while the electrically/manually-traversed turret is a cast unit with a welded roof plate.

Six prototypes were completed before the end of the Second World War, but though these were shipped to Germany, they arrived too late to see combat. An extended period of development followed the war as the concept of a battlefield team of cruiser and infantry tanks faded in the face of the notion of the single battle tank that could undertake both halves of what was becoming a unified role, and the initial Centurion Mk 1 began to enter service only in 1949 with the 17-pdr (76.2-mm/3-in) Mk 3 gun as main armament. This was the ultimate development of this Second World War weapon, which was a formidable weapon by the standards of the time: though the L/55.15 bore length remained unaltered, at 2,032 lb (972 kg) and 184.05 in (4.675 m) the gun was both heavier and longer than its predecessors, and could fire the new APDS round, whose 8.15-lb (3.7-kg) projectile left the muzzle at a velocity of 3,950 ft (1,204 m) per second for a penetration of 186 mm (7.32 in) of armour at an angle of 30° at a range of 500 yards (455 m). Compared with the 17-pdr Mk 2 used in the Sherman 'Firefly', this represented a 55 per cent improvement in penetrative capability, while the equivalent improvement over the slightly shorter 77-mm Mk 2 used in the Comet was no less than 73.4 per cent.

Further development of the baseline model produced the Centurion Mk 2 with improved armour, but a major change came with the Centurion Mk 3, armed with the 20-pdr (83.4-mm/3.28-in) Tank Gun Mk 1. This offered still greater armour-penetration capability and, at a weight of 2,885 lb (1,309 kg) and overall length of 220 in (5.59 m), used its L/64.1 barrel to fire a 20-lb (9.07-kg) APCBC shot with a muzzle velocity of 3,300 ft (1,006 m) per second. The Centurion Mk 4 was to have been the close-support counterpart of the Mk 3 with a 94-mm (3.7-in) Tank Howitzer Mk 1, but was not built, so the next production variant was the Centurion Mk 5, which was the first definitive version. It was a Vickers-designed counterpart to the Mk 3, which were all brought up to this operationally-improved standard. Further development produced the up armoured Centurion Mk 5/1, and the Centurion Mk 5/2 which entered service in 1959 and was armed with the magnificent 105-mm (4.13-in) Tank Gun L7, a product of the Royal Ordnance Factories, fitted in a mounting that provided full stabilization in elevation to complement the turret's stabilization in azimuth. The basic details of the L7 include a weight of 2,826 lb (1,282 kg) and an overall length of 231.9 in (5.89 m). The L7 is notable for its high degree of accuracy and consistency, and is the standard weapon that entered widespread service in the Western world as the British L7 series, the US Watervliet Arsenal M68 series and the West German Rheinmetall Rh-105-60 series. The development of improved weapons continues, as does that of upgraded ammunition types. The success of the L7 series helped to standardize the 105-mm (4.13-in) calibre as the norm for Western tanks in the 1960s and 1970s, and thus prompted development of the GIAT CN105 series in France, an OTO Melara weapon of the same calibre in Italy, and a number of modification programmes in countries such as Austria.

Even with the comparatively long recoil of the L7, it was possible to install the weapon with an elevation arc that ran from a maximum of +20° to a minimum of -10°, and this latter proved invaluable in combat. The Centurion has been used in anger in many wars (most notably the Korean, various Middle Eastern, Indo-Pakistani and Vietnam conflicts), and the main gun's large depression angle has allowed the tank to adopt a hull-down tactical position for maximum concealment and protection. This had proved very useful in operations against Soviet tanks, which have a main gun depression limit of about -3°, meaning that they cannot readily hide themselves, even in shallow dips. The 105-mm (4.13-in) gun in the Centurion is provided with 64 rounds of ammunition, and was aimed in these initial models with the aid of a 0.5-in (12.7-mm) spotting machine-gun with 600 rounds: this coaxial machine-gun was ballistically matched to the 105-mm (4.13-in) weapon, and after machine-gun rounds had been seen to hit the target, the main gun could be fired with a high probability of scoring a decisive first-round hit, even when the tank was moving, thanks to the provision of

Centurion Mk 5 battle tanks of the Canadian army on manoeuvres. (*Canadian Armed Forces.*)

two-axis stabilization. The standard 0.3-in (7.62-mm) coaxial machine-gun was retained, as was a similar weapon in the 360° vision commander's cupola, and 4,750 rounds of ammunition were carried for these weapons. Extra tactical capability was offered by the provision of six dischargers for smoke grenades on each side of the turret. The Mk 5 could also tow a 200-Imp.gal. (909-litre) monowheel fuel trailer as an expedient to boost range.

The Centurion was probably produced in more variants than any other tank of the post-war period, and after the Mk 5 variants the sequence continued with the Centurion Mk 6, which was the Mk 5/2 uparmoured and fitted with additional fuel tankage, increasing overall capacity to 228 Imp.gal. (1,037 litres) and range to 118 miles (190 km); variants of the Mk 6 were the Centurion Mk 6/1 with a stowage

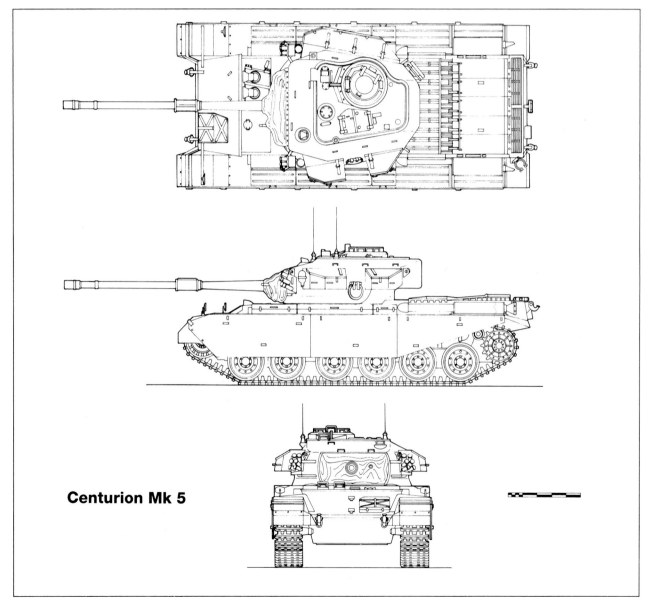

Centurion Mk 5

ROF Leeds/ROF Woolwich/Vickers Centurion Mk 5/2
(UK)

Type: main battle tank
Crew: 4
Combat weight: 111,835 lb (50,728 kg)
Dimensions: length, gun forward 32.25 ft (9.829 m) and hull 24.79 ft (7.556 m); width 11,12 ft (3.39 m) over skirts; height 9.65 ft (2.94 m) to top of cupola
Armament system: one 105-mm (4.13-in) ROF L7 rifled gun with 64 rounds, two 7.62-mm (0.3-in) Browning machine-guns (one co-axial and one AA) with 4,750 rounds, and six smoke-dischargers on each side of the turret; the turret is electrically powered, the main gun is stabilized in elevation (− 10° to + 20°) and azimuth (360°), and an optical fire-control system is fitted
Armour: cast and welded steel varying in thickness from 0.66 to 6 in (17 to 152 mm)
Powerplant: one 650-hp (485-kW) Rolls-Royce Meteor Mk IVB petrol engine with 101 Imp. gal (458 litres) of internal fuel
Performance: speed, road 21.5 mph (34.6 km/h); range, road 64 miles (102 km); fording 4.75 ft (1.45 m) without preparation and 9.0 ft (2.74 m) with preparation; gradient 60%; side slope 30%; vertical obstacle 3.0 ft (0.91 m); trench 11.0 ft (3.35 m); ground clearance 18 in (0.46 m)

basket on the turret rear and infra-red equipment to provide a limited night-driving and night-fighting capability, and the Centurion Mk 6/2, which introduced the ranging machine-gun for the main armament. The Centurion Mk 7 was a Leyland model with the 20-pdr (83.4-mm/3.28-in) gun fitted with a fume extractor and carrying 61 main-armament rounds, and was subsequently designated FV4007 in the Fighting Vehicle designation system; variants of the Mk 7 were the Centurion Mk 7/1 (FV4012) with improved armour, and the Centurion Mk 7/2 with the L7 gun. The Centurion Mk 8 was essentially the Mk 7 with a revised gun mounting, contra-rotating commander's cupola and provision for the commander's twin hatch covers to be raised for overhead protection with the commander's torso out of the turret; standard variants of the Mk 8 were the Centurion Mk 8/1 with improved armour, and the Centurion Mk 8/2 with the L7 gun. The Centurion Mk 9 (FV4015) was the Mk 7 with thicker armour and the L7 gun; variants of the Mk 9 were the Centurion Mk 9/1 with the stowage basket and infra-red vision devices, and the Centurion Mk 9/2 had the ranging machine-gun. Next came the Centurion Mk 10 (FV4017), essentially the Mk 8 with improved armour and the L7 gun plus 70 rounds; stan-

In Swiss service the Centurion Mk 7 is designated Pz 57. (*Swiss Army*)

Armoured vehicles since the First World War have been developed increasingly as families of battlefield types with approximately the same performance and agility. These are a Centurion AVRE 165 and two Centurion AVLBs. (*MARS*)

dard variants of the Mk 10 were the Centurion Mk 10/1 with stowage basket and infra-red vision devices, and the Centurion Mk 10/2 with the ranging machine-gun. The Centurion Mk 11 was the Mk 6 with stowage basket, infra-red vision devices and ranging machine-gun, while the Centurion Mk 12 was the Mk 9 with the same improvements, and the final Centurion

Mk 13 was the Mk 10 with infra-red vision devices and the ranging machine-gun.

The Centurion was also used as the basis of several specialized vehicles, such as two armoured vehicle-launched bridges, an armoured recovery vehicle, an assault engineer vehicle and a beach armoured recovery vehicle. There were also several projected

The Centurion ARV is essentially a battle tank with its turret replaced by a fixed superstructure topped by a rotating commander's cupola. A mass of repair and engine-change equipment is carried. (*MARS*)

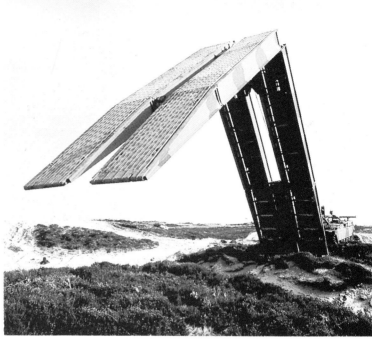

Above   The Centurion AVLB has an 80-ft (24.38-m) bridge launched in between 3 and 5 minutes and recoverable from either end. (*MoD*)

Above left   A Centurion AVRE 105, fitted with mine ploughs, of the 32nd Armoured Engineer Regiment, Royal Engineers, during 1984. This AVRE model retains the 105-mm (4.13-in) main armament of the gun tank, but has much of the Centurion AVRE 165's specialized combat engineer equipment. (*MARS*)

Left   A Centurion AVRE 165 of 32 Armoured Engineer Regiment, Royal Engineers, is put through its paces with the new mine ploughs during 1980. The main armament is a 165-mm (6.5-in) demolition gun, which has only a short range but fires a devastating demolition projectile. (*MARS*)

models, such as two types of self-propelled gun and two types of tank destroyer with 120- or 180-mm (4.72- or 7.09-in) guns. As the basic gun tank is still in service, Vickers and a number of overseas companies have offered retrofit programmes or kits ranging from a completely new diesel powerpack to modern fire-control systems (laser rangefinder and ballistic computer) for the main armament.

The Centurion remains one of the classic tanks of all time, and finally proved that the UK could produce a tank matching the best anywhere in the world. The same cannot be said of the A45, which was conceived as the Centurion's heavy companion and then planned as the baseline model in the Universal Tank series, which would have used the same hull as the basis of the flame-throwing, dozing and amphibious variants. The first FV201 prototype of the A45 was delivered in 1948, and was a massive machine on running gear fitted with Horstmann suspension (four twin-wheel units, each with three concentric springs on each side), the turret of the Centurion with its 17-pdr (76.2-mm/3-in) gun, and a remotely-controlled machine-gun barbette on the left-hand track guard. It became clear during the A45's prototype trials that this unwieldy tank's role could be fulfilled without difficulty by the Centurion, and in 1949 the A45 was cancelled. However, its chassis became the core of a new heavy tank planned to tackle the IS-3 and its successors in Soviet service. This was developed as the Conqueror (FV214), initial proof of the concept being undertaken in a model called

the Caernarvon (FV221), which was the hull of the Conqueror and the turret of the Centurion. The definitive Conqueror appeared in 1950, and the obsolescence of the concept that led to its development is indicated by the fact that production of only 180 vehicles was undertaken in the period between 1956 and 1959. At a weight of 145,600 lb (66,044 kg), attributable mostly to armour of 178-mm (7-in) maximum thickness, the Conqueror attained a speed of 21 mph (33.8 km/h) on its 810-hp (604-kW) Meteor 120 No. 2 Mk 1A petrol engine. The crew was four, and the massive cast turret accommodated a 120-mm (4.72-in) Tank Gun

FV214 Conqueror Mk 2
(UK)

Type: heavy tank
Crew: 4
Combat weight: 145,600 lb (66,044 kg)
Dimensions: length, gun forward 38.00 ft (11.58 m) and hull 25.33 ft (7.72 m); width 13.08 ft (3.99 m); height 11.00 ft (3.35 m)
Armament system: one 120-mm (4.72-in) gun with 35 rounds, two 0.3-in (7.62-mm) machine-guns with 7,500 rounds, and two sextuple smoke-dischargers
Armour: 178 mm (7 in) maximum
Powerplant: one 810-hp (604-kW) Rolls-Royce M120 No.2 Mk 1A petrol engine
Performance: speed, road 21.3 mph (34.3 km/h) range, road 95 miles (153 km); fording 4.75 ft (1.45 m) without preparation; gradient 60%; vertical obstacle 3.0 ft (0.91 m); trench 11.0 ft (3.35 m); ground clearance 20 in (0.51 m)

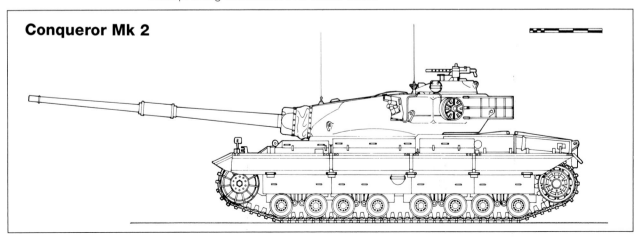

Conqueror Mk 2

Undoubtedly the most successful operator of the Centurion has been the Israeli army, which has used the type's protection and firepower to engage Arab-operated tanks from hull-down positions of a number of tactical advantages. Surviving Centurions have been upgraded considerably and give far superior performance through the adoption of a diesel engine and new transmission. (*Camera Press*)

L11 with 35 rounds, one 0.3-in (7.62-mm) coaxial machine-gun and one 0.3-in (7.62-mm) machine-gun on the commander's cupola. The L11 weighed 3,926 lb (1,781 kg) and was 270.2 in (6.86 m) long with an L/55.3 bore. The Conqueror was allocated at the rate of nine vehicles to each of the British armoured regiments in West Germany, and was designed to provide Centurion units with long-range fire and anti-tank support. But in addition to its conceptual obsolescence, the Conqueror was unreliable, and was phased out of service in 1966.

French tank developments had effectively ceased on all but the covert level in June 1940, resuming fully only after the liberation of France had started in 1944. However, the Free French were already fighting on the Allied side, and in 1943 the first steps had been taken towards the creation of a Free French armoured force based on the *division blindée* (armoured division). This was modelled on US practice, as indicated in the Appendix. Such divisions fought for the rest of the Second World War, and the basic establishment remained unaltered, even when the formation

became the *division mobile* (mobile division) in 1950.

As proved by the composition of their armoured division, the French subscribed initially to the US concept of separate tank destroyer units, to leave the tank units proper free for infantry support and/or exploitation tasks. This began to alter in 1953, when dedicated tank destroyers were phased out of service in favour of M46 medium tanks. The shift in emphasis is proved by the adoption of the AMX-13 light tank as part of the reconnaissance regiment's complement, providing this deep-probing element of the division with a lightly protected but moderately heavily armed and highly mobile vehicle for reconnaissance and tank destroying. In 1955 this tendency was taken one step farther with the turning of some *divisions mobiles* into *divisions mécaniques rapides* (fast mechanized divisions). Each of these divisions comprised one reconnaissance regiment with EBR 4/8-wheeled armoured cars, two *régiments inter-armes* (all-arms regiments), one infantry regiment, one artillery regiment with single self-propelled 105-mm (4.13-in) howitzer and

263

anti-aircraft artillery battalions, and an engineer battalion. The *régiment inter-armes* had been pioneered in the previous year within the experimental Javelot Brigade, and was a fixed grouping of one reconnaissance squadron with jeeps, two regiments of AMX-13s, two infantry companies mounted in tracked personnel carriers, and one battery of 120-mm (4.72-in) mortars for heavy fire support. The combination of the *division mobile* and *division mécanique rapide* was thought by the French to offer the right all-arms blend.

Just before the fall of France, designers had completed preliminary work on the ARL-40, a project originated in 1938 for a Char B1 successor, using the same hull but with the 75-mm (2.95-in) gun located in the revolving turret, rather than in a limited-traverse hull mounting. During the war the design was modified and modernized at the Atelier de Construction de Rueil (ARL) with a different hull (retaining the Char B1's running gear and tracks) and a revised power-traversed Schneider turret accommodating a 90-mm (3.54-in) gun, and after the liberation this was placed in production as the Char de Transition ARL-44. The prototype appeared in 1946 as a 48,000-kg (105,820-lb) heavy tank with armour to a maximum thickness of 120 mm (4.72 in) and with a 700-hp (522-kW) Maybach petrol engine for a speed of 37 km/h (23 mph). In the event only 60 out of a planned 300 were built, and these served between 1947 and 1953,

eventually being replaced, not by the proposed AMX-50, but by US medium tanks, as France came to develop its own concept of combined-arms warfare and the new type of tank to go with it.

The Char AMX-50 heavy tank was an interesting machine, with its hull and running gear modelled on those of the Panther, which was widely used by France after the war, with a wholly French turret. This was a fascinating oscillating unit mounting a 90-mm (3.54-in), then a 100-mm (3.94-in) and finally a 120-mm (4.72-in) main gun in the AMX-50, AMX-50A and AMX-50B variants respectively. Large-scale production plans were laid, but the

Char de Transition ARL-44
(France)

Type: heavy tank
Crew: 5
Combat weight: 48,000 kg (105,820 lb)
Dimensions: length, gun forward 10.52 m (34.51 ft); width 3.40 m (11.15 ft); height 3.20 m (10.50 ft)
Armament system: one 90-mm (3.54-in) gun and one 7.5-mm (0.295-mm) machine-gun
Armour: 120 mm (4.72 in) maximum
Powerplant: one 522-kW (700-hp) Maybach petrol engine
Performance: speed, road 40 km/h (24.9 mph); range, road 150 km (93 miles); gradient 50%; vertical obstacle 0.93 m (3.05 ft); trench 2.75 m (9.02 ft)

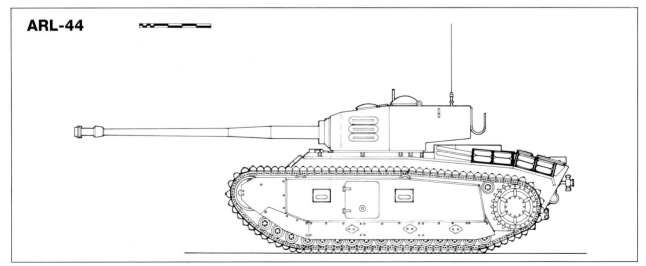

ARL-44

availability of the M47 under the US Military Aid Program resulted in the cancellation of the production-standard AMX-50B, which had a weight of about 56,000 kg (123,457 lb), was powered by a 1,000-hp (746-kW) petrol engine, was armoured to a maximum thickness of 120 mm (4.72 in) and possessed a secondary armament of three 7.5-mm (0.295-in) machine-guns, two of them cupola-mounted for anti-aircraft defence.

Thus the first French tank of wholly post-war design to enter production and service was the Char AMX-13 light tank, designed at the Atelier de Construction d'Issy-les-Moulineaux (AMX), but built first by the Atelier de Construction de Roanne before construction was transferred to Creusot-Loire at Chalon-sur-Saône. The AMX-13 is not currently being built, but production facilities remain in existence so that the total of some 4,500 chassis (including about

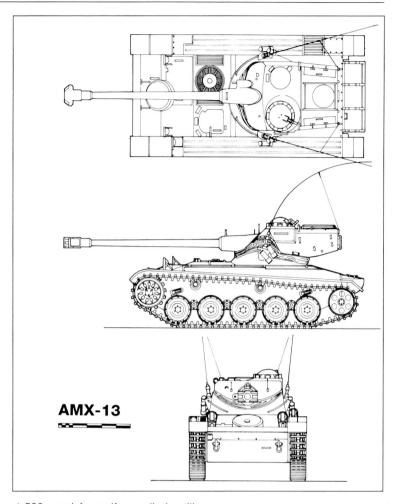

AMX-13

Creusot-Loire AMX–13 Modèle 1951/75
(France)

Type: light tank
Crew: 3
Combat weight: 15,000 kg (33,069 lb)
Dimensions: length, gun forward 6.36 m (20.87 ft) and hull 4.88 m (16.01 ft); width 2.50 m (8.20 ft); height 2.30 m (7.55 ft) to commander's hatch
Armament system: one 75-mm (2.95-in) GIAT rifled gun with 37 rounds (in the hull and six in each of the two revolver cylinders of the automatic loading system), two 7.5- or 7.62-mm (0.295- or 0.3-in) FN1 machine-guns (one coaxial and one AA) with 3,600 rounds, and two smoke-dischargers on each side of the turret; the turret is hydraulically powered, the main gun is stabilized in neither elevation (−5° to +12.5°) nor azimuth (360°), and an optical fire-control system is fitted
Armour: welded steel varying in thickness between 10 and 25 mm (0.39 and 1 in)
Powerplant: one 186-kW (250-hp) SOFAM 8Gxb petrol engine with 480 litres (105.6 Imp. gal.) of fuel
Performance: speed, road 60 km/h (37.3 mph); range, road 400 km (249 miles); fording 0.6 m (23.6 in); gradient 60%; side slope 30%; vertical obstacle 0.65 m (2.1 ft); trench 1.6 m (5.25 ft); ground clearance 0.37 m (14.6 in)

1,500 used for self-propelled artillery mountings and other specialized roles) can be supplemented if required. The origins of the AMX-13 lay with a 1946 requirement of the French airborne forces for a tank that could provide their forces with medium fire-support: the requirement therefore demanded a high-velocity 75-mm (2.95-in) gun, air-portability and a maximum weight of 13,000 kg (28,660 lb). This attractive combination of features appealed to the French army, which thus became the major operator of the resultant type for the reconnaissance and tank-destroying roles, and also to a number of armies round the world, who appreciated the AMX-13's heavy firepower and modest cost. This latter combined with the vehicle's simplicity and reliability to urge its purchase by ar-

One of the most successful tanks developed since the Second World War, the French AMX-13 light tank has been evolved through various marks with its innovatory oscillating turret. This is a vehicle fitted with a Fives-Cail Babcock turret and a 105-mm (4.13-in) gun. (*ECP Armées, France*)

mies that were in the process of establishing armoured forces for the first time.

The prototype appeared in 1948, and revealed its origins not only in its lightweight construction but also in its configuration and the use of a low-profile oscillating turret. The hull is of all-welded construction, using armour between 10 and 20 mm (0.39 and 0.79 in) thick, and is supported on each side by five road wheels with torsion bar suspension. The hull locates the driver (left) and engine (right) at the front, together with the transmission to the front drive sprockets; there are two or three track-return rollers on each side. This leaves the centre and rear of the hull for the Fives-Cail Babcock FL-10 turret, an oscillating type whose fixed lower portion (located on the turret ring) has the trunnions that carry the oscillating upper portion together with the fixed gun plus the commander (left) and gunner (right). Thus traverse is achieved hydraulically or manually by the complete turret, while elevation between -5° and +12.5° is achieved hydraulically or manually by the upper portion. This has the advantage of keeping down the overall height of the vehicle, and permits the use of an automatic loader for the main gun:

this loading system occupies the turret bustle, and comprises in addition to the loader itself two six-round revolver magazines. After each round has been fired the spent case is ejected automatically, but once all 12 rounds have been fired the magazines have to be reloaded from outside the tank, using the tank's reserve supply of 25 rounds. The adoption of an automatic loader means that no tactical capability is lost in having only a three-man crew, which in turn allowed the designers to keep the tank smaller and lighter than would have been the case with a four-man crew. In addition to a 12.5-kg (27.55-lb) HE round, the gun can fire a 14.4-kg (31.75-lb) APC shell whose projectile leaves the muzzle at 1,000 m (3,281 ft) per second and can penetrate 170 mm (6.7 in) of armour at 2,000 m (2,185 yards). A variant of the AMX-13 intended for North African operations had the FL-11 turret with a manually loaded gun, and was distinguishable by its lack of a turret bustle.

The next variant was fitted with the FL-12 turret and its 105-mm (4.13-in) GIAT CN105/57, a rifled weapon designed to fire non-rotating rounds: the most important of these is the 17.3-kg (38.14-lb) HEAT type, whose 10.95-kg (24.14-lb) projectile is launched with a velocity of 800 m (2.625 ft) per second to penetrate 360 mm (14.17 in) of armour at an angle of 0°, or 150 mm (5.91 in) of armour at an angle of 65°, regardless of range. In the early 1960s the French army adopted a version with the FL-10 turret modified to accept the 90-mm (3.54-in) GIAT CN90F3 gun. This has a thermal sleeve and a single-baffle muzzle brake, and can fire Canister, HE, HEAT and Smoke rounds: the most important anti-tank round is the 8.9-kg (19.62-lb) HEAT type, whose 3.65-kg (8.05-lb) projectile leaves the muzzle at 950 m (3,117 ft) per second to penetrate 320 mm (12.6 in) of armour at an angle of 0°, or 120 mm (4.72 in) of armour at an angle of 65° at any range. However, the pace of development in amunition has been such that this 1950s' vintage weapon can fire the recent APFSDS round, whose fin-stabilized projectile can pierce a triple target of 10-, 25- and 60-mm (0.39-, 0.98- and 2.36-in) armour at an angle of 60° at a range of 2,000 m (2,185 yards). Most older AMX-13s in French service were revised with the 90-mm (3.54-in) gun, but some retained the smaller gun and in recompense gained four SS.11 wire-guided anti-tank missiles, which were replaced in the late 1960s by six more advanced HOT anti-tank missiles. As noted above, the AMX-13 was used as the basis of a number of specialized vehicles, and such is the number still in service that several upgrade packages have been offered, these generally centering on replacement of the original petrol engine with a more economical diesel, and the addition of a laser rangefinder.

The only other nation in the Western alliance to develop new tanks in the second half of the 1940s and in the 1950s was inevitably the USA, which unlike the USSR had ended the Second World War with a vast number of vehicles designed largely in the early 1940s and thus approaching obsolescence. The USA could therefore not allow any delay in the development of the new types, based largely on the few types that entered service late in the war, but revised in the light of analysis of Second World War operations and the emergence of the USSR as the main threat. The older tanks found a ready home in the newly-created armoured forces of American allies all over the world, and the way was left clear for the quick adoption of a new generation of armoured fighting vehicles.

As far as organization was concerned, the Armored Force retained the 1943 armoured division with slight modification as the 1947 armoured division, whose establishment is detailed in the Appendix. The basic organization of the divisions was still into three combat commands (each comprising one medium tank battalion, one armoured infantry battalion and one battalion of 105-mm/4.13-in self-propelled howitzers), the additional heavy tank, armoured infantry and 155-mm (6.1-in) self-propelled howitzer battalions being allocated by divisional headquarters as required. Subsequent thinking replaced the disliked heavy tank battalion with an additional medium tank battalion, allowing the creation of four combat commands, each of one medium tank and one armoured infantry battalion plus self-propelled howitzer support as dictated by divisional headquarters.

The most important of the late-Second World War vehicles was the Heavy Tank M26 Pershing, which was reclassified as a medium tank in May 1946 as part of the final American recognition that the wartime classification of vehicles as medium tanks for the 'maid-of-all-work' roles, heavy tanks for the support role and tank destroyers for the tank-killing role, was spurious. The new medium tank classification used for the Pershing paved the way for what is now universally known as the main battle tank.

In 1947 it was decided to modify the Pershing to a more workmanlike standard, with the improved 90-mm (3.54-in) M3A1 gun in place of the original M3, and the 810-hp (604-kW) Continental AV-1790-5A petrol engine and Allison cross-drive transmission/steering in place of the original Ford GAF petrol engine with mechanical transmission and separate controlled-differential steering. In this guise the tank began to enter service in 1948 as the Medium Tank M46 Patton. The Patton was planned as an interim type, pending deliveries of a new medium tank based on the T42 development model, but this latter was still unavailable when the Korean War broke

An M46 medium tank of the 6th Medium Tank Battalion, US 24th Infantry Division, delivers the mail to front-line units in Korea during December 1951. (*US Army*)

out in 1950, and the M26 and M46 therefore bore the brunt of operations in that war.

In 1949 the US Army decided to develop a new series of tanks to replace all Second World War types and their derivatives still in service. These were placed under development as the Light Tank T41, the Medium Tank T42 and the Heavy Tank T43. The makings of the T41 were available in the T37 light tank, whose design as a development model had been launched shortly after the Second World War. The T37 Phase I prototype with the 76.2-mm (3-in) M32 gun was completed in 1949, but already the T37 was involved in a development programme whose fruits were the T37 Phase II, with a redesignated cast/welded turret, a new mantlet, revised ammunition stowage, and a fire-control system that integrated a coincidence rangefinder with a Vickers stabilizer for the gun mounting, and the T27 Phase III with an automatic loader for the main armament, and an IBM stabilizer for the gun mounting. The T37 Phase II became the starting point for the T41, which was finally standardized in 1950 as the Light Tank M41 Little Bulldog, though the name was subsequently changed to Walker Bulldog in honour

of the small but pugnacious US commander in Korea, who had been killed in 1951. Production began in 1950, and some 5,500 M41 series vehicles were built before the production line closed.

In design, the M41 made full use of US combat experience in the Second World War, but is in many ways similar to the M24 it was designed to replace. The all-welded hull is divided into the standard three compartments, with the driver in the forward compartment, the commander, gunner and loader in the turret-basket assembly over the central compartment, and the 500-hp (373-kW) Continental AOS-895-3 petrol engine in the rear compartment to power, via the cross-drive transmission, the rear drive sprockets. The running gear consists on each side of five road wheels with independent torsion bar suspension, and there are three track-return rollers and a front idler. The powered turret is mainly of cast construction with a welded roof and bustle, and accommodates the M32 unstabilized gun, which weighs 1,321 lb (599 kg) and has an overall length of 187 in (4.75 m), its L/52.1 bore firing the armour-piercing projectile with a muzzle velocity of 3,200 ft (975 m) per second.

Later variants of the Walker Bulldog were the M41A1, M41A2 and M41A3 which differed only in detail, including an increase in main armament stowage from 57 to 65 rounds. The last variants also had the AOSI-895-5 engine, a fuel-injected version of the standard unit. Subsequent variants were to have had a 90-mm (3.54-in) or even 105-mm (4.13-in) main gun, but these were not procured. Variants that did appear, however, were the M42 Duster with twin 40-mm anti-aircraft guns, the M44 155-mm (6.1-in) self-propelled howitzer, the M52 105-mm (4.13-in) self-propelled howitzer and the M75 armoured personnel carrier.

The M41 and its derivatives are still in extensive service, current update packages centring on the engine and armament, for which a diesel and a 90-mm (3.54-in) weapon are offered.

The T42 medium tank did not enjoy as successful a career, at least in so direct a fashion, as the M41. It had been realized from fairly early in the M26's life that the turret lacked the ballistic shaping to provide adequate protection against the best anti-tank projectiles beginning to appear in the mid-1940s, and the T42 project was designed to remedy this deficiency. However, when the Korean War broke out, the hull of the T42 was still not ready for production and it was decided to produce another interim type by combining the hull of the M46 with the turret of the T42, complete with its 90-mm (3.54-in) M36 gun, to produce the M46A1 (converted models) and then the

Light Tank M41 Walker Bulldog (USA)

Type: light tank
Crew: 4
Combat weight: 51,800 lb (23,496 kg)
Dimensions: length, gun forward 26.92 ft (8.20 m) and hull 19.08 ft (5.82 m); width 10.50 ft (3.20 ft); height 10.08 ft (3.07 m) including AA machine-gun
Armament system: one 76-mm (3-in) gun with 65 rounds, one 0.5-in (12.7-mm) Browning machine-gun with 2,175 rounds and one 0.3-in (7.62-mm) Browning machine-gun with 5,000 rounds
Armour: between 9.25 and 31.75 mm (0.35 and 1.25 in)
Powerplant: one 500-hp (373-kW) Continental AOS–895–3 petrol engine with 140 US gal. (530 litres) of fuel
Performance: speed, road 45 mph (72.4 km/h); range, road 100 miles (161 km); fording 3.33 ft (1.02 m); gradient 60%; side slope 30%; vertical obstacle 2.33 ft (0.71 m); trench 6.0 ft (1.83 m); ground clearance 17.75 in (0.45 m)

Medium Tank M47 Patton 1 (production models). The better turret shape further highlighted the Americans' fairly rapid move towards the Soviet pattern of battle tank with a more curvaceous turret located well forward on the tank in front of an extensive rear decking: the increased length of current tank guns dictated that when the tank was out of combat the turret was generally traversed to the rear as a means of reducing the vehicle's overall

M41 Walker Bulldog

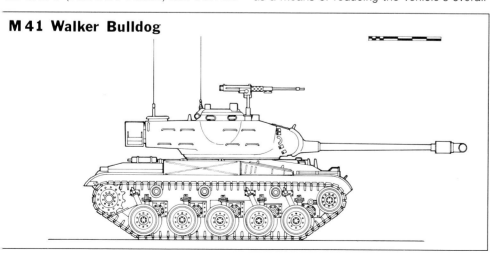

M 47 Patton

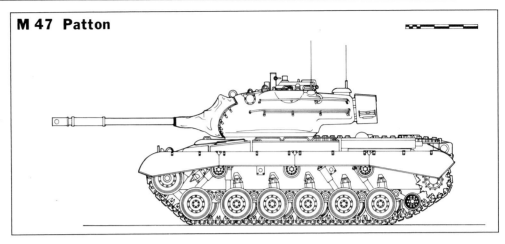

length. Despite its interim nature, the M47 was produced to the tune of 8,576 examples. The M36 gun was a fairly straightforward development of the M1 anti-aircraft gun and, at a weight of 2,652 lb (1,203 kg) and overall length of 203.4 in (5.166 m), had an L/43.1 bore that fired the standard armour-piercing projectile with a muzzle velocity of 2,700 ft (823 m) per second.

The M47 began to enter service with the US Army in 1952, but as an interim type it did not remain in service for particularly long. As soon as supplies of M48s began to arrive in useful numbers, the M47 was withdrawn and reallocated to the USA's allies under the Military Aid Program. The tank is still in widespread service, and in many countries has been upgraded with a diesel powerplant and improved armament, the latter sometimes including the 105-mm (4.13-in) M68 gun with a more modern fire-control system.

Development of the Medium Tank M48 Patton 2 began in October 1950 at the Detroit Arsenal, and as its name suggests, this is an evolutionary development of the M46 and M47. The first T48 prototype appeared in December 1951, and the type was ordered into production during the following March at two major construction facilities, some 11,700 being built before production ended in 1959. The production commitment occurred at a time when the Americans were worried that the Korean War could escalate towards a third world war, and this demanded the rapid production of new battle tanks. However, when the tank began to reach service units in 1953 it became clear that the production decision had been reached too quickly, and most of the early M48s had to be virtually rebuilt in a costly programme to eliminate the mechanical teething problems that had not been obviated by the development programme.

By comparison with the M47, the M48 introduced a cast hull and a cast turret of revised shape, for a vehicle that is slightly shorter, wider and lower than its predecessor. The

Medium Tank M47 Patton 1
(USA)

Type: medium (battle) tank
Crew: 5
Combat weight: 101,775 lb (46,165 kg)
Dimensions: length, gun forward 28.08 ft (8.56 m) and hull 20.90 ft (6.37 m); width 10.50 ft (3.20 m); height 11.00 ft (3.35 m) including AA machine-gun
Armament system: one 90-mm (3.54-in) gun with 71 rounds, two 0.5-in (12.7-mm) Browning machine-guns with 3,440 rounds and one 0.3-in (7.62-mm) Browning machine-gun with 4,125 rounds
Armour: between 12.7 and 115 mm (0.5 and 4.6 in)
Powerplant: one 810-hp (604-kW) Continental AVDS–1790–5B petrol engine with 233 US gal. (882 litres) of fuel
Performance: speed, road 30 mph (48.3 km/h); range, road 80 miles (128.75 km); fording 4.0 ft (1.22 m); gradient 60%; vertical obstacle 3.0 ft (0.91 m); trench 8.5 ft (2.59 m); ground clearance 12.8 in (0.325 m)

An M47 Patton 1 of the Italian army reveals the type's basic similarity to the M26, from which it inherited the hull in combination with the T26's turret and a 90-mm (3.54-in) gun. (*Italian Army*)

Below Generally evident in photographs of main battle tanks firing their main armaments is the low angle of elevation normal for such activities: this reflects the high velocity of the projectile and the short range of most tank-against-tank engagements. This is an M47 Patton 1 of the US 2nd Armored division on manoeuvres in West Germany during 1955. (*US Army*)

Though still in limited service and subject to a number of update programmes, the M47 Patton 1 has always been identifiable as a product of Second World War design philosophies with its high layout and comparatively simple armament configuration. (*Belgian Defence Ministry*)

same engine and transmission are used, but despite a 2,225-lb (1,009-kg) increase in combat weight compared with the M47, the M48 is slightly faster. But the M48 resembles the M47 in possessing the wholly inadequate range of 70 miles (113 km) on its 200-US gal. (757-litre) internal fuel capacity. The running gear comprises, on each side, six road wheels with independent torsion bar suspension, between three and five track-return rollers depending on variant, a rear drive sprocket and a front idler; there is also a small track-tensioning wheel behind the rear road wheel on some variants. The capability of the anti-tank weapons of the 1950s is reflected in the armour thicknesses, which vary from a minimum of 25 mm (0.98 in) to maxima of 110 mm (4.33 in) on the hull and 120 mm (4.72 in) on the turret fronts.

The baseline M48 was followed by the M48A1 with detail improvements, the M48A2 with a fuel-injected engine with 335 US gal. (1,268 litres) of fuel for a range of 160 miles (258 km) and a speed of 30 mph (48.2 km/h), rather than 26 mph (41.8 km/h), the M48A3 (rebuilt M48A1 and M48A2) with the 750-hp (559-kW) AVDS-1790-2A diesel engine with 375 US gal. (1,420 litres) of fuel for a range of

288 miles (463 km), and the M48A5 (rebuilt M48A1 and M48A3) with the host of improvements pioneered on other models and a 105-mm (4.13-in) L68 main gun. Like other battle tanks of its period, the M48 was successively improved with operational additions such as infra-red lights and upgraded fire-control systems. In more recent years, several manufacturers in the USA and elsewhere have offered upgrade packages including a modern diesel engine, a 105-mm (4.13-in) gun and other advanced features. The M48 series has also been used as the basis for many specialized vehicles, such as the M67 flamethrower and M48 armoured vehicle-launched bridge, and in both its standard and modernized versions is likely to remain in service with US allies for some years to come.

By the mid-1950s the M48 was maturing into a powerful battle tank, but in 1956 it was decided to press ahead with the development of an M48 derivative with greater firepower, superior mobility, better reliability and enhanced range. Greater firepower and superior mobility were clearly desirable in a tank whose primary object was to tackle and defeat main battle tanks of the type epitomized all too capably by the Soviet T-54 and T-55 series with

their 100-mm (3.94-in) L/54 guns, while better reliability and enhanced range offered significant battlefield advantages at all operational levels. The Americans had previously been comparatively unworried by deficiencies in range and, to a lesser extent, reliability: in the Second World War they had deployed so large a logistical back-up capability that any such shortfalls in their tanks did not seriously affect the tempo of operations. But the changing nature of warfare persuaded the Americans by the mid-1950s that greater unrefuelled range (and thus a greater reliability) were required, for it could no longer be guaranteed that these services could be made constantly available to front-line forces in the type of fluid warfare that seemed most likely.

The hull and running gear of the M48 were deemed more than adequate as the basis of the new tank, which was thus an evolutionary development rather than a completely new design, with all the financial advantages and low technical risks of such a concept. In November 1956, therefore, an M48 hull was re-engined with the AVDS-1790-P diesel engine, and this was extensively tested with highly successful results during the next months. In February 1958 the concept was taken a step further, when three M48A2s were re-engined with the diesel powerplant as the prototypes for the XM60 series, and these were extensively and again successfully tested under a whole range of operational climatic and geographical conditions.

The final part of the improvement package over the M48 rested with the new tank's firepower, which had to be markedly superior to that of the 90-mm (3.54-in) M41 L/48 gun of the M48 series, and in October and November 1958 a number of candidate weapons were trialled, before the decision was made in favour of the 105-mm (4.13-in) M68 that combined the barrel of the British L7 with an American breech. Work had been developing on the refinement of the complete package, and the selection of the main armament allowed the Main Battle Tank M60 to be standardized in March 1959, with the initial production contract let to the Chrysler Corporation in June 1959 for 180 examples of the M60 to be built at the Delaware Defense Plant, though production later switched to the Detroit Tank Plant, which then became the USA's only major tank production facility.

The inherent limitations of this system are revealed by the USA's attempts to increase

An M48 Patton 2 tank on the driver training course at Fort Benning, Georgia. (*US Army*)

273

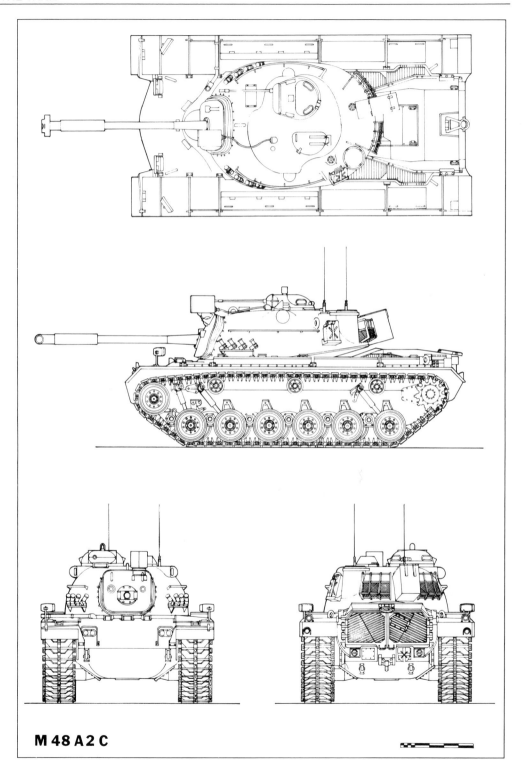

M 48 A 2 C

Chrysler (General Dynamics) M48A5 Patton 2
(USA)

Type: main battle tank
Crew: 4
Combat weight: 108,000 lb (48,989 kg)
Dimensions: length, gun forward 30.53 ft (9.306 m) and hull 20.06 ft (6.419 m); width 11.91 ft (3.63 m); height 10.12 ft (3.09 m)
Armament: one 105-mm (4.13-in) M68E1 rifled gun with 54 rounds, three 7.62-mm (0.3-in) M60D machine-guns (one coaxial and two AA) with 10,000 rounds, and smoke-dischargers; the type can also generate smoke by injecting fuel into the exhaust system; the turret is electro-hydraulically powered, the main gun is stabilized in neither elevation (−90° to +19°) nor azimuth (360°), and an optical fire-control system is fitted
Armour: welded and cast steel varying in thickness between 0.5 and 4.72 in (12.7 and 120 mm)
Powerplant: one 750-bhp (559 kW) Teledyne Continental Motors AVDS–1790–2A/D diesel engine with 375 US gal (1420 litres) of fuel
Performance: speed, road 30 mph (48.3 km/h); range, road 310 miles (499 km); fording 4.0 ft (1.22 m) without preparation and 8.0 ft (2.44 m) with preparation; gradient 60%; side slope 30%; vertical obstacle 3.0 ft (0.91 m); trench 8.5 ft (2.59 m); ground clearance 16.5 in (0.39 m)

the rate of tank production in the 1970s: this was a period when the US Army realized that its tank stocks were too low, especially when it was faced by demands for replacement vehicles from Allies such as Israel which suffered severe M60 losses in the 1973 Yom Kippur War. The limitation that most affected M60A1 production in this period was the time needed to produce large castings of the type used in the M60's hull and turret. By 1975 the production rate had risen from the initial 30 to a better 48 tanks per month, thereafter climbing slowly to a maximum of 129 tanks delivered in October 1978, a rate maintained only until April 1979, when production slowed towards 50 vehicles per month in the summer of 1980. Production continued into mid-1985, when the M60 production line was closed after the delivery of slightly more than 15,000 vehicles for the US and export markets. Building rates and overall production figures compare most unfavourably with those for the Soviets' main battle tanks.

The M60 began to enter service with the US Army in 1960, and in numerical terms remains the most important US tank, though it has been supplemented during the 1980s by the M1 Abrams, which will eventually supplant the M60 fleet in its entirety. The initial M60 variant

The M60 was essentially the M48 with its turret revised for the British-designed 105-mm (4.13-in) gun produced in the USA with modification as the M68. (*MARS*)

weighed 102,000 lb (46,267 kg), and with a 750-hp (559-kW) AVDS-1790-2A diesel plus 385 US gal. (1,457 litres) of internal fuel attained a maximum speed of 30 mph (48.3 km/h) and maximum range of 310 miles (499 km). The M60 can be regarded only as an interim model, for it retained the basic turret of the M48, that was recognized as failing to provide adequate levels of ballistic protection. In October 1962, therefore, the M60 was replaced in production by the M60A1 with the new 'needle-nosed' turret that offered not only superior ballistic protection, but also greater internal volume. This helped to modify the main armament's ammunition stowage from 60 to 63 rounds, and just as importantly, to increase its elevation arc from the range between -9° and +20° in the M60 to the range between -10° and +20° in the M60A1. The modified turret also alters the ammunition capacities for the 7.62-mm (0.3-in) coaxial and 0.5-in (12.7-mm) anti-aircraft machine-guns, the latter located in a trim commander's cupola with 360° traverse and excellent fields of vision, from 5,950 and 600 rounds respectively to 5,500 and 1,040 rounds respectively. The overall weight of the M60A1 is 108,000 lb (48,989 kg), but the engine and performance remain unaltered, despite a fractional reduction in fuel capacity.

The M60A1 was the initial definitive produc-

General Dynamics M60A1
(USA)

Type: main battle tank
Crew: 4
Combat weight: 116,000 lb (52,618 kg)
Dimensions: length, gun forward 30.96 ft (9.436 m) and hull 22.79 ft (6.946 m); width 11.91 ft (3.631 m); height overall 10.73 ft (3.27 m)
Armament system: one 105-mm (4.13-in) M68E1 rifled gun with 63 rounds (26 in the hull and 37 in the turret), one 7.62-mm (0.3-in) M240 coaxial machine-gun with 5,950 rounds, one 0.5-in (12.7-mm) M85 AA machine-gun with 940 rounds, and six smoke-dischargers on each side of the turret; the type can also generate smoke by injecting fuel into the exhaust system; the turret is electro-hydraulically powered, the main gun is stabilized in elevation (−10° to +20°) and azimuth (360°), and an advanced optical fire-control system is fitted; this last combines day/night optical sights, a laser rangefinder, various sensors and a ballistic computer
Armour: cast and welded steel
Powerplant: one 750-bhp (559-kW) Teledyne Continental Motors AVDS−1790−2A diesel engine with 375 US gal (1,420 litres) of fuel
Performance: speed, road 30 mph (48.3 km/h); range, road 300 miles (483 km); fording 4.0 ft (1.22 m) without preparation and 8.0 ft (2.44 m) with preparation; gradient 60%; side slope 30%; vertical obstacle 3.0 ft (0.91 m); trench 8.5 ft (2.59 m); ground clearance 18.25 in (0.46 m)

An M60A1 battle tank moves up past a group of M113 halftracks. (*US Army*)

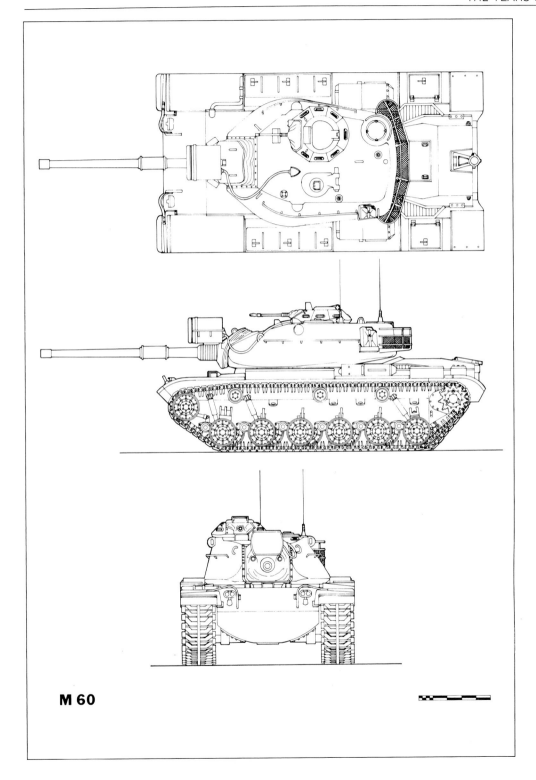

M 60

tion model, and was made of large castings welded together to create the hull and turret. The driver is located in the forward compartment, while the commander, gunner and loader occupy the turret/turret basket arrangement located centrally over the hull with an electro-hydraulic/manual traverse system. The engine and transmission are in the rear compartment, driving rear sprockets for the tracks that run round an arrangement on each side of a front idler, six dual rubber-tyred road wheels with independent torsion bar suspension, and between three and five track-return rollers, depending on specific variant. There is no stabilization system for the gun in either elevation or azimuth, but the necessities of modern war are reflected in the provision of night-vision equipment and, most importantly of all, a central filtration system that supplies air cleaned of NBC (nuclear, biological and chemical) warfare agents to the four crew members via individual tubes. The requirements of independent operations are further reflected in the provision of dozer blade attachments for the preparation of fire positions, and in the provision of deep-wading capability: 4 ft (1.22 m) without preparation, 8 ft (2.44 m) with preparation and 13.5 ft (4.11 m) with a detachable snorkel attached to the commander's cupola.

The M60 was still at a comparatively early stage of its career, which has seen development right up to the present, but as its basic design lies with the philosophies of the 1950s, it is worth treating the tank's complete history here, rather than dividing it in separate sections for treatment in different chapters.

At much the same time that the M68 gun was being developed and accepted, the US Army was considering alternative anti-tank weapons for future armoured fighting vehicles, and decided that a surer method of defeating modern armour might lie with the guided missile, and this resulted in the development by Philco-Ford of the MGM-51 Shillelagh tube-launched missile for use by the M551 Sheridan, often called a light tank, though the US Army is right to designate it a reconnaissance vehicle. The missile was designed to be fired from a 152-mm (6-in) gun/launcher, and was 45.5 in (1.155 m) long with its solid-propellant rocket that burned for 1.18 seconds to provide an effective range of 2,500 yards (2,285 m). The missile weighed 59 lb (26.76 kg), and after leaving the gun/launcher deployed its control surfaces for guidance by an infra-red system that required the gunner merely to keep the crosshairs of his sight centred on the target until the missile impacted and the HEAT warhead detonated. Considerable development problems were encountered with the missile and also with the ammunition designed for use with the same gun/launcher. This ammunition used a semi-combustible cartridge case, and was available in HEAT, White Phosphorus and Canister varieties.

M551 Sheridan
(USA)

Type: reconnaissance and anti-tank vehicle (light tank)
Crew: 4
Combat weight: 34,898 lb (15,830 kg)
Dimensions: length overall 20.67 ft (6.30 m); width 9.25 ft (2.82 m); height 9.67 ft (2.95 m)
Armament system: one 152-mm (6-in) combined gun/missile launcher with 20/8 rounds, one 0.5-in (12.7-mm) Browning machine-gun with 1,000 rounds, one 7.62-mm (0.3-in) machine-gun with 3,000 rounds, and two quadruple smoke-dischargers
Armour: not revealed
Powerplant: one 300-hp (224-kW) Detroit Diesel 6V-53T diesel engine
Performance: speed, road 45 mph (72.4 km/h); range, road 373 miles (600 km); gradient 60%; side slope 30%; vertical obstacle 2.75 ft (0.84 m); trench 8.33 ft (2.54 m)

M 551 Sheridan

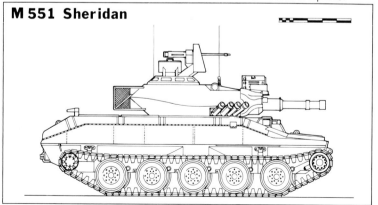

It was decided to instal the same gun/launcher in an M60 variant with 13 missiles and 33 conventional rounds of ammunition. This M60A2 model was developed in 1964 and 1965 for its production debut in 1966: some indication of the gun/launcher and ammunition/missile development problems can be gained from the facts that the first M60A2 unit became operational only in 1972, and that total M60A2 production was a mere 526 vehicles, which have now been withdrawn for conversion, as required, in specialized derivatives of the M60 series such as the M60 Armoured Vehicle-Launched Bridge and M728 Combat Engineer Vehicle.

Service experience with the M60 and M60A1 had meanwhile suggested a number of ways in which the basic tank could be upgraded mechanically, and a number of retrofit packages were developed. The most significant of these are the so-called RISE (Reliability Improved Selected Equipment) modification of the engine, two-axis stabilization for the main armament, an upgraded fire-control system and improved night-vision equipment. These and other modifications are the hallmarks of the final variant, the M60A3, that is in essence a product-improved M60A1 that began to enter production in February 1978. New-production examples are complemented in service by M60A1 retrofitted to virtually the same standard with items such as a thermal sleeve to reduce main armament barrel distortion caused by differential heating, a top-loading air cleaner, and passive night-vision devices.

The M60A3 incorporates all of these features, as well as British-type smoke-dischargers on each side of the turret, an engine smoke generator, an automatic engine fire-extinguishing system, and a much improved fire-control system. This last was developed by Hughes with a laser rather than optical rangefinder and a solid-state digital rather than mechanical analog computer. The laser rangefinder is more accurate than the optical type, and works instantly, while the computer stores information about a maximum six types of ammunition and is automatically fed with information from the laser rangefinder, traversing/elevating rate subsystem, crosswind sensor and cant sensor, leaving the gunner to enter values for air temperature, pressure altitude and (in event of laser failure) range. This allows the generation of a high-quality fire-control solution for the engagement of targets with a high probability of a hit even when the tank is moving. The fire-control system also possesses a self-test sub-

The M60A2 was the variant of the US Army's main battle tank carrying the Launcher for Shillelagh missiles and conventional ammunition but, like the M551 Sheridan light tank, proved inadequate for effective operational service. (*Chrysler Corporation*)

M60A3 battle tanks of the Israeli army begin their evacuation of Sinai in 1975, a token of their desire to reach a permanent accord with Egypt. (*Camera Press*)

Far right A monster past its time, the M103 heavy tank was a thoroughly unsatisfactory vehicle, even after an extensive development programme, and was ill-suited to the needs of the US Marine Corps. (*US Army*)

system: if the system becomes inoperative, manual inputs can be used for insertion of relevant data. From 1980 the system has been further upgraded with the Tank Thermal Sight system, which uses Texas Instruments infrared equipment to provide the ability to fight at night and in smoke against targets that cannot be effectively disguised by ground cover.

An interesting defensive feature developed by Israel Military Industries and now being widely copied on main battle tanks of both power blocs is reactive armour. This was developed by IAI as the Blazer system, and comprises shaped blocks of explosive bolted to the outside of the tank in vulnerable spots: the explosive is triggered by the formation of a HEAT warhead's penetrating jet of vaporized metal and superhot gas, its explosion disrupting the jet and so preventing a catastrophic penetration of the defended tank's main armour. Israel is the M60 operator with greatest operational experience of the tank in modern battlefield conditions, and the overall success of the type in Israeli hands is striking evidence of its capabilities. Like British tanks, the M60's success rests mainly with its good protection and firepower, though some reservations have been expressed about mobility and the M60's high silhouette, a factor exacerbated by the substantial commander's cupola.

The heavyweight companion to the M41

light and M60 medium (now main battle) tanks was the Heavy Tank M103. After the Second World War, the US Army continued trials with

---

Heavy Tank M103
(USA)

Type: heavy tank
Crew: 5
Combat weight: 125,000 lb (56,700 kg)
Dimensions: length, gun forward 37.375 ft (11.39 m) and hull 33.17 ft (10.11 m); width 12.33 ft (3.76 m); height overall 11.67 ft (3.56 m)
Armament system: one 120-mm (4.72-in) M58 L/60 rifled gun with 38 rounds, one 0.3-in (7.62-mm) Browning M37 or M1919A4 coaxial machine-gun with 5,250 rounds, and one 0.5-in (12.7-mm) Browning M2HB AA machine-gun with 1,000 rounds; the turret was electrically operated, the main gun was stabilized in neither elevation (−8° to +15°) nor azimuth (360°), and an optical fire-control system was fitted
Armour: cast and welded steel varying in thickness between 12.7 and 178 mm (0.5 and 7 in)
Powerplant: one 810-hp (604-kW) Continental AV–1790–5B or −7C petrol engine with 268 US gal (1,014.5 litres) of fuel
Performance: speed, road 21 mph (33.8 km/h); range, road 80 miles (128.75 km); fording 4.0 ft (1.22 m) without preparation and 8.0 ft (2.44 m) with preparation; gradient 60%; vertical obstacle 3.0 ft (0.91 m); trench 7.5 ft (2.29 m); ground clearance 15.5 in (0.39 m)

the prototypes of the comparatively large number of heavy tanks developed in the closing stages of that war, but in 1947 decided to concentrate its efforts on a new T43 development model with a weight of 120,960 lb (54,867 kg), a maximum armour thickness of 127 mm (5 in),an 800-hp (596-kW) engine for a speed of 20 mph (32.2 km/h, and a 120-mm (4.72-in) gun as main armament. The urgency attached to the programme was at first low, the US Army having already decided that the heavy tank was not ideally suited to its operational concepts. But it was felt that a useful purpose would be served by producing an American counter to the Soviet IS-3 (in much the same way that the British decided to develop the Conqueror), and the so-called 'Cold War' at the time of the Soviet blockade of Berlin in 1948 inspired a higher level of urgency and, indeed, a rather too hasty develop-

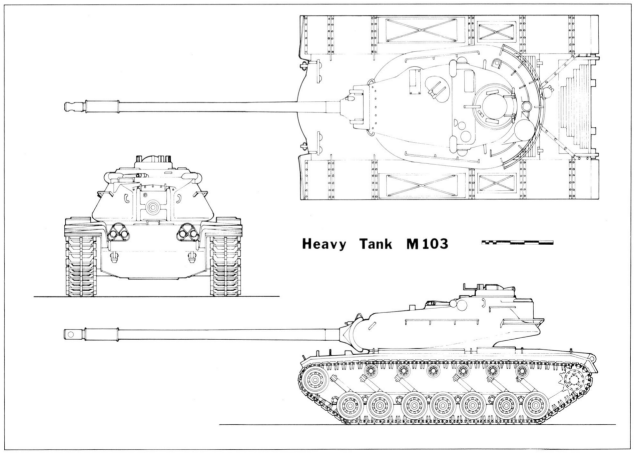

Heavy Tank M103

ment of so large a vehicle. The first two T43 prototypes appeared in 1948, and these were followed by four T43E1 prototypes, which marked the standard approved for production after the beginning of the Korean War in 1950, when 200 T43E1s were ordered from Chrysler.

The cast hull was basically that of the M48 lengthened by the addition of an extra track-return roller and two road wheels on each side, and the turret was a very large cast unit that accommodated a crew of four (commander located immediately behind the gun, gunner and two loaders) and the massive 120-mm (4.72-in) M58 gun, an L/60 weapon for which 38 rounds were provided. The capabilities of this weapon are indicated by provision of three sight systems: direct sighting via rangefinder and periscopic sight, direct sighting via telescopic sight, and indirect sighting via azimuth indicator and gunner's quadrant. An analog mechanical computer was used for solution of the fire-control problem.

The T43E1 was built between 1952 and 1954, and standardized as the M103 in 1953. The vehicle was armoured to thicknesses between 12 and 178 mm (0.47 and 7.12 in) and therefore weighed 125,000 lb (56,700 kg). It was underpowered to a serious degree and so lacked mobility: the engine and transmission combination originally designed for the 101,775-lb (46,165-kg) M47 was also overstressed, and the result was an abysmal level of mechanical reliability. Some 150 improvements were required on each vehicle to produce a battleworthy but indifferent tank, and it was 1957 before the type was finally cleared for service as the M103A1, which was soon replaced by the M60. The other main operator of the type was the US Marine Corps, which used 156 M103A2 tanks, produced by converting surplus M103A1s with AVDS-1790-2AD diesel engines. Given the

An unusual feature of the Pz 61 as built was its 20-mm coaxial cannon, replaced in the AA9 version with a 7.5-mm (0.295-in) machine-gun. (*Swiss Federal Construction Works, Thun*)

weight and size of the M103 series, its allocation to the US Marine Corps seems odd, for that service's logistical capabilities would have been more than severely taxed by trying to field the M103 in amphibious assault operations.

The only other Western nation to develop an indigenous tank in the 1950s was Switzerland, a country with a long record of tank operation, though until the development of the first Swiss tank in the 1950s, these had all been imported or licence-built machines. The Swiss tank arm had been formed in 1919 with Renault FT-17 light tanks, supplemented in the mid-1930s by a very small number of Carden-Loyd tankettes and in the late 1930s by a number of TNH light tanks from Czechoslovakia, assembled in Switzerland with Swiss engines and armament. During the Second World War, in which the country remained firmly neutral, the indigenous NK I self-propelled 75-mm (2.95-in) anti-tank gun and NK II 75-mm (2.95-in) assault gun were designed, though neither entered production. Between 1947 and 1952 some 150 Jagdpanzer 38(t) Hetzer self-propelled anti-tank guns were procured from Czechoslovakia, remaining in service until 1974. These were bolstered by about 200 AMX-13 light tanks, which remained in service up to 1981

with the local designation Leichte Panzer 51, plus 300 Centurion battle tanks, which remain in service with the local designations Pz 55 (Centurion Mk 5) and Pz 57 (Centurion Mk 7). However, from the early 1950s the Swiss made determined efforts to produce an indigenous battle tank, and this resulted in the KW 30 prototype that appeared in 1958 with a Swiss-designed 90-mm (3.54-in) main gun and Belleville washer suspension for its arrangement of six road wheels on each side. The KW 30 was joined by a similar prototype in the following year, and then by 10 examples of the Pz 58 pre-production version with the British 20-pdr (83.4-mm/3.28-in) gun. But the pace of tank development in this period was unrelenting, and the Pz 61 production model that began to enter service in 1965 mounted a British 105-mm (4.13-in) L7 gun. This model had a cast hull and turret, each an impressive single-piece casting, and weighed 38,000 kg (83,774 lb). Power was provided by 630-hp (470-kW) MTU MB 837 diesel, which allowed for a maximum speed of 50 km/h (31.1 mph) and a range of 300 km (186 miles) on 760 litres (167 Imp. gal.) of fuel.

After 150 Pz 61s, the production line switched to the improved Pz 68, which first appeared in 1968 and was then built to the extent of 170

Far left Notable on this Pz 57 (Centurion Mk 7) of the Swiss army are the turret bustle for the radio equipment, the turret side panniers, and the sextuple dischargers for smoke grenades on the turret front. (*Swiss Army*)

The Swiss Pz 61 tank has comparatively modern armament, but is in many respects typical of the tank technology of the late 1940s and early 1950s. (*Eidgenössische Konstrucktionswerkstatte, Berne*)

enterprising but not altogether successful attempt to break into main battle tank design and construction. The protection is only modest, at thicknesses varying from 20 to 60 mm (0.79 to 2.36 in), the armament is in itself adequate but let down by lack of any type of stabilization system, and the type lacks features, such as an NBC system, that are now judged essential.

On the other side of the Iron Curtain all tank development was concentrated in Soviet hands, and pressed ahead with an almost monomaniacal intensity on the basis of late Second World War developments. As noted in

tanks. This model is similar to the Pz 61 in all essential details but the addition of a two-axis stabilization system for the main gun, and a 650-hp (485-kW) MB 837 diesel for superior performance, including a speed of 55 km/h (34.2 mph) despite an increase in weight to 39,700 kg (87,522 lb). Gun-armed variants of this initial model, which was redesignated the Pz 68 Mk 1 when the later variants appeared, are the Pz 68 Mk 2 with a thermal sleeve for the main armament (50 built) and Pz 68 Mk 3 based on the Mk 2 but with a larger turret (110 built) and the Pz 68 Mk 4 based on the Mk 3 (60 built). There are also armoured recovery and armoured vehicle-launched bridge versions of the Pz 68, which may be summarized as an

Pz 68 Mk 2
(Switzerland)

Type: main battle tank
Crew: 4
Combat weight: 39,700 kg (87,522 lb)
Dimensions: length, gun forward 9.49 m (31.14 ft) and hull 6.98 m (22.90 ft); width 3.14 m (10.30 ft); height 2.75 m (9.02 ft) to top of commander's cupola
Armament system: one 105-mm (4.13-in) gun with 56 rounds, two 7.5-mm (0.295-in) machine-guns with 5,400 rounds, and two triple smoke-dischargers
Armour: between 20 and 60 mm (0.79 and 2.36 in)
Powerplant: one 492-kW (660-hp) MTU MB 837 diesel engine with 710 litres (156 Imp. gal.) of fuel
Performance: speed, road 55 km/h (34 mph); range, road 350 km (217 miles); fording 1.1 m (3.6 ft) without preparation and 2.3 m (7.5 ft) with preparation; gradient 70%; side slope 30%; vertical obstacle 1.0 m (3.28 ft); trench 2.6 m (8.5 ft); ground clearance 0.41 m (16 in)

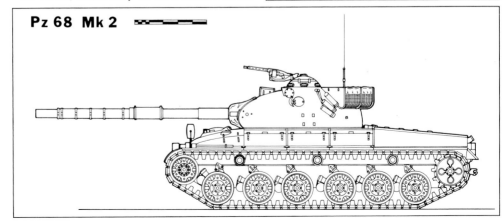

Pz 68 Mk 2

the previous chapter, the two most important types in Soviet service at the end of the Second World War were the T-34/85 medium tank and IS-3 heavy tank, which were deemed adequate for first-line service through the rest of the decade. But the Soviets were not content to rest on their laurels, and a classic new tank was developed from the T-44 medium tank that was built in small numbers during 1945 and 1946, but proved mechanically unreliable. This was the T-54 main battle tank, which appeared in prototype form during 1946 and entered production at Kharkov in 1947 for service in 1949 or 1950. The T-54 and its Main Battle Tank T-55 derivative were built in larger numbers than any other tank of the post-war period, and it is estimated that before production ceased in 1981, more than 50,000 examples had come off the main production lines in Kharkov and Omsk in the USSR, and off other lines in China (as the Type 59), Czechoslovakia and Poland.

The hull of the T-54 is made of welded armour, and varies in thickness between 20 and 99 mm (0.79 and 3.9 in). The sides are vertical, but the front is well angled, the lower plate at 55° and the upper plate at 58°. The driver is seated in a forward compartment on the left; there is a fixed 7.62-mm (0.3-in) machine-gun for use by the driver. To the driver's right, instead of the bow machine-gun and its gunner of earlier tanks, are main armament ammunition stowage, the vehicle's batteries and a modest quantity of fuel. At the rear of the vehicle is the compartment for the 520-hp (388-kW) V-54 diesel engine and transmission, which drive the tracks via rear sprockets. The running gear is of well proved torsion bar type with five unequally spaced road wheels on each side; there are no track-return rollers, and the idlers are at the front. This overall arrangement leaves the centre of the vehicle for the fighting compartment, whose elegantly shaped turret had a manual traverse system in early models. The turret is a single casting with a welded two-piece roof and a rotating floor rather than a turret basket, and accommodates in somewhat cramped conditions the

The Pz 68 Mk 3 has the same armament as the Mk 2 tank, but this is fitted in a larger and ergonomically superior turret. (*Swiss Federal Construction Works, Thun*)

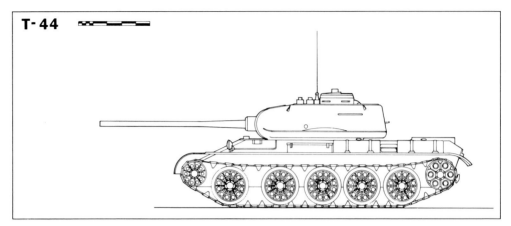

T-44/100
(USSR)

Type: medium tank
Crew: 4
Combat weight: 34,550 kg (76,168 lb)
Dimensions: length, gun forward 8.08 m (26.51 ft) and hull 6.05 m (19.85 ft); width 3.10 m (10.17 ft); height 2.40 m (7.87 ft)
Armament system: one 100-mm (3.94-in) gun with 34 rounds and three 7.62-mm (0.3-in) DT machine-guns with 1,890 rounds
Armour: between 20 and 120 mm (0.79 and 4.72 in)
Powerplant: one 381.75-kW (512-hp) V–2–44 diesel engine with 1,035 litres (228 Imp. gal.) of fuel
Performance: speed, road 51.5 km/h (32 mph); range, road 300 km (186 miles); fording 1.3 m (4.3 ft); gradient 30°; vertical obstacle 1.0 m (3.28 ft); trench 2.5 m (8.2 ft); ground clearance 0.5 m (19.7 in)

commander, gunner and loader together with the 100-mm (3.94-in) D-10T gun.

The gun was developed from a high-velocity naval weapon, and at a weight of 1,948 kg (4,294 lb) has an overall length of 5.608 m (220.79 in). The gun has an L/54 bore that fires a variety of projectiles including a 15.69-kg (34.59-lb) AP projectile with a muzzle velocity of 1,000 m (3,281 ft) per second to penetrate 150 mm (5.91 in) of armour at an angle of 0° at a range of 1,000 m (1,095 yards), or a 16-kg (35.27-lb) APC projectile with a muzzle velocity of 1,000 m (3,281 ft) per second to penetrate 185 mm (7.28 in) of armour at an angle of 0° at 1,000 m (1,095 yards). These initial anti-tank rounds were complemented by HE and FRAG-HE projectiles, and later joined by more advanced anti-tank projectiles: the 12.36-kg (27.25-lb) HEAT-FS projectile has a muzzle velocity of 900 m (2,953 ft) per second and can penetrate 380 mm (14.96 in) of armour at an angle of 0° at any range, while the 5.69-kg (12.54-lb) HVAPDS projectile has the high muzzle velocity of 1,415 m (4,642 ft) per second and can penetrate 200 mm (7.87 in) or more of armour at an angle of 0° at a range of 1,000 m (1,095 yards).

The D-10T is still a useful weapon, but in the T-54 is now let down by its simple fire-control system, which relies on optical sighting by the commander and gunner. This was adequate, but never more than that, when the T-54 was introduced, but increasingly became a limiting feature as the type remained in service. The other main limitations suffered by T-54 crews are the small main armament ammunition stowage of 34 rounds, the use of external (and thus highly vulnerable) fuel tanks to boost range beyond the barely adequate, and the poor elevation arc of the main gun: this has an adequate upper limit of + 17°, but the lower limit of -4° makes it all but impossible for the T-54 to adopt a hull-down tactical position, and this places great emphasis on the good ballistic protection provided by the tank's shaping.

Given the longevity of its production and service careers, the T-54 has inevitably undergone a number of modifications and improvements including, on later models, an

Introduced in the late 1950s, the T-55 is essentially a late-production T-54 with greater power, a D-10T2S main gun with two-axis stabilization plus a bore evacuator, greater ammunition stowage and a rotating turret floor.(*Finnish Army*)

NBC system that was then retrofitted to earlier models. The first T-54s cannot be fitted with a snorkel for deep wading, and the turret is fitted with two cupolas and a wide mantlet. Later examples of this first production model have what is now the standard turret without a bulged rear, and the right-hand cupola has a 12.7-mm (0.5-in) machine-gun; most were later fitted with infra-red driving equipment and received the revised designation T-54(M). First

seen in the mid-1950s, the T-54A has improved main armament in the form of the D-10TG gun with a bore evacuator, stabilization in the vertical plane and powered elevation; when retrofitted with infra-red driving lights it is designated the T-54A(M). In 1957 the Soviets introduced the T-54B and, apart from being the first model produced with infra-red night-vision devices as standard, it has the D-10T2S main gun with two-axis stabilization. Variously

The T-54 was the embodiment of all the USSR's vast experience of armoured warfare in the Second World War, and at the time of its introduction in the late 1940s marked a high point in tank firepower, protection and mobility. This is a basic T-54 of the Finnish army, and has the unstabilized D-10T without a bore evacuator. (*Finnish Army*)

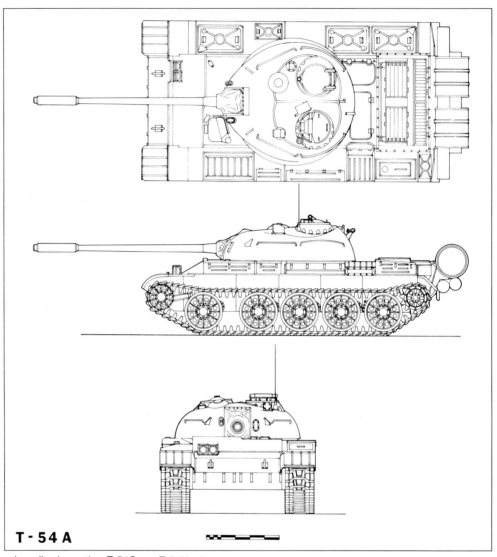

T-54A

described as the T-54C or T-54X, the next model is identical with the T-54B, except that the gunner's cupola is replaced by a plain forward-opening hatch.

These collective modifications resulted in a basically similar tank with the revised designation T-55 main battle tank, which was introduced in the late 1950s with standard features such as no loader's cupola with its 12.7-mm (0.5-in) anti-aircraft machine-gun, no turret dome ventilator, a 580-hp (432-kW) V-55 diesel with 960 litres (211 Imp. gal.) rather than 812 litres (179 Imp. gal.) of internal fuel for a range of 500 km (311 miles) rather than 400 km (249 miles), and 37 rounds of ammunition for the D-10T2S gun which is stabilized in two planes; the 12.7-mm (0.5-in) machine-gun has been reinstated on some tanks, which are then designated T-55(M). Seen for the first time in 1963, the T-55A is the final production version, and is similar to the T-55 apart from having a 7.62-mm (0.3-in) PKT coaxial machine-gun in place of the original SGMT of the same calibre, no bow machine-gun to allow an increase in main armament ammunition stowage to 43 rounds, and a number of

T–54A
(USSR)

Type: main battle tank
Crew: 4
Combat weight: 36,000 kg (79,365 lb)
Dimensions: length, gun forward 9.00 m (29.53 ft) and hull 6.45 m (21.16 ft); width 3.27 m (10.73 ft); height 2.40 m (7.87 ft) to turret top
Armament system: one 100-mm (3.94-in) D–10TG L/54 rifled gun with 34 rounds, one 7.62-mm (0.3-in) SGMT coaxial machine-gun with 3,500 rounds, and one 12.7-mm (0.5-in) DShKM AA machine-gun with 500 rounds; the turret is electro-hyraulically powered, the main gun is stabilized in elevation (– 4° to + 17°) but not in azimuth, and an optical fire-control system is fitted; the type can generate smoke by injecting fuel into the exhaust system
Armour: cast and welded steel varying in thickness between 20 and 210 mm (0.79 and 8.27 in)
Powerplant: one 425-kW (570-hp) V–2–54 diesel engine with 530 litres (117 Imp. gal.) of fuel and provision for 300 litres (66 Imp. gal.) in external tanks plus 400 litres (88 Imp. gal.) in two jettisonable external tanks
Performance: speed, road 50 km/h (31 mph); range, road 500 km (311 miles) on internal fuel and 600 km (373 miles) with external fuel; fording 1.4 m (4.6 ft) without preparation and 4.546 m (14.9 ft) with snorkel; gradient 58%; vertical obstacle 0.8 m (2.625 ft); trench 2.7 m (8.85 ft); ground clearance 0.425 m (16.7 in)

detail improvements such as an anti-radiation lining; when fitted with the 12.7-mm (0.5-in) anti-aircraft machine-gun, this model is designated the T-55A(M).

The T-54 and T-55 have been used as the bases for a number of specialized types such as armoured recovery vehicles, armoured vehicle-launched bridges, mineclearers, a combat engineer vehicle, a flamethrower and a dozer vehicle. The T-54 and T-55 are now only in limited service with the Soviet forces, but are widely used by many of the USSR's clients and allies, who have often carried out their own modification and update programmes. The most important of these have included replacement of the Soviet 100-mm (3.94-in) main gun with a British or American 105-mm (4.13-in) weapon. Despite its tactical failings

by comparison with the latest Western tanks, the T-54 and T-55 remain important weapons for the many emergent nations which have turned to the USSR for military support: the tanks are thoroughly reliable, their armament is effective, and the very simplicity that makes them obsolescent against the West is an invaluable asset in countries with limited mechanical resources and trained manpower. In general the T-54 and T-55 can be equated with the American M60A1.

The Soviets' best heavy tank at the end of the Second World War was the IS-3. Immediately after the end of the war the Soviet army began to receive an improved model with the same 122-mm (4.8-in) main gun, namely the IS-4. This was the starting point for IS-5, IS-6, IS-7, IS-8 and IS-9 prototypes in the late 1940s and early 1950s. In 1953 Stalin died, and when the IS-9 was placed in production during 1956 the letter prefix was altered to 'T' so that the service version of the IS-9 became the T-10, whch began to reach operational units in 1957. Production amounted to some 2,500 such tanks in the late 1950s, and its role was heavy support for the T-54 and T-55. The hull was of the same rolled armour construction as the IS-3, but was lengthened by the addition of a seventh road wheel on each side. The main armament was an improved version of the IS-3's 122-mm (4.8-in) D-25 L/43 gun, in this instance designated D-74, and the ammunition supply was 30 separate-loading rounds: the projectiles were a 25-kg (55.1-lb) APC type fired with a muzzle velocity of 885 m (2,094 ft) per second to penetrate 185 mm (7.28 in) of armour at a range of 1,000 m (1,095 yards) and a 27.2-kg (60-lb) HE type fired with a muzzle velocity of 885 m (2,904 ft) per second. The other armament was a pair of 12.7-mm (0.5-in) machine-guns, one located coaxially and the other on the turret roof as an anti-aircraft weapon.

The 49,800-kg (109,788-lb) T-10 was succeeded by the more capable T-10M with 14.5-mm (0.57-in) rather than 12.7-mm (0.5-in) machine-guns, a multi-baffle rather than double-baffle muzzle brake on the main armament, two-axis stabilization for the main armament, another ammunition type in the form of a HEAT projectile fired with a muzzle velocity of

T-10M

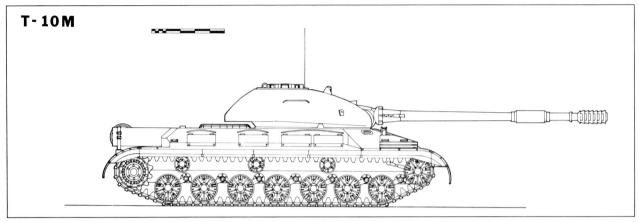

T-10M
(USSR)

Type: heavy tank
Crew: 4
Combat weight: 46,230 kg (101,918 lb)
Dimensions: length, gun forward 10.31 m (33.83 ft) and hull 7.675 m (25.18 ft); width 3.50 m (11.48 ft); height 2.40 m (7.87 ft)
Armament system: one 122-mm (4.8-in) gun with 50 rounds and two 14.5-mm (0.57-in) KPV machine-guns with 1,000 rounds
Armour: between 10 and 273 mm (0.79 and 10.75 in)
Powerplant: one 514.5-kW (690-hp) V–2–IS diesel engine with 840 litres (185 Imp. gal.) of fuel
Performance: speed, road 50 km/h (31.1 mph); range, road 350 km (217 miles); fording 1.3 m (4.25 ft); gradient 32°; vertical obstacle 1.0 m (3.28 ft); trench 3.0 m (9.85 ft); ground clearance 0.46 m (18 in)

900 m (2,953 ft) per second to penetrate 460 mm (18.1 in) of armour at any range, enhanced night-vision capability, and an NBC system. The revised T-10M weighed 46,250 kg (101,962 lb), and maintained the T-10's striking resemblance to the IS-3, though its armour was revised and thickened to minimum and maximum thicknesses of 20 and 273 mm (0.79 and 10.75 in), while the use of a 690-hp (515-kW) V-2-IS (otherwise V-2K) diesel provided for a maximum speed of 42 km/h (26.1 mph). The range was only 250 km (155 miles), a poor figure by Soviet standards, but one reflecting the type's operational role as a breakthrough and support tank commit-

ted for specific reasons, rather than for deep penetration purposes. The T-10 and T-10M are no longer in front-line Soviet service, but remain in reserve for use should the situation demand.

PT-76
(USSR)

Type: light tank
Crew: 3
Combat weight: 14,000 kg (30,864 lb)
Dimensions: length, gun forward 7.625 m (25.02 ft) and hull 6.91 m (22.67 ft); width 3.14 m (10.30 ft); height, early model 2.255 m (7.40 ft) and late model 2.195 m (7.20 ft)
Armament system: one 76.2-mm (3-in) D–56T rifled gun with 40 rounds, one 7.62-mm (0.3-in) SGMT coaxial machine-gun with 1,000 rounds, and in some vehicles one 12.7-mm (0.5-in) DShKM AA machine-gun; the turret is electrically powered, the main gun is stabilized in neither elevation (− 4° to + 30°) nor azimuth (360°), and an optical fire-control system is fitted; the type can generate smoke by injecting fuel into the exhaust system
Armour: welded steel varying in thickness between 5 and 17 mm (0.2 and 0.67 in)
Powerplant: one 180-kW (241-hp) Model V–6 diesel engine with 250 litres (55 Imp. gal.) of fuel plus provision for 180 litres (40 Imp. gal.) of additional fuel in external tankage
Performance: speed, road 44 km/h (27.3 mph) and water 10 km/h (6.2 mph) driven by two waterjets; range, road 450 km (280 miles) with maximum fuel and water 65 km (40 miles); fording amphibious; gradient 70%; vertical obstacle 1.1 m (3.6 ft); trench 2.8 m (9.2 ft); ground clearance 0.37 m (14.6 in)

The most common PT-76 variant is that seen here in Finnish service, with a double-baffle muzzle brake and a bore evacuator for the D-56T main armament. (*Finnish Army*)

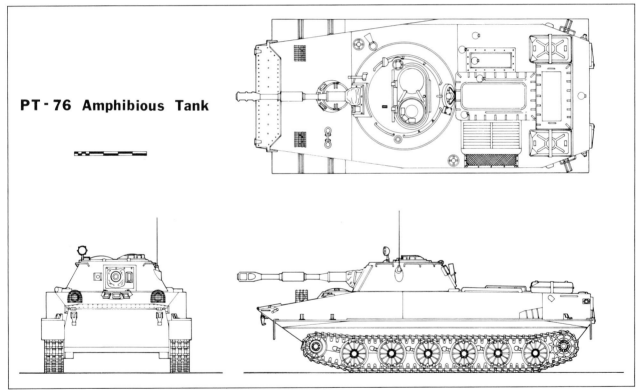

PT-76 Amphibious Tank

Falling somewhat beyond this main sequence of the development is the PT-76 light tank, which appeared in service during 1952 as evidence of the Soviets' return to the concept of a light amphibious vehicle for deep reconnaissance. Developed from a lightweight cross-country vehicle and Soviet light tanks of the late Second World War period such as the T-80, the PT-76 has the advantages of simplicity with moderate offensive capability, and this has made the type popular with Soviet client states requiring a machine matched to their poor communications and lack of a large industrialized base for the support and maintenance of more advanced tanks. On the other side of the coin, of course, are the main failings of the PT-76 and other amphibious light tanks: large size to provide

291

The Soviets have always placed great emphasis on tanks with amphibious or river-crossing capabilities, and still in widespread service despite its technical obsolescence is the PT-76 amphibious light tank such as these vehicles of the USSR's Naval Infantry (marine corps). Notable in this view are the snorkel on the turret rear and the openings in the hull rear for the twin waterjets. (*MARS*)

adequate volume for buoyancy, armour varying in thickness between 5 and 17 mm (0.2 and 0.67 in) making the PT-76 vulnerable to heavy machine-gun fire, and the sacrifice to weight-saving of features such as an NBC system and night-vision equipment.

The welded hull of the 14,000-kg (30,864-lb) PT-76 accommodates the driver in a forward compartment, the fighting compartment in the centre and the engine compartment at the rear. The 240-hp (179-kW) V-6 diesel engine is half of the V-2 used in the T-54/T-55 series, and provides maximum land and water speeds of 44 and 10 km/h (27.3 and 6.2 mph) respectively. The transmission powers two rear drive sprockets. The running gear on each side comprises six road wheels with torsion bar suspension, and there is a front idler. Water propulsion is provided by a pair of engine-driven waterjets, and the only preparations required before the tank enters the water are the erection of a trim vane on the nose plate and the activation of two electrically powered bilge pumps. The electrically/manually-powered turret is again of welded steel, and accommodates the commander, who doubles as

gunner, and the loader for the 76.2-mm (3-in) D-56T gun. This is a development of the weapon used in the T-34 and KV-1 tanks of the Second World War, and fires five types of ammunition, of which 40 rounds are carried. The ammunition types are one HE and four armour-piercing types, the best of the latter being a HEAT type capable of penetrating 120 mm (4.72 in) of armour at an angle of 0° at any range.

The PT-76 has appeared in a number of forms as the PT-76 Model 1 with a multiply-slotted muzzle brake, the PT-76 Model 2 with a double-baffle muzzle brake and a bore evacuator, the PT-76 Model 3, similar to the Model 2 but without a bore evacuator, and the PT-76 Model 4 (or PT-76B) with the D-56TM gun with two-axis stabilization. The D-56TM gun has probably been retrofitted to all Warsaw Pact PT-76s, but fire on the move is still limited by the tank's simple optical fire-control system. The PT-76 is still in very widespread service, and is likely to remain so for some years to come for lack of an adequate replacement in such key roles as support of the Soviet navy's marine arm.

New Beginnings

The tanks of the 1950s may be characterized as logical developments of the best features to emerge from the Second World War: new features did appear, but in almost every instance these were grafted on to tanks which could have been (and indeed often had been) developed in that war. Tanks were extensively used in the period up to 1960, especially by the Soviets in dealing with revolts and revolutions by their eastern European subjects, but true warfare had been sparse. The Korean War (1950–53) saw considerable use of tanks by the United Nations' forces, though mainly in the support rather than anti-tank role, and the most significant episodes of tank warfare in the period were thus the Arab-Israeli wars of 1947–48 and 1956. In these wars the Israelis secured major victories over larger and theoretically more powerful foes, through the adventurous use of high-quality armoured forces in deep outflanking and penetration movements, destroying the Arab forces', cohesion and lines of communication to hasten their inevitable dissolution. These were essentially the tactics of the Second World War with their pace speeded by ideal tank terrain, and confirmed the continued dominance of the tank under conditions of air superiority.

By 1960, however, there had begun to emerge a new generation of tanks which, while building on previous experience and practice, were notable for their adoption during the design phase of the best of modern features that had been retrofitted into the tanks of the 1950s. Hand in hand with these largely technical features (two-axis gun stabilization systems, computer-aided fire-control systems, night-vision equipment, NBC protection, advanced ammunition and the like) went improvements in protection, mobility and firepower. Armour continued to increase in thickness, but was also better conceived and designed for superior protection against the diversity of modern ammunition types, increasingly complemented by surface- and air-launched guided missiles. Mobility was enhanced by the adoption of increasingly powerful yet compact engines to improve power-to-weight ratios, and firepower was increased by the adoption of larger-calibre main guns, firing improved projectiles with the aid of increasingly sophisticated fire-control systems to create a significantly higher first-round hit probability. Typical of the improved projectiles are the comparatively slow-moving HEAT warhead, designed to generate an armour-piercing jet of super-hot gas and molten metal that can burn its way through the protective armour, and the extremely fast-moving APFSDS, designed as a fin-stabilized dart of heavy metal (normally tungsten or depleted uranium) that discards its supporting sabots on leaving the gun barrel, to deliver a devastating kinetic blow to the target armour.

Of course all was not new, and the early 1960s were marked by the continued evolution of unremarkable, but nonetheless workmanlike tanks. Typical of the breed is the Vickers Main Battle Tank, which was planned and developed as a private venture largely to meet the needs of countries with a requirement for a capable battle tank that lacked the outright sophistication (and thus cost and advanced maintenance requirements) of the latest Western offerings. To this extent the Vickers Main Battle Tank was planned as the successor to the Centurion for those countries that neither needed nor could afford the Chieftain being developed as the Centurion's successor in British service. The actual spur for the development was India's 1961 requirement for an 85,120-lb (38,610-kg) replacement for the miscellany of AMX-13 light tanks, M4 Sherman medium tanks and Centurion battle tanks operated by India during the 1950s: the new Vickers Main Battle Tank (now designated

Vickers Mk I MBT

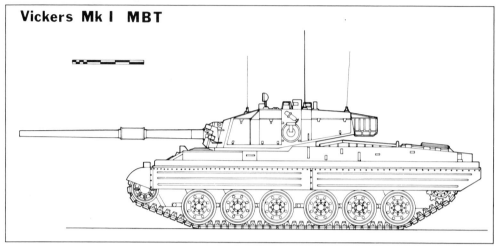

Vickers Main Battle Tank Mk 1
(UK)

Type: main battle tank
Crew: 4
Combat weight: 85,120 lb (38,610 kg)
Dimensions: length, gun forward 31.92 ft (9.73 m) and hull 26.00 ft (7.92 m); width 10.42 ft (3.175 m); height 8.67 ft (2.64 m) to commander's cupola
Armament system: one 105-mm (4.13-in) gun with 44 rounds, one 0.5-in (12.7-mm) ranging machine-gun with 600 rounds, two 7.62-mm (0.3-in) machine-guns with 3,000 rounds and two sextuple smoke-dischargers
Armour: 80 mm (3.16 in) maximum
Powerplant: one 650-hp (485-kW) Leyland L60 Mk 4B multi-fuel engine with 220 Imp. gal. (1,000 litres) of fuel
Performance: speed, road 35 mph (56.3 km/h); range, road 300 miles (483 km); fording 3.75 ft (1.14 m); gradient 60%; side slope 30%; vertical obstacle 3.0 ft (0.91 m); trench 8.0 ft (2.44 m); ground clearance 17 in (0.43 m)

the Main Battle Tank Mk 1) was designed as a conventional machine using as many proven components as possible (including the L7 main gun and 0.5-in/12.7-mm ranging machine-gun of the Centurion with a two-axis stabilization system, and the 650-hp/485-kW Leyland L60 multi-fuel engine, David Brown TN12 transmission and running gear of the Chieftain) in a package that was admirably suited to the capabilities of a nascent tank-production industry such as that being estab-

lished by India, outside Madras. To provide maximum flexibility, the type was also offered with optional features such night-vision equipment, an NBC system, an air-conditioning system and an amphibious kit.

The Vickers Main Battle Tank was sold in this form to India, where the type was built under licence as the Vijayanta, and to Kuwait. The Vijayanta began to enter service with the Indian army in 1965, and was thus too late for major use in the 1st Indo-Pakistani War of that year, but was deployed successfully in the 2nd Indo-Pakistani War of 1971. Production continued into the late 1980s, despite Indian dissatisfaction with the powerpack, and the 1,500 Vijayantas have been improved considerably in recent years. It is also likely that much of the Vijayanta fleet will be upgraded with new composite armour and a diesel engine.

Vickers proposed a Main Battle Tank Mk 2, with four launchers for the Swingfire heavy-weight anti-tank missile, but this concept came to nothing and the next variant was therefore the Main Battle Tank Mk 3 for Kenya and Nigeria. This retains the basic all-welded hull of the Main Battle Tank Mk 1, but the engine has been changed to a 750-hp (559-kW) General Motors 12V-71T diesel; this provides slightly improved speed and greater range on the same 220-Imp. gal. (1,000-litre) internal fuel capacity, but also provides greater reliability and ease of maintenance. The turret retains the basic armament of the Main Battle Tank

Mk 1, but instead of being an all-welded unit now combines a cast front with welded sides, rear and roof with provision for a number of alternative fire-control systems, including the Marconi Simplified Fire-Control System for a high first-round hit probability. The ranging machine-gun is retained to provide a cost-effective weapon for the engagement of light armoured fighting vehicles, and as a back-up ranger for the main armament.

Further development has produced a still more potent variant of the Main Battle Tank, and this is covered below.

The British army required an altogether more sophisticated machine in its search for a Centurion replacement, and this led to the development of the Chieftain (FV4201). At much the same time, the newly re-formed West German army was pressing ahead with the development of an indigenous tank design to supersede its initial complement of American tanks.

Reflecting as they do the same basic levels of armoured warfare technology, but at the same time exemplifying two different conceptual approaches to basically similar operational needs, the Royal Ordnance Factories Chieftain and Krauss-Maffei/Krupp MaK Leopard (now Leopard 1) are worth examining in parallel. The threat which both types were designed to meet is that of Soviet armoured advances westwards across the North German Plain: as key components of NATO's Central Army Group, the British Army of the Rhine and the West German army would in this circumstance be faced with a defensive campaign against an opponent enjoying the benefits of numerical superiority, at the cost of only modest technical inferiority. In this situation the allied countries could hope to meet the challenge only by optimum use of its slight technical superiority on battlefields they had chosen and surveyed in advance of actual combat. In this situation, therefore, the advantages offered by mobility to the Soviets could perhaps be balanced by allied advantages in protection and firepower.

During the early 1950s the main tanks in service with the British forces were the Centurion medium and Conqueror heavy types. These were recognized as amongst the best

vehicles in their classes, but it was also appreciated that Soviet developments would soon redress the USSR's qualititative inferiority, and the search was therefore initiated for a single type to supersede both the Centurion and Conqueror, offering the mobility of the former with the firepower of the latter in a modern package in which overall capability would be greater than the sum of the two parts. Various experimental designs were drawn up, but none of these progressed past the drawing board stage until Leyland produced two examples of its FV4202. This was perceived as a research rather than pre-production design, but pioneered two of the key features later adopted for the Chieftain: a turret without a gun mantlet, and a semi-reclined driver position, allowing considerable reduction in hull height.

In August 1958 the War Office issued a statement of the desired military characteristics for the new vehicle. The preface established some guiding principles, of which the most important was the need for an effective gun/armour combination, followed by agility and the capability for sustained operations (good habitability, high ammunition capacity and considerable fuel capacity) in the possibly chaotic conditions posited for modern warfare. The gun/armour portion of the specification reflected operational lessons from the Korean War in calling for the engagement of the enemy at long range (requiring a larger than normal gun elevation angle, as well as the UK's traditional large gun depression angle to allow the use of hull-down tactical firing positions) and the ability to withstand medium artillery attack at modest range (requiring better protection over the frontal arc). The pace of modern battlefield operations demanded a high rate of fire from the main gun (10 rounds in the first minute and six rounds per minute for the following four minutes), a maximum speed of at least 26 mph (41.8 km/h) and a range of at least 300 miles (483 km) at 15 mph (24.1 km/h). Yet this advanced package was to be combined in a vehicle weighing not more than 100,800 lb (45,723 kg), though realization of the impossible constraints this would impose on the design soon led to an easing of the weight limit to 116,000 lb (52,618 kg).

295

Definitive design work began at Leyland during 1958, but late in that year primary responsibility for the turret was allocated to Vickers-Armstrongs, who also assumed control of integration of the weapon package, the key component of which was the new 120-mm (4.72-in) Royal Ordnance Factories L11 rifled gun firing an extensive range of advanced ammunition types (APDS, HESH, Smoke-White Phosphorus, two practice types and finally APFSDS). It was decided to power the new tank with the Leyland L.60 series multi-fuel engine, used in conjunction with a TN12 semi-automatic transmission, and by March 1959 a full specification had been tentatively agreed: a weight of 100,000 lb (45,360 kg), a hull length of 22.25 ft (6.78 m), a height of 7.83 ft (3.55 m), a ground clearance of 17 in (0.43 m), 60 rounds of main armament ammunition, a fuel capacity of 250 Imp. gal. (1136.5 litres) for a 700-hp (522-kW) engine, to provide a modest power/weight ratio of 15.5 hp/ton (11.37 kW/tonne).

Slight changes to the specification were made as the first prototype was built during 1959, and the turret was simulated by a circular weight as this core of the fighting system inevitably took longer to evolve than the automotive components. The Chieftain prototype was first revealed in 1961 with a fairing to disguise the advanced shaping of its low glacis, and a further six prototypes were produced between July 1961 and April 1962. Extensive trials confirmed the advantages of this heavily-armed vehicle, and in May 1963 the Chieftain was accepted for service. Production lines were established at the Royal Ordnance Factory in Leeds and at the Vickers-Armstrongs plant at Elswick outside Newcastle.

When it was re-created in 1956, the West German army was equipped largely with US weapons, including the M47 and M48A2 tanks: the M47 was already in widespread service, and was thus cheap, and presented even an inexperienced service with no problems, while the smaller number of M48A2s offered superior combat capabilities to crews who had mastered the M47. From the beginning, however, the West German army realized that its tactical concepts, inherited from its vast experience of European armoured warfare in the Second World War, were at variance with US concepts, which stressed firepower and protection, to the detriment of agility and the battlefield advantages of modest weight and low overall silhouette. The US main battle tanks of the period turned the scales at about 112,000 lb (50,803 kg) but the West German army thought that a figure nearer 30,000 kg (66,138 lb) should be the norm for operations in Western Europe. In 1957, therefore, the West German army called for a new tank weighing a maximum of 30 tonnes, powered by an air-cooled multi-fuel engine for a minimum power/weight ratio of 22 kW/tonne (30 hp/ton) and possessing the fuel tankage for a 350-km (217.5-mile) radius of action. The new vehicle was to possess an overall height of 2.2 m (7.22 ft) or less, and be armed with a main gun capable of penetrating 150 mm (5.91 in) of armour at an angle of 60° at optimum range and possessing a maximum effective range of 2,250 m (2,460 yards). A constraint on the weight of the vehicle was the large number of European bridges limited to a maximum of 40 tonnes, and with the width of these bridges also limited width to a maximum of 3.15 m (10.33 ft). Defensive capability was clearly important, but the West Germans opted for a different concept to the British: acceleration, agility and cross-country performance in preference to thick armour, and this capability was sought in the new tank's light overall weight, high power/weight ratio and advanced suspension, for which torsion bar or hydropneumatic types were specified.

France and Italy had reached much the same conclusions as the West Germans, and with France the West Germans were able to sign an interim understanding about the development of the new vehicle. Thus two prototypes were produced in France by AMX, and two different prototypes by each of the West German consortia: Gruppe A led by Porsche and Gruppe B by Ruhrstahl. A turret to suit all these prototypes was ordered from Rheinmetall. The two Gruppe A vehicles were delivered in January 1961 and the two Gruppe B machines in September of the same year. Given the nature of the specification, it was hardly surprising that the two vehicle types were similar in overall line, and powered by the same Daimler-Benz MB 838 multi-fuel engine.

The machines were exhaustively evaluated in 1961, together with the Rheinmetall turret, which was offered with a choice between two 105-mm (4.13-in) rifled guns in the forms of the British L7 and the West German Rheinmetall Rh-105. The situation was then complicated by the French decision to adopt a GIAT main gun of the same calibre but firing only a HESH round in the anti-tank role, whereas the West Germans placed great store of NATO standardization of the British L7 firing APDS, HEAT and HESH anti-tank rounds. Ultimately it was realized that while the Gruppe B hull and automotive system were more advanced than those of the Gruppe A vehicle, it would take too long to bring them to production and service standards, and the Gruppe A vehicle with the Rheinmetall turret and L7 series main gun was standardized as the Leopard in 1963, the French having meanwhile opted to go their own way. Thus the Leopard series began to enter production while an intensive programme of innovative development was

pressed ahead with for the introduction of more advanced derivatives and for the retrofit of in-service tanks.

Though ordered in 1962, the Chieftain began to enter service only in 1967, after delays occasioned by problems with the powerplant, transmission and suspension. At the time of its introduction the Chieftain was the best protected and most powerfully armed tank in the world, a position it enjoyed until the advent of the West Germans' Leopard II in 1980. Given that the Chieftain was designed primarily for head-on operations against tanks, the heaviest protection is fitted on the frontal arc: a cast front for the otherwise welded hull and the thickest portion of the cast turret at the front. These frontal sections are well sloped as well as thick, offering an exceptional combination of protection against kinetic- as well as chemical-energy weapons. Overall layout is typical of modern tank practice: the forward compartment accommodates the centrally-located driver, the central compartment is the fighting compartment with the commander and gunner located on the right of the turret

The Chieftain battle tank is typical of modern British practice, which emphasizes protection and firepower at the expense of mobility. On the left of the turret is a large white light/infra-red searchlight. (*MARS*)

A Chieftain battle tank in a hull-down firing position in typical Northern European winter conditions. (*MoD*)

Far right The radio operator's station of a Chieftain battle tank. (*COI*)

Bottom right Seen here in typical wooded terrain, the Chieftain was designed for mobile warfare on the North European plain, and in this context British operational doctrine emphasized firepower and protection over outright mobility. This thinking was based largely on the feeling that highly mobile operations would not be possible in terrain such as this.

and the loader for the 64 separate-loading rounds of 120-mm (4.72-in) ammunition on the left, and the rear compartment is devoted to the powerpack (engine and transmission). The vehicle is supported on wide tracks that ride over an arrangement, on each side, of six road wheels with Horstmann suspension, three track-return rollers, a rear drive sprocket and a front idler. Modern tank tactics stress the importance of securing a 'mobility kill' if the target tank cannot be destroyed entirely, and to reduce the chances of sustaining such damage the Chieftain is fitted with substantial skirt armour over all but the lower halves of the road wheels, idlers and drive sprockets: this is designed to protect the suspension and lower hull from the effect of HEAT warheads.

Full provision was made for the warfare in modern conditions, and the Chieftain therefore has passive night-vision equipment, a sextuple discharger for smoke grenades on each side of the turret, and an overpressure NBC system with its main unit in the large turret bustle. This last is an altogether more ef-

fective type of defence against nuclear, biological and chemical agents than the original individual projection type, the overpressure concept removing the need for individual face masks, with all its constraints on movement and endurance under adverse conditions.

The armament of the Chieftain is the L11A5, which has an elevation arc between -10° and + 20° in a turret that can be traversed through 360° in primary electrical or secondary manual modes. The gun is fully stabilized in elevation and azimuth for high first-round hit probability even when the tank is moving, and is fitted as standard with a bore evacuator and thermal sleeve. The use of separate-loading ammunition greatly eases the task of the loader, and additional safety is provided by the location of all the bagged propellant charges in water-filled containers below the level of the turret ring to reduce the chances of an explosion if the turret is pierced. The secondary armament comprises two 7.62-mm (0.3-in) machine-guns, one located coaxially and the other for anti-aircraft defence on the commander's cupola. The cupola can be traversed entirely independently of the turret, and the commander can operate the machine-gun from his closed-down position. In early models of the Chieftain, ranging for the main gun was achieved by a method similar to that used in the later Centurions, namely a 0.5-in (12.7-mm) ranging machine-gun over the barrel, used in conjunction with a Marconi gun-control unit that offered stabilized power, unstabilized power, emergency battery and manual control modes. From the early 1970s the ranging machine-gun was superseded by a Barr & Stroud laser rangefinder, and the gun-control unit has been supplemented by a Marconi Improved Fire-Control System with a digital computer to integrate stored data (ammunition types and performance etc) with data from sensors to create a high-quality solution to the fire-control problem.

In the course of a production run up to 1978 of about 900 vehicles for the British army, and in its subsequent service career, the Chieftain has gone through various marks of notably improved quality. The Chieftain Mk 1 had only a 585-hp (436-kW) engine, and only 40 were built

in 1965 and 1966 for training purposes; the Mk 1s were subsequently improved as the Chieftain Mk 1/2 brought up to Mk 2 standard, the Chieftain Mk 1/3 with a new powerpack, and the Chieftain Mk 1/4 which is the Mk 1/3 with a modified ranging machine-gun. The first operational version was the Chieftain Mk 2, which began to reach service units in 1967 with a 650-hp (485-kW) engine. In 1969 the Mk 2 was complemented by the Chieftain Mk 3 with an improved auxiliary engine and a number of secondary armament, suspension and equipment modifications; service variants of the Mk 3 included the Chieftain Mk 3/S, evolved from the Mk 3/G prototype with turret air breathing and a firing switch for the commander, the Chieftain Mk 3/3 with a 720-hp (537-kW) engine and a number of operational improvements (an extended-range ranging machine-gun, provision for a laser range-finder, a modified NBC pack etc), and the Chieftain Mk 3/3P export version of the Mk 3/3 for Iran. The Chieftain Mk 4 was a development model with greater fuel capacity. The Chieftain Mk 5 may be regarded as the definitive production model based on the Mk 3/3 with many operational improvements such as greater APDS stowage at the expense of ammunition capacity for the ranging machine-gun; the two export variants of the Mk 5 were the Chieftain Mk 5/2K for Kuwait and the Chieftain Mk 5/3P for Iran. The Chieftain Mk 6 is a Mk 2 with a new powerpack. The Chieftain Mk 7 is the Mk 3 and Mk 3/S with an improved engine and modified ranging machine-gun. The Chieftain Mk 8 is the Mk 3/3 with Mk 7 modifications. The Chieftains Mk 9, Mk 10, Mk 11 and Mk 12 are the Mk 6, Mk 7, Mk 8 and Mk 5 respectively with the Improved Fire-Control System.

An important development for in-service Chieftains is the Barr & Stroud TOGS (Thermal Observation and Gunnery Sight), an external retrofit package developed from the system used in the Challenger that replaces the current white light/infra-red searchlight to produce an observation and gunnery capability in smoke and at night. Another Chieftain enhancement is the so-called Stillbrew armour, which comprises appliqué plates added over the frontal arc to improve protection and additionally to shield the vulnerable interface between the hull and turret from frontal fire. The Stillbrew armour is added at base workshops, and though it improves protection to a marked degree through its multi-layer nature (classified, but believed to be a steel outer layer over a ceramic composite) it is comparatively light and so affects mobility only slightly. This is particularly important, since the Chieftain's mobility has always been its weakest point. Mobility was admittedly placed behind firepower and protection in the formulation of the Chieftain specification, but the engine reached the planned power output only

Vickers Defence Systems (ROF Leeds) FV4201 Chieftain Mk 5 (UK)

Type: main battle tank
Crew: 4
Combat weight: 121,250 lb (55,000 kg)
Dimensions: length, gun forward 35.42 ft (10.795 m) and hull 24.67 ft (7.518 m); width 11.50 ft (3.504 m) over skirts; height 9.50 ft (2.895 m) overall
Armament system: one 120-mm (4.72-in) ROF L11A5 rifled gun with 64 rounds, one 0.5-in (12.7-mm) L21A1 coaxial ranging machine-gun with 300 rounds (not fitted in vehicles with the IFCS with laser rangefinder), two 7.62-mm (0.3-in) machine-guns (one L8A1 coaxial and one L37A1 AA) with 6,000 rounds, and six smoke-dischargers on each side of the turret; the turret is electrically powered, the main gun is stabilized in elevation (−10° to +20°) and azimuth (360°), and a Barr & Stroud Tank Laser Sight Unit or Marconi Improved Fire-Control System is fitted; this latter combines stabilized day/night optical sights, a laser rangefinder, various sensors and a ballistic computer
Armour: cast and welded steel; all in-service Chieftains are being retrofitted with the Stillbrew appliqué armour system (an outer layer of steel on top of an inner laminate layer) over the most vunerable sections of the frontal arc
Powerplant: one 750-bhp (559-kW) Leyland L60 No.4 Mk 8A multi-fuel engine with 210 Imp. gal. (955 litres) of fuel
Performance: speed, road 30 mph (48 km/h); range, road 310 miles (499 km); fording 3.5 ft (1.07 m) without preparation; gradient 70%; side slope 30%; vertical obstacle 3.0 ft (0.91 m); trench 10.33 ft (3.15 m); ground clearance 20 in (0.51 m)

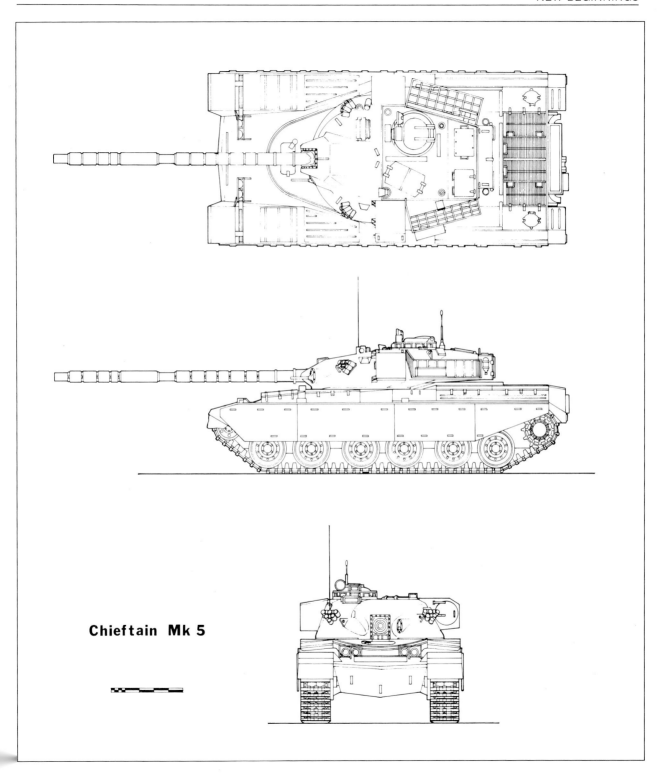

Chieftain Mk 5

A Chieftain AVLB lays its No.8 bridge, a folding unit laid over the front of the launcher's hull to span a gap of up to 75 ft (22.68-m). In military bridging operations, speed and reliability are prime requisites. The Chieftain AVLB can lay its bridge in about five minutes using hydraulic power and controlling the operation from within the hull, uncouple itself from the bridge automatically, and recover a bridge in about 10 minutes. *(COI)*

in later models, which had risen considerably above the legend weight of the early models designed for 750 hp (559 kW) but produced with only 585 hp (436 kW).

There have been a number of experimental models of the Chieftain with uprated engines or indeed a gas turbine powerplant, but the only other models to have entered service are two armoured vehicle-launched bridges, an AVRE (Armoured Vehicle Royal Engineers) and an armoured recovery vehicle. It is conceivable, however, that as the Chieftain is phased out of first-line service as a battle tank in the later 1990s, other variants will be developed on surplus chassis.

As noted above, the Chieftain secured initial export sales to Iran (707 Chieftain Mk 3/3Ps, Mk 5/3Ps, armoured recovery vehicles and bridgelayers all delivered in 1978) and to Kuwait (Mk 5/2Ks). Oman later ordered 15

The Chieftain ARV is based on the hull of the Chieftain Mk 5 battle tank, and carries a full range of equipment for the vitally important armoured recovery role. *(BAOR)*

Chieftain Mk 15s, which have the local designation Qayis al Ardh. Iran also received 187 examples of the Improved Chieftain (FV4030/1) with additional fuel capacity, better protection against mines and improved suspension. Plans to re-engine Iran's fleet with an 800-hp (596.5-kW) Rolls-Royce diesel were abandoned after the imperial regime was overthrown in 1979 in favour of a fundamentalist Muslim republic.

By this time, though, Iran had ordered 125 examples of the Shir 1 (FV4030/2) and 1,225 examples of the Shir 2 (FV4030/3), and when the order was cancelled by the new Iranian government in 1979, production of the Shir1 was under way, while development of the Shir 2 was almost complete. The Shir 1 then became the Khalid for Jordan, which received 274 examples, and the Shir 2 formed the basis for the British army's Chieftain successor, the Challenger. The Khalid is basically a late-model Chieftain with a Perkins (Rolls-Royce) Condor 12V 1200 diesel developing 1,200 hp (895 kW) through a TN37 fully automatic transmission for superior performance and mobility, in combination with improved suspension, and with the Computer Sighting System developed from the Chieftain's Improved Fire-Control System.

The Challenger is an altogether more formidable machine that is nonetheless an evolu-

tionary development of the Chieftain, with all the advantages that accrue from such a practice in terms of low technical risk, reduced development cost and contracted development time. Work on the vehicle was started in the late 1960s, but then halted in 1970 when an Anglo-West German agreement was signed for a collaborative main battle tank. This latter project was bedevilled by a divergence of timetable and operational requirements, and

The Chieftain ARV has a front-mounted earth anchor and twin winches for the recovery of disabled or ditched vehicles. (*P. Griffiths*)

An FV434 armoured repair vehicle prepares to lower a complete powerpack into a Chieftain battle tank. (*BAOR*)

The Challenger battle tank is essentially an upgraded Chieftain hull with a more powerful engine and a revised turret fitted with laminate armour. (*BAOR*)

was abandoned in 1977 in favour of separate national efforts. The British thereupon decided to produce a so-called MBT-80 with a 120-mm (4.72-in) high-pressure main gun. But in 1980 the MBT-80 was cancelled on grounds of rising cost and slipping schedules, and the British army had therefore to look elsewhere for its Chieftain replacement.

The result was the Challenger, which began to enter service in 1983 and is essentially the Shir 2 revised to accord with British operational requirements and fitted with the Chobham composite armour first trialled during 1971 on a Chieftain derivative, the FV4211 prototype. Though based on the Chieftain in its structure and basic layout, the Challenger has a different appearance through the use of the special Chobham laminate armour, which comprises layers of special ceramics, metal and other material to provide a very high level of impenetrability to anti-armour weapons of both the chemical and kinetic varieties. Chobham armour can be produced only in flat sheets so far, and this means that specially shaped panels have to be laid over a steel inner structure to produce hull and turret contours less curvaceous than those of the Chieftain. The Challenger also uses the Condor 12V 1200 diesel and TN37 transmission in an easily removed powerpack, hydropneumatic rather than Horstmann suspension, with in-

creased wheel travel for a better cross-country ride, the TOGS sight and the IFCS fire-control system. The armament is currently the L11A5 gun with 64 rounds, though the production version of the XL30 high-pressure gun is planned for retrofit as soon as possible: the L11A5 weighs 3,930 lb (1,783 kg) and is 285.75 in (7.258 m) long, while the XL30

FV4030/4 Challenger
(UK)

Type: main battle tank
Crew: 4
Combat weight: 136,685 lb (62,000 kg)
Dimensions: length, gun forward 37.89 ft (11.55 m) and hull 27.53 ft (8.39 m); width 11.54 ft (3.518 m); height 9.48 ft (2.89 m) to top of commander's sight
Armament system: one 120-mm (4.72-in) gun with 64 rounds, two 7.62-mm (0.3-in) machine-guns with 4,000 rounds and two quintuple smoke-dischargers
Armour: not revealed
Powerplant: one 1,200-hp (895-kW) Rolls-Royce Condor 12V 1200 diesel engine with 395 Imp. gal. (1797 litres) of fuel
Performance: speed, road 35 mph (56.3 km/h); range, road not revealed; fording 3.5 ft (1.07 m) without preparation; gradient 58%; vertical obstacle 3.0 ft (0.91 m); trench 10.33 ft (3.15 m); ground clearance 19.7 in (0.5 m)

The main armament of the Challenger is the well proved but accurate and devastating 120-mm (4.72-in) L11A5 rifled gun. *(P. Griffiths)*

weighs 4,410 lb (2,000 kg) but is only 223.6 in (5.68 m) long, and the barrel is rated at slightly more than 4.5 times the number of fired rounds, with all the financial and operational advantages of this fact.

A number of improvements have already been developed as part of the Challenger Improvement Programme, but the exact extent to which these features will be adopted depends on the willingness of the British government to allocate the required funding. After considerable pressure from inside the Army and from industrial organizations, the

British government decided in 1989 to hedge its bets for a Challenger successor by ordering prototypes of the private-venture Challenger II from Vickers Shipbuilding and Engineering Ltd (VSEL), while maintaining a watching brief over the service and development capabilities of the M1A1 Abrams. It seems that the Army would have preferred early delivery of the American M1A1, with its proved capabilities and 120-mm (4.72-in) smooth-bore gun, while political and economic considerations persuaded the government to opt, at least in the short term, for development of the Challenger

FV 4030/3 Challenger

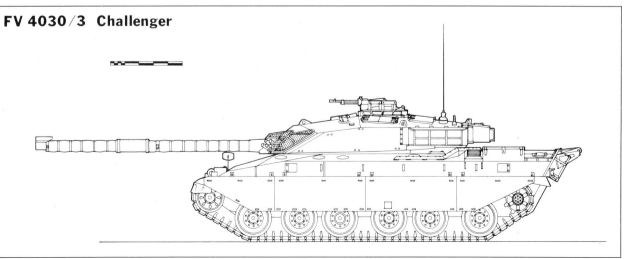

II with a new turret and high-pressure 120-mm (4.72-in) rifled gun on the hull of the basic Challenger. The government's compromise committed VSEL to an exacting schedule of development and prototype trials before any production order was forthcoming: should the company or its product have failed to meet the schedule or requirements, the government would have switched its commitment to the American tank. The main criticism levelled at the Challenger has been its poor fire-control system, which in its current form is an add-on type that has proved to be inadequately integrated into the Challenger as a complete system: in the Challenger II this criticism has been overcome by the development of a new turret and armament combination into which the advanced fire-control and associated gun-control systems will be fully integrated.

This leaves the issue of smooth-bore versus rifled main gun, which is a question that has exercised military planners very deeply in the last couple of decades or so. The smooth-bore gun is ideal for the anti-tank role, allowing the potent APFSDS (Armour-Piercing Fin-Stabilized Discarding-Sabot) kinetic-energy dart to be fired under optimum conditions: the primary protagonists of this type of weapon are the French, West Germans and Americans, the former with a GIAT gun and the latter two with a Rheinmetall weapon. The British, on the other hand, have historically seen their tanks more as multi-role types, in which a rifled gun offers better capabilities for a combined complement of kinetic- and chemical-energy projectiles. There appears to be a switch in the British army's tactical thinking at the moment, favouring the advantages of logistic commonality with their NATO allies over the more problematic advantages of a multi-role capability when ploughing a singleton logistic furrow.

Introduced in 1965, the Leopard 1 is in marked contrast with the Chieftain: whereas the priority list for the British tank was firepower, protection and mobility last by a considerable margin, that for the West German tank was firepower and mobility as equal first and only then protection. Since that time the Leopard 1 has proved eminently successful, the total of 2,437 vehicles built for the West German army being complemented by export sales to Australia (90 vehicles), Belgium (334 vehicles), Canada (114 vehicles), Denmark (120 vehicles), Greece (106 vehicles), Italy (920 vehicles), the Netherlands (468 vehicles) Norway (78 vehicles) and Turkey (77 vehicles)

Like the Chieftain, the Leopard 1 is of conventional layout, but with only two compartments: that for the crew of four (the driver in the hull, and the commander, gunner and loader in the turret) at the front and that for the powerpack at the rear. The manual transmission drives rear sprockets, and the running gear comprises on each side seven dual road wheels with independent torsion bar suspension, and four track-return rollers. Like the

Krauss-Maffei/Krupp MaK Leopard 1
(West Germany)

Type: main battle tank
Crew: 4
Combat weight: 40,000 kg (88,184 lb)
Dimensions: length, gun forward 9.543 m (31.31 ft) and hull 7.09 m (23.26 ft); width 3.37 m (11.06 ft) over skirts; height 2.764 m (9.07 ft) to top of commander's periscope
Armament system: one 105-mm (4.13-in) ROF/Rheinmetall L7A3 rifled gun with 60 rounds, two 7.62-mm (0.3-in) MG3A1 machine-guns (one coaxial and one AA) with 5,500 rounds, and four smoke-dischargers on each side of the turret; the turret is electro-hydraulically powered, the main gun is stabilized in elevation ($-9°$ to $+20°$) and azimuth (360°), and an EMES 12 fire-control system is fitted; this combines stabilized optical sights, a computer-controlled rangefinder and a ballistic computer
Armour: cast and welded steel varying in thickness between 10 and 70 mm (0.39 and 2.76 in)
Powerplant: one 619-kW (830-hp) MTU MB 838 Ca-M500 multi-fuel engine with 955 litres (210 Imp. gal.) of fuel
Performance: speed, road 65 km/h (40.4 mph); range, road 600 km (373 miles); fording 1.2 m (3.9 ft) without preparation, 2.25 m (7.4 ft) with preparation and 4.0 m (13.1 ft) with snorkel; gradient 60%; side slope 30%; vertical obstacle 1.15 m (3.77 ft); trench 3.0 m (9.8 ft); ground clearance 0.44 m (17.3 in)

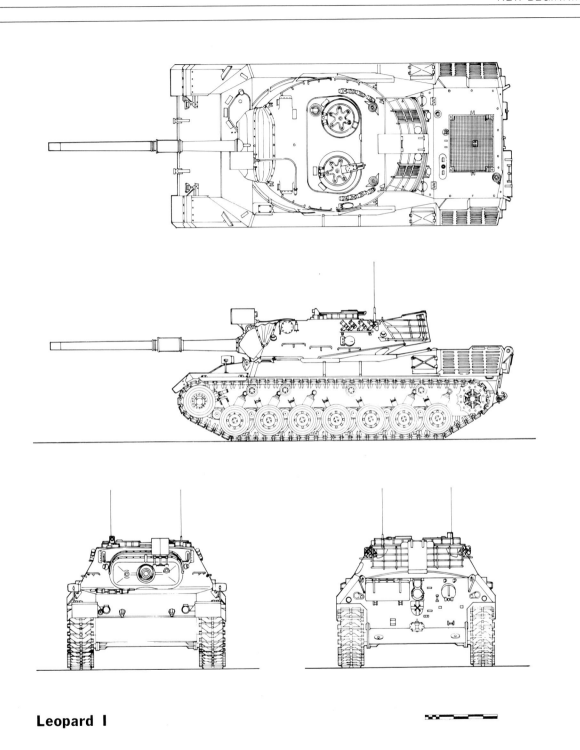

Leopard I

The first production
Leopard 1 for the West
German army clearly
reveals the type's
ancestry in German
Second World War
experience, married to
modern concepts of
ballistic shaping. (*Krauss-
Maffei AG*)

Chieftain, the Leopard 1 has night-vision devices, smoke-dischargers on each side of the
turret (in this instance triple units), an overpressure NBC system, and skirts, these last
being metal-reinforced rubber units. The armament is a British-supplied 105-mm (4.13-in)
L7A3 weapon firing the standard range of

NATO ammunition, of which 55 rounds are
carried, but as first delivered, the Leopard 1
lacked any gun stabilization or a sophisticated
fire-control system.

Given that low weight was important to the
Leopard 1, modest armour was inevitable: this
varies from a minimum of 10 mm (0.39 in) to a

Belgium was the first
country after West
Germany to order the
Leopard 1. Such a vehicle
is seen before the
mid-1970s update that
added a thermal sleeve to
the main armament and,
less visibly, a Cadillac
Gage main armament
stabilization system.
(*Belgian Defence Ministry*)

Italian Leopard 1 battle tanks were slow to reach operator units as production tool-up at OTO Melara was slow. (*Italian Army*)

Dutch Leopard 1 battle tanks are similar to West Germany's Leopard 1A2s but have different equipment (including Dutch smoke dischargers) and three stowage panniers. (*Netherlands Army*)

maximum of 70 mm (2.76 in). In shape, the Leopard 1 has much in common with the German battle tanks of the Second World War, being fairly angular and possessing sharply angled armour only on the hull front and upper sides. The hull is of welded construction, while the turret is a cast unit.

The initial variant was the Leopard 1, as described above, and 1,845 of this basic variant were built in the first four production batches; from 1971 these were retrofitted with a two-axis stabilization system and thermal sleeve for the main armament, thereby becoming Leopard 1A1 tanks or, with Blohm und Voss appliqué spaced armour for the turret and mantlet, Leopard 1A1A1 tanks. Next in

production came 232 examples of the Leopard 1A2 with the modifications of the Leopard 1A1 as well as a cast turret of stronger armour, a better NBC system and passive night-vision devices. The Leopard 1A2s formed the bulk of the fifth production batch, which was completed by 110 examples of the Leopard 1A3 to Leopard 1A2 standard but with a new turret fabricated of welded spaced armour and fitted with a wedge-shaped mantlet; the Greek and Turkish vehicles are to this standard, which incorporates a stowage basket built into the turret structure, rather than appended to its rear. The final new-build model was the Leopard 1A4, comprising a sixth production batch of 250 tanks, basically similar to the Leopard 1A3

The Leopard 1A3
introduced a completely
new turret of spaced
armour with a wedge-
shaped mantlet. (*Krauss-
Maffei AG*)

apart from the installation of an integrated fire-control system complete with ballistic computer. From 1986 some 1,300 Leopard 1s have been virtually remanufactured to Leopard 1A5 standard, with a more capable Krupp-Atlas EMES 18 fire-control system, Carl Zeiss thermal imaging system for continued operational capability in smoke and at night, appliqué armour and a number of secondary defensive features, such as an explosion-suppressing system in the crew compartment.

The export and licence-built versions of the Leopard have been developed to different pitches in their operator countries, generally with better fire-control systems and other operationally advantageous items. The Leopard 1 family of armoured vehicles is completed by an armoured recovery vehicle, an armoured engineer vehicle, an armoured vehicle-launched bridge, a driver training tank and the Gepard anti-aircraft vehicle carrying twin 35-mm radar-controlled cannon in its turret.

The Leopard 1A4 is
similar to the 1A3 but has
a fully integrated fire-
control system with
stabilized optics, a
stabilized main gun and a
ballistic computer.
(*Krauss-Maffei AG*)

Just as the Chieftain paved the way for the Challenger in British service, the Leopard 1 paved the way for the Leopard 2 in West German service. According to plans laid in the 1960s, the West German Leopard 1 and US M60 series were to have been replaced by the MBT-70, a joint West German and American vehicle using the 152-mm (5.98-in) gun/launcher for the Shillelagh anti-tank missile. But in 1970 the MBT-70 was cancelled because of rising cost and an increasing divergence of West German and American requirements, leaving West Germany with a potentially devastating gap in its armoured force's inventory as the Leopard 1 began to show its age. There had been separate Porsche and Krauss-Maffei development programmes under way before the cancellation of the MBT-70, but after the cancellation the West Germans decided to develop a new main battle tank using MBT-70 components wherever possible: the most significant of these were the MTU MB 873 multi-fuel engine and the Renk transmission. Improved Leopard 1 components had also been developed, and wherever possible these too were worked into the design of the Krauss-Maffei Leopard 2, which may be compared favourably to the T-34 as being the only tank of its period to combine firepower, protection and mobility in equal and unparalleled proportions. The Leopard 2's main European rivals are the Chieftain and AMX-30. The Chieftain, as discussed above, has good firepower, good

protection and poor mobility, while the AMX-30, as discussed below, has good mobility, adequate firepower and poor protection.

West Germany had come to the conclusion during the 1960s that smooth-bore main guns offered significant advantages over rifled weapons, largely in the anti-tank role firing APFSDS and HEAT ammunition, which both function better when not spinning. Rheinmetall therefore produced smooth-bore weapons in 105- and 120-mm (4.13- and 4.72-in) calibres,

The frontal contours of the Leopard 1A4's turret offer a high level of ballistic protection though the wedge-shaped mantlet provides a shot trap between itself and the hull roof. (*Krauss-Maffei AG*)

The Australian army's main battle tank is the Leopard AS 1, essentially a tropicalized Leopard 1A3 with the Belgian SABCA fire-control system. (*Australian Defence Ministry*)

The Leopard AEV is the armoured engineer vehicle member of the Leopard family, and though quite similar to the Bergepanzer Leopard armoured recovery vehicle carries an earth auger in place of the spare powerpack on the rear decking. (*Krauss-Maffei AG*)

Krauss-Maffei/Krupp MaK Leopard 2

(West Germany)

Type: main battle tank
Crew: 4
Combat weight: 55,150 kg (121,583 lb)
Dimensions: length, gun forward 9.668 m (31.72 ft) and hull 7.722 m (25.33 ft); width 3.70 m (12.14 ft) over skirts; height 2.46 m (8.07 ft) to turret top
Armament system: one 120-mm (4.72-in) Rheinmetall Rh–120 smooth-bore gun with 42 rounds, two 7.62-mm (0.3-in) MG3A1 machine-guns (one coaxial and one AA) with 4,750 rounds, and eight smoke-dischargers on each side of the turret; the turret is electro-hydraulically powered, the main gun is stabilized in elevation (– 19° to + 20°) and azimuth (360°), and an EMES 15 fire-control system is fitted; this last combines stabilized optical sights, thermal sights, a laser rangefinder and a ballistic computer
Armour: spaced multi-layer type
Powerplant: one 1120-kW (1,502-hp) MTU MB 873 Ka–501 diesel engine with 1,200 litres (264 Imp. gal.) of fuel
Performance: speed, road 72 km/h (44.7 mph); range, road 550 km (342 miles); fording 1.0 m (3.3 ft) without preparation, 2.25 m (7.4 ft) with preparation and 4.0 m (13.1 ft) with snorkel; gradient 60%; side slope 30%; vertical obstacle 1.1 m (3.61 ft); trench 3.0 m (9.8 ft); ground clearance 0.63 m (24.8 in)

and these were installed in 10 and six of the 16 prototype Leopard 2s. Trials with the weapons confirmed the overall superiority of the 120-mm (4.72-in) Rh-120 weapon, which has a total system weight (including the shield) of 3,655 kg (8,058 lb) including the 1,905-kg (4,200-lb) ordnance, and an overall length of 6.168 m (242.84 in) including the 5.3-m (208.66-in) barrel. The gun fires two types of operational ammunition, both of the fixed type: the APFSDS round weighs 19 kg (41.89 lb) and fires its 7.1-kg (15.65-lb) projectile with a muzzle velocity of 1,650 m (5,413 ft) per second, which gives the 32-mm (1.26-in) diameter projectile enormous kinetic energy on the target. The HEAT round weighs 23 kg (50.71 lb) and fires a 13.5-kg (29.76-lb) projectile whose full-bore diameter gives the warhead's focussed jet very considerable penetrative power on the target. From the late 1980s Rheinmetall was working on a more advanced APFSDS projectile launched with a muzzle velocity in the order of 1,800 m (5,906 ft) per second.

The prototypes were completed between 1972 and 1974, two of them with hydropneumatic suspension but the other 14 with the advanced friction-damped torsion bar type that was adopted for the production variant. The prototypes underwent a period of intense evaluation before the West German army announced an order for 1,800 vehicles with the 120-mm (4.72-in) gun during 1977. The first of these was delivered in 1978 and the last in mid-1987, an order for 150 more arriving just too late to ensure an uninterrupted production programme. The Leopard 2 has also been ordered by the Netherlands (445 vehicles) and Switzerland (380 vehicles, including 345 made under licence by Contraves and the Federal Construction Works).

In overall configuration the Leopard 2 is unexceptional, with the driver's compartment at the front, the fighting compartment in the centre, and the power compartment at the rear, with the transmission powering rear drive sprockets for tracks that run round an arrangement of seven dual road wheels, a front idler and four track-return rollers on each side. The large turret accommodates the commander and gunner on the right, and the loader plus his hydraulically-assisted loading system on the left. It was initially thought that the Leopard 2

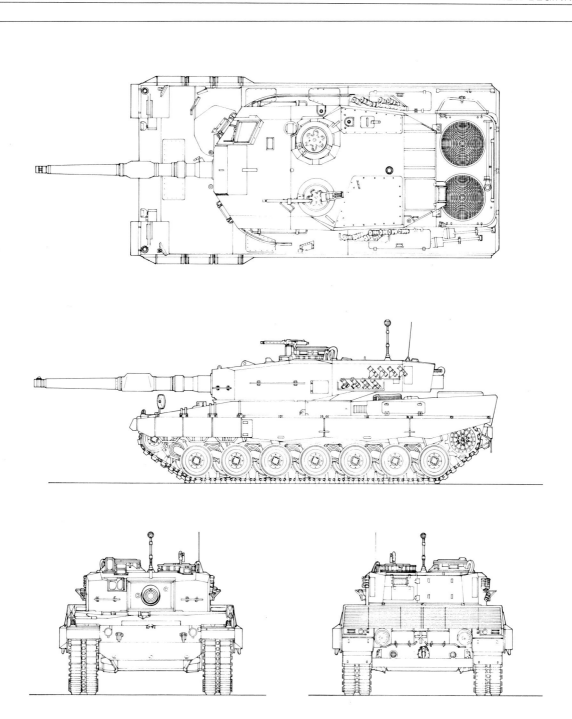

Leopard 2

An AMX-30 fitted for deep wading emerges from a river. This battle tank is typical of modern French practice, which emphasizes firepower and mobility at the expense of protection, resulting in a light and comparatively cheap vehicle. (*ECP armées, France*)

The AMX-30 lacks gun stabilization and an advanced fire-control system, but has standard features such as an NBC system and night-vision equipment. This results in a tank that is somewhat cheaper to buy and easier to maintain than equivalent American, British and West German main battle tanks, with consequent advantages in the export market to less developed countries: AMX-30 operators therefore include (in addition to France) Chile, Cyprus, Greece, Iraq, Qatar, Saudi Arabia, Spain, the United Arab Emirates and Venezuela.

The series is still in production, the current variant being the upgraded AMX-30 B2 with improved transmission, a COTAC integrated fire-control system (with a laser rangefinder, low-light-level TV and lead-generating computer) and other operational enhancements, such as skirts and appliqué armour for the turret. The basic chassis is highly capable, and this is reflected in the number of alternative roles in which the type is found: the AMX-30D armoured recovery vehicle, an armoured vehicle-launched bridge, a combat engineer tractor, the Pluton surface-to-surface missile launcher, the Roland SAM vehicle, the Shahine SAM vehicle, an anti-aircraft vehicle with twin 30-mm radar-controlled cannon in the turret, and the GCT 155-mm (6.1-in) self-propelled howitzer.

The French also realized in the 1970s that export sales of the AMX-30 might be curtailed by the type's comparatively poor armament and protection, and therefore evolved the 43,000-kg (94,797-lb) AMX-32 derivative with thicker and better-arranged armour, and a 120-mm (4.72-in) GIAT smooth-bore gun designed for installation interchangeability with the 105-mm (4.13-in) weapon. The 120-mm (4.72-in) gun weighs 2,620 kg (5,776 lb) and possesses an overall length of 7.15 m (281.5 in). The two primary ammunition types associated with this weapon are a HEAT round firing its 13.9-kg (30.64-lb) projectile with a muzzle velocity of 1,100 m (3,609 ft) per second, and an APFSDS round firing its 6.2-kg (13.67-lb) projectile with a muzzle velocity of 1,700 m (5,577 ft) per second to release a 3.78-kg (8.33-lb) dart with very high kinetic energy. Two prototypes of the AMX-32 were built in 1979 and 1981, but no orders have

great kinetic energy as the dart, which has a diameter of 26 mm (1.02 in) and a weight of 3.8 kg (8.38 lb), impacts the target for the penetration of 150 mm (5.91 in) of armour at an angle of 60° at a range of 5,000 m (5,470 yards). The AMX-30 possesses an unusual secondary armament, for though the coaxial weapon was the standard 0.5-in (12.7-mm) heavy machine-gun when the AMX-30 began to enter service, this was soon replaced by a 20-mm GIAT M693 dual-feed cannon (with API and HEI ammunition) to provide a potent capability against lightly-armoured targets and helicopters. Against this latter type of target the cannon's maximum independent elevation angle of +40° is a useful asset.

been placed. The type remains available for production, but now only with the 105-mm (4.13-in) rifled gun carried by the first prototype.

Another export model that had yet to secure a production order is the AMX-40. Unlike the AMX-32, which was an AMX-30 derivative, the 43,700-kg (96,340-lb) AMX-40 is an all-new design with laminate armour over the frontal arc and conventional protection in all other areas. The type retains many clear similarities

GIAT AMX-32
(France)

Type: main battle tank prototype
Crew: 4
Combat weight: 43,000 kg (94,797 lb)
Dimensions: length, gun forward 9.45 m (31.00 ft) and hull 6.59 m (21.62 ft); width 3.24 m (10.6 ft); height 2.29 m (7.51 ft) to top of turret
Armament system: one 105-mm (4.13-in) gun with 47 rounds. One 20-mm cannon with 480 rounds, one 7.62-mm (0.3-in) machine-gun with 2,170 rounds and two triple smoke-dischargers
Armour: unrevealed thicknesses of welded and cast steel, spaced steel and composite
Powerplant: one 595-kW (798-hp) Hispano-Suiza HS 110–2–SR multi-fuel engine with 920 litres (202 Imp. gal.) of fuel
Performance: speed, road 65 km/h (40.4 moh); range, road 530 km (329 miles); fording 1.3 m (4.3 ft) without preparation and 2.2 m (7.2 ft) with preparation; gradient 60%; side slope 30%; vertical obstacle 0.9 m (2.95 ft); trench 2.9 m (9.5 ft); ground clearance 0.44 m (17.3 in)

AMX-32

2nd Prototype

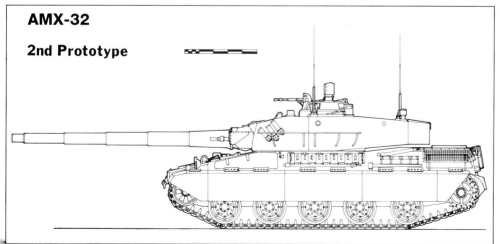

Ammunition for the modern battle tank: seen with this AMX-40 export tank are 20-mm ammunition for the coaxial weapon, and 120-mm (4.72-in) combustible-case ammunition for the smooth-bore main armament including, towards the front, APFSDS rounds whose projectiles leave the muzzle at 1,630-m (5,348 ft) per second and towards the rear, HE anti-tank rounds whose projectiles leave the muzzle at 1,050-m (3,445 ft) per second. (*MARS*)

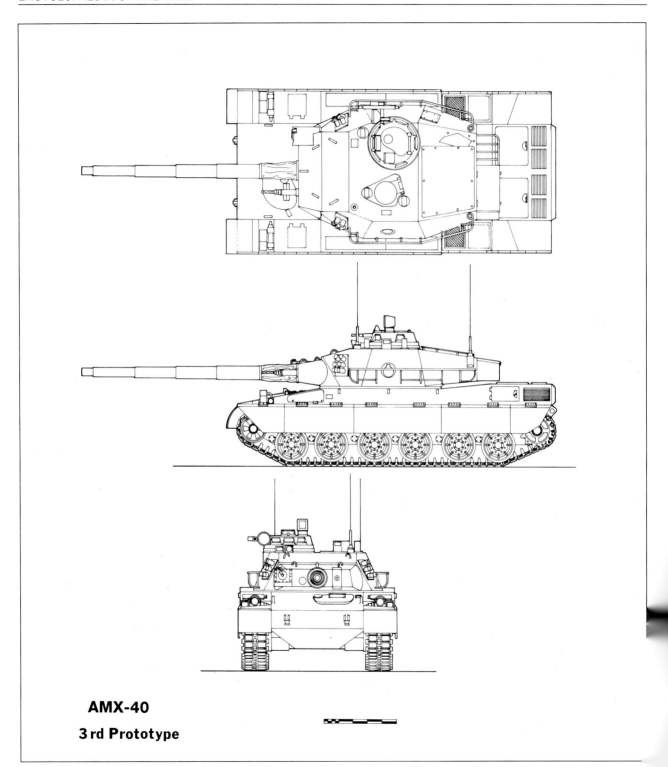

AMX-40

3 rd Prototype

GIAT AMX-40
(France)

Type: main battle tank
Crew: 4
Combat weight: 43,700 kg (96,340 lb)
Dimensions: length, gun forward 10.05 m (32.97 ft) and hull 6.80 m (22.31 ft); width 3.35 m (10.99 ft) over skirts; height 2.38 m (7.81 ft) to turret top and 3.10 m (10.17 ft) to commander's sight
Armament system: one 120-mm (4.72-in) GIAT smooth-bore gun with 40 rounds, one 20-mm GIAT M693 (F2) coaxial cannon with 578 rounds, one 7.62-mm (0.3-in) NF1 AA machine-gun with 2,170 rounds, and three smoke-dischargers on each side of the turret; the turret is electro-hydraulically powered, the main gun is stabilized in elevation (− 8° to + 20°) and azimuth (360°), and a COTAC fire-control system is fitted; this last combines optical sights, a low-light-level TV sight, various sensors, a laser rangefinder and a ballistic computer
Armour: welded and laminate
Powerplant: one 970-kW (1,301-hp) Poyaud V12X diesel engine with 1100 litres (242 Imp. gal.) of internal fuel plus provision for additional fuel in two jettisonable external tanks
Performance: speed, road 70 km/h (43.5 mph); range, road 600 km (373 miles) on standard fuel and 850 km (528 miles) with auxiliary fuel; fording 1.3 m (4.3 ft) without preparation, 2.3 m (7.5 ft) with preparation and 4.0 m (13.1 ft) with snorkel; gradient 70%; side slope 30%; vertical obstacle 1.0 m (3.28 ft); trench 3.2 m (10.5 ft); ground clearance 0.45 m (17.7 in)

to the AMX-30 and AMX-32 in concept and layout, but offers significantly improved firepower in the form of the 120-mm (4.72-in) smooth-bore gun, much better protection and superior mobility through the use of a 1,301-hp (970-kW) Poyaud V12X diesel driving an automatic transmission.

As replacement for the AMX-30 and AMX-30 B2 in national service (and also for export), France is developing a new main battle tank as the AMX-48 Leclerc. This entered into the design phase in 1983 after the failure in 1982 of a Franco-West German collaborative venture, and appeared in test-rig form during 1985 (one for the armament, one for the suspension and three for the automotive system). Production is scheduled to begin in 1990 for a service entry date of 1992. Current plans envisage the building of between 1,100 and 1,400 Leclercs, for service well into the next century. The specification is as yet unrevealed in its details, but a weight in the order of 53,000 kg (116,843 lb) seems likely, and the 1,500-hp (1118-kW) Uni Diesel V8X-1500 engine and automatic transmission will provide the power-to-weight ratio for high performance and considerable agility. The main armament is the 120-mm (4.72-in) smooth-bore weapon originally offered on the AMX-32, though in this instance modified with an automatic loader located in the turret bustle with 22 rounds. The bustle is separated from the rest of the turret by an armoured bulkhead, and its roof is a blow-out panel to mitigate the effect of any explosion. The use of such a loader in an electrically powered turret (with emergency manual controls) reduces the crew requirement to three, and in combination with an advanced fire-control system (including a digital computer, various sensors, stabilized optics, a laser rangefinder and a thermal-imaging system), this allows the engagement of five separate targets within one minute. The protection system was initially thought to be an innovative type, with comparatively thin steel armour covered completely with reactive panels, but it is now clear that laminate armour is being used in combination with reactive panels. A useful feature of the tank's high power-to-weight ratio is the possibility of considerable uparmouring without significant loss of agility. The running gear comprises six road wheels, a rear drive sprocket and a front idler on each side, but it has not yet been revealed if the suspension will be of the rotary-damped torsion bar or hydropneumatic type.

The Swedish contemporary of the AMX-30 is the Strv 103, a fascinating machine that in many respects falls outside the normal concept of a main battle tank as it lacks a turret, the 105-mm (4.13-in) main gun being fixed in the hull for traverse by movement of the complete vehicle, and elevation by differential adjustment of the suspension. Such a system greatly simplifies the vehicle, reduces its silhouette to a marked degree, and allows excellently angled armour of considerable thickness within an overall weight of only 39,700 kg

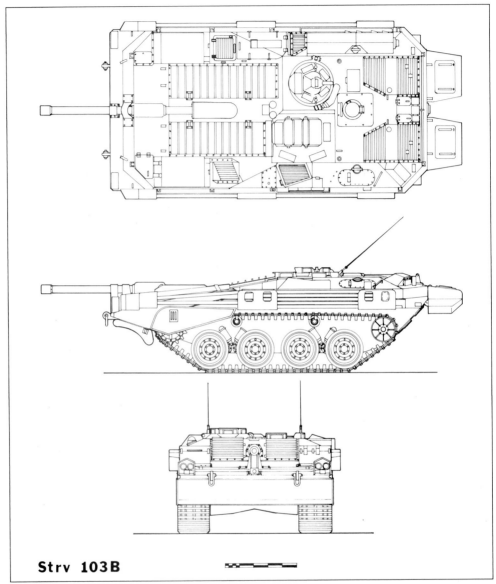

Strv 103B

(87,522 lb). The gun elevation arc lies between −10° and +12°.

The origins of the Strv 103 go back to the 1950s, when the Swedish army was reliant mainly on imported medium and main battle tanks (notably 300 Centurions) as it began to phase out its indigenous Strv m/40 and Strv m/41 light tanks. While development of their KRV heavy tank with a 150-mm (5.91-in) smooth-bore gun was proceeding, the Swedes began to develop a keen interest in the AMX-13's oscillating turret. This led rapidly to the notion of the main gun fixed in the hull, and in the late 1950s development of the KRV was halted to allow total concentration on the Strv 103, which was ordered in 1960, even though the first two prototypes did not appear until 1961. Production by Bofors lasted from 1966 to 1971, and 300 vehicles were completed.

The Strv 103 is of unusual configuration, with the engine and transmission at the front, the fighting compartment in the centre, and

Designed in the early stages of the Second World War, the Swedish 22,850-kg (50,375-lb) Strv m/42 with a short-barrel 75-mm (2.95-in) gun and remained in service right into the 1960s. It was even rebuilt as the modernized Strv 74 weighing 26,425-kg (58,256-lb) with a longer-barrel gun. (*Försvarets Materièlverk, Sweden*)

Bofors Stridsvagn 103B
(Sweden)

Type: main battle tank
Crew: 3
Combat weight: 39,700 kg (87,522 lb)
Dimensions: length overall 8.99 m (29.49 ft) and hull 7.04 m (23.10 ft); width 3.63 m (11.91 ft); height 2.14 m (7.02 ft) to top of cupola
Armament system: one 105-mm (4.13-in) Bofors L74 (ROF L7) rifled gun with 50 rounds in an automatic loader with 10 racks of five rounds, three 7.62-mm (0.3-in) FFV ksp58 machine-guns (two coaxial and one AA) with 2,750 rounds, and four smoke-dischargers on each side of the hull; the gun has no stabilization for its elevation arc of -10° to +12° (and is fixed in azimuth), and a simple fire-control system with stabilized optical sights is fitted
Armour: welded steel
Powerplant: one 240-bhp (179-kW) Rolls-Royce K60 multi-fuel engine and one 490-shp (365-kW) Boeing 553 gas turbine with 960 litres (211 Imp. gal.) of fuel
Performance: speed, road 50 km/h (31 mph); range, road 390 km (242 miles); fording 1.5 m (4.9 ft) without preparation and with preparation amphibious; gradient 58%; side slope 70%; vertical obstacle 0.9 m (2.95 ft); trench 2.3 m (7.5 ft); ground clearance 0.4 m (15.75 in)

the automatic loader and magazine at the rear. The powerplant is in itself unusual, comprising a 240-hp (179-kW) Rolls-Royce K.60 multi-fuel engine and a 490-shp (365-kW) Boeing 553 gas turbine: these two engines are geared to a common output, allowing the multi-fuel engine to be complemented in action by the gas turbine. A comparatively simple gearbox is used to drive the two front sprockets, the rest of the running gear comprising, on each side, four twin road wheels identical with those of the Centurion, two track-return rollers and a rear idler. The suspension is hydropneumatic, a pump being used to move fluid between the units to lift or lower the suspension at front or back and so alter the hull and thus the armament angles to exactly the desired degree.

No details of the Strv 103's armour have been released, but this is believed to be simple steel plate whose sections are welded to make the hull of the tank. The crew comprises the driver, who can also lay and fire the main armament, on the left of the fighting compartment, the radio operator/reverse driver on the right of the compartment facing the rear, and the commander behind the radio operator under a raised and azimuth-stabilized cupola

that is used to acquire the target. The commander then uses the steering tillers to lay the tank on the target: once the target has been acquired the commander selects the appropriate ammunition type, loads the main gun and fires. The main gun is the L74, an L/62 Swedish development of the British L7 rifled gun with an automatic loader and 50-round magazine, whose combination of ammunition types is selected to reflect the current tactical situation: the loader also provides the impressive fire rate of 15 rounds per minute. The secondary armament comprises a 7.62-mm (0.3-in) machine-gun on the cupola, and two fixed machine-guns of the same calibre on the left-hand side of the hull. The initial Strv 103A had no flotation screen to provide an amphibious capability, but the improved Strv 103B featured such a screen, which has since been retrofitted to Strv 103As: in the water the Strv 103 is propelled by its tracks. The Strv 103 series lacks an NBC system and night-vision equipment, but is fitted with a hydraulically actuated dozer blade for the creation of its own fire positions.

Above Though resembling a self-propelled gun in physical concept, the Strv 103B is in fact a true tank with gun elevation and traverse arcs restored by the considerable agility and speed of the chassis/hull combination. (*Försvarets Materielverk*)

Right Members of the Swedish army's armoured warfare team: the revolutionary Strv 103B turretless tank and the PBv 302 armoured personnel carrier. (*Swedish Army*)

TAM

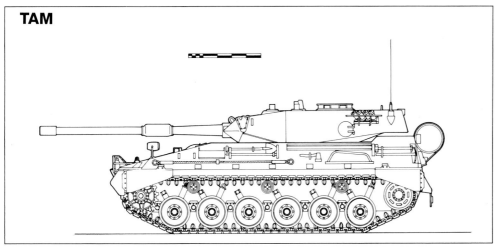

In the late 1980s the Strv 103 fleet was modernized with a 290-hp (216-kW) Detroit Diesel 6V-71T diesel in place of the Rolls-Royce unit, an automatic transmission, a laser rangefinder and other updated features. Current investigation of further enhancement of this Strv 103C variant is centred on the retrofit of an advanced fire-control system and, as possibilities, an NBC system and night-vision equipment.

No other European main battle tanks were developed during the 1960s, though the 1970s saw the development of the Thyssen Henschel TAM to an Argentine requirement, the OTO Melara/Fiat OF-40 to meet a perceived export need, and the Israeli Ordnance Corps Merkava to a purely Israeli requirement. The TAM is one of the few modern examples of the medium tank, and was designed in West Germany on the basis of the Marder mechanized infantry combat vehicle to provide the Argentine army with a tank that was light enough to be unlimited by Argentina's poor internal communication network and straightforward enough for local construction, yet possessing the firepower and mobility to match better-protected main battle tanks. This decided the designers to opt for a 105-mm (4.13-in) gun, the eventual type selected being an Argentine weapon, though the Rh-105-30 remains an option. This main armament is installed in a mounting with two-axis stabilization, which is located in the three-man welded turret placed at the rear of the vehicle in a position that

minimizes the gun's forward overhang. Only a comparatively simple fire-control system is fitted. The 720-hp (537-kW) MTU MB 833 diesel provides the 30,500-kg (67,240-lb) vehicle with a good power-to-weight ratio and lively performance, while the six-wheel torsion bar suspension and welded hull inherited from the Marder provide a good cross-country ride and well-proved structural strength.

TAM
(Argentina/West Germany)

Type: medium tank
Crew: 4
Combat weight: 30,500 kg (67,240 lb)
Dimensions: length, gun forward 8.23 m (27.00 ft) and hull 6.775 m (22.23 ft); width 3.12 m (10.24 ft); height 2.42 m (7.94 ft)
Armament system: one 105-mm (4.13-in) gun with 50 rounds, two 7.62-mm (0.3-in) machine-guns with 6,000 rounds and two quadruple smoke-dischargers
Armour: not revealed
Powerplant: one 537-kW (720-hp) MTU 833 Ka-500 diesel engine with 640 litres (143 Imp. gal.) of fuel excluding 400 litres (88 Imp. gal.) in external tanks
Performance: speed, road 75 km/h (46.6 mph); range, road 550 km (342 miles) on internal fuel and 900 km (559 miles) with external fuel; fording 1.4 m (4.6 ft) without preparation, 2.25 m (7.4 ft) with preparation and 4.0 m (13.12 ft) with a snorkel; gradient 65%; vertical obstacle 1.0 m (3.28 ft) trench 2.5 m (8.2 ft); ground clearance 0.44 m (17.3 in)

OF 40 Mk I

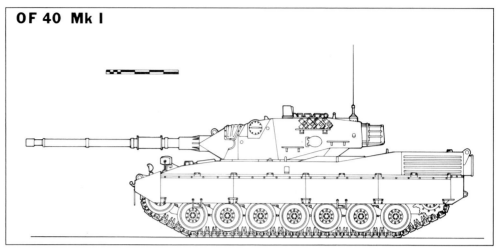

Thyssen Henschel has also offered the type on the export market (so far without success) in a revised version known as the TH 301: this is externally similar to the TAM, but has the Rh-105-30 gun, a more capable fire-control system (laser rangefinder, low-light-level TV, sensors and computer) and a 750-hp (559-kW) diesel to maintain performance at the increased weight of 31,000 kg (68,342 lb)

The Italian OF-40 was developed so that OTO Melara and Fiat, the two companies most heavily involved in the Italian licence-building programme for the Leopard 1 main battle tank, could capitalize on their experience. The Leopard 1 licence forbade export production, so from 1977 the Italian companies produced a perfectly conventional four-man main battle tank of welded construction weighing 45,500 kg (100,309 lb), powered by an 830-hp (619-kW) MTU 90° diesel and carrying as main armament an OTO Melara 105-mm (4.13-in) L/52 rifled gun that fires the full range of NATO tank ammunition with the aid of an Officine Galileo OG14LR fire-control system. This latter combines a computer and a laser rangefinder, and with the optional two-axis gun stabilization system offers a high first-round hit probability, even with the tank on the move. The first deliveries were made to the United Arab Emirates in 1981; and variants of the basic vehicle are the OF-40 Mk 2 with the improved OG14L2 fire-control system and gun stabilization, and the OF-40 armoured recovery vehicle. The basic design still has growth potential,

OTO Melara/Fiat OF–40 Mk 1
(Italy)

Type: main battle tank
Crew: 4
Combat weight: 45,500 kg (100,309 lb)
Dimensions: length, gun forward 9.222 m (30.26 ft) and hull 6.893 m (22.615 ft); width 3.35 m (10.99 ft) with skirts; height 2.76 m (9.06 ft) to top of sight
Armament system: one 105-mm (4.13-in) gun with 57 rounds, two 7.62-mm (0.3 in) machine-guns with 5,700 rounds and two quadruple smoke-dischargers
Armour: not revealed
Powerplant: one 620-kW (831.5-hp) MTU 90° diesel engine with 1000 litres (220 Imp. gal.) of fuel
Performance: speed, road 60 km/h (37.3 mph); range, road 600 km (373 miles); fording 1.2 m (3.94 ft) without preparation, 2.25 m (7.38 ft) with preparation and 4.0 m (13.12 ft) with snorkel; gradient 60%; side slope 30% vertical obstacle 1.1 m (3.61 ft); trench 3.0 m (9.85 ft); ground clearance 0.44 m (17.3 in)

and has been used as the basis for self-propelled artillery (surface-to-surface and surface-to-air).

Far more capable, however, is the Merkava (chariot) designed in the light of Israel's unparalleled experience with modern armoured warfare, and produced by the Israel Ordnance Corps for the Israeli armoured corps. Up to 1973 Israel obtained most of its armour initially from France and the UK, and then from the

USA. In all cases the tanks were modified extensively to meet Israel's particular requirements, and emerged as vehicles somewhat different from the baseline models in service with the originating countries. Even before their problems in the 1967 'Six-Day-War', the Israelis had become increasingly concerned about their vulnerability when losses outstripped the ability and/or the willingness of the originating countries to supply replacements, which would then have to be modified in a time-consuming process to Israeli standards. Time has always been a commodity in short supply for the Israeli armed forces, so an indigenous tank clearly offered advantages in this situation. At the same time an indigenous tank design provided the chance for the Israeli army to develop and procure a main battle tank tailored exactly to its needs: for the Israeli armoured corps this meant a priority list that placed protection of its invaluable crews first, firepower second and mobility a poor third.

Design work on the new tank, which was to use as many M48, M60 and Centurion components as possible, began as early as 1967, with detail design beginning in 1970. The Israelis' priority list conditioned the layout of

the vehicle, which is unusual in locating the engine, transmission, cooling system and fuel at the very front of the hull as additional protection from head-on fire. It also provides for a highly angled nose plate and glacis, which are complemented by the excellent ballistic shaping of the turret against head-on fire. The turret also possesses low frontal area and is thus a harder target than the substantial turrets of other Western main battle tanks: this reflects the Israeli's frequent use of the hull-down tactical position for the ambush of enemy tanks. Both the hull and the turret are of cast and welded construction, though details and thicknesses have not been revealed. The gunner is located just in front and to the left of the turret, with the powerful diesel engine to his right: the engine is an uprated version of that used in the M48 and M60 series, and in combination with the same basic transmission offers high reliability and useful commonality with other parts of Israel's tank fleet. The turret is home to the three-man tactical crew (the commander and gunner on the right and the loader on the left) and the main armament, which is a 105-mm (4.13-in) M68 gun identical with that of the M60 and stabilized in two axes for max-

A rear view of the Merkava Mk 1 battle tank reveals the twin access hatches to the useful rear compartment of this Israeli battle tank, which has the transmission system at the front to improve frontal protection. (*Israeli Defence Forces*)

imum accuracy with the tank on the move: the gun has an elevation arc between -8.5° and +20°, and is used in conjunction with the Elbit Matador Mk 1 fire-control system (laser rangefinder, stabilized optics, computer and sensors).

Long-range operations are important in Israeli tactical doctrine, and the Merkava's substantial fuel load is balanced by a large ammunition capacity: 92 rounds are carried in special containers, and to reduce vulnerability, none of these are located above the turret ring or in the front of the hull. Further protection is provided by features such as an NBC system and an explosion-suppressing system, and standard features include night-vision equipment. The Merkava is also unusual amongst modern tanks in having a rear compartment: this was originally thought to be for the carriage of an infantry squad, but is now known to be for the carriage of a 60-mm Soltam mortar with 30 bombs, or of additional 105-mm (4.13-in) ammunition. The compartment can carry three commandos by the sacrifice of 25 main-armament rounds, or 10 infantrymen by the sacrifice of 45 main-armament rounds, but this last is a capability used only under exceptional circumstances: the Merkava is a battle tank par excellence, not an armoured personnel carrier.

The Merkava possesses a poor power-to-weight ratio and thus has only indifferent performance in comparison with the best of the Western battle tanks, but this reflects the Israelis' operational philosophy, rather than a failing in the design process. Agility is better than the performance, the Merkava's running gear comprising on each side six Centurion-type road wheels with independent helical spring suspension; there are four track-return rollers on each side, and the drive sprocket and idler are at the front and rear respectively. The running gear is protected by skirt plates, and additional protection on the Merkava includes closely shaped chains under the turret bustle to prevent the ingress of HEAT warheads to this potentially vulnerable area.

The Merkava Mk 1 prototype was completed in 1977, and the type began to enter service in 1979. In 1983 the improved Merkava Mk 2 began to enter service. This has a layer of 'special armour' over the hull front and the tur-

Israeli Ordnance Corps Merkava Mk 1
(Israel)

Type: main battle tank
Crew: 4
Combat weight: 60,000 kg (132,275 lb)
Dimensions: length, gun forward 8.63 m (28.31 ft) and hull 7.45 m (24.44 ft); width 3.70 m (12.14 ft); height to turret top 2.64 m (8.66 ft) and to commander's cupola 2.75 m (9.02 ft)
Armament system: one 105-mm (4.13-in) IMI M68 rifled gun with 85 rounds, one optional 0.5-in (12.7-mm) Browning M2HB heavy machine-gun over the main armament, three 7.62-mm (0.3-in) FN-MAG machine-guns (one coaxial and two roof-mounted) with 10,000 rounds, and one 60-mm (2.36-in) Soltam Commando mortar with 30 rounds; the turret is electro-hydraulically powered, the main gun is stabilized in elevation (−8.5° to +20°) and azimuth (360°), and an Elbit Matador Mk 1 fire-control system is fitted; this last combines optical sights, various sensors, a laser rangefinder and a digital ballistic computer
Armour: cast and welded steel
Powerplant: one 900-hp (671-kW) Teledyne Continental AVDS–1790–6A diesel engine with 900 litres (198 Imp. gal.) of fuel
Performance: speed, road 46 km/h (28.6 mph); range, road 400 km (249 miles); fording 1.38 m (4.5 ft) without preparation and 2.0 m (6.6 ft) with preparation; gradient 60%; side slope 38%; vertical obstacle 0.95 m (3.12 ft); trench 3.0 m (9.8 ft); ground clearance 0.47 m (18.5 in)

ret front and sides, the mortar relocated to the left of the turret with provision for loading and firing from within the turret, the Matador Mk 2 fire-control system with better laser rangefinder and enhanced computer, and an Israeli transmission system that improves range by 25 per cent with only a slight increase in fuel capacity. Some sources suggest that the original AVDS-1790 engine has been replaced by a 1,200-hp (895-kW) version of the same basic unit, but this remains unconfirmed. All Merkava Mk 1 tanks are being brought up to Mk 2 standard. The latest model is the Merkava Mk 3, which entered production in 1987: this has a 1,500-hp (1,118-kW) powerpack, a 120-mm (4.72-in) smooth-bore gun, the Matador Mk 3 fire-control system offering 100

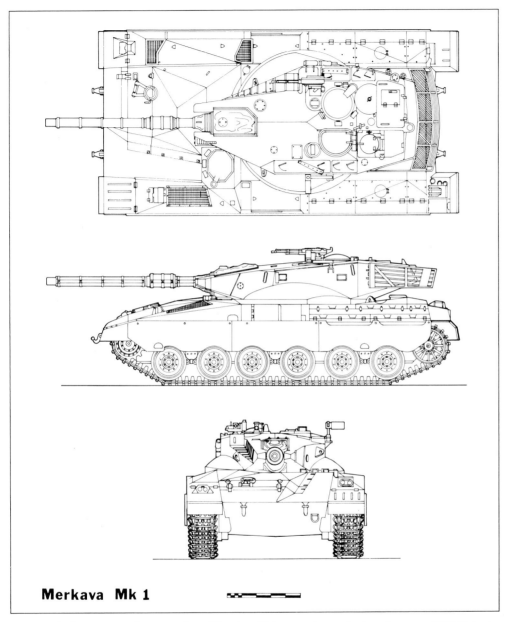

Merkava Mk 1

per cent improvement over the Mk 1, hydropneumatic suspension and new armour integrated with the vehicle's overall protective system

Working on the basis of their experience with the OF-40 export tank, the Italian consortium of OTO Melara and Fiat (Iveco) has developed a main battle tank tailored specifically to the requirements of the Italian army.

This was planned primarily as an OTO Melara responsibility, with Iveco undertaking the chief responsibility for a companion vehicle, an 8 x 8 wheeled tank destroyer with as much commonality as possible with the OTO Melara/Iveco C1 Ariete main battle tank. The C1 is basically conventional in structure and configuration, with a welded steel armour structure covered, over its frontal arc, with

327

composite armour. The driver is located in the hull front, with the commander, gunner and loader behind him in the turret, which also accommodates the 120-mm (4.72-in) OTO Melara smooth-bore main gun and the Officine Galileo TURMS OG14L3 fire-control system. The fire-control system includes a laser rangefinder, stabilized optics, a thermal imager, a computer and a number of sensors to allow the calculation of a high-quality fire-control solution for the main gun, which is stabilized in two axes. The rear compartment is occupied by the powerplant, comprising a 1,200-hp (895-kW) Fiat V-12 MTCA diesel engine and its automatic transmission. The running gear comprises rear drive sprockets, front idlers, and on each side an arrangement of seven road wheels (with torsion bar suspension) and an unspecified number of track-return rollers; the running gear is protected in standard fashion by skirts. Prototype C1s were completed in 1987, and production began in 1988 against a total Italian requirement for possibly 250 vehicles. In 1987 it was revealed that the Spanish army had decided to adopt the C1 as replacement for some of its older main battle tanks, and Spain has since become a development and production partner in the programme. Production will be undertaken by Santa Barbara in succession to the AMX-30 and in preference to the scaled-down Leopard 2 proposed by Krauss-Maffei as the Lince.

Other Western-oriented countries that have in recent years entered the main battle tank production market are Brazil, Japan and South Korea. Brazil's effort has been centred on two somewhat differing vehicles, the 43,700-kg (96,340-lb) ENGESA EE-T1 Osorio and the 30,000-kg (66,138-lb) Bernardini MB-3 Tamoyo (sometimes rendered Tamoio). The Osorio was designed to meet both domestic and export requirements, and uses either of two turrets designed by Vickers Defence Systems in the UK: the first of these accommodates a 105-mm (4.13-in) L7A3 gun with its recoil system modified for low recoil, and the second

ENGESA EE-T1 Osorio
(Brazil)

Type: main battle tank
Crew: 4
Combat weight: 43,700 kg (96,340 lb)
Dimensions: length, gun forward 9.36 m (30.71 ft) and hull 7.13 m (23.39 ft); width 3.256 m (10.68 ft); height 2.37 m (7.78 ft) to turret top
Armament system: one 105-mm (4.13-in) gun with 45 rounds, two 7.62-mm (0.3-in) machine-guns with 5,000 rounds, and two quadruple smoke-dischargers
Armour: not revealed
Powerplant: one 746-kW (1,000-hp) MWM TBD 234-V12 diesel engine
Performance: speed, road 70 km/h (43.5 mph); range 550 km (342 miles); fording 1.2 m (3.9 ft) without preparation and 2.0 m (6.6 ft) with preparation; gradient 60%; side slope 40%; vertical obstacle 1.15 m (3.77 ft); trench 3.0 m (9.85 ft); ground clearance 0.46 m (18.1 in)

Engesa EE-T1 Osorio

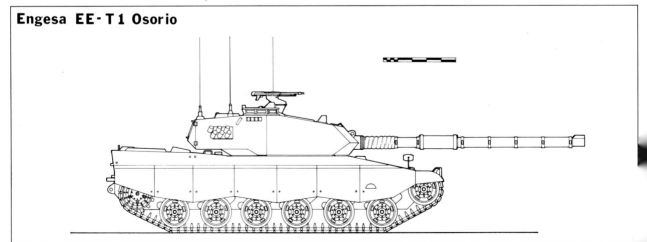

has a 120-mm (4.72-in) GIAT smooth-bore gun. Prototypes were completed in 1984 and 1985, and though considerable interest has been displayed by Arab nations as well as by the Brazilian army, no production examples had been ordered by the early 1990s. The type is basically unexceptional in layout and general concept, though the structure is unusual for main battle tanks in using ENGESA's special bi-metallic armour as the primary medium, with an ENGESA-developed composite over the most vulnerable area. To suit the type for the export market the Osorio is offered with a choice of two fire-control systems: a simple type with a laser rangefinder and unstabilized optics, and an advanced type with a laser rangefinder, thermal imaging, stabilized optics and a multi-sensor input to the computer.

The Tamoyo is an altogether lighter and simpler machine that, like the Argentine/West German TAM, should perhaps be classified as a medium tank rather than a main battle tank. The Tamoyo results from Bernardini's extensive experience in updating (through a process of complete rebuilding) obsolete and obsolescent light tanks of US origins but still extensively used in Brazil and other parts of the world. The Tamoyo was conceived as partner to these vehicles, and the prototype first appeared in 1983. Like the Osorio, the Tamoyo is conventional in configuration and construction, with welded steel hull and turret, including spaced armour and, in production vehicles, the option of laminate armour. The turret accommodates the Bernardini 90-mm

(3.54-in) main gun. Torsion bar suspension is used for the arrangement of six road wheels on each side, and the 500-hp (373-kW) Saab-Scania DSI-14 diesel drives the rear sprockets via a manual or optional automatic transmission. In 1987 Bernardini revealed the upgraded Tamoyo III with a 736-hp (549-kW) Detroit Diesel 8V-92TA engine, automatic transmission and a 105-mm (4.13-in) L7A3 main gun. This offers considerably greater firepower than the 90-mm (3.54-in) weapon. By the early 1990s neither variant had been ordered into production.

Bernardini MB–3 Tamoyo
(Brazil)

Type: battle tank
Crew: 4
Combat weight: 30,000 kg (66,138 lb)
Dimensions: length, gun forward 8.77 m (28.77 ft) and hull 6.50 m (21.325 ft); width 3.22 m (10.56 ft); height 2.50 m (8.20 ft)
Armament system: one 90-mm (3.54-in) gun with 68 rounds, one 0.5-in (12.7-mm) Browning machine-gun with 600 rounds, one 7.62-mm (0.3-in) FN-MAG machine-gun with 3,000 rounds and two quadruple smoke-dischargers
Armour: not revealed
Powerplant: one 375-kW (503-hp) Saab-Scania DSI–14 diesel engine with 700 litres (154 Imp. gal.) of fuel
Performance: speed, road 67 km/h (41.6 mph); range, road 550 km (342 miles); fording 1.3 m (4.625 ft); gradient 60%; side slope 30%; vertical obstacle 0.71 m (2.33 ft); trench 2.4 m (6.56 ft); ground clearance 0.5 m (19.7 in)

MB 3 Tamoyo

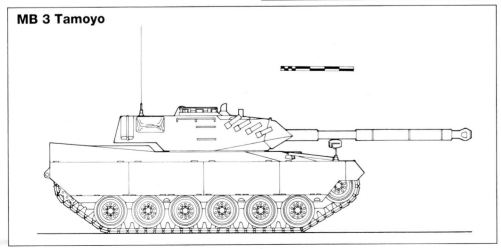

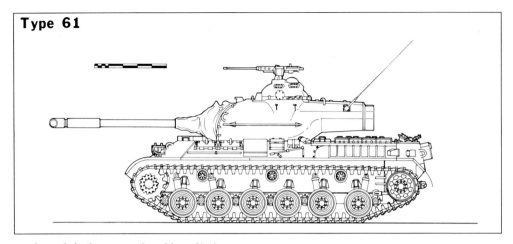

Type 61

Japan is in the unusual position of being prohibited by its post-Second World War constitution from possessing offensive military capability, or offering its weapons for export. This has placed singular constraints on the Japanese defence establishment and industry, which are unwilling for national and economic reasons to undertake large-scale imports and yet lack the large domestic or any export market for the cost-effective design and construction of primary equipment such as battle tanks. Nonetheless the Japanese have opted to produce such tanks for the limited market offered by their army. The first main battle tank designed by the Japanese after the Second World War was the Type 61, which was standardized for production in 1961 after a protracted development phase from 1954: four prototypes appeared in 1957, and were followed by 12 pre-production vehicles. Service deliveries began in 1962, and by the time production was completed by Mitsubishi in 1970, some 560 Type 61s had been completed.

The 35,000-kg (77,160-lb) Type 61 is still in service, but thoroughly obsolete. In overall design the tank is similar to American tanks of the same period, with a welded hull, cast turret, torsion bar suspension and 600-hp (447-kW) Mitsubishi Type 12 HM 21 WT diesel engine plus mechanical transmission. The main armament is unstabilized and provided with a simple optical fire-control system, and comprises a 90-mm (3.54-in) Japan Steel Works Type 61 rifled gun. Signs of the design's

Type 61
(Japan)

Type: main battle tank
Crew: 4
Combat weight: 35,000 kg (77,160 lb)
Dimensions: length, gun forward 8.19 m (26.87 ft) and hull 6.30 m (20.57 ft); width 2.95 m (9.68 ft); height 2.49 m (8.17 ft) to turret roof
Armament system: one 90-mm (3.54-in) gun, one 0.5-in (12.7-mm) Browning machine-gun, one 0.3-in (7.62-mm) Browning machine-gun, and two triple smoke-dischargers
Armour: between 15 and 64 mm (0.59 and 2.52 in)
Powerplant: one 447-kW (600-hp) Mitsubishi Type 12 HM 21 WT diesel engine
Performance: speed, road 45 km/h (28 mph); range, road 200 km (124 miles); fording 0.99 m (3.25 ft) without preparation; gradient 60%; vertical obstacle 0.685 m (2.25 ft); trench 2.489 m (8.17 ft); ground clearance 0.4 m (15.75 in)

age can be seen in the Type 61's lack of standard features such as NBC protection and passive night-vision equipment. Variants of the basic type were produced as the Type 67 armoured vehicle-launched bridge, the Type 67 armoured engineer vehicle and the Type 70 armoured recovery vehicle.

Design of a Type 61 successor began in the same year that this first type began to enter service. But whereas Type 61 had been conceived almost entirely by the Ground Armaments Directorate of the Technical Research and Development Headquarters, the new Type 74 was planned by the army in collaboration with Mitsubishi, the designated manufacturer. Various test rigs were built and trialled to validate the main features between 1964 and 1967, and construction of prototypes was launched in 1968. These were the 1969 STB-1 variant with an automatically loaded 105-mm (4.13-in) L7A1 gun, licence-built by Japan Steel Works, and a remotely controlled 0.5-in (12.7-mm) machine-gun, and the 1971 STB-3 with a manually loaded main gun, manually-operated machine-gun and an elongated turret with a stretched bustle. This latter variant was standardized for production in 1973, the first Type 74s appearing in the following year. Production lasted in to the late 1980s, resulting in some 850 tanks.

Like the Type 61, the 38,000-kg (83,774-lb) Type 74 is entirely conventional in layout and construction, with a welded hull and cast turret, the latter accommodating the commander, gunner and loader as well as the 105-mm (4.13-in) main ordnance firing the standard NATO range of ammunition, supplemented from 1985 by the American M735 APFSDS round. A new recoil mechanism was developed for the licence-built weapon, reducing the frontal area of the turret to a tactically advantageous degree. The main armament has two-axis stabilization, and is used with a moderately advanced fire-control system with sensors, a laser rangefinder and a ballistic computer. The main armament can be elevated in an arc between -6.5° and +9.5°, though maximum depression and elevation angles of -12.5° and +15° can be obtained with the aid of differential adjustment of the 'kneeling' hydropneumatic suspension for the five road wheels on each side: this suspension can also be adjusted collectively to modify ground clearance between 0.2 and 0.65 m (7.87 and 25.6 in) to suit the ground being crossed, and laterally to tilt the tank a maximum of 9° left and right. Standard equipment for the four-man Type 74 includes the NBC system and active night-vision equipment. The same basic hull is used for the Type 78 armoured recovery vehicle and a self-propelled anti-aircraft vehicle under development with two radar-controlled 35-mm cannon.

The latest Japanese tank entered production as the Type 90, after development as the TK-X. Development of this modern vehicle was begun during 1976 by the Technical Research Headquarters of the Japanese Self-Defence Agency, with collaboration by Mitsubishi (tank and fire-control system) and Japan Steel Works (main armament). Prototypes appeared in 1986, and the Type 90 entered production in the early 1990s as a considerably more advanced main battle tank than those previously fielded by the Japanese Ground Self-Defence Force, as the army is officially designated. The new tank has a 1,500-hp (1,118-kW) Mitsubishi 10ZG diesel for a high power-to-weight ratio at a combat weight of about 50,000 kg (110,229 lb), and has multilayer armour with ceramic pockets for a high level of protection against all types of weapon. It was originally planned to fit the Type 90 with a Japanese-designed 120-mm (4.72-in) main gun, but it was finally decided to adopt the West German Rheinmetall Rh-120 weapon

The Type 74 battle tank is a useful but not very advanced vehicle that has nonetheless served the Japanese army well and paved the way for more ambitious vehicles. (*Japanese Defense Forces*)

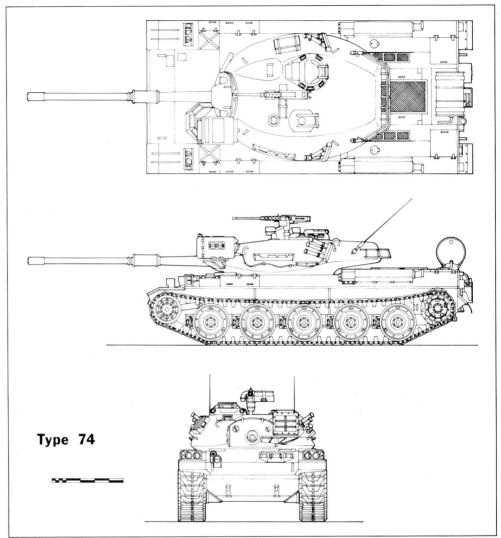

Type 74

with an automatic loader so that the total crew requirement is only three. The main armament has two-axis stabilization, and the advanced fire-control system includes a high-speed digital computer, laser range-finder stabilized optics and a number of other sensors.

Though South Korea is now producing its own main battle tank as the Hyundai K-1, this vehicle was in fact designed in the USA to an exacting South Korean specification by Chrysler Defense (now the General Dynamics Land Systems Division). The K-1 has strong conceptual affinity to the Americans' M1

Abrams, which is not surprising, given the involvement of General Dynamics in both designs, but is a lighter and smaller vehicle, better suited to the mountainous terrain of the border region between North and South Korea. It is believed that the South Korean requirement is for some 700 K-1s, but like the Brazilian Osorio the type will almost certainly be offered for export at a highly competitive price. Details of the protection have not been released, but it is believed that composites feature strongly in the overall scheme. In layout the K-1 is conventional, with the driver in the forward compartment, the commander,

Mitsubishi Type 74
(Japan)

Type: main battle tank
Crew: 4
Combat weight: 38,000 kg (83,774 lb)
Dimensions: length, gun forward 9.41 m (30.87 ft) and hull 6.70 m (21.98 ft); width 3.18 m (10.43 ft); height to turret top 2.48 m (8.14 ft)
Armament system: one 105-mm (4.13-in) ROF L7A1 rifled gun with 55 rounds, one 7.62-mm (0.3-in) Type 74 coaxial machine-gun with 4,500 rounds, one 0.5-in (12.7-mm) Browning M2HB AA machine-gun with 660 rounds, and three smoke-dischargers on each side of the turret, the turret is electrically powered, the main gun is stabilized in elevation (− 12.5° to + 15° using the suspension or − 6.5° to + 9.5° mechanically) and in azimuth (360°), and a Mitsubishi fire-control system is fitted; this last combines optical sights, a laser rangefinder and a ballistic computer.
Armour: cast and welded steel
Powerplant: one 559-kW (750-hp) Mitsubishi 10ZF Type 22 WT diesel engine with 950 litres (209 Imp. gal.) of fuel
Performance: speed, road 53 km/h (33.0 mph); range, road 300 km (186 miles); fording 1.0 m (3.3 ft) without preparation and 2.0 m (6.6 ft) with preparation; gradient 60%; side slope 40%; vertical obstacle 1.0 m (3.28 ft); trench 2.7 m (8.9 ft); ground clearance adjustable from 0.2 to 0.65 m (7.9 to 25.6 in)

transmission also used in the Brazilian Osorio, French AMX-40 and Italian C1. The suspension is a hybrid type with torsion bars for the central road wheels and hydropneumatic units for the front and rear road wheels: differential use of the hyrdropneumatic units is believed to add 3° more to the main armament's maximum mechanical depression of -7°. A special fire-control system with advanced sensors and features has been developed by Hughes Aircraft. The K-1 clearly offers very considerable operational capability, and production in South Korea will certainly combine quality and economy.

K-1
(South Korea)

Type: main battle tank
Crew: 4
Combat weight: 52,000 kg (114,638 lb)
Dimensions: length, gun forward 9.58 m (31.43 ft) and hull 7.39 m (24.25 ft); width 3.59 m (11.79 ft) with skirts; height 2.25 m (7.38 ft)
Armament system: one 105-mm (4.13-in) gun with 47 rounds, one 0.5-in (12.7-mm) Browning machine-gun with 1,000 rounds, two 7.62-mm (0.3-in) machine-guns with 11,400 rounds, and one sextuple smoke-discharger
Armour: not revealed
Powerplant: one 1,200-hp (895-kW) MTU 871 Ka-501 diesel engine
Performance: speed, road 65 kn/h; range, road 500 km (311 miles); fording 1.2 m (3.9 ft) without preparation and 1.8 m (5.9 ft) with preparation; gradient 50%; verticle obstacle 1.0 m (3.3 ft); trench 2.74 m (9.0 ft); ground clearance 0.46 m (18 in)

gunner and loader in the turret complete with the 105-mm (4.13-in) M68 main armament, and the 1,200-hp (895-kW) MTU MB 871 Ka-501 diesel in the rear compartment, together with the popular West German

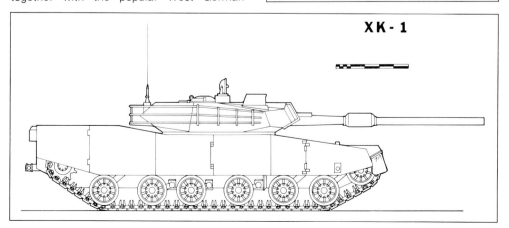

XK-1

The only other main battle tank in Western service is the Americans' most important weapon of this type, the M1 Abrams. This vehicle marks a turning point in main battle tank design, as it is the world's first such machine to use a gas turbine as its sole automotive engine. The origins of the type lie with West Germany's 1970 decision to pull out of the German-American MBT-70 programme and to concentrate instead on an indigenous tank (the Leopard 2). This left the Americans with the need to develop an M60-series successor as rapidly as possible: the MBT-70 had offered considerable firepower in the form of the 152-mm (5.98-in) gun/launcher for conventional ammunition and the MGM-51 Shillelagh anti-tank missile, a three-man crew through the use of an automatic loader, and a maximum speed of 44 mph (70.8 km/h) through the use of a 1,500-hp (1,118-kW) engine. The apparently logical starting point was a so-called 'austere' version of the MBT-70, designated XM803, but this was cancelled by the US Congress late in 1971 on the ground of its great cost and exorbitantly high levels of sophistication.

In December 1971 the US Army therefore decided to start from scratch with an altogether new programme resulting in XM1 prototypes from the Chrysler Corporation (M60-series contractor) and the Detroit Diesel Allison Division of the General Motors Corporation (MBT-70 contractor). The army needed competitive prototypes of a tank that would provide significantly better protection and mobility than those possessed by the M60, while in the short term at least the same main armament was retained, though with a superior fire-control system to generate a higher first-round hit probability with the tank on the move. The competing prototypes were delivered in February 1976, and a period of exhaustive trials was started. In November of the same year it was announced that the Chrysler prototype had been chosen for full-scale engineering development, though the Leopard 2AV (Austere Version) was kept under test to provide a back-up design in the event of the American tank's subsequent failure. Some 11 XM1 pre-production vehicles were completed between February and July 1978, and the first M1 Abrams main battle tanks emerged from the Lima Army Tank Plant in February 1980, a second supply source coming on stream in 1982 at the Detroit Arsenal Tank Plant, whose operation was sold by Chrysler to General Dynamics in March 1982. Production totals for the Abrams rose steadily from the initial 3,312 to 7,058 by the end of Fiscal Year 1988, and this figure was increased during 1984 to 7,467

The MBT-70 programme eventually came to nothing, though the design and technology efforts paid off with dividends in the M1 Abrams. This is the second prototype, seen at the Aberdeen Proving Grounds with the 152-mm (6-in) launcher for Shillelagh missiles and conventional projectiles. (US Army)

to be delivered by the same date: production ran at 30 vehicles per month in 1981, then at 60 vehicles a month from January 1982 to December 1983, and finally at 70 vehicles per month from January 1984. This provides striking evidence of the importance attached to the Abrams' programme by the US Army, which planned to field 89 M1 battalions by the early 1990s.

In basic layout the Abrams is completely conventional, but in structure the tank reflects advances made in recent years with protection: the Abrams is thus made of the same type of composite armour as the Challenger and Leopard 2, and this explains the angularity of the tank's external contours, which are conditioned by the inflexibility of the protective material added over the core structure.

The driver is located in the centre of the vehicle's forward compartment, and is seated in a semi-reclining position so that the hull front can be kept low and well angled against head-on fire. Behind the driver's position is the turret, which had electro-hydraulic traverse with manual control for emergency use. The main armament is the 105-mm (4.13-in) M68

rifled gun, which is stabilized in two axes and has power elevation in an arc between -9° and +20°; the commander and gunner are located to the right of the weapon, and the loader to its left. The fire-control system includes a Computing Devices of Canada high-speed solid-state digital computer, a Hughes Aircraft Company laser rangefinder, a Hughes Aircraft Company stabilized day/night sight and automatic sensors for static cant and wind direction/speed. The inputs from these sensors go directly to the computer, and the crew have then to add figures for battle sight range, ammunition type, ammunition temperature, barrel wear, muzzle reference compensation and barometric pressure, so that the fire-control solution can be integrated for a high first-round hit probability that has become one of the cornerstones of modern armoured tactics, where there is seldom a chance for a second aimed shot.

Protection within the turret is to a very high order, with sliding doors and spall-protected boxes complemented by a fast-acting fire/explosion-suppressing system and all ready-use ammunition is located behind doors

The XM1's angular shape is necessitated by the extensive use of compositer armour, which can be produced only in flat plates. (*Chrysler Corporation*)

in the turret bustle. The upper surface of the bustle is designed to blow off in two panels during an explosion and so allow the ammunition's main destructive potential to be dissipated upwards and backwards.

Under the raised rear decking typical of most modern battle tanks is the unusual engine, a 1,500-shp (1,118-ekW) Avco Lycoming AGT-1500 gas turbine. The power delivered to the rear drive sprockets by the gas turbine is greater than that from a similarly rated diesel, because of the gas turbine's reduced cooling requirement and, together with its compact size and supposedly high levels of reliability, this was one of the reasons for this engine type's selection. The greater power of the gas turbine does give the M1 far livelier performance that the M60A3, however, and another advantage is the fact that the engine can be run on diesel oil or kerosene, or in an emergency on petrol; the fuel tanks are separated from the crew compartment by an armoured bulkhead for increased safety. On the debit side of the account, however, are the engine's comparative lack of ruggedness, its high thermal signature which makes the M1 more vulnerable to heat-seeking missiles than diesel-engined tanks, and a specific fuel consumption high enough to offset the additional fuel capacity made possible by the smaller engine: thus the M1 attains a range of 310 miles (499 km) on 504 US gal. (1,908 litres) of fuel, while the comparable figures for the M60A3 are 300 miles (483 km) on 375 US gal. (1,420 litres).

The engine drives the sprockets via a fully automatic transmission, which also offers integral braking, variable hydrostatic steering and pivot steering. On each side, the running gear comprises seven road wheels, two track-return rollers and a forward idler, and the use of an improved torsion bar suspension allows independent vertical movement of 15 in (0.381 m) to each road wheel, compared to only 6.4 in (0.163 m) on the M60 series: this translates into far superior ride at speed and across country. The upper part of the trackwork and suspension is protected by skirts. Standard features are NBC protection by an overpressure system, passive night-vision equipment, and a bank of six dischargers for smoke grenades on each side of the

General Dynamics M1 Abrams (USA)

Type: main battle tank
Crew: 4
Combat weight: 120,250 lb (54,545 kg)
Dimensions: length, gun forward 32.04 ft (9.766 m) and hull 25.98 ft (7.918 m); width 11.98 ft (3.653 m); height overall 9.465 ft (2.885 m)
Armament system: one 105-mm (4.13-in) M68E1 rifled gun with 55 rounds, two M240 7.62-mm (0.3-in) machine-guns (one coaxial and one AA) with 12,400 rounds, one 0.5-in (12.7-mm) Browning M2HB AA machine-gun with 1,000 rounds, and six smoke-dischargers on each side of the turret; the type can also generate smoke by injecting fuel into the exhaust system; the turret is electro-hydraulically powered, the main gun is stabilized in elevation (−9° to +20°) and azimuth (360°), and a Computing Devices/Hughes/Kollmorgen advanced fire-control system is fitted; this last combines stabilized day/night optical and thermal sights, a laser rangefinder, various sensors and a ballistic computer
Armour: laminate and steel
Powerplant: one 1,500-hp (1118-kW) Avco Lycoming AGT-1500 gas turbine with 504 US gal. (1908 litres) of fuel
Performance: speed, road 45 mph (72.4 km/h); range, road 310 miles (499 km); fording 4.0 ft (1.22 m) without preparation and 7.8 ft (2.375 m) with preparation; gradient 60%; side slope 40%; vertical obstacle 4.08ft (1.244 m); trench 9.0 ft (2.74 m); ground clearance 17 in (0.43 m)

turret.

The last 894 M1s were completed to the Improved M1 Abrams standard with enhanced protection.

Production then switched to the definitive M1A1 Abrams, which began to enter service in August 1985. This has the enhanced protection of the Improved M1, a number of detail improvements, three rather than two blow-off panels in the turret roof, integral engine smoke generators, an integrated NBC system that provides the standard conditioned breathing air and also heating or cooling for those occasions when the crew are using NBC suits and face masks. The most important modification, however, is the use of the 120-mm (4.72-in) Rheinmetall Rh-120 smooth-bore gun in place

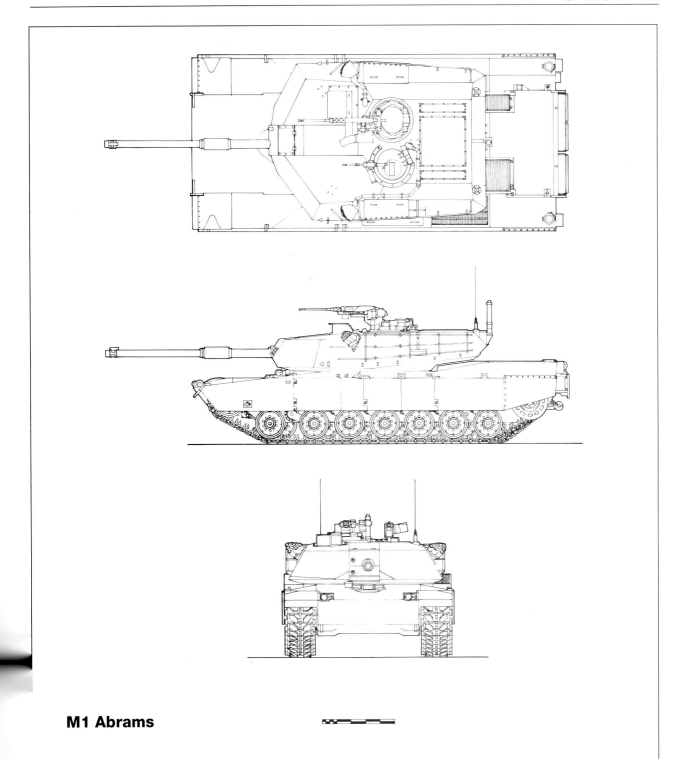

M1 Abrams

The M1 Abrams battle tank at speed, emphasizing the type's low silhouette. (*US Army*)

of the original 105-mm (4.13-in) M68 rifled weapon for greater offensive capability and longer range. The gun mounting was designed with this change in view, so the disruption to production caused by the armament change was minimal. The considerably larger ammunition of the 120-mm (4.72-in) gun made a reduction in ammunition capacities inevitable: in the M1, stowage is provided for 55 rounds (44 in left- and right-hand bustle compartments each surmounted by a blow-off panel, eight in a hull compartment and three in spallproof boxes on the turret basket) while in the M1A1 this declines to 40 rounds (36 in left-hand, central and right-hand bustle compartments, each surmounted by a blow-off panel, and four in a rear hull box).

Enhancement of the M1A1 has continued at a steady pace. M1A1 Block II vehicles have a number of detail improvements as well as an improved commander's position with an independent thermal viewer, and the M1A1 Block III is a General Dynamics proposal with a three-man crew made possible by the addition of an automatic loading system, rapid refuelling and reammunitioning capabilities and improved suspension. The Abrams has suffered its fair share of problems as it entered service, but in its M1A1 form is certainly one of the best tanks in the world today, with a large measure of development capacity still ahead of it.

On the other side of the political divide separating the two superpowers and their blocs of adherents and clients, the development of main battle tanks proceeded apace in the 1960s and 1970s. In the communist bloc the capability to design heavy armour was retained exclusively by the USSR, which in the late 1950s began to plan the T-62 main battle tank as the successor to the T-55 and T-55 series with the same levels of protection and mobility, but usefully increased firepower in the form of a 115-mm (4.53-in) U-5TS (or 2A20) smooth-bore gun fitted with a fume extractor and two-axis stabilization: an unusual feature of this gun is its integral spent case ejection system, activated by the recoil of the gun. This is a useful feature, but had to be bought by a limitation in fire rate to only four rounds per minute with the tank stationary, as the gun has to be brought to an elevation of exactly + 3° 30° for the ejection system to function. The gun fires fin-stabilized projectiles, the FRAG-HE type leaving the muzzle at 750 m (2,461 ft) per second, the HEAT type at 900 m (2,953 ft) per second to penetrate 430 mm (16.9 in) of armour at any range, and the APFS-DS type with a muzzle velocity of 1,680 m (5,512 ft) per second, to penetrate 330 mm (13 in) of armour at a range of 1,000 m (1,095 yards). Turret risks are reduced by the carriage of only four ready-use rounds actually in the turret, the balance of 36 rounds being carried below the turret ring (16 to the right of the driver and 20 in the rear of the fighting compartment).

The cast turret resembles that of the T-54 and T-55 series, but the welded hull is both longer and wider than that of the earlier series, with a different spacing of the road wheels. In other essential respects the T-62 is very similar to the T-55 it succeeded, and began to enter production during 1961 for service in 1963. The construction programme in the USSR lasted until 1975 and accounted for about 20,000 tanks, complemented by another 1,500 from a Czech line between 1973 and 1978, and an unknown number from a North Korean line that is currently producing tanks for the domestic and continued export markets.

The T-62 is still in very widespread service, and continues as one of the East European forces' most important first-line assets. The standard features of the tank include an NBC system, active night-vision equipment and a snorkel to permit wading to a maximum depth of 5.5 m (18.05 ft), and its adequate range on internal fuel can be boosted by up to 200 km (124 miles) with an additional 685 litres (151 Imp. gal.) of fuel carried in main and supplementary external tankage. The T-62 has been extensively used in combat, especially in the Middle East. The type has acquitted itself well, the high level of protection provided by its well-sloped armour being particularly notable. However, in common with other Soviet tanks this protective capability is made all the more valuable (or perhaps invaluable) by the main armament's poor elevation arc of -4° to + 17°: the former figure means that a hull-down firing position is difficult to obtain. The T-62 is also limited in offensive capability by its

Compared with the T-54/T-55 series, the T-62 has a comparatively wider and lower hull, and its main armament is fitted with a fume extractor. These are T-62A tanks on their way to the southern USSR as part of the Soviet withdrawal from Afghanistan in 1988. (*Novosti Press Agency*)

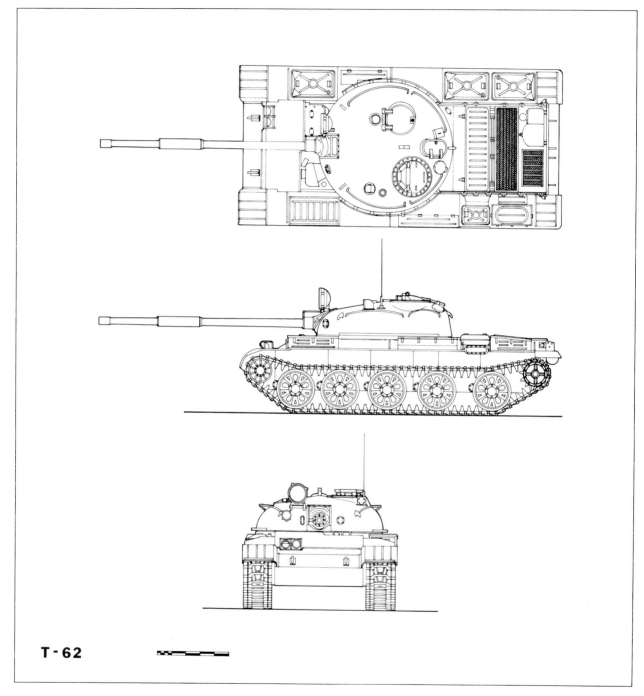

T-62

comparatively simple fire-control system.

Given its importance and longevity, it is hardly surprising that the T-62 has appeared in variant form, but perhaps surprisingly these variants are relatively few in number. Numerically the most important of these is the T-62A, which has a turret of revised shape and different size, together with a rotating cupola mounting (plus external 12.7-mm/0.5-in machine-gun) in place of the fixed loader's hatch of the T-62. It is also believed that an improved fire-control system and night-vision equipment have been fitted, the former to a standard comparable with that of the M60A1 with a ballistic computer, laser rangefinder and various sensors. A derivative of the T-62A is the T-62M with 'live' tracks for longer life and better performance. In common with other Soviet gun tanks in service with erstwhile Soviet allies, the T-62 can now be revised with Western main armament, in the form principally of the 105-mm (4.13-in) L7 series rifled gun produced by the Royal Ordnance Factories (now Royal Ordnance); modification of the main armament and mounting is generally accompanied by wholesale revision, updating or replacement of the fire-control system. As an

alternative to the L7 gun, moreover, Royal Ordnance offers a British-designed 115-mm (4.53-in) smooth-bore barrel with higher performance than the Soviet original.

Other T-62 variants include a T-62K command tank with a land navigation system and extra communications equipment, a T-62 flamethrower with a flame gun located coaxially with the main armament in place of the standard 7.62-mm (0.3-in) machine-gun, and the M1977 armoured recovery vehicle.

Like the Americans and other major tank-producing nations, the USSR has for some time operated on the principle of starting the search for a successor as soon as any major type has entered production. In the case of the T-62 this process led to the development of the T-64. Several prototypes were trialled in the period up to 1966, when the decision was made to place the best in production as the T-64, which was designated the M1970 in Western terminology for lack of information about the proper designation. It is uncertain when the T-64 began to enter service, but the type is operated only by the Soviet forces and is believed to have been manufactured between 1966 and 1971, though the production

T-62
(USSR)

Type: main battle tank
Crew: 4
Combat weight: 40,000 kg (88,183 lb)
Dimensions: length, gun forward 9.335 m (30.63 ft) and hull 6.63 m (21.75 ft); width 3.30 m (10.83 ft); height 2.395 m (7.86 ft)
Armament system: one 115-mm (4.53-in) U–5TS (2A20) smooth-bore gun with 40 rounds (16 in the hull and 24 in the turret), and one 7.62-mm (0.3-in) PKT coaxial machine-gun with 2,500 rounds; the turret is electro-hydraulically powered, the main gun is stabilized in elevation − 4° to + 17°) and azimuth (360°), and an optical fire-control system is fitted; the type can generate smoke by injecting fuel into the exhaust system
Armour: cast and welded steel varying in thickness between 14 and 242 mm (0.59 and 9.53 in)
Powerplant: one 432-kW (580-hp) V–55 diesel engine with 675 litres (148 Imp. gal.) of fuel provision for 285 litres (63 Imp. gal.) of external fuel and additional provision for 400 litres (88 Imp. gal.) of supplementary external fuel in two jettisonable tanks
Performance: speed, road 50 km/h (31 mph); range, road 450 km (280 miles) on internal fuel and 650 km (404 miles) with external fuel; fording 1.4 m (4.6 ft) without preparation and 5.5 m (18.0 ft) with snorkel; gradient 60%; vertical obstacle 0.8 m (2.625 ft); trench 2.85 m (9.35 ft); ground clearance 0.43 m (17 in)

The T-62 is the final expression of the design concept pioneered with the T-54, and began to enter service in the early 1960s. It is admirably low in silhouette, but this tactical advantage has to be bought at the expense of a main armament depression angle limited to -4°, effectively negating the vehicle's chances of adopting a genuine hull-down position. (*US Army*)

The M1970 is fitted with a 115-mm (4.53-in) smooth-bore gun, but the T-64 'definitive' production version has a 125-mm (4.92-in) D-81TM Rapira 3 (or 2A46) smooth-bore gun, an altogether more powerful weapon fitted with an automatic loader to allow a reduction in crew from the M1970's four to the T-64's three. The carousel automatic loader contains 24 separate-loading rounds with semi-combustible cases, and the main fin-stabilized projectile types associated with the Rapira 3 gun are FRAG-HE fired with a muzzle velocity of 850 m (2,789 ft) per second, HEAT fired with a muzzle velocity of 900 m (2,952 ft) per second to penetrate 475 mm (18.7 in) of armour at a range of 1,000 m (1,095 yards), and APFS-DS fired with a muzzle velocity of 1,615 m (5,299 ft) per second to penetrate 300 mm (11.8 in) of armour at a range of 1,000 m

One of the most important features of Soviet tank design in the period after the end of the Second World War has been the retention, on vehicles such as these T-62s, of the excellently shaped turret without shot traps. The basic turret shape allows the installation of a large-calibre gun and provides very good ballistic protection, while its poorer features include comparatively little internal volume and a limited depression angle for the main gun.

line remained open until 1981 for the remanufacture of earlier vehicles. Total production is thought to have been in the order of 8,000 vehicles. Taken in combination, factors such as a comparatively small production run, a late service entry date and an extensive remanufacturing programme suggest that there were severe problems with the type. It is also probable that the Soviets had a high expectation of the type, which resulted in remanufacture rather than cancellation of the project.

The initial M1970 version was probably a large-scale pre-production type with a turret basically similar to that of the T-64, but considerably different hull, running gear and engine. The turret is located slightly farther to the rear, and the welded hull uses a more advanced type of armour than the rolled plate used in the T-62. Whereas the T-54 and its immediate successors have medium-diameter road wheels without track-return rollers, the M1970 and its progeny have six small-diameter road wheels per side instead of the earlier tanks' five larger wheels, four track-return rollers per side to support the inside of the track, and hydropneumatic rather than torsion bar suspension. The idlers are at the front, leaving the drive sprockets to be located at the rear where they are powered by hydraulically-assisted transmission driven by a new type of engine, a five-cylinder opposed-piston diesel engine.

T-64
(USSR)

Type: main battle tank
Crew: 3
Combat weight: 42,000 kg (92,593 lb)
Dimensions: length, gun forward 9.90 m (32.48 ft) and hull 7.40 m (24.28 ft); width 4.64 m (15.22 ft) over skirts; height 2.20 m (7.22 ft) to top of cupola
Armament system: one 125-mm (4.92-in) 2A46 Rapira 3 smooth-bore gun with 40 rounds, one 7.62-mm (0.3-in) PKT coaxial machine-gun with 3,000 rounds, and one 12.7-mm (0.5-in) NSVT AA machine-gun with 500 rounds; the turret is electrically powered, the main gun is stabilized in elevation (−5° to +18°) and azimuth (360°), and a fire-control system is fitted; the last combines optical sights and a ballistic computer; the type can generate smoke by injecting fuel into the exhaust system
Armour: cast and composite
Powerplant: one 559-kW (750-hp) five-cylinder diesel engine with 1,000 litres (220 Imp. gal.) of fuel plus provision for 400 litres (88 Imp. gal.) of additional fuel in two jettisonable external tanks
Performance: speed, road 75 km/h (46.6 mph); range, road 400 km (249 miles) on internal fuel and 600 km (373 miles) with auxiliary fuel; fording 1.4 m (4.6 ft) without preparation and 5.5 m (18.0 ft) with snorkel; gradient 60%; side slope 40%; vertical obstacle 0.915 m (3.0 ft); trench 2.72 m (8.9 ft); ground clearance 0.377 m (14.8 in)

(1,095 yards). The gun is stabilized in two axes, has a larger-than-usual elevation arc (from -5° to +18°) and is used with an advanced fire-control system including a ballistic computer, stabilized optics and a laser rangefinder. Other standard features are an NBC system, night-vision equipment and a snorkel for deep wading; it is also possible that a laser-warning receiver is fitted to provide the crew with advanced warning of attack by a tank fitted with a laser rangefinder, or by an air-launched 'smart' weapon with passive laser guidance to home on to any tank laser-illuminated by a third party.

There were considerable problems associated with the T-64's engine, suspension, automatic loader and fire-control system, and the type has evolved through a number of variants, known only by their hybrid Western designations. Thus the initial T-64 was followed by the T-64A (M1981/1) with a revised gunner's sight, smoke-grenade dispensers on the turret and hinges for the attachment of skirt armour; there is also an M1981/2 subvariant fitted with permanent skirts, rather than the optional skirts of the M1981/1.

The next variant is believed to have been the most important production model, built as

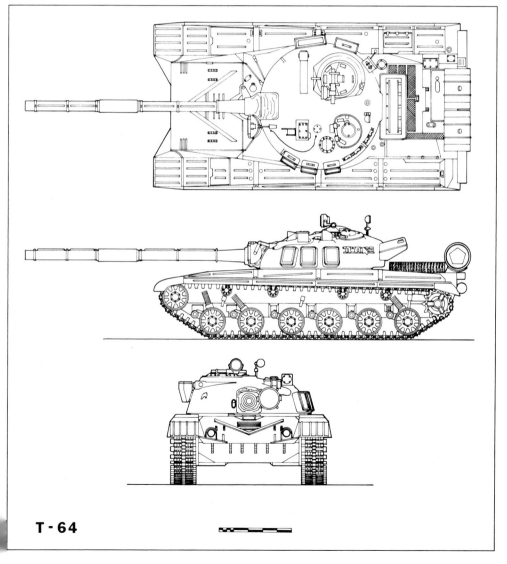

T-64

such but perhaps supplemented by older tanks remanufactured to the improved standard. This variant is the T-64B, which has the improved 125-mm (4.92-in) weapon carried by the T-72 and T-80 together with a revised and more reliable automatic loading system. The gun can also fire the AT-8 'Songster' missile, which is a dual-role weapon for use against tanks to a range of 4,000 m (4,375 yards) and against helicopters to a range of perhaps 8,000 m (8,750 yards). This missile weighs about 25 kg (55.1 lb) at launch, and leaves the barrel at about 125 m (410 ft) per second under the impulse of a solid-propellant booster, speed thereupon increasing to 500 m (1,640 ft) per second under the power of the missile's solid-propellant sustainer. The warhead is of the HEAT type and is thought capable of penetrating 600 mm (23.6 in) of conventional armour, while the guidance is thought to be of the semi-active laser type with the target illuminated by the tank's special laser designation system, carried in a removable but armoured box on the turret front. The missile is carried in the automatic loader in two sections, and fed into the main ordnance in exactly the same way as the conventional ammunition. The precise balance of missiles and conventional ammunition will clearly depend on the tactical situation, but it is likely that at least some tanks in any given unit will be tasked with a primary anti-helicopter role and therefore field a higher-than-normal complement of missiles. Some US sources have claimed that the T-64B also possesses an electronic package to detect helicopters out to slightly more than the AT-8's maximum range. Other features of the T-64B are an improved laser rangefinder and reactive armour: this latter comprises 111 HE plates attached over the glacis, the hull sides as far back as the turret rear, and the turret front, roof and sides. The T-64B became operational in 1980, with reactive armour first appearing in 1984.

The problems faced by the T-64 series persuaded the Soviet authorities at an early date to hedge their bet with a comparable but lower-risk version powered by a conventional diesel engine and fitted with torsion bar suspension for an arrangement of six larger-diameter road wheels on each side, together with only three track-return rollers. The hull was revised accordingly, with slightly less length, marginally more width and a modestly increased height. The result is the T-72, a main battle tank generally similar to the T-64 in operational capability, but offering greater reliability in its automotive system and as a result of its lighter weight (and improved power-to-weight ratio), superior mobility and

The vehicle known to the Americans as the T-64A is known in Europe as the T-64 M1981/1, and differs only in small respects from the baseline T-64. (*MARS*)

The T-72 battle tank has a long-base optical rangefinder in the turret just forward of the commander's cupola, and an infra-red searchlight to the right of the main armament. (*MARS*)

performance.

The T-72 began to reach service operations in 1971, and is still in production at four Soviet plants and single plants in Czechoslovakia, India, Poland and Yugoslavia. Whereas the T-64 is used exclusively by the USSR, the T-72 has no provision for AT-8 missiles and is operated by the Warsaw Pact countries, and non-Warsaw Pact operators ranging from Algeria to Yugoslavia via Angola, Cuba, Finland, India, Iraq, Libya and Syria, with other countries pro-bably to be added as this excellent main battle tank continues in production.

The T-72 has been developed in a number of forms and variants, and while some of these are known by their true Soviet designations, others are best individualized by Western designations. The baseline model is the T-72 discussed above, and has an infra-red searchlight to the left of the main gun; there is also a T-72K command model. The T-72M is the main production variant, with the searchlight moved

The T-72 is essentially a version of the T-64 revised for greater mechanical reliability through the use of a V-12 diesel in place of the T-64 series' 5-cylinder opposed engine. The 125-mm (4.92-in) main gun cannot fire the AT-8 'Songster' anti-tank missile, but the combination of a carousel-fed autoloader and advanced fire-control system provides the T-72 with a very high first-round kill probability, even on the move. Notable in this photograph are the spring-loaded skirts to protect the upper run of the tracks, and the smoke dischargers located on the turret front (seven on the left and five on the right). (*US Dept. of Defense*).

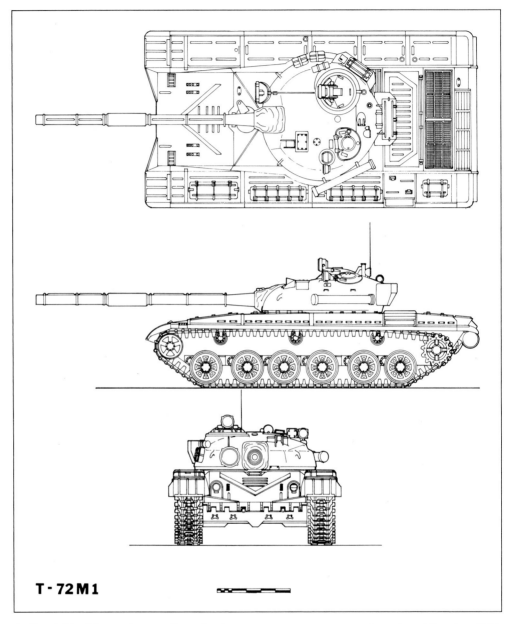

T-72M1

to the right of the main gun; there is also a T-72MK command model. The designation T-72 (M1981/2) is used for older T-72s retrofitted with side armour to prevent effective top attack of the engine compartment. The next model has the overall designation T-74, and has been produced in several sub-variants. The initial version lacks the optics port in the right-hand side of the turret front (presumably for a laser rangefinder), while the T-74 (M1980/1) is similar but has fabric skirt armour over the suspension and side containers. The T-74 (M1981/3) has appeared in two models, the initial type resembling the T-72 (M1980/1) but with thicker frontal armour, and the later type having smoke-grenade launchers. The latest model is the T-74 (T-72 M1984 or T-74M) based on the previous type but with appliqué

T-72M
(USSR)

Type: main battle tank
Crew: 3
Combat weight: 41,000 kg (90,388 lb)
Dimensions: length, gun forward 9.24 m (30.31 ft) and hull 6.95 m (22.80 ft); width 4.75 m (15.58 ft) over skirts; height 2.37 m (7.78 ft) to top of cupola
Armament system: one 125-mm (4.92-in) 2A46 Rapira 3 smooth-bore gun with 39 rounds (15 in the hull and 24 in the autoloader), one 7.62-mm (0.3-in) PKT coaxial machine-gun with 3,000 rounds, one 12.7-mm (0.5-in) NSVT AA machine-gun with 500 rounds, and 12 smoke-dischargers (five on the right of the turret and seven on the left; the type can also generate smoke by injecting fuel into the exhaust; the turret is electrically operated, the main gun is stabilized in elevation (−5° to +18°) and azimuth (360°), and an advanced fire-control system is fitted; this last combines optical sights, a laser rangefinder and a ballistic computer
Armour: cast, welded and composite to a maximum thickness of 280 mm (11.02 in)
Powerplant: one 585-kW (785-hp) V–46 diesel engine with 1,000 litres (220 Imp. gal.) of fuel plus provision for 400 litres (88 Imp. gal.) of additional fuel in two jettisonable external tanks
Performance: speed, road 80 km/h (49.7 mph); range, road 480 km (298 miles) on internal fuel and 700 km (435 miles) with auxiliary fuel; fording 1.4 m (4.6 ft) without preparation and 5.5 m (18.0 ft) with snorkel; gradient 60%; side slope 40%; vertical obstacle 0.85 m (2.79 ft); trench 2.8 m (9.2 ft); ground clearance 0.47 m (18.5 ft)

armour and anti-radiation cladding. Beyond the conventional gun tank series there are a number of specialized-role derivatives, such as the BREM-1 armoured recovery vehicle, the IMR combat engineer tractor and the ZSU-30-2 self-propelled anti-aircraft mounting with two radar-directed 30-mm cannon.

The latest main battle tank from the Soviet stable is the T-80, which is now known to be a further development of the missile-capable T-64B, and began to enter production in the early 1980s for service deliveries in 1984. Large-scale production is under way, and by the end of 1987 it is believed that some 7,000 T-80s had been produced exclusively for the Soviet forces.

The tank is basically similar in configuration and shape to the T-64, with the driver's compartment at the front, the two-man turret in the centre and the engine compartment at the rear. But the T-80 has a considerable number of detail differences from the T-64B. Working from the front towards the rear, the most important of these are a laminate glacis for improved protection against both kinetic and chemical attack, a dozer blade retracting under the nose, a new pattern of road wheel with torsion bar suspension, a cast steel turret with an inside layer of 'special armour', a modified commander's hatch, revised stowage on the outside of the turret, a modified rear decking and, perhaps most significantly of all, a new powerplant in the form of a 985-shp (734-ekW) gas turbine with a manual transmission featuring five forward

The Soviets' latest T-80 main battle tank is an advanced derivative of the T-64 with a laminate glacis plate, other advanced protective features and a gas turbine powerplant. Notable in this photograph are the jettisonable fuel drum at the rear and the snorkel stowed on the turret rear. (*MARS*)

and one reverse gears, compared with the diesel-engined T-64's synchromesh transmission with seven forward and one reverse gears. The only known variant of the T-80 is the so-called T-80 M1984, which is the basic vehicle fitted with a large area of reactive armour, varying in extent from 185 to 211 specially-shaped plates to protect the tank's frontal arc against gun-fired or missile-borne HEAT warheads.

The T-64 and T-80 are currently the most important main battle tank types in Soviet service, but are more than ably backed by massive numbers of T-72s, T-62s and even T-54s and T-55s. The T-80 is still at a comparatively early stage of its service life, and like the M1 Abrams in American service, can be expected to evolve through steadily improved variants until it reaches obsolescence in the next century.

The only other designer of main battle tanks in the communist bloc is China, a massive and populous nation that has begun to develop and flex its industrial muscle only in recent years. During and after the revolution that brought them to power in 1949, the communists used some captured Japanese equipment, but relied increasingly on Soviet-supplied tanks. As China tried to secure a limited independence from Soviet sources of supply, an indigenous tank industry was established, and this at first produced licensed copies of Soviet equipment.

The first of these vehicles is the Type 59, which is the Chinese copy of the T-54. The tank is still in extremely widespread service with China and a growing number of Asian and African countries. The baseline Type 59 is essentially similar to the T-54 and the T-54A with a fume extractor, but in recent years much of the fleet has been updated slightly with night-vision equipment and a laser rangefinder. As befits an elderly design in large-scale service, the Type 59 is now offered a growing range of retrofit packages, ranging from that by the Chinese armaments organization NORINCO for a 730-hp (544-kW) diesel in place of the original 520-hp (388-kW) unit, to a British package that can fit a 105-mm (4.13-in) L7 series gun, a Belgian OIP LRS-5 fire-control system and a British thermal imager for full night-fighting capability. The Type 59 has also

T-80
(USSR)

Type: main battle tank
Crew: 3
Combat weight: 42,000 kg (92,593 lb)
Dimensions: length, gun forward 9.90 m (32.48 ft) and hull 7.40 m (24.28 ft); width 3.40 m (11.15 ft) over skirts; height 2.20 m (7.22 ft) excluding AA machine-gun
Armament system: one 125-mm (4.92-in) combined gun/missile-launcher with 40 rounds, one 12.7-mm (0.5-in) NSVT machine-gun with 500 rounds, one 7.62-mm (0.3-in) PKT machine-gun with 2,000 rounds, and between eight and 12 smoke-dischargers
Armour: not revealed
Powerplant: one 735-kW (986-hp) gas turbine with 1,000 litres (220 Imp. gal.) of fuel excluding 400 litres (88 Imp. gal.) in jettisonable external tanks
Performance: speed, road 75 km/h (46.6 mph); range, road 400 km (249 miles) without external fuel; fording 1.4 m (4.6 ft) without preparation and 5.5 m (18.0 ft) with preparation; gradient 60%; side slope 40%; vertical obstacle 0.9 m (2.95 ft); trench 2.9 m (9.51 ft); ground clearance 0.38 m (15 in)

Main Battle Tank Type 59
(China)

Type: main battle tank
Crew: 4
Combat weight: 36,000 kg (79,365 lb)
Dimensions: length, gun forward 9.00 m (29.53 ft) and hull 6.04 m (19.82 ft); width 3.27 m (10.73 ft); height 2.59 m (8.50 ft)
Armament system: one 100-mm (3.94-in) gun with 34 rounds, one 12.7-mm (0.5-in) Type 54 machine-gun with 200 rounds and two 7.62-mm (0.3-in) Type 59T machine-guns with 3,500 rounds
Armour: between 20 and 203 mm (0.79 and 8 in)
Powerplant: one 390-kW (523-hp) Type 12150L diesel engine with 815 litres (179 Imp. gal.) of fuel excluding 400 litres (88 Imp. gal.) in jettisonable external tanks
Performance: speed, road 50 km/h (31.1 mph); range, road 600 km (373 miles) with external fuel; fording 1.4 m (4.6 ft) without preparation and 5.5 m (18.04 ft) with snorkel; gradient 60%; vertical obstacle 0.79 m (2.59 ft); trench 2.7 m (8.86 ft); ground clearance 0.425 m (16.75 in)

This poor-quality photograph nonetheless reveals the rear exhaust for the gas turbine and the external stowage on the turret of the T-80 battle tank. (*MARS*)

T-80

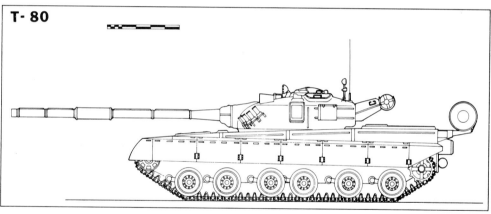

Type 59

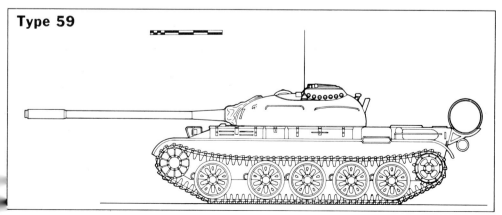

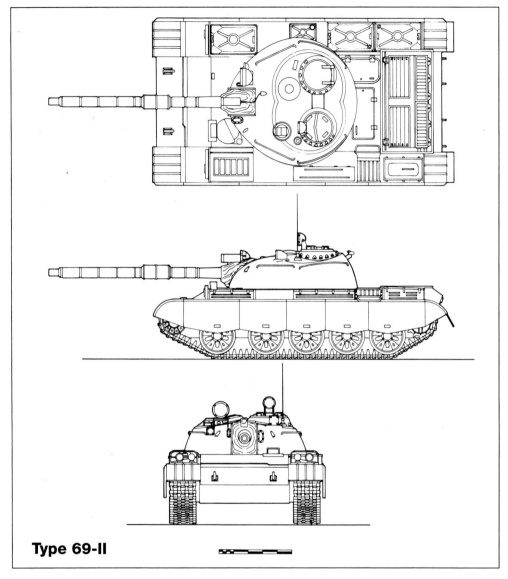

Type 69-II

been used as the basis for a simple armoured recovery vehicle, and for a self-propelled anti-aircraft mounting with twin optically-controlled 37-mm guns.

Further development of the Type 59 resulted in the Type 69, which apparently began to enter production in the early 1980s. This resembles the Type 59 closely in external features, but has a new main gun (a 100-mm/3.94-in smooth-bore weapon in the Type 69-I and a rifled weapon of the same calibre in the Type 69-II, each weapon with its

own type of fire-control system), an NBC system, a semi-automatic fire-extinguishing system and improved protection.

In 1985 the Chinese revealed another offshoot from the same stock in the form of the Type 69-III, later renamed the Type 80. This has a new all-welded hull with six rather than five road wheels and three track-return rollers on each side (the standard torsion bar suspension being retained), a layer of composite armour at the front and a more powerful 730-hp (544-kW) diesel that is probably a turbocharg-

Main Battle Tank Type 69-II
(China)

Type: main battle tank
Crew: 4
Combat weight: 36,500/37,000 kg (80,467/ 81,570 lb)
Dimensions: length, gun forward 8.657 m (28.40 ft) and hull 6.243 m (20.48 ft); width 3.298 m (10.82 ft); height with AA gun at full elevation 3.909 m (12.825 ft)
Armament system: one 100-mm (3.94-in) rifled gun, two 7.62-mm (0.3-in) Type 59T machine-guns (one coaxial and one bow), and one 12.7-mm (0.5-in) Type 54 AA machine-gun; the turret is electro-hydraulically powered, the main gun is stabilized in elevation and azimuth, and a Tank Simplified Fire-Control System—Laser is fitted, this last incorporating a laser rangefinder, optical sights and a ballistic computer; an optional fit for export models is the TSFCS–C which adds sensors for variables such as crosswind, ambient temperature and propellant-charge temperature; the type can also generate smoke by injecting fuel into the exhaust system
Armour: cast and welded steel varying in thickness between 20 and 203 mm (0.79 and 8 in)
Powerplant: one 435-kW (583-hp) Model 12150L–7BW diesel engine
Performance: speed, road 50 km/h (31.1 mph); range, road 440 km (273 miles); fording 1.4 m (4.6 ft); gradient 60%; side slope 40%; vertical obstacle 0.8 m (2.625 ft); trench 2.7 m (8.9 ft); ground clearance 0.425 m (16.75 in)

CO ISFCS-212 fire-control system that includes a laser rangefinder, stabilized optics, a ballistic computer and a number of sensors.

China is only just beginning to find its feet as a designer rather than just a builder of tanks. Considerable experience has been gained from development of the Type 54, and a substantial expertise in modern tank technology has accrued from the purchase of Western equipment and a number of collaborative ventures in lighter armoured vehicles. This probably opens the way for the development of a purely Chinese tank in the

Main Battle Tank Type 80
(China)

Type: main battle tank
Crew: 4
Combat weight: 38,000 kg (83,774 lb)
Dimensions: length, gun forward 9.328 m (30.60 ft) and hull 6.325 m (20.75 ft); width 3.372 m (11.06 ft); height 2.874 m (9.43 ft) including AA machine-gun
Armament system: one 105-mm (4.13-in) gun with 44 rounds, one 12.7-mm (0.5-in) Type 54 machine-gun with 500 rounds, one 7.62-mm (0.3-in) Type 59T machine-gun with 2,250 rounds, and two quadruple smoke-dischargers
Armour: not revealed
Powerplant: one 545-kW (731-hp) Model 12150L–7BW diesel engine with 1,400 litres (308 Imp. gal.) of fuel, excluding an unknown quantity of fuel in jettisonable external tanks
Performance: speed, road 60 km/h (37.3 mph); range, road 430 km (267 miles); fording 0.8 m (2.6 ft) without preparation and 5.0 m (16.4 ft) with snorkel; gradient 60%; side slope 40%; vertical obstacle 0.8 m (2.63 ft); trench 2.7 m (8.9 ft); ground clearance 0.48 m (18.9 in)

ed version of the 580-hp (432-kW) unit used in the Type 69. On this hull is located a cast turret based on that of the Type 69, but fitted in this instance with a fully stabilized 105-mm (4.13-in) rifled gun and the advanced NORIN-

Type 80

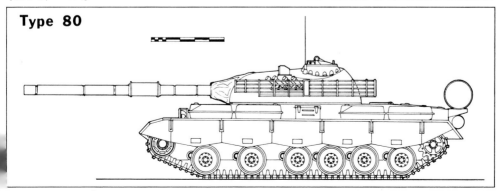

Steyr SK 105 Kürassier

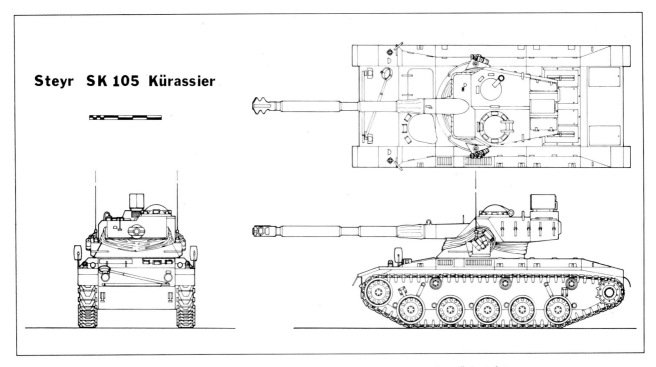

Steyr SK105/A1 Kürassier
(Austria)

Type: light tank/tank destroyer
Crew: 3
Combat weight: 17,500 kg (38,580 lb)
Dimensions: length, gun forward 7.763 m (25.47 ft) and hull 5.582 m (18.31 ft); width 2.50 m (8.20 ft); height 2.53 m (8.30 ft) to top of commander's cupola
Armament system: one 105-mm (4.13-in) GIAT CN–105–57 rifled gun with 44 rounds (32 in the hull and six in each of the two revolving cylinders of the semi-automatic loading system), one 7.62-mm (0.3-in) MG74 coaxial machine-gun with 2,000 rounds, and three smoke-dischargers on each side of the turret; the turret is hydraulically powered, the main gun is stabilized in neither elevation (– 8° to + 12°) nor azimuth (360°), and the day/night optical/thermal fire-control system is supported by a laser rangefinder
Powerplant: one 239-kW (320-hp) Steyr 7FA diesel with 400 litres (88 Imp. gal.) of fuel
Performance: speed, road 65.3 km/h (40.6 mph); range, road 520 km (323 miles); fording 1.0 m (3.3 ft); gradient 75%; side slope 40%; vertical obstacle 0.8 m (2.62 in); trench 2.41 m (7.9 ft); ground clearance 0.4 m (15.75 in)

none-too-distant future.

Such, then, is the current state of play in main battle tank production and service. With the exception of the few examples treated above with the main battle tanks, the medium tank has all but disappeared. So too in modern armies has the light tank, principally on the grounds that a light tank is a non-survivable type on the modern battlefield. Main battle tanks can be designed with adequate provision for all three essential features (firepower, protection and mobility) but the very constraints imposed upon any light tank mean that it is possible to include adequate provision for only two of these components, most generally firepower and mobility, to the exclusion of protection. There are a number of vehicles in this category, but though these are sometimes graced with the designation light tank, they are better described as tank destroyers: typical of the breed are the 17,500-kg (38,580-lb) Steyr SK105 Kürassier from Austria with a 105-mm (4.13-in) rifled gun on the chassis of an armoured personnel carrier, the 17,800-lb (8,074-kg) Alvis Scorpion from the UK with a 76-mm (3-in) gun on a multi-purpose chassis, the 18,000-kg (39,683-lb) Hagglund Ikv-9

Alvis FV101 Scorpion CVR(T)
(UK)

Type: tracked reconnaissance vehicle (light tank)
Crew: 3
Combat weight: 17,548 lb (7,960 kg)
Dimensions: length overall 15.73 ft (4.79 m); width 7.33 ft (2.235 m); height 6.90 ft (2.102 m)
Armament system: one 76-mm (3-in) gun with 40 rounds, one 7.62-mm (0.3-in) machine-gun with 3,000 rounds, and two quadruple smoke-dischargers
Armour: not revealed
Powerplant: one 190-hp (142-kW) Jaguar J60 No.1 Mk 100B petrol engine with 93 Imp. gal. (423 litres) of fuel
Performance: speed, road 50 mph (80 km/h); range, road 400 miles (644 km); fording 3.5 ft (1.07 m) without preparation and amphibious with preparation; gradient 60%; vertical obstacle 1.65 ft (0.5 m); trench 6.75 ft (2.06 m); ground clearance 14 in (0.36 m)

FV 101 Scorpion CVR(T)

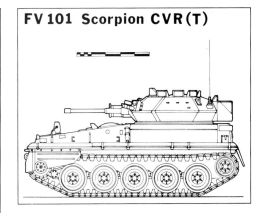

from Sweden with a 90-mm (3.54-mm) gun, and the now-obsolete 34,900-lb (15,831-kg) M551 from the USA with the 152-mm (6-in) gun/launcher for conventional ammunition and the MGM-51 Shillelagh anti-tank missile. These all resemble main battle tanks in being fully tracked and having their main armament

The concept of a launcher for MGM-51 Shillelagh anti-tank missiles and low-velocity 152-mm (6-in) projectiles did not prove altogether successful, and the M551 Sheridan enjoyed only a comparatively short first-line career. This missile guidance box is located above the barrel, and is seen with its front cover closed. (*Detroit Diesel Allison*)

Bernardini X1A2

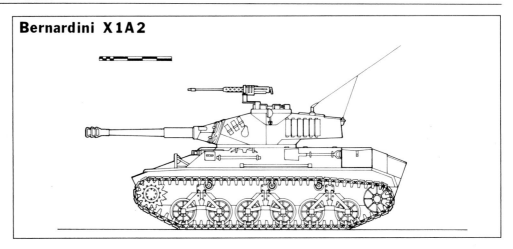

Bernardini X1A2
(Brazil)

Type: light tank
Crew: 3
Combat weight: 19,000 kg (41,887 lb)
Dimensions: length, gun forward 7.10 m (23.29 ft) and hull 6.50 m (21.33 ft); width 2.60 m (8.53 ft); height 2.45 m (8.04 ft)
Armament system: one 90-mm (3.54-in) gun with 66 rounds, one 0.5-in (12.7-mm) Browning machine-gun with 750 rounds, one 7.62-mm (0.3-in) machine-gun with 2,500 rounds, and two triple smoke-dischargers
Armour: not revealed
Powerplant: one 225-kW (302-hp) Saab-Scania DS–11 diesel engine with 600 litres (132 Imp. gal.) of fuel
Performance: speed, road 55 km/h (34.2 mph); range, road 600 km (373 miles); fording 1.3 m (4.3 ft); gradient 70%; side slope 30%; vertical obstacle 0.7 m (2.3 ft); trench 2.1 m (6.9 ft); ground clearance 0.5 m (19.7 in)

in the 360° traverse turret, but are conceptually more akin to recognized tank destroyers such as the West Germans' gun-equipped Jagdpanzer Kanone and the Soviets' ASU-85, which both feature high-velocity guns in a superstructure mounting that provides only limited traverse.

Genuine light tanks do still serve in some parts of the world, generally where there is a special reason for their existence. Some of these are considerably updated or even re-manufactured examples of obsolete light tanks (typically the X1A1 and X1A2 versions of

the M3 Stuart from the Brazilian manufacturer Bernardini) while others are reworkings of slightly less elderly designs (typically the Modernized M24 used by Norway and the Type 64

Cadillac Gage Stingray
(USA)

Type: light tank
Crew: 4
Combat weight: 44,600 lb (20231 kg)
Dimensions: length, gun forward 30.67 ft (9.35 m) and hull 20.67 ft (6.229 m); width 8.92 ft (2.71 m); height 8.33 ft (2.55 m) overall
Armament system: one 105-mm (4.13-in) ROF L7A3 rifled Low Recoil Force Gun with 36 rounds (28 in the hull and eight in the turret), one 7.62-mm (0.3-in) M240 coaxial machine-gun with 2,400 rounds, one 0.5-in (12.7-mm) Browning M2HB AA machine-gun with 1,100 rounds, and four smoke-dischargers on each side of the turret; the turret is electro-hydraulically operated, the main gun is stabilized in elevation (− 7.5° to + 20°) and azimuth (360°), and a Marconi Digital Fire-Control System is fitted; this last combines OEC day/night optical and thermal sights, a laser rangefinder, various sensors and a Cadillac Gage ballistic computer
Armour: welded steel
Powerplant: one 535-hp (339-kW) Detroit Diesel 8V–92TA diesel engine with 200 US gal. (757 litres) of fuel
Performance: speed, road 41.5 mph (67 km/h); range, road 300 miles (483 km); fording 4.0 ft (1.22 m); gradient 60%; side slope 40%; vertical obstacle 2.5 ft (0.76 m); trench 7.0 ft (2.13 m); ground clearance 18 in (0.46 in)

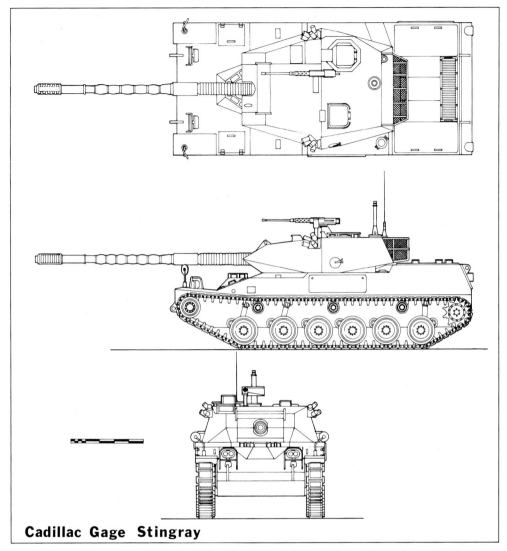

Cadillac Gage Stingray

developed in Taiwan on the basis of the M41 Walker Bulldog).

Apart from types already discussed, as they were developed in the 1950s, the only light tanks of comparatively recent design are the Type 63 and Type 62 from China, a North Korean light tank, and the Cadillac Gage Commando Stingray from the USA. The Type 63 was developed in the early 1960s for amphibious operations, and is an 18,700-kg (41,226-lb) vehicle with a welded hull based on that of the Type 77 armoured personnel carrier to carry a cast turret resembling that of the Type 59 main battle tank but scaled down and

carrying an 85-mm (3.35-in) gun. The Type 62, a heavier 21,000-kg (46,296-lb) vehicle resembling a scaled-down Type 59 main battle tank, was designed in the early 1980s for operations in mountainous terrain, and like the Type 62 is armed with an 85-mm (3.35-in) gun. Little is known of the North Korean tank, which resembles the Type 63 and is armed with an 85-mm (3.35-in) gun at a weight believed to be in the order of 20,000 kg (44,092 lb). The most modern and by far the most impressive of current light tanks is the Commando Stingray, a 44,600-lb (20,231-kg) vehicle armed with the Low Recoil Force version of the 105-mm

355

Light Tank Type 63

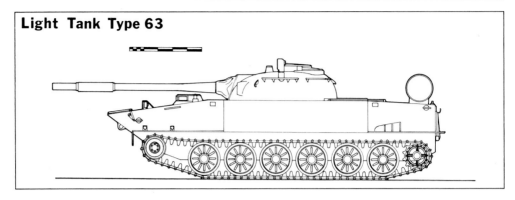

Light Amphibious Tank Type 63
(China)

Type: amphibious light tank
Crew: 4
Combat weight: 18,700 kg (41,226 lb)
Dimensions: length, gun forward 8.437 m (27.68 ft) and hull 7.15 m (23.46 ft); width 3.20 m (10.50 ft); height 3.122 m (10.24 ft) including AA machine-gun
Armament system: one 85-mm (3.35-in) gun with 47 rounds, one 12.7-mm (0.5-in) Type 54 machine-gun with 500 rounds and one 7.62-mm (0.3-in) machine-gun with 1,000 rounds
Armour: between 10 and 14 mm (0.39 and 0.55 in)
Powerplant: one 300-kW (402-hp) Model 12150-L diesel engine with 545 litres (120 Imp. gal.) of fuel
Performance: speed, road 64 km/h (39.8 mph) and water 12 km/h (7.5 mph); range, road 370 km (230 miles); fording amphibious; gradient 60%; vertical obstacle 0.87 m (2.85 ft); trench 2.9 m (9.5 ft); ground clearance 0.4 m (15.75 in)

(4.13-in) L7A3 rifled gun with optional two-axis stabilization and a choice of fire-control systems. The type has been ordered by Thailand, which has need of a tank offering high firepower and considerable range but only modest protection.

It is worth noting, moreover, that considerable design effort is being devoted to large-calibre weapons of the Low Recoil Force type, which offer the possibility of heavyweight armament in comparatively lightweight chassis types.

Afterword: The Future

The tank is currently at a crossroads in its history. It still has an army of proponents to extol its unparalleled combination of offensive/defensive attributes combined in a single package. But it also has a growing numbers of opponents who see the tank as an increasingly sophisticated (and therefore unreliable) white elephant that swallows vast amounts of the tank nations' limited research, procurement and maintenance budgets, yet as a combat type is increasingly vulnerable to the whole gamut of modern anti-tank weapons. These latter range from cheap and easily laid mines, through chemical- or kinetic-energy warheads launched by an increasing variety of surface weapons (artillery, rockets and missiles), to air-launched weapons that themselves range from the unsophisticated and cheap anti-tank bomblet via the medium-price guided bomb to the expensive guided missile.

The threat posed to the tank by these weapons is indeed potent, and is therefore worth considering in detail. The APFS-DS and HEAT projectiles fired by other tanks have long been considered the most important battlefield dangers faced by the tank, but in recent years these two weapons have been joined by the other types mentioned above. These latter have the twin advantages of destructive power at least equal to that of tank-fired projectiles, and in most cases the considerably greater range that puts their launch platforms well out of the range of the gun tank's own weapon. The last factor provides a useful level of self-protection capability for the launch platforms, which are often warplanes such as attack fighters and dedicated anti-tank helicopters that also enjoy the advantages of greater speed and agility. The higher speed of these aerial launch platforms provides them with the vital opportunity to close to firing range and launch their weapons before the target tank can detect them and thus manoeuvre out of the way or implement other defensive features. Also the superior three-dimensional agility of these aerial launch platforms allows them to make use of terrain and other features to conceal

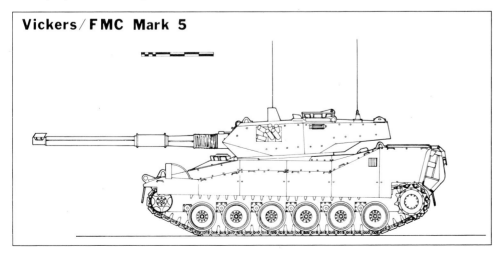

Vickers/FMC Mark 5

Vickers/FMC VFM 5
(UK/USA)

Type: light battle tank
Crew: 4
Combat weight: 19,750 kg (43,541 lb)
Dimensions: length, gun forward 8.61 m (28.25 ft) and hull 6.20 m (20.34 ft); width 2.69 m (8.83 ft); height 2.62 m (8.60 ft)
Armament system: one 105-mm (4.13-in) gun with 41 rounds, one 0.5-in (12.7-mm) Browning machine-gun with 1,000 rounds, one 7.62-mm (0.3-in) machine-gun with 5,000 rounds and two sextuple smoke-dischargers
Armour: not revealed
Powerplant: one 552-hp (412-kW) Detroit Diesel 6V–92TA6 diesel engine with 570 litres (125 Imp. gal.) of fuel
Performance: speed, road 70 km/h (43.5 mph); range, road 483 km (300 miles); fording 1.0 m (3.28 ft); gradient 60%; side slope 40%; vertical obstacle 0.76 m (2.5 ft); trench 2.13 m (7.0 ft); ground clearance 0.41 m (16 in)

their approach to firing range, where they 'unmask' only long enough to acquire their target, unleash their weapon or weapons and, when these last are of the guided variety, control their flight unless the weapon or weapons are of the 'fire-and-forget' type that use an autonomous guidance package that requires no further input from the launch platform after release.

The simplest and cheapest of these weapons, and often the most effective in tactical terms, is the anti-tank mine. This is generally laid in specially designed fields that are designed to cripple tank forces trying to move across them or, in fact more generally and effectively, divert tank advances towards natural chokepoints where they are easier targets for individual weapons. The mines themselves are designed to be triggered by a single sensor (pressure, acoustic or magnetic for the most part) or a combination of sensors, and their explosion is directed upward to penetrate the comparatively thin belly armour of the tank or at worst knock off one of the tracks and so secure a 'mobility kill'.

Such mines have been in existence for some time, and modern mines resemble the weapons of the Second World War in most features but their very high level of sophistication. Their casings, for example, are often made largely of plastic to reduce the chances of their detection, their single or combination triggering systems are more capable and can also be fitted with delay subsystems to permit the tank force to penetrate well into the minefield before the first weapon is activated fully, and the capability of their explosive charges has been considerably enhanced.

The very latest generations of such mines, moreover, are planned round a 'bounding' payload: when triggered, the mine fires a submunition into the air, where the submunition's infra-red sensor system searches for a target, aligns the 'self-forging fragment' warhead at it, and then detonates the warhead. The SFF warhead comprises a shaped explosive charge and a disc of copper alloy. When the warhead is initiated, the shaped charge explodes behind the copper disc, which is forged into a high-density penetrator that hits the upper surface of the target tank with devastating force. Typical of the weapons designed round this principle is an American type, the air-launched ERAM (Extended-Range Anti-armor Mine) that is scattered in nine-round batches in the path of the targeted armoured force. Each ERAM carries two Avco Skeet submunitions, and its sensor system can detect a tank at the range of some 165 yards (150 m), thereupon swivelling its upper section to bring one of the two Skeets onto the right bearing before firing the submunition. The Skeet's sensor then acquires its target and at a range of some 50 ft (15 m) detonates its warhead so that the SFF impacts the target with a velocity of up to 9,000 ft (2,743 m) per second.

Artillery has long been a mainstay of any army's defence against tank attack. In the Second World War and the period immediately after it, such artillery was generally of two types: the dedicated anti-tank gun was generally of comparatively small calibre and fired a solid kinetic-energy shot with a very high velocity for the flat-trajectory engagement of target tanks at short range, while field artillery of slightly larger calibres were used to fire chemical-energy projectiles for the

engagement of target tanks at longer ranges. The dedicated anti-tank gun is now something of a rarity, but field artillery is now fairly standardized at the somewhat larger calibre of 155 mm (6.1 in) and is capable of more devastating attacks at short and medium ranges as a result of the improved targeting systems and projectiles now used. The former can include radar as well as visual systems, and the latter include the 'traditional' HEAT as well as more modern cargo-carrying and guided projectiles.

As its name implies, the cargo-carrying round is a shell capable of carrying submunitions such as anti-tank mines, which means that minefields can be laid rapidly and accurately to meet an evolving tactical situation. For the French 155-mm (6.1-in) TR gun, for instance, there is a round that can deliver six 0.55-kg (1.2-lb) mines each capable of penetrating 50 mm (1.47 in) of armour. Comparable projectiles have been developed by other nations including the USA, whose equivalent is the RAAMS (Remote Anti-Armor Mine System) with either of two projectiles carrying nine 5-lb (2.27-kg) mines that are released in the air over the target area. The M741 projectile carries mines that self-destruct if they are not triggered within 24 hours, while the M718 projectile has mines that self-destruct after a

longer non-triggered interval.

The most important artillery-launched guided projectile is another American weapon, the Martin Marietta Copperhead cannon-launched guided projectile. This is fired in exactly the same way as a standard artillery projectile, but after emerging from the gun barrel deploys its cruciform set of tail-mounted control fins to stabilize the weapon as it undertakes the ballistic first part of its flight toward the predetermined area of the target. As the weapon approaches the target area, the cruciform set of mid-set wings is deployed and the guidance package is activated. The latter is based on an optronic sensor located in the nose: this searches for the laser light reflected from the target tank 'illuminated' by a forward observer on the ground or in a scouting helicopter. The Copperhead then homes onto the target tank and hits it, the impact initiating the detonation of the large shaped-charge warhead located between the guidance package and the wings. The Copperhead weighs 140 lb (63.5 kg), has a maximum range of 21,875 yards (20,000 m), and has proved its ability to strike moving as well as stationary targets with pinpoint accuracy.

The rocket started to mature as an effective anti-tank weapon during the Second World

Developed as a private venture, the Vickers Main Battle Tank series has enjoyed somewhat varied export success. This is an MBT Mk 3 of the type sold to Nigeria. (*Vickers Ltd*)

359

The AAI Universal Turret with its 75-mm (2.95-in) gun is typical of the possible way forward, with a high technology gun (firing a projectile at high velocity for the same kinetic energy as a large projectile fired with lower velocity) in a low-profile turret and auto loader. (*MARS*)

War, when ground-launched weapons such as the American 'Bazooka' and air-launched weapons such as the British 60-lb (27.2-kg) rocket began to inflict decisive losses on German tanks. Progress in surface-to-surface and air-to-surface rockets continued in the years after the war, initial emphasis being placed on 'Bazooka' type weapons to improve infantry anti-tank capabilities. Such weapons are essentially simple, and comprise a tube from which a rocket is launched at fairly short range against a tank which is crippled if not destroyed by a HEAT warhead. The use of a tube-launched rocket removes recoil problems, and as the HEAT warhead works best if it reaches the target at low velocity and with as little spin as possible, launch weight and system complexity are much reduced. This means that infantry-launched anti-tank rockets are now one-man weapons such as the Soviet RPG-18 whose rocket weighs 2.5 kg (5.5 lb) and can penetrate 250 mm (9.84 in) of armour at a range of 200 m (218 yards), the French Strim LRAC 89 whose rocket weighs 2.2 kg (4.85 lb) and can penetrate 120 mm (4.7 in) of armour at 600 m (656 yards), and the US M72 LAW (Light Anti-

tank Weapon) whose rocket weighs 2.2 lb (1.0 kg) and can penetrate 300 mm (11.8 in) of armour at 330 yards (300 m).

The artillery rocket also came into its own during the Second World War, and though the type fell into temporary abeyance after that war, except in the USSR where large-scale development and deployment continued, it underwent something of a revival at an area-saturation weapon from the later 1950s. The type is now seen as an important adjunct to conventional artillery, and its area-saturation capability has now been exploited by the Americans to create a truly devastating weapon system in the form of the Vought Multiple-Launch Rocket System. This is based on the same tracked chassis as the M2 Bradley infantry fighting vehicle for a high-level of battlefield mobility, and carries on its rear decking a traversing and elevating launcher assembly able to accommodate two six-rocket packs reloaded from the accompanying Heavy Expanded-Mobility Tactical Truck's complement of four packs. The MLRS is fielded in a firing platoon of nine launcher vehicles each supported by two HEMTTs each towing a Heavy Expanded-Mobility

Ammunition Trailer carrying another four reload packs. This gives the firing platoon a prodigious fire capability, and each launcher can ripple-fire between two and twelve rockets in less than one minute, each rocket being individually aimed by the high-quality fire-control system to ensure great accuracy. The fin-stabilized rocket has a diameter of 8.94 in (227 mm) and a length of 12.92 ft (3.937 m), and weighs 680 lb (308.4 kg) complete with a 340-lb (154.2-kg) warhead. This last is essentially of the cargo-carrying type, and typical loads include 644 shaped-charge submunitions of the M77 dual-role anti-personnel/anti-armour type delivered to a maximum range of 33,000 yards (30,175 m) or 26 AT-2 parachute-retarded anti-tank mines delivered to a range of 43,750 yards (40,005 m). Under development but then discarded was a still more capable anti-tank warhead with six shaped-charge submunitions each incorporating an active radar terminal guidance system and delivered to a range of 45,925 yards (41,995 m). In overall terms, therefore, the MLRS can lay down a dense carpet of anti-tank munitions with great accuracy at long range, and the standard rocket's supersonic speed means that fast tactical response to an evolving armoured threat is possible.

The MLRS marks the current high point in artillery rocket capability for the anti-tank role, and despite its very high cost is operated by a number of American allies in addition to the army of the originating country. It is worth noting, however, that effective if less capable systems have also been developed elsewhere in the world, and these smaller and therefore considerably more affordable systems include the Forges de Zeebrugge LAU-97 from Belgium, the Avibras ASTROS II/SS-60 and SS-40 from Brazil, the CPMIEC WS-1 and Type 74 from China, the SAKR-18 from Egypt, the LARS-2 from Germany, the IMI LAR-160 from Israel, the SNIA FIROS 25 from Italy, the Santa Barbara Teruel-2 from Spain, and the BM-22 Uragzy from the USSR (now CIS).

Surface-to-surface artillery rockets carrying submunition payloads therefore pose a considerable threat to armoured forces, and a comparable threat is posed by air-to-surface rockets carried in multiple (four- to 22-tube) launchers under the wings of attack warplanes and anti-tank helicopters. These rockets are generally of smaller diameter than their ground-launched counterparts, but are faster as the velocity imparted by their rocket motors is incremental to the speed of the launching warplane. In its anti-tank forms, the air-launched rocket is generally used with a hollow-charge or dart warhead for chemical- or kinetic-energy effect respectively. The Thomson Brandt 100-mm (3.94-in) rocket from France is typical of the breed, and has been developed and produced in two basic variants.

The AAI RDF/LT shows what can be achieved in the form of firepower and mobility through the full exploitation of modern technologies. (*AAI Corp*)

The guided missile is now one of the tank's most potent enemies, and the adoption of such a weapon turns an armoured personnel carrier into a highly capable tank-killer. This is an AMX-10P mechanized infantry combat vehicle of the French army with a Lancelot turret carrying two twin-tube missile launchers and the optics for the missile guidance system. The vehicle carries 18 HOT missiles (four in the launcher tubes and 14 reload missiles in the hull). (*MARS*)

The earlier of these variants is the TBA 100, which is based on a core section (rocket motor and stabilizing fin assembly) weighing 24 kg (52.9 lb). To this can be added one of several warhead types to create a weapon 2.48 m (97.6 in) long. The primary anti-armour warheads are the 14-kg (30.9-lb) Type ESP semi-armour-piercing unit with a hard steel core surrounded by 0.7 kg (1.54 lb) of explosive and able to penetrate 150 mm (5.9 in) of armour, and the 14.4-kg (31.75-lb) Type ECC armour-piercing unit whose shaped-charge warhead can penetrate 500 mm (19.7 in) of armour. The later variant is the Multi-Dart 100, which is based on the same core section but carries any of three specialized anti-armour warheads somewhat longer than those of the TBA 100. The 15.5-kg (34.2-lb) Type AB 24 unit contains six 1.65-kg (3.64-lb) steel flechettes each with a diameter of 24 mm (0.94 in) and the ability to penetrate 80 mm (3.15 in) of armour. The 14.5-kg (32.0-lb) Type ABL unit contains 36 0.19-kg (0.42-lb) steel flechettes each with a diameter of 13.5 mm (0.53 in) and the ability to penetrate 15 mm (0.6 in) of armour. The 14-kg (30.9-lb) Type AMV unit contains 192 0.35-kg (0.77-lb) steel flechettes each with a diameter of 9 mm (0.35 in) and the ability to penetrate 8 mm (0.315 in) of armour.

In several respects this French 100-mm (3.94-in) air-to-surface rocket is atypical of the mainstream of current thinking about such weapons, most notably in its calibre. Although the Soviets (now the Russians) have developed a number of air-to-surface unguided rockets of somewhat larger calibre, the Western practice has been to concentrate on air-to-surface rockets of slightly smaller diameter than the TBA 100/Multi-Dart 100 series. However, this should not disguise the fact that there are considerably larger-calibre Western weapons such as the 122-mm (4.8-in) SNIA Falco from Italy, the 5-in (127-mm) Zuni from the USA, and the 135-mm (5.315-in) Bofors M70 from Sweden, moderately large-diameter weapons such as the 82-mm (3.2-in) SNIA Medusa from Italy and 82-mm (3.2-in) Oerlikon-Bührle SNORA from Switzerland, and indeed smaller-calibre weapons with diameters as minimal as 50 or even 37 mm (1.97 or even 1.46 in).

However, the 'standard' diameter for Western air-to-surface rockets may be regarded as 68 mm (2.68 in) or 2.75 in (70 mm). The most prolific weapon in the former calibre is the Thomson Brandt SNEB 68/TBA68 and Multi-Dart 260 series from France, which may be regarded as the smaller half-brother of the TBA 100/Multi-Dart 100 series. The latter calibre is epitomized by the US (and now Belgian) FFAR/Hydra 70 series and the Canadian CRV7 weapon.

The Folding-Fin Air Rocket series is a very widely used tactical rocket. The type was developed in the USA as the 'Mighty Mouse' series in the air-to-air role with a 6-lb (2.72-kg) warhead, evolving in the 1960s to a 10-lb (4.54-kg) warhead and ultimately to a 17-lb (7.7-kg) warhead. The original FFAR (Mk 4) is based on the Mk 4 rocket motor core section, which is a unit weighing 11.4 lb (5.17 kg) and providing a thrust of 750 lb (340 kg). This is sufficient to give the rocket minimum and maximum ranges of 550 and 6,500 yards (505 and 5,945 m) respectively, 3,750 yards (3,430 m) being the maximum effective range, but its modest velocity is insufficient to free the weapon from the worst effects of gravity drop and crosswind. The rockets based on the Mk 4 rocket motor section are designed for use with high-performance fixed-wing warplanes.

The FFAR (Mk 40) is the Mk 4 variant optimized for use by helicopters. It thus has a scarfed nozzle that provides spin stabilization (and thus greater accuracy) after launch from a low-speed platform. There are nine warheads associated with the Mk 4 and Mk 40 versions of the original FFAR, and of these the only anti-tank type is the 5.8-lb (2.63-kg) Mk 5.

The WAFAR (Mk 66) is the most important of current weapons, produced in the USA as part of the BEI Defense Systems Hydra 70 system. This model is based on the Mk 66 WAFAR (Wrap-Around Fin Air Rocket) rocket motor core section, which weighs 13.6 lb (6.17 kg). The core section contains a higher-impulse rocket motor which gives a higher burn-out velocity than that provided by the rocket motors of the Mk 4 and Mk 40 core sections, and in addition to its greater thrust this motor offers advantages such as lower smoke emission, enhanced accuracy, and a 40 per cent increase in range. Unguided rockets based on the Mk 66 core section can be used by fixed- and rotary-wing warplanes, and can carry a useful assortment of warhead types. Of the 20 possible warheads for the FFAR and WAFAR series, seven are in service during the early 2000s: the only one of these optimized for use against armour is the 13.5-lb (6.12-kg) M261, a multi-purpose submunition warhead carrying nine M73 hollow-charge fragmentation submunitions, which are released in the air (thereafter descending under spring-opened retarders) by the action of a fuse remotely set from the cockpit to provide optimum bursting conditions to create an aerial 'wall in space' of submunitions that then fall towards the most vulnerable upper surfaces of a tank or other armoured target. The combination of the Mk 66 WAFAR core section and the M261 warhead with its integral fuse results in a weapon weighing 27.1 lb (12.29 kg) with a burn-out speed of 2,605 mph (4,192 km/h) and a range that varies from a minimum figure of

Reconnaissance vehicles such as this French AMX-10RC are little short of wheeled tanks. Though its protection is scanty by real tank standards, its combination of a high power/weight ratio and 6 x 6 drive layout provides good cross-country mobility and speed, while its firepower is comparable with that of modern medium tanks in its reliance on a 105-mm (4.13-in) gun and an advanced fire-control system. (*MARS*)

550 yards (505 m) to a maximum figure of 9,650 yards (8,825 m).

Produced by Bristol Aerospace, the Canadian Rocket Vehicle 7 was designed for full compatibility with the FFAR type, especially in warheads and launchers, but offers a considerably higher velocity for a flatter (and therefore more 'aimable') trajectory, less susceptibility to gravity and crosswind effects, and some three times greater kinetic energy at impact. The rocket is spin-stabilized by a fluted exhaust nozzle, has three wraparound fins which are spring-opened immediately after launch for maximum stability and accuracy, and is notable for its excellent combination of multiple warhead options, considerable range and low angular dispersion. The warheads intended for employment against armoured targets are the 8-lb (3.63-kg) WAU-5001/B containing a plastic-cased tungsten rod penetrator for use against heavy tanks, the 8-lb (3.63-kg) BAH-002 warhead containing a plastic-cased steel rod penetrator for use against light and medium tanks, the 5-lb (2.27-kg) BAH-004 under development with a plastic-cased tungsten penetrator for long-range use against heavy tanks, and the 10-lb (4.54-kg) WDU-5002/B under development with six low-drag tungsten rod flechette penetrators ejected at motor burn-out for use against armour.

The CVR7 has a maximum speed of 2,798 mph (4,503 km/h) when carrying a 10-lb (4.54-kg) warhead after launch from a warplane flying at 622 mph (1,001 km/h) and a typical range of 7,100 yards (6,490 m) in the air-to-surface role.

As may be deduced from the figures above for the speed and warhead weights of air-to-surface unguided rockets, their kinetic energy on impact with the target is considerable. But such rockets are difficult to launch with fine accuracy, so there remains scope for other air-launched weapons for use against tanks. The cheapest of these is, of course, the free-fall bomb, which is merely a fin-stabilized streamlined metal casing containing an explosive charge together with its fuse system. Experience has shown that the effect of a 500-lb (227-kg) bomb on a tank is lethal, but the problem of hitting so small a target, especially when it is moving, is considerably more difficult with a bomb than with a salvo of rockets.

But a bomb aimed at a tank with the aid of a modestly advanced fire-control system will land in the vicinity of the target, and this area accuracy prompted the development of the cluster bomb, in which the bomb casing is filled not with a unitary charge of explosive but with a number of specialized anti-tank submunitions. The bomb casing splits in the air at a predetermined moment, spilling its submunitions to fall to the ground in a pattern that effectively saturates an area including the target tank.

Typical of such cluster bombs is a British weapon, the Hunting BL755 that was introduced in 1972. The weapon weighs 582 lb (264 kg), and its casing contains 147 submunitions to provide a high 'kill' probability. When the bomb is dropped the primary striker is armed and, after a set interval, this fires the primary cartridge which rapidly generates the gas pressure to blow off the two-part bomb body skins and then fires the main gas cartridge: this latter ejects the submunitions, which are accommodated seven to each of the weapon's 21 bays. Submunition ejection from each of the bays is varied in velocity to ensure the attainment of the desired pattern on the ground. Each submunition has a diameter of 2.68 in (68 mm) and length of 5.91 in (0.15 m) as it is fired increasing to 1 ft 2 in (0.356 m) as the spring tail and nose probe deploy. The submunition is armed as it falls, and detonates on impact: the shaped-charge warhead can penetrate at least 250 mm (9.84 in) of armour.

Entering the service in 1987, the Improved BL755 is a much enhanced version of the original BL755 (and possessing the same external dimensions and weights) but carrying considerably more powerful bomblets using the latest shaped-charge techniques. Each bomblet is still of 2.68-in (68-mm) diameter, but is 5.87 in (0.149 m) long as it is fired, lengthening to 2 ft 0.69 in (0.627 m) complete with extending nose probe and retarding parachute. The system makes full use of increased launch warplane attack accuracy, and the submunitions are retarded to increase their angle of attack, and thus their

Known in Italian army service as the VCC-1 Camillino, the Infantry Armoured Fighting Vehicle was evolved by OTO Melara from an American armoured personnel carrier, the prolific M113. The vehicle has two machine-guns (one 0.5-in/12.7-mm weapon for the main gunner located alongside the commander at the front of the fighting compartment, and one 0.3-in/7.62-mm weapon for a machine-gunner above the rear of the fighting compartment), and the five embarked infantrymen can also fire their weapons from inside the close-down vehicle. In this guise the AIFV is a mechanized Infantry Fighting Vehicle of only limited capability, but greater firepower derives from the installation of an Emerson Improved TOW System with an elevating twin-tube launcher/sight system for the BGM-71 anti-tank missile. (*MARS*)

armour-penetrating capability.

The US Air Forces' equivalent to the BL755 is the 'Rockeye II' cluster bomb, but the American forces also have a number of considerably more advanced weapons at their disposal. Typical of these latest anti-armour weapons is the CBU-97/B cluster bomb. This is the 914-lb (414.6-kg) so-called Sensor-Fused Weapon (SFW) intended to enter production in the 1990s to provide US tactical warplanes with the ability to make direct attacks on armoured formations. Each SFW is 7 ft 8 in (2.337 m) long and comprises an SUU-64/B Tactical Munitions Dispenser carrying a load of ten BLU-108/B submunitions: when released by the dispenser (under the control of a timer or altitude fuse) each of these deploys a parachute to slow its descent to a pre-set altitude, where a retro-rocket is fired to drive the pack upwards again, spinning rapidly so that the BLU-108/B's four Avo Skeet warheads are articulated outward on levers and then released to fall individually, oscillating so that each unit's infra-red sensor can search for a target within

an area of about 4,800 sq yards (4,015 m^2) immediately below it; if no target is detected, the Skeet detonates just above the ground to cause blast and fragment damage to any soft-skinned target in the vicinity.

The Skeet is the world's first production weapon of the 'self-forging fragment' variety, wobbling through the air so that its onboard sensor can detect the heat of a tank, whereupon the guidance system aligns the Skeet with the target and then detonates a transverse explosive sheet that imparts very high velocity to a 5.25-in (133-m) diameter slab of copper, iron, tantalum and uranium alloy, at the same time turning it into a streamlined self-forging fragment that hits the tank's weakest armour with a speed of up to 9,000 ft (2,743 m) per second.

As indicated above, the cluster bomb was developed largely to provide an area-saturation weapon that would obviate the lack of terminal accuracy with free-fall bombs. Yet the ready availability and comparative cheapness of such unitary free-fall weapons was still attractive and early experience in the

365

Vietnam War, in which the USA was involved between 1961 and 1973, persuaded the US Air Force to expend considerable effort from the mid-1960s in the creation of a programme to improve the terminal accuracy of 'free-fall bombs. This led to the Texas Instruments 'Paveway' series of laser-guided bombs, of which the first were introduced in 1967 after the initial release of a laser-guided development weapon in 1965.

The designation 'Paveway I' is used for a series of add-on laser-homing kits, which are marked-target seekers and associated control surfaces. Each kit, designed to be added on the nose of the basic bomb, weighed about 30 lb (13.6 kg) and increased the bomb's overall length by some 6 in (0.15 m): the complete unit was in fact 3 ft 4 in (1.01 m) long, but this was offset by a reduction in the length of the tail surfaces, which were fixed surfaces of trapezoidal planform. The kit could be fitted to standard low-drag bombs for maximum accuracy when used in conjunction with an air- or ground-based laser designator. Several prototype kits were evolved, but the only two to enter service were the KMU-351A/B and KMU-388A/B, resulting in two weapons in the Guided Bomb Unit category, namely the GBU-10 'Paveway I' with the KMU-351A/B on the 2,000-lb

(907-kg) Mk 84 bomb and the GBU-12 'Paveway I' with the KMU-388A/B on the 500-lb (227-kg) Mk 82 bomb. The 'Paveway I' soon proved in operations from 1968 that its primary benefit, other than the very high degree of terminal accuracy, was that the launch warplane needed no modification to carry the weapon and after weapon release could depart from the target area unless it was the laser-designator machine.

Entering service in 1980, the 'Paveway II' is an improved series based on the same basic concept but with a simpler (thus cheaper) guidance package and a folding wing group (comprising spring-open extensions to the fixed tail fins for extra manoeuvrability and additional horizontal range) added at the tail. There are several members of this important family, but the only one used in the anti-tank role is the GBU-12B/C/D 'Paveway II' based on the Mk 82 bomb. In each case the weapon functions in a manner basically similar to that of the 'Paveway I' series: the gimballed laser seeker at the extreme nose is aligned by its ring tail with the velocity vector of the falling bomb, and detects laser radiation reflected from the 'illuminated' target, the different strengths of the reflections on each of its four internal quadrants being passed to the computer for the generation of commands

The USSR was one of the first proponents of the mechanized infantry fighting vehicle concept with machines such as these BMP-1s. The main armament is a turreted 73-mm (2.87-in) low-pressure gun firing a HEAT projectile in the anti-tank role. Further capability is provided by the installation of a launcher for the AT-3 'Sagger' or AT-4 'Spigot' anti-tank missile. (*MARS*)

The West German army's Marder heavyweight mechanized infantry combat vehicle is now elderly in basic design but is still a potent fighting vehicle. In addition to its crew of three and six embarked infantrymen, the Marder has a turreted 20-mm cannon forward of the infantry compartment and a remotely controlled 7.62-mm (0.3-in) machine-gun above the right rear of the infantry compartment. (*MARS*)

signalled to the cruciform of canard control fins. Operational service revealed that while the system was extremely accurate, the use of a 'bang/bang' control system, in which the control surfaces are moved to their maximum deflection position each time a command is received, increased drag and therefore reduced range.

The 'Paveway III' series entered service in 1987 for use mainly in high-threat areas and therefore fitted with fold-out rear wings for increased stand-off launch range.

These terminally guided bombs are in effect unpowered guided missiles, but greater stand-off range and higher short-range terminal velocity can be achieved with true guided missiles. Typical of the Western air-to-surface missile used in the anti-tank role by warplanes such as the Fairchild Republic A-10A Thunderbolt II, which can carry two triplets of such weapons under its wings, is the Hughes AGM-65 Maverick that is still in large-scale production and development. Authorization to proceed with this small but exceptionally capable multi-role ASM was given in 1965, the object being the creation, production and deployment of a more advanced but still subsonic type to replace the Martin Marietta AGM-12 Bullpup. Development and initial production proceeded without undue problem, and the AGM-65A entered service with the US Air Force during 1972 as the first production variant. The Maverick adheres to the standard config-

uration of Hughes missiles in its large cylindrical body carrying a cruciform of swept low-aspect-ratio delta wings, and a cruciform of rectangular control surfaces close-coupled to the rear of the wings. The AGM-65 series is the smallest fully guided ASM family in the US inventory, and certainly the West's most important weapon of its type, largely because in all its versions it is a completely fire-and-forget type. The AGM-65A is the initial TV imaging version (often known as the TV Maverick), and suffers the tactical disadvantage of low magnification for its nose-mounted camera, forcing the pilot of the launch warplane to fly close to the target before he can secure a solid lock before missile launch and subsequent automatic attack. Once he is in the vicinity of the target, the pilot selects a missile and this process initiates the missile's gyro, which illuminates a light in the cockpit as it runs up to speed. The pilot then acquires a target optically and activates the nose-mounted TV camera. The image from this camera is displayed on a cockpit screen, the pilot brings the target image into this display by slewing the camera in the missile nose or aligning his warplane so that the target appears in his sight or HUD, depresses the tracking switch and waits until the target image is centred on the cockpit display before releasing the switch to lock the image into the missile's guidance package, and finally fires the missile for its autonomous attack. The AGM-65A's data include a diame-

A vehicle similar to the AMX-10RC in its approximation to a wheeled tank is another French machine, the ERC armoured car. This has appeared in a number of forms, but is here epitomized by ERC 90 F1 Lynx vehicles of the Mexican army. In this model, the standard 6 x 6 hull is topped by a manually operated turret accommodating a 90-mm (3.54-in) gun controlled via a modestly advanced fire-control system. (*MARS*)

seeker and digital processing as well as a more powerful 300-lb (136-kg) Avco penetrating blast/fragmentation warhead.

The Maverick may be taken as typical of the modern ASM in its anti-tank capability, and other such weapons have been developed by France and the USSR (now CIS). Another type of ASM for the anti-tank role is the wire-guided missile originally intended for ground-launched use over medium ranges, and thus considerably lighter than the purpose-designed ASM. The capabilities of such weapons matured rapidly, and the type was then adapted for air launch by dedicated anti-tank helicopters now epitomized by the Bell AH-1 HueyCobra and McDonnell Douglas Helicopters AH-64 Apache from the USA, the Westland Lynx from the UK, the Aérospatiale AS 565 Panther from France, the Eurocopter Tiger/Tiger from France and Germany, the Agusta A 129 Mangusta from Italy, and the Mil Mi-24 'Hind' from the USSR (now CIS). The ease with which such missiles and their guidance packages can be attached to light helicopters, moreover, means that small machines such as the Aérospatiale SA 341/342 Gazelle, MBB BO 105 and McDonnel Douglas Helicopters MD-500 Defender can be outfitted with four or six missiles such as the Euromissile MILAN and the Hughes BGM-71 TOW. These are based on semi-automatic command to line-of-sight guidance, which requires the operator to keep his sight on the target: the guidance package thus watches the flare on the missile's tail and issues commands to make the missile and target coincide in space to ensure impact and the optimum detonation of the anti-tank warhead.

The TOW (Tube-launched Optically-tracked Wire-guided) weapon is currently the anti-tank missile most widely used in ground- and air-launched applications. The earliest model was the BGM-71A Basic TOW that entered service in 1970. The missile is a heavyweight of its type, and has proved its capabilities in several wars as a result of its reliability, high degree of accuracy, and a warhead that has shown itself able to penetrate 600 mm (23.6 in) of armour, but the range of this initial model is limited to 3,280

ter of 1 ft 0 in (0.305 m) and length of 8 ft 2 in (2.49 m), weights of 463 lb (210 kg) for the complete missile and 125 lb (56.7 kg) for the shaped-charge warhead containing 83 lb (37.6 kg) of explosive, supersonic speed and range that varies from a minimum figure of 985 yards (900 m) to a maximum figure of 26,400 yards (24,140 m).

The Maverick has also been developed and produced in a number of variants with a larger warhead and/or different guidance packages suiting the type for a number of other roles, but the variants used most frequently for the anti-tank role as the AGM-65A, the AGM-65B or Scene-Magnification Maverick introduced in 1980 with double the image magnification of the AGM-65A to overcome some of the earlier version's tactical disadvantages and provide target acquisition, lock-on and firing at a longer slant range and more quickly than is possible with the AGM-65A, the AGM-65D or Imaging Infra-Red Maverick for superior operational capability at night or in rain and mist as well as features such as a lock-on range of at least twice that of the AGM-65A/B and the ability to distinguish between live (and therefore hot) targets and dead (and therefore cold) decoys or hulks, and the AGM-65E or Laser Maverick with the Hughes tri-service laser

yards (3,000 m) by the length of its guidance wires. The BGM-71A has a diameter of 6 in (152 mm) and a length of 3 ft 10.25 in (1.174 m), its weights are 49.6 lb (22.5 kg) for the complete missile and 8.6 lb (3.9 kg) for the warhead that includes a 5.3-lb (2.4-kg) shaped charge, and performance figures comprising a speed of 700 mph (1,127 km/h) and a range that varies from a minimum figure of 70 yards (65 m) to a maximum figure of 3,280 yards (3000 m)

The BGM-71B Extended-Range TOW is the improved version produced from 1976 with greater range through the lengthening of the guidance wires to 4,100 yards (3,750 m). Introduced during 1981 in response to the development of Soviet tanks with improved armour, the BGM-71C Improved TOW is an interim model carrying an updated and improved warhead with LX-14 explosive and a telescoping nose probe 1 ft 3 in (381 mm) long: this latter extends in flight to ensure a perfect stand-off distance for the detonation of the improved shaped-charge warhead, which can puncture 700 mm (27.6 in) of armour. The model has a length of 5 ft 10 in (1.778 m) with the probe extended, and weighs 56.65 lb (25.7 kg). Introduced in 1983

as the standard US weapon for tackling the latest Soviet tanks at long range, the BGM-71D TOW 2 has a guidance system hardened against countermeasures, an improved double-base motor offering about 30 per cent greater impulse, and a 13.2-lb (6-kg) warhead increased in diameter from 5 to 6 in (127 to 152 mm) and provided with a nose probe 1 ft 9.25 in (540 mm) long to ensure optimum stand-off detonation distance for an armour penetration figure of 800 mm (31.5 in). This significant variant weighs 61.95 lb (28.1 kg) and, though it can be fired from the original analog-electronics launcher, it is designed for use with an improved digital-electronics launcher fitted with thermal as well as optical sights, and with a more advanced guidance package.

During the 1980s Hughes proposed three developments of the already powerful TOW 2 weapon. The first of these to enter service, in 1987, was the BGM-71E TOW 2A with an improved direct-attack warhead with tandem charges to defeat reactive and then core armour: a small explosive charge on the nose probe is designed to trigger the detonation of the target's ERA (Explosive Reactive Armour), so opening the way for the

One of the primary advantages offered by the creation of a well-designed armoured personnel carrier or mechanized infantry vehicle is its ready adaptability to alternative roles. This concept provides virtual identity of battlefield mobility, simplified crew training, and reduced logistic holding. This vehicle is the Radarpanzer TÜR, a derivative of the German Marder MICV with an elevating arm carrying the antenna of a surveillance radar, and the infantry compartment heightened and adapted for the radar display and control units. (*MARS*)

By adding an FL-13 oscillating turret with its 105-mm (4.13-in) gun to the chassis of the Saurer 4K 7FA tracked armoured personnel carrier, the Austrians have developed the SK 105 Küassier as a simple yet effective light tank offering moderately good firepower and good cross-country mobility. (*MARS*)

gas/metal vapour jet of the missile's main HEAT charge. The variant is externally identical to the BGM-71D, but later weapons also introduced the British-developed FITOW guidance and fusing improvements for an additional 'pop up' top attack as the missile overflies the target tank: the tandem warheads (using explosively created self-forging fragment technology) are therefore arranged to fire obliquely forward and downward, the first triggering the target's reactive armour and the second thus having a clear path to penetrate the armour proper. The warhead package also contains a dual-mode sensor package for optimum detonation of the warheads. This sensor package includes optronic and magnetic components, the former to acquire the target by shape and the latter by its iron content. Though the TOW 2A works in its basic elements, doubts about its real operational utility have been expressed as operators have found it very difficult to control the nose-heavy missile.

Entering service in 1991 as the second improved variant of the TOW 2, the BGM-71F TOW 2B has a blunt nose carrying a dual guidance package (passive IR and active millimetric-wavelength radar) and a dual warhead system employing explosively formed penetrators. The third improvement proposed by Hughes has a wire-less command system of unspecified type, supersonic speed and a range of 10,000 yards (9,145 m). Other improvements in the pipeline for the TOW series include a new motor to reduce the missile's time of flight, and hence the launch helicopter's window of vulnerability. The new motor will also extend range and prevent the 'pitch up' that occurs as current missiles reach their maximum range.

It is also worth noting that in addition to their basic infantry-operated ground role, weapons such as the TOW and MILAN have also been adopted for tank destroyer versions of armoured personnel carriers and infantry fighting vehicles. These generally carry a launcher unit (complete with sight) that can be raised above the hull so that the vehicle can attack its prey from a hull-down position. Once a target has been destroyed, the launcher unit is retracted so that the crew can dispose of the launcher for the expended round and load a fresh round from the ready-use supply embarked in the erstwhile infantry volume.

As can be seen from the section above, the types and characteristics of modern anti-tank weapons, both air and ground-launched, are great and formidable in the extreme. The overall performance of such modern weapons has persuaded some people that the day of the tank is effectively at an end. The tank, such critics argue, has lost its freedom to operate effectively on the battlefield because minefields (either permanent or laid in short order by special vehicles or even by fixed-wing warplanes or helicopters in times of crisis) can be used to channel tank formations into killing zones where they can be engaged decisively be heavy artillery, air and ground-launched missiles, and the increasingly sophisticated range of air-launched dispenser weapons. To such critics, the decisive factor is basically the cost-effectiveness equation that places on one side the vulnerable tank that is expensive and therefore impossible to produce in adequate numbers, and on the other the diversity and increasing effectiveness of anti-tank weapons of all varieties, which are comparatively cheap and can therefore be produced in relatively vast quantities for static, land-mobile and air-mobile use.

The argument of the tank critics is a telling one, and clearly reflects a true tactical situation. But the tank proponents claim that for the lack of the concrete evidence provided by modern high-intensity battlefield operations with the latest weapons on each side, the position of the critics has been overstated. The proponents of the tank therefore aver that the tank is not as vulnerable as its critics claim, and that its vulnerability is in fact declining as new technology is brought into play. This technology is of an increasingly sophisticated nature and is claimed to offer new levels of firepower, protection and mobility. There is no doubting that the tank proponents' claim is also true to a very large degree: for example, the HEAT warhead has long been thought to provide the key to the tank's destruction at medium and long range, but the efficiency of this type of warhead has been steadily eroded by the adoption of features such as skirts, spaced armour, composite armour, laminate armour and reactive armour. The technological battle between the tank and its killers sways back and fourth, as is always the case with weapons and their counters, and while any improvement in tank technology calls forth the skills of the anti-tank weapon designer to produce a solution, that in turn spurs the tank designer to further effort, etc.

That most armies do not necessarily share the optimism of those who claim the tank is obsolete as a primary weapon seems to be indicated by the pace with which they continue to press ahead with tank development. This is now a lengthy and highly complex business, and the advent in recent years of a number of major battle tanks has produced a temporary plateau in the development cycle in which designers are using their time to investigate a number of alternatives to the conventional, weighty and expensive main

Air-to-surface missiles such as this Hughes AGM-65E Maverick now give modern warplanes a potent anti-tank capability. Whereas older ASMs had to be guided to their target by an operator in the launch warplane, modern weapons, such as the Maverick, are of the 'fire-and-forget' type using either an internal guidance system or, in the case of the Laser Maverick, a semi-active system relying on laser-illumination of the target by a third-party designator. (*MARS*)

battle tank. This reflects in part the potential lethality of the latest anti-tank weapons, but also the emergence of new technologies that may allow the designers to strike off at a profitable tangent.

From the mid-1980s West Germany (just Germany since the unification of the previous separate East Germany and West Germany in 1990) was looking seriously at the possibilities for a new main battle tank of the highest qualitative standard for service towards the end of the century. West Germany was collaborating with France on a main battle tank for the 1990s, but this project fell through in 1982 when the differing service entry dates required by the partners became too great: France wanted an in-service date of 1991 while West Germany thought in terms of 1996. After the collapse of the collaborative project the West German defence ministry called for submissions for a new Leopard 3 main battle tank, Krauss-Maffei and Krupp MaK each submitting five different options: an altogether new tank, a Leopard 2 revised with a low-profile turret accommodating a two-man crew and an automatically loaded 120-mm (4.72-in) gun, a Leopard 2 revised with a low-profile turret accommodating a three-man

crew including a seated gunner supported by a loading-assistance device, a modified version of the Leopard 2, and an additional batch of Leopard 2 including all the current developments. In 1984 Krauss-Maffei was contracted to study three developments on the Leopard 2 chassis, while Krupp MaK was alternatively contracted to study an all-new vehicle. West Germany planned to complete the studies by 1989, with full-scale development of the best option following between 1990 and 1995 for a production launch in 1988 to replace the Leopard 1 with 1,300 of these Kampfwagen 90 main battle tanks. No other details have been released, though West Germany did announce that the KW 90 would be the last of a series of new armoured vehicles to include a tank-destroyer with a 120-mm (4.72-in) smooth-bore gun, a missile-armed anti-tank/helicopter vehicle, and a mechanized infantry fighting vehicle. The programme was later cancelled.

India is typical of the countries that are now entering the field of main battle tank design, in India's case after cutting its teeth on licensed production (the Vijayanta followed by the T-72). The requirement for the Arjun was issued as far back as 1972 and work began in

1974. The first prototype was revealed in 1985 with an Indian-developed 120-mm (4.72-in) rifled gun, an Indian fire-control system based on that developed for the Vijayanta upgrade programme and including a laser rangefinder and thermal imaging sights, hydropneumatic suspension and a weight in the order of 60,000 kg (132,275 lb). It had originally been planned to use a 1,500-shp (1,118-ekW) gas turbine, but the plan was then revised to a diesel engine of similar rating. With turbo-charging, however, current models of this Indian engine are rated at only 1,000 hp (746 kW), and even if tardy development increases this figure to the originally specified figure the 15,000-kg (33,069-lb) increase in the tank's weights will result in performance and agility far inferior to the desired levels. The Arjun prototypes were in fact completed with German engines, transmissions and tracks, which were retained for the early production tanks, which entered initial service at about the turn of the century. The Arjun weighs 58,500 kg (128,968 lb) and is powered by an MTU 838 Ka-501 diesel engine rated at 1,400 hp (1,044 kW).

The increasing cost of tank development has promoted continued efforts towards international programmes. These have been singularly unsuccessful to date, but nationally inspired efforts have recently been largely supplanted by commercially led attempts to develop tanks with a broader base of international market appeal. Typical of this approach to shared risk-taking and lower unit costs through large-scale sales to smaller countries were the Franco-German Clovis multi-role combat tank, the Anglo-American VFM 5 main battle tank, and the Anglo-German Main Battle Tank Mk 7. The 32,100-kg (70,767-lb) Clovis was a comparatively lightweight competitor that combined a West German hull (based on that of the Marder mechanized infantry combat vehicle) with the French Fives-Cail Babcock FL-20 two-man turret mounting a 105-mm (4.13-in) main gun and a 20-mm co-axial cannon. The Clovis reached only the prototype stage, and the same applied to the VFM 5. This was another lightweight turning the scales at only 43,550 lb (19,754 kg), and combined the

FMC-produced hull of the Close Combat Vehicle (Light) with a Vickers Defence systems three-man turret armed with a 105-mm (4.13-in) Low Recoil Force gun and fitted with a Marconi integrated fore-control system that provided full gun stabilization and a high-quality fire-control solution based on a laser rangefinder, stabilized day and night sight, a muzzle reference system and a ballistic computer. The Main Battle Tank Mk 7 was an altogether more formidable piece of equipment that combined a hull based on that of the West German Leopard 2 with the turret designed by Vickers for its abortive Valiant main battle tank. The result weighed 54,640 kg (120,459 lb), and the turret carried a 120-mm (4.72-in) L11 series rifled gun provided with full stabilization and control by a Marconi Centaur advanced fire-control system. The turret was fitted with Chobham laminate armour over its front and sides, and other advanced items were an NBC system and an automatic fire- and explosion-suppression system. The Vickers Main Battle Tank Mk 7 completed exhaustive trials with excellent results, but was not ordered into production.

Though the USSR was obviously committed to the development of new tanks closing still further, or indeed eliminating the quali-

Long-range rocket systems such as the Multiple-Launch Rocket System use a high-quality fire-control system to ensure that its unguided rockets deliver their multiple payloads with great accuracy over long ranges. (*MARS*)

tative gap between its service tanks and those of the Western alliance, no details of such Soviet developments have been released in the open literature on the subject. It is likely, however, that they parallel American developments along a number of interesting avenues. During the late 1980s the economic pressure of trying to match the American defence capability finally caught up with the Soviets at a time when there were increasing demands for political reform, and this resulted in the end of the USSR. This was transformed into the Commonwealth of Independent States, a loose federation of autonomous republics that has since been riven by civil and 'international' wars, fundamental political, economic and nationalistic disagreements between Russia and the new states on its eastern and southern borders, and devastating financial problems and the new political grouping seeks to adopt a capitalist free-market economy in place of the earlier communist centralized economy.

This has in itself devastated the current military potential of the states of the erstwhile USSR, and has meant the wholesale cancellation of many military development programmes. Moreover, most of the USSR's previous satellites in the Warsaw Pact have now become independent in fact as well as in theory, and have in general turned their backs on new Russian military equipment as and when their original Soviet weapons begin to wear out or become obsolete. This reduced market for Russian weapons has further eroded the numbers of each type which the Russian factories can hope to produce, increasing unit cost to the point at which such weapons become less and less affordable.

The net effect of these totally fundamental changes, evidenced by the creation of the CIS out of the USSR, has been to end the 'Cold War' between the two previous superpowers and bring to an end some 40 years of military confrontation between the alliances headed by the USA and the USSR. An immediate consequence of this easing of world tension has been the so-called 'peace dividend', resulting from drastically curtailed military expenditure on each side of the now-fallen 'Iron Curtain'. The effect of this on the CIS has been mentioned above, and a similar result is readily discernible in the countries of the North Atlantic Treaty Organization alliance, who have all trimmed their military establishments in accordance with, if not in fact further than, the levels deemed adequate for a time of eased tensions. So far as the tank is

The interior of any modern tank is inevitably cramped and cluttered as the designers try to cram the maximum amount of equipment into the smallest possible volume. The very sophistication of modern sighting and fire-control systems complicates this problem, for such equipments need frequent servicing, and the skill of the design team is taxed to the limit in using ergonomic design principles to ensure that the crew men have enough comfort to avoid early degradation of their combat performance. (*MARS*)

concerned, this trimming of the military establishment had also meant a drastic cut in research and development budgets as finance ministries decide that armies must now make do with current equipment rather than anticipate large-scale production of more advanced weapon systems intended to provide a qualitative edge over the USSR.

It is as yet uncertain what effect this curtailment will have on the US Army's armoured equipment. Well satisfied with its current M1 Abrams and its development potential, the Americans were pushing forward with the evolution of a number of slimmed-down tank concepts to provide lightweight operational vehicles that also opened the way for other developments: the rationale for these lightweight vehicles is greater tactical mobility combined with a high level of operational and strategic air-portability so that far-flung forces can be equipped from centralized stocks in the USA rather than having to rely on prepositioned heavy weapons as is now the case, for example, with the US Marine Corps force earmarked for operations in Norway or the Central Common (née Rapid-Deployment Joint Task Force) earmarked for larger-scale operations in the Middle and Near Easts.

The service that has led the way in calling for the new vehicles is the US Army, whose programme centred on the unfunded but potentially profitable Armored Gun System requirement. FMC, a major producer of the lighter types of armoured vehicle, responded with its Close Combat Vehicle (Light) prototype, which could perhaps be linked to a tank destroyer in many respects as it had a heavy turret-mounted gun on a lightweight tracked chassis for an overall weight of 42,800 lb (19,414 kg). The design requirement called for mobility equal to that of the M1 main battle tank and M2 Bradley infantry fighting vehicle, a main gun capable of defeating any vehicle able to engage it, air-portability in the Lockheed C-141 StarLifter logistic and Lockheed C-5 Galaxy strategic transport aircraft, and the facility for LAPES (Low-Altitude Parachute Extraction System) delivery by the Lockheed C-130 Hercules tactical transport aircraft. Additional requirements were high reliability and an early in-service date by use of proved components wherever possible.

The first CCVL prototype was completed in August 1985. The hull was of welded aluminium armour with a layer of steel, and made extensive use of components from the M113 armoured personnel carrier and M2 infantry fighting vehicle. The easily removed power-pack comprised a 575-hp (429-kW) Detriot Diesel 6V-92TA diesel and a General Electric hydromechanical transmission as used respectively in the Heavy Expanded Mobility Tactical Truck and M2. The low-profile turret was again built of welded aluminium armour with a layer of steel, and was armed with a 105-mm (4.13-in) M68A1 rifled gun as used in the M60A3 and M1, firing the standard US range of ammunition for this ordnance. The commander and gunner were located to the left of the weapon, the area to its right being occupied by the FMC Northern Ordnance Division automatic loader that held 19 of the CCVL's 43 rounds and allowed a fire rate of twelve rounds per minute. The turret and gun drives were basically similar to those supplied by Cadillac Gage for the M1A1, and the fire-control system was similar to that in the M1 series with a Computing Devices of Canada computer, various sensors, a laser rangefinder and stablized thermal imaging and optical sights supplied by Hughes Aircraft.

To the same basic requirement Teledyne Continental produced another three-man machine, the 42,000-lb (19,051-kg) Direct Fire Support Vehicle. The prototype was first trialled as a complete unit in 1985 after separate evaluation of the hull and turret. Though the DFSV had the same conceptual feature as the CCVL in its use of a 105-mm (4.13-in) rifled gun with an automatic loader, higher levels of crew survivability were provided by making the main armament an unmanned, trunnion-mounted system above the hull, so that most of the armour could be reserved for protection of the crew compartment. The powerpack was located in the extreme front to provide extra protection for the crew, and comprised a 500-hp (373-kW) Cummins VTA-903T diesel and the same hydro-mechanical transmission as used in the CCVL. The drive sprockets were at the front,

375

The AAI Rapid-Deployment Light Tank is perhaps a harbinger of future tank development practices, for the crew are all located under cover in the low hull, and the armament is a 75-mm (2.95-in) ARES high-velocity gun in a remotely controlled mounting and fed from a 60-round magazine/automatic loader system. (*MARS*)

and the running gear on each side comprised five road wheels with hydropneumatic suspension, two track-return rollers and a rear idler. The hull was made of steel, steel and ceramic composite, aluminium armour and Kevlar, with applique ceramic for enhanced protection in key areas, and accommodated the drive at the front with the commander and gunner side-by-side behind and slightly above him. The remotely controlled main gun was located above the hull rear, and had a long-recoil system and automatic loader developed by ARES: the latter was a 9-round unit between the commander and gunner in the turret basket, feeding rounds automatically to the loader behind the gun breech and being itself topped up from two 10-round revolver magazines in the hull rear; there was also a reserve supply of 15 rounds for manual loading into the revolvers as required. The turret and gun drives were basically those of the M2 Bradley, while the fire-control system was that of the M60A3 augmented as required by thermal sights.

A lighter vehicle was developed entirely as a private venture by the AAI Corporation to meet the supposed needs of the Rapid Deployment Force. This Rapid Deployment Force Light Tank (RDF/LT) used experience gained by the manufacturer with its High Survivability Test Vehicle (Light), and was an all-aluminium vehicle with a crew of three, a weight of 29,600 lb (13,427 kg) and armed with a 75-mm

(2.95-in) ARES cannon and automatic loader (fed from a 60-round hull magazine) in a low mounting immediately behind the crew compartment, or in a one-man turret of very low profile. High performance was claimed for the vehicle and its armament, and for possible export orders the manufacturer developed a revised model with a two-man turret and 76-mm (3-in) M32 gun as fitted in the M41 Walker Bulldog light tank.

All these vehicles were notable for their standard suspension systems, high power-to-weight ratios for great agility and good all-round performance, low-profile weapon mountings with automatic loaders, high levels of protection through the use of composite armour of different types, and generally solid-state electronics in their advanced systems. The result, even at this largely experimental level, was a series of vehicles offering great fire-power relative to vehicle weight, good protection, high levels of mobility and performance, and low observability through their adoption of a low-profile silhouette and an increasing level of thermal mitigation. Such tendencies are certain to follow in the next generation of main battle tanks, to be joined later by more advanced guns (perhaps using liquid propellants and firing more capable projectiles with the possibility of terminal guidance).

As the longer-term importance of developing more advanced and therefore more expensive tanks is questioned in the light of decreased international tensions, a greater emphasis is being placed on simpler and therefore less costly machines. A case in point is the 'peacekeeping' effort undertaken from the early 1990s by the United Nations in the former Yugoslavia, where several civil wars have and are being waged between the Bosnian, Croat and Serb minorities after the collapse of the federal state. Heavy armour would be inappropriate at the psychological as well as the technical level for the peace-keeping role, but the British, French and Ukrainian contingents have made effective use of machines such as heavyweight wheeled reconnaissance vehicles and mechanized infantry combat vehicles.

The wheeled reconnaissance vehicles can be regarded as the modern counterpart of the armoured car that remained useful up to the period immediately following the Second World War, and has all-wheel drive for good cross-country mobility. But whereas the armoured car was generally armed to light tank standard, the modern reconnaissance vehicle is armed to medium tank standard and, in some cases, even to main battle tank standard. The type is usually outfitted with a modern fire-control system, but is compar-atively lightly protected as it relies on speed and agility rather than armour as its primary means of defence. The calibre of the armament and the sophistication of the associated fire-control system also mean that such reconnaissance vehicles can gainfully be employed in the complementary fire-support and tank destroyer roles.

Typical of modern reconnaissance vehicles are the Belgian 17,500-kg (38,580-lb) BN Constructions SIBMAS AFSV-90 with 6 x 6 drive and a 90-mm (3.54-in) gun, the Brazilian 13,400-kg (29,541-lb) ENGESA EE-9 Cascavel Mk IV with 6 x 6 drive and a 90-mm (3.54-in) gun, the French 15,880-kg (35,009-lb) GIAT AMX-10RC with 6 x 6 layout and a 105-mm (4.13-in) gun, the French 10,000-kg (22,046-lb) Panhard ERC 90 F4 Sagaie 2 with 6 x 6 drive and a 90-mm (3.54-in) gun, the French 13,500-kg (29,762-lb) Renault VBC 90 with 6 x 6 drive and a 90-mm (3.54-in) gun, and the Italian 8,000-kg (17,637-lb) IVECO Tipo 6616/90 with 4 x 4 drive and a 90-mm (3.54-in) gun.

The mechanized infantry fighting vehicle is really the modern development of the armoured personnel carrier with the same provision for an embarked detachment of infantry, but with the APC's small manually operated machine-gun turret replaced by a larger powered turret accommodating the

The latest British light armoured fighting vehicle is the Warrior MICV, which carries as its main armament the powerful 30-mm RARDEN cannon with excellent capabilities against other light AFVs. (MARS)

An important feature in the design of any AFV turret is the angle of depression it allows the main armament: the larger this angle, the more effectively the vehicle can adopt a hull-down position. Such a hull-down position reduces the vehicle's detectability and vulnerability without sacrifice of firepower. This is an ERC reconnaissance vehicle, whose gun can be depressed to − 8°. (*MARS*)

commander and gunner, a cannon between 20 and 30 mm in calibre and often fitted with a two-axis stabilization system for accurate fire on the move, and a modestly advanced fire-control system. There are a number of wheeled MICVs, but the most capable vehicles of this type are based on a fully tracked chassis. Typical of this breed are the British 24,494-kg (54,000-lb) GKN Warrior with a 30-mm cannon, Chinese/British 16,000-kg (35,273-lb) NORINCO/Vickers NVH-1 with a 25-mm cannon, the French 14,500-kg (31,996-lb) GIAT AMX-10P with a 20-mm cannon, the German 30,000-kg (66,138-lb) Thyssen Henschel/Krupp MaK Marder with a 20-mm cannon and a remotely controlled 7.62-mm (0.3-in) machine-gun, the Italian 19,000-kg (41,887-lb) IVECO/OTO Melara VCC-80 with a 25-mm cannon, the Italian 14,650-kg (32,297-lb) OTO Melara C13 with a 20- or 25-mm cannon, the Swiss 22,300-kg (49,162-lb) MOWAG Improved Tornado with a 25-mm cannon, the Soviet 14,600-kg (32,187-lb) BMP-2 with a 30-mm cannon, and the US 22,590-kg (49,800-lb) FMC M2 Bradley with a 25-mm cannon and a two-tube launcher for seven Hughes BGM-71 TOW anti-tank missiles.

Such reconnaissance vehicles and MICVs can in no way replace the tank under conditions of high-intensity warfare, but certainly have an important role to play as tank substitute under the current peacekeeping and other low-intensity warfare conditions.

The disappearance of the USSR and its allies as a threat to the other superpower bloc headed by the USA has eased world tensions, but has certainly not done anything to reduce the number of smaller wars, which have indeed flared in many areas. Quite apart from those in the southern republics of the erstwhile USSR and in the former Yugoslavia, the mid-1990s witnessed warfare in Rwanda and Aden, and 1991 saw a successful UN-led effort to expel the Iraqi forces which had invaded and occupied Kuwait in 1990.

The front-line between the Iraqis and the US coalition extended west from Kuwait in ideal terrain for tank fighting, and the area witnessed the world's greatest ever concentration of armour. Yet there was to be little tank-against-tank combat, for Iraq's ability to wage a sustained land battle was virtually eliminated by the coalition's overwhelming air strength even before the coalition launched its 100-hour land offensive on 4 February 1991. Spearheaded by US, British, French, Saudi Arabian and Egyptian armoured units, the coalition army swept forward against negligible opposition and scored an overwhelming victory.

The war with Iraq saw the heaviest armoured fighting since the Second World War, but was so one-sided that few lessons could be drawn from it. Even so, the fighting confirmed that the tank was still very far from dead.

One of the countries that is still developing and producing main battle tanks in substantial numbers at the beginning of the 21st century is China. The country's chief exponent of tank design and manufacture is NORINCO, otherwise known as the China North Industries Corporation, which operates on what can be described as an evolutionary rather than innovative basis.

Thus the Type 69-II was further developed as the Type 79, initially known as the Type 69-III and still described by this designation in some publications. Only about 800 of the Type 79 were produced for the Chinese army, and this number was possibly as low as 520 tanks, although export orders were also solicited. The vehicle is basically a development of the Type 69-II with improvements in aspects such as firepower, fire-control system, night-vision equipment and communications equipment. The changes raise the tank's weight by 1,500 kg (3,307 lb) to 37,500 kg (82,672 lb), yielding a maximum road speed of 50 km/h (31 mph). The armament comprises a 105-mm (4.13-in) rifled gun fitted with a thermal sleeve and a fume extractor, one 7.62-mm (0.3-in) coaxial machine-gun and one 12.7-mm (0.5-in) local-defence and anti-aircraft machine-gun on the loader's cupola.

It was in 1978 that NORINCO began concept studies for a second-generation Chinese main battle tank, and the first prototypes started their trials in 1985. The new type is generally known as the Type 80, although the alternative designations Type 88 and Type 69-III have also been used for it. The primary improvements over the Types 69 and 79 incorporated in the Type 80 include the installation of a new computerized fire-control system for increased first-round hit probability, a laser rangefinder, a gun-stabilization system, passive night-vision equipment, a 105-mm rifled main gun, a new suspension system of the torsion-bar type with six road wheels on each side for increased cross-country mobility, an up-graded powerplant based on a more powerful diesel engine for increased power/weight ratio, and provision for the installation of a snorkel for deep fording. Among the Type 80's capabilities is the ability to engage a moving target from a stationary firing position.

Manufacture of the Type 80 (500 tanks for China and 20 or more vehicles for Burma) was completed by NORINCO during the 1990s, and China's export effort is now concentrated on more modern tanks such as the Type 85 and the Type 90 together with their variants.

In basic concept the 38,000-kg (83,774-lb) Type 80 is still very closely related to the Soviet tanks of the 1950s and 1960s. The hull is of all-welded steel construction with the driver's compartment at the front, the fighting compartment in the centre, and the engine and transmission at the rear. The driver sits at the front of the hull on the left-hand side under a single-piece hatch cover, which lifts and swings to the left when opened. The driver has two forward-vision periscopes for daylight operations, and one of these can be replaced by an infra-red or passive periscope for nocturnal operations.

Located in the centre of the vehicle, the cast turret carries the commander on the left with the gunner forward and below the commander and the loader on the right. As with the glacis, composite armour can be added for improved protection. The commander's cupola can be manually traversed through 360°, and has a

Created by General Dynamics Land System, a newcomer to the complex world of the armoured amphibious assault vehicle, the AAAV (Armored Amphibious Assault Vehicle) beat a design by United Defense LP, the previous incumbent in the field, to be selected for further development as successor to the current in-service AAV7A1. The AAAV(P) personnel transport will carry 17 or 18 US Marines in addition to its 3-man crew. The driver is located at the front of the hull on the left-hand side, and the two-man turret on the right-hand side carries a 30-mm cannon with two-axis stabilization and also a 7.62-mm (0.3-in) machine-gun. (*General Dynamics Land Systems*)

forward-opening hatch cover with two integral periscopes for observation to the sides. Ahead of the hatch cover are three day periscopes for observation over the frontal arc. The loader has a circular hatch cover opening to the left. The main armament comprises a 105-mm (4.13-in) rifled gun with 44 rounds of ammunition and is characterized by powered elevation in the arc between − 4.5° and +18°. The gun is basically similar in appearance to the Western L7 and M68 series weapons, and is fitted with both a fume extractor and a thermal sleeve. The gun can fire Western as well as Chinese ammunition whose types include the following NORINCO-developed rounds: APFSDS-T with a muzzle velocity of 1,455 m (4,774 ft) per second, HEAT-T with a muzzle velocity of 1,173.5 m (3,850 ft) per second, HESH with a muzzle velocity of 731.5m (2,400 ft) per second, HE with a muzzle velocity of 850 m (2,789 ft) per second and, the two more recently NORINCO-developed types, the Type 105-I and Type 105-II. Both of these employ a brass cartridge case: the Type 105-I ammunition produces a muzzle velocity of 1,455 m (4,774 ft) per second and has the claimed capability to penetrate 150 mm (5.91 in) of armour at an angle of 60° at a range of 2,000 m (2,185 yards), while the Type 105-II produces a muzzle velocity of 1,530 m (5,020 ft) per second for a claimed armour-

penetration capability of 150 mm at an angle of 71° at a range of 2,000 m (2,185 yards).

The secondary armament comprises the standard fit of one 7.62-mm (0.3-in) coaxial machine-gun to the right of the main gun with 2,250 rounds of ammunition, and one 12.7-mm (0.5-in) machine-gun on the loader's hatch for local-defence and anti-aircraft use with 500 rounds of ammunition. Located on each side of the turret are four forward-firing dischargers for smoke grenades, and a stowage basket runs around the sides and rear of the turret. As well as providing external carriage for non-combat equipment, the basket offers a measure of protection against HEAT projectiles, which would be detonated away from the turret's main armour.

The fire-control system includes a ballistic computer, a laser rangefinder integrated into a stabilized sight, sensors and a gun stabilization system, and the standard night-vision equipment is of the second-generation image intensification type.

The Type 80 is powered by a 700-hp (522-kW) Model VR36 diesel engine, up-graded to 730 hp (544 kW) in late-production vehicles. The engine exhausts via two circular outlets on the right-hand side of the hull, and fuel can be injected into these exhausts for the generation of a smoke screen. Two large and jettisonable drum tanks can be mounted over the hull's rear for additional range, and provision is made for an unditching beam at the rear of the hull under these tanks.

The torsion-bar suspension is based on the combination of six dual rubber-tyred road wheels, three track-return rollers, a rear-mounted drive sprocket and a front-mounted idler on each side. The upper part of the track on each side is covered by skirt armour. The tank's standard equipment includes an NBC system of the overpressure type, night-vision equipment for the commander, gunner and driver, internal and external communications gear, and an automatic explosion-suppression and fire-extinguishing system.

The sole variant of the Type 80 is the Type 80-II, otherwise known as the Type 88B, which differs from the baseline model only in its greater combat weight of 38,500 kg (84,877 lb), slightly increased length, and possibly a semi-

The AAAV is fabricated of welded aluminium alloy armour providing protection against 14.5-mm (0.57-in) machine-gun fire as well as shell fragments, and its space frame configuration allows for the addition of ceramic armour. Powered by an MTU 883 Ka-523 diesel engine, the AAAV will have a maximum land speed of 45 mph (72 km/h) with 850 hp (634 kW) delivered to the standard transmission, and a maximum water speed of 23 mph (37 km/h) with 2,700 hp (2,013 kW) delivered to two waterjets. (*General Dynamics Land Systems*)

AAAV
LEADING THE WAY

The bow wave and wake of this AAAV prototype provides telling evidence of the vehicle's high water speed, which will allow troops to be delivered from their ships to the beach in the smallest possible time of vulnerability. (*General Dynamics Land Systems*)

automatic transmission in place of the standard manual transmission. Both the Type 80 and the Type 80-II can be fitted with a different fire-control system, which consists of a projecting sight, laser rangefinder, ballistic computer, and a two-axis stabilization system.

Early on in 1989 NORINCO revealed its development of two new main battle tanks based on the Type 80, namely the Type 85-II and Type 85-IIA, to satisfy the operational needs of the Chinese army. The primary conceptual difference between the two Type 85 models and all earlier Chinese main battle tanks was their use of a welded rather than cast-steel turret, this incorporating compound armour to provide a higher level of battlefield survivability. The two models also introduced a more capable computerized fire-control system permitting the gunner to tackle a moving target with his own tank in motion rather than stationary.

The differences between the Type 85-II and Type 85-IIA have not been revealed, although the Type 85-IIA weighs 39,500 kg (87,081 lb), which is slightly more than the figure for the Type 85-II, and has a slightly shorter hull. The main armament of the two Type 85 models is the same 105-mm (4.13-in) rifled gun as used in the Type 80, and while the Type 85-II carries

46 rounds for this gun the Type 85-IIA carries only 44 rounds. The Type 85 models, as well as the Type 80-II, have an overpressure NBC system, but this is of the collective variety rather than the individual variety employed in the Type 80 tank.

In 1991 it was announced that the Type 85-II was to be co-manufactured in Pakistan with the local designation Type 85-IIAP. Deliveries of the Type 85 to Pakistan from China are thought to have amounted to just under 270 vehicles as well as 20 examples of an armoured recovery variant. Late in 1992 NORINCO revealed that it is also building another version of the Type 85 as the Type 85-IIM. This is similar to the earlier models but is heavier, at 41,000 kg (90,388 lb), and is significantly more heavily armed with a 125-mm (4.92-in) rifled gun, for which 40 separate-loading rounds are carried and fed into the breech by an automatic loader, the presence of which allows the crew to be trimmed from four to three.

It was early in 1995 that NORINCO unveiled a new version of its Type 85 as the Type 85-III. Not yet placed in production, this is a development of the Type 85-II and Type 85-IIM with improvements including a new powerpack consisting of a transversely mounted V-type diesel engine developing 1,000 hp (746 kW), and changeable in less than 40 minutes under field conditions; an improved and hydraulically operated transmission operable in automatic, semi-automatic and manual modes; composite armour panels on the turret (replaceable) and the front of the hull (fixed) to provide excellent protection against kinetic and chemical energy attack; roof-mounted day/night sights stabilized in two axes for the commander and gunner and tied into a computerized fire-control system to provide a high first-round hit probability on fixed and moving targets while the Type 85-III is under way; and a 125-mm (4.92-in) smooth-bore main gun with an automatic loader allowing a maximum rate of fire of 8 rounds per minute with 42 rounds of separate-loading ammunition including a charge with a semi-combustible cartridge case.

The main gun can fire three types of 125-mm (4.92-in) ammunition, namely APFSDS, HEAT and HE-FRAG. The two subvariants of the APFSDS ammunition are the NORINCO-developed Type 125-I and Type 125-II: both used a variable-density tungsten alloy as their core material: the 7.37-kg (16.25-lb) Type 125-I projectile has a diameter of 28 mm (1.1 in) and leaves the muzzle at 1,730 m (5,676 ft) per second to penetrate 460 mm (18.1 in) of armour at 2,000 m (2,185 yards), while the 7.44-kg (16.4-lb) Type 125-II projectile has a diameter of 26 mm (1.02 in) and leaves the muzzle at 1,740 m (5,709 ft) per second to 600 mm (23.6 in) of armour at 2,000 m (2,185 yards).

It was in 1991 that NORINCO revealed the availability, for the export rather than internal market, of another new main battle tank. By comparison with earlier Chinese main battle tanks, this Type 90-II marks a new level in overall sophistication and capability in all three major aspects of tank design, namely firepower, protection and mobility. In May 1990 Pakistan signed an agreement for licensed production of the Type 90-II, which was then further developed locally as the Khalid (otherwise known as the MBT-2000 and P-90) for fuller compliance with the needs of the Pakistani army. At the beginning of the 21st century the Type 90-II had not entered production in China.

The most advanced main battle tank yet to have entered service with the Chinese army is the Type 98, which was first revealed late in 1999 and features major improvements in the areas of firepower, protection and mobility. The new tank has sometimes been called the Type 90-III and is probably related to the baseline Type 90, although it uses a different hull that is longer than that of the Type 90.

In overall configuration the Type 98 is wholly conventional, with the driver's compartment at the front, the fighting compartment and turret in the centre, and the powerpack (engine and transmission) at the rear. The driver is seated on the centreline under a single-piece roof hatch lifting and opening to the right, and the driver's forward fields of vision are provided by day periscopes, of which the central unit can be replaced by a passive night-vision periscope. The turret is of a new design providing good levels of protection over its frontal arc, largely through the use of modular and therefore field-replaceable armour packages to each side of the 125-mm (4.92-in) main gun. The gunner is located on the left-hand side of the turret and has a single-piece hatch cover opening to the front, and ahead of this is the stabilized day/night sight that also includes a laser rangefinder feeding range data to the computerized fire-control system. The commander is seated on the right-hand side of the turret and has a roof-mounted stabilized day/night sight. The commander operates the 12.7-mm (0.5-in) machine-gun for local and anti-aircraft defence. Located on each side of the turret is a bank of five forward-firing dischargers for smoke grenades.

The 125-mm (4.92-in) smooth-bore gun is supplied with separate-loading ammunition by an automatic loader below the turret. The secondary armament comprises the standard combination of one 7.62-mm (0.3-in) coaxial machine-gun and one 12.7-mm (0.5-in) local-defence machine-gun on the turret roof.

The hull is reminiscent of that used by the Soviet T-72, with a well-sloped glacis plate characterized by a V-type splash board, horizontal ribs and a dozer/entrenching blade located below the vehicle's nose. The suspension is probably of the torsion-bar type, and on each side there are six large dual rubber-tyred road wheels, track-return rollers, a front-mounted idler and a rear-mounted drive sprocket.

On the right- and left-hand sides of the turret respectively are what are probably a laser detector and a laser dazzle device, the latter for use against the optronic sensors now associated with many ground- and helicopter-launched anti-tank weapons. A stowage basket extends round the turret, providing a measure of protection against incoming HEAT warheads, and the rear of the turret carries a snorkel for deep fording. The Type 98's standard equipment includes an NBC system.

In the late 1970s Czechoslovakia began licensed production of a Soviet main battle tank, the T-72 in its T-72M1 version, but both the factories involved in this process are in the area of the country that later became the Slovak Republic. The other portion of the former Czechoslovakia still wished to continue procurement of a main battle tank based closely on the T-72, however, and in 1995 started work on a locally developed version as the T-72CZ. Two different standards were trialled as the T-72CZ M3 and T-72CZ M4, and the latter formed the basis of the T-72CZ upgrade package with an Israeli NIMDA powerpack (1,000-hp/746-kW Perkins CV-12 diesel engine and Allison fully automatic transmission), an Italian fire-control system and Polish-developed explosive reactive armour over the frontal arc.

France continues manufacture of the Leclerc main battle tank for the domestic and export markets, currently amounting to 310 and 436 tanks respectively, the latter for the United Arab Emirates. The two main tank variants are the Leclerc Mk 1 for European service and the Leclerc Mk 2 optimized with an air-conditioning system for operations in countries with a high ambient temperature. GIAT, the manufacturer of the Leclerc, has completed studies for a three-phase upgrade of the Leclerc for improved capability in the first quarter of the 21st century, but it remains to be seen if any or all of these packages will be introduced. Another possible improvement is the adoption of a 140-mm (5.51-in) smooth-bore main gun supplied with ammunition from an automatic loading system located in the turret bustle: GIAT has completed design of this new turret, which has not yet reached the hardware stage. The Leclerc main battle tank has also been used as the basis of a number of specialized battlefield vehicles such as an armoured recovery vehicle with or without a mineclearing kit, and the EPG armoured engineer vehicle.

The main battle tank that forms the mainstay of the German army's land warfare capability is still the Leopard 2, which entered service with what was then the West German army in the course of 1978. The Leopard 2 is rightly regarded as one of the classic main battle tanks of the period following the Second World War, and is still a formidable weapon in its earlier forms. Germany has not stood still on the development of the Leopard 2, however, and there are two upgrade programmes planned for the Leopard. The KWS I programme is concerned with the installation of a new 120-mm (4.72-in) Rheinmetall L/55 smooth-bore weapon in place of the original 120-mm (4.72-in) Rheinmetall L/44 smooth-bore weapon and firing, in addition to the shorter gun's range of ammunition, the improved DM53 improved kinetic-energy ammunition with increased armour-penetration capability. The KWS II programme is already being implemented on Leopard 2 tanks of the German and Dutch armies to create the Leopard 2A5, while further improvement to the same basic standard are characteristic of the latest production examples of the Leopard 2 for the Swedish army.

The first of three Leopard 2A5 prototypes was completed by Krauss Maffei late in 1990, just before this company's January 1999 merger with Wegmann to create Krauss Maffei Wegmann, with funding from the Dutch, German and Swiss defence ministries. Krauss Maffei Wegmann received a contract to upgrade the Leopard 2 to Leopard 2A5 standard in January 1994, and it was in September 1995 that the German army started to receive an initial 225 but later 350 Leopard 2 main battle tanks that are being upgraded to Leopard 2A5 (originally Leopard 2 [Improved]) standard. In March 1994 the Dutch army decided to upgrade 180 of its Leopard 2 tanks to the Leopard 2A5 standard with an option on

Germany's Leopard 2 main battle tank offers excellent overall capabilities for the modern battlefield, but the flat front of its standard turret has led to a measure of criticism. This resulted in the development of the Leopard 2A5 with a wedge-shaped turret front offering improved ballistic protection, and also a better range of ammunition types for the 120-mm (4.72-in) main gun. (*KMW*)

a further 150 vehicles, and the first deliveries were made in March 1996. Switzerland received the last of its Leopard 2 tanks only in 1993, and later decided to put off any decision on an upgrade. With a number of other improvements, especially to the armour and to the command and control element, the Leopard 2A5 has been ordered by the Spanish and Swedish armies.

In overall configuration the Leopard 2A5 is very similar to Leopard 2, and the main improvements incorporated in the Leopard 2A5 are the equipment of the commander's roof-mounted periscope with a thermal sight, with the image transmitted to a monitor inside the turret, permitting the commander and gunner to engage targets under all weather conditions and opening the way for these two members of the crew to function as a hunter/killer team; the installation of new all-electric gun-control equipment in place of the original hydraulic equipment with advantages in reduced noise, easier maintenance and less demand on electricity; superior armour over the frontal arc (characterized by a distinctive arrowhead shaping of the protection on the turret's front) for a major enhancement of protection against kinetic- and chemical-energy warheads; the installation of spall liners inside the turret; the incorporation of composite materials on the skirt armour; the installation of a TV camera at the rear of the hull with monitor for the driver; the introduction of a hybrid

navigation system with GPS upgrade of the basic optical fibre gyroscopic system; and the upgrade of the laser rangefinder's data processor for greater versatility.

In Swedish service the Leopard 2 is designated as the Strv 122, and this type features a number of additional improvements increasing the weight from the 59,700-kg (131,614-lb) figure of the German army's vehicles to 62,000 kg (136,684 lb). The improvements include enhanced protection (similar to that of the turret) for the front and sides of the chassis, enhanced protection for the turret roof against the effects of anti-armour bomblets; the introduction of a modular and databus-based command and control system connected to the tank's subsystems, the navigation system and the radio equipment; and the introduction of an eye-safe laser rangefinder.

In March 2001 the manufacturer delivered to the German army the first of a planned 350 Leopard 2A6 main battle tanks upgraded with the L/55 main gun. Used with the DM53 APFSDS-T ammunition, based on a non-depleted uranium penetrator, the L/55 gun gives the Leopard 2A6 an additional 1,600 m (1,750 yards) of combat striking range in combination with significantly improved armour-penetration capability. The L/55 barrel weighs 1,347 kg (2,970 lb) by comparison with the L/44 barrel's 1,190 kg (2,625 lb).

The Dutch army is also upgrading its Leopard 2 tanks to the Leopard 2A6 standard, while the first army to order new-build Leopard 2A6 tanks was that of Spain, which ordered 219 such vehicles. In addition to the five countries mentioned above, the other operators of Leopard 2 series main battle tanks comprise Austria and Denmark, while the operators of the older-generation Leopard 1 comprise Australia, Belgium, Canada, Denmark, Germany, Greece, Italy, the Netherlands, Norway and Turkey.

Effectively isolated from the Western world and wishing to develop its own defence industries as a means of avoiding reliance on imports that can be halted by exterior political considerations, Iran has made considerable strides since the early 1980s in the creation and expansion of its capabilities for the design and manufacture of indigenous weapons. One result of this process is the Defence Industries Organization Zulfiqar main battle tank, which was first revealed in 1994 as a type created by the 'Construction Crusade' arm of the Islamic Revolutionary Guards Corps. Russia delivered a number of T-72 tanks to Iran, where the T-72S export model with explosive reactive armour is also manufactured under licence, and it is likely that the Zulfiqar uses T-72 components, these including the 125-mm (4.92-in) smooth-bore main gun supplied with ammunition by an automatic loader.

The Zulfiqar is based on a hull and turret of welded steel, and is powered by a diesel engine. In its configuration the Zulfiqar is wholly conventional, with the driver's compartment at the front of the vehicle on the left-hand side, the turret in the centre, and the engine and transmission compartment at the rear. The driver is seated under a single-piece hatch cover that opens to the right, and has three day periscopes.

The suspension seems to be of the torsion-bar type, and is characterized on each side by six dual rubber-tyred road wheels, five return rollers, a front-mounted idler and a rear-mounted drive sprocket. The road wheels and other elements of the suspension seem to possess a considerable similarity to those of the American M60 tank, a series that has been in service with the Iranian army for some time, but whereas the hull of the M60 is basically boat-shaped that of the Zulfiqar is box-shaped.

The turret front is well sloped, and accommodates the commander and gunner on the right- and left-hand sides respectively. As noted above, the primary armament is a Soviet-developed 125-mm (4.92-in) smooth-bore gun, fitted with a fume extractor and in all probability supplied with ammunition by an automatic loader. The gun is installed in a mantlet of notably small width, and there appears to be no coaxial machine-gun. There is provision for a 12.7-mm (0.5-in) machine-gun on the commander's cupola for anti-aircraft and local defence.

Iran has revealed no specification for the Zulfiqar, which may have entered production in 1999, but it is believed that the tank has a weight of 40,000 kg (88,183 lb) and is powered by a 1,000-hp (746-kW) diesel engine for a

maximum speed of 70 km/h (43.5 mph). Information from inside Iran claims that the Zulfiqar has a main gun stabilization system, a computer-based fire-control system including a laser rangefinder, night-vision equipment, and an NBC system.

The most important main battle tank of the Israeli army is the Merkava, designed indigenously to satisfy the very particular requirements of the units that would have to operate the vehicle. The original 60,000-kg (132,275-lb) Merkava Mk 1 is powered by a 900-hp (671-kW) diesel engine with a semi-automatic transmission, and the electro-hydraulically operated turret carries a 105-mm (4.13-in) rifled main gun, from which 62 rounds of ammunition are fired with the aid of a computer-based fire-control system incorporating a laser rangefinder and night-vision equipment. There followed the 61,000-kg (134,480-lb) Merkava Mk 2 with the same main armament and engine, the latter now driving an automatic transmission, but with a second- rather than first-generation suspension system, and add-on special armour in addition to the basic spaced armour. Then came the much enhanced 65,000-kg (143,298-lb) Merkava Mk 3 with a 1,200-hp (895-kW) diesel engine driving an automatic transmission, an electronically controlled and electrically powered turret carrying a 120-mm (4.72-in) smooth-bore gun with 48 rounds fired with the aid of an improved fire-control system

It is expected in the first part of the 21st century that considerably greater emphasis will be placed on the mechanized infantry combat vehicle than the main battle tank, for there seems to be a declining need for any MBTS more advanced than the current generation. Armed with a cannon of up to 35-mm calibre, or possibly larger, and firing advanced ammunition with the aid of a highly capable fire-control system, the MICV also carries embarked troops and offers a greater degree of battlefield flexibility. The tracked MICV offers better battlefield mobility but is considerably more expensive to buy and operate than the wheeled MICV, which is faster and produced in a variety of configurations including, at the upper end as illustrated here in the Singapore Technologies Kinetics Terrex AV81 proposed for sale to Belgium and Turkey, the 8 x 8 layout. (*S.T. Kinetics*)

incorporating stabilized horizontal and vertical lines of sight as well as an automatic target tracker, main armament ammunition stowage that provides resistance to chain detonation as well as heat detonation, special modular armour, crew air-conditioning as well as the standard overpressure NBC system, and an improved electro-magnetic warning system.

In June 2002 Israel revealed the latest iteration of the series, the Merkava Mk 4, which was developed over a nine-year period and is seen as a significant improvement over the Merkava Mk 3 introduced in 1990. Intended to enter full service by 2004, the Merkava Mk 4 has a 1,500-hp (1,118-kW) General Dynamics 883 powerpack based on a diesel engine, the components of which are made by MTU in Germany before being shipped to the USA for assembly by General Dynamics Land Systems. As on earlier marks of the Merkava, the engine is installed in the front of the hull to provide additional protection for the crew against head-on attack, and is supplied with fuel from a system that combines one front- and two rear-mounted tanks. The Merkava Mk 4 is armed with the same 120-mm (4.72-in)

smooth-bore main gun as the Merkava Mk 3, and this is supplied with ammunition by a semi-automatic loading system that selects one of several ammunition types including new advanced high-penetration projectiles. The Merkava Mk 4 is slightly larger than the Merkava Mk 3 and, significantly, has a turret characterized by only a single hatch for the use of the commander. Both the turret and the main gun's fire-control system are better than those of the Merkava Mk 3, the fire-control system incorporating a second-generation TV/thermal automatic target tracker as well as an advanced thermal night-vision and stabilized panoramic sight for day/night target engagement capability. A camera is mounted at the rear of the vehicle to give the driver a rearward field of vision. The mobility and firepower enhancements are combined with improvements in the protection, whose features include an advanced electro-magnetic threat identification warning system and modular special armour, which, for the first time, covers the turret as well as the hull.

Italy's latest main battle tank is the Ariete, which results from a requirement issued in

The Ariete is the latest Italian tank, armed with a 120-mm (4.72-in) smooth-bore gun firing advanced projectiles such as the APFSDS (Armour-Piercing Fin-Stabilized Discarding-Sabot) type in which a kinetic-energy penetrator of heavy metal and small diameter is released at the muzzle to travel at extremely high velocity in a very flat trajectory. (*Otobreda*)

The Ariete is of all-welded steel armour construction, with the protection over the frontal arc (nose, glacis and turret front and sides) enhanced by the addition of advanced armour. (*Otobreda*)

1982 for an advanced vehicle to be designed and manufactured in Italy. By 1984 there had emerged a consensus between the authorities and industry about a detailed specification, and work was already well under way on the design of the required powerpack and armament. In 1984 IVECO and Otobreda reached agreement on forming a consortium to undertake the design and manufacture of the latest generation of tracked and wheeled fighting vehicles needed by the Italian army. Otobreda was allocated primacy in the creation of the new main battle tank, with IVECO responsible for the powerpack and suspension.

The Ariete's first prototype was completed in 1986, and by 1988 all six of the prototype vehicles that had been ordered were under evaluation, leading to an eventual order for 200 examples of the Ariete. The first tank off the production line was handed over in the later part of 1995. Studies for a proposed 'Ariete Mk 2' have already started, and envisage the use of an uprated powerpack based on a turbocharged diesel engine, a hydro-pneumatic suspension arrangement, an automatic loader for the 120-mm (4.72-in) smooth-bore main gun, a more advanced fire-control system, and enhanced protective

features. However, there are as yet no firm plans for production of this more advanced main battle tank.

The 54,000-kg (119,048-lb) Ariete is based on a hull and turret of all-welded steel construction with an additional covering of advanced armour over the vehicle's frontal arc. The configuration of the Ariete is basically standard for Western main battle tanks, with the driver located in a compartment to the right of the centreline in the front of the hull, the turret in the centre, and the powerpack (engine and transmission) in a compartment at the rear of the hull. The driver is seated on a hydraulically adjustable seat under a single-piece hatch cover lifting and swinging to the right to provide access and egress, and the driver's compartment is fitted with three integral forward-facing day periscopes, of which the central unit can be replaced by a passive periscope for night driving. To the left of the driver is stowage for 27 of the 42 rounds of ammunition for the main gun.

Characterized by vertical sides and rear but a well-sloped front, the turret carries the commander on the right with the gunner below and ahead of him, and the loader on the left. The commander has a single-piece hatch that opens to the rear above a ring of eight day

387

The Leopard 2A5 marks one of the high points in the current sophistication of the main battle tank, but the role for which it was created has largely disappeared. (*KMW*)

ASCOD, otherwise Austrian Spanish Co-Operative Development as a collaborative undertaking by Steyr and Santa Barbara, is developing an advanced armoured infantry fighting vehicle of the tracked type. Manned by a three-man crew and carrying eight infantrymen, the type has been ordered by the Austrian army as the Ulan and also by the Spanish with a two-man turret armed with a 30-mm cannon. This development model, intended to appeal to non-European nations requiring a fire-support and tank destroyer capability, has its weapons station occupied by a 105-mm (4.13-in) rifled gun with an automatic loader. (*LIW/ASCOD*)

periscopes providing all-round fields of vision. The loader has a rearward-opening single-piece hatch cover and two roof-mounted day periscopes providing fields of vision ahead and to the left of the vehicle, and ahead of this man's hatch is a laser warning sensor with the display at the commander's station. There are blow-out panels in the turret roof to vent any ammunition explosion upward and away from the turret crew, plus an ammunition resupply hatch in the left side and a large stowage basket at the rear of the bustle.

The commander's and gunner's periscopes are part of the TURMS (Tank Universal Modular System) manufactured by Officine Galileo. The fire-control system's other main elements are the commander's primary stabilized panoramic day/night sight of the image intensification type, the gunner's primary stabilized periscope laser sight, a ballistic computer with input from a number of sensors, a muzzle reference system, and the control panel. The commander's sight has magnifications of x 2.5 and x 10. This roof-mounted sight can be traversed through 360° and elevated in an arc between −10° and +60°. The gunner's roof-mounted sight is based on a primary stabilized head mirror, a visual unit, a laser rangefinder and a thermal imaging unit all contained in one housing protected by armoured shutters. The x 5 daylight sight and thermal night-vision sight, the latter with wide and narrow fields of vision, are routed through the common head mirror.

The ballistic computer performs all computation, and also controls and manages the optical sight, laser rangefinder and servos as well as the sensors, which provide barrel wear information, vehicle attitude information and also wind speed/direction and temperature data, the last two from sensors mounted on the turret's roof. Its fire-control system makes it feasible for the Ariete to tackle moving as well as stationary targets while it is in motion or at a halt.

The main armament is an Otobreda 120-mm (4.72-in) smooth-bore gun, an L/44 weapon fitted with a muzzle reference system, a thermal sleeve and a fume extractor. The gun's chamber is dimensionally identical to that of the guns in the German Leopard 2 and the American M1A1 and M1A2 Abrams main battle tanks, and can therefore fire the same range of separate-loading ammunition types. Some 15 rounds of ammunition are carried in the turret's bustle. The secondary armament comprises a 7.62-mm (0.3-in) coaxial machine-gun and another 7.62-mm (0.3-in) machine-gun on the turret roof for anti-aircraft and local defence; 4,200 rounds of ammunition are carried for the two machine-guns.

Traverse of the turret and elevation of the main gun are entrusted to an electro-hydraulic system with a manual back-up. An all-electric gun control and stabilization system is now offered for the tank.

The powerpack, comprising the 1,300-hp (969-kW) diesel engine, transmission and cooling system, is produced by IVECO and delivered as a single unit for ease or installation and/or replacement, which can be completed in less than an hour. Fuel is delivered from two glassfibre-reinforced plastic tanks installed as one on each side of the fighting compartment. The torsion-bar suspension comprises, on each side, seven dual rubber-tyred road wheels, four track-return rollers, a front-mounted idler and a rear-mounted drive sprocket. The upper part of the suspension is covered by skirts.

The Mitsubishi Type 90 is the most recent main battle tank to enter service with the Japanese army. The programme that led to this vehicle started in 1976, and with the single

The all-steel Dardo is an Italian infantry fighting vehicle with accommodation for seven infantrymen as well as a three-man crew, including the commander and gunner in a turret armed with one 25-mm cannon and one 7.62-mm (0.3-in) coaxial machine-gun. (*IVECO OTO*)

exception of the 120-mm (4.72-in) main gun manufactured under licence from Rheinmetall of Germany, the Type 90 and all its other elements are of Japanese design as well as manufacture.

The detailed requirement for the Type 90 was finalized in 1980, leading to the construction of two prototypes by 1982. These were each armed with a 120-mm (4.72-in) smooth-bore gun of Japanese design and firing Japanese ammunition. Trials of these two prototypes were undertaken between 1982 and 1986, and paved the way for an additional four prototypes completed by 1988 to a standard that differed from that of its predecessors in being armed with the German gun. The Type 90 was accepted for service in 1991, and by the end of the decade some 175 Type 90 tanks had been delivered with production continuing.

Although there are no concrete details available about the exact nature of the Type 90's armour, it is all but certain that composite armour is used over the frontal section of the tank. The Type 90 is orthodox in its configuration, with the driver's compartment at the front of the hull, the turret in the centre, and powerplant (1,500-hp/1,118-kW) Mitsubishi 10ZG diesel engine and automatic

transmission) at the rear of the hull. The driver is seated to the left of the centreline under a single-piece hatch cover with three day periscopes of which the central unit can be replaced by a passive periscope, for nocturnal movement. To the right of the driver is stowed part of the ammunition for the main gun.

The turret appears to have been inspired by that of the Leopard 2, for it is an angular unit with vertical faces on all four sides and a substantial bustle extending to the rear over the engine compartment. Located under individual roof hatches, the commander and gunner are on the right- and left-hand sides of the turret respectively, and the main gun's Mitsubishi-designed automatic loader is fitted to their rear in the bustle, which incorporates blow-out panels in its upper surface to mitigate the effects of an ammunition explosion. The commander has day-vision blocks for all-round fields of view. The 120-mm (4.72-in) smooth-bore main gun is fitted with a thermal sleeve, a fume extractor and a muzzle reference system: while the gun is identical to the baseline German weapon, the recoil system and gun mount are of Japanese design. Traverse of the turret and elevation of the main gun are entrusted to an electrically powered system,

The cost and weight of the modern type of advanced main battle tank has led to the resurgence of interest in less capable but considerably cheaper light tanks. This is a Swedish prototype that can be considered a hybrid between the light tank and the infantry fighting vehicle, for this CV 90120 has a small rear-set compartment for four infantrymen or additional ammunition for the main armament. The four-man crew comprises a driver in the front of the hull, and a commander, gunner and loader in the turret. This last carries the main armament, which is a Swedish-developed 120-mm (4.72-in) smooth-bore gun with a semi-automatic loader and a recoil-attenuation system. The hull and turret fronts are notably well sloped, but the generally thin armour provides protection again projectiles up to a calibre of only 30 mm. (*Hägglunds Vehicle AB*)

with manual controls available for emergency situations. It is believed that the loader carries 16 rounds of ready-use APFSDS-T or HEAT-MP ammunition. These two types have a semi-combustible cartridge case. After it has been fired, the main gun moves to 0° elevation for reloading, and then automatically returns to the firing elevation.

A 7.62-mm (0.3-in) coaxial machine-gun is installed to the left of the main gun, and there is also a 12.7-mm (0.5-in) machine-gun on the turret roof for anti-aircraft and local defence in the hands of the commander or the gunner. On each side of the turret there is a bank of three forward-firing dischargers for smoke grenades.

The fire-control system of the Type 90 includes the gunner's periscopic sight which is stabilized in azimuth, the commander's periscopic sight with 180° traverse and two-axis stabilization, and a digital fire-control computer. The gunner's sight incorporates a daylight channel, a thermal sensor and a laser range-finder. Data from these sights, together with information about ambient wind and temperature conditions as well as barrel bend and trunnion tilt, are supplied to the fire-control system's digital computer for the generation of a fire-control solution offering a high probability of a first-round hit on a moving or stationary target even when the Type 90 itself is in motion.

The Type 90 tank's suspension is a hybrid type using torsion bars for the central pair of road wheels and hydro-pneumatic units for the forward and rear pairs of road wheels. This combination of six dual rubber-tyred road wheels on each side is complemented by return rollers, a front-mounted idler and a rear-mounted drive sprocket. The upper part of the track on each side is protected by a skirt.

Mounted on the forward part of the turret's upper surface is a laser detector, an NBC system is standard, and there is provision for the installation of a dozer blade or mine-clearing roller at the front of the vehicle. The same basic hull is used in two specialized battlefield vehicles, namely the Type 90 armoured recovery vehicle and the Type 91 armoured vehicle-launched bridge.

Despite the collapse of the USSR into the CIS, Russia retains a formidable military design capability but is hampered in production

terms by the CIS's economic problems. Even so, the period since the emergence of the CIS has been characterized by the appearance of three new main battle tanks, one of them in production and the other two only at the prototype stage.

The first of these, stemming from development work started during the existence of the USSR, is the T-90 created at the Kartsev/-Venediktov Bureau (Vagonka) under the supervision of V. Potkin. The new tank was revealed in 1993, and it is believed that the vehicle entered production in the following year.

The T-90 is essentially an evolutionary development of the T-72BM, also designed and manufactured at Nizhnyi Tagil with some of the advanced features of the late-production T-80, most notably in the defensive aids systems, fire-control system and Kontakt-5 explosive reactive armour system. The T-90 is also offered for export in T-90S and T-90E variants, and early in 2001 India contracted for a total of 310 T-90S tanks: the initial 124 are being delivered from Russia and the other 186 are to be assembled by the Heavy Vehicle Factory at Avadi in southern India.

In configuration the 46,500-kg (102,513-lb) T-90 is virtually identical to the T-72, with the driver's compartment at the front of the hull, the turret in the centre and the powerplant (840-hp/626-kW Model V-84MS multi-fuel diesel engine and manual transmission) in a

A side view of the all-steel CV 90120, which is based on the hull of the CV 9030/9040 armoured personnel carriers, shows the well-sloped frontal armour (glacis and turret front) of this interesting armoured fighting vehicle. The main gun has two-axis stabilization and is fired with the aid of a capable fire-control system. (*Hägglunds Vehicle AB*)

The CV 9030 was developed by the Swedish company Hägglunds (now owned by Alvis of the UK) as an export derivative of the CV 9040 in service with the Swedish army. The CV 9030 is an infantry fighting vehicle with accommodation for eight infantrymen as well as a three-man crew, including two operating the turret, which is armed with a 30-mm cannon and a 7.62-mm (0.3-in) coaxial machine-gun. Useful numbers have been sold to the armies of Finland, Norway and Switzerland. (*Hägglunds Vehicle AB*)

compartment at the rear of the hull. The T-90's hull and turret are fitted over their frontal arcs with Kontakt-5 explosive reactive armour providing a high level of protection against APFSDS and HEAT projectiles. ERA panels are also installed on each side of the hull front in line with the driver's compartment for enhanced lateral protection.

Seated on the vehicle's centreline, the driver is located under a hatch cover that lifts and swings open to the right, and for forward vision is provided with a day periscope that can be replaced by a night-vision device for nocturnal operations. Located in the turret, the other two members of the crew are the commander and gunner, who are positioned respectively in the right- and left-hand sides of this unit. The commander's contra-rotating cupola is covered by a forward-opening hatch, and the associated vision equipment comprises two rear-facing day-vision blocks and, in the cupola's forward part, an Agat-S stabilized day/image-intensification sight flanked by a pair of day periscopes. The gunner's forward-opening hatch incorporates the mounting for the snorkel provided for a deep-fording capability, and there are also two day-vision blocks, one in the hatch cover and the other ahead of it.

The gunner has a day/thermal sight system, and the commander is provided with a screen to monitor the gunner's thermal view. Fire-control is based on an integrated computer system known as the 1A45T, which makes it possible for the commander and the gunner to lay and fire the main armament under day and/or night conditions with the T-90 on the move or stationary. The gunner's sight system includes a day sight with two-axis stabil-ization and a laser rangefinder, a day sight rangefinder with missile guidance channel, a digital ballistic computer, a wind gauge, infra-red vision equipment and a Buran-PA sight that can be replaced by an Agava-2 roof-mounted stabilized thermal sight.

The T-90's main armament is a 125-mm (4.92-in) 2A46M1 (otherwise D-81TM) smooth-bore gun with a fume extractor and thermal sleeve. The gun had two-axis automatic stabilization, and is supplied with separate-loading ammunition by an automatic loader carrying 2 of the tank's 43 rounds of 125-mm (4.92-in) ammunition and providing a maximum rate of fire of 7 rounds per minute. The T-90's ammunition types are the same as those of the T-80 supplemented by a special high-explosive fragmentation projectile that can be detonated over the target with the aid of the tank's fire-control system. The gun can also fire the 9M119 and 9M119M laser-guided projectiles to a range of 5,000 m (5,470 yards): the T-90 carries six examples of the 9M119, which has the NATO reporting designation AT-11 'Sniper' and in its 9M114M variant has a tandem warhead to defeat explosive reactive armour.

To the right of the main gun is a 7.62-mm (0.3-in) PKT coaxial machine-gun, and on the commander's cupola is a 12.7-mm (0.5-in) NVST machine-gun for anti-aircraft and local defence. On each side of the turret is a bank of six dischargers for smoke grenades. There are also other defensive aids including a laser warning system to trigger aerosol-forming grenades, an infra-red countermeasures system, a smoke-laying system using fuel injected into the exhaust, and an NBC system. There is also a fire detection and suppression system.

The Model V-84MS engine runs mainly on diesel fuel, but can also use other fuels in pure or blended forms. The tank's suspension is of the torsion-bar type, and the running gear on each side comprises six dual rubber-tyred road wheels, three track-return rollers, a front-mounted idler and a rear-mounted drive sprocket. The standard equipment includes a nose-mounted dozer blade, provision for two

fuel drums carried under the rear of the hull, and provision for two types of mineclearing equipment.

An enhanced development of the T-90 evolved to meet the needs of Asian countries is the T-90S. This has an air-conditioning system to cater for operations in high ambient temperatures, and an upgraded sight/fire-control system using many equipment items manufactured by the French company Thales. There is also the BMR-3M armoured demining vehicle, which is based on a much modified T-72 or T-90 hull with the turret replaced by an enclosed raised super-structure. Mounted on the front of the vehicle is a roller mineclearing system which includes a device to trigger magnetically fused anti-tank mines.

Early in 2000, the Russians revealed the existence of the completely new T-95 main battle tank which, unlike the T-90, has not yet progressed past the prototype stage. No details of this new 50,000-kg (110,229-lb) type have been released, but it is known that the key to its capabilities rests with its radial layout with the main gun installed in a small unmanned turret and supplied with separate-loading ammunition by an automatic loader below the turret. The crew of three comprises the driver, gunner and commander, all located

Now an independent state within the CIS rather than an intrinsic part of the USSR, Ukraine has its own tank design and production facilities, the former in the shape of the Kharkov Morozov Design Bureau that was the A.A. Morozov Design Bureau. It was this agency that developed the USSR's T-64 with its opposed multi-fuel engine and its T-80UD derivative with a diesel engine, and further development led to the Ukrainian T-84 with a 125-mm (4.92-in) KBA-3 smooth-bore gun with an automatic loader. Seen here, however, is the T-84-120 Oplot, intended for the export market with the standard type of NATO tank gun, namely a 120-mm (4.72-in) smooth-bore weapon. (*Malyshev Plant*)

in an armoured capsule that is separated from the turret and automatic loader by an armoured bulkhead. The tank's concept has made it possible not only to lower the overall height and thereby improve battlefield survivability, but also to enhance the safety of the crew.

It is thought that the T-95 is armed with a 135-mm (5.31-in) gun, probably of the smooth-bore type and operated via an advanced fire-control system using optical, thermal and infra-red imaging.

Late in 1997 the Russians revealed another new main battle tank that has still, it is believed, not passed the development stage. In its first definitive form, this Chiorny Oriol (Black Eagle) has a longer hull than the T-80, and the running gear on each side comprises seven rather than six road wheels, an undetermined number of track-return rollers, a front-mounted idler and a rear-mounted drive-sprocket. The hull's layout is conventional, with the driver at the front, the turret in the centre and the 1,200-hp (895-kW) turbocharged diesel engine and transmission at the rear, but the additional length has allowed a significant increase in the armour protection worked into the front of the hull.

The two-man turret is stabilized in azimuth and carries a 125-mm (4.92-in) gun stabilized in elevation. This gun is a 2A46M smooth-bore weapon supplied with separate-loading ammunition by an automatic loader in the turret's bustle. The loader is divided from the turret crew by an armoured

bulkhead, and there are blow-out panels in the turret roof for further mitigation of the effects of any ammunition explosion. The installation of an advanced computer fire-control system provides a high probability of a first-round hit on a moving or stationary target, and the provision of an automatic fuse-setting system makes it feasible to set HE fragmentation projectiles to explode directly over the target.

The dissolution of the USSR into a number of independent states grouped under Russian leadership as the CIS resulted in the partial fragmentation of the erstwhile USSR's tank designing and manufacturing capabilities. One result of this process is the emergence of the Ukraine as a 'tank nation', for the A.A. Morizov Design Bureau was located at Kharkov, now in the Ukraine and known as the Kharkov Morizov Machine-Building Design Bureau. This bureau designed and built the T-64 main battle tank used exclusively by the Soviet army, and then its T-64A and T-64B developments before moving forward in 1986 to manufacture of the T-80UD diesel-engined version of this gas turbine-powered tank, but manufacture was terminated in about 1990 as just under three-quarters of the tank's assemblies and components had to be imported. In 1993 the Ukrainian authorities decided to develop an improved T-80UD as the T-84, which was designed by the St Petersburg (formerly Leningrad) Kirov Plant in Russia for Ukrainian production.

The 46,000-kg (101,411-lb) T-84 is derived directly from the T-80UD with a Ukrainian-manufactured welded-steel turret in place of the T-80UD's Russian-made cast-steel turret, and a choice between the 1,200-hp (896-kW) Model 6TD-2 or 1,000-hp (746-kW) Model 6TD diesel engines. The latter was selected for the tanks for the Pakistani army, which ordered 320 such vehicles delivered between 1997 and 1999, and the higher-rated engine is used in the tanks of the Ukrainian army.

Late in 2000 the Ukraine revealed the preliminary details of a T-84 development armed with a 120-mm (4.72-in) smooth-bore gun in place of the basic tank's 125-mm (4.92-in) KBA-3 smooth-bore weapon. This

The most advanced main battle tank in service with the US Army in the first years of the 21st century is the M1 Abrams, seen here in the form of the M1A2, its definitive production variant. (*General Dynamics Land Systems*)

The British army's equivalent of the Americans' M1A2 is the Challenger 2, a type that offers excellent capabilities in firepower and protection, although only at the expense of a weight that inevitably has an effect on the weapon's overall mobility. (*Vickers Defence Systems*)

T-84-120 Oplot was demonstrated to the Turkish army in 2001, but has not yet been ordered into production.

The 48,000-kg (105,820-lb) T-84-120 is virtually identical to the baseline T-84 except for its gun and associated ammunition-handling system. Whereas the T-84 has a 125-mm (4.92-in) gun with 43 rounds of ammunition, of which 28 are accommodated in the automatic loader below the turret, the T-84-120 has a 120-mm (4.72-in) gun with 40 rounds of ammunition, of which 22 are accommodated in the automatic loader in the turret bustle, a position that operational experience has revealed to be significantly safer than that below the turret.

The standard main battle tank of the British army is the Challenger, whose latest version is the 62,500-kg (137,787-lb) Challenger 2 that entered full service in 1994 as a development of what is now designated as the Challenger 1. The hull, powerpack (engine and transmission) and running gear remain essentially unaltered, but above them is a new three-man turret incorporating second-generation Chobham (composite) armour for much enhanced resistance to the effects of kinetic- and

chemical-energy projectiles, improved sighting and fire-control systems, and in place of the original 120-mm (4.92-in) L115A5 smooth-bore gun with 64 separate-loading rounds the superior L30A1 smooth-bore gun of the same calibre but with 50 separate-loading rounds of improved ammunition. The gun and its ammunition were developed by RO Defence, a

This M1A2SEP is a development vehicle for the System Enhancement Package planned as a means of further upgrading the operational capabilities of the M1A2 by the addition of improved computer equipment, advanced navigation system, under-armour auxiliary power unit, improved crew compartment cooling and air-conditioning, and great component reliability. (*General Dynamics Land Systems*)

EuroPowerPack also used in the Leclerc main battle tank manufactured in France.

The main variant of the Challenger 2 is the so-called Engineer Tank System, whose two members are the Titan armoured bridgelaying vehicle and Trojan flexible obstacle/mineclearing vehicle.

The most advanced tank fielded by the US Army is the M1A2 variant of the Abrams main battle tank. The changes effected to turn the M1A1 into the M1A2 with enhanced 'fightability' include an Improved Commander's Weapon Station, a Commander's Independent Thermal Viewer, an Inter-Vehicular Information System, Position/Navigation System, and several survivability features. The first M1A2 tanks came off the production line late in 1992, and large numbers of earlier M1 tanks have been upgraded to the new standard, in this instance with new turrets.

In September 1994 the Department of Defence contracted with General Dynamics Land Systems for the design of the M1A2 SEP (System Enhancement Package), which was to be introduced into the programme to upgrade M1, M1A1 and M1A2 tanks to an enhanced M1A2 standard. The planned improvements comprised a coloured tactical display, keyboard for data entry, voice synthesis, digital terrain maps, increased memory, upgraded processors, updated command and control capability, a GPS receiver, improved internal communications, standard army computer architecture, an under-armour auxiliary power unit, crew compartment cooling and air-conditioning, improved power distribution, improved component reliability, CITV second-generation FLIR, OPS second-generation FLIR, battle combat identification system, multi-purpose integrated chemical agent detector, and eye-safe laser rangefinder.

In overall terms, though, there are signs that the pace at which tank design and upgrade are being pushed forward is slowing dramatically, at least in the Western world. With the removal of the USSR as a significant element in the thinking of the major powers, the countries of the Western world feel that they have a comfortable edge in main battle tank superiority. Thus the emergence of a spate of

The standard infantry fighting vehicle of the British army is the Warrior, seen here under evaluation in Switzerland. Carrying seven infantrymen, the Warrior has a three-man crew including two persons in a turret armed with a 30-mm cannon and 7.62-mm (0.3-in) coaxial machine-gun. (*Alvis Vehicles Ltd*)

BAE Systems company, in its CHARM programme, and the L30A1 can fire new APFSDS-T rounds based on depleted uranium or conventional penetrator.

The Challenger 2 is powered by a 1,200-hp (895-kW) Perkins CV-12 TCA Condor diesel engine, and a variant of this same engine, modified to allow the maintenance of rated power under hot ambient conditions, is used in the 38 Challenger 2 tanks delivered to Oman. The Challenger 2 is also offered for export as the Challenger 2E with a different powerplant, the Perkins engine and David Brown transmission being replaced by a 1,500-hp (1,118-kW) MTU 883 diesel engine and Renk automatic transmission: this combination is the

Seen above and below in the form of its M1A1 and M1A2 SEP forms respectively, the M1 Abrams is perhaps the last main battle tank that will be developed in the USA for the foreseeable future. The M1A1 was the most potent element of the US Central Command forces involved in the 1991 war to expel Iraqi occupation forces from Kuwait, and in that conflict proved itself a truly formidable MBT. Even in the absence of another superpower likely to threaten the USA's overwhelming dominance of the land battlefield, the US Army pressed ahead with the improved M1A2 programme and then with the SEP (System Enhancement Program) for the M1A2. (*General Dynamics Land Systems*)

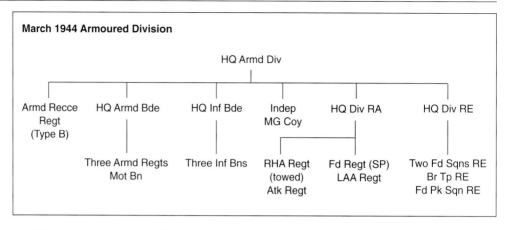

March 1944 Armoured Division

HQ Armd Div

- Armd Recce Regt (Type B)
- HQ Armd Bde — Three Armd Regts Mot Bn
- HQ Inf Bde — Three Inf Bns
- Indep MG Coy
- HQ Div RA — RHA Regt (towed) Atk Regt / Fd Regt (SP) LAA Regt
- HQ Div RE — Two Fd Sqns RE Br Tp RE Fd Pk Sqn RE

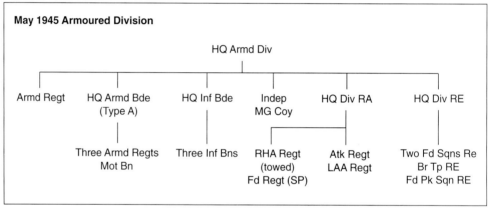

May 1945 Armoured Division

HQ Armd Div

- Armd Regt
- HQ Armd Bde (Type A) — Three Armd Regts Mot Bn
- HQ Inf Bde — Three Inf Bns
- Indep MG Coy
- HQ Div RA — RHA Regt (towed) Fd Regt (SP) / Atk Regt LAA Regt
- HQ Div RE — Two Fd Sqns Re Br Tp RE Fd Pk Sqn RE

2 US Armored Organization, 1940–7

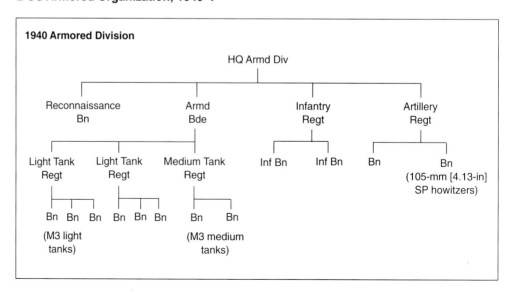

1940 Armored Division

HQ Armd Div

- Reconnaissance Bn
- Armd Bde — Light Tank Regt (Bn Bn Bn — M3 light tanks), Light Tank Regt (Bn Bn Bn), Medium Tank Regt (Bn Bn — M3 medium tanks)
- Infantry Regt — Inf Bn / Inf Bn
- Artillery Regt — Bn / Bn (105-mm [4.13-in] SP howitzers)

1941 Armored Division

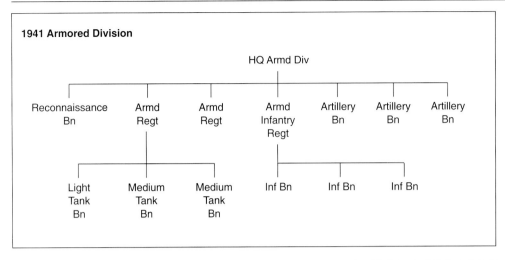

1943 Armored Division

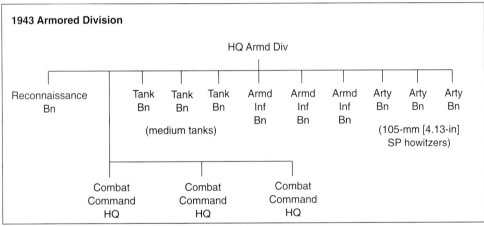

3 German Armoured Organization, 1935–43

1935 Panzer Division

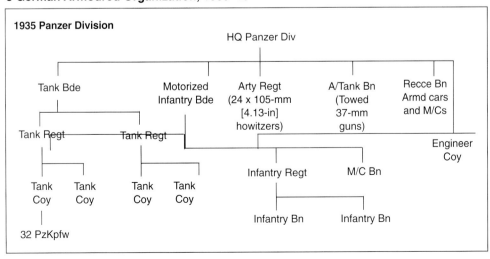

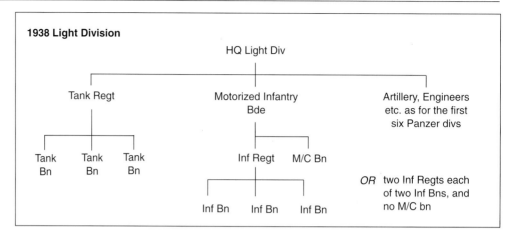

1938 Light Division

HQ Light Div

Tank Regt — Motorized Infantry Bde — Artillery, Engineers etc. as for the first six Panzer divs

Tank Bn   Tank Bn   Tank Bn

Inf Regt   M/C Bn

Inf Bn   Inf Bn   Inf Bn

OR two Inf Regts each of two Inf Bns, and no M/C bn

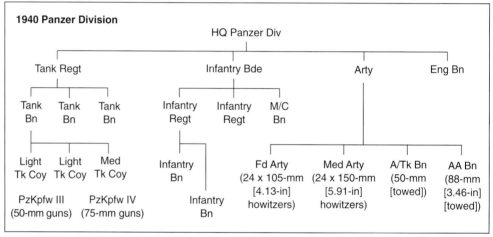

1940 Panzer Division

HQ Panzer Div

Tank Regt — Infantry Bde — Arty — Eng Bn

Tank Bn   Tank Bn   Tank Bn

Light Tk Coy   Light Tk Coy   Med Tk Coy

PzKpfw III (50-mm guns)   PzKpfw IV (75-mm guns)

Infantry Regt   Infantry Regt   M/C Bn

Infantry Bn

Infantry Bn

Fd Arty (24 x 105-mm [4.13-in] howitzers)   Med Arty (24 x 150-mm [5.91-in] howitzers)   A/Tk Bn (50-mm [towed])   AA Bn (88-mm [3.46-in] [towed])

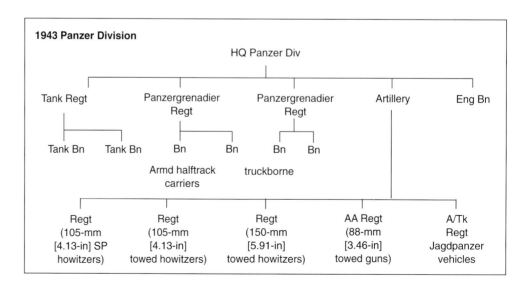

1943 Panzer Division

HQ Panzer Div

Tank Regt — Panzergrenadier Regt — Panzergrenadier Regt — Artillery — Eng Bn

Tank Bn   Tank Bn

Bn   Bn
Armd halftrack carriers

Bn   Bn
truckborne

Regt (105-mm [4.13-in] SP howitzers)   Regt (105-mm [4.13-in] towed howitzers)   Regt (150-mm [5.91-in] towed howitzers)   AA Regt (88-mm [3.46-in] towed guns)   A/Tk Regt Jagdpanzer vehicles

4 Italian Armoured Organization, February 1942

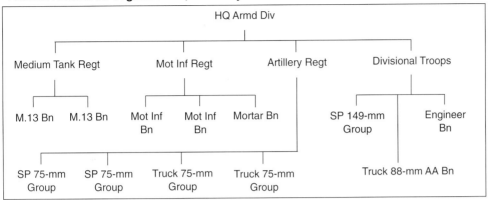

5 French Armoured Organization, 1917–55

1934 Division Légère Mécanique (DLM)

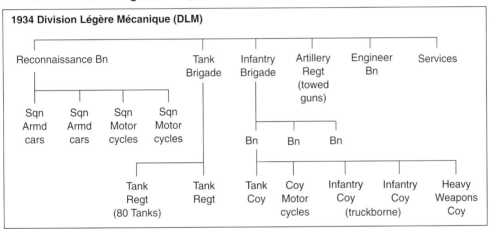

1939 Division Cuirassée (DCR)

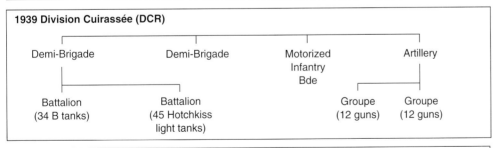

1943 Division Blindée (DB)

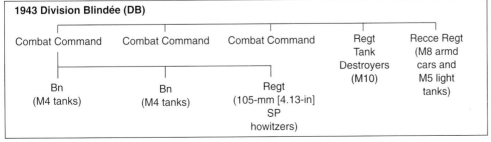

6 Soviet Armoured Organization, 1940–5

1940 Tank Division

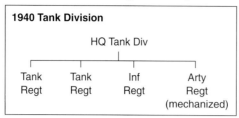

HQ Tank Div

Tank Regt — Tank Regt — Inf Regt — Arty Regt (mechanized)

1940 Motor Rifle Division

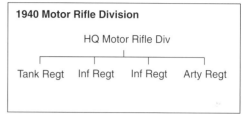

HQ Motor Rifle Div

Tank Regt — Inf Regt — Inf Regt — Arty Regt

1942 Tank Brigade

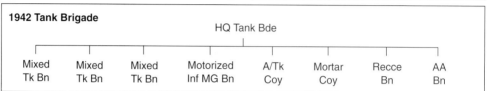

HQ Tank Bde

Mixed Tk Bn — Mixed Tk Bn — Mixed Tk Bn — Motorized Inf MG Bn — A/Tk Coy — Mortar Coy — Recce Bn — AA Bn

1944 Tank Corps

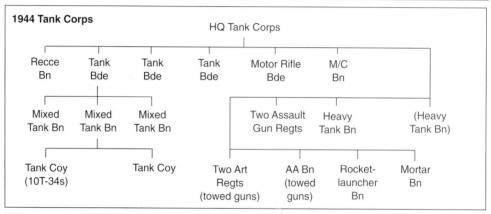

HQ Tank Corps

Recce Bn — Tank Bde — Tank Bde — Tank Bde — Motor Rifle Bde — M/C Bn

Mixed Tank Bn — Mixed Tank Bn — Mixed Tank Bn

Two Assault Gun Regts — Heavy Tank Bn — (Heavy Tank Bn)

Tank Coy (10T-34s) — Tank Coy

Two Art Regts (towed guns) — AA Bn (towed guns) — Rocket-launcher Bn — Mortar Bn

1945 Tank Division

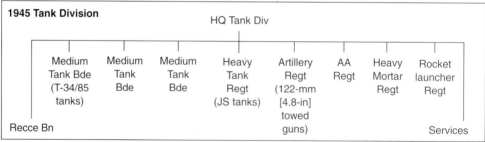

HQ Tank Div

Medium Tank Bde (T-34/85 tanks) — Medium Tank Bde — Medium Tank Bde — Heavy Tank Regt (JS tanks) — Artillery Regt (122-mm [4.8-in] towed guns) — AA Regt — Heavy Mortar Regt — Rocket launcher Regt

Recce Bn

Services

1945 Motor Rifle Division

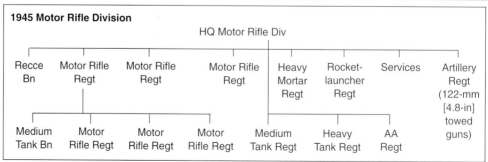

HQ Motor Rifle Div

Recce Bn — Motor Rifle Regt — Motor Rifle Regt — Motor Rifle Regt — Heavy Mortar Regt — Rocket-launcher Regt — Services — Artillery Regt (122-mm [4.8-in] towed guns)

Medium Tank Bn — Motor Rifle Regt — Motor Rifle Regt — Motor Rifle Regt — Medium Tank Regt — Heavy Tank Regt — AA Regt

Index